P9-CLZ-533

QUEEN OF THE WORLD

Also by Robert Hardman

Her Majesty: Queen Elizabeth II and her Court
Monarchy: The Royal Family at Work

QUEEN OF THE WORLD

ROBERT HARDMAN

PEGASUS BOOKS
NEW YORK LONDON

Queen of the World

Pegasus Books, Ltd.
148 West 37th Street, 13th Floor
New York, NY 10018

First Pegasus Books hardcover edition January 2019

ISBN: 978-1-64313-002-6

10 9 8 7 6 5 4 3 2 1

Printed in the United States of America
Distributed by W. W. Norton & Company, Inc.

To Matilda, Phoebe and Hal

Contents

Acknowledgements ix

Introduction 1
Chapter One: On Tour 19
Chapter Two: Welcoming the World 66
Chapter Three: Setting Sail 105
Chapter Four: Head of the Commonwealth 138
Chapter Five: The Realms 181
Chapter Six: The Special Relationship 237
Chapter Seven: Europe 273
Chapter Eight: African Queen 307
Chapter Nine: The Yacht 341
Chapter Ten: Elizabeth, Margaret and Nelson 374
Chapter Eleven: Breaking the Ice 423
Chapter Twelve: The Prince of Wales 464
Chapter Thirteen: The Family 507

Appendix 534

Sources and Bibliography 547

Picture Permissions 553

Index 556

ACKNOWLEDGEMENTS

In a matter of months, between the spring and autumn of 1994, the Queen had hosted the President of the United States and had become the first and only British monarch in history to visit Russia. She had completed a three-week, ocean-going tour of eight Commonwealth nations in Central and South America and the Caribbean. She had led a Yacht-load of world leaders across the Channel to reinvade France, where she was saluted on the Normandy beaches by thousands of old soldiers, in one of the most moving military parades of her life (and theirs). Just one month earlier, along with the French President, she had opened a project first dreamed up during the Napoleonic era – the Channel Tunnel.

It was not merely a case of turning up. These were all state occasions that required that blend of diplomacy, gravitas and charm which, in a person of a certain age, is called statesmanship. Just two years short of her seventieth birthday, here was a stateswoman at the height of her powers. The world seemed impressed. And yet, in Britain, the Queen's central role in all this was largely eclipsed by a series of marital and financial crises that, according to some, threatened the monarchy's very existence.

This was the state of play in the mid-Nineties. Covering all these events as a relatively new royal-cum-political correspondent, I was intrigued – and have been ever since. At home, modernity and 'Cool Britannia' were in the ascendant, whereas the monarchy was painted as out of date and out of touch, its useful functions taken for granted and its more decorative ones questioned and criticised. Royalty didn't seem to matter. Overseas, however, it had lost none of its prestige. It really did matter. The monarchy might be something of a curiosity at times, but the Queen was seen as a unique and benign bulwark of stability.

That view holds true today. Whatever the prevailing mood in Britain might be, the rest of the world has not really changed its mind about the monarchy at all. So how and why is it that the best-known head of state on Earth has made such a mark on it? Many people have helped me answer that question. I am grateful to them all.

In the first instance, I would like to thank Her Majesty The Queen for access to the Royal Archives and for privileged access to events and people at Buckingham Palace and Windsor Castle. I would like to thank HRH The Princess Royal and HRH The Countess of Wessex for their time. The idea for this project has evolved from many conversations in many countries, but it was the decision to hold the 2018 biennial summit of Commonwealth nations in Britain that brought things to a head. As a benchmark by which to assess the Queen's global standing, this seemed as good as any. I am most grateful to Samantha Cohen, former Assistant Private Secretary to the Queen and now Private Secretary to TRH The Duke and Duchess of Sussex, who was one of the main architects of that summit, for seeing merit in both a book and a documentary on the monarchy's international role. This is not in any way an official or authorised project, but I would like to thank the many members of the Royal Household who have facilitated the process, including Lord Geidt, Her Majesty's former Principal Private Secretary, and his successor, Edward Young; Captain Nick Wright, Private Secretary to the Princess Royal; Vice Admiral Anthony Johnstone-Burt, the Master of the Household; Alistair Harrison, the Marshal of the Diplomatic Corps; Oliver Urquhart Irvine, the Royal Librarian; and others. I am equally grateful to many former members of the Private Office who have been so generous with their time and advice, including Sir William Heseltine, Lord Fellowes, Lord Janvrin, Simon Gimson and Charles Anson. No study of roving royalty would be complete without that honorary member of the Royal Family, HMY *Britannia*. My thanks go to Sir Jock Slater, Sir Robert Woodard, Commodore Anthony Morrow and others who have kindly shared their memories of royal life at sea.

Particular thanks go to Sally Osman and Colette Saunders in the Royal Communications department at Buckingham Palace, together with their colleagues Steve Kingstone, Marnie Gaffney, Hannah Howard, Laura King, David Pogson, Louise Tait and Daisy Northway. For their help both at home and overseas, especially on the royal tour of Asia, I should like to thank the Household of TRH the Prince of Wales and The Duchess of Cornwall, notably Clive Alderton, Julian Payne, Eva Williams, Amanda Foster, Natalie Forster, Constantine Innemee and Lucy Mathews. At Kensington Palace, I am grateful to Miguel Head, Jason Knauf, Katrina McKeever, Amy Pickerill, James Holt, Charlotte Pool, Ciara Berry and Naomi Smith. Within the Royal Collection, I should like to thank Frances Dunkels, Caroline de Guitaut, Sarah Davis and Sally Goodsir.

Many members of the British government, past and present, have been kind enough to talk to me about the monarchy's global role. Of the Queen's British Prime Ministers, I should like to thank Theresa May, David Cameron and Sir John Major; among her Foreign Secretaries, I should like to thank Boris Johnson, Lord Hague, Dame Margaret Beckett, Jack Straw, Sir Malcolm Rifkind and Lord Owen. I am most grateful to Lord Howell, former Cabinet minister, ex-Commonwealth Minister and now President of the Royal Commonwealth Society; to Baroness Chalker, the former Minister of State for Overseas Development; and to Lord Judd, the former Minister of State at the Foreign Office. I am grateful, too, for the thoughts of Sir Simon Fraser, the former Head of the Diplomatic Service, and to Lord Butler of Brockwell, the former Cabinet Secretary.

Britain is just one of sixteen of the Queen's realms and one of fifty-three Commonwealth nations. Among those I would like to thank from these countries are Justin Trudeau, Prime Minister of Canada; Jacinda Ardern, Prime Minister of New Zealand; Sir John Key, former Prime Minister of New Zealand; Sir Jerry Mateparae, former Governor-General of New Zealand and High Commissioner to London; Alexander Downer, former Foreign Affairs Minister of Australia, former High Commissioner to London and now Chairman of Policy Exchange. In her capacity as Head of the Commonwealth, the Queen has been served by six Secretaries-General at Marlborough House, of whom the surviving five have all been kind enough to share their thoughts with me: Sir Sonny Ramphal, Chief Emeka Anyaoku, Sir Don McKinnon, Kamalesh Sharma and Baroness Scotland. Within the secretariat, David Banks has been an invaluable guide to all things Commonwealth, as have Marlborough House alumni including Sir Peter Marshall, Patsy Robertson and Stuart Mole. I am also grateful to Neil Ford and Barney Choudhury; to Sir Tim Hitchens, chief executive of the Commonwealth Summit, and his Cabinet Office team; to Lord Marland, the chairman of the Commonwealth Enterprise and Investment Council; and to Peter Francis and Tim Brearley at the Commonwealth War Graves Commission for their help.

Every state visit and royal tour is both the culmination and distillation of many months of planning by an ambassador, high commissioner or governor-general and a team who have discussed little else for months. Many distinguished former members of the British Diplomatic Service have been good enough to discuss their experiences, among them Sir David Manning, now senior adviser to TRH the Duke and Duchess of Cambridge and the Duke and Duchess of Sussex, Sir Brian and Lady [Delmar] Fall, Sir Antony Acland, Sir Roger du Boulay, Sir Francis Richards, Sir Julian King and Tom Fletcher, as well as others who cannot be named but to whom I am equally grateful. Thanks, too, to Matthew Barzun, the former United States Ambassador to the Court of St James, whose observation that the Queen was also a symbol 'for the rest of us' was one of the catalysts for this project.

This has been a broad canvas. I have not attempted to cover every state visit or royal tour, since that would require many volumes. Rather, I have selected some of the most interesting and significant moments of modern royal diplomacy, assisted by the personal recollections of many people with a seat in the front row. They include the Most Reverend Dr John Sentamu, Archbishop of York; Sir Nicholas Soames, MP; Brigadier Andrew Parker Bowles; Robin, Countess of Onslow; Alastair Bruce of Crionaich; and Reginald Davis.

Queen of the World has also evolved, in parallel, as an ITV documentary series. It has been a great pleasure working with Oxford Films once again as writer/producer. I am especially grateful to Nicholas Kent, Faye Hamilton, Matt Hill, Floury Crum and Marisa Erftemeijer, who have all been friends and allies from the outset.

I should also like to thank Peter Wilkinson, the Queen's Cameraman, and Jo Clinton-Davis at ITV.

For their company, their humour and their resourcefulness on so many tours over the years, I should like to salute all my brothers and sisters in the royal press corps. Ditto all those Foreign Office staff deployed to work with us and help us make it from A to B, while occasionally rescuing us from C along the way. It may have seemed a thankless task at the time, but I thank them now. Thanks, too, as ever, to Paul Dacre, Leaf Kalfayan and the *Daily Mail* Features team.

After following more than eighty royal tours of more than sixty countries, I should like to thank my old friend and colleague Ian Jones, the award-winning photographer, with whom I covered most of them. I should like to toast the memories of James Whitaker and Alan Hamilton, two much-missed travelling companions and masters of the art of royal reporting *in extremis*. Equally important has been the perspective from the other side of the street. I am most grateful to Marc Roche, doyen of the French media in the UK and the biographer of the Queen in French; and to Thomas Kielinger, *primus inter pares* among German correspondents, and the biographer of the Queen in German.

Many people have been generous with their time, their suggestions and their hospitality. I would like to thank Wesley Kerr, Zaki Cooper, John Armah, Tara Douglas-Home, Susan Gilchrist, Judith Slater, Claire Popplewell, Elizabeth Addy, Duncan Jeffery, Tim and Penny Harvey-Samuel, Lizzie Pitman, Dean Godson, Jacob Rees-Mogg, Ian Cowley, Barbara Stevens, Dinesh Patnaik, the Earl of Onslow, Sir Alan Parker, Tom Burns, Commander Tim Jones, Johnny Hewitson, Andy Goodsir, Robbie Lyle, Lady [Annie] Slater, Dr Christopher McCreery, James Bethell, Simone Finn, John Bridcut, Chris and Natasha Owen, Mark Roberts, Anthony and Susannah Frieze, Jennifer Williams and others.

I have been particularly fortunate to draw on the expertise and sage advice of many distinguished historians, biographers and academics, notably Andrew Roberts, Simon Sebag Montefiore, William Shawcross, Charles Moore, Dr Amanda Foreman, Professor Joseph Nye and Richard Fitzgerald.

This book would be thinner and duller without the custodians on whom our trade depends. I am most grateful to Oliver Urquhart

Irvine's team at Windsor Castle, to Bill Stockting, the Archives Manager of the Royal Archives, and to his colleagues.

Andrew Riley and his team at the Churchill Archives Centre, Cambridge – home of so many important collections – have been most thoughtful and wise. I am grateful to the family of Sir Alan Lascelles for permission to quote from his papers, which reside at Churchill, and to Emma Soames for permitting access to the papers of her father, Lord Soames. Hilary McEwan, the archivist and librarian at the Commonwealth Secretariat, has provided invaluable help with my research at Marlborough House. I am always impressed by the speed and friendliness of the staff of the National Archives at Kew. They run an excellent operation. I would also like to thank the Foreign & Commonwealth Office's Historical Freedom of Information Team inside the 'Knowledge Management Department' at Hanslope Park. I have never met them, but they have always been courteous and professional in their dealings with my numerous FOI requests, many of which have been successful. Thank you, whoever you are.

At Penguin Random House, particular thanks go to my publisher, Selina Walker, for her enthusiasm and shrewd advice from the very start of this project, and to Tom Monson for bringing *Queen of the World* together. Thanks to my excellent copy editor, Mandy Greenfield, my indexer, Alex Bell, along with Grace Long, Joanna Taylor, Rachel Kennedy, Natalia Cacciatore and Linda Hodgson. As ever, nothing has been too much trouble for my agent, Charles Walker, and his assistant, Florence Hyde.

Friends and family have been pivotal, as this endeavour has increasingly consumed weekends, holidays and all available spare time. I am greatly indebted to Richard and Dinah Hardman, Marion Cowley, Hugo and Victoria Hardman and Justin and Victoria Zawoda. I am, furthermore, especially grateful to my sister, Harriet Hewitson, for devoting so much of her time to transcription and proofreading and, likewise, to Melanie Johnson for the expert eye she has cast over the entire manuscript. These have been tall orders. Finally, it is my wife, Diana, who deserves the greatest thanks, forever taking up the slack as another book has usurped precious family life once more. *Queen of the World* is dedicated to our children.

INTRODUCTION

'I am the last bastion of standards'

Buckingham Palace is in the middle of one of the busiest days anyone around here can remember – including the Queen. And no one has a longer memory than the monarch's.

In the Palace ballroom, representatives of every faith and major organisation across the Commonwealth are taking their seats for the opening ceremony of the biggest summit the Commonwealth has ever known. In the Blue Drawing Room, leaders from fifty-three nations of what was once called the British Empire are being welcomed by the Queen, the Prince of Wales and the rest of the Royal Family. The atmosphere is upbeat, informal, noisy and familiar. Most of the time, visitors to the Palace's state apartments treat these rooms with reverence and awe, much as they might a great museum, taking great care not to touch a thing. Yet this lot are lounging around on George IV's blue silk-damask Regency sofas and chairs, feet up, gossiping and cracking jokes. They could almost be at home. In a sense, they are. This is, after all, where the Head of the Commonwealth lives.

In the 1844 Room, staff are preparing the Queen's lunchtime reception for those leaders attending their first Commonwealth meeting. Meanwhile, the Royal Chef and his team are already preparing for this evening's banquet for 135. For such a multinational crowd, the Queen has approved a meat-free menu of watercress panna cotta, halibut and rhubarb-and-ginger mousseline. It is a pity that the Duke of Edinburgh will not be there, as he continues to recover from a hip operation. For tonight will also be the moment of truth for his latest experiment on the Windsor Estate. As Ranger of the Great Park, the Duke has overseen the planting of a new vineyard. This will be the first state occasion at which the Queen and her guests raise a toast using Windsor sparkling wine rather than champagne.

The 2018 Commonwealth Heads of Government Meeting will be one of the most important gatherings in recent royal history – and a moment of great poignancy, too. Commonwealth leaders have never assembled in this sort of strength before, but they are all conscious that this represents a crossroads for the 'family of nations' to which Princess Elizabeth dedicated herself at the age of twenty-one.

Two days short of her ninety-second birthday, the Queen is opening what is almost certainly her last Commonwealth summit. She is in a lively, even skittish mood as she chats to the leaders, some of whom she has known since they were children. These events happen every other year, but because the event moves to a different part of the planet each time, it will almost certainly not return to Britain for at least another twenty years. The Queen has announced that she will no longer be flying long distances, so she will certainly not be attending the 2020 summit, scheduled for Rwanda, or the 2022 gathering in Samoa. Come the 2024 event – which may very well be somewhere in the Caribbean – she will be ninety-eight.

It means that this event will be a very curious gathering – a farewell of sorts for someone who is not leaving and is not retiring, either. The Commonwealth has always been the odd one out among the world's great geopolitical groupings. This is an organisation with an evolving, unwritten constitution, just like Britain's. The nearest it has to a rulebook is a list of enlightened aspirations embodied in a single charter, which has just one signature: the Queen's. Its members – most of them republics – owe her no allegiance. She has no say in their affairs. Her role as Head of the Commonwealth is to embody a free association of equals, to provide continuity, dignity and calm. As the former New Zealand Prime Minister, David Lange, once remarked: 'We do the fighting. She does the unifying.' The Commonwealth has never had quite such a family feel at one of these gatherings, with three generations of the Royal Family on hand to welcome the leaders to London. And today will be exceptional for another reason. In seven decades, the Queen has never once openly interfered with the internal workings of the organisation. On this occasion, though, she will do so for the first time. She will ask the Commonwealth leaders to endorse the Prince of Wales as her successor, telling them that it is her 'sincere wish'. No one is going to begrudge the request of the person who has done more than anyone to ensure the very survival of what many still call 'the club'.

It has long been fashionable in some political and diplomatic circles to dismiss the Commonwealth as irrelevant and outdated, its supporters as deluded and sentimental. Its champions point to the queue of nations that want to join, and the myriad number of global civic organisations in its orbit.

It is self-evident that the Queen is very fond of the Commonwealth. What today's events at the Palace will show is just how fond the Commonwealth is of the Queen. Her reign will go down in history for many reasons, not least the fact that it exceeded the duration of all others before it, one of so many royal records smashed by Elizabeth II. Future historians, however, will credit her with a great deal more than longevity. From the Norman Conquest to the end of the Second World War, British monarchs were cast as rulers. Foreign policy was about either expansion or consolidation in the name of the Crown, reaching its apotheosis in the British Empire. Our Queen is unique. She has been the first monarch who, from the moment of her accession, was expected to reverse that process. However, this has not been a story of reluctant decline. Rather, it has been about redefining the role of Britain and the monarchy itself in a post-imperial world of equals. It is a role reversal that hasn't always been easy. The Queen may have inherited her Crown, her Church and her Forces, but her 'family of nations' was different. She had to earn its approval, often in the face of thinly veiled opposition from her ministers in Britain. That process would help transform Britain into today's multicultural society, a process in which the Queen herself has had a key role. It was her task to offset the pain felt by old Commonwealth cousins when Britain embraced a new European future in the Seventies. Following the UK's 2016 vote to detach itself from the European project, it would also fall to the Queen and her family to help provide some soothing balm once more, both at home and across the continent.

There are those all over the world, even in countries that have no connection with the Crown she wears, who feel a close affinity for this unchanging global figure. As the Queen approached her ninetieth birthday, the American Ambassador to Britain reflected on her transnational – if not universal – appeal, at the end of an evening at Buckingham Palace. 'Not only is the Queen the constant for this country,' Matthew Barzun observed, 'but for the rest of us.'

Thomas Kielinger, the Queen's German-language biographer and long-standing London correspondent for *Die Welt*, says that many Germans view her as a 'global' monarch. 'I can't begin to think what the German *Bundespraesident* would do if he was also head of state of Canada and Australia,' says Kielinger, a former academic, adding that the Queen is one of a handful of British institutions for which his compatriots have long felt a proprietorial sense of shared ownership. 'The German language has imbibed three main sources: the Bible, Goethe and Shakespeare. So Shakespeare is virtually German! The Queen is our Queen in the same way that Shakespeare is our author. We don't think she is *actually* German but we feel familiar, we feel close. Like Shakespeare, she is a figure in our imagination and in our heart.'

A former Private Secretary found a similar reaction during the Queen's trips across the Channel: 'Visits to France were always very moving. When you walk down a street and hear cries of "*Vive la reine!*" it does make the hairs stand on the back of your neck.' No one in France would ever specify which *reine* they had in mind. There was no need.

Former Prime Minister Sir John Major has had the same experience on his travels. 'Everybody in the world has seen the Queen as part of their lives since they were born,' he says. 'I was in Zambia some years ago and went to a village very close to the Zambesi. I went in to see the head man who turned out to be a head woman. This very distinguished elderly lady put out her hand and said: "My name is Elizabeth – just like our Queen".'

Following the 1981 state visit to Sri Lanka, the British High Commissioner in Colombo, Sir John Nicholas, reported that many people had still not accepted the ex-colony's transition to a socialist republic nine years earlier. 'The placards saying "God bless our Queen" were not written in ignorance of the constitutional changes,' he reported to the Foreign Office, 'but reflected a genuine feeling that in spite of these changes, Her Majesty still in a sense belonged to the people of Sri Lanka.' Sir John went on to describe the remarkable scenes when the Queen had arrived in Kandy, once a kingdom in its own right. She was greeted by 'fifty caparisoned elephants and richly clothed Kandyan Chiefs' as part of a 'royal welcome from the Kandyan Kingdom to a monarch who, in the eyes of many in Sri Lanka, not least the President, is considered to be the last in the royal line dating back 2,500 years'.

William Hague* points to the opening night of the 2012 Olympics as an example of the Queen's global stature. Unlike most people, he is not thinking about her appearance alongside 007 in a spoof mini-Bond film,† but of the Buckingham Palace reception for heads of state a few hours earlier. No previous Olympiad had attracted quite so many world leaders. No other city had staged three games – 1908, 1948 and 2012 – let alone with the same family presiding over the opening ceremony each time. As Hague recalls: 'The Queen was able to give a speech saying she was about to open an Olympic Games, like her father and great-grandfather, which is a totally unique thing to be able to say. There was a gasp as everyone realised: "This is serious".' The main organiser of the Games, former Olympian Lord (Sebastian) Coe, had used the monarchy to seduce the International Olympic Committee (IOC) during the original Olympic bidding process, taking the IOC's evaluation team to meet the Queen at the Palace. Even so, it was not until 2012 that Coe fully appreciated her pulling power. 'I didn't quite understand the global reach until we got to the business end of the Olympic Games,' he explains. 'We had 205

* William Hague was MP for Richmond, Yorkshire from 1989-2015, Conservative leader from 1997-2001, Foreign Secretary from 2010-2014 and ennobled as Lord Hague of Richmond in 2015.

† For many people around the world, the most memorable moment of the London Olympics was not a sporting one. It came during the opening ceremony when the Queen and James Bond actor Daniel Craig appeared to parachute into the Olympic stadium. The cameo role was such a closely guarded secret that even the Royal Family were taken by surprise. Games chief Lord Coe, sitting with Princes William and Harry, remembers the cry of: 'Go, Granny!' The Queen is also the only person in history to have opened two Olympiads: London 2012 and Montreal 1976.

Olympic committees all wanting to come to the UK and saying, above and beyond anything, that it was Her Majesty The Queen who they wanted to see, not Usain Bolt.'

It was the Harvard political scientist Professor Joseph Nye who developed the theory of 'soft power' as 'the ability to produce outcomes through attraction rather than coercion or payment'. As more and more of the world is shaped along democratic lines, he argues, so soft power becomes more important. The monarchy, Nye believes, is one of the factors which help to keep Britain up at the top of the 'soft power charts' regardless of passing political storms. 'Britain is in the top rank, it really is. Despite things like Brexit, there are other soft power assets and one of them is the Royal Family,' he says, pointing to the global interest in the 2018 royal wedding. 'We had Americans staying up in the middle of the night to watch this. It was quite remarkable. Not just Anglophiles who were committed devotees of Britain but all sorts of people.' Nye believes that it is 'one of the great ironies of this century' that this ancient hierarchy is 'a very cost-effective way of attracting attention for Britain today.'

The global success of *The Crown*, the Netflix dramatisation of the Queen's life, is another example. Beautifully produced and with fistfuls of awards, much of its success is down to the brilliance of the creative team involved. Yet its core appeal is that it is based on a true person who also happens to be the most famous woman in the world. Some of *The Crown*'s plotlines are far-fetched, others wholly fabricated, and yet they are a portrait of someone who is not only alive but still in office. It is perhaps unsurprising then, that some people feel that the series has pushed the bounds of dramatic licence, not to mention taste, to the limit.

Asked to place the Queen in the pantheon of post-war world figures, former Labour Foreign Secretary Jack Straw replies instantly: 'At the top – not just in terms of longevity but the way she's handled herself over more than sixty-five years.' He calls her the 'epitome' of soft power. 'She has been able to promote the United Kingdom in a way that goes above and beyond what a politician can do. Diplomacy is still about projecting power,' says Straw. 'You have to do it in a physical way and I am afraid size matters. We are in a world where twenty countries have populations bigger than ours. The metrics are changing and wealth is being shared more which is good but projecting power is very, very important. If you're lucky, you've got a head of state who is able to symbolise your power and influence.'

Successive prime ministers have had good reason to be thankful for this very substantial extra diplomatic asset. In March 2016, President Barack Obama left British diplomats crestfallen as he witheringly described British foreign policy in Libya as 'a shit show'. Prime Minister, David Cameron, he said disparagingly, was 'distracted by a range of other things'. No US President had been quite so caustic about the UK for years. Might the fabled 'special relationship' be in peril? If it was, it wasn't for long. A month later, Obama would record a special message for an ITV documentary to mark the Queen's ninetieth birthday. 'I'm glad to be the very first president of the United States to wish Her Majesty a happy Ninetieth Birthday,' he announced. Describing her as 'a source of strength and inspiration not only for the people of Britain but for millions of people around the world', he added: 'The United States is extremely grateful for a steady and energetic leadership.' To cap it all, he then flew into Britain just one day after the Queen's birthday to be the first world leader to congratulate her. 'He was devoted to her,' says David Cameron. 'He was really keen to come and be one of the first to wish her Happy Birthday. He talked about her a lot. It's rather intriguing how devoted he was.' In others words, here was soft power at its hardest.

The former Foreign Secretary, Boris Johnson, remembers listening to President Obama's speech at the funeral of the former Israeli leader, Shimon Peres. 'It was very striking when Barack Obama was trying to think of other great leaders in the world today,' he says. 'The first one he reached for was Queen Elizabeth II.' Another former Foreign Secretary, Margaret Beckett, believes that the Queen and the BBC World Service are Britain's two greatest soft power weapons. It is why she takes issue with politicians and civil servants who believe that Britain should offload grand old assets on cost grounds, whether it is a palatial embassy building or the Royal Yacht. 'I do think the Treasury has a very silly attitude to a lot of this stuff,' she says. 'There have always been bean counters who say: "You've got this residence. Sell it." But ambassadors will tell you that people genuinely want to come to the Queen's birthday party at the old embassy.' Together with several former foreign secretaries, she managed to dissuade a successor, David Miliband, from selling off the Foreign Secretary's official London residence, 1 Carlton Gardens (a former home of Prince Louis Napoleon, later Napoleon III of France).

The Queen provides similar continuity for the Commonwealth. Lord Howell,* the President of the Royal Commonwealth Society, points to a royal paradox: the monarchy has become more influential as its power has declined. He says that an organisation like the Commonwealth is perfectly suited for a digital age, quoting another Joseph Nye maxim: 'Military resources may produce the outcome you want in a tank battle but not on the internet.'

Howell points out that the Commonwealth includes seven of the world's fastest-growing economies, offers smaller nations a platform and serves as the 'ultimate network', with self-help groups covering almost every conceivable requirement for a modern nation state, from dentistry to higher education. That, in turn, offers larger members like Britain a chance to deploy their various sources of soft power: culture, non-governmental organisations, the judiciary, the arts, design, and so on. Underpinning all that, in turn, is the Queen. When it comes to engaging with the world, the Commonwealth is her ideal conduit.

A few months ahead of the big 2018 London summit, the Queen and Prince Harry are having a reception to get her latest Commonwealth venture under way. The Queen's Commonwealth Trust will bypass the politicians and give direct grants to help enterprising young people in all member states. It will be similar to the original Prince's Trust, which started out using the Prince of Wales's Royal Navy pension pot to make small grants, and went on to become Britain's biggest youth-charity network. The Queen is no mere figurehead. The fact that she has appointed two of her outgoing Private Secretaries, Sir Christopher Geidt† and Samantha Cohen, as founding trustees shows how seriously she takes this.

* Former Cabinet Minister David Howell is the only person to have been a minister in the governments of Edward Heath, Margaret Thatcher and David Cameron. As an MP, he spent ten years as chairman of the House of Commons Foreign Affairs Committee.

† Knighted four times by the Queen, Sir Christopher Geidt was ennobled as Lord Geidt after leaving the Palace in 2017. He used his maiden speech in the Lords to promote the work of the Commonwealth.

Among the first cluster of beneficiaries here tonight is Joannes Yimbesalu, a young scientist from Cameroon who used his savings to set up Hope for Children Cameroon, a tiny organisation building lavatories in rural schools. He knew that the absence of toilets was keeping both teachers and students, particularly girls, away from school, as well as causing disease. His government wasn't interested, but the trust has now come up with a £35,000 grant, enabling him to build latrines for seven schools, covering 1,300 children. The results have been both swift and astonishing: school absence down by 27 per cent and a similar reduction in sickness. The Queen knows all about it. It's hard to imagine a previous monarch talking toilets with a guest at a Palace reception, but she is fully briefed on Joannes's work. 'It's splendid, isn't it? Harry was telling me all about your exploits and how well you've been doing,' she tells him brightly. Prince Harry is busy pushing Joannes's story to a cluster of would-be donors who have been asked tonight. 'God knows how many ideas are being wasted every day because young people don't have the support,' he says crossly. Joannes still cannot quite believe that the Queen, her family and her staff are all promoting his tiny charity at the Palace. 'She doesn't only believe in young people. She sees us as stewards of development,' he says. After this evening, he hopes that someone from the Cameroon government might finally return his call.

Joannes has already been recognised by another one of the monarch's Commonwealth initiatives, her Queen's Young Leaders. At the same time, great swathes of the planet are being designated as protected forest under a different scheme, the Queen's Commonwealth Canopy. She and her family have been endorsing Commonwealth projects with patronage and support throughout her reign. So why this recent run of initiatives in her name? It turns out that since her Diamond Jubilee in 2012, there has been a fresh strategy to reflect her personal dedication to the Commonwealth and its people directly, rather than going through institutions, bureaucracies and governments.

It has been the politicians, not the public, who have caused the greatest problems for the Commonwealth. The Queen wants to lend her name to lean, purposeful organisations and initiatives that do not get bogged down in politics. After all, as we shall see, it has been the

Queen who has been called upon, time and again, to clear up the mess caused by others, to do the healing and the fence-mending.

The writer and broadcaster Andrew Marr has described her as Britain's 'slightly mysterious Department of Friendliness'. It has required a lot more than a smile and innocuous conversation, however. That wise old Commonwealth *consigliere* Sir Sonny Ramphal,* who steered the organisation through its most tempestuous years, talks admiringly of the Queen's 'quiet insistence' when it comes to resolving quarrels within her 'family of nations'.

On several occasions, the Queen has found herself and her loyalties pulled in different directions, not least when it comes to Europe.

David Cameron, who resigned as Prime Minister following Britain's decision to leave the European Union, still believes that, for the Queen, the greater challenge was not Brexit, but Brentry – when Britain was determined to join the European Economic Community (EEC) in the Sixties and Seventies, to the dismay of the Commonwealth realms. 'That would have been much harder,' says Cameron.

Today, Europe might continue to divide Britain. No longer, though, does it drive a wedge between Britain and the Commonwealth, which must be a source of considerable relief to the Head of the Commonwealth. The former Prime Minister of New Zealand, Sir John Key, believes that the Queen has played a crucial part in the way that people in his country have come to terms with a difficult moment in post-war relations with the old 'mother country'. 'They can understand that Britain was doing what's best for Britain at the time,' he says, adding that it was the monarch who prevented a deeper rift between New Zealand and the UK. 'The Queen has been the one consistent voice – and the glue.'

So what are the Queen's own views on Europe? David Cameron says that the Queen remained steadfastly non-committal when he discussed his negotiations with the EU. 'I explained to her every week where we'd got to. She was very sympathetic. I never got the impression that she had a very strong view,' he says. Caution, he believes, would be the default position for the whole Royal Family. 'My sense

* Sonny Ramphal, former Foreign Affairs Minister of Guyana, was Commonwealth Secretary-General from 1975-1990.

is that they are risk averse. I don't think they were ever Heathite Euro-enthusiasts, as it were, because it had been a painful choice,' he says. 'That is the point about Europe. It has always been a painful choice for Britain. We've always been the reluctant member.' Those who confidently place the Queen squarely on a particular side of a polarising issue like Brexit are being short-sighted. They neglect the quiet pragmatism of someone who has remained steadfastly neutral for longer than the vast majority of human beings have been alive, someone who really has seen it all before. In any discussion of the Queen's long reign, the same question is always asked: 'what's she really like?' It is to her great credit that, in her tenth decade, the question is still unanswered.

The former Labour Foreign Secretary, David (now Lord) Owen, praises what he calls her 'courage to be boring'. He says it is fundamental to the separation of powers under a system of constitutional monarchy. 'Everybody likes to be interesting but you have to be disciplined to be boring. You aren't going to get the real person on display at a formal dinner, nor should you.' During his years as a minister, often in attendance on engagements and overseas tours, he saw a different, private side of the Queen. 'It is a really remarkable privilege to have seen her in her own setting and to realise that there is a huge amount to this woman. She'd have got a first-class degree if she'd gone to university, I have no doubt about that.'

In order to assess the Queen's place in the world and her own view of it, as this book aims to do, it is necessary first to appreciate her own perspective.

This is a monarch whose father served in the First World War and who, with her husband, served in the Second. Yet today she meets members of her Armed Forces who were unborn at the turn of the millennium. On her first tour of southern Africa, in 1947, she met the seventy-eight-year-old nephew of the great Victorian explorer, Dr David Livingstone. On her first tour of Australia, the Queen held receptions for Boer War veterans in every city and met a veteran who had served in Sudan in 1885, the year in which General Gordon was killed at Khartoum. On her first tour of Canada, in 1951, she was introduced to Benjamin Mansell, an old soldier of such advanced years that he had been too old for the Boer War. Mansell, of Springfield

Junction, Nova Scotia, had served in Afghanistan during the 1870s and had gone on to meet Queen Victoria, Edward VII, George V and George VI. The Queen must, therefore, be the only person who has heard first-hand accounts of both the Anglo-Afghan War of 1878 and the twenty-first-century Afghan war against the Taliban.

By any measure, her life and reign comprise a vault of experience unrivalled by any world leader. It is one of the reasons that even those who are not royalists by inclination applaud her dedication to duty. 'I'm not a believer in the hereditary principle and I'm not a monarchist,' says Lord Owen. 'But if monarchies suit countries, then have monarchies. Seeing her handle it so brilliantly, you realise it is a huge skill.'

'She was of the generation that saw the Commonwealth grow up,' says Sir Sonny Ramphal, listing many of the founding fathers of post-colonial nations like Tanzania and Zambia. 'They were her age group – and so was I – and I think the Queen grew with the Commonwealth.' He places great significance on the fact that the pivotal moment in the Queen's life – her accession to the Throne – occurred in the heart of Africa, as she visited Treetops in Kenya's newly created Aberdare National Park. 'It made a big impact on the other leaders,' says Ramphal. 'It made it so much easier for her to be a player in their midst. She really became a player at Treetops. She was a child of the Commonwealth too!'

The Princess Royal, who visited the site on her first overseas tour, aged twenty, has always been intrigued by what it was like for her twenty-five-year-old mother to succeed to the Throne in a remote part of Kenya. 'It must have been really weird. What an extraordinarily fundamental environment to be in to be told that your father has died – and what that meant.'

The Cold War was in its infancy, and the Jet Age had only just begun. The Space Age was years off, while the Digital Age had not even occurred to writers of science fiction. Yet the Queen would reign through it all. Of all the changes that have occurred on her watch, says the Princess, one of the most infuriating, from a royal point of view, is the advent of the mobile phone and its ilk. 'I'm glad I'm not starting now because at least you had people to talk to,' she says. 'Now you don't really. Phones are bad enough, but the iPads – you can't even see their heads! You have no idea who you're talking to.' The Princess Royal has a blunt response to people who put a camera in her face: 'I either don't bother or just say: "If you want to meet somebody, I suggest you put that down." It is weird. When you're standing immediately in front of them, it makes it almost impossible to have any kind of chat with them. People don't believe that they've experienced the event unless they've taken a photograph.'

The Queen certainly regrets the way in which technology has erected this new barrier between her and the public, as she told incoming US Ambassador, Matthew Barzun, when he came to the Palace to present his credentials. The new Ambassador mentioned the crowds who had been taking photographs of him as he sat in his top hat being driven through London in the Queen's horse-drawn carriage. As Barzun recalls: 'The Queen said: "There've always been tourists and they always used to have regular cameras. They'd put them up, take a picture and then put them down. Now . . ." – and then she put her hand over her face – "they put these things up and they never take them down. And I miss seeing their eyes." I thought that was just the sweetest thing – she missed their eyes. You think it's a one-way thing, snapping a famous person. But it's a two-way thing. There's a connection and an energy. And technology is getting in the way of that now.'

The Queen is a traditionalist, but she is not a sentimentalist. Her former Prime Minister of New Zealand, Sir John Key, says he once asked her why she still wore formal dress on occasions when there were no crowds or cameras around. 'I am the last bastion of standards,' she replied. It was not doing things for the sake of it, Key realised. It was just part of the job. He explains 'People ask me: "Who was the most impressive person you met?" I say: "The Queen". What you see is what you get. Equally, she really is a tireless worker. When you are prime minister, you work horrendous hours but you are elected to do that. When your time is over, it really is over. It's different. We've got Barack [Obama] coming out for a few weeks and he'll play a bit of golf. We'll have a nice time. For the Queen, it's a lifetime of dedication. It's a lifetime of service.'

Sir John Key remains genuinely astonished by her power of recall, arguing that it proves the Queen does not regard being monarch as a mere job. 'I had lots of discussions over the years with her and her knowledge and understanding goes vastly beyond any briefing note anyone can write for her. There are a million things I can't repeat.

But it's the difference between going through the motions of a job and really having a deep, passionate belief in what you do.'

Those who have worked with the Queen have often talked of her elephantine memory. Republicans and cynics dismiss such talk as oleaginous nonsense. Peter Morgan, the writer of the fictional Netflix series, *The Crown*, echoed the modish agnosticism of some sections of the commentariat in 2017 when he described the Queen as a 'countryside woman with limited intelligence'. No one – least of all the Queen herself – has ever suggested that she is an intellectual. Yet unlike many intellectuals, she has a genuine interest in and innate grasp of what makes other people tick – often more so than her own prime ministers. Sir John Birch, former Ambassador to Hungary, had only met the Queen a couple of times before she arrived in Budapest in 1993 for her first state visit behind the former Iron Curtain. He certainly wasn't expecting what he found, as he told the British Diplomatic Oral History Programme after his retirement: 'She knew a lot about Eastern Europe. It was a rather strange contrast with Mrs Thatcher.' On her visit in 1990, Mrs Thatcher had quizzed him at length about every aspect of post-war communism. 'People say she never listened, she just talked. Actually she did listen. She wanted really to know these things,' says Birch. 'But I was surprised – perhaps a comparison one shouldn't make – between the Queen's knowledge and the Prime Minister's knowledge. On that occasion, and on that subject, the Queen had the edge.'

The Queen likes to remember the past. Yet she does not like to dwell in it, a luxury reserved for those who have retired. And she has no plans to do that – 'unless I get Alzheimer's,' as she told her cousin Margaret Rhodes. As a serving head of state, she wants to live in the present and look to the future. It is why, in later life, the pattern of her engagements has seen a marked shift towards young people, a sentiment that is fully reciprocated. On the first day of her Diamond Jubilee tour of Great Britain, her initial port of call was a university campus in Leicester, where huge student crowds turned out to welcome her. In any speech about the Commonwealth, she likes to remind her audience that the majority of its people are under the age of thirty.

'Everyone can agree she's super-important and someone to aspire to be like,' explains the British-South African celebrity youth 'vlogger' Caspar Lee, during a Buckingham Palace reception for the

Queen's Young Leaders programme. He calls her 'a mother figure to us, somebody who has everything in the world but also gives everything'. Just a few feet away the Queen is discussing the initiative with one of its supporters, the philanthropist Bill Holroyd. 'It's rather exciting. I'm trying to involve the young,' she explains brightly. 'I couldn't think of a better legacy,' says Holroyd. 'They've got wonderful go-ahead ideas,' says the Queen, pointing admiringly at her younger guests. 'Wonderful people who've already done a lot.' Members of the Royal Family and their staff prefer not to use the word 'legacy'. 'Do you go through life trying to make a legacy?' the Duke of Edinburgh told the author in 2005. 'I'd rather other people decided what legacy I'd left. I mean I'm not trying to create one!'

Yet the Queen has always thought about what she will be handing on. Her observations on the first President of independent Ghana, Kwame Nkrumah, were as revealing about her as they were about him. Writing to her friend, Lord Porchester, she said Nkrumah was 'naïve and vainglorious' and 'unable to look beyond his own lifetime'. That was in 1961, when she was barely thirty-five.

In fairness to Nkrumah, looking beyond one's own lifetime comes more naturally when you are the custodian of a thousand-year-old institution whose core purpose is continuity. The first duty of each successor is to ensure a safe handover to the next one. The monarchy has had its wobbles on the Queen's watch, of course. During the darker days of the 1990s, the republican-minded political theorist and commentator Dr Stephen Haseler wrote confidently of the Queen as 'Elizabeth The Last'. By the end of the 2002 Golden Jubilee his argument seemed, at best, eccentric. By the end of the 2012 Diamond Jubilee it was preposterous.

It is why, in recent years, the Queen has appeared as happy as those who know her best can recall. She is the first monarch since Queen Victoria to be able to look three reigns into the future. The Royal Mail stamp to mark her ninetieth birthday featured a delightful shot of the Queen in the White Drawing Room of Buckingham Palace, flanked by the Prince of Wales, the Duke of Cambridge and a beaming two-year-old Prince George, standing on a pile of box files to ensure a level eyeline. It is a scene that exudes permanence.

'She has been there all my life. I can't imagine her not being there. I just can't,' says the actress Dame Maggie Smith (of whom some might say much the same). The *Downton Abbey* star – who regards the Queen as the 'best of Britain' – has joined her at Hampton Court Palace to mark the centenary of the Order of the Companions of Honour. The 'CH' was created by George V for distinguished people who deserved national recognition but did not necessarily want the 'opprobrium of a title'. The current crop of Companions of Honour – who include ex-politicians Sir John Major, George Osborne and Lords Howard, Heseltine and Owen, plus eminent national treasures like Sir David Attenborough, Dame Judi Dench and Lord Coe – join the Queen in the small Chapel Royal for a service of thanksgiving. The address is delivered by the former Bishop of London, Dr Richard Chartres, who reminds his illustrious congregation that 'the order stands not merely for public achievements but for the kind of integrity and unshakeable commitment to principle which comes from obeying a calling beyond our immediate self-interest'. Dr Chartres notes: 'Some members of the order have been household names but this is not an order for celebrities who are well-known for their well-known-ness but for practitioners with a sustained record of service of national importance.' It is pretty clear whom he has in mind. The Queen looks on, utterly expressionless. 'I suppose it's a contradiction in terms but the word that comes to mind is modest,' Sir David Attenborough says afterwards. 'She's not flamboyant.'

These are precisely the qualities that have made this assiduous non-celebrity the most celebrated woman on Earth (one whose face has been reprinted more than that of any person since Jesus Christ, be it on stamps, in the media or via more than thirty currencies in the course of her reign). Thomas Kielinger says that, to the outside world and his German compatriots in particular, she is increasingly Britain's greatest asset. 'She appears to be the last man standing,' he says. 'Everything else seems to be collapsing. Democratic institutions appear to be crumbling. The monarchy suddenly stands tall and that translates into respect for her.'

He says that when the Queen made the first state visit to Germany in 1965, she was seen as the representative of 'a glorious country'. Today, he argues, that is no longer the case; that Britain is now regarded as a diminished, damaged nation, particularly post-Brexit. Yet he is not unduly pessimistic. 'History shows the British always get through these things,' says Kielinger. 'In Germany, we can't live with such uncertainty. We'd have a mental breakdown. You have a maritime mentality.' He quotes Nelson: 'Something must be left to chance; nothing is sure in a sea fight.' What underpins that mentality today, he believes, is a sense of stability personified by the Queen herself.

To most people in Britain, her legacy will be to have led the nation and the monarchy through more change – demographic, social and scientific – than that experienced by any British monarch in history. Globally, however, her legacy will take many forms. To some nations, the Queen has been an old friend. To others, she has been the genuine face of reconciliation. To those emerging from a painful totalitarian past, she has been a symbol of encouragement. To large parts of the old British Empire, however, she has served as a bridge during the transition from subjugation to self-determination and independence. That the vast majority of ex-colonies should choose to remain enthusiastic members of her Commonwealth has been, in no small part, down to her. That it should have survived intact and gone on to do some great things – from the battle against apartheid to the ongoing struggle against avoidable blindness – is to her credit, too.

In 2018, it emerged that some of the smaller nations of the Commonwealth were talking about nominating the Queen for the Nobel Peace Prize. Some would probably dismiss the idea as ludicrous. Others regarded it as original and wholly appropriate, pointing to former Nobel recipients such as US Secretary of State Henry Kissinger, former US Vice-President Al Gore, President Barack Obama (within days of taking office) and the European Union. Nor would the Queen be the first member of the family to be nominated. Princess Anne was once proposed for her work with Save the Children, and Prince Philip for his role in founding the World Wildlife Fund and the Duke of Edinburgh's Award.

The only prizes that the Queen has received to date have been for her horses and livestock – plus a gold disc from the recording industry for CD sales of her Golden Jubilee concert at the Palace. As the 'Fountain of Honour', she sees it as her role to give out awards rather than receive them. Like Alfred Nobel, she has now created a prize of global pre-eminence in one field that Nobel himself overlooked, as he drafted his legacy to the world in 1895. Founded in 2013, the Queen Elizabeth Prize for Engineering recognises 'ground-breaking innovation' that has 'a major impact on humanity', with a cheque for £1 million (30 per cent more than a Nobel Prize). Like the Nobel, it is open to all-comers from all nations.

There are many people all over the world who feel a connection with someone to whom they have no lineal, historical or linguistic connection at all. The notion of her as 'Queen of the World' might seem a tad presumptuous (even un-British) to some of her understated British subjects – and, no doubt, to the subject of this book herself. It is not, though, an idea that originated in Britain. It was inspired by countless conversations and observations all over the globe. It has encountered no resistance whatsoever overseas, merely unsurprised acknowledgement of a sentiment widely held and deeply felt.

In 2015, on the first full day of her fifth state visit to Germany, the Queen and Prince Philip visited the Berlin University of Technology. During her first state visit in 1965 she had instituted an annual address in her name. Now she was back for the fiftieth anniversary of 'The Queen's Lecture'. The university had invited Neil MacGregor, outgoing director of the British Museum and incoming director of Berlin's Humboldt Forum, to deliver it. Moments before he started, there was mild panic at the door. To the delight of both the organisers and British diplomats, the German Chancellor, Angela Merkel, had suddenly arrived unexpectedly. Exasperated by the lack of progress in a meeting to discuss the eurozone crisis, she had bailed out in order to spend a little extra time with the royal visitors. MacGregor gave the packed theatre a witty talk on 'symbols of a nation', exploring shared Anglo-German tastes in pets, politics and gardens, before turning to the ultimate symbol, the Queen herself. What's more, he added, Elizabeth II had now officially entered the German language. MacGregor pointed to the latest edition of *Duden*, the definitive reference work on German grammar. The correct word for a 'queen' had always been '*die Königin*', he said. However, new editions now carry an additional entry: '*die Queen*'. As *Duden* states clearly: 'There is no plural.'

Chapter 1

ON TOUR

'There are no harems in active use . . .'

THE JOURNEY

As duty officer of the day, Lieutenant Jock Slater was keeping a close eye on the movements along the quayside. It was a sultry West African evening. The Royal Yacht *Britannia* was berthed in the Gambian capital, Bathurst, the point at which the Gambia River meets the Atlantic. The Queen was nearing the end of her 1961 tour of West Africa, following a tense trip to newly independent Ghana. Despite bomb threats and the mood-swings of Ghana's President, Kwame Nkrumah, it had turned into a great success. From there, the Queen and the Duke of Edinburgh had sailed on to Sierra Leone and Liberia, where they had been received by President William Tubman, dressed in thick morning coat and black top hat, as he came out to greet them in his own presidential yacht. Finally, *Britannia* had reached Bathurst (today known as Banjul). Spirits were high at the end of a long tour. The Queen had just knighted the captain of *Britannia*, ahead of his impending retirement. A steady stream of dignitaries was arriving for the Queen's farewell dinner before she sailed on to the Senegalese capital of Dakar, and her plane home. Suddenly Slater was approached by a visitor who was definitely not on the guest list, a young boy clutching a biscuit tin with holes in the lid. He explained to Slater that it was a present for the Queen and required a certain amount of care. The lid opened to reveal a baby crocodile. Slater thanked the boy and went to seek the advice of the Queen's omniscient deputy Private Secretary, Martin Charteris. 'Martin instructed me to put it in his bath,' Slater recalls. And there it remained all the way back to Britain, where more suitable accommodation was arranged. As Slater* remembers: 'It became quite a size in London Zoo.'

The records show that the Queen has visited at least 126 nations and territories, many of them several times. No one is entirely sure how many miles she has travelled. The Royal Yacht alone logged more than one million nautical miles during more than four decades at sea, and royal flights have covered many times that distance. The number of countries visited is debatable, too, since many of those states would change their name and status in between visits by the Queen. It is why Buckingham Palace will not produce an official figure.

Southern Rhodesia was a colony when the Queen first visited as a princess in 1947. It was the proud Republic of Zimbabwe when she returned as Queen forty-four years later. The Pakistan that the Queen visited in 1997 was significantly smaller than the one she saw in 1961, much of it having broken away to become Bangladesh – which she also visited in 1983. Of her five state visits to Germany, two were to the former West Germany and three to the Federal Republic. The Caribbean island of Anguilla had gone from being a colony to independence within a federation and then back to colonial status again, by the time the Queen visited in 1994 (and met nearly a quarter of the population in a couple of days). Few things better illustrate the scale of change during this reign than the fact that most of the nations on Earth today have only come into existence since the Queen came to the Throne. Yet she has visited most of them.

In 2017, when the Royal Collection wanted to stage an exhibition marking the Queen's interaction with an ever-changing world over sixty-five years, it chose to do so through the prism of gifts. Even a tiny cross-section of the presents she has received still managed to occupy all the state apartments at Buckingham Palace. Put together,

* He would go on to be an equerry to the Queen and later become Admiral Sir Jock Slater, First Sea Lord and Chief of the Naval Staff. His great-uncle, Admiral of the Fleet Viscount Cunningham of Hyndhope, was Prince Philip's wartime commanding officer at the Battle of Cape Matapan.

they represented a spectacular answer to a question people have been asking themselves since 1952: what do you give the woman who has everything? In the case of Russia's President, Boris Yeltsin, the answer was a silver samovar. Pope Francis settled for a copy of a seventeenth-century decree canonising King Edward the Confessor. In 2012, the people of the Marshall Islands in the Pacific decided that the Queen should receive a Jackie Kennedy-style Kili handbag, made entirely of coconut leaves. Six decades earlier, the Girl Guides of New Zealand had given her a giant jigsaw puzzle of New Zealand, along with a delightful book inscribed with a handwritten message from every single Girl Guide. On her travels through Africa the Queen has often received seats – the concept of the Throne is by no means unique to Britain – including an intricate beaded stool from Kenya and a brightly painted kitchen-style chair, her seat for the 2007 Commonwealth meeting in Uganda.

The world, and in particular the Commonwealth, has been extremely generous, with the result that the Queen has a very personal selection of 'E II R' Crown jewels in addition to the inherited collection. They include the 'Flame Lily' brooch that she received as a Princess from the children of Southern Rhodesia in 1947, the 203-carat Andamooka Opal given to her by Australia in 1954, the golden porcupine brooch presented by the King of the Ashanti in 1961 and the exquisite sapphire-and-diamond snowflake that she received from the people of Canada in 2017. Be it the engraved glass cup that the Queen received on her first state visit to the USA in 1957, or the gold camels resting beneath silver palm trees hung with amethyst dates that she received from a Saudi prince in 1997, or a stunning portrait of herself in Rwandan banana leaves, every last gift has been logged and noted and put somewhere safe for future generations. Perhaps, one day, someone will put them all in a museum dedicated to the longest reign in British history.

There are plenty of gifts that have never made it through the doors of Buckingham Palace. That baby crocodile in a biscuit tin was by no means the most exotic. In 1968, during her state visit to Brazil, the Queen was given two jaguars, Marquis and Aizita. In 1972, President Ahidjo of Cameroon gave her an elephant. Like the jaguars and the crocodile, it went to London Zoo. Sadly, not all these kind gestures would have happy endings. The Princess Royal remembers receiving two gazelles in Djibouti. 'That was a tragic story. There are sometimes things that you really don't want to be given,' she says. 'No cloven-footed animals have been imported from the Horn of Africa for over forty years. And they turned up at London airport where they were very nearly shot on the runway. We persuaded Air France to take them back to Paris. They passed through the zoo and ended up finally back in the game park in Nairobi but they didn't last very long, I'm afraid.' The Princess now leaves any living gifts *in situ*. 'I've got, I think, three Mongolian horses – but they're still in Mongolia, fortunately.'

When the Queen was given a pair of trumpeter swans in Canada in 1956, she presented them to Sir Peter Scott's bird sanctuary in Gloucestershire. Few countries have been as generous or thoughtful as Canada, but then she has visited it more often than any other country outside Britain. Her much-loved mare Burmese was a gift from the Royal Canadian Mounted Police.*

It was also in Canada that the Queen was presented with the largest gift she has ever received (not including 170,000 square miles of Antarctica, renamed Queen Elizabeth Land in her honour). It is a 12-ton, 100-foot totem pole from the Chief of the Kwakiutl people, to mark British Columbia's centenary in 1958. After it was presented to the Queen, it embarked on a long journey by ship down the Pacific coast, through the Panama Canal and across the Atlantic. A barge took it some of the way up the Thames, before two lorries moving at walking speed deposited it in Windsor Great Park. There the Royal Engineers were given the task of erecting it, 4,600 miles from its birthplace. The pole's sacred status means that only a relative of the original creator may conduct maintenance work on it, as happened in the spring of 2018. Fearing that other provinces might feel compelled to come up with something even larger, the Palace issued some gentle guidance, ahead of the Queen's next visit to Canada. In future, said her officials, she would be happier if any larger gifts could be translated into endowments for scholarships. The Queen Elizabeth II Canadian Research Fund has been going strong ever since. The basic human urge to present a powerful and important visitor with a present has never changed.

* When Burmese retired in 1986, the Queen gave up riding at her Birthday Parade. Thereafter she would travel to Trooping the Colour in a phaeton from the Royal Mews.

No monarch – perhaps no world leader – has seen as much of the planet and its peoples as Queen Elizabeth II. From the earliest days of her reign to her latest overseas visit, less than six months before her ninetieth birthday, every trip has had its own unexpected challenges and pleasures. The objectives and priorities have changed from year to year. The Foreign Office mandarins who thought it would be a good idea for the Queen to befriend autocrats, or invite Idi Amin to lunch, or go tiger-hunting in Nepal have long since retired or moved on to an eternal embassy in the hereafter. To view newsreel footage or diplomatic files chronicling some of her earlier travels is to view a world and a mindset that sometimes seem more in tune with Edwardian thinking than the present day. Yet so much else has a strikingly contemporary feel. As the years progress, so the people around the Queen get younger, her Commonwealth grows larger and the fascination with her grows exponentially.

The core business of international monarchy has not changed one bit. With a handful of exceptions that can be counted in single figures – all of them connected to racehorses – the Queen has never travelled overseas for pleasure. Other members of the Royal Family, from Queen Victoria to Prince William and Prince Harry, might have enjoyed the idea of a foreign holiday. For the Queen, holidays have always been synonymous with Scotland. Abroad equals duty. She has also welcomed more fellow heads of state and other world leaders to Britain than anyone, too. Of course much of this is down to longevity – and to Sir Frank Whittle's invention of the jet engine. It is also down to the sheer pulling power of a world leader who has been doing the same job in very much the same way since before most people were born; and who continues to do so, with the support of her son and heir and the rest of her family, very happily. So how does this constant presence continue to engage with an ever-changing world and its people?

THE DESTINATION

Long before any visit is ever decided, a discreet group of some of the most senior public servants in the land will have assembled in a Foreign and Commonwealth Office (FCO) conference room for the quarterly meeting of the Royal Visits Committee. Chaired by the head of the Diplomatic Service, the Permanent Under-Secretary, it also includes the Private Secretaries to the Queen, the Prince of Wales and the Duke of Cambridge. There, too, is the Vice-Marshal of the Diplomatic Corps, otherwise known as the Director of Protocol, who acts as the intermediary between the Palace and the Foreign Office. Sir Roger du Boulay, himself a former Vice-Marshal, recalls that in the Seventies the committee also involved the two supreme mandarins, the Cabinet Secretary and the Head of the Civil Service. It has to be a balancing act between the demands of the British government, with its UK-centric focus, and the expectations of the Queen's fifteen other realms. Little thought is given to where the Royal Family might actually *want* to go. However, the committee still needs to be aware of anywhere they are *not* keen to visit.

'We started with British foreign policy: where did we want to go, and in what order?' says Sir Roger. Ahead of these meetings, the Foreign & Commonwealth Office would assemble its own internal committee to work out which leaders might be appropriate as either a host or guest of the Queen and her family. Even at the height of the Cold War, it transpires that Margaret Thatcher's government was pondering the idea of sending the Queen behind the Iron Curtain. Minutes of the FCO's sub-committee meeting in October 1979 show that the Royal Visits Committee was exploring royal tours of 'China, the USSR and Eastern Europe'. The FCO wanted to invite the Soviet leader, Leonid Brezhnev, for a state visit in 1982 or 1983, and that would have required a reciprocal visit by the Queen. Having just entertained the loathsome Romanian dictator, Nicolae Ceausescu, it seems that the Queen was not wildly keen on going to the Eastern Bloc. 'The main problem lay with the USSR,' it was noted. 'The Queen was unlikely to want to go there, although she wanted to go to China.'*

Forthcoming trips to Italy, Norway and Sweden were on the cards in 1979, but a long-standing proposal to send the Queen to Egypt was dropped as 'too controversial'. Perhaps that would explain why the Prince and Princess of Wales were asked to incorporate a dinner with President Sadat into their honeymoon plans two years later.

In terms of royal guests, President Portillo of Mexico was a front-runner, while President Marcos of the Philippines was among a list of

* Seven years later the Queen would get her wish and would visit China. She would successfully avoid the Eastern Bloc countries until after the collapse of communism.

possible reserves. It was then decided that, on balance, he should drop back down the list until at least 1982, not because of his kleptomania or his autocratic rule or his human-rights record, but 'because of the instability of his regime'. In any event, Marcos would be gone by 1986 without ever enjoying a state visit.

As for a proposed visit by the thirty-ninth US President, Jimmy Carter, it was decided not to make any firm plans until after the upcoming US presidential election. 'Any visit by the President can always be arranged on an "ad hoc" basis,' the committee concluded. Planning a US state visit would turn out to be somewhat more problematic by the time the forty-fifth President, Donald Trump, began his administration in 2017.

Over the years, financial imperatives would start to be of greater importance when planning trips. Today, the Royal Visits Committee also includes the Keeper of the Privy Purse, with responsibility for royal finances, and the chief executive of UK Trade and Investment. Where possible, royal trips must pay their way – commercially as well as politically. 'They are an important diplomatic asset, so therefore I saw it as my responsibility to make the best possible diplomatic use,' says Sir Simon Fraser, who was head of the Diplomatic Service from 2010 to 2015. 'In particular I was very keen to link it to the agenda of the time, which was about the post-economic crisis and international economic relationships. Clearly, for state visits, you have to look for things that are materially adding political and diplomatic value and not just maturing a friendship.'

Following the economic crash of 2008, there was a heavy emphasis on the Gulf, China, Indonesia and Mexico. Once the Queen had decided to curtail long-haul travel, at the time of her 2012 Diamond Jubilee, it was a case of inviting long-haul heads of state from faraway countries to visit her in London. She would then make short-haul state visits to places like Germany, Italy and France, while other members of the family ensured a regular royal presence in realms like Australia, Canada and New Zealand. None of this happens without the closest consultation at the very top. The Queen would be constitutionally obliged to visit Timbuktu*, if her Prime Minister

* Though the Queen has never made it to Mali or its famously remote regional capital, Timbuktu, she has visited the neighbouring states of Senegal and Algeria.

advised her to do so, but her governments have, with some exceptions, ensured that the Queen visits – or is visited by – people she actually wants to see.

Every world leader, says David Cameron, is delighted to see her, especially if things are not going too well on the home front. He points to the way in which France's President François Hollande arranged several events marking the seventieth anniversary of D-Day, in 2014, around the Queen, even hosting the main international ceremony in what had been the British sector in June 1944. 'If you are suffering, like President Hollande was suffering, what is better than sitting with the Queen on Sword Beach? They did it very well.' On those occasions, Cameron explains, the Royal Family are in much greater demand than UK politicians anyway. 'God, they throw themselves into it. There were royals everywhere,' he says. 'I went home before they had finished.'

THE INVITATION

Before the Queen can go anywhere, she requires an invitation. She has never travelled anywhere unless asked. Acceptances would not always be straightforward, either. It was all very well saying that the Queen would be happy to visit Country A, but its neighbour, Country B, might be deeply offended that it was being overlooked. So the leader of Country B might require an invitation to visit London at a later date, perhaps, or an assurance of a visit by the Prince of Wales. When Kenya fell off the list of the Queen's African destinations in 1979, it was no surprise that President Moi of Kenya found himself riding down the Mall in a carriage with the Queen a few months later. In 1996, according to a telegram from the British Ambassador in Bangkok, the King of Thailand was not only thrilled that the Queen was paying him a state visit in his fiftieth year on the Throne, but regarded it as a 'special honour' that she was not going anywhere else. Every detail of every visit would be scrutinised by protocol pathologists for the tiniest indication of either preferment or a snub.

If the Queen was due to visit multiple countries on the same tour, there would be diplomatic jostling for position. Long before any formal announcement about the Queen's 1968 tour of South America – the first there by any reigning monarch – there was turmoil in

British embassies across the entire continent when confidential plans were circulated. The Queen, it transpired, would visit Brazil and Chile. Chile was a little upset to discover that it would not be the Queen's only destination. As the British Ambassador, Frederick Mason, informed his bosses, President Frei 'appeared to think that the visit would be Chile only'. If President Frei was miffed to learn that Brazil was also included, he was even more displeased to learn that Brazil would also be the first port of call. The Brazilian Foreign Minister had been adamant that his country had to come first or else the visit to Brazil would be seen as an 'appendage' to a visit to Chile.

Chilean rivalry with Brazil was the least of the Foreign Office's worries. Internal documents show that there had also been considerable pressure on the Foreign Office to include Argentina in the trip, not least from the Duke of Edinburgh, who had recently been there himself. Though he had been a target of nationalist anger against British ownership of the Falkland Islands – shots had been fired at the British Embassy residence, and someone had tried to pelt him with fruit – he was still keen to return. The Queen's Private Secretary, Martin Charteris, wrote to the head of the Diplomatic Service, Sir Paul Gore-Booth, saying that the Duke feared that omitting Buenos Aires from the tour 'could be taken very much amiss by the Argentinians'. As Sir Michael Creswell, British Ambassador to Buenos Aires, put it, if the Queen did not go to Argentina, it would be regarded as 'a gratuitous snub and evidence of ill-will'.

No details of the tour had yet been made public. The Queen's view was that sensitive travel plans should be under wraps for as long as possible, though Gore-Booth was wary of such a delay. 'The risk of a leakage among some excited Latins would be considerable,' he warned in an internal Foreign Office memo.

When news of the tour was finally released in April 1968, there was a compromise over Argentina. A visit there was still a 'possibility'. This, in turn, created new problems. The British Ambassador in Montevideo wrote to his masters warning that Uruguay was 'deeply disappointed' to learn of a possible visit to its larger neighbour, but not to Uruguay itself. The Foreign Office duly issued instructions to all the other British embassies in South America on what to say when affronted presidents and dictators started asking them why the Queen was not visiting their particular country.

In May, John Beith, Assistant Under-Secretary at the Foreign Office, wrote to Creswell, the Ambassador in Buenos Aires, with word from the Palace. The Queen could not possibly go to Argentina without also visiting her British subjects in the Falkland Islands. Creswell was appalled. Out of the question, he harrumphed to London the following day. The Argentinians, he warned, would regard such a move as an 'unbelievably clumsy step or else, more probably, as deliberately provocative'. If the Queen set foot on her islands, 'it would have a lastingly harmful effect on our relations and trade with this country'. The files show that Creswell was already busy trying to negotiate a memorandum of understanding with Argentina, as the first step towards sharing or even surrendering British sovereignty of the Falkland Islands. Since he was doing so behind the backs of the islanders, he argued, they were bound to be furious when they found out. This would have the 'most undesirable consequences' for any visit by the Queen and would embroil her in a politically embarrassing situation. Writing to Gore-Booth on 22nd May, the Queen's Private Secretary, Sir Michael Adeane, said that he had discussed it all with her and she had very clear views on the matter. It would be 'inexpedient' to visit the Falkland Islands, wrote Adeane, 'without also going to the Argentine'. He went on: 'From the point of view of opinion in this country, it would be even worse to visit [the] Argentine and not the Falkland Islands.'

On top of all this, there were some serious practical problems, too. The islands lacked a runway suitable for a royal flight, which would mean 'a good deal of probably rough sea travel' in the Royal Yacht, and the Queen would not be home until 30th November. 'This would create various administrative difficulties which, though not insurmountable, would be awkward,' wrote Adeane, noting that the biggest indoor event in the Palace calendar, the Diplomatic Reception, had already been arranged for 28th November. For all these reasons, Adeane concluded, 'The Queen is not prepared to undertake a visit to the Falkland Islands by sea.' In which case, Argentina was out of the question, too.

The grumbling continued for weeks afterwards. 'By advising the Queen not to visit the Falklands, the Government acts disgracefully,' thundered the *Daily Express*, beneath the headline 'Do Not Betray Them'. It went on: 'There should be no thought of the Queen visiting that part of the world without receiving the homage of 2,000

Falkland Islanders. It matters not at all if the Argentinos [*sic*] object.' In reality, the Queen had dodged an insoluble diplomatic problem by cleverly blaming logistical issues.

THE 'RECCE'

The next phase of any visit would be the reconnaissance or 'recce' mission by a small cross-section of the Royal Household. Leading the team would be one of the Queen's three Private Secretaries, her trio of senior advisers, at least one of whom is in attendance every day of the year, anywhere in the world. Some might have been drawn from the Civil Service, the Foreign Office or business. Several have been promoted from within the Palace press office. It is a job that requires the skill set of a diplomat, a constitutional lawyer, a public-relations executive, a charity worker and a drill sergeant – plus a touch of Jeeves. 'It is no use thinking you are a mandarin. You are also a nanny,' Sir Michael Adeane, a former principal Private Secretary, once explained, with typical private-secretarial modesty. 'One moment you may be writing to the PM. The next, you are carrying a small boy's mac.' The Private Secretary might be trying to work out the right blend of civic worthies, good causes and youth for the Queen's away-day to Manchester, while also juggling fifteen different governments, in addition to the British one. It is the Private Secretary who is the direct conduit between the Queen and all her realms. If a government does something of which the Queen heartily disapproves – like Tony Blair's attempt to abolish the position of Lord Chancellor in 2003 – it is the Private Secretary who will contact his or her opposite number in government and try to head off trouble. It will all be done as discreetly as possible. The Private Secretary's ultimate role in all things is to be an unobtrusive lubricant.

Ahead of each recce, the Private Secretary would already have received a suggested itinerary from the host government. If it was a state visit to a foreign country, the British Ambassador or High Commissioner* would have been closely involved. If it was a visit to a

* An ambassador from one Commonwealth country to another is called a High Commissioner.

realm, things were rather more straightforward. The Palace could deal directly with the host government via the Queen's representative, the Governor-General. This would usually involve officials whom the Queen's staff knew well. Sir William 'Bill' Heseltine, who originally joined the Palace from the Australian Civil Service and became the Queen's principal Private Secretary, recalls the very different atmosphere in somewhere like the Fijian capital, Suva, in the days when this was still a realm. 'Fiji had begun to feel like home to me,' he says, explaining that everyone from the long-serving Prime Minister, Ratu Mara, to the Lord Mayor and the editor of *The Fiji Times* had become old friends.

Wherever the trip was heading, the Queen and the Duke would have a good look at the schedule in its early stages and make appropriate comments. So, for example, when the Queen and Prince Philip were planning their tour of Africa in 1979, the Zambian government had been keen to include an ambitious safari on the only 'rest' day on the entire itinerary. As the Private Secretary in charge of that particular trip, Bill Heseltine was deputed to pass on his boss's hopes for a 'rest' day that was precisely that. 'I said that neither Her Majesty nor His Royal Highness had any particular wish to go out in search of wildlife but would be content to spend a restful day in pleasant surroundings, without the attentions, however well intended, of their hosts,' he says.

As the years progressed and the Queen grew a little older, Heseltine would try to build more gaps into the schedule, though he found that she was not always keen on the idea. 'I often tried in my latter days to make programmes a bit lighter,' he explains. 'But both the Queen and the Duke felt that it was preferable to go full steam ahead for however long was required, and get back to Windsor, or Sandringham or Balmoral for a few days off to relax and recover, than to try and do this in the middle of a long visit. We quite often did insert a day or two without engagements in the course of a long tour but I think both of the principals thought that it was better to press on and get home.'

Along with a Private Secretary, the 'recce' team would also include a police officer and a press officer, who would need to map out every step of the itinerary from their own perspectives. The Queen's equerry would often be asked to attend, too. A promising youngish officer chosen from one of the three Services in rotation, the equerry would be in uniform alongside the Queen throughout the visit, as an extra pair of eyes, ears and – more often – hands, receiving and logging gifts, checking on timings and clearing a path through the crowds. Sir Jock Slater, who would serve as equerry from 1968 to 1971, recalls being sent to check arrangements ahead of the Queen's 1969 trip to Norway. She was due to travel there in the Royal Yacht, stopping off in the Shetland Isles, where she was to inspect an exhibition of local products. Scrupulously going over every detail, Slater asked about the arrangements for a gift presentation at which the Duke of Edinburgh was to be given a pair of shooting stockings. He was even introduced to the elderly woman who was still knitting the royal gift and who was anxious to know at which point she was supposed to present the results. Slater promised her that he would give her a wink at the appropriate moment, and duly made a note to do so. Come the day, he did exactly that. 'Before I could stop her,' he recalls, 'she shuffled up to Prince Philip and, in a loud voice, said: "Here's your socks!"'

If the Queen was likely to be entertaining, as she usually was, then the recce team would also include a senior member of the Master of the Royal Household's department, if not the Queen's chef, to check on everything from cooking facilities to crockery and the water supply. The Palace team would usually be welcomed with open arms by any ambassador nervously awaiting the arrival of the ultimate boss. 'They were full of good ideas,' says Sir Francis Richards, High Commissioner to Namibia when the Queen paid her first (and, thus far, only) visit to the country in 1991. What might seem a relatively straightforward event – like a garden party on the High Commission lawn – could suddenly morph into a protocol minefield when it included the Queen. Even crowd control could be an issue. 'The Palace had lots of answers,' Richards recalls, 'like putting two lines of whitewashed stones through the grounds to create a pathway for the Queen. Brilliant.'

THE LOGISTICS

Ask any ambassador or high commissioner who has hosted the monarch about the trickier aspects of the visit, and guest lists always feature prominently. Having served in various capacities from Moscow to Gibraltar (where he was Governor), Sir Francis Richards is a firm believer in what he calls 'Richards's law' of royal visits. 'It's very simple. The number of people you offend is always double the number of those you invite to things,' he explains, 'so you try not to invite the wrong people.'

Ahead of that state visit to Namibia, Richards would have to explain, as diplomatically as possible, that the Queen did not like to travel in the same way as some other heads of state. The Namibian President, Sam Nujoma, and his staff had already ordered a ring of anti-aircraft defences to be installed around the capital, Windhoek, for the Queen's seventy-two-hour stay. The Namibians had also assumed that speed was of the essence, when it came to royal travel. 'Their plan was to have the Queen brought in to town at 100 mph with outriders zig-zagging in front. I had to explain that the Queen wouldn't like that,' says Richards. 'So I went with them to the racecourse to agree the right sort of convoy speed.' On most tours, the Queen would make a point of asking the police escorts to stay fore and aft, but not alongside her car, on the basis that any crowds lining the street were probably there to catch a glimpse of her and not to look at motorbikes.

Of greater importance was the way in which the Queen would travel from Britain to the host country. As the only G7 head of state without her own dedicated aircraft, the Queen has relied on the Royal Air Force or the charter market for most of her overseas trips. In recent years, until David Cameron designated a multi-purpose RAF Voyager aircraft for government and royal VIP use in 2014, the Palace would charter a variety of British Airways airliners, depending on the distance and the size of the royal party. Throughout the reign the entourage has been around thirty-five for a typical state visit, including the Foreign Secretary, two ladies-in-waiting, two Private Secretaries, an equerry, a doctor, a press office team, four police officers, the Queen's dresser, the Duke of Edinburgh's valet, a hairdresser, several secretaries (previously known as 'lady clerks'), plus a page or two and a handful of luggage orderlies. That might rise if the Queen was going to be entertaining on a major scale, as she might at a Commonwealth summit, and did not have the Royal Yacht at her disposal. In which case, the entourage might top fifty, with footmen and chefs at the back of the plane, too.

Even a chartered airliner with room for 150 could look full, by the time uniforms, gifts and commemorative poppy wreaths had started to fill the seats. As well as reconfiguring the layout to give the Queen and the Duke some extra space, any chartered plane would require two extra items: a full-length mirror and a St Christopher's medallion. The Queen is famously stoical about the inherent dangers of royal life—keeping motorcades to a minimum; refusing to budge from Buckingham Palace when informed of a possible terrorist mortar attack; nonchalantly responding to a lump of concrete, being dropped on her car with the remark: 'It's a strong car'. However, she has never been a great fan of air travel. If St Christopher, the patron saint of travellers, can afford any extra protection, then so much the better. The photographer, Reginald Davis, who covered many of the Queen's tours in the earlier years of her reign, well remembers discussing it with her at a reception. 'I'm never relaxed flying,' she told him. She has always been particularly wary of helicopters, despite the fact that two sons and two grandsons (Princes Charles, Andrew, William and Harry) have all served as professional helicopter pilots. It was only after twenty-five years on the Throne that she finally climbed into a helicopter and, even then, without any great enthusiasm. Security considerations during her Silver Jubilee meant that it was the safest way of getting to and from Northern Ireland at a time when the terrorist threat was grave. Today, she is a regular user of the Sikorsky helicopter leased by the Royal Household for general royal use. Even so, she tries not to use it between October and March when fog, mist and bad light are more common. The monarch who stole the show and wowed billions at the opening of the 2012 London Olympics by 'jumping' out of a helicopter with James Bond much prefers fixed-wing aviation.

For much of the reign, she preferred to travel in a trusty Vickers VC10, either from the Royal Air Force's Air Support Command or from BOAC (the state-owned precursor to British Airways), stopping off every 2,000–3,000 miles to refuel. The RAF operation manual for Royal Flight 1007, for the 1972 state visit to France, shows a typical layout. The Queen and Prince Philip had the front quarter of the RAF VC10 Mk 1, with a C-shaped sofa on the starboard side and a four-seat dining table to port, plus a galley and bar and screened-off fold-out beds on either side of the aisle. The 'VIP' toilet, just behind the cockpit, was twice the size of the adjacent 'crew' toilet. The largest compartment on the aircraft was the royal 'dressing room', sealed off behind a curtain. To the rear of the royal quarters were thirty-eight rear-facing seats for royal staff and air crew, including a smaller dressing room.

Though her trip to Paris was a short daytime flight of no more than an hour, the RAF inventory included 'VIP china, glassware, linen napkins, tablecloths' and a 'comprehensive' bar. Although this was to include whisky, gin, brandy, vodka, sherry, sweet and dry Martini, beer and cigarettes, plus mixers including Angostura Bitters, bitter lemon, tonic and Worcestershire sauce, there was not a drop of wine on board, let alone a glass of champagne. Perhaps it was felt surplus to requirements on a trip to France.

At the start of her reign, the emphasis was very much on long tours of British colonies and Commonwealth realms or protectorates. In her first three years on the Throne, the Queen would spend nearly six months in her own territories and just six days in non-Commonwealth countries (three of them with Britain's old friend, the King of Norway). Commonwealth republics like India, however, had to wait nine years before they received a visit. There was a marked upturn in royal attention towards European nations in the run-up to Britain's various attempts to join the Common Market. As the reign progressed and jet engines improved, tours and journey times became considerably shorter. The Queen's return from Australia in 1970, for example, would involve just over twenty-six hours of flying time in a BOAC Super VC10, with an extra three hours on the ground at four different refuelling stops. The BOAC flight details show that the Queen flew for four hours from Sydney to Nandi (during which dinner was served: smoked salmon, steak and Neapolitan cassata), six hours and twenty minutes from Nandi to Honolulu (a late supper of cold duckling and orange salad), five hours and twenty-five minutes from Honolulu to Vancouver (with a full English breakfast), six hours and twenty minutes from Vancouver to Gander (during which lunch became afternoon tea, followed by a dinner of Canadian salmon mayonnaise and veal Marsala) and finally four hours and forty-five minutes from Gander to London (with another cooked breakfast). Unlike the trip to France, a wine list was included: a 1967 Chablis, a 1964 Château Mouton and Mumm Cordon Rouge throughout.

It is unlikely, though, that the Queen will have consumed very much of anything. A firm believer in the philosophy of all things in moderation, she would always be abstemious on a long tour packed with official lunches and dinners. Frank Judd* was the Foreign Office minister accompanying the Queen for the latter part of her 1979 tour of the Middle East. Flying home on the royal plane (a chartered British Airways jet), he was delighted to be invited to join the Queen for dinner. 'The plane was divided up with a sort of business class for officials and a special sealed off-part for the Queen,' he recalls. 'There were six of us round the table there. British Airways had really bust a gut and produced this magnificent menu and we were all looking at it. The Queen looked round the table, smiled disarmingly at us and said: "After all that hospitality on this trip, I am having one course!" We had to do the same.'

Some tours could indeed become an ordeal by gluttony. Sir William Heseltine remembers the voyage home in the Royal Yacht after the 1972 state visit to France. 'President Pompidou and Sir Christopher Soames [the British Ambassador] were both vying to make it the success of the century. Both were gourmets and were absolutely determined to outdo each other in the splendour of the meals. As we left, I remember saying to the Queen: "Do you mind if I don't come to dinner?" I couldn't eat another bite. I couldn't face it.'

THE BRIEFING

As all the politicians and diplomats who have accompanied the Queen on her travels are aware, she does her homework. The former Foreign Secretary, Jack Straw, learned that when he accompanied the Queen to Lagos in 2003. 'On my way to Nigeria, I had lunch with the Queen, the Duke and the doctor on the plane,' he says. 'She was very well-briefed and I knew that I needed to be very well-briefed. It was not that she'd try to catch you out, but you had to have a base of knowledge. We talked about developments in Nigeria and the fact that it is divided into the Muslim North and Christian South – a direct legacy of empire.'

* A Labour MP for thirteen years and a minister in the governments of Harold Wilson and Jim Callaghan, Frank Judd was later director of Oxfam and was made a peer in 1991.

He noticed that the Queen had spent much of the flight working her way through a thick ring-binder file with a labelled finger-index. 'It was just for her and she read it,' says Straw. These manuals would usually include the nuts and bolts of particular engagements, including timings (to the nearest second). They would also be leavened by the personality notes compiled by the FCO. In the days before emails and instant leakage, the FCO authors did not hold back. Of an early Zimbabwean Foreign Affairs Minister, Dr the Hon. Witness Mangwende, the FCO notes observed: 'A bad foreign minister. He probably owes his position to personal connections. A large, bluff man of limited intelligence and a ponderous sense of humour. His world view is one of knee-jerk "anti-imperialism" notably anti-Americanism. Suspicious of Britain. Identifies almost unthinkingly with almost all radical causes. Intelligent and attractive wife, Elen.'

A set of briefing notes ahead of the 1979 Commonwealth summit in Lusaka reads like a cast of characters from a soap opera. There was the African Cabinet minister who 'divides his time between his office and his mineral water factory ... fond of la dolce vita, his excitable and probably xenophobic personality make him less than pleasant company. His present wife is a schemer'; the Malaysian foreign minister – 'he is friendly, likeable and honest with the mannerisms of an English country squire. One son at Cheltenham, one daughter at Benenden'; and a certain Cabinet minister from Papua New Guinea who 'has a drink problem which gives rise to appalling behaviour. This is often overlooked in PNG.'

Many entries could be as revealing about the mindset of the author as that of the subject. Ahead of the 1971 state visit to Turkey, the Queen's host, President Cevdet Sunay, was described as a 'soldier of the old school; efficient; loyal; solid and unimaginative; underlying warmth of personality and pawky [*sic*] sense of humour which can emerge attractively ... an intelligent interest in international affairs ... much less of a backwoodsman than he looks'.

As well as enjoying her pre-tour briefing notes, the Queen would be even more interested in a list of 'Topics to be avoided'. 'She found that they would often get a good conversation going,' says a former Private Secretary. In the case of Turkey, for example, the Foreign Office files show that the following were no-go areas in 1971:

'Minorities. In particular, there are no Kurds in Turkey as far as the Turks are concerned. There are perhaps people (3 million) of 'rather special origin' in the extreme south east but they are 'Turks' . . .
Turkish antiquities.
British Occupation of Istanbul after the First World War. Mention of President Sunay's time as a British prisoner of war should also probably be avoided unless he brings it up . . .
Islamic Turkey. There are strict laws against religious propaganda . . . Turkey's civil law allows only one wife and outlaws the turban and the fez.
Cyprus.
Place names: Istanbul – never Constantinople.
The Turks are not Arabs.
There are no harems in active use . . .'

Jack Straw was already familiar with what he calls the Queen's 'encyclopaedic knowledge' of places and people. During his days as Home Secretary, he had been formally required to attend her swearing-in of bishops and had been astonished by her capacity to recall diocesan minutiae. Now, as Foreign Secretary, he was seeing it all over again. On that 2003 visit to Nigeria, the Queen's briefing notes reminded her that she had been presented with a bouquet of flowers by a nine-year-old princess on her first visit in 1957. The same princess was to be re-presented to her again. 'She remembered her!' says Straw.

The Queen also enjoyed tossing the odd question in the direction of Prince Philip, who would usually be immersed in a book or paperwork. Sometimes she was just being mischievous. Former Foreign Secretary Sir Malcolm Rifkind recalls travelling to Prague alongside the Queen and the Duke in 1996, when a member of the RAF crew handed them a copy of the flight path. 'Philip,' murmured the Queen, 'what's this place – Praha?' 'It's Prague,' the Duke retorted. 'Why don't they call it Prague?' the Queen went on. 'It's like "Paree" and "Paris",' said the Duke, immersed in his book. Rifkind wasn't sure where to look. 'My wife and I were pretending we couldn't hear but it was like Monty Python,' he chuckles. 'I think the Queen was having some fun. She is far too bright to be remotely puzzled as to why it's called "Praha".'

The Queen would also use these opportunities to pick up extra nuggets of information, which she might not be receiving from her Prime Minister. 'There was a feeling that you must be careful not to interfere with the Prime Minister's audiences but she was always wanting to talk, especially on plane trips. That's the best time to talk to her,' says David Owen, her Foreign Secretary in the late Seventies.

MAKING AN ENTRANCE

Once on the ground, the Queen would usually be greeted by her ambassador for a short series of introductions along the red carpet at the airport. Most heads of state, including the Queen herself, prefer to lay on a formal state welcome somewhere more telegenic and atmospheric than an airport – be it the White House lawn in Washington or the Quirinale in Rome. Some, like King Bhumibol of Thailand, liked to do both. When the Queen arrived on her state visit in 1996, he and his family travelled to greet the Queen and Duke at the airport. There was momentary embarrassment when the chartered British Airways 767 overshot the red carpet and clipped the steps. The two royal families then drove at speed through Bangkok in one of the longest motorcades the Queen had ever seen, comprising more than fifty vehicles, many of them Rolls-Royces in the Thai royal livery (yellow), to another welcome ceremony.

As the years progressed, these grand arrivals would become more demanding for the monarch. When the Queen first visited Thailand in 1972, she arrived on board the Royal Yacht at the start of a relatively leisurely six-week tour of South East Asia. Jet lag was a minor concern. In 1996, the year of her seventieth birthday, and having just crossed seven time zones, the Queen had to hit the ground running. Within hours of landing she was at a state banquet, saluting the Golden Jubilee of a monarch whom she addressed as 'my brother'. It was the same form of address with which Queen Victoria had addressed King Bhumibol's forebear, King Rama IV. If there were moments of fatigue, she could perhaps reflect on her own good fortune compared to that of her fellow monarch. Bhumibol had reigned through seventeen military coups, twenty-one prime ministers and fifteen different constitutions since acceding to the Throne half a century earlier, following the mysterious death of his elder brother ('whether by murder, accident or suicide has never been finally established,' noted a Foreign Office internal assessment).

Day One would be a test of all the main requirements of every tour: speech-writing, gift-giving, providing the media with something to report, and the royal wardrobe. Not for nothing did that royal VC10 have such a large changing area. Newcomers to the Royal Household are always taken aback by the number of times a change of clothes can be required on official duties. Dame Margaret Beckett, Britain's first female Foreign Secretary, remembers when she and her husband, Leo, found themselves on a plane with the Queen and the Duke for the first time. 'What I hadn't expected was that we were up at the front of the plane,' she recalls. 'My husband was impressed by the speed with which the Queen changes outfit. There's this place at the end of the plane and she disappears in to it and – zip-zip-zip – out she reappears in a completely different outfit for a different event.'

During the Thai tour, in 95-degree heat, the Queen would appear in at least four different outfits in the course of a day, all of them chosen with the help of her dresser, Angela Kelly. The Queen's dresser has always been a figure of considerable power and influence at the court of Elizabeth II. From her earliest years, Princess Elizabeth was devoted to Bobo MacDonald, the Scottish farmer's daughter who shared a room with her as a baby and grew up to share her confidences throughout her life. When the Princess went on her honeymoon, she also took her corgi, Susan, and Bobo with her. 'Look after the Princess for me, Bobo,' King George VI had whispered as he waved his daughter off for the last time in 1952. Bobo could tell the Queen things that no one else – with the possible exception of Prince Philip – would dare to raise. New royal staff would be warned: 'Don't upset Miss MacDonald or you'll ruin the Queen's day.'

On board the Royal Yacht, where she was known as 'The QE3', Bobo had her own cabin, which would be locked and never used by anyone else if she was not on board. For much of the reign, it would be Bobo who mapped out the day-dresses, ballgowns and jewellery for every step of every royal visit. The most senior members of the entourage and of the government would defer to her, while also enlisting her help. One former Private Secretary chuckles at the memory of a tricky moment ahead of a grand dinner in Canada. 'The Queen said that she didn't want to wear a tiara as it would mean having her hair done all over again. Unfortunately, the Canadians were expecting the full works,' he recalls. 'Someone said: "Talk to Bobo." So, I did and I remember she said: "Och, my wee small girl's getting spoiled!" That sorted it out. And sure enough, the Queen came down to dinner looking a million dollars.' Bobo, who never married, continued to live above the Queen's Buckingham Palace apartment until her dying day in 1993, aged eighty-nine.

No matter how illustrious the dress designer, if 'Miss MacDonald' did not like something – or someone – then the outfit was doomed. On the first post-Coronation world tour, Bobo was responsible for more than 100 dresses, including the Coronation dress itself, which the Queen would wear three times. Its creator, Norman Hartnell, had produced a large part of the tour wardrobe, including the Queen's 'wattle' dress, the emblematic crinoline gown decorated with the Australian national flower and immortalised in Sir William Dargie's portrait of the Australian Queen. From her earliest travels, she was keen to deploy fashion as a diplomatic tool in a way completely beyond the reach of kings and princes. So, for the 1956 tour of Nigeria, Hartnell created a duchesse-satin evening gown for the Queen's address to the House of Representatives. He also used pearls and beads to create what the Royal Collection calls 'a long encrustation around the neckline in a style reminiscent of African tribal necklaces'. For the 1961 tour of India and Pakistan, Hartnell produced a pearl-encrusted evening gown in the pattern of an Indian lotus flower for her first evening in New Delhi. On the Queen's first evening in Pakistan, the effect was even more dramatic. Hartnell had designed a duchesse-satin gown in ivory and emerald green, perfectly matching the insignia of the Order of Pakistan, which she had been given by President Ayub Khan earlier in the day. To cap it all, she was wearing the Vladimir Tiara hung with the Cambridge emeralds. Bobo had excelled herself that night.

Another Hartnell classic was the turquoise silk-crêpe dress for the Queen's 1976 trip to Canada and the Montreal Olympics, complete with interlocking rings (even the famously litigious International Olympic Committee was not going to prosecute the Canadian head of state for copyright infringement at her own Games).

As the years passed, Hartnell would gradually lose ground to Hardy Amies, another old-school designer whose name became synonymous with royal fashion. 'It's quite simple,' Amies said of Hartnell years later. 'He was a silly old queen and I'm a clever old queen.' Amies, like his most important client, was unmoved by what might or might not be in fashion at any particular moment, well aware that a monarch should neither be in nor out of fashion but, rather, above it. 'The Queen's attitude is that she must always dress for the occasion, usually for a large mob of middle-class people towards whom she wishes to seem friendly,' he said in 1997, six years before his death. 'There's always something cold and rather cruel about chic clothes which she wants to avoid.' Chic or not, Amies was not cheap. 'Thank you for the enormous bill which will take a little time to pay', the Queen wrote back after receiving one invoice. It was through Amies that the Queen met the man who would design her hats for decades, Australian-born Freddie Fox. Ahead of their first meeting, Amies gave him three pieces of advice: 'Don't touch the Queen, don't ask questions and don't turn your back.' In due course, Fox would have the distinction of designing for three generations – the Queen Mother, the Queen and the Princess of Wales. His chief aim with all the Queen's hats was to ensure that the brim would keep the sun off the monarch's face, while not obscuring the public's view of her.

Fox's work was much in evidence on that steamy 1996 tour of Thailand, along with dresses by Jon Moore, who had taken over as design director of the Hardy Amies label following the founder's retirement.*

On a tour of somewhere as colourful as Thailand, a designer could have something of a free rein with colours – with royal ensembles in white, tangerine, light blue, raspberry and gold on a single day. As usual, the state banquet would require the Queen to wear the decoration bestowed on her by her host. Moore created a white beaded evening dress to offset the mustard sash, grand cross and collar of the Most Illustrious Order of the Royal House of Chakri.

* Both Hartnell and Amies received knighthoods in later life. 'When I was eighty,' Amies told an interviewer, 'I said to my studio that an octogenarian can't go crawling around the Queen's t**s, for God's sake. So I wrote to her and said: "Ma'am I shall always be watching carefully what is going on, but I think you should have the younger generation to wait on you".'

By now the mantle of Bobo had passed to the new dresser, Angela Kelly, another close confidante and straight-talking guardian of the royal wardrobe, who would show great talent as a designer in her own right. It was Miss Kelly (whom the Queen calls 'Angela') who would come up with what the Queen has described as her 'very useful dress', and what others at the Palace call 'credit-crunch couture'. For a number of state occasions the Queen has had the same dress redesigned with different emblems to suit the location – such as maple leafs in Canada and national birds in the Caribbean. Other outfits are simply recycled. One favourite dusky-pink Angela Kelly coat trimmed with plum has been seen on at least a dozen different occasions.

Fashion commentators have been unkind at some stages of the Queen's reign. More recently, though, her obvious confidence in her personal style – like her loyalty to her Walsall-made Launer handbags and her London-made Rayne shoes, with their square heels (better for spreading the pressure on the foot) – would see off her critics. During the Queen's 2000 state visit to Italy, she attended a Milan reception for clothing-industry giants including Prada, Krizia, Fendi, Missoni and Ferré. Nervous Palace press officials attempted to keep British reporters away from the fashion gods, for fear of withering remarks. Fortunately for the Queen, they failed. The brand names were unstoppable in their praise. 'She is so perfect in the clothes she wears,' was the verdict of Gianfranco Ferré on the Queen's silver-blue dress and jacket by Karl-Ludwig Rehse with a matching straw hat by Philip Somerville. 'The Queen is above fashion,' proclaimed Mariuccia Krizia. 'She is, simply, one of the most elegant women in the world,' concurred Miuccia Prada.

Other trusted designers of recent years include milliner Rachel Trevor-Morgan and designer Stewart Parvin. 'She has an amazing complexion which means I can put her in any colour,' Parvin has said, although the Queen tends to choose colours that help her stand out. As she once told a milliner: 'I can't wear beige because people won't know who I am.' She was not being vain. As the Countess of Wessex has pointed out, it is out of consideration for the public: 'Don't forget, when she turns up somewhere, the crowds are ten, fifteen deep – and somebody wants to be able to say that they saw a bit of the Queen's hat as she went past. She needs to stand out for people to be able to say: "I saw the Queen".' Ahead of the Diamond Jubilee of 2012, *Vogue* magazine carried out a survey of the Queen's clothes over a twelve-month period and discovered a marked preference for shades of blue (29 per cent), followed by floral (13) and green and cream (both 11).

The Queen is also very conscious of the need for her tour wardrobe to hang well. Angela Kelly is adept at finding fabrics and designs that do not show creases. On those occasions when her clothes have been caught in a downpour, she has preferred to dry out standing up, knowing that sitting down will increase the chance of creasing. Stewart Parvin has said that he learned an important tip from his predecessors. He buys small lead weights from the curtain department at Peter Jones and sews them into the royal hemlines, not only to maintain the shape of the Queen's clothes, but to prevent what would now be called a 'wardrobe malfunction'. During the 1963 tour of New Zealand, a gust of wind raised the royal skirt in the capital and created 'Windy Wellington' headlines around the world. The photographer Reginald Davis captured the moment for the British press – 'it only showed her slip' – yet when he submitted it for the 1963 Photographer of the Year awards, the judges refused to accept it, on grounds of taste. In 1991 exactly the same thing happened as the Queen arrived in Namibia, and her skirt was caught in a gust as she descended from her plane. The wind has been an occupational hazard on tour for most of her reign. However, the lead weights have served her well.

THE PRESS

They might periodically infuriate diplomats and Palace officials but the Queen has always understood the role of the media on her travels. A regular fixture at the start of most royal tours would be the media reception, at which all the press covering the visit would be invited to down their cameras and notebooks and spend an hour or so meeting the Queen and the Duke privately. In the early years of the reign there would even be a pre-tour press reception at Buckingham Palace (without a royal presence), which could become so well refreshed that a 1961 gathering ended with photographers racing their cars around the Palace quadrangle.

Despite the best efforts of local security forces, ardent royalists and more deferential elements at the Foreign Office to obstruct the media over the years, in the belief that they are doing the Queen some sort of favour, the Royal Family do not actually want the press excluded from their travels. There might be occasions when the Royal Family wish the ground would swallow up the press enclosure. The Duke of Edinburgh would have periodic run-ins with the press for most of his life, going back to the eve of his 1947 wedding, when he and his friends ripped the flashbulbs from the photographers' cameras outside his Dorchester Hotel stag party. However, the Royal Family know that there is little point promoting Britain overseas if no one knows they are there. In his confidential despatch on the 1991 state visit to the USA, the British Ambassador, Sir Antony Acland, reminded his Foreign Office colleagues: 'Those arranging a visit and those reporting it have a shared interest in obtaining as full coverage for the visit as possible.' Giving the press 'at least one good story each day', he advised, 'kept them busy and discouraged them from looking for silly stories to which they might otherwise have resorted.'

In the early years of the reign, royal officials were fond of quoting Walter Bagehot's Victorian warning that 'we must not let in daylight upon magic', and yet the Queen is equally fond of saying, 'I have to be seen to be believed.' She and her Private Secretaries are mindful of another great Victorian, Lord Salisbury. 'Seclusion is one of the few luxuries in which royal personages may not indulge,' the future Prime Minister wrote. 'The power which is derived from affection or from loyalty needs a life of almost unintermitted publicity to sustain it.' As the Queen's wiser advisers have always acknowledged, the greatest threat to the institution is not republicanism but irrelevance and indifference.

The balance between what the press would call 'public interest' and what the Palace old guard would call 'intrusion' continues to be in flux. For the first sixteen years of her reign, the Queen's press secretary was Commander Richard Colville, DSC, an Old Harrovian ex-Royal Navy officer who made little attempt to disguise his contempt for the press, let alone to woo them. 'I am not what you North Americans would call a public relations officer,' he once declared, getting another tour off to a winning start. As Philip Murphy, Professor of British and Commonwealth History at the University of

London, has pointed out, the press were not the only people who found Colville exasperating. In September 1948, the Colonial Office was arranging a conference of African leaders in London and the Permanent Under-Secretary asked if the delegates might be photographed with the King. Colville sniffily responded that this was impossible and would set a dangerous precedent. The Colonial Office went straight over Colville's head and complained to the Private Secretary, Sir Alan Lascelles. It was pointed out that, since the King had been happy to pose for a recent photograph with the Australian cricket team, it would go down extremely badly if he could not bring himself to do the same with the African leaders. The King agreed and the Colonial Office was happy to report 'considerable fervour and loyalty' in the colonies, following publication.

Colville would remain in post for more than twenty years, before retiring in 1968. Ahead of his departure, the Foreign Office produced a withering report on the Palace's lack of imagination and its feeble efforts with the international media. George Littlejohn Cook, the head of the Foreign Office's information department, wrote that 'severe restrictions on press and photographers' and dull engagements 'tend to produce a certain degree of apathy and a feeling that "we've seen it all before".' He cited a serious lack of media interest in the Queen's 1965 state visit to Belgium. The derisory coverage had offended the hosts and 'was not commensurate with the great efforts expended both by us and by the Belgians'.

Worse still was the fact that Colville allowed 'practically no press photography at the Palace', to the point that the only picture taken of a visiting prime minister from the Congo was of the back of the man's head. 'What are really required are warm, friendly informal pictures showing the Queen and Duke tête-à-tête with their guests,' he wrote. The official royal photographs for Foreign Office distribution were so out of date that they showed the Queen with just three children (omitting Prince Edward, born in 1964).

However, the cumulative effect of the cultural, political and social changes on public life during the Sixties had not gone unnoticed at the Palace. Television was becoming more popular while deference was heading the other way. In 1968, the Comptroller of the Lord Chamberlain's Office (the ceremonial department of Buckingham Palace) finally gave up his historic role as censor of all theatre productions, an anomaly dating back to 1737. The Comptroller and his team were somewhat relieved. Even ardent royalists had to admit that it should not be left to a retired Army officer at the Palace to adjudicate on dramatic depictions of God or homosexuality or police corruption. In that same year, the Queen promoted Colville's deputy, that unstuffy Australian ex-civil servant, to replace the Commander. Originally talent-spotted by the Australian Prime Minister, Sir Robert Menzies, William Heseltine had an intuitive grasp of the importance of both tradition and of public relations. Colour television had just arrived and both Prince Charles and Princess Anne were about to enter mainstream public life. Heseltine was alert to the dangers of the Monarchy slipping apart from the society it was there to represent. Over at the Foreign Office, there were many who could not wait to see the back of the man the press called the 'Abominable "No" Man'.

Concluding his report, Littlejohn Cook wrote: 'The image which we are presenting of a modern Monarchy is central to our whole effort to project the right image of Britain of today overseas, not only in the Commonwealth but in the sophisticated European and American markets.' His one hope, he said, was that 'the appointment of Mr Heseltine as Press Secretary may usher in a new era'.

Heseltine would certainly do things differently. He would oversee the first royal television documentary, *Royal Family*, and frequently had to deal with local media who had never encountered royalty before. One of his most vivid memories, he says, is still the Queen's 1971 state visit to Turkey, as the Turkish photographers ran riot ahead of a trip to Ephesus. 'I addressed them from the stage of the amphitheatre in Ephesus, from where Paul had preached to the Ephesians!' he says. Unlike St Paul, Heseltine had a rather simpler message: if the photographers would only congregate on one side of the auditorium, they would all get a photograph of the Queen and the Duke on the other. And it worked.

The graph line of Palace–press relations continued to climb once again through the Seventies and Eighties, as the Royal Family kept expanding in number, giving Britain something to cheer about during a turbulent political period. Then the graph line crashed. Few remember that 1992 was actually the Queen's Ruby Jubilee. She herself called it her '*annus horribilis*' – a year of marital dramas, public debates about the royal finances and then the Windsor Castle fire. Five years later, the death of Diana, Princess of Wales would mark the low point in royal relations with the media. At the public service to mark the Queen's golden-wedding anniversary three months later, Palace hostility towards the media was such that the British press was allocated a single seat in a congregation of 2,000. The Golden Jubilee of 2002, however, would mark the start of a new era of workmanlike coexistence, which has continued to the present, through three royal weddings (those of the Prince of Wales and both his sons) and the Diamond Jubilee.

On every tour, to the eternal dismay of the Foreign Office, the media might easily be more interested in the trivia than in the grand bilateral strategy. Food has often been a distraction, particularly the roasted gibnut – a jungle rodent – served by the Governor-General of Belize in 1985 (prompting 'Queen eats rat' headlines) and the sea slug served a year later in China. On the 2000 state visit to Italy, the Queen's tour of Rome's ancient Forum was eclipsed by the fact that she was served goat by the Italian Prime Minister. There were no complaints from the Queen. Her staff always advise against shellfish and spicy or messy food, but she could be forgiven for wanting the occasional note of variety on tour. Yet the menus seldom change from one decade to the next. The Queen's lunch with her High Commissioners on her 1963 tour of Australia ('Scotch salmon, breast of chicken') was little different from her 1970 lunch in Botany Bay, Australia ('Cold salmon, braised lamb') or her 2000 lunch in Ballarat, Australia ('Tasmanian salmon, loin of lamb'). Another unchanging feature of every royal tour would be the drinking water – always Malvern Water, regardless of the calibre of the local water supply. On longer tours, whenever possible, there would also be a barbecue, cooked by Prince Philip, with the Queen on salad duty. Offers of help would not be welcome.*

* The Queen's 'signature dish' is the salad dressing she prepares at picnics and barbecues. The former Governor-General of Canada, Michaëlle Jean, recalled a Balmoral barbecue where she was given a tip: praise the dressing. Not only had the monarch made it herself, but it was her own recipe. The tip had come from Prince Philip.

TEAMWORK

Though the Queen will receive all sorts of gifts on her travels, she will bring many of her own, both for her hosts and for the staff, 'She is very attentive on gifts,' says one official. It was entirely down to the Queen when it came to picking the gift for the Queen of Spain during King Felipe's 2017 state visit to Britain. 'It was her choice of a Burberry scarf for Queen Letizia. She said: "She is a very fashionable young woman" and she asked to look through a selection.'

There can be a lot of present-buying to do ahead of a big tour. On her 1996 state visit of Thailand, for example, the Queen was presented with silks and gold. In return, she gave the King a sterling-silver charger dish, engraved with royal ciphers, along with a Crown Derby tea service for Queen Sirikit. There were other members of the family to remember, too. For the Thai Crown Prince – something of a bon viveur – there was a pair of claret jugs. For Princess Sirindhorn, a well-known academic, there was an Edwardian ink-stand and an original copy of Alan Turing's groundbreaking article on artificial intelligence. One Palace veteran recalls how much the Queen has enjoyed giving toys to the children of her hosts, be it the offspring of the erratic King Hassan of Morocco, or Justin, the 'very lively' young son of her fourth Canadian Prime Minister, Pierre Trudeau. Years later, the same boy would become her twelfth Canadian Prime Minister, saluting her at the 2015 Commonwealth summit as a 'constant presence in the life of Canada', who had 'seen more of Canada than almost any Canadian'.

As well as gifts, the Queen has enjoyed adding personal touches to her itinerary – a card and cake on a host's birthday, for example. During her 1976 state visit to Luxembourg, she held a dinner to thank the Grand Duke for his hospitality and had a little surprise. The Anglophile Grand Duke had served with the British during the war and was immensely proud of his honorary position as Colonel of the Irish Guards. When dinner was over, the Queen suddenly produced the regimental pipers of the Irish Guards to perform around the table. 'The Grand Duke couldn't believe it,' says Sir Antony Acland, the British Ambassador at the time. 'He said: "Those are my pipers!" If one could organise touches like that, which were personal to the head of state, it meant a great deal.' Sir Antony would observe the power of the pipes once again while serving as British Ambassador to the United States during the Queen's 1991 state visit to Washington. Among the presents for her host was a new piece of music which her piper, Jim Motherwell, had composed in President George Bush's honour. The Queen had named it after the recent Allied victory in the Gulf War. Reporting back to the Foreign Office, Acland noted that Bush had been 'genuinely delighted with the pipe march "Desert Storm" (for which its surprised composer and performer, Pipe Sergeant Motherwell, received a handwritten note from the President the next morning.)'

The vast majority of presents on any royal visit would be for the staff and officials who had made it all happen. The inventory of gifts for the 1963 tour of Australia and New Zealand ran to several pages, including an engraved silver cigarette box for Lady Menzies, the wife of the Australian Prime Minister; an ashtray for Ernest Veniard, the royal butler in Adelaide; a book on George III's Merino sheep for the chairman of the New Zealand Wool Board; even a scarf for the Queen's chambermaid at the Grand Hotel, Dunedin. On state visits there would also be decorations for the British diplomats involved in the visit. Diplomats usually receive their honours via the Foreign Office's Order of St Michael and St George but on these occasions they come from the monarch herself, via the Royal Victorian Order. It means, as a general rule, that any diplomats with the letters VO after their name will have helped organise a royal visit at some point. Heads of mission in a large country have usually received a knighthood, becoming a knight commander (KCVO) or dame commander (DCVO); in a smaller country, the ambassador might become a commander (CVO). For the next rungs down on the diplomatic ladder there would be the LVO (lieutenant) and MVO (member).

What remains etched in the minds of so many of the Queen's staff, past and present, is her sense of teamwork on these tours. Those close to her point out that the Queen has spent her entire life in a military environment. As well as being Head of the Armed Forces, her father, husband, sons and grandsons have all been officers, and she seldom leaves home without a uniformed equerry at her side. Her annual birthday party is a military parade. Though her own career in the Forces was a short one, she remains very proud that she served in uniform during the Second World War. And when she is on tour, she feels very much like the commanding officer of her unit. Lynda Chalker,* the Minister for Overseas Development, was in attendance during part of the Queen's 1994 tour of the Caribbean. They were walking to a church service when Chalker put her foot through a piece of plyboard covering a hole in the pavement. 'The coppers hauled me out and we went into the church. The Queen asked if I was OK. I said: "It hurts a bit". And the Queen said: "Gentlemen, some ice". Her care for other people is tremendous. There are loads of anecdotes like this.'

As a commanding officer, the Queen would have little time for 'girl talk' on tour. All members of the entourage were treated much the same, and there could be little sympathy for those struggling to maintain the pace. Canadian politician Alvin Hamilton told author Sally Bedell Smith of a long day touring Saskatchewan, during which the Queen never requested a 'health break'. 'You need not worry,' the Private Secretary told him. 'Her Majesty is trained for eight hours.' On a handful of occasions, however, the Queen has insisted on all-women company. After the Dunblane primary-school massacre of 1996, she asked her assistant Private Secretary, Mary Francis, to accompany her to meet the families and staff. 'She really did break down there,' says one of her team. 'She said: "I want a woman with me because they understand". She knew how she would feel.'

Though never one for idle chat with staff going about their business on a normal day at the office, the monarch is often in a very different frame of mind on tour. Every member of the team, however, is well aware that, at any official engagement, the spotlight should always remain on the Queen.

Frank Judd recalls the moment when he himself broke this cast-iron rule during the 1979 royal tour of the Gulf. He had been asked by the Foreign Secretary, David Owen, to break off from the tour for a few hours, to deliver a private reprimand to a local emir who had been breaching international sanctions against Rhodesia. Judd had also been authorised to give an off-the-record background briefing to a journalist. The following day, however, his remarks had been printed in full, and Judd

* One of just four ministers to serve through all eighteen years of the Thatcher/Major Conservative administrations, Lynda Chalker became Baroness Chalker of Wallasey on losing her seat in 1992.

suddenly found himself and his secret meeting all over the news. The royal tour had been eclipsed. 'All I can say is that nobody in the Queen's entourage or the Queen said anything to me,' he recalls. 'But I had the distinct impression that she was encouraging me to keep closer to her.' Judd had been doing his job, he had been let down by a journalist and the Queen was making it very clear that she did not hold it against him. He was part of the team – *her* team. 'I was very moved by that,' he says. 'I thought: "That's my monarch!" if you know what I mean.'

When on board the Royal Yacht, the minister in attendance was always treated as part of the Royal Household. Judd remembers being asked to join the Royal Family for one of Prince Philip's barbecues on an empty beach as *Britannia* cruised the Persian Gulf. He would be touched, once again, when he went round to Buckingham Palace a few months later. Margaret Thatcher's Conservatives had just won the 1979 election and Judd, along with all the other outgoing Labour ex-ministers, was invited to receive a formal farewell from the Queen. After a long and punitive election campaign, he recalls that the atmosphere was rather jolly as the jobless politicians stood around gossiping before the Queen's arrival. 'We were almost demob happy and very relaxed,' he says. 'And I suddenly became aware there was someone outside the group waiting and it was the Queen. I said "Hello, Ma'am" and she said: "I've got something here for you, a memory of happier times". And she gave me an envelope addressed to me, with the words "Memories of a happier occasion" in her handwriting. And in there were photographs which *she* took of the barbecue. And there were photographs of me and her Private Secretary sitting in our deck chairs eating steak – very funny photographs – which I treasure to this day.'

A lifelong 'international socialist non-conformist', Judd had been intrigued by what he discovered as he travelled through the Gulf with the Queen. It was abundantly clear that, for all the diplomatic niceties, the warm words and the gifts of precious carpets, she was keenly aware of the problems in the countries she was visiting. It is an old Palace joke that members of the Royal Family think the whole world smells of fresh paint. Judd found that the Queen was under no such illusions. 'Let me say that I became very convinced of her liberal humanity on that trip,' he says. 'She did not have the wool pulled over her eyes. And she saw some of the underlying – what we would now call human rights – issues very clearly on her own account. And in private would give vent to her feelings.'

He will not divulge what was said, out of respect for the Queen's neutrality, but he remains a great admirer of the way she handled herself, both overseas and at home. 'The whole point of a constitutional monarchy is that it is entirely irrational. It has no logical basis whatsoever,' he argues. 'It is the lock in the constitution. By accident someone is monarch and by accident they have this role. Now disaster could follow from that situation but our Queen has been anything but a disaster.'

THE UNEXPECTED

There are so many parts of the royal calendar that work like clockwork, year in, year out. It is during tours and state visits that things tend to go off-script. It might be an innocent remark, like that of the mayor showing the Queen some ancient civic regalia in a display case. 'When do you wear it?' she asked, by way of small talk. 'Only on special occasions,' came the mayoral reply, a line which would be gleefully recalled for a good deal longer than the regalia. Like all members of the Royal Family, the Queen enjoys those moments when things don't go entirely to plan.

In 1982 she was invited to Canada to sign the new Canada Act, embodying key constitutional changes, in a grand public ceremony. Members of the Canadian government then had to sign an associated document but, in doing so, Prime Minister Pierre Trudeau managed to break the nib of the official pen. Next up was the Justice Minister, Jean Chrétien, who found that he couldn't sign a thing. '*Merde!*' he muttered within royal earshot, then suddenly remembered himself and looked up. The Queen was highly amused. And on her 1952 tour of Kenya, she was introduced to a little boy born on the same day as Prince Charles and named Prince as a result. If anyone thought he was going to surrender the bunch of flowers that he was supposed to present to the guest of honour, they could think again. Bouquet presentations – and non-presentations – have been a rich source of royal entertainment over the years, as have power cuts.

'It's awful getting dressed in the dark. I was just putting on my tiara!' the Queen joked as the Governor-General of Jamaica, Sir Howard Cooke, led her to dinner by candlelight at his residence in

Kingston during her 2002 Golden Jubilee visit. The power had gone off twice during the course of the evening – at one point official cars were lined up outside, to illuminate the hall with their headlights – but it seemed that the guest of honour was thoroughly enjoying the unexpected drama.

After all, what often gets overlooked in the planning and execution of a state visit is the fact that the two heads of state are supposed to be enjoying themselves. David Owen's happiest memory of his 1979 tour of Saudi Arabia is the dinner the Queen gave for King Khalid on the Royal Yacht in Dhahran. 'We had a really good party and everyone felt it had gone really well,' Lord Owen remembers. 'The old king hobbles down the steps with the Duke of Edinburgh and I'm standing with the Queen. The King gets in this Rolls-Royce and suddenly this stick appears out of the window. And for about 300 yards this stick is waving out of the window and he's obviously had a hell of a time.'

These are occasions when outsiders catch a glimpse of the real Queen. One quality that many have noted is her calmness. Even on her way to one of the most important and sensitive tours of the entire reign, the 2011 state visit to Ireland, the Queen gave no indication of any nerves, though the rest of her entourage were decidedly on edge. 'There were no signs of tension,' recalls William Hague, her Foreign Secretary on that adventure. 'You could have imagined that we were just going for a nice day out. She was quite calm. She had already mastered everything.'

Her first Commonwealth Secretary-General, Arnold Smith, would write of her 'calm acceptance' of any reverse. He would often have to inform her that yet another of her colonies was about to seek independence and did not want the Queen as its head of state. He contrasted the Queen's 'natural' reaction with the possessive rage of her grandfather, George V, who could explode over the smallest challenge to his regal authority. He was absolutely furious in 1923 when he learned that Canada had had the temerity to sign a halibut fishing treaty with the United States and had not consulted him first.

Behind the gentle, non-confrontational façade there has always been a steely sense of purpose, the 'quiet insistence' that Commonwealth Secretary-General Sonny Ramphal has observed. Those around her would never take the Queen or her opinion for granted. 'I was always very nervous with the Queen. In fact, I still am,' says Lynda Chalker. 'I think she has always been very conscious that if she says something in just a few words and in just a few seconds, it will have a dramatic effect.'

One of the more arrogant Commonwealth leaders during the Nineties was also the world's youngest head of state at the time. Valentine Strasser had been a junior officer in the army of Sierra Leone in 1992 when he turned up at the presidential palace with a few other soldiers to complain about the lack of pay and equipment for his men. Fearing the worst, the President jumped in a helicopter and fled, whereupon Strasser decided to declare himself leader at the age of twenty-five – the same age as the Queen, in fact, when she had become head of state herself.

The following year, he arrived at the Commonwealth summit in Cyprus and, like all leaders, was invited to a reception with the Queen on board the Royal Yacht. Sir Robert Woodard, *Britannia*'s captain, remembers that Strasser 'behaved very badly', ignoring his outstretched hand, and thus missing Woodard's polite warning about the step on his way into the reception. He went flat on his face. 'I couldn't have been more pleased really,' says Woodard. The following day Strasser returned for his one-on-one audience with the Queen. 'This time, he came on board and shook my hand and it was like a wet kipper,' says Woodard. 'He was overcome with nerves because he realised he was going to be alone with Her Majesty.'

Like all audiences, it was a private affair, but it would later emerge that the Queen had given the hot-headed young dictator some stern advice. He would need to embrace democracy, she told him, if he was to stay in the Commonwealth and, indeed, if he was to stay alive. She also told Strasser that she would help him by introducing him to someone who knew about reforming his ways. A few hours later, at the Queen's banquet for the leaders, her strategy was clear: Strasser found himself seated next to Zimbabwe's Robert Mugabe, who had already been primed by the hostess to give the young man a talking-to.*

* Strasser, who developed a fondness for clothes from the royal tailor, Turnbull & Asser, failed to follow the Queen's advice and was ousted in a coup in 1996. Britain attempted to rehabilitate him by enrolling him on a law course at Warwick University, but he dropped out after fellow students complained about sharing lectures with an ex-dictator accused of war crimes. After turning to drink and living on friends' sofas for a couple of years, he returned to Sierra Leone, where he now lives in a rundown area of Freetown with his mother.

There have been occasional moments when the Queen has decided to let off steam, such as the night she surprised fellow guests by taking to the drums after a jolly dinner during that 1976 state visit to Luxembourg. Her entourage, however, would never take such moments as a cue for over-familiarity.

Nor would they be in any doubt when they had let her down. During a royal cruise back from Finland in May 1976, as *Britannia* was passing from the Baltic through the Kiel Canal, the crew were asked to alert the Queen when the Yacht was passing a well-known stud.

The request went astray and the Queen missed her horses. Her quiet fury was obvious the moment she appeared for dinner. A chilly silence prevailed as the officers present nervously took their seats, whereupon they were treated to a fascinating display of royal anger-management. The Queen suddenly put her napkin over her face. She then slowly peeled it down to reveal a monarch transformed, smiling warmly and changing the subject. 'It was like a magic trick,' says one of the guests. 'Suddenly, here was this new smiley Queen. It was quite extraordinary. And Prince Philip did the same thing.' It was not merely a revealing illustration of iron self-control but also provides a sense of the way the Queen feels that life is one unending performance, even on home territory among close confidantes. Though reprieved, the crew of *Britannia* would never make that mistake again.

Though she may be the most famous woman in the world, the Queen has always been, at heart, a shy person, much like her father; fiercely protective and conscious of her position, while modest about her own abilities. 'What do I know?' she sighed to one of her ministers over a *Britannia* lunch. 'I'm just a woman about the place.'

It has always helped her identify with those for whom a royal encounter is a source of terror. It may be an old cliché that the Queen puts others 'at their ease', but it is a phrase that has kept recurring over the years. The veteran royal photographer Reginald Davis recalls that the Queen could be disarmingly bashful at her media receptions on tour. 'She was marvellous but she always looked down at your feet at a press reception. Maybe it was a nervous thing,' he says. Many have remarked on how the Queen prefers to gloss over awkward accidents. During that 1961 tour of West Africa, there was an embarrassing moment at the state banquet on board the Royal Yacht in Bathurst when the wife of one Gambian VIP, on being offered gravy, proceeded to pour it in to her wine glass. The Queen did not flinch.

Similarly, when a photographer dropped a glass of sherry all over the carpet during a press reception in *Britannia* in 1981, she pretended not to notice. A few hours later there was a sharp clattering noise as the same photographer was attempting to capture her arrival at an evening event and dropped a lens. 'Oh, dear. It just really hasn't been your day,' the Queen remarked by way of consolation.

Sir Jock Slater, serving as the Queen's equerry during the 1970 tour of Australia, remembers lining up the guests for an investiture. One recipient was becoming increasingly perplexed about what he should do and say as he went up to receive his honour, so Slater attempted to calm him by explaining that the easiest way to get it right was to do exactly the same as the person ahead of him in the queue. By the time Slater had discovered that the recipient was following a woman, it was too late. The man did 'as good a curtsey as he could manage,' says Slater. 'To this day, I don't think he knew what he had done as Her Majesty was marvellous and held out her hand to help him up as if it was the most natural thing in the world.'

As well as putting people 'at their ease', another quality singled out time and again is the Queen's ability to make them feel as if they are the most fascinating person in the room. Tom Fletcher, a former British Ambassador, recalls his first meeting with the Queen at a Commonwealth summit while working as Foreign Office Private Secretary. He showed the Queen a photograph of his grandfather meeting her during her 1956 tour of Nigeria. 'I know everyone has one of those stories,' he says, 'but her eyes lit up and you got a few seconds when she was completely in the moment and her eyes sparkled and fizzed.'

'When you're talking to her, you are the only person who exists,' says Kamalesh Sharma, the Queen's fifth Commonwealth Secretary-General. 'I have seen her talk to millions of people and it's all about focus on the person.'

THE CHOICE OF WORDS

Like the gifts, clothes and so much else, another aspect of any tour that will require plenty of thought are the speeches. Traditionally, there might be a major one at the state banquet on the first evening, plus one or two shorter addresses during a visit. If the Queen is in one of her realms, this will be a matter for her government in that country, and the British Foreign Office will have no more say in the matter than an ambassador from Brussels or Bogotá. If she is on tour as Queen of the United Kingdom, then the local British Embassy and the Foreign Secretary will have produced a draft version of the speech. It is unlikely to survive intact, after the royal red pen has been run over it. It is a sacred convention that, with the exception of her Christmas broadcast, anything the Queen does or says in public is approved by her democratically elected ministers. This is known as speaking or acting 'on advice'. However, it certainly does not mean that she is an automaton reading a government script. 'You got a draft from an ambassador or the Foreign Office and then the Queen had views,' says Sir William Heseltine. What might sound suitably regal to an ambassador did not always chime with the monarch, and a speech could come back severely tweaked. 'Martin Charteris used to say that it had been "Queenised",' says Heseltine, adding that flowery metaphors and effusive adjectives 'wouldn't last a minute'. As we shall see, when the Foreign Office attempted to pack the Queen's speech with effusive praise for the EEC, ahead of Britain's entry into the Common Market, the final version was decidedly more workmanlike.

A key influence in all the Queen's speeches would often be the Duke of Edinburgh. Constitutionally, of course, he could have no say in their substance. The Queen, though, greatly valued his advice. Sir Robert Woodard recalls a typical rest day on board *Britannia* when the royal couple would work as a team from their studies on either side of the Upper Deck – her brightly decorated sitting room on the starboard side, and his teak-panelled study to port. 'The Queen was writing her speech for the next day and she was padding to and from his study, giving him rewrites,' says Woodard.

The Queen could use her speeches to make important points that no ambassador or politician could hope to make – and she was happy to do so. Ahead of her 1979 visit to Malawi, the British High Commissioner, Mike Scott, wrote to the Foreign Office complaining that the President, Dr Hastings Banda, was very reluctant to make any sort of public acknowledgement of British financial support.

Since being granted independence in 1964, the former British colony had trousered £140 million in aid, easily the largest contribution from any foreign nation, with barely a word of thanks. 'A more serious aspect lies in the failure of President Banda to mention this when he so often makes comparisons between conditions in colonial times and those which exist today,' wrote Scott. Might the Queen work on the President's amnesia? Come the night of the state banquet, she duly saluted Malawi's 'rapid economic and social development' under Dr Banda, adding: 'My country is proud to be a chief contributor to this important work.' And just in case anyone had not got the message, the Queen added: 'We have demonstrated the genuineness of our concern for your future by the provision of one hundred and forty million pounds of capital aid.'

The Queen's speeches could also force other leaders to try a little harder, too. Former Foreign Secretary William Hague says that he would only 'fiddle with little things here and there' when he was in attendance. But he recalls a certain degree of panic among the hosts during the Queen's 2014 state visit to France, following the commemorations to mark the seventieth anniversary of D-Day. Having received a copy of the speech that President François Hollande was preparing to deliver later in the day, Hague sent a draft of the Queen's speech across to the Elysée Palace. 'When President Hollande saw the Queen's speech for the banquet he asked for his own speech to be rewritten. He had to raise his game and increase the quality. He was going to say "Welcome to France, Cheers", that sort of thing. He definitely had to make the speech more *profonde.*'

TWO PACES BEHIND

The Duke of Edinburgh's pivotal role on tour would extend far beyond speech-writing. As she herself has made clear often enough, she would not have achieved all that she has without her 'liege man of life and limb'. Whenever the Queen was on tour, the Duke would be there too, sharing the walkabouts and receptions, while always conscious that the Queen was the main attraction. If he spotted any children trying not to look too disappointed that they had picked his side of any given walkabout route, he would help them over the barriers to present their flowers to the Queen.

Once the big set-piece features of a state visit were out of the way, the Duke was available to maximise diplomatic impact with a programme of his own. On Day Two of the Queen's 1996 state visit to the Czech Republic, for example, as she met vast crowds in the second city of Brno, the Duke toured the old silver-mining town of Kutná Hora. The following day he broke off from the main tour to visit the country's largest brewery. One of the Queen's former Private Secretaries points out that the monarch would always be wary of overdoing any commercial activity during a state visit. 'We always had to be careful about the trade side because you didn't want to destroy the special atmosphere,' he says. The Duke, however, could not only do more for the commercial section of any embassy, but usually enjoyed it, too. The media would always be on the lookout for any chance remarks that could join the long anthology of ducal 'gaffes'. Some were, manifestly, a joke. 'It's a pleasure to be in a country that isn't ruled by its people,' he is reported to have told the Paraguayan dictator Alfredo Stroessner in 1963. Others would be an attempt to jolly along a sticky conversation. Every now and then they might backfire, like the fabled conversation with a Brazilian admiral in the capital, Brasília. Had the admiral won his medals on the local lake, he asked? 'Yes, sir,' came the reply. 'Not by marriage.'

In most cases, however, the local reaction to a gaffe would bear little comparison to the banner headlines in Britain. A joke about the food in Hungary – 'You can't have been here that long. You haven't got a pot belly' – was big news back home, but passed virtually unnoticed in Budapest. The Governor of the Cayman Islands, Michael Gore, was irked that the only international media coverage from an otherwise dizzying royal visit in 1994 was the Duke's joke, at an exhibition about a famous shipwreck, that the islanders were descended from pirates. 'This caused no offence locally because, just as Australians prefer to be descended from convicts rather than warders, Caymanians are not averse to being labelled as descendants of pirates,' Gore wrote in his telegram to London. 'I often pull their legs that the Wreck of the Ten Sails came about as a result of Caymanians having learnt from their Cornish forefathers!' As the Duke once admitted to a biographer, there were moments when he might be 'skating on very thin ice', adding: 'I go through occasionally.'

The focus on trivia would leave the Duke's staff and former staff wearily disappointed, but unsurprised. They would see a boss whose career in international public life had eclipsed that of most politicians. The World Wildlife Fund (WWF), of which the Duke was a co-founder and international president, has been a catalyst for the likes of Greenpeace and Friends of the Earth. The Duke of Edinburgh's Award for young people has been embraced in more than 140 countries around the world. Award-seekers and award-holders are to be found everywhere, as the Duke has discovered himself. He told Sir Malcolm Rifkind of the day he spent hours stalking a stag across a Scottish hillside at Balmoral. He was about to take aim when his quarry suddenly ran away at speed. Moments later, a band of ramblers came over the brow of the hill. 'What they bloody hell are you doing?' he thundered. 'The Duke of Edinburgh's,' came the reply. 'He likes to tell that story against himself,' says Sir Malcolm, with a laugh.

Added to all the other 700 international charities and organisations that he supported until his retirement in 2017, at the age of ninety-five, it means that the Duke would leave an imprint on the wider world for longer than almost any post-war figure alive. In that context, it is not so surprising there was that discreet campaign some years ago, by a handful of friends from different countries, to put his name forward for a Nobel Prize.

For most of his life, however, his role has been that of the Royal Family's (and the world's) longest-serving supporting act, always walking two paces behind his wife. Jack Straw was struck by the fact that, on a long flight, the Duke would sit in the row of seats behind the Queen, too. He would also help to keep the rest of the entourage alert, even if he was not always wholly convinced of their reason for being there. 'He would bring a virile dimension to a tour. His temper could keep things cracking along quite nicely,' recalls a former member of the Royal Household. 'Because when the Duke went travelling on his own, it would just be him and a policeman and his private secretary. So on these tours, he'd come in and see all these dressers and footmen and so on. "What are all these people doing here?" he'd say.' It helped that the Duke had travelled so widely. 'When the Queen went to somewhere she'd never been like Hungary, he'd been before,' says a former Private Secretary. 'He knew the place and that helped. And if anything went wrong, he'd say: "Who organised this bloody shambles?"' He could also lighten the mood in a crisis, like the Normandy veterans' parade on the sandy beach at Arromanches in 1994. An incoming tide was already cutting things fine when the royal party were informed that President Mitterrand was running an hour late. 'Who does he bloody think he is?' roared the Duke. 'King Canute?' The parade stuck to the original timings.

The Duke was not averse to taking on the Foreign Office, either. The Queen's 1972 state visit to France was one of the most important of her reign, effectively paving the way for Britain's entry to the European Common Market. Having been invited to address the joint chamber of commerce in Paris, the Duke prepared a speech gently arguing that some issues – notably the challenges facing the world's poorest nations, and the threat of global pollution to the environment – were of even greater significance than Britain's impending entry to Europe. 'I do not believe we need to be mesmerised by the great debate about Britain and the Common Market,' he wrote, noting that Britain's entry had been 'hotly debated' and was still under discussion. He was concerned that 'Europe has achieved a level of prosperity far higher than many other countries', adding that he wanted to see Europe help the 'less fortunate regions of the world'.

Although few would quibble with his thesis today, it was viewed as dangerous heresy at the Foreign Office. William Adams, then head of the Foreign Office's European integration department, wrote to his bosses warning that the Duke's speech was 'a gift to the anti-marketeers in Parliament and the country'. He added: 'I wonder whether the Duke of Edinburgh really wishes to make what amounts to a policy statement about Europe's attitude to the Third World.' Lees Mayall, the Foreign Office's head of protocol, was given the task of writing a blunt letter to the Duke's office, warning that 'we have to be careful not to play into the hands of the anti-marketeers'. He wanted some drastic changes, including the removal of the section about Britain being 'mesmerised' by the Common Market. The Duke was clearly having none of it because, come the day, he said exactly what he was going to say. 'Mesmerised' was not edited out. Rather than cause a stir, it ended up receiving extensive and favourable coverage across the British media. 'Duke tells Europe not to forget needy nations,' declared the *Financial Times*. Under the headline 'Don't be mesmerised by the Market, says Prince', *The Daily Telegraph* reported that the Duke, 'speaking in excellent French', had delivered a speech 'refreshingly free of official platitudes'.

As a rule, if the Duke was happy, then the Queen was happy. On occasion, though, she would intervene to avert the odd local difficulty. The Labour politician and diarist, Chris Mullin, accompanied the Queen and Duke during a trip to Nigeria in his days as a junior Foreign Office minister. During a visit to the local offices of the British Council, the Duke was unimpressed by a jargon-filled speech of welcome from the director and turned to a group of expat staff. 'You're teachers, aren't you?' he said, within Mullin's earshot. 'Can you tell me what all that meant?' One of the teachers – 'a bit right-on,' Mullin observed – replied: 'No, sir. We're not actually teachers.' 'Not teachers?' said the Duke. 'What are you then?' 'Well, sir, we empower people.' It was precisely the sort of flaccid modern management-speak guaranteed to irritate the Duke, who has been known to bridle at the mere mention of 'human resources', 'affordable housing' and 'stakeholder'. '*Empower?*' he snorted. 'Doesn't sound like English to me.' By now the Queen's finely tuned early warning system was emitting signals. 'Look,' she said brightly, pointing over a balcony, '... at the pottery.' After the royal party had moved on, Mullin went to look over the balcony. There was no pottery.

Though the Duke would announce his retirement from public life in 2017, he would continue to accompany the Queen to important events and to remain central to the way she arranges her programme. At the end of a busy morning, she has been known to say: 'Now I must give Philip his lunch.' As the longest-serving double-act in royal history, they are unrivalled. No other royal duo have done so much together around the world. On her 1954 Coronation tour of Australia, it was estimated that seven million people saw the Queen and the Duke with their own eyes; a million on a single drive through Accra in 1999. The overall viewing figures remain incalculable, the overall impact unquantifiable, and yet the effect, in terms of soft power, is unquestionable.

THE AFTERMATH

After most tours, the Ambassador or High Commissioner would send a confidential report to the Foreign Office assessing the impact of the royal visit. With a new knighthood, damehood or CVO, and knowing that a copy would usually find its way to the Palace, the authors were seldom critical. On the other hand, they would not be thanked for treacly hyperbole. These reports would be circulated confidentially inside the Foreign Office and used by those planning future tours, as well as by those keen for a post-mortem. In his 1996 despatch, Sir James Hodge reported proudly that when the King of Thailand attended the Queen's dinner at the British Embassy, it had been the first time in history that he had visited a foreign embassy. It had not all been plain sailing, however. 'There were a few ragged edges,' Sir James added. 'The normal Thai practice of having dozens of senior officials accompany senior members of the Royal Family – including the Crown Prince's Hat Bearer and Pipe Carrier – was not easy to manage, particularly for the return dinner.'

In his report on the 1956 state visit to Sweden, the British Ambassador, Sir Robert Hankey, reported unsurprisingly that the visit had been greeted with 'breathless interest by the whole of Sweden'. His assertion was supported by facts, however. He quoted the Swedish press, noting that even the anti-royal papers had covered the events with enthusiasm. The Ambassador observed that 'the strongly socialist and feminist' Welfare Minister, Ulla Lindström, had been very respectful towards the Queen, but had 'elected as a matter of principle to bow rather than curtsey which earned her a certain amount of humorous comment in the press'.

He also quoted reports that the visit had even 'saved the Swedish Monarchy', in the face of rising republicanism. The increase in antipathy towards the monarchy stemmed in part from 'the rational and materialist cast of mind of the Swedes', but was largely down to scandal surrounding the late King Gustav V and 'the peculiarities of the King's private life'. The report did not go into the details of Gustav's widely rumoured gay past, or the prosecution of an alleged lover for blackmail following the King's death in 1950, but it was emphatic that the presence of the British monarchy had 'made Swedes more proud of their monarchy'. Sweden, Sir Robert added, was now 'a country in which Great Britain is held in higher esteem than any other power'. No small boast.

It was to be expected that all these visits would entail plenty of flag-waving and brand promotion on behalf of the UK but, equally, the

Queen well understood that these occasions were about boosting the self-esteem of the hosts, particularly in countries recovering from war or oppression. Reflecting on the 1993 state visit to Hungary – the Queen's first behind the former Iron Curtain (and less than four years after the fall of the Berlin Wall) – the British Ambassador, Sir John Birch, wrote to the Foreign Secretary: 'There is still a lack of self-confidence in the country's future, tinged with some shame about the past. The presence of the Queen and the Duke of Edinburgh struck a deep chord with Hungarians and showed that Britain cared about them.'

These visits could preoccupy an entire embassy or high commission for months in advance, as the Queen herself was well aware. That is why her luggage would contain all those decorations, medals, photo frames and commemorative pens for the embassy staff. She likes to see that everyone is recognised, so she must have enjoyed the despatch of Alan Shave, the Governor of Anguilla, after her visit in 1994. As well as commending his team, he particularly wanted to place on record his thanks to Mrs Shave. Extensive renovation work on Government House had only just finished, giving Lidia Shave a mere three days to prepare for the royal visit. 'To prepare a reception for 400 people is reasonable; to do so while living in our third temporary home in as many months was a challenge. To convert bedrooms into royal rest areas and reorganise an entire house and then instantly reconstruct gardens from builders' rubble was her most outstanding achievement of a thirty-two-year unpaid diplomatic support career.'

Other diplomats might be chided for the tone of their despatches. After the 1979 state visit to Tanzania, the Queen's Private Secretary, Philip Moore, was distinctly underwhelmed by the report of the High Commissioner, Sir Peter Moon. 'I was slightly surprised to find plenty of compliments for President Nyrere, the Tanzanians and also the High Commission staff but none for the Queen!' Moore wrote rather crossly to Roger du Boulay at the Foreign Office. As the man in charge of royal liaison, du Boulay circulated a memo to his colleagues. 'The Palace do not seek or enjoy sycophantic gush,' he assured them, 'but I thought when I first read the despatch, and still think, that it betrays a tendency to take the Queen and her personal entourage and their achievements for granted. Sir P. Moore's note sounds a timely note of warning.'

There was no shortage of praise, and humour too, in the lively 1968 despatch from Brazil by Sir John Russell. Brazilians, he said, had found the Queen to be '*multo simpatica*' while the Duke had received the ultimate accolade of being hailed as a '*pao*' (literally, a cheese roll, but also slang for an elegant young man). 'The modernity of his style, his technological interests, the ready if at times caustic wit, the easy elegant clothes, all this endeared him to the Brazilians,' wrote Sir John. The Ambassador wrote of 'a thousand little points', which had created a riotous triumph: 'lights fusing at the Governor's Palace and the party continuing with candles; the Governor's black umbrella held against the sun, as often as not over his own rather than the Queen's head; the vulgar mobbing in Congress; the Queen's speech at the Banquet; the Gadarene rush of 5,000 guests to the buffet at the President's reception where spurs and a lit cigar came in very handy and I realised that in a previous incarnation I must have been a police horse . . .' This was a visit that had 'real impact not alone on the upper crust but also on the great mass of the poor', notably at the Maracaña stadium, where the Queen had honoured the Brazilian national religion – football – in front of 140,000. 'The seal was set by pictures of a smiling Queen shaking hands with Pelé, Brazil's black "King".'

There had been glitches. Sir John was especially irritated by the behaviour of the crowd in São Paolo, 'where I lost two buttons and a CMG'. At one point, the officer of the cavalry escort had been forced to take on an unidentified car with 'the business edge of his sword'.

Politically, however, the visit had been 'a direct blessing to Brazil' in so many ways. 'The students called off their riots and the right wing suspended their retaliations; all parties are in much improved humour, united by the feeling their country has been greatly distinguished and has behaved well.' He concluded by quoting the words of an eminent Brazilian: 'It was the greatest event here since 1822 – independence.'

Chapter 2

WELCOMING THE WORLD

'That frightful little man'

THE GUEST LIST

As well as visiting more of the world and its people than any other monarch, the same is true in reverse. The Queen has welcomed more world leaders, organised more banquets and carriage processions and held more receptions than any of her predecessors. Her diplomatic duties at home, on behalf of both the UK and the Commonwealth, have been just as important to her as her overseas expeditions in envoy mode. On paper, she has organised at least 110 state visits for 108 different heads of state (two were invited twice). Each one would involve every section of the Royal Household in months of the most intricate planning, followed by a few days of faultless execution. Those figures understate the true picture. The official total does not include many other equally elaborate visits, including those by one of Britain's oldest and closest allies. Presidents of the United States of America might have been visiting Britain ever since Woodrow Wilson arrived in December 1918, but none formally accepted an invitation for a full state visit until George W. Bush in 2003. The celebrated 1982 visit of President Ronald Reagan might have looked like a state visit in every regard, with a white-tie banquet at Windsor and a ride with the Queen through Windsor Great Park. In protocol terms, however, it was not a state visit, merely an 'official' one. Similarly, although the Pope is a head of state, neither Pope John Paul II nor Pope Benedict (the only two Popes to set foot on British soil) made state visits. They were classified as 'papal' visits.

It does not, of course, require carriages, tiaras, flummery and bling to deliver a historic bilateral hit. UK–Soviet relations were still well short of the diplomatic intimacy required for a state visit when the Soviet leader, Mikhail Gorbachev, and his wife, Raisa, made an historic thirty-six-hour visit to Britain in 1989. The trip would be a key moment in bringing about the end of the Cold War and the fall of the Iron Curtain. The symbolic high point was Gorbachev's visit to Windsor Castle and a luncheon for thirty-four, including Prime Minister Margaret Thatcher and the Archbishop of Canterbury. The dress code might have been rudimentary – 'lounge suit' – but the Queen and her staff were keen to push things to the limit. A guard of honour from the Coldstream Guards greeted the Gorbachevs, ahead of a tour of the state apartments and a lunch of smoked salmon stuffed with crab and fillets of beef and duck. Afterwards, the Queen led her guests through to a special exhibition that she had laid on in their honour, courtesy of the Royal Library. It featured a careful mix of Russian royal artefacts, including works by the great imperial favourite, Carl Fabergé, but also Soviet-era correspondence from George VI concerning the Sword of Stalingrad, the King's gift to Stalin as a mark of respect at the height of the Second World War. By the time the Gorbachevs departed, there had been two further milestones: Gorbachev's invitation to the Queen to make a state visit to Moscow at some point in the future – and her acceptance. That one lunch had achieved a more powerful diplomatic impact than so many of those 110 sumptuous state visits before or since.

Some world leaders can never have a state visit, however much they and the Queen would both like one, for the simple reason that they are not heads of state. The Indian Prime Minister, Narendra Modi, is a case in point. He might control the rising economic powerhouse of both Asia and the English-speaking world, but he is not the head of state. As in Germany, Italy and elsewhere, that post is occupied by a non-executive President. That did not stop the British government giving Modi full royal face-time – with lunch at the Palace and tea at Clarence House – during his 2018 visit ahead of the Commonwealth summit.

'One of the constraints that has emerged in recent years is that the Queen is less inclined to do long-haul overseas travel,' says Sir Simon Fraser, head of the Diplomatic Service during the Cameron years, from 2010 to 2015. In deference to her advancing years, the world has come to the Queen, instead. Hence, during that period, the leaders of Qatar, the USA, Indonesia, Kuwait, the United Arab Emirates, South Korea, Singapore, Mexico and China (as well as a couple of short-haul Presidents - Ireland and Turkey) were all welcomed either to Buckingham Palace or Windsor Castle by the octogenarian monarch and her nonagenarian consort.

Though the invitation is ultimately a matter for the government, David Cameron says that he would always be guided by the Queen's thoughts: 'I used to talk to her Majesty a lot to make them the best possible success. Who would be next? If they can't make it, who else? I might say: "We have the Ghanaians coming and obviously we want to emphasise this and that". She always had her own reflections on what they were like and she often had done an outward state visit to that country so she was hugely knowledgeable. She sees all our ambassadors who are about to leave and all their ambassadors who are coming in, so if you do that every week of your life, you are very well informed.'

Cameron has found that a summons from the Queen has never been in greater demand. 'State visits have always been a tool. As she has become more iconic, so they have become more powerful,' says the former Prime Minister. 'And I think some of the recent ones have been game changers.'

'Even in fully functioning modern democracies – and most countries are not well-functioning democracies – the way leaders are treated and how they feel they have been treated matters hugely,' says former Foreign Secretary Jack Straw. 'Anybody in a leadership position will have a larger ego than the generality of the population so it really matters. And we do incoming visits really well.' Among the guests during his term of office was the only Russian state visitor the Queen has ever received, Vladimir Putin. Though relations would subsequently nosedive over Syria, Ukraine and assassination attempts on Putin's enemies in the UK, Straw insists that it was a worthwhile exercise. 'Relations had been strained but everyone was on their best behaviour, trying to make the visit work. I think it made a difference at the time. Relations were straightforward for a period; it gives you a platform on which to build. It was later that things started to go sour.'

THE ARRIVAL

Britain can make no greater diplomatic gesture to another country than by inviting the head of state to stay with the Queen. All receive the same treatment, whether friend or borderline foe. State visit number 110, by King Felipe of Spain, was in many ways identical to state visit number one back in 1954. That, too, involved a European monarch, King Gustav VI of Sweden, though he had sailed to London in a Swedish navy cruiser, the *Tre Kronor*. In 2017, King Felipe arrived by private jet. The Queen's invitation to Felipe was a strategic move by the British government, part of a royal charm offensive designed to offset some of the political fallout from the UK's 2016 Brexit vote. The Prince of Wales and the Duchess of Cornwall, Duke and Duchess of Cambridge and the Duke and Duchess of Sussex were also asked to play their part in this healing process, undertaking a series of European tours to emphasise continuity and to promote the same message: the UK might be leaving the EU, but it is still the same old UK.

No such grand strategy lay behind the invitation to the King and Queen of Sweden in 1954. The Queen's international focus in the early years of the reign was very much on cementing bonds with the Commonwealth realms, of which she herself was head of state. Since she could hardly pay a state visit to herself, this left room for a few inward state visits by non-Commonwealth leaders. Why not start with a friendly fellow monarch, particularly one who happened to be married to Prince Philip's aunt?* The Swedish royal party came ashore at Westminster Pier, where they were formally welcomed by the Queen before the state procession to Buckingham Palace. Neither the state and semi-state landaus from the Royal Mews nor the uniforms of the Household Cavalry had changed by the time the Queen welcomed King Felipe on Horse Guards more than six decades later in 2017.

* During private visits to London, Queen Louise, who was Lord Mountbatten's sister, would carry a note in her handbag, just in case she was hit by a bus. It stated, quite correctly: 'I am the Queen of Sweden.'

For many years, state visitors would fly into London's Gatwick Airport and travel in the Royal Train to Victoria Station, where the Queen would greet them on the platform. Eventually the welcome ceremony would move to the more elegant and ancient setting of Horse Guards. Wherever it took place, the programme was always the same for every visitor: royal introductions, a government greeting line and an inspection of the guard of honour. Any variation or omission ran the risk of a diplomatic incident, particularly with more protocol-minded visitors. David Cameron remembers negotiating the long list of demands from the Chinese delegation ahead of the 2015 state visit of President Xi Jinping. Some were out of the question. 'They wanted a five-mile exclusion zone around Buckingham Palace and no protests,' Cameron recalls. He could not agree to that, as they well knew. On other matters, though, there would be no compromise. 'The Chinese are very conscious about protocol,' Cameron continues. 'They said: "We must have a full honour guard with two bands of the Household Division." I said: "That's ridiculous". And they said: "No – it is protocol. Go check." I checked. They were right. They really do spot these things!'

It is the smallest details that can sometimes upset the grandest people. Ahead of the 1960 state visit of King Bhumibol of Thailand, the Queen sent a note via her Private Secretary to all the bands involved in the visit. 'Not a note of "The King and I" is to be played,' she wrote. The Rodgers and Hammerstein hit musical about an earlier Thai monarch might have been wildly popular in London, but the Queen was well aware that her guest had banned it in Thailand for being disrespectful.

The welcome completed, the most dramatic and telegenic element of every state visit has always been the carriage procession to the Palace. Accompanied by the Sovereign's Escort from the Household Cavalry, the Queen and her guest would travel in the first carriage, while the Duke would steer the visiting spouse to carriage number two. Other members of the family and the rest of the entourage would bring up the rear.

The procession always draws a crowd and, from time to time, a protest, too. All three Chinese state visits have enjoyed rival demonstrations with Tibetan flags and human-rights banners on one side of the Mall and a pro-government counter-demonstration on the other.

The arrival of Japan's wartime leader, Emperor Hirohito, in 1971 was attended by many British war veterans who had survived the brutality of Japanese prisoner-of-war camps (and some of the families of those who had not). There were a few boos and one man was detained for throwing his coat at the procession, but most stood in contemptuous silence as the Queen's carriage passed by. Sir Jock Slater was travelling in one of the rear carriages, as the Queen's equerry at the time, and remembers the strange lack of noise. 'When I commented to my opposite number from the Japanese Embassy that I hoped the Emperor was not offended by the silence, he looked at me, smiled and pointed out that silence in Tokyo was a sign of respect.'

The Duke of Edinburgh had a particularly memorable carriage ride during the state visit of President Urho Kekkonen of Finland in 1969, although it is unlikely the same could be said for his opposite number. The first lady of Finland, Sylvi Kekkonen, had been so nervous ahead of the formal arrival that she had accidentally taken a sleeping pill instead of her heart medication. No sooner had she got into her carriage than she started to nod off while her travelling companions, the Duke and Princess Anne, were left struggling to keep her conscious and prop her upright all the way back to the Palace.

Once inside Buckingham Palace, the Queen would show her state visitors through to the Belgian Suite, the main guest rooms adjacent to the royal swimming pool. Named after Queen Victoria's uncle, King Leopold of the Belgians, the suite has as its main bedroom the blue-draped Orleans Room, an airy upper-ground-floor bedchamber with Victorian portraits and (nowadays) a large flat-screen television. It is, however, the only head of state accommodation in the Western world without en-suite facilities. The two bathrooms – one green and one pink – are across a corridor and are very much designed for those who prefer a hot bath to a shower. When one Middle Eastern monarch was due to stay some years ago, his advance party insisted that their (amply proportioned) king required a spacious shower, instead of a showerhead attached to the bath tap. At great expense, a temporary shower chamber – nicknamed 'the Tardis' – was installed in the middle of one of the bathrooms (all paid for by the visiting king). It was used for just two nights and then removed.

Once settled in, the state visitors then join the Royal Family for a small welcome lunch and the exchange of gifts and decorations. In

2017, just as on that first state visit in 1954, the Queen made King Felipe an honorary Knight of the Order of the Garter, with its famous blue sash. The 'KG' is a rare accolade reserved for fellow monarchs. Non-royal heads of state usually receive the regalia and red sash of an honorary GCB, a Knight Grand Cross of the Order of the Bath. The Queen has added an extra touch to her welcome arrangements in recent years, however, just as she did with Mikhail Gorbachev. A special exhibition is usually laid out in the Picture Gallery, featuring a cross-section of royal treasures and souvenirs that have a connection to the guest nation. In the case of the King and Queen of Spain, the Royal Librarian, Oliver Urquhart Irvine, was spoiled for choice as he prepared an exhibition which ranged from a woodcut of Charles I of Spain visiting England in 1520 to a Salvador Dalí watercolour that Dalí had given to the Duke of Edinburgh in person. Based on the British coat of arms, it featured a unicorn with a bloodstained horn and a British crown looking suspiciously like the Rock of Gibraltar. 'A very amusing deconstruction of the British royal arms,' observed Urquhart Irvine diplomatically. Alongside the diaries and photographs of earlier royal visitors to Spain was the text of the Queen's speech in Madrid during her 1988 state visit, the first by a reigning British monarch. Saluting Spain as both a 'formidable adversary and a true and brave ally', she had cracked a Spanish Armada joke: 'My country has experience of both!'

THE BANQUET

If a state visit is all about dazzling the visitor, then it is the state banquet that generates optimum dazzle – an occasion for tiaras, decorations and the unrivalled collection of gold and silver tableware amassed by George IV. Voluminous flower arrangements are prepared, to reflect the colours of the visiting nation, and the flowers at the very top of the U-shaped table will conceal microphones for the speeches. As with the carriage procession, the spectacle has remained largely unchanged since the reigns of earlier monarchs. However, the Queen has made a few subtle tweaks over the years. The menu at that first state banquet had been a four-course affair, starting with turtle soup, followed by 'Délice de Sole Elizabeth', chicken 'Gustav' with peas and new potatoes and 'Soufflé Glacé Louise'. By 2017 it was down to three courses: fillet of salmon trout, medallion of Scottish beef and a chocolate-and-raspberry tart.

The Queen has never liked long meals. So when, later in the reign, the Master of the Royal Household suggested that banquets could be shortened by twenty minutes if there was no soup, the Queen readily agreed to the idea. Another marked difference in the last two decades has been protocol. On that first state visit in 1954 – and for many years to come – the Palace adhered to the official order of precedence laid down by the Lord Chamberlain's Office and the Foreign Office. This gloriously arcane index of social hierarchy had a clearly defined place for everyone in relation to everyone else, be they a duchess, a bishop, a Cabinet minister, the younger son of a baronet or a commodore. Arranging the table according to preordained rules certainly made things easier. However, it meant that members of the Royal Family were inevitably concentrated at the top end of the table, often sitting next to each other, while all the rest of the 170-strong guest list could determine their place in the social spectrum simply by their distance from the Queen. There was also little scope for mixing up the nationalities, which was, after all, the whole point of a state visit in the first place. The Queen would always sit next to her fellow head of state, of course. Yet with the Swedes in 1954, for example, there was an unbroken line of British guests, stretching from Princess Margaret at the top end of the table a full fourteen places, via the Archbishop of Canterbury, all the way down to the Lord Privy Seal, before a foreign guest (the Swedish Ambassador) finally appeared on the seating plan. The Foreign Secretary, for whom a state banquet might have been a logical opportunity to promote bilateral relations, spent the evening in an all-British sandwich between the Countess of Scarborough and the Countess of Onslow.

The starchiness of these occasions could, inevitably, leave regulars yearning for a spot of drama. One member of the Royal Household recalls the night that Helen Adeane, the free-spirited wife of the Queen's famously reserved Private Secretary, Sir Michael Adeane, decided to enliven proceedings by dropping a fake dog-mess on the carpet mid-banquet. The liveried footmen were agog. How had a corgi sneaked inside a state banquet? While the joke was much enjoyed afterwards, staff were less amused by the behaviour of some of the visiting entourage during the 2005 state banquet for President

Hu Jintao of China. 'The Queen remarked they were all whipping out their laptops during the state banquet and doing emails at the table,' says David Cameron. 'Very bad manners.' The behaviour of some Chinese officials during the 2015 visit by President Xi Jinping did not impress the Queen, either. She was later filmed commiserating with the senior Metropolitan Police officer in charge of security for the visit. 'Oh, bad luck,' she told Commander Lucy D'Orsi at a garden party, noting that some of the Chinese delegation had been 'very rude' to the British Ambassador.*

As a rule, however, the Royal Household will do all they can to accommodate every special request, though little can now be done for smokers, since a 2016 ban on all smoking on royal premises. Heads of state who dislike the rigmarole of white tie can opt for a dress code of black tie, lounge suit or national dress. If guests are running late, there will be no embarrassing gap at the table. A 'reserve' banquet is held for surplus members of both entourages in the Royal Household Dining Room. They will eat the same food, be dressed in the same clothes and, in the event of a no-show, will despatch one of their number to make up the numbers. Perhaps the most original excuse for a late appearance came at the 1989 state banquet for President Babangida of Nigeria. According to Sir Patrick (now Lord) Wright, former head of the Diplomatic Service, one of the President's senior officials arrived just as dinner was over. He apologised immediately to the Queen, explaining that he had missed the presidential jet earlier in the day because he was unmarried. As a result, there had been no wife to wake him up in time.

The order of precedence was finally set aside as the world entered the twenty-first century. At the state banquet for the Queen of Denmark in 2000, the Queen decided to spread her family around the table. That way no one would feel 'below the salt'. In 2017, it would mean that every member of the British Royal Family and government was seated next to a member of the King of Spain's

* The Queen does not mince her words when she senses disrespect towards those serving in her name. During the chaotic 1980 royal tour of the Maghreb, the King of Morocco loftily ignored the schedule, repeatedly kept the Queen waiting and then informed her that it was the fault of her assistant Private Secretary, Robert Fellowes. 'I'll thank you not to speak about my staff like that,' she replied firmly.

entourage. Prince Harry, for example, was next to the Spanish Prime Minister's chief of staff.

Another adjustment – one that has proved extremely popular with all the Queen's guests – has been the shifting of the speeches from the end of dinner to the start. The Queen set this precedent, in unhappy circumstances, just after the Windsor fire of 1992. She was due to address a City of London luncheon marking the fortieth anniversary of her accession to the Throne, but she had a cold and a sore throat. The damage to her family home, on top of months of wounding headlines about royal marriages and royal finances, had left her at a low ebb. She had wanted Prince Philip to make the speech on her behalf. Her Private Secretary insisted that the words had to come from her. The compromise was that she would speak before, and not after, the meal; and she has been keen to stick to that arrangement ever since. It not only means that both heads of state can enjoy their dinner rather more, but also ensures that their words reach a wider audience, since the press can include them in earlier newspaper editions and the broadcasters have more chance of hitting the evening news bulletins. Not so at that first state banquet in 1954, however. On that occasion the guests had already worked their way through a wine list of Tarifa sherry, Johannisberger Erntebringer Riesling 1949, Château Lafite Rothschild 1937, Krug Private Cuvée Vintage 1937 and were on to the Sandeman vintage 1935 port by the time the Queen rose to address her guests, and an international radio audience, on the historical ties between the two nations. 'We thrive and prosper on the same liberal institutions which we have slowly built up through the years,' she told the King of Sweden. 'We share an abiding love of the sea which both separates and unites us.' In reply, the King saluted Britain's 'stout defence' and 'immense sacrifice' during long years of war.

In 2017 the wine list flattered both nations – with a Camel Valley sparkling rosé from Cornwall and a Spanish Bodegas Alión, Ribera del Duero 2000 – but the guests had hardly sat down when the Queen opened the speeches. 'With such a remarkable shared history, it is inevitable that there are matters on which we have not always seen eye to eye,' she said, in an oblique reference to Gibraltar. The King of Spain had already raised that issue in an earlier speech to the Houses of Parliament. No more needed to be said on the subject here. The Queen went on: 'The strength of our friendship has bred a resilient spirit of cooperation and goodwill. We deeply appreciate the significant contribution that Spain continues to make to this country.' After a toast from the world's longest-reigning monarch, Europe's newest (and tallest) monarch rose to thank her. Acknowledging the 'different choices' made by Britain and Spain over membership of the European Union, the King added that this was 'an integral part of our democratic tradition, rooted in the values of the European civilisation to which our two countries will always belong'.

The media would certainly give this occasion plenty of coverage, not least because of the jewellery on display. All state banquets bring out prized pieces from the Royal Family vaults, but, with two royal houses on parade, this proved to be one of the most glamorous in years. The following day's papers would all feature pictures of Queen Letizia wearing her 1906 Fleur de Lys Tiara, and the Duchess of Cambridge in a pink Marchesa gown and the diamond-and-pearl Lover's Knot Tiara.

Having attended plenty of state dinners all over the world, David Cameron still believes there is nothing quite like a Palace banquet for wowing even the most modern world leader: 'They are brilliant, ruthlessly efficient. Drinks beforehand, the receiving line, everyone gets to shake hands with the Queen, you go into dinner, you do the speeches and the toast, you eat your three courses, have a drink and you are out. Bang, bang, bang. You don't feel you are being rushed at all. It's done in good time. Even though we all know Buckingham Palace is falling apart, it all looks beautiful and it's everything you could wish for.'

After the old-world formalities of the first day of a state visit, most visitors then follow a well-trodden route over the next few days: a mandatory visit to Downing Street for talks and lunch, some glad-handing with the financial sector in the City of London, a visit to a university. Some of these excursions might conclude with a trade agreement or political deal, but that has never really been the main aim of a state visit. The emphasis is on mood, ambience and bilateral warmth.

Another traditional feature of a state visit has been the return banquet, when the host repays some of the Queen's hospitality.

During the first state visit by a Chinese leader, in 1999, President Jiang Zemin had arranged an elaborate banquet for the Queen at the Chinese Embassy. Those expecting an earnest, rigidly formal occasion were in for a shock. Protocol (and this was the protocol-obsessed Chinese, after all) dictates that there are no speeches at a return banquet. Yet once dinner was over, the seventy-three-year-old president rose to his feet and promptly burst into song. Dame Margaret Beckett, then Leader of the Commons and a future Foreign Secretary, still chuckles at the thought of the Queen unexpectedly finding herself next to a cabaret turn. 'The Chinese president decided to serenade the guests. He sang very well actually,' she recalls. 'I was opposite the Thatchers, and Denis Thatcher was appalled. He was like a little volcano bubbling up and down. And then the President said: "There's got to be a reply". Everyone looked at the Queen and we all thought: "You're kidding me". But further down the table, on the Thatchers' side, was the Speaker of the Commons, Betty Boothroyd.* Betty, God bless her, can sing and, one way or another, the President asked her to sing.'

As Jiang Zemin and Betty Boothroyd performed a duet of 'Our Hearts Were Young and Gay', Sir Denis grew ever more apoplectic. 'We were just hoping Denis Thatcher wasn't going to explode,' says Dame Margaret. 'He kept saying: "I've never seen anything like this in all my life!"' The royal guests, on the other hand, were enjoying every moment. Dame Margaret adds 'It was clear that the Queen and the Duke of Edinburgh were on the brink of hysteria for quite some time.'

Of all the changes the Queen has observed in seven decades of entertaining world leaders, one of the most noticeable has been the shrinking diary. Earlier in the reign, she would lay on a gala evening for her guests at the Royal Opera House – a production of *Le Coq d'Or* for the Swedes in 1954, for example. As the years went by, few world leaders would have either the time or the appetite for a whole night at the opera. There was, however, one musical evening in 2004 when President Chirac and his wife, Bernardette, came to Windsor

* A former professional dancer and member of the Tiller Girls troupe, Betty Boothroyd was elected as Labour MP for West Bromwich in 1973 and became the first female Speaker of the House of Commons in 1992. Following her retirement in 2000, she joined the House of Lords as Baroness Boothroyd.

Castle to celebrate the centenary of the Entente Cordiale. After the banquet in St George's Hall, the Queen escorted her guests through to the Waterloo Chamber for coffee and a compressed version of the hit musical, *Les Misérables*. It was a long evening for the cast, who had to finish their regular performance in London's West End, jump on a coach with police outriders and dash to Windsor – still in costume and make-up – for their royal encore. They made it just as the guests were having coffee, and the evening was a triumph. Its success, however, was also due to the fact that the Queen had paid attention to those small details, just as she had done with the King of Thailand all those years before. Mindful that this was an evening to mark 100 years of Franco-British bonhomie, she realised that it would be highly inappropriate to entertain her guests in a room named after France's greatest defeat. For one night only, Windsor Castle's Waterloo Chamber officially became 'The Music Room'.

ROYAL RELATIONSHIPS

Those who have worked for the Queen over many years say that she genuinely enjoys her role as a host. She is extremely proud of her Royal Household team and of the way they unfailingly rise to the occasion, whoever happens to be visiting. Her former Private Secretary, Sir William Heseltine, points to the way visits have reflected British foreign policy over the years: 'You can see a pattern: a concentration on the important countries of Europe at various times as negotiations for entry waxed and waned; an increasing interest in the Arab nations – remarkably, it seems now, one of the earliest visitors was King Faisal of Iraq, in July 1956, just before the Suez crisis; occasionally interspersed with "family visits" from other European monarchs.' Visits from the last, he says, were 'undoubtedly the most enjoyable', from a royal point of view.

Aside from the familiarity and the family connections, fellow monarchs could understand each other's challenges and problems in a way that an elected politician or a dictator could not. Only a fellow monarch might feel able to seek or offer advice on anything from succession to prime-ministerial interference; from coinage or heraldic orders, to interesting destinations for a royal yacht. Queen Margrethe of Denmark, who was educated in Britain, enjoys regular low-key private trips to London and always drops in on her cousin at Buckingham Palace. She has even admitted that she 'dreams in English' when she is in Britain. The fact that Britain and its Royal Family provided shelter to so many refugee monarchies during the Second World War remains etched in the collective European royal memory.

Monarch-to-monarch visits are much enjoyed by the staff, too, since they also know their opposite numbers. From time to time, all the European royal Private Secretaries get together to swap notes. Similarly, there are annual get-togethers for all the European royal press officers, royal chefs and royal protection officers. The royal trade union seems to be in good shape, despite the gloomy prediction of King Farouk of Egypt, shortly before the collapse of his own monarchy in 1953: 'There will soon be only five kings left – the Kings of Diamonds, Heart, Spades and Clubs, and the King of England.' In 2018, there were still twenty-seven monarchs reigning over forty-three nations. At the same time, the latest available United Nations Human Development Index listed all 188 countries according to a combination of life expectancy, education and income. Of the top twenty, more than half had a constitutional monarch as head of state, with Norway in first place (Britain was at number sixteen). As far as the Queen is concerned, even deposed monarchs are still part of the regal trade union. During her Diamond Jubilee in 2012 she invited all the world's monarchs to lunch at Windsor. Working out the seating plan for the official photograph could have been an insuperable challenge, even for a professor of protocol. After all, where do you put a fully-fledged emperor like Akihito of Japan? The Queen had a very simple solution. She would sit in the middle and all the other monarchs would be placed according to the date of their accession. As a result, she was flanked by the King of Romania and the King of the Bulgarians. Both had lost their thrones many years before, and both their nations were now avowedly republican. Nonetheless the Queen's view is: once a monarch, always a monarch – unless you abdicate.

Sir Antony Acland, former British Ambassador to Spain and latterly to the USA, remembers the Queen's enthusiastic support for Spain's King Juan Carlos during the years immediately after the restoration of the Spanish monarchy in 1975. 'The King had a tremendous respect for the Queen and used to telephone her quite often,' he says. 'I remember one of the things she told him was he needed to get out and about around the country. She'd been persuaded to do walkabouts in parts of Britain and he should do the same. He very much took her advice and went down to Andalusia. He was initially quite retiring, though he played a tremendously important part in establishing democratic modern Spain.' The closeness between the monarchs was certainly a bonus for Sir Antony, as British Ambassador. 'I saw the King often. He was very open. I remember going to see him and telling him I was about to go on a trip back to London and he said: "Do give the Queen my love when you see her". I didn't admit that I didn't automatically bowl in to Buckingham Palace and have a cup of tea.'

Sir Antony's boss during the same period was David Owen. The former Foreign Secretary remembers the way that the Spanish monarchy helped Spain regain its place in the democratic fold, thanks to Juan Carlos. 'He was very, very good and playing a skilful hand. He definitely stopped a military coup.' Lord Owen was less impressed by another young monarch who would not regain his throne, despite the Queen's active encouragement. 'The Queen was very supportive of the young King of Serbia – she's his godmother. But he couldn't speak Serbian at the time that he was trying to get back in to power. I did say to him: "I think the best thing is you should learn Serbian!" '

The Queen was stoical about the outbreak of abdication-itis that began in 2013. Four monarchs, including Juan Carlos, plus the Pope would step down in the space of a year. The Queen, however, had made a Coronation oath before the Almighty. Prior to that, aged twenty-one, she had dedicated herself to her royal duty 'for the whole of my life'. So, she would not be abdicating.

DIFFICULT GUESTS

If fellow monarchs have always been very welcome, the Queen has also had some atrocious guests to stay over the years, more so than any previous sovereign. Interestingly, most of them turned up during the same period. Look through the Palace visitors' book and, when it comes to the objectionable, the rude and the downright psychotic, the Seventies stand out.

Not that the British government seemed to harbour any great concerns about Major-General Idi Amin of the Ugandan army, when he first came to power in 1971. Uganda had been a British colony until 1962, when Prime Minister Milton Obote led it to independence. By 1966, Obote had also assumed the presidency and was a vocal critic of British foreign policy in Africa, particularly the decision by Edward Heath's Conservative government, on coming to power in 1970, to resume arms sales to South Africa. Uganda even threatened to leave the Commonwealth at its tempestuous 1971 summit in Singapore. Obote's mistake, however, was to go there in the first place. While he was out of the country, Amin, as head of the army, saw his opportunity and launched a swift and successful military coup. Britain wasted no time in recognising the new regime. Amin might have been a fantasist – he claimed to have fought in the Second World War, despite joining the King's African Rifles as a cook in 1946 – but British diplomats were keen to get him onside as quickly as possible. In July 1971, he let it be known that he wanted to come to London to meet the Queen, the Prime Minister and the Commonwealth Secretary-General, Arnold Smith. Although Britain was already aware of terrible human-rights abuses by Amin's gangsters, the Foreign Office readily agreed. At their request, the Queen went one better than an audience and gave him lunch at Buckingham Palace. She quickly realised that she was dealing with a maniac when he took her into his confidence. He told her that he was planning to start a war. What's more, he was planning to invade a neighbouring Commonwealth nation, Tanzania, to establish a corridor to the sea. As Arnold Smith recorded later: 'He shocked her by saying he wanted to cut a strip of territory from his landlocked country down to the Indian Ocean.' The Queen might normally regard her lunch conversations as confidential. On this occasion, however, she felt morally obliged to report what Amin was up to. She had a high regard for Tanzania's President, Julius Nyerere, and was appalled that Amin felt entitled to invade his neighbour's sovereign territory to grab a 450-mile section of northern Tanzania.

As soon as lunch was over, she asked her officials to contact the Foreign Secretary, Sir Alec Douglas-Home, and warn him what Amin had said. Douglas-Home was already aware that Amin was rearming because, quite separately, the newly-installed dictator had asked him for British assistance in obtaining new weapons, including a fleet of armoured cars. Douglas-Home duly shared all this information later with Arnold Smith. 'It was obvious that Amin could be a very dangerous man, puffing out these grandiose dreams,' Smith wrote in his memoirs.

Despite this, Amin was still on the Queen's Christmas-card list at the end of 1971, although a clerical error meant that her card was late. 'When I gave the card to the president yesterday he was delighted but would have been even more delighted if it had arrived before Christmas,' a frustrated Harry Brind, British High Commissioner to Uganda, wrote to Lees Mayall, Vice-Marshal of the Diplomatic Corps, in January 1972. A few days later, Amin invited the Queen to attend the tenth-anniversary celebrations of Ugandan independence. The Queen replied that she was 'most disappointed', but other commitments precluded a visit. At this stage she was still signing her correspondence to him: 'Your Good Friend, Elizabeth R.'

Within months, however, it was clear that relations with Amin were doomed, as he announced the expulsion of 80,000 Ugandan Asians, many of whom had close ties with Britain. Their properties and businesses were seized, and 28,000 of them would move to the UK as stories mounted of atrocities against all forms of opposition to Amin. Edward Heath's government, which had been so ready to embrace the enemy of the irritating Milton Obote, now began lobbying for Uganda to be expelled from the Commonwealth. Arnold Smith warned that this would be regarded by many African leaders as a case of Britain reverting to its old imperial ways. Amin might be a monster, but at least he was *their* monster.

He failed to appear at the 1973 and 1975 Commonwealth meetings, sending ministers in his place as the charge sheet of human-rights abuses stacked up. By the time of the 1977 meeting, most of the world had learned about Amin's massacres and torture squads. Some 300,000 people in a country of twelve million were executed, often in the most grotesque fashion – forced to bludgeon each other to death, or pushed from aircraft or over a precipice. His behaviour was demonstrably worse than that of the pariah state of South Africa. Yet Uganda could still rely on Pan-African solidarity to maintain his membership of the club. Commonwealth double-standards had reached a new low.

So there was alarm bordering on panic when Amin let it be known that he was planning to attend the 1977 Commonwealth Heads of Government Meeting in London. It had originally been earmarked for Zambia but, at the Queen's personal request, had shifted to Britain to coincide with her Silver Jubilee celebrations. Amin's presence would not only be hugely embarrassing for the British government, now led by Labour's Jim Callaghan, but would be deeply embarrassing for the more democratic Commonwealth member states and, in particular, for the Queen. If he came, she would be duty bound to meet him, in her capacity as Head of the Commonwealth.

Pressure would have to be applied from various quarters to keep him away from London. Would Amin listen, though? Sir William Heseltine, former Private Secretary to the Queen, recalls that Buckingham Palace tried using the old-boy network by despatching an officer who, like Amin, had been in the King's African Rifles. 'He was sent to talk some sense and I remember him saying that it was hopeless,' says Heseltine. 'He'd been received in some sort of mud hut with a drain as an entrance and he'd been made to crawl through this to have his audience with Amin. It was a very unsuccessful attempt at diplomacy.'

Amin was never going to listen to the despised imperialist British government. So the Foreign Secretary, David Owen, attempted to persuade other African nations to keep him away from the Queen's party in London. That was a fruitless mission, too.

Jim Callaghan consulted the new Commonwealth Secretary-General, Sonny Ramphal, for his advice. 'He was terrified,' says Ramphal. 'I warned him: "You cannot turn Amin away". After all, Ted Heath received him at Downing Street.' Ramphal set off for Uganda, for what would be one of the most bizarre encounters during his entire fifteen years as Secretary-General. 'Amin invited us to the opening of a tourist hotel in the Queen Elizabeth game park and offered us this helicopter,' recalls Patsy Robertson, Ramphal's press secretary. 'I remember someone said "that's the helicopter he throws people out of" which was a worry. Then one of the press said: "Why have they brought these children?" They turned out to be Amin's troupe of pygmy dancers.'

Ramphal gently but firmly advised Amin that if he came to London, he would only embarrass the Queen and alienate his allies within the Commonwealth.

Amin seemed to relish the guessing game and all the attention. He vanished from public view just as the Commonwealth leaders began arriving in London, fuelling inevitable rumours. Might he really be on his way to upstage the Queen at her own party? Even as the heads of government were gathering at St Paul's Cathedral for the service of thanksgiving to mark her twenty-five years on the Throne, there was palpable unease that Amin might make a last-minute appearance. Earl Mountbatten recorded in his diary that the Queen was not her normal self. 'I asked her afterwards why she had looked rather cross and worried,' he wrote. 'She laughed and said: "I was just thinking how awful it would be if Amin were to gatecrash the party".' Mountbatten ventured to ask what she would have done. Noting that the Lord Mayor's Pearl Sword had been placed before her, the Queen replied that she would have 'hit him hard over the head' with it.

Though there was no sign of Amin at St Paul's, tension mounted as the guests moved on to the Lord Mayor's lunch that followed. The press had picked up word that Amin's plane had just entered Irish air space. He might yet arrive in time for pudding. Jim Callaghan and his ministers were certainly not enjoying their lunch, as former Foreign Secretary David Owen recalls: 'Merlyn Rees [the Home Secretary] came up to me and said: "David, Amin is about to land at London Airport!" We had made plans in case he was crazy enough to fly in so I said: "We will push him to a remote part of the airfield and just not allow him to get off the airplane". Merlyn was on the phone for most of the banquet.' In the event, Amin was having them all on. He had never left Uganda.

Owen would have the last laugh a year later. 'Amin was a menace and I got rid of him,' he says proudly, adding, 'I'd be in jail now for what I did!' When Amin finally launched an invasion of Tanzania, as he had warned the Queen he would in 1971, Tanzania's President Julius Nyerere came to Britain for help. 'Nyerere was not a mild man by any means but he didn't have any ammunition,' says Owen. 'I said: "I can't buy you ammunition but I can increase your aid budget so you can buy ammunition". You'd go to jail now for using aid money to buy ammunition. But there was nothing on paper.' Armed with new British-funded weaponry, Tanzania went on to launch its own offensive against Uganda, forcing Amin into exile, never to return.

Though he was a volatile and brutal dictator at home, Amin retained an abiding respect and affection for the Queen. Sonny Ramphal believes that is why he stayed away from her Jubilee. It would be a similar story with Zimbabwe's megalomaniacal President, Robert Mugabe. Even in the latter stages of his regime, as he ranted and raved against the evils of the British government and the empire that had imprisoned him for eleven years, he never had a bad word to say about the Queen. While he led his country in the earlier years after independence, he was a firm royal favourite. One former member of the Royal Household remembers being mesmerised by him – 'the longest fingers I'd ever seen on a man'. In 1994, the Queen formally invited Mugabe to pay a state visit to Britain and he even made a little bit of ceremonial history. That traditional state welcome at Victoria railway station was finally abandoned, for the novelty value of state visits had worn off over the years and the crowds along Victoria Street were getting thinner. For a sensitive head of state like Mugabe, a small, unenthusiastic crowd could be taken as a grave insult. So the Queen approved a plan to greet Mugabe on Horse Guards, at the other end of the Mall from the Palace. Not only did the grand old parade ground look smarter, but the route would be much shorter. It was such a success that the Queen has stuck to that format ever since.

British diplomats of the period recall that Mugabe was already morphing into a different character. His first wife, Sally, a teacher from Ghana, was widely regarded as a crucial, steadying influence in his life. 'She was a remarkable woman, Sally Mugabe,' says Sir Nicholas Soames, MP, whose father, Lord Soames, had come to know the Mugabes well as the last Governor of Rhodesia. 'He never put a foot wrong while she was alive and then it went bad.' Many who knew him chart Mugabe's decline from Sally's death, after a long history of renal failure, in 1992. 'Sally was a tremendous support,' says Sonny Ramphal. 'My wife saw a lot of her and we knew the strength she was to him.'

In 1996, Mugabe married Grace, a former secretary forty-one years his junior, by whom he had fathered two children while Sally was still alive. He was a changed man, according to another royal insider who had got to know him well: 'Money got to him. He lost touch with reality. I asked his second wife what her main interests were outside of her husband's political career? "Shopping!" she said.'

Mugabe grew increasingly hostile to Britain after 1997, when the new government of Tony Blair announced that it would no longer fund a Zimbabwean land-reform programme. The scheme was supposed to help small farmers, but was very clearly enriching members of Mugabe's family and his inner circle instead. As Blair remarked to the new Commonwealth Secretary-General, Don McKinnon: 'He's really an old-style Marxist.' The New Zealander recalls Mugabe's increasingly manic demeanour as Zimbabwe entered the twenty-first century. 'He jiggled incessantly, hands flapping, head bobbing, I've never seen such a level of nervous energy in one person,' McKinnon wrote in his memoirs. To this day, though, he remains in awe of Mugabe's brainpower. 'Never underestimate his intelligence,' says McKinnon at his home in New Zealand. 'And never underestimate his ability to know more than anyone about Commonwealth cricket scores.' He believes that Mugabe had become increasingly embittered after the release from prison and subsequent election of Nelson Mandela in South Africa. Mandela enjoyed a global respect that had eluded the Zimbabwean leader, and Mugabe loathed being overlooked as the standard-bearer for black African self-determination. By 2003, after umpteen violations of Commonwealth rules, Mugabe had removed Zimbabwe from the Commonwealth before it could be expelled. McKinnon is confident that it will return in the new post-Mugabe era – and that the Queen will be thrilled when it happens. Yet, through it all, Mugabe never voiced any criticism of the Queen. Baroness Chalker, former Minister for Overseas Development, also got to know Mugabe well. She says that he always made a very clear distinction between the monarch and her ministers: 'One of the things he would tell you is: "She is one of the most wonderful women. Pity about the politicians".'

Another African visitor of that period was less respectful of the Queen, however. At around the same time as the Queen's shocking lunch with Idi Amin in 1971, Edward Heath's government invited Mobutu Sese Seko, the fearfully corrupt President of Zaire, to pay a state visit to Britain. The date was fixed for 1973 and Mobutu arrived at Buckingham Palace with his wife, Marie-Antoinette, who exhibited a similar lack of tact and common sense to her ill-starred French namesake of a previous age. She had smuggled her pet dog into

Britain in the presidential luggage. Given the strict quarantine laws and the prevalence of rabies in mainland Europe, it was a very serious breach of the law. Mrs Mobutu's subterfuge was soon discovered when she requested some steak from the Palace kitchens to feed her pet. The Queen's staff say that no one has ever seen her angrier than the moment she learned of the four-legged contraband hiding in the Belgian Suite. 'Get that dog out of my house!' she bellowed at the Deputy Master of the Household, and ordered the instant removal of the royal corgis to Windsor for safekeeping. Mrs Mobutu's pet was promptly quarantined while the state visit continued in a glacial atmosphere.

Despite this flagrant abuse of royal hospitality, the Mobutus are still not remembered as the worst guests of the Queen's reign. That honour would go to the couple from Eastern Europe who arrived five years later.

THE NADIR

After a lot of thought, the Queen had prepared what she imagined would be the perfect present for her communist guest. President Ceausescu of Romania might be one of the nastiest state visitors ever invited to Buckingham Palace but there were still standards to maintain ahead of his arrival in the summer of 1978. So her officials had consulted the Romanian Ambassador for gift suggestions. Back came the reply that Ceausescu would like nothing more than a hunting rifle from a famous British gunmaker. The Queen had not only commissioned a rifle, with telescopic sight, but also a handsome leather case embossed with her 'E II R' cypher and the name 'Nicolai Ceausescu'. On the eve of the visit, her deputy Private Secretary, William Heseltine, invited the Ambassador round to the Palace to check the final arrangements and to see the Queen's present. 'His face fell and he went ashen grey,' Heseltine recalls. 'He said: "You've spelt Nicolai in the Russian way." I could plainly see he thought his head was going to be taken off if it was handed over with this misspelling. Fortunately, we had an amazing craftsman down at Windsor who was able to turn the 'i' into an 'e' overnight.'

The Ambassador was not the only nervous wreck ahead of this visit. Over at the Foreign Office, David Lambert in the Eastern

European & Soviet Union department had spent months trying to arrange a much trickier gift for the Romanian first lady, Elena Ceausescu. The volatile, semi-literate self-styled 'academic' had let it be known that she was expecting to receive an honorary degree from a prestigious British university during her stay with the Queen. The state visit would clearly be deemed a painful failure if her academic brilliance went unrecognised. Unfortunately, British seats of learning were not queuing up.

Even more astonishingly, we now learn that Lambert's boss, the Foreign Secretary, was actually in favour of calling the whole thing off. David Owen had been sent a confidential memo from his Private Secretary, Ewen Fergusson, warning that the media were becoming increasingly hostile to the first state visit by a dictator from communist Eastern Europe. Owen's private response, though honest, was extraordinary, given that the state visit was just two days away. For the Foreign Office files reveal that he, too, was appalled by the prospect of welcoming the Ceausescus. 'Who agreed to this visit?' he scribbled on the side of Fergusson's memo. 'Did I? If I did, I regret it.' As for the media, Owen had no quarrel. 'They have some fair points of criticism,' he added.

At least he would not have to give the Ceausescus board and lodging. That unenviable task fell to the Queen. That is the way it always is when world leaders come to the United Kingdom. The government issues the invitation and the monarch delivers the royal magic. She and her staff would arrange Ceausescu's state visit uncomplainingly because that has always been her duty, though she would surely have been displeased to learn that David Owen, the very minister responsible for imposing the guest from hell on her, now thought that the whole thing was a terrible idea. It was too late, anyway. There could be no going back. The horses and carriages were arranged, the banquet planned, the Palace's Belgian Suite cleaned and prepared with fresh flowers. Finally, on June 13th, 1978, the Queen and the Duke of Edinburgh opened their home to their two unforgettably disagreeable guests.

The Ceausescus' state visit is a vivid illustration of British diplomatic priorities at the height of the Cold War. In those days, the government was willing to turn a blind eye to almost any misdemeanour and even embarrass the Queen, if a short-term political deal might be struck. In this case, it was all about selling a few British planes. The fact that the buyer was the most repressive dictator among the Warsaw Pact nations (even the Soviets regarded him as authoritarian) mattered not one jot.

The Ceausescus would arrive during the last year of Jim Callaghan's troubled Labour premiership. This, though, was yet another visit that, like so many questionable invitations, had its origins in the Tory administration of Edward Heath. Foreign Office files show that Britain first suggested an official or state visit to the Romanians as far back as 1973, courtesy of Foreign Office Minister of State Julian Amery. Although a staunch member of the very right-wing Monday Club, Amery had been struck by Ceausescu's willingness to stand apart from the rest of the communist Eastern Bloc nations. Romania had not supported the Soviet invasion of Czechoslovakia in 1968. Here was a leader who was keen to pursue his own trade and political agendas, regardless of what the Soviet Union might think. By engaging with Ceausescu, the argument went, Britain might gain some sort of foothold inside the Warsaw Pact and derive some sort of commercial advantage, too.

The Labour leader, Harold Wilson, had already had similar thoughts during a visit to Romania in 1972, while returning from Moscow as leader of the opposition. Shortly after ousting Edward Heath as Prime Minister in February 1974, Wilson made fresh overtures to the Romanian dictator. On 3rd May he had a Downing Street meeting with some of the most senior figures in the Ceausescu regime, including Stefan Andrei, secretary of the Romanian communist party. According to a classified minute of the meeting: 'Mr Andrei said that President Ceausescu would like to visit the Prime Minister in London but would need an official invitation from the Queen.' Wilson replied that Ceausescu would be very welcome, but a state visit was 'difficult to arrange', and that 'he could come much sooner' if he made an ordinary 'official' visit. The Romanian leader, however, clearly wanted the full royal treatment. As the Cabinet papers reveal: 'Mr Andrei did not reply to these remarks but at the end of the meeting took Mr Wilson to one side and emphasised the importance which President Ceausescu attached to a state visit.'

Relations continued to strengthen. Ceausescu made a brief official visit to Britain in 1975, when he dropped in at Chequers to discuss several issues, including British support for a new Romanian aerospace programme. The President let it be known that he still wanted a state visit and was very happy to wait for a gap in the Queen's diary. In the same year, Wilson became the first British Prime Minister since the war to visit Romania. The time had finally come to fix a date for Ceausescu to stay with the Queen: June 1978. Unusually for a state visit, this one had a very clear and straightforward commercial imperative. Ceausescu would sign a £200 million contract to build eighty-two BAC 1-11 aircraft* in Romania, under licence from the British Aircraft Corporation (soon to become British Aerospace), plus another £100 million contract for 225 Rolls-Royce Spey engines to power them. At a time when Britain's ailing economy was lurching from one crisis to the next, amid almost constant industrial unrest (and just six months before the 'winter of discontent' that would eject Labour from office for the next eighteen years), this was a substantial win for the Callaghan government. Yet it all hinged on the Queen. For, in return, Britain would lay on the grandest welcome the Romanian despot had ever received. Though Ceausescu might have been entertained at the Vatican, by Pope Paul VI, and at the White House, by President Jimmy Carter, nothing would portray his stature as a global statesman quite as spectacularly as a full royal welcome in London.

'We thought that Romania was rather liberal,' recalls Sir Simon Fraser, former head of the Diplomatic Service. 'It just shows how careful you have to be about these things.'

Files from Downing Street and the Foreign Office show the extent to which Britain's politicians, diplomats and commercial sector were happy to pander to Ceausescu's ego and paranoia in almost every way in order to ensure that the visit ran smoothly. There was even an offer from British Aerospace to fly Ceausescu home to Bucharest at the end of the visit in Concorde. Roger du Boulay, the man in charge of protocol and royal liaison at the Foreign Office – and himself a Second World War fighter pilot -was quick to advise caution. It would, he wrote to his colleagues, 'set up a very awkward precedent'

* Introduced in 1965, the BAC 1-11 was a short-haul passenger jet that was soon superseded by the Boeing 737.

for future state visitors, who would all demand a ride home in Concorde. However, he added: 'Of course, if it could be shown that a free ride in Concorde would turn the scale in the BAC 1-11 negotiations, we might have to think again.'

What would go down even better, however, would be that honorary degree for the President's wife. The signals were coming loud and clear from the British Embassy in Romania that this was very much what Elena Ceausescu was expecting, not least because Harold Wilson had apparently mooted the idea during his 1975 visit to Romania. Though Wilson had since retired from politics, he had become Chancellor of the University of Bradford. So, in December 1977, the Foreign Office wrote to Wilson's Private Secretary, Baroness (Marcia) Falkender, with a candid proposal. Since Wilson had come up with this idea in the first place, would he please ask Bradford University if they would consider an honorary degree for Mrs Ceausescu, in recognition of her 'distinguished work' in the fields of 'polymer science and scientific education'. The following month, Andrew Burns, First Secretary at the British Embassy in Bucharest, informed his bosses that the Romanian council for science and technology had again 'dropped a number of strong hints that Mrs Ceausescu would be pleased to receive some kind of academic distinction' during the state visit. Very soon, an entire team of Foreign Office talents would be applying themselves to this Herculean task. Lady Falkender reported back that Bradford would need to put any such proposal to a vote, and that Wilson was pessimistic about the result. Realising that a rejection would be a diplomatic disaster, the Foreign Secretary, David Owen, decided not to take things any further with Bradford.

The Foreign Office files reveal a mounting sense of panic. Anthony Figgis, in the Eastern European department, attempted to woo Heriot-Watt University. No luck there, either. It was the same with Sussex and Liverpool. Andrew Burns in Bucharest wrote to his opposite number in London, David Lambert. 'Surely Imperial College could help?' pleaded Burns, noting that one of the Ceausescus' sons had studied there. They could not. Lambert, meanwhile, had been rebuffed by the Royal Society, but was chasing Southampton University, having heard that they were pursuing new international partnerships. They might just be willing to give Mrs Ceausescu a robe and a scroll 'as a means of putting themselves on the map in Romania'.

Kenneth Scott, head of the Eastern European department, was nervous about all these rejections. On 15th February 1978, he wrote to the British Ambassador in Romania, Reggie Secondé, saying that it might be better to have no degree than face hideous embarrassment 'if some disgruntled member of a university council chooses to leak that the FCO are hawking Madame Ceausescu's somewhat dubious wares around several universities'.

If British academe was proving unfriendly to the forthcoming visitors, other organisations were not. The chairman of National Westminster Bank, Robin Leigh-Pemberton, and his board wanted to invite Ceausescu to lunch. The Labour Mayor of Coventry was begging the Foreign Office to send the Ceausescus there. Sir John Russell, now foreign-affairs adviser to Rolls-Royce, wrote to Roger du Boulay at the FCO insisting that the company should be included in all the 'major protocol functions'. He added that the company's chairman, Sir Kenneth Keith, had been Ceausescu's guest 'at a bear shoot – not that I imagine there will be anything similar in London in June'. Du Boulay replied that guest lists were still being discussed. 'As for bear shoots, we could I suppose round up the stray dogs in Hyde Park but I am inclined to think we will have to seek other ways of diverting the President.'

ALARM BELLS

From the outset, the Foreign Office planners were keen to ensure that everyone at the Palace and in Whitehall was aware of what a thin-skinned egomaniac they were dealing with. Here was a man with such a carefully controlled personality cult that the Romanian media could not even mention Ceausescu's height (5 feet 6 inches) for fear of reprisals. British diplomats offered some hilarious guidance on what not to say in the presidential presence. There was to be no mention of the former Romanian Royal Family (because 'the present regime might not look too favourably on the reference'). Romanians should not be described as 'Eastern Europeans', but as '*sui generis* Romanians'. And hosts should 'refer to the respect with which the President is held for his dynamic and imaginative foreign policies'. In particular, demonstrations should be discouraged. Ceausescu's head of protocol was 'very touchy' on the subject, and the President had recently refused to leave his embassy in the USA until a crowd of protestors had been dispersed.

The Foreign Office was also picking up warning signals of some Mobutu-style bad behaviour. In March 1978, David Lambert received a tip-off from Ivor Rawlinson in the FCO's Southern European department that one of Ceausescu's sons, believed to be Nicu, had caused great offence by running up a string of unpaid bills while accompanying his father on a visit to Greece. Rawlinson added: 'Perhaps if he comes, we could organise some parachute jumping with the Prince of Wales!'

Staff at the Palace had complained to Roger du Boulay about the size of the Romanian entourage. In mid-March, the Romanian Ambassador had informed them that Ceausescu was planning to bring a team of fifty-five – including ten pet journalists, his personal aircrew and four extra bodyguards – who would all need to stay at the Palace. Royal staff replied that these hangers-on would have to sleep elsewhere, because even Buckingham Palace could not possibly accommodate such numbers.

And still the quest for an honorary degree was getting nowhere. On 7th April, Kenneth Scott wrote to the British Embassy in Bucharest with further bad news: a thumbs-down from the University of Southampton. David Lambert in the FCO's Eastern European department was still not giving up, though. Next stop: the University of York.

On 24th April, the British Ambassador, Reggie Secondé, sent two very frank telegrams with his own impressions of the Queen's guests. The first, to the Foreign Secretary, David Owen (and thence to the Palace), was a candid if somewhat admiring pen portrait of Ceausescu. 'He is as absolute a dictator as could be found in the world today,' the Ambassador warned, adding that Elena Ceausescu was a 'viper', their children were 'feckless' and that Ceausescu's endless speech-making to slavish, chanting party apparatchiks resembled a cross between Adolf Hitler and George Orwell. 'The sinister aspect is that a shrewd and accomplished statesman like Ceausescu can accept such orchestrated adulation. It is all too reminiscent of 1938 and 1984,' wrote Secondé. He warned of 'disastrous' scenes on some of the President's previous tours, including one to Belgium, where his guards had roughed up the locals and 'scrambled for places at the dinner table'. On the plus side, Ceausescu was 'well-disposed towards Britain and, despite attacks of anxiety, there is every chance that he will restrain his natural instinct to erupt if crossed or provoked by his public reception'. Secondé concluded: 'We are lucky to have President Ceausescu in the saddle. He is courageous, independent-minded and prepared to treat in all fields with the West.' To which one senior mandarin added a wry note in the margin: 'Help!'

Secondé also wrote to Roger du Boulay with some useful American intelligence on protocol. He had just received a briefing from the American Embassy in Romania on how to handle this most prickly of guests, based on Ceausescu's visit to the USA. For one thing, grace should be avoided before all meals. 'He will not stand for any religious invocations,' Secondé wrote, adding that, at one American event, Ceausescu had simply walked out of the room during grace and walked back in afterwards. 'It is very important to keep Mrs Ceausescu happy,' he added. 'Madame likes shopping. She apparently pays but the payment aspect should be made clear; she gladly accepts anything which is presented.' The staff were another matter: 'The Americans had some trouble with the Romanian advance guard who gave shameless instructions about the delivery of fur coats etc.' Ceausescu was also acutely sensitive to being patronised in any way – what the British Ambassador called 'being high-hatted' – although he could easily be seduced by extravagant ceremonial and a decent guard of honour.

The golden rule, to be observed at all times, was the need for profuse sycophancy. 'Constant praise for Ceausescu's international statesmanship is very much in order,' Secondé advised. 'There is no better lubricant and it can be poured on in unlimited quantities.' The Ambassador's advice was circulated around the Foreign Office and Buckingham Palace. 'Useful,' noted Kenneth Scott, who would one day end up at the Palace as a deputy Private Secretary to the Queen. He quickly passed on all these tips to the Lord Mayor of London, Peter Vanneck, who had been wondering what on earth to say in his traditional welcome to the state visitor. Back came the Lord Mayor's draft speech for Scott's approval. Hailing Ceausescu's 'universal reputation as an experienced international statesman', the Lord Mayor added that Mrs Ceausescu was 'not only a scientist and chemical engineer of international repute but a great exponent of women's rights'. The sharpest satirist would have been pushed to match his fawning conclusion, complete with a quote from Theodore Roosevelt: 'We need leaders to whom are granted great visions . . . who can kindle people with the fire from their burning soul. You, Sir, are such a person.' Even Kenneth Scott felt this was taking things a little too far. 'Not as I would have written it,' he wrote on the draft, 'but perhaps we'll all be too drunk to notice!' The Lord Mayor's hyperbole, however, would pale before some of the drivel that was to come.

Ahead of any state visit, the British Embassy would normally send the Palace some briefing notes on the state visitor's entourage. Andrew Burns, First Secretary in Bucharest, was decidedly restrained about Mrs Ceausescu – 'tough-minded and puritanical' – but more outspoken on other members of the inner circle. Ion Avram, the 'Minister of the Machine Building Industry', was 'short fat and bald; a rather jolly man whose ungainly exterior hides a good intelligence'. The one to watch, however, was Nicolae Ecobescu, head of protocol. As well as causing 'considerable offence' on many foreign visits, 'he has been known to exercise some physical violence in his efforts to restrain Ambassadors or journalists seeking to approach unnecessarily close to the President'.

And then came a diplomatic miracle. At last, a British seat of learning had decided that Mme Ceausescu was worthy of an academic laurel. On 3rd May, Professor Terence Burlin, of the Polytechnic of Central London, wrote to David Lambert saying that the court of governors was minded to present the first lady not merely with an honorary degree, but with an honorary professorship, no less. 'We do not anticipate any problems,' he added. There was yet more good news to follow. While the University of York had refused to countenance an honour, its professor of chemistry, Richard Norman, also happened to be President of the Royal Institute of Chemistry. Wearing that hat, he had every confidence that he could persuade his fellow chemists that they should not merely confer an honorary award on the first lady, but a bona-fide fellowship. As soon as the news had reached Bucharest, Mrs Ceausescu accepted both offers instantly and cancelled her visits to the other academic institutions on her itinerary.

With just days to go before the arrival, the Romanians were still demanding further kowtowing from the UK, in deference to the presidential ego. As the British Ambassador, Reggie Secondé noted,

Ceausescu always liked to round off a visit with 'an endless and turgid Joint Declaration'. There was nothing to make a declaration about, beyond the aircraft deal, but Jim Callaghan and his ministers were happy to go along with the charade. So Downing Street drafted some meaningless 'memoranda of understanding' about the importance of cultural and educational ties. Yet Cabinet papers show that there was virtually no attempt to mention the human rights record of a country where torture and persecution were a regular fact of life. The Foreign Office did not object when the Romanians handed them a list of undesirable dissidents and 'irredentists' whom they wanted expelled from Britain for the duration of the visit. The Romanian government even warned the British authorities about a 'Hungarian' member of the House of Lords, Lord Balogh, in case he might cause trouble. Instead of rejecting this shameless affront to British justice, the Foreign Office Minister of State, Lord Goronwy-Roberts, simply 'welcomed the information'. As for Lord Balogh, he assured the Romanians that 'British parliamentarians would not behave in an undignified manner'.

RED CARPET

For the Foreign Office, the pressing issue now was guest lists. The chairmen of Shell, ICI and Hawker Siddeley were among those in the top tier, with invitations to the Queen's state banquet, along with the director-general of the BBC. Next down in the pecking order were those invited to the Prime Minister's lunch (including the editor of *The Sunday Times*, Harold Evans, and ITN's head of current affairs, Peter Snow). Then came the Lord Mayor's banquet, followed by various receptions. Years later, the British establishment would pour vitriol over the very mention of Ceausescu, but the great and good were queuing up to shake his hand in 1978. Kenneth Scott received a delightful begging letter from Sir Leslie Glass, former Ambassador to Romania and chairman of the Anglo-Romanian Bank, pointing out that he had yet to receive an invitation to anything. 'I didn't expect to be invited to any meal at the Palace but if there is any larger reception, I wonder if I could suggest our names,' he wrote from his home in Leominster, adding that he had no great desire to leave it at the height of the fly-fishing season. 'It is a wrench to leave Herefordshire when the mayfly are out but I think that the Romanians might be a little surprised if we weren't included.' Such was the demand for invitations that Sir Leslie would remain on his Herefordshire riverbank for the duration of the visit.

The Foreign Office was also fielding an increasing number of complaints from MPs and members of the public. Why were they inflicting another despot on the Queen? Geoffrey Howe wrote to the Foreign Secretary, David Owen (whose position he himself would occupy a few years later), complaining about Romanian persecution of Christians. An eminent Bristol physicist relayed warnings from a senior Romanian professor that Elena Ceausescu had 'no serious reputation as a chemist'. The FCO memo records, with a certain snobbish relish, that the physicist was greatly relieved to learn that the only seat of learning hoodwinked by Mrs Ceausescu's bogus achievements was Central London Poly.

By now, the Queen was receiving some reliable inside information from a fellow head of state. President Valéry Giscard d'Estaing of France called the Palace to warn her about the conduct of Ceausescu's entourage during a visit to Paris a few months before. The official deputed to look after the Romanians had never seen anything like it. As the President later recalled: 'He came to see me, appalled, and said: "It's frightful. The place has been wrecked. They have taken everything away." There were lots of lamps, vases, ashtrays and bathroom fittings. After their departure the place had been emptied. Everything had been unscrewed. It was as if burglars had moved in for a whole summer.' To make matters worse, Ceausescu's minders had even hacked out holes in the walls, looking for hidden wires and bugging devices.

The Queen warned the Master of the Household to ensure that any remotely valuable loose items in the Belgian Suite were removed. As Lord Butler, former Private Secretary to three prime ministers, recalls: 'They were advised to move the silver brushes from the Palace dressing table or the Romanians would pinch the lot.' And criticism was mounting in the press. With two days to go, the Foreign Secretary, David Owen, scribbled that bizarre note on his Foreign Office memo, deploring the visit and wishing it was not about to take place. Looking back on it, he explains that he had no choice. The invitation had been extended by another government long before he took the job: 'I had to defend this decision that was made by [Conservative minister] Julian Amery who had made it to get an order in for BAC 1-11s. So I just had to sit tight while papers like the *Daily Telegraph* poured filth on the Foreign Secretary for arrogantly making this decision. There was b***** all I could do!'

Ceausescu was getting some favourable reviews, however, in the left-wing media. Just before leaving Romania, he rambled on at great length in an exclusive interview with the *Guardian*'s Hella Pick. There was a cursory discussion of human rights. 'How do you feel about criticism that has been voiced in the West?' he was asked. Ceausescu replied that Romania took a 'democratic humanistic' approach to human rights and that 'the entire people fully support the policies of our country'. The following day the *Guardian* carried a 'Letter from Bucharest' about Britain's next state visitor: 'He and more so his wife appear to have won genuine popular affection. Mr Ceausescu is a small, taut man who always seems to hold himself under tight control. He has shown immense courage in asserting Romania's independence from the Russians and encouraging Romania's nationalism. They appear to accept Romania's stringent austerity with good humour and believe that deliverance will come.' It would indeed come, eleven years later – via a firing squad.

On the same day, writing in *The Times*, Bernard Levin delivered a scathing attack on Ceausescu's persecution of Christians, in which he added: 'Before you finish this column, there will be a Foreign Office official telling his opposite number in President Ceausescu's entourage that "the Times is getting frightfully unreliable these days".' His prediction would also prove correct.

On that bright June day in 1978 the Ceausescus flew into London's Gatwick airport to be greeted by the Duke and Duchess of Kent, who escorted them to the Royal Train for their journey to Victoria Station. The Queen and Prince Philip, with Prince Charles and Princess Anne, were waiting to greet them, along with the Prime Minister, the Foreign and Home Secretaries, the chiefs of the Armed Forces and a guard of honour from the 1st Battalion, Grenadier Guards. Seven carriages lined up to bring the honoured guests to Buckingham Palace, with the Queen and the President leading the way and the combative Nicolae Ecobescu, director of protocol, bringing up the rear in carriage number seven, with the Queen's equerry.

There were just two small, silent demonstrations outside Victoria Station. One was formed by a group with a banner saying, 'Human rights for Romanian Christians'. The other was made up of members and supporters of Romania's persecuted Hungarian minority – two million people, who could be imprisoned or even executed merely for celebrating their Hungarian cultural identity.

At Buckingham Palace the Royal Household staff were already discovering that they were looking after a very odd guest, when the presidential luggage was delivered. The Ceausescus had brought all their clothes in hermetically sealed containers, to prevent secret British agents posing as footmen from impregnating their clothes with poison or bugging devices. There were the usual rituals of the welcome lunch at the Palace, followed by the exchange of gifts. Ceausescu, by all accounts, was thrilled with his rifle and personalised gun case; ditto Elena with the gold brooch that the Queen gave her. In return, the Ceausescus presented two hand-made rugs. There was the laying of the state visitor's wreath at the Grave of the Unknown Warrior in Westminster Abbey, followed by tea with the Queen Mother and an address from the Lord Mayor and councillors of the City of Westminster.

Ostensibly, everything was exactly the same as for any other state visit, although beady-eyed veterans of these gatherings will have detected a few nods and winks in the preparations for the state banquet. Most state visitors could expect to be served the best claret from the Palace cellars – a first-growth (premier cru) or similar – to go with their dinner. For President de Gaulle in 1960 the Queen had produced a Château Lafite 1949, while Presidents of Germany have been served, variously, Château Lafite and Château La Fleur-Petrus. For Ceausescu, however, the Queen started with a perfectly respectable if unexciting white, an Ockfener Bockstein Spätlese 1971, to go with the fish, followed by a decidedly pedestrian (in state-banquet terms) claret: a fifth-growth Château Croizet-Bages 1966. There was some mischievous code in the menu, too. Despite the Foreign Office ban on all references to Romanian royalty, the Queen was not going to let timid diplomats airbrush altogether her own Romanian/Hungarian ancestry from the proceedings. Coming between the pea soup and the 'Selle d'Agneau Windsor', the fish course was called 'Paupiettes de Sole Claudine'. The Queen would regularly name dishes in honour of her guests – 'Aiguilette de Sole Tehran' for the Shah of Iran; that 'Soufflé Glacé Louise' for the King and Queen of Sweden; and so on. The only nod to Romania at this banquet was this reference to the Transylvanian-born Countess Claudine Rhédey, who also happened to be the Queen's great-great-grandmother.* Neither Ceausescu nor his abrasive head of protocol, Ecobescu, appeared to notice that the Queen was committing a capital offence by thus celebrating her own Hungarian cultural identity. Even if they did, they were not going to cause a scene. For once, Ceausescu was cowed, as the Foreign Office had hoped he would be all along. 'We wanted to overawe him and make it very clear this was a very special, incredible privilege,' says Sir Roger du Boulay, then Ecobescu's opposite number. 'He did exactly what he was told to do. We would say: "Now, sir, you need to spend a penny because we don't want you caught short during dinner" and he would. He had a whole load of us around him.'

The banquet would be a somewhat lopsided affair. The British guests wore white tie – the Queen was wearing Queen Alexandra's Russian Fringe Tiara – while the Romanians chose to remain in their lounge suits. The President wore the badge of the GCB (Knight Grand Cross of the Order of the Bath), which the Queen had given him earlier, while she wore the sash of the Order of Socialist Romania (First Class), which he had given her. It fell to the Royal Family to do the hard work over dinner, with Ceausescu sandwiched between the Queen and the Queen Mother, and Mrs Ceausescu sitting between the Duke of Edinburgh and the Prince of Wales.

Once the lamb and the 'Bombe Glacée aux Mangoes' had been cleared, the Queen rose to begin the speeches. They would prove as unexceptional as the wine. Reading words prepared by her ministers, she noted that she was glad to be offering the President a full state visit. Her main themes were the fact that Ceausescu was something of a free spirit within the Soviet orbit and was about to buy a lot of

* Claudia Rhédey, known as Claudine, was born into Hungarian nobility and married Duke Alexander of Württemberg. Their son, Francis, was Queen Mary's father. Aged just twenty-nine, Claudine was trampled to death watching a military parade in Austria.

planes. Praising Romania's 'heroic struggle' for independence, she admired 'the resolute stand you have taken to sustain that independence'. Stretching this flimsiest of bilateral relationships to the extreme, she added: 'We have enjoyed excellent co-operation with your country for many years, particularly in the field of aviation.' Ceausescu's formulaic, five-paragraph reply noted that he looked forward to further bilateral collaboration.

THE DEAL

The press coverage in Romania was, predictably, effusive. The following day, Ceausescu had his talks with Jim Callaghan at Downing Street. The highlight of the day, however, was the acclamation for Mrs Ceausescu as one of the greatest scientific brains of the age. At the Royal Institute of Chemistry, Professor Richard Norman could almost have been welcoming a Nobel laureate as he saluted this 'distinguished' expert in 'the stereospecific polymerisation of isoprene', for 'work which has the dual merit both of increasing our fundamental understanding of chemical processes and of increasing our effectiveness in exploiting chemistry for the benefit of mankind'. Norman told her that she was joining the world's oldest professional body for chemistry and that he looked forward to working with her in the future. Curiously, within five years, Norman would be chief scientific adviser to the Ministry of Defence and closely involved in Ronald Reagan's anti-Soviet 'Star Wars' programme. Yet here he was eulogising a ruthless and corrupt non-scientist from the wrong side of the Iron Curtain.

If the Royal Institute of Chemistry was being naïve, the Polytechnic of Central London appeared to have taken leave of its senses. Among the trio of speeches hymning the brilliance of the guest of honour was that of the rector, Colin Adamson, who saluted the 'renowned Romanian skills in international relationships and diplomacy'. Nothing could match the presentation address of the senior pro-rector, Professor Terence Burlin, who heralded Mrs Ceausescu as 'a fine example of Heisenberg's epigram: "Science clears the field on which technology can build".' Burlin charted the first lady's meteoric rise through Romanian academe. 'From the National Council for Scientific Research, it was a short step to the Central Commission on Socio-Economic Forecasting,' he declared, without a hint of irony.

Here was 'a woman of discernment', he concluded, adding: 'Did she not discern the calibre of Mr Ceausescu long before the other Romanians?'

Back at Buckingham Palace, another woman of discernment had seen quite enough of the state visitors already. While out walking her dogs in the Buckingham Palace garden, the Queen spotted the Ceausescus coming the other way (they preferred to talk outdoors, fearing secret bugging devices inside the Palace). As the Queen later revealed to the writer, Sir Antony Jay, she hid behind a bush in her own garden to avoid them.

There was no avoiding them later that day as she attended the mandatory return banquet that Ceausescu had arranged in her honour at Claridge's. It was there that the British government's behaviour reached its lowest point. When a small demonstration gathered outside the hotel, led by the British-based Romanian dissident Ion Ratiu, the police not only parked a coach between the demonstrators and the building, but arrested Ratiu for 'obstructing the police'. He was taken away in a van and was not released until the banquet was over. Though Ratiu received an absolute discharge at Marlborough Street magistrates' court the following day, the case would later be singled out by the *New Law Journal* as a 'deplorable' example of 'political policing'.

That the government was nervous was understandable. Ceausescu had yet to sign the contract for the aircraft. In his despatch on the visit, Reggie Secondé, the British Ambassador to Romania, admitted that the contracts with BAC and Rolls-Royce 'were cliff-hangers until the last moment'. The British had taken Ceausescu down to the BAC factory at Filton near Bristol for a celebratory lunch and a formal signing in front of the television cameras. As Secondé put it, there was so much last-minute haggling on all sides that the lunch 'looked like an anthill that had been poked with a stick'. The visit would conclude with the signing of various pointless communiqués that were every bit as 'turgid' as expected. Ceausescu grandly informed Jim Callaghan that trade with Britain would rise from £133 million in 1977 to £1 billion by 1985. 'You have set a very ambitious target,' Callaghan replied politely. Foreign Office papers show that, privately, the British government thought he was talking rubbish – as indeed he was. At the time, however, British diplomats felt extremely pleased with themselves. 'The President's satisfaction at his visit has been reflected in Romania by a colossal and quite unprecedented amount of publicity,' Secondé noted in his despatch. 'President Ceausescu was a tricky customer,' he admitted, noting with 'relief' that 'there were very few anti-Romanian placard-bearers and no embarrassing demonstrations'. The chief villains – as ever, in the eyes of the Foreign Office – were the British press. In this case, Bernard Levin was singled out in particular for his 'unbalanced and offensive articles' about Ceausescu's persecution of Romanian Christians.

That the visit went so well, Secondé went on, was down to the fact that the Romanians had been so well looked after by the Queen: 'On the British side, no corners were cut in either dress or formality. The Romanians wore dark lounge suits throughout. But any misgivings they may have had about being high-hatted by their hosts must have been immediately dispelled by the unmistakeable wish of Her Majesty, the Duke of Edinburgh and all the Royal Family that their guests should feel welcome. Our star rides high and it is conceded all round that, when it comes to State Visits, Britain has a secret weapon that no one else can match.'

The warm afterglow continued long after the Ceausescus had returned home. Four months later, the leader of the Liberal Party, David Steel, visited Romania and presented the President with an album of photographs from the state visit. He was invited shooting with Ceausescu and so enjoyed himself that he sent him a black Labrador puppy called 'Gladstone'. The dictator adored the dog, which was renamed 'Corbu' (meaning 'raven') and given the honorary rank of colonel.

The Queen, however, wanted nothing more to do with a visitor she would often refer to as 'that frightful little man'. Ceausescu may not have ransacked the Palace's Belgian Suite, as President Giscard d'Estaing had predicted, but the Queen had not remotely enjoyed being her government's 'secret weapon'. 'She made it very clear that she intensely disliked having Ceausescu to stay. He was just a dreadful guest,' says David Owen. Despite being Foreign Secretary through it all, Lord Owen's memoirs fail to make any mention of the state visit whatsoever. When asked why, this veteran of half a century of international politics shakes his head, laughs and replies: 'I try to pretend it never happened!'

It would remain engraved on the Queen's mind, however. When she finally made her first state visit to Eastern Europe fifteen years later, touring Hungary in 1993, she learned that the British Ambassador, John Birch, had previously served in Bucharest. 'She talked about the dreadful experience of having Ceausescu to stay,' he told the British Diplomatic Oral History Programme. 'She was interested in what had gone on in Romania after the War and she knew all about King Michael.'*

All her efforts, however – not to mention those of so many staff in the Eastern European department of the Foreign Office – would come to nothing. Despite those great hopes of building a new British-backed aerospace industry in Eastern Europe, the 'ROMBAC' alliance between BAC and Romania was a dismal failure. More than a decade after the grand signing of the contracts, just nine aircraft had been built, instead of the projected eighty-two. When, in 1989, the Queen's former house guests were put up against a wall and shot, they took ROMBAC with them. By then, Ceausescu had already been stripped of his GCB, following a campaign by the Conservative peer and human-rights campaigner Lord Bethell.† Some months later, the Polytechnic of Central London got round to stripping Mrs Ceausescu of her professorship, as 'a mark of revulsion'. To this day the Ceausescu visit is still regarded as the most regrettable entry in the Queen's visitors' book. It also shows how far public and social attitudes have changed in the intervening years. No wonder the Queen is entirely unfazed by public mood-swings. She really has seen it all before.

* The Queen's interest is shared by her eldest son. Following his 1998 tour of Romania, the Prince of Wales was so enchanted by the Saxon villages of Transylvania, and so concerned about their plight, that he bought two farmhouses as holiday homes and now rents them out to the public.

† Lord Bethell continued his quest to retrieve the gold-and-silver collar that comes with each GCB and is the property of the monarch in perpetuity, to be returned on death. In 1994 it was found in a drawer in Bucharest and returned to the Queen.

Chapter 3

SETTING SAIL

'A touch of healing'.

YOUNG LEADERS

The state apartments at Buckingham Palace are packed once more. The Queen will shake every hand in a 300-strong greeting line, which takes thirty minutes to file past her, and then she will work her way through her drawing rooms and picture gallery. When the events to mark the sixtieth anniversary of her accession to the Throne generated a £100 million pot of money from across the Commonwealth, she created the Queen Elizabeth Diamond Jubilee Trust. It would not be a long-term endowment. Rather, the idea was to distribute all the money in a few years on two priorities: eliminating avoidable blindness across the Commonwealth and identifying exceptional Commonwealth leaders of the future. Younger members of the family would get stuck in, too. Overall, the impact has been swift and impressive. In October 2017, for example, it was announced that every child in Botswana would receive an eye test for the first time.

At the same time, the scheme to unearth the 'Queen's Young Leaders' has identified hundreds of outstanding young people, all of whom have been flown to London for a week of mentoring, a meeting with the Queen and an awards ceremony. All come with stories and CVs that never fail to move the organisers. 'I'll be very surprised if some are not leaders of their countries in twenty or thirty years,' says

Sir John Major, chairman of the trustees. 'Some of their stories almost defy belief. In a world that is very displeased with itself, these young people are a beacon of hope.' They range from the young man running a rescue programme for child soldiers in Sierra Leone, to Elizabeth Kite, twenty-six, from Tonga. She runs courses for the disabled and a radio programme educating Tongan girls about women's health. It is an emotional moment for her as she prepares to meet the Queen. Her mother has sent her to London with a bark-cloth dress that has been passed down through female members of the family for generations. Elizabeth (who is named after the Queen) says that her mother wore it when the Queen visited Tonga in 1953. Now it is coming out again for the Queen, a generation later.

Once again, the rest of the family are here in numbers tonight to support the monarch. Prince Harry introduces the Queen to the champion Olympic long-distance runner, Sir Mo Farah, an ambassador for the Young Leaders programme. 'He's retiring at the end of the year,' Prince Harry reminds his grandmother, who needs no reminding. 'Well, he has run an awful long way,' says the Queen, to Farah's obvious delight. 'I've probably gone to Africa and back,' he tells her.

The Palace Ballroom is laid out as it would be for an investiture. The Young Leaders queue up to receive their awards from the Queen, ahead of a photo and a grand reception. They will then attend a dinner hosted by Prince Harry. The next day a handful are invited back for an audience with the Queen, including Elizabeth Kite. 'Nice to see you again,' the Queen tells them. 'You're not too exhausted?' They are in the same study where the Queen meets her prime ministers and other world leaders. The Governor-General of Papua New Guinea has been in moments earlier to receive his knighthood. The Queen immediately strikes an informal, chatty note. 'The programme is an interesting one isn't it?' she says, turning to Rahat Hossain from Bangladesh. He runs an emergency first-aid network that has now trained 2,600 volunteers. 'Did you start this?' the Queen asks. Rahat explains that he set it up after 1,500 compatriots were killed when a building collapsed. 'That changed my life, I had to start something for the people,' he says. The Queen is sympathetic. 'I think Bangladesh has probably been the unluckiest country in the world, hasn't it, over the years?' she says, before reminiscing more happily about her own visit in 1983. 'I thought one of the interesting things about Bangladesh is the difference between the cities and the country. It's amazing. It's very – citifed, isn't it?' Indeed it is, Rahat concurs.

Turning to Elizabeth, the Queen apologises for not having been to her home lately. 'Tonga – I'm afraid, I haven't been for a very long time,' she says. 'I know, but you have come!' says Elizabeth. 'I've watched the documentaries. Did you enjoy your time there?' 'Oh yes, it was wonderful,' the Queen replies, cheerfully debunking the old myth that one should never ask the monarch a question. 'We had people playing their nose flutes outside the window. It was the most extraordinary thing to do. It sounds awfully uncomfortable but they do it rather well.' She casts her mind back to the vast picnic laid on for her by Tonga's Queen Salote in 1953. 'The only thing I found difficult was sitting cross-legged – a lot,' says the Queen. 'It's quite painful for people who are not built in the same direction.'

Elizabeth asks her about Queen Salote.* 'Of course, I'd met her here,' says the Queen, mentally ticking off Tongan monarchs she has met. 'I've met both the kings – oh, but I haven't met the new one.' She is almost apologetic. 'Having been here such a long time, I've met an awful lot of people!' Whereupon talk turns to Twitter.

As she leaves the Palace, Elizabeth and her friends are still trying to take it all in. 'The best doesn't even capture how we feel right now,' she says. 'I'm going to wake up tomorrow and think: "Did that happen?" We are so lucky to have ended our trip like that.' All have been struck by the fact that the Queen has such vivid memories of their countries. Elizabeth cannot wait to call her mother. 'I'm going to get teary, that's for sure. I already got teary in there.' She will return to Tonga armed with a message for the young girls to whom she broadcasts: 'Anything really is possible, anything you dream. I have always dreamed of meeting Her Majesty for tea. I got to meet her one on one – and that is amazing.'

It is another illustration of that pattern in the Queen's diary over recent years. The older she has become, the more she has surrounded herself with young people and their work. It is why, when the Queen's Young Leaders programme had run its course in 2018, she swiftly followed it up with The Queen's Commonwealth Trust, with Prince

* Queen Salote of Tonga greatly endeared herself to the British public at the Queen's Coronation, famously refusing to raise the roof on her carriage during a downpour, for fear of obstructing the view of the crowd.

Harry as her right-hand man. Why, in her tenth decade, does she keep on inventing new forms of Commonwealth patronage like this? Perhaps because, just like Elizabeth Kite and the others, Elizabeth II was the original Commonwealth young leader who has never really stopped.

THE WORLD BEYOND

It was on her twenty-first birthday in 1947 that Princess Elizabeth delivered her famous pledge: 'My whole life whether it be long or short shall be devoted to your service and the service of our great imperial family.' As we shall see, there is now a fascinating little mystery attached to this celebrated address to the world. Yet she has remained unswervingly true to her word. Her message was aimed particularly at her contemporaries. 'I am thinking especially today of all the young men and women who were born about the same time as myself,' she said. It was also very pointedly directed at 'all the peoples of the British Commonwealth and Empire, wherever they live, whatever race they come from, and whatever language they speak'. The reference to 'peoples' in the plural, and her explicitly multiracial target audience, would set the tone for the new Commonwealth that was to follow. Within two years the 'British Commonwealth and Empire' – as it was officially described -would already start to shed both 'British' and 'Empire' from its name. From then on, it would be a very different organisation that would occupy and shape so much of the life and the thoughts of Elizabeth II.

Compared to her children and grandchildren, who would travel the world at a very early age, the most-travelled monarch in history was a late-starter. Princess Elizabeth was twenty before she left Britain for the first time, on what would be her only overseas tour with her parents. Yet it would be a journey that not only taught her the art of royal diplomacy, but also laid the foundations for her record-breaking reign, thanks to that speech which might today be called her 'mission statement'.

In the aftermath of the Second World War, Britain was exhausted, virtually bankrupt and viewing the impending dismantling of its Empire with melancholy and alarm. India was well on the way to becoming an independent republic. The Union of South Africa, run by its white minority, was making republican noises, too. King George VI was in dire need of a break, after the stresses of war and ill health. He himself wanted to thank South Africa for its loyalty during the war and to show his support for its Prime Minister, Field Marshal Jan Smuts, the onetime Boer commando leader,* who had gone on to be a great imperial commander in the First World War and a Churchillian elder statesman in the Second. It was Smuts who, in 1945, had drafted and pushed through the preamble to the Charter of the United Nations. His Anglophile Unionists were heading for an election showdown with the far-right Afrikaans-speaking Nationalists the following year. Though ostensibly above politics, the King would do no harm to the prospects of his favourite South African politician by paying him a visit.

So on 31st January 1947, the King and Queen, together with Princess Elizabeth and Princess Margaret, took the train to Portsmouth and boarded the battleship HMS *Vanguard*, the pride of the British fleet.† The weather was atrocious as the royal party headed south with two Private Secretaries, three ladies-in-waiting and a small Royal Household team. The King's press secretary, Captain Lewis Ritchie, RN, kept an official tour diary, which has remained locked away in the Royal Archives until now.

After many years at sea, Ritchie was certainly impressed by the special facilities for royal passengers. 'It should be noted that coat hangers are not provided automatically in a man-of-war,' he wrote. The Royal Family were clearly suffering. For the first few days, the King and Princesses did not leave their cabins. 'A good deal of movement. Fifteen-degree roll during the afternoon,' Ritchie wrote on 2nd February.

* Smuts was on the Boer side at the 1900 Battle of Spion Kop, which surely ranks as one of the great small battles in modern history. It not only involved two future prime ministers, Smuts himself and Winston Churchill (a war correspondent with the British), but one Mahatma Gandhi was also in the thick of it (and decorated for his role as a stretcher-bearer). This modest mountain in Natal then entered British sporting vernacular as the nickname for a steep grandstand. To this day, Liverpool's most ardent fans still congregate on 'the Kop'.

† HMS *Vanguard* was the largest – and last – battleship built by the Royal Navy. Launched by Princess Elizabeth in 1944 and commissioned in 1946, at a total cost of £11.5 million, it had eight 15-inch guns, a top speed of 30 knots and a crew of nearly 2,000 officers and men. It would have been called HMS *Home Guard* if the King had had his way. The Admiralty thought otherwise.

Three days later, the royal party had discovered their sea legs well enough to dance an eightsome reel with ships' officers on the quarterdeck and watch a film – *Odd Man Out*. But it was still bracing weather. 'Domestic note,' wrote Ritchie. 'Ashtrays in any places where there is a breeze should be filled with sand.'

A week later it was 'insufferably hot' but raining and Sunday morning service had to be conducted under an awning outside. The King's Private Secretary, Sir Alan 'Tommy' Lascelles, passed any spare time rereading the later works of Trollope. *Mr Scarborough's Family* had proved 'ideal reading for the tropics, though they give me nostalgia for the relatively cloudless days of the early 1900s'. A brilliant, waspish classicist, who won the Military Cross in the Great War and served four monarchs before his retirement in 1953, Lascelles wrote letters home (now lodged with the rest of his papers at Churchill College, Cambridge) that provide an astute, if occasionally irritable, commentary on one of the great royal adventures of all time.

As *Vanguard* crossed the Equator, her less well-travelled passengers were expected to take part in the traditional 'Crossing the Line' ceremony for those entering the southern hemisphere for the first time. For the sailors, that meant being smothered in shaving foam, dunked in water and eating soap. The ship's officer dressed as 'King Neptune' was rather more lenient to the Princesses. 'Razor brush and lather too / Have been debarred for use on you,' he declared. 'Elizabeth and Margaret Rose / Accept some powder on each nose.' The Princesses were forced to eat a candied cherry instead of soap. As they continued south, the crew rigged up a swimming tank for the Princesses, who also enjoyed treasure hunts, yet more films and cocktails with the midshipmen in the Gun Room. The guns would not see much action on this trip. The ship's commanding officer, Captain Agnew had already received orders forbidding gun salutes on arrival 'owing to [the] danger of untrained police horses stampeding'.

The royal party found Cape Town in a state of euphoria, with 1,200 schoolchildren lined up in 105-degree heat on Signal Hill to spell out the word 'Welcome'. 'A real Bombay Day,' wrote Lascelles. 'Unexpectedly large and enthusiastic crowds . . . a state banquet in a hall as hot as Hades and a terribly slow and dreary dinner, through which we had to sit on very hard little chairs. In thirty years of public dinners, I can't recall one that caused me greater misery. However, the King spoke well and made a deep impression, and to my great surprise, I found when we got home that the royals had enjoyed it and thought it great fun – especially the young ones.'

Even on the initial day of her first foreign tour, Princess Elizabeth was already showing an aptitude for the royal diplomatic role that would take up so much of her life. 'Princess Elizabeth is delightfully enthusiastic and interested,' wrote Lascelles. 'She has her grandmother's passion for punctuality and, to my delight, goes bounding furiously up the stairs to jolt her parents when they are more than usually late.' He was less impressed with the accommodation. 'This is one of those incredibly uncomfortable government houses with good rooms but lacking all the essentials like writing tables, tooth glasses etc. and staffed by servants who don't know if it's Christmas or Easter.'

The King's high regard for Jan Smuts was illustrated from the outset as he awarded him the Order of Merit. Later, at a private dinner, the King and Queen would also give him a famous Afrikaner Bible, looted by the British during the Boer War.

Captain Ritchie reported an 'almost incredulous admiration' among the guests at a garden party. The Royal Family had made it clear that they wanted to meet all sections of South African life, even if their hosts had organised these events on both racially segregated and class lines. There were 'receptions' and 'balls' for 'Europeans' (divided into 'British' and 'Afrikaans') and 'non-Europeans'. For 'Africans' or 'natives' there were 'rallies' and '*indabas*'. 'The most interesting feature of the ball for the non-European community was folk singing by three little Malay girls,' wrote Captain Ritchie. 'The City Hall was packed to suffocation.'

The King was already finding it stressful, Lascelles noted, and suffered 'repeated spasms of stage fright which gave me much trouble'. Yet George VI battled on through the state opening of parliament, even managing to 'get out his few sentences of Afrikaans to his own satisfaction'. The Queen, for her part, had worn a 'too massive tiara which she felt obliged to wear because it is made of the chippings of the Cullinan Diamond.'*

* The Cullinan Diamond, the world's largest, was a 3,106-carat specimen named after the manager of the South African mine that discovered it in 1905. It was so big that an Amsterdam cutter was commissioned to break it into several usable pieces. 'I'd love to have been there,' the Queen told the royal commentator, Alastair Bruce, in 2018. The largest stone, Cullinan 1, sits in the Sceptre; Cullinan 2 is in the Imperial State Crown; numbers 3–9 are in brooches and other royal jewellery.

From Cape Town, the royal party set off across the country by rail in the air-conditioned 'White Train', which would be their home for much of the next two months. In between major towns there would be picnics, bathing parties and random stops, with some often touching and unexpected results. At one remote halt, wrote Ritchie, 'a huge old man with an intractable obstinate face' galloped up on a Basuto pony. He was Henry Dreyer, an old Boer farmer, who promptly undid the ancient leather belt that he himself had been given by a Central African tribe many years earlier. 'Give it to the King,' he said. The tour diary adds: 'The incident is the more interesting in that he was a rebel in 1914 and fought the British in the Boer War.'

At Camper, an old man asked Princess Elizabeth if she would look in the direction of his disabled son, Clive, who was at the back of the crowd. The Queen promptly asked for the barrier to be lowered and went over with her daughters to say hello. 'The father was so overwhelmed with gratitude that he broke down,' Ritchie noted. The royal party were impressed by the town of Graaff-Reinet in the Great Karoo. Though it had 'not seen rain for three years', its floral displays 'were the best so far'.

As word spread, so did the expectations of the crowds. When the train failed to stop at Uitenhage, the mayor cabled the train to say that he feared a breakdown of public order. The King swiftly agreed to retrace his steps, with a 20-mile round trip by car back to Uitenhage. The incident rapidly became a topic of national debate, the Natal *Daily News* warning that there could be no repeat 'or official time tables will be seriously upset', while *The Star* congratulated the King, noting that 'he overrode the authors of his itinerary'.

Having originally called for a boycott, the Natal Indian community had decided on a 'first-class welcome' ahead of the royal arrival in Durban. One newspaper quoted a stern-faced Boer farmer in Worcester who summed up a popular Afrikaner sentiment: 'I still don't like the English but, man, I like the King and Queen'. The view was echoed in the Nationalist press. The *New Era* said that the royal party would be 'received with courtesy for they are respected for their personal qualities', though this should not be misinterpreted as 'a sudden upsurge of enthusiasm for the Union's affiliations with Great Britain'. The ultra-conservative Afrikaans newspaper, *Die Burger*, however, criticised the King for playing tennis on a Sunday.

As for the left-wing press in both South Africa and Britain, there was dismay at 'the apathy and complacency induced by the Royal Visit'. *The Guardian* warned the oppressed not to 'take a holiday from the struggle' or to be duped by 'feudal devices'. Yet none of this translated into any sort of hostility along the royal route. In fact, the crowds kept on getting larger.

In Lovedale, Princess Elizabeth heard, for the first time, a piece of music that she would much enjoy hearing again nearly half a century later. A choir of 5,000 black students sang the Bantu national anthem, 'Nkosi Sikelel' iAfrika', later to become the first half of the anthem of Nelson Mandela's multiracial South Africa. 'In perfect tune,' wrote Ritchie admiringly, 'with the basses coming in like an organ, wild and sad – not unlike the songs of Cornish miners and certain Welsh hymns'.

On 3rd March, the Princess made her first speech of the tour when she opened a dock in the Eastern Cape. 'This is a young country and everywhere there is a feeling of youth and strength,' she told an audience who heard almost nothing due to a faulty microphone. The Princess received a casket of cut diamonds – a theme of this tour – for her troubles. There were even a few biblical moments. At Frere General Hospital it was recorded that 'her presence stimulated a paralysed man into talking at some length although the doctor had not previously heard him say anything but yes and no'.

One of the largest gathering of 'natives' – more than 15,000 – turned out to greet the King in Transkei. Speaking in Xhosa, Chief Jeremiah Moshesh explained that they were in Western dress rather than traditional costume 'lest the King should think we are naked savages', to which the diary adds: 'which was a pity'. The chief then issued the traditional prayer for '*pula!*' – 'rain!' – which promptly followed. 'The King will get the credit for it,' wrote Lascelles.

Like his master, Lascelles was delighted by the warmth of the welcome in the Boer heartlands of the Orange Free State. 'What fun it is in the OFS discussing the Boer War with old Boer fighters,' he wrote. 'They are rolling up in their thousands to give Their Majesties an amazingly good welcome.' The government minister in attendance, Colin Steyn, regaled the royal party with the story of how his Boer commander father escaped from a British cavalry patrol 'in nothing but his nightshirt and beard'.

The high point of this leg of the tour came in Kroonstadt. The royal entourage always love it when something unexpected breaks the monotony. Here, they were gripped by the sight of a local dignitary covered in bees, thanks to his hair lacquer. 'It was observed that one of the Councillors' hair was full of bees,' wrote Ritchie. 'He was unmoved.' Lascelles was overjoyed. 'Knowing the Family,' he wrote home, 'you can imagine the instantaneous success this had with them. I was able to set off, in a whisper, a quick one about "bees in the bonnet being better than ants in the pants" which the King used as his own, to the unbridled delight of the rest of the assembly. From that moment, the proceedings at Kroonstad were a Wow.'

Some days later, in Commondale, the King was similarly struck by the sight of a gigantic local farmer, Cornelius Mostert, and asked for a tape measure to confirm his height: 7 feet 3 inches. A less welcome surprise was the stray firework that burned a hole in Princess Elizabeth's dress in Ladybrand. Other unusual spectacles included a trip to an ostrich farm and an encounter with a 'liger' – a cross between a lion and a tiger – in a zoo. It was more successful than a visit to the Kruger National Park to view the lions. So many unwanted hangers-on, and their vehicles, had latched onto the royal convoy that every living creature for miles around had vanished. A peevish diary entry concluded: 'The King observed at the end of the day that the only member of the feline species he had seen was a ginger cat at Pretoriuskop.'

Meanwhile the rallies kept on growing larger. For all the daily discrimination suffered by the 'natives', old tribal patriarchal social structures meant that the hereditary King Emperor was viewed as a wholly different and essentially benign symbolic leader, unlike the colonial oppressors governing in his name. Almost 70,000 Basuto tribesmen, many of whom had ridden for several days, greeted the King in Maseru, in modern-day Lesotho, while an eager crowd of prisoners and lepers watched from the slopes of a nearby hill. In order to make it easier for large crowds to identify him at 'native' events, the King made a point of wearing white naval uniform with the Garter ribbon, while the other male members of the entourage were told to wear dark suits.

The great Maseru rally would, in turn, be eclipsed by the royal greeting from the King and Queen Mother of Swaziland. 'The gathering of the natives was the most impressive to date,' wrote Ritchie, 'a sea of raised knobkerries behind a frieze of naked torsos, shields and leopard skins, an enthralling spectacle. It was said to be a representation of the sea breaking on the shore – the more remarkable as none of the participants had ever seen the sea.'

By mid-March it was time for a rest. Smuts arranged a few days of fishing and walking at a government hostel in the Drakensberg Mountains. He also gave the King an 'entirely neutral' guided tour of the Battle of Spion Kop, adding his own side of the story of Winston Churchill's celebrated escape. Having been taken prisoner during the battle, Churchill wrote a bestselling book about his exploits and his hair-raising journey through enemy territory to freedom. Yet Smuts explained that he himself had already secured Churchill's release, on the grounds that the young Englishman was merely a war correspondent. Canny young Churchill had escaped regardless and had turned the whole escapade into a spiffing *Boy's Own* yarn. Smuts noted that it had 'earned him £9,000 and allowed him to get married'.

Hundreds of thousands of all races turned out to greet the royal entry into Durban. Fighting broke out between 100,000 Africans and 65,000 Indians around the Curries Fountain stadium, due to a lack of water and crowd control. The crowds were even greater on April Fool's Day in Johannesburg as the Royal Family drove through the 'native settlements' around the main gold mines. 'It is estimated that a million people saw Their Majesties. This is probably the peak day for the tour in all that it has asked of the King and Queen,' wrote Ritchie. Lascelles agreed: 'We are just finishing the most exhausting day of the whole trip having left Government House at 9 a.m. and been yelled at by vast crowds, black and white, ever since. I've never seen larger, noisier crowds save perhaps in Montreal in 1939 . . . but I don't like the "City of Gold".'

After six weeks on tour, tempers were at breaking point. The following day, an excruciating episode occurred as the royal party drove through crowds in the East Rand district. 'A Zulu rushed out and appeared to board the Royal car,' the official diary noted. 'The Queen fended him off with her umbrella and he was arrested.' It was only after the man had been roughed up by the police that the truth emerged. 'It turned out his motive was to present ten shillings to Princess Elizabeth,' wrote Ritchie. 'He was apparently a harmless religious crank.'

THE PROMISE

A change of scene was well overdue, as the tour moved on to the British colony of Southern Rhodesia. Although the Queen had lobbied hard against travelling by plane, they flew to Salisbury. In case of an accident, it was standard practice for the King and Princess Margaret to fly in one aircraft while the Queen with the Heir Presumptive flew in the other, precisely two minutes behind (the order of precedence even applied in the air). In Southern Rhodesia, the racial segregation was fractionally less rigorous. The Princess was given that platinum-and-diamond 'Flame Lily' brooch as an early twenty-first-birthday present from children of all races ('European, Asiatic and Coloured' children contributed one shilling each, while 'Africans' gave a penny). The royal party felt considerably more relaxed. The Queen 'shopped in the town' while the King met 2,500 servicemen, including two holders of the VC. The Princesses were taken to a Girl Guides rally in a strangely empty spot, whereupon the District Commissioner gave a signal and girls 'came rushing down the hillside'.

Tommy Lascelles liked it so much that he wrote home to his wife talking wistfully of 'spending our declining years' there. 'The servant problem doesn't exist, the housewife has no worries, the air is like wine; the gardens bloom,' he told her, adding that he had a 'delicious humming bird' outside his window.

The tour resumed by train to Victoria Falls, where the Royal Family marvelled at one of the great sights of Africa and then travelled across the Zambesi River for a day-trip to Northern Rhodesia (now Zambia). They were escorted on their crossing by the state barge of Imwiko, the British-educated Paramount Chief of Barotseland, whose father had asked the Crown to protect his lands half a century before. A drummer kept the forty paddlers in time. The notes for the royal party explained that 'in former times, if a paddler in the State Barge did not pull his weight, he was thrown overboard and risked death from the crocodiles'.

The most fascinating entry in the official diary concerns what happened next. Back at the Victoria Falls Hotel, in what is now Zimbabwe, the royal party spent a quiet weekend, albeit a very historic one. For, on Sunday 13th April, Ritchie wrote: 'At the Victoria

Falls Hotel. Princess Elizabeth read her 21st Birthday speech for the newsreel photographer; Horton and Boland [two of the travelling press] also took photographs.' Following 'Divine Service' in the drawing room, held by the Bishop of Pretoria, it was back to work. 'Princess Elizabeth went through her speech with Frank Gillard [of the BBC] in the presence of the King and Queen,' the official diary continues. There was a break for lunch followed by an afternoon walk and a swim. The diary continues: 'At 6 p.m., Princess Elizabeth recorded her speech for the BBC. It was afterwards played off for Her Royal Highness to hear and was a great triumph.' And so it would prove to be – even if it now appears that her pledge to devote her whole life to 'our great imperial family' was delivered in Southern Rhodesia rather than South Africa, as has been universally accepted ever since.

The Royal Family left Victoria Falls that evening for Bulawayo. Here, once again, there was a clear sense of tribal kinship with the Royal Family, as the warriors of the Matabele Nation performed their first royal *indaba* since the death of Chief Lobengula fifty years earlier. The King and his family went on to visit World's View, the hilltop grave of the colonial founding father, Cecil Rhodes, a place of 'almost primeval grandeur', according to Ritchie. When the Queen struggled to make it up the hill in high heels, Princess Elizabeth gave her mother her own shoes and walked in her stockings, a telling gesture that attracted considerably more media attention than the view.

Finally the royal party returned to South Africa via the famous 'Big Hole' diamond mines of Kimberley, where they were shown a selection of diamonds worth £3 million (£110 million today) and were given a small selection to take home. After travelling 6,942 miles across Africa for over two months, it was back to Cape Town in time for the Princess's twenty-first birthday on 21st April. There was a certain theme to all her presents: a diamond flower brooch from the Royal Household, diamond earrings from the Diplomatic Corps, a diamond brooch from the Grenadier Guards ... Later that night, at one of a series of birthday parties, she would receive a diamond necklace from the South African Prime Minister. Before that, the Princess reviewed a parade of 10,000 troops at 3 p.m., followed by a 'youth rally' at the Rosebank Showgrounds.

So what about that famous twenty-first-birthday speech? The tour diary made one brief reference to what was by far the most important event of the day, if not of the whole tour: 'At 7 p.m., Princess Elizabeth broadcast a speech to the Empire.' Of this famous address, Captain Lewis Ritchie wrote only that 'reception in the UK, and America was excellent' and that 'HRH spoke beautifully'. It is an oddly understated diary entry, presumably because the BBC was transmitting the version which the Princess had recorded with Frank Gillard at the Victoria Falls Hotel. The famous newsreel footage of the moment shows the Princess uttering her famous declaration while sitting outdoors at a table in the shade of a tree. The stonework behind her is speckled with sunlight. Yet the official diary says it all happened 'at 7 p.m.' However, the Cape Town sun sets well before 7 p.m. in April. It is, therefore, clear that this must have been filmed on another occasion – and with good reason. The schedule had been unrelenting all day and the Princess had a long evening of official engagements ahead of her. These were hardly the best circumstances in which to be making an historic broadcast to the world. Buckingham Palace can provide no further information on the speech, although we do know that the BBC had started using new 'Magnetophone' high quality tape recorders the previous year. None of which makes a jot of difference either to the content or relevance of this great speech. However, it has always been a source of enormous pride to South Africans – and a key part of the modern Commonwealth narrative – that the future Queen made her selfless act of dedication in South Africa. It would now seem that Zimbabweans can stake a claim, too.

Having glossed over the radio broadcast, the diary of that 21st birthday goes on to discuss the evening's social events in much greater detail. Dinner at the Governor-General's residence was followed by two balls, which went on into the night. The Princess, it was noted, danced with Lieutenant Commander M. G. McLeod of HMS *Nigeria*.

Two days after the birthday celebrations, the royal party boarded HMS *Vanguard* for the voyage home. There was one final presentation of gifts, including a gold teaset for the Queen and a gold box for the King, containing yet more diamonds to create a new Garter Star for the Sovereign. By now Sir Alan Lascelles had an awful lot of jewels in his care. 'To me fell the task of guarding them. I am not used to looking after £200,000 worth of diamonds,' he wrote. He was in good spirits, however. 'I feel refreshed and even a bit exhilarated by the tremendous success of the whole thing and of Princess Elizabeth's speech on which I have lavished much care.' He was also pleased with the 'loot' he had bought for his wife – 48 pounds of marmalade for a guinea and a 'ham or two'.

Emotions were running high. 'We had a great send-off with everybody crying,' said Lascelles. The tour diary called it 'the last upsurging of a people's love and loyalty . . . a triumph beyond all expectations'. The parting editorial in the *Cape Times* saluted the King in heroic terms: 'It is only too apparent that he did not come to sunny Africa to get away from the hardships of England. His troubles can be seen on his noble, thoughtful face. Rather he came – they all came – the better to get acquainted with their larger family. And who of us does not now respect England a thousand times more than we did?'

Once they were under way, almost all the royal party came down with colds. The highlight of the return journey was the first visit by a reigning monarch to St Helena and a trip up to Longwood, the final home of the exiled Napoleon Bonaparte. 'I have never found a place so permeated with melancholy – it gave us all the heeby-jeebies,' wrote Lascelles, deploring the way the French government – to whom Britain had donated the property – had allowed it to fall apart.

Reflecting at length on this colossal undertaking as *Vanguard* returned to Portsmouth – where half a million people lined the shore to welcome their returning King – Lascelles was proud of his handiwork: 'It has been an immense success and amply achieved its only object (at least from my point of view) – to convince the South African people that the British monarchy is an investment worth keeping.' He was wrong in that regard. The following year, Britain's friend and ally, Jan Smuts, would be ousted by the Nationalists. They would go on to create the reviled system of apartheid and, in due course, to abolish the monarchy.

Yet this tour had undoubtedly been a success for another reason, one that Lascelles touched upon in a shrewd and candid pen portrait of the future Queen. It is an assessment that holds fast today, more than seventy years later, as surely as that great act of self-dedication on (or at least around) her twenty-first birthday. 'From the inside,' Lascelles wrote to his wife, 'the most satisfactory feature of the whole business is the remarkable development of Princess Elizabeth. She has come on in the most surprising way ... Not a great sense of humour, but a healthy sense of fun. Moreover, when necessary, she can take on the old bores with much of her mother's skill, and never spares herself in that exhausting part of royal duty. For a child of her years, she has got an astonishing solicitude for other people's comfort; such unselfishness is not a normal characteristic of that family. But what delights me especially is that she has become extremely businesslike and understands what a burden it is to the Staff if some regard is not paid to the clock. She has developed an admirable technique of going up behind her mother and prodding her in the Achilles tendon with the point of her umbrella when time is being wasted in unnecessary conversation. And, when necessary – not infrequently – she tells her father off to rights.' In short, she would certainly have what it took, when the time came.

As *Vanguard* sailed up the English Channel on its last night at sea, the tour finished with a boisterous wardroom dinner, followed by a final conga – and a sorry end for one feathered stowaway. 'At 11.30 p.m., the dottrell – which the better informed have decided is a young golden plover – was still on the quarterdeck being stalked by cats,' Ritchie noted in the official diary. 'At midnight, it was no longer visible.'

END OF EMPIRE

The British Empire had started with the transatlantic warrior-explorers of Elizabeth I's age. British expansion to the west gathered momentum across the Caribbean and the Americas until the American Declaration of Independence in 1776, followed by the eventual loss of the American colonies in 1783. The empire then redirected its focus in the direction of Asia, the Pacific and, latterly, Africa, creating a global network of colonies, protectorates and allied states, all under the Crown, but enjoying varying degrees of self-determination. Empire it might have been, but the monarch remained a 'monarch'. 'Emperor' was a foreign concept, carrying unhappy associations with the mad and bad – from Julius Caesar to Napoleon. In 1858, following the bloody anti-British uprising known as the Indian Mutiny, control of India passed from the East India Company to the British government. Given its size and composition, India could claim to be an 'empire' of states in its own right. The Tory Prime Minister, Benjamin Disraeli, would eventually create Queen Victoria 'Empress of India' in 1876. The idea was, in part, to glamorise and reinforce India's bond with Britain, but also to enhance public affection for the Queen after several years of widowed seclusion. Any form of self-government, however, was still a long way off.

In honour of Victoria's Golden Jubilee in 1887, the leaders of those colonies with their own governments were summoned to London for a colonial conference, an event that might be described as the first Commonwealth summit. Occasional conferences thereafter, usually in honour of royal landmarks, would lead to the Balfour Declaration of 1926 – the year of the Queen's birth – which formally established these (all-white) colonies as dominions. They were defined as 'autonomous communities within the British Empire, equal in status' and 'united by a common allegiance to the Crown'. All were free and equal members of what was now the 'British Commonwealth of Nations', an idea that was formally enshrined in law five years later when the UK Parliament passed the 1931 Statute of Westminster. Britain had, effectively, relinquished all control over these dominions. They were now sovereign nations within this new Commonwealth – the same one that Princess Elizabeth was talking about in 1947 when she made that twenty-first-birthday speech.

Today the Commonwealth might exude a rather dated feel, just like its palatial eighteenth-century red-brick headquarters. Marlborough House, sandwiched between a row of royal residences on one side and the gentlemen's clubs of Pall Mall on the other, still feels like a blend between the two. Before he became King Edward VII, this was the home of Queen Victoria's rakish heir, Bertie, Prince of Wales. It was the birthplace of George V, whose widow, Queen Mary, would be the last member of the Royal Family to live in it, since when it has been home to the 'family of nations'. It still has royal portraits on the walls, and much remains as it was in the days when the Queen was a little girl and knew this place as 'Granny's house'.

There is little indication of the original, often radical thinking that has driven so many deliberations in these somnolent state rooms. Queen Mary was still in residence in 1947 when her son, King George

VI, and his ministers were gloomily pondering the new, existential threat to the entire Empire. India, the most prized of all the Crown's colonial possessions – the one upon which the British Empire was founded – was not only heading for independence, but also for Partition.

When George VI had come to the Throne in 1936, following the abdication of Edward VIII, the new King had great ambitions for a 'durbar', a spectacular Coronation-style gathering of all India's princely rulers. His father had been crowned Emperor of India in this way in 1911, and George VI adored royal ritual. Rising Indian nationalism, followed in short order by the Second World War, soon quashed any lingering royal dreams of an assembly of bejewelled, elephant-borne maharajahs and princelings paying homage to their King Emperor. Like Queen Victoria, George VI regarded the Indian nobility as kindred spirits who could be relied upon in times of trouble, unlike some of India's politicians. The King's views would be reinforced as Britain fought for its very survival.

In 1942, with Japanese forces sweeping through Burma towards the Indian border, many Congress Party politicians were demanding instant British withdrawal from all of India – and were interned for their troubles. By contrast, the racing-mad Maharajah of Rajpipla, a friend of the Royal Family, commissioned three Spitfires and a Hurricane for the Royal Air Force. Come the end of the war, however, it was the politicians, not the princes, who represented the majority of the population and they wanted independence. A new Labour government in Britain, urged on by the United States, was committed to the idea. But the Indian nationalists were not prepared to settle for dominion status – like, say, Australia or Canada – whereby India would be entirely self-governing, yet retain the King as head of state. They wanted a fully independent republic. The King had grave fears about the speed and direction of travel. In December 1946, he met the two key players in the Indian power struggle, Jawaharlal Nehru, leader of the Hindu-dominated Congress Party, and Muhammad Ali Jinnah, leader of the Muslim League. With deadlock in India, they had come to London for a crisis meeting.

'The leaders of the two parties, I feel, will never agree. We have gone too fast for them,' the King wrote afterwards in his diary. 'I could see no alternative to civil war between Hindus and Moslems [*sic*] for which we should be held responsible.'

George VI was, at least, reassured when the British Prime Minister, Clement Attlee, suggested a man who might come up with that alternative. Lord Mountbatten, the King's cousin and close friend, was appointed Viceroy in early 1947 and soon insisted on clarity and speed if civil war was, indeed, to be averted. There had to be a clear date after which British imperial rule – the British Raj – would cease. He was also clear that the two rival factions were never going to create a viable, united nation. In just a matter of months, on 15th August 1947, the subcontinent was divided between a shrunken Hindu-dominated India and the new Islamic Pakistan, amid terrible bloodshed. As up to fifteen million people moved between either side, hundreds of thousands were killed in sectarian violence. Nehru would famously call the moment 'a tryst with destiny'. The King was stoical and yet, undeniably, diminished. Having signed letters and documents with 'GRI' – George Rex Imperator – throughout his reign, he was now officially reduced to 'GR', under the terms of the Indian Independence Act. A trivial point perhaps, but not to a monarch who was so punctilious about such matters. After receiving a letter from the King three days later, Queen Mary scribbled her own forlorn postscript on it: 'The first time Bertie wrote me a letter with the I for Emperor of India left out, very sad.'

Both India and Pakistan would start off as dominions while they sorted out their new constitutions. India was already preparing to adopt a republican system, at which point it would jettison the King. But that raised a further question, one of the greatest concern to the King: what about the Commonwealth?

Under the existing rules, any member of the Commonwealth had to recognise the King as its head of state. If not, it was out. On 4th January 1948, after a short and bitter independence struggle, Burma became the first British colony since the American war of independence to leave the British Empire. It had opted to become a republic and, thus, severed its link with the Crown. It was automatically expelled from the Commonwealth at the same time. Ireland would do the same the following year. Neither the King nor the British government wanted that to happen with India or Pakistan. Quite apart from personal and national pride, the King had a deep affection for the 'brightest jewel' in the imperial crown. He had warmed to Nehru greatly when the Indian Prime Minister had come to London in 1948. 'I liked him very much,' he told Lord Mountbatten. Like many others, the King was having trouble keeping up with all the comings and goings in his Commonwealth. Burma might just have gone, but newly independent Ceylon had just become a dominion. The Royal Archives contain a copy of the King's speech at his dinner for them all in October 1948. 'It gives me great pleasure to welcome here tonight my Prime Ministers or their representatives from the eight independent countries of the Commonwealth,' it begins. Except that the King has crossed out 'eight' and scribbled 'nine'. He was especially pleased, he said, to welcome India, Pakistan and Ceylon to the 'councils of the Brotherhood of Nations'. At this stage, Pakistan and Ceylon were still happy to retain the King as head of state. The problem was India.

The King's personal feelings were one thing. Of far greater concern were the Cold War implications of an Indian exit from the post-colonial fold. As Clement Attlee wrote to the King in early 1949: 'If India against her will is obliged to leave the Commonwealth, it would encourage Russia in her efforts to disrupt South East Asia.'

The fact was that Nehru did not want to lead India out of the Commonwealth anyway. An internationalist at heart, he argued that the Commonwealth would 'enable us to contribute to the peace of the world'. Many within his Congress Party thought otherwise. They wanted to sever all post-colonial ties with Britain. As the former Commonwealth Secretary-General Kamalesh Sharma points out, they feared lingering imperial interference. 'At home, there wasn't much support,' he says, pointing to people like the future Indian Prime Minister, Atal Bihari Vajpayee, who was 'vehemently' opposed to having anything to with 'the old dominions'. So how to resolve the contradiction of being a republic, yet somehow owing allegiance to the Crown?

A meeting of all the dominions, old and new, was finally convened in London in April 1949. Some of the 'old Commonwealth', like Australia and New Zealand, were deeply hostile to any changes that appeared to dilute their loyalty to the Crown. South Africa's new nationalist Prime Minister, Daniel 'DF' Malan, who had beaten Smuts in the 1948 election, took a different line. An Afrikaans-speaking former church minister and no royalist, he was wary of giving the King any enhanced role. After much heated debate, an ingenious solution was finally agreed. To be a member of the Commonwealth, countries did not have to recognise the King as head of state. Instead they had to acknowledge that he was 'the symbol of the free association of its independent member nations and as such the Head of the Commonwealth'. Those two little words – 'as such' – were inserted to reassure India and South Africa that the King had no constitutional authority at all. In just four paragraphs of text, the 1949 London Declaration also quietly removed the word 'British' from what would now be the 'Commonwealth of Nations'.

'British Empire to British Commonwealth to Commonwealth of Nations,' wrote the Canadian Prime Minister, Lester Pearson. 'Emperor to King to Head. This was one of the most important landmarks in the history of the Commonwealth.' Sir Peter Marshall, former Deputy Secretary-General of the Commonwealth, believes it was one of the shortest, cleverest political compositions of modern times: 'It emphasised that nothing had changed. In fact just about everything changed.'

Nehru had a deal, but he still had to sell it to his anti-British hotheads. He returned home and assured the Indian Constituent Assembly that 'it was made perfectly clear that the King has no functions at all' (even if the King's daughter would make a mockery of that claim in years to come). In what would become one of his most famous speeches, he spoke of the Commonwealth as 'this new type of association with a touch of healing'. Of all the attempts to capture the essence of the Commonwealth over the years – and there have been some good, bad and incomprehensible ones – none quite captures the spirit of those early days as well as Nehru's 'touch of healing'.

In the end, says Kamalesh Sharma, it was Nehru's greatness and force of personality that propelled India into this new Commonwealth, rather than the arguments. If a man who had served nine British prison sentences and nearly nine years in jail was championing the idea, could it really be such a bad one? Another former Secretary-General, Sir Sonny Ramphal, says that George VI should take a share of the credit. 'The emotion and the argument was all about the King and it was managed with great skill.'

The most ardent royalists could go home happy, too. To this day, veteran diplomats and civil servants marvel at the way that a serious post-war crisis had been averted by a few carefully drafted words.

In the process, the King would stop talking about his 'kingdoms' and 'dominions' and would use the more understated word 'realms' instead. And then the finest minds in the Civil Service, including the Cabinet Secretary himself, started tackling the really pressing issue of the day: how should the 'Head of the Commonwealth' be translated into Latin, for ceremonial use? Professor Philip Murphy chronicles the gloriously esoteric academic process that toured the common rooms of Oxbridge, taking far longer than the actual Commonwealth conference itself. Though the Latin for 'head' was *caput*, for example, it was deemed an insufficiently 'honorific' term for the King. There was, of course, no possibility of using *rex*, the Latin word for 'king' since the whole point of the exercise was to include nations which did not want a *rex*. In the end, they opted for *princeps*, a multi-purpose word for both a 'leader' and a 'prince'. The King would be '*Consortionis Populorum Princeps*'.

Whatever his title, George VI had succeeded in creating something unique, enduring and forward-looking in a turbulent, war-weary world. Seven decades later, the current Secretary-General of the Commonwealth, Baroness Scotland, says that his legacy remains 'a thing of wonder'. The King, though, would never live to see his handiwork. Soon after postponing plans for another grand tour of his realms, the new 'Head of the Commonwealth' died in his sleep at Sandringham on 6th February 1952.

SUCCESSION

Having famously climbed that giant Kenyan fig tree as a Princess, Elizabeth came down it as Queen on the morning of 6th February 1952. She had succeeded to the Throne while spending a night watching wild animals. Having pledged her life to her peoples while touring the Commonwealth five years earlier, she had now become their Queen in the heart of Africa, too. 'I have very special reasons for feeling a special affection for Africa,' she told Commonwealth leaders at their 1999 meeting in Durban. 'My life was transformed by those events.'

Before she had even returned to London, to be greeted by her first British Prime Minister, Winston Churchill, the well-oiled machinery of royal succession was under way. Elizabeth II would automatically become Head of the Armed Forces, Supreme Governor of the Church of England, Duke of Lancaster, and much else. But there was a problem. What about the Commonwealth?

In all the careful negotiations and political pirouettes that had produced this new creation, no one had clarified what happened after a change of reign. Was the title of Head of the Commonwealth hereditary or finite? To this day, some constitutional experts like to argue that it is hereditary, on the basis that the London Declaration refers to 'The King' in generic terms and not specifically to George VI. Yet the accepted position today, reinforced at the 2018 summit, is the same as it was in 1952 – namely, that being Head is not automatic. The new Queen would, therefore, need to be endorsed by all the nations of the Commonwealth, and by one in particular. What if India argued that the London Declaration only applied to the late King? This potential diplomatic nightmare was averted on 8th February, when Nehru sent a formal message of condolence to the new monarch. 'May I welcome your Majesty as the new head of the Commonwealth and earnestly trust that this great fellowship will continue to work for the cause of human understanding and peace,' he wrote, solving the problem in a single sentence. If Nehru was happy, no one else was going to step out of line. At the Coronation the following year, the Queen was the first monarch to be crowned with the style and title of 'Head of the Commonwealth', while her gown was embroidered with the floral emblems of every Commonwealth nation. The Queen's designer, Norman Hartnell, had included the lotus flower of India and wheat, cotton and jute to represent Pakistan. Still some years away from becoming a republic, Pakistan had even despatched a contingent of troops to take part in Changing the Guard on the day itself.

The Coronation gown was the most prized item in the eight tons of luggage loaded aboard the cargo-liner, the SS *Gothic*, for the great Coronation tour of 1953–4. The dress would appear at the opening of parliament in New Zealand, Australia and finally Ceylon, where the glass beads got so hot that the Queen said it was 'like being in a radiator'. From there, she crossed the Indian Ocean to Africa, before her triumphal homecoming voyage in the new Royal Yacht.

The newsreels and picture books present this as a joyous, stately progress through an old empire happily adjusting to life in the new Commonwealth. Yet the cracks were already there, for those who cared to look. Even on the night she acceded to the Throne in Kenya's Aberdare National Park, Princess Elizabeth was a terrorist target. She and the Duke of Edinburgh were under the protection of a big-game hunter whose primary concern was not the threat from wild animals. Jim Corbett, famous for bagging two of the deadliest man-eating tigers in Indian history, was more alert to the dangers of the Mau Mau guerrilla movement, which was already operating in the area. The royal presence was neither overlooked nor forgotten. In 1954, in the very same month that her Coronation tour brought the Queen back to Africa for the first time since her accession, Mau Mau insurgents returned to Treetops. They torched the giant fig tree to the ground and then led away the five domestic staff who had looked after the royal couple during their stay. Four were never seen again. Only Nahashon Mureithi, a handyman and porter, managed to escape into the undergrowth, albeit with a bullet wound to his arm. This was the unreported postscript to the enchanting story of the Princess who went up a tree and came down a Queen. From the outset, there was a dark side to the fairytale.

'A HOLIDAY FEEL'

During the early years of her reign, with the jet engine in its infancy, most royal travel was still by sea. The emphasis was still firmly on visiting those parts of the world where the Queen was Queen, plus near-neighbours in Europe. The rest of the world would have to wait, especially when it was learned, in 1959, that the Queen was expecting her third child. All that would change, however, in 1961, as a result of two events. One was the arrival of Prince Andrew in 1960. The other was the British government's enthusiasm for joining the new European Economic Community. The UK's increasingly energetic flirtation with the EEC had gone down badly with the Commonwealth. Britain needed to show that it still cared, especially if ex-colonies were not to be wooed by predatory rogues like the USSR. The easiest way of doing that was to despatch the Queen. As a result, she would spend more than a quarter of 1961 visiting eleven nations on three continents.

Nothing, though, would match the drama and colour awaiting her in the former lodestar of British imperialism. India was the reason the modern Commonwealth had come into existence. Now the Queen was going to visit the man who had effectively anointed her as its head. 'I have a holiday feeling,' Prime Minister Jawaharlal Nehru declared as he waited for his guest to land in Delhi in January 1961. Nehru and his government wanted to show the Queen – and the world – how far post-imperial India had progressed. Though that might be the Indian government's ambition, how would the people of India be feeling, little more than a decade after the blood and pain of Partition? Would they still bear a grudge?

The answer to that was clear enough as more than two million people lined the road into Delhi from the airfield where the Queen's BOAC Britannia landed on 21st January 1961. All along the 12-mile route there were vivid scenes of welcome, not least a 'durbar' of 800 carts with their oxen and camels draped in Union flags. Mounted police had to hold back the crowds at Connaught Place. 'I have never seen so many people in my life. I became quite worried. I thought they would fall off the trees and roofs,' the Queen told Nehru, over tea. He gleefully revealed to her that she had actually drawn a larger crowd than the recent visit of America's President Dwight Eisenhower. Those who have travelled with the Queen often say that she has a photographer's eye for detail in a crowd. While this was one of the most tumultuous welcomes of her entire life, what had made a deep impression on her, she told Nehru, was not the crowd, but the deadpan faces of the water buffalo.

Her first major engagement of a forty-four-day, 20,000-mile tour – which would include Pakistan and Nepal – was to lay a wreath of 500 white roses at the tomb of the founding father of Indian independence, Mahatma Gandhi. It was an act that epitomised Nehru's famous dictum about the Commonwealth's capacity to administer 'a touch of healing'.

Though a giant in the pantheon of Commonwealth leaders – and a man whom the Queen's father had held in the highest esteem – Nehru was not her host. Protocol dictated that this was the role of the head of state, India's non-executive President, Rajendra Prasad. At his state banquet on the first evening, Prasad set an upbeat tone that came as a relief both to the Queen and the British government. 'We welcome you not only as head of the oldest democracy in the world but also as head of the great Commonwealth,' he told her, adding that it was 'perhaps the most suitable and effective organisational expression of the world's independence'.

For the Queen, this was a visit that had to blend the forward-looking egalitarianism of the new India with a nod to those who had been most loyal to her late father – India's own royalty. In all his dealings with his British ministers during the moves towards Partition, the King's firmest intervention had been to seek 'fair play' for the princes and nobility. Dressed in a white gown and the same Russian Fringe Tiara that she had worn at her own wedding, the Queen spoke of the 'free partnership' of the Commonwealth, before gently reminding India not to jettison its past. 'You do not wish India in all the fierce rush and strain of the modern world to become oblivious of the best traditions and the great legacy from former generations,' she said.

Underlining that point, the royal couple were promptly transported back to the past a day later. Having flown into modern Delhi, they then travelled to Rajasthan to spend a couple of days rooted in Raj-era India with the Maharajah of Jaipur. As the royal car approached Jaipur, the couple switched to a pair of elephants. 'Fasten your seatbelt,' yelled the Duke of Edinburgh as the Queen set off on top of a richly decorated, hand-painted creature called Beauty. Royal photographer Reginald Davis, by now struck down with dysentery, took what he still regards as one of his best-ever pictures: an image of the Queen, beaming down from Beauty's back. At the palace, the Maharajah presented 200 local noblemen, all dressed in the same extravagantly elaborate ceremonial garb in which their forebears had greeted George V at the great Delhi Durbar of 1911. The women present were expected to watch through peepholes in the alcoves above. The only nod to the twentieth century was that the official programme omitted the word 'durbar' and called this a 'reception' instead.

The Maharajah was very clear about the main purpose of the visit: the Duke of Edinburgh was going to shoot a tiger. At that very moment the Duke was in the process of establishing the World Wildlife Fund, which would be founded four months later. Yet in the India of 1961, the tiger was still seen as a dangerous pest and a very desirable trophy. There was certainly no secrecy about the exercise.

'Of course I plan to shoot a tiger if possible. Why not?' the Duke had told reporters at an earlier reception in Delhi. The Maharajah had even erected a special press tent in the jungle, complete with bar and telegraphing facilities, to enable the world's media to report on progress. In Britain, the League Against Cruel Sports was objecting loudly. It was not the killing of tigers that upset many members of the British public nearly as much as the fact that the hunt involved a tethered buffalo as bait. It was hardly sport. Ever sensitive to opinions overseas, the Indian authorities were irritated by the criticism. 'How can the English fuss when they spend their time hunting stags and foxes and happily watch their hounds tearing the animals to pieces?' a government spokesman told the *Evening Standard*. 'At least we don't sit and watch the buffalo.' One Indian commentator complained to the *Guardian* that Western critics were wrong in portraying this as a purely aristocratic pursuit, pointing out that many heroes of the left had also pursued tigers: 'Why give a sport which Tito and Nasser enjoyed an imperialistic flavour?' According to this argument, tiger-shooting was every bit as proletarian as darts or rugby league.

Day and night, the Queen, the Duke and their hosts waited in a *machan* or tree platform while 200 beaters scoured the jungle below. Finally, on their third outing, the Duke bagged a tigress just as it was time to return to Delhi.

The episode had done little to temper Indian excitement about the visit. *The Times of India* said that the Queen had 'aroused fabulous enthusiasm in republican India', attributing this both to the legacy of Gandhi and to the fact that 'Britain had the courage and the good sense to be essentially liberal in her Indian empire'. There was, however, irritation among the new political establishment that the old aristocracy were peddling an outdated image of India; that the media were focusing on clichés like tiger-hunting instead of the country's exciting new steel industry. *The Indian Express* voiced what it called a 'trenchant criticism of the Maharajah'. Nehru had a more restrained dig at the old grandee, telling politicians: 'In the past, people thought of India as a country of snakes and snake charmers, the rope trick and gay Maharajahs. Well, they are still there but they are fading, and rightly so.'

The British press preferred to blame the royal advisers, rather than the royal couple, for the dead tigress in Jaipur. Elsewhere in the

Commonwealth, however, the reaction was scathing. Noting that the Queen was present throughout the tiger hunt, the Melbourne *Age* lamented: 'The presence of the Queen unhappily sets the stamp of her approval' on 'a grotesque revival from the magic-lantern days of potentates and sahibs'. It 'lacked only the Duke's right foot planted melodramatically on the sacrificial beast's neck to bring back days we thought were dead beyond recall'.

India was much more interested in another sight. The Queen agreed to attend the country's Republic Day parade in Delhi, the first time a foreign head of state had joined the President as he received the salutes. Not even Eisenhower had done that. Old India and new were competing for attention once again, as costumed elephants paraded past the presidential dais while a helicopter hovered overhead, dropping marigold petals on the VIP area.

Back in Britain, there was fresh grumbling. It had nothing to do with wildlife. Why was the Queen driving around in both a Mercedes and a Cadillac, but not a Rolls-Royce? Might this be some sort of nose-rubbing exercise by the Indians? Why, the London *Evening Standard* demanded, was the Queen not promoting British industry? It turned out that the hosts had, in fact, contacted Rolls-Royce the previous year to order a new open-topped vehicle, but the company had replied that making one in six months would be 'out of the question'. The Indians had then spoken to Mercedes, which found it no problem at all. Here was another small illustration of the dismal state of Britain's post-war productivity.

Before leaving Delhi for a moonlit inspection of the Taj Mahal, the Queen reaffirmed her belief in the Commonwealth as 'a practical example of the kind of relationship which human beings can have if only they will listen to the good of their own hearts'. Addressing the Mayor of Delhi, she added that she was excited to be visiting 'the new factories, the power stations ... signs of an ampler life in the towns and the villages'. There would be plenty of that during royal visits to major industrial cities like Ahmedabad and Bombay. In Calcutta, she was greeted by what was perhaps the largest single crowd that has ever turned out for her. Not even her Coronation had drawn the estimated 3.5 million who gathered on the streets of the capital of West Bengal. The British press gleefully reported (and no doubt the Foreign Office gleefully noted) that this was considerably more than the three million who had turned out for Khrushchev when the Soviet leader visited Calcutta the previous year.

It was essential for the Queen to honour both sides of the Partition divide. However, the tone of the visit was entirely different in Pakistan, where the Queen's host was General Ayub Khan, by now three years into a military dictatorship. Instead of a focus on industry and civic development, the emphasis was on martial might. The tour involved a review of Pakistan's fleet and several army tattoos. If the lack of democracy ran counter to the Commonwealth's mantra of enlightened fellowship, it did not show. The Queen certainly wasn't going to criticise this particular host for taking power at the point of a gun. At the state banquet in Karachi,* she said 'it should not come as a surprise' if British forms of government had been modified since independence. 'The forms are not sacred but the ideals behind them are,' she noted. Her effective endorsement of military rule delighted Pakistan's leadership. Though her words had obviously been prepared by the Foreign Office rather than the Queen herself, the royal couple clearly got on well with their Sandhurst-trained host, who delighted in organising more shooting parties and polo matches for the Duke of Edinburgh.

Having been struck by the extremes between rich and poor in India, the British media were struck by the great divide between the sexes in Pakistan, as well as the Queen's capacity to bridge it. In Peshawar, it was noted that thousands of women ignored the norms of purdah and happily fought their way to the front of predominantly male crowds to catch a glimpse of the Queen. At the Lahore Fort, men were excluded from the Queen's tea party, though one or two women were barred as well. The government had insisted that all 200 lady guests had to provide a doctor's certificate confirming that they had undergone both a medical test and an X-ray, if they were to be permitted within 15 feet of the Queen, let alone introduced. One crestfallen Lahore matriarch was excluded because she was deemed to have a sore throat. Had she been aware of the poor woman's predicament, the Queen would hardly have objected. Just three days earlier she herself had pulled out of the Wali of Swat's goat hunt, thanks to a cold of her own.

* Pakistan's modern capital, Islamabad, had not yet been built, though the Queen was shown the proposed site from an aircraft. By the time of her next visit, in 1997, Islamabad was a sprawling conurbation of two million people.

The pursuit of wildlife had certainly been an international public-relations challenge in India. It was threatening to be a disaster on the third leg of the tour. The King of Nepal was preparing a big-game expedition that would make the Maharajah of Jaipur's tiger hunt look like a rabbit shoot. More than 2,000 workers had been drafted in to build 12 miles of road and a new airstrip in the Tarai jungle. The ground beneath a town-sized campsite had been dug up to a depth of one foot, in order to remove all scorpions that might sting a royal toe. It was then relaid with fresh turf. This time the royal couple would not be sitting in a tree. They would be hunting tigers – and a rhino or two – from the top of elephants, of which the King had mustered more than 300. Under the circumstances, cancellation was not an option, whatever the growing noise and fury back in Britain.

Come the day of the shoot, however, there was a bizarre if fortuitous development. The Duke had mysteriously developed an infection in his trigger finger, which had been encased in a thick bandage. While a Palace spokesman confirmed that he was responding well to penicillin, there was no way the Duke could shoot anything. When a tethered buffalo finally lured a tigress out of the jungle, 327 elephants and a long canvas screen encircled the animal in the royal line of fire. It fell to the most senior non-royal member of the party, the Foreign Secretary, the Earl of Home,* to take a shot. Eight times the tigress was driven in front of his gun. Five times he failed to take a shot and three times he missed. Finally, at the ninth attempt, the animal was felled by Sir Christopher Bonham-Carter, the Duke's treasurer.

There were, predictably, no complaints in Nepal. There was also an important military background to the tour. Although Nepal has never been part of the Commonwealth, having never been under British rule, it is from this country that the British Army has drawn some of its finest troops over two centuries. The Queen and the Duke travelled to the hill regions from where the Royal Gurkha Rifles have always recruited their elite infantrymen.

The royal couple returned home in early March, with an equally groundbreaking state visit to Iran – and the ancient ruins of

* He would disclaim his earldom in 1963 on becoming Prime Minister. He sat in the Commons as Sir Alec Douglas-Home until he returned to the Lords, with a new life peerage, as Baron Home, in 1974.

Persepolis – on the way back. Both in Britain and in Asia, the trip had been viewed as an outstanding diplomatic result, by the public, politicians and press alike. There had been some obvious lapses of judgement on the part of both the hosts and the Palace. The *Herald*'s Anthony Carthew called the tiger shoot 'silly, undignified, a bad mistake by the Queen's advisers'. However, he wrote that it was to India's credit that 'the Queen could see the poor and they could see her'. The *Guardian*'s Michael Wall described the tour as an 'unqualified success'. India and Pakistan, he observed, had been deeply impressed by the contrast between the 'small young woman in simple dresses who perches on the back of an open car waving and smiling and the austere statues of her grandfather'.

All this had taken place less than fifteen years after British rule had come to a close, in violent and bloody circumstances. Yet the atmosphere on that first visit had been unfailingly warm and cordial. An important line had been drawn under the central chapter in Britain's imperial story. As the editorial in the Hindustan Times proclaimed, the tour had 'stirred an intimate chord of memory'.

WIND OF CHANGE

Within months of that epic tour of the India sub-continent, the Queen would embark on that equally important but challenging tour of Africa. She had originally been due to visit Ghana in 1960. The impending arrival of Prince Andrew had forced her to abandon that trip but it would only be a postponement. There were major upheavals underway across Africa and the Queen wanted to play her part.

The former colony of Gold Coast had been the first African colony to obtain independence when it became Ghana in 1957. Though it retained the Queen in the beginning, it was already planning to remove her as head of state and become a republic. It had also opted for one-party rule under the volatile Kwame Nkrumah. This was always going to be a challenging assignment for the Queen. Despite his socialist credentials, however, Nkrumah retained a deep personal affection for her and was keen to keep his country in the Commonwealth, if only for the sake of 'that young girl', as he called her. With the Soviet Union and China ready and willing to fill any goodwill deficit towards this brand new African nation, the pressure was on the Queen to keep the balance tipped towards the West. So when her pregnancy precluded all travelling, she invited Nkrumah to Balmoral by way of an apology for cancelling that trip earmarked for 1960. She also made him a Privy Councillor for good measure. At the same time the British government embarked on a charm offensive aimed at Nkrumah's key lieutenants. One of his closest aides was the urbane Kwesi Armah, posted to the Ghanaian High Commission in London. Armah's family recall the way that he was feted by the British establishment, with shooting and fishing invitations from the Duke of Devonshire, nephew of Prime Minister Harold Macmillan. Africa might be changing but, as the Queen well understood, it had to be kept close.

1960 was the same year in which Harold Macmillan travelled to Cape Town to deliver his famous address to the white-dominated South African parliament, warning that 'the wind of change is blowing through the continent'. The National Party government of the new Prime Minister, Hendrik Verwoerd, was wedded to white supremacy and racial segregation and heading in a very different direction from the rest of the Commonwealth. It was also planning to dispense with the Queen, too. When South Africa voted 52:48 to become a republic later in the year (only whites were eligible to vote), the rules meant that it would now have to reapply for Commonwealth membership. Rather than face humiliation, it announced that it had left of its own volition.

This was a watershed in so many regards. The balance of power in the Commonwealth was shifting away from the cosy consensus of old white realms towards the newly independent nations, many of which had chosen a presidential constitution rather than a royal one. As Professor Philip Murphy has demonstrated, the British government was actually urging colonies to abandon the Queen and opt for a republican model, for fear that she might end up being caught in some constitutional crossfire. The Queen would not complain – as long as these ex-colonies stayed inside her Commonwealth.

'When Macmillan talked about the "winds of change", the Queen was presiding over an empire evolving into a Commonwealth of Nations. That cannot be done unless the "winds of change" change you as well,' says the Archbishop of York, John Sentamu, a Ugandan schoolboy at the time. 'The Queen is not into revolution but she is into very deep evolution. She's evolved with the Commonwealth and the Commonwealth has evolved with her.'

It had not gone unnoticed by the Commonwealth states that, during the Queen's 'maternity leave', she had staged a particularly lavish welcome for the French President, General Charles de Gaulle. The UK had laid on opera, fireworks and even state trumpeters to herald his speech to Parliament, all in the (ultimately vain) hope that he would welcome Britain into the EEC. A few weeks later, the Commonwealth prime ministers met in London, feeling a little spurned and making it clear that even among those nations that had abolished the Crown, there was still a great affection for the Queen. That is why she set off for India in 1961 and why, eight months later, she would leave Britain and her infant son once more to fulfil her promise to President (as he had now become) Nkrumah. She was on her way to Ghana, despite serious civil unrest and bombings in the capital, Accra. In Britain, there had been parliamentary calls for her to cancel the trip. The Queen was unperturbed.

According to *The Crown*, the fictionalised Netflix drama about her life, the Queen's chief motive for visiting Ghana was because she felt inadequate compared to the impossibly glamorous American first lady, Jackie Kennedy. This thoroughly misleading portrayal of a scorned royal diva ignores the Queen's astute grasp of realpolitik. Jackie Kennedy had played no part whatsoever in the Queen's decision to visit Ghana. First, the trip had already been agreed two years before. More importantly, the Russian premier, Nikita Khrushchev, was keen to make new friends in West Africa and the Queen was determined to exclude him. 'How silly I should look if I was scared to visit Ghana and then Khrushchev went and had a good reception,' she told Macmillan. Splashed across newspapers around the world were historic pictures of the black independence leader dancing with the smiling white Queen whom he had just removed as head of state. Here was living proof of that 'wind of change' sweeping through Africa, even if the media in one corner of the continent pretended not to notice. Just fourteen years before, South Africa had showered her in diamonds. Now, its media simply ignored her.

Chapter 4

HEAD OF THE COMMONWEALTH

'They all love a bit of royal jelly on their toast'

THE BEEHIVE

Exotic dancers are lighting up the East Front of Buckingham Palace. A giant illuminated peacock has been projected over the central arch, its wings fanning out across the very balcony where the Queen and her family appear on special occasions. In the kitchens the Royal Chef, Mark Flanagan, and his team are preparing 5,000 Indian-themed canapés with help from chefs from Britain's oldest Indian restaurant, Veeraswamy. The Queen is holding a reception to mark the 2017 UK–India Year of Culture, a series of events designed to honour the seventieth anniversary of Indian independence in 1947. That was the moment when the subcontinent was divided into modern India and Pakistan, marking the formal end of the British Empire. It also led to the birth of the modern Commonwealth. These, though, were tumultuous events that left enduring scars. For tonight's anniversary party, the Queen is treading carefully. This will be a sensitive celebration of contemporary ties between two great nations. A selection of Indian music had been played during the Changing the Guard ceremony earlier in the day. There is a modest exhibition of uncontroversial gifts from the Indian subcontinent, such as the shawl that Mahatma Gandhi wove for Princess Elizabeth as a wedding present and the garland the Queen received on her first visit to India in 1961. This is not a moment to evoke memories of the British Raj.

The Royal Family are here to help the Queen with a 300-strong guest list, which includes an eminent cross-section of UK/Indian life. Word has clearly gone round to keep things demure and 'culturally appropriate'. The Duchess of Cambridge and the other royal ladies have all steered clear of anything resembling a sari. The Duchess is wearing a below-the-knee metallic dress by Erdem and sparkling Oscar de la Renta shoes.

'What do you do?' the Queen asks Kapil Dev. 'I used to play cricket,' replies the man named by the cricketing bible, *Wisden*, as 'Indian cricketer of the century'. The Duke of Cambridge chats to Dev about Indian food and about his alma mater, St Andrew's University in Scotland. It transpires that the revered sportsman knows it well, because his daughter is currently a student there. Here is just one more reminder of the intricate web of personal connections, networks and historical ties that make up the Commonwealth.

For this evening is honouring much more than a seventieth-birthday party for modern India. It is also a celebration of one of the oldest and quirkiest multilateral international organisations in the world, which is why the Queen is making such a big fuss of the occasion. The Commonwealth is one of the Queen's greatest achievements. It is the key to any understanding of her world view and her engagement with the rest of the planet.

Anyone with a close working knowledge of this post-imperial 'family' of fifty-three nations – covering what used to be the footprint of the British Empire – will readily concede that were it not for the Queen, the Commonwealth might very well have disappeared long ago. And if it had not been for India, it might never have existed in the first place. For, as we have seen, it was India that forced the expiring British Empire to reinvent itself as a unique and benign alliance of equal and independent nations.

To some, the Commonwealth might now seem like a sepia-tinted relic, superseded by shiny new talking shops like the G7 or the G20, and dwarfed by that great behemoth, the United Nations. That is how it is seen by many within the Foreign & Commonwealth Office, an institution that sometimes gives the impression of having jettisoned the 'C' in FCO. Yet everyone knows that the Queen adores *her*

Commonwealth, which helps explain why it enjoys an unusual ambience and range of perks. Its ambassadors are called High Commissioners and get invitations denied to the rest of the diplomatic pack. 'People are not quite foreigners. It's a subtle difference,' says Lord Howell, former Cabinet and Foreign Office minister and President of the Royal Commonwealth Society. 'It is an association which starts with a prejudice in favour of friendship,' the former Prime Minister, Sir Alec Douglas-Home, said in later life, 'and that, in this modern world, is a good start.'

Yet the Commonwealth is often its own worst enemy, squabbling ineffectively over membership rules and the allocation of its small, ever-dwindling budget. 'I think we are struggling to find a role for it,' says former Conservative Foreign Secretary, Lord Hague. 'You do have to think: in fifty years' time are all the leaders going to be sitting at those meetings? Are they going to find that there's value in that? But I do think it is worth trying to keep such a network going because you don't know what networks will survive.'

The more the former British Empire recedes into the past, the more it seems to be demonised as a force for evil. At Oxford University, a perennial student campaign calls for the removal of all traces (except the vast financial endowment) of the colonial adventurer Cecil Rhodes. When Nigel Biggar, Oxford's Regius Professor of Moral and Pastoral Theology, embarked on a study of imperial rights and wrongs in 2017, he was denounced as 'racist' for suggesting that there could be any positives at all. Yet the overwhelming majority of countries which once constituted that empire still resolutely insist on staying inside – and celebrating – this association of Empire alumni, hand-in-hand with the original imperial power. Whatever their divisions, the one thing on which they all agree is their respect for the old Emperor's daughter. No wonder foreign observers are baffled, while the Commonwealth's critics ask despairingly: why don't these countries get it? By way of an answer, one Commonwealth official points to Monty Python's cult film, *Life of Brian*, as the armchair revolutionary asks: 'What have the Romans ever done for us?'*

* At a meeting of the People's Front of Judea, its leader, Reg, played by John Cleese, asks: 'What have the Romans ever done for us?' To which comes a series of unhelpful replies: 'sanitation', 'medicine', 'education', 'roads' ...

Most complaints about the Commonwealth are not about glossing over imperial wrongdoing – which no one denies – but about hypocrisy. Often fully justified, these criticisms focus on the Commonwealth's high-minded preaching about human rights while ignoring flagrant abuses by member governments. Yet that is to overlook its immense advantages as a network that operates in umpteen ways at a human level.

After a distinguished diplomatic career spanning the Foreign Office, the United Nations and the Commonwealth, former Deputy Secretary-General of the latter, Sir Peter Marshall, has 'lost count of the number of times I have heard its demise confidently predicted or stridently recommended'. It continues to flourish, he says, because it is many things at once: 'The experts debate whether the Commonwealth is a church, a club or a beehive. The only possible diplomatic answer is that it is all three, simultaneously and interactively.'

Whatever the political row of the moment – and there have been some spectacular ones over the years – the practical, human side of the Commonwealth cheerfully gets on with its own thing. It is the 'beehive' aspect that the Queen most enjoys. Indeed, she even takes a keen interest in the work of the Commonwealth Beekeepers' Association and has warmly approved its proposals for a new fund to assist beekeepers in poorer parts of the Commonwealth, like the honey-gathering Batwa Pygmies of Uganda. On being informed it would be called the Sir Edmund Hillary Fund, after the beekeeping Kiwi conqueror of Everest, the Queen is said to have clapped her hands in delight.

The G7 cannot boast an association of beekeepers, or a club of more than 500 universities on every continent that talk to each other every day, as the Association of Commonwealth Universities does. Neither the G20 nor OPEC can connect paediatricians or tax inspectors or teachers or police officers in the Caribbean with their equals in the South Pacific. Set aside the politicians, and here is a network of people who may all be delighted to see the back of the British Empire but who, as a result, nonetheless have a shared language, a shared legal system, a very similar civil service and a very similar system of parliamentary democracy.

Sir David Manning, former Ambassador to the United States and a senior adviser to the Duke and Duchess of Cambridge and The

Duke and Duchess of Sussex calls the Commonwealth a 'surprising' organisation. 'It sticks together because, on the whole, there is no one overwhelmingly in charge,' he says. Lord Howell believes that hierarchical, geographical blocks like the European Union are gradually losing ground in the digital age. Not so the Commonwealth, as he argues in his book, *Old Links and New Ties*: 'Take a planet-wide common working language, similar legal systems, a new weave of business alliances in friendly and familiar markets, a cross-pollinating stream of educational linkages, a plethora of professional associations and mix all these in with the age of broadband and the internet. An extraordinary new trans-continental brew of connections and exchanges emerges. That is the new Commonwealth case.'

It is a view shared by the Queen, which explains why she has quietly spent the last few years creating so many new Commonwealth organisations in her own name. They have been carefully designed to keep politicians at a distance, keep the costs down and focus on young people. It all goes back to why she is making a big fuss of India at the Palace tonight. For India is the economic powerhouse of her Commonwealth, not to mention the home of half of its 2.4 billion citizens. This reception is the first of many events leading up to what will be one of the most glamorous and poignant occasions in the organisation's history, the 2018 Commonwealth Summit in London. That will be an event where, on the eve of her ninety-second birthday, the Queen will discreetly hand the baton on to the next royal generation, secure in the knowledge that her Commonwealth is back on an upward trajectory. It still needs the British monarchy to provide lustre and continuity, though. 'There is no doubt that the Queen provides the magnet,' says the then Foreign Secretary, Boris Johnson, mingling with the guests at the Indian reception. 'The lunar pull of royal charisma is incredibly important for the Commonwealth, always has been, always will be.'

It has, though, been a very bumpy journey.

GANGING UP

Those landmark royal tours to places like India and Ghana had captured the mood across a fast-expanding Commonwealth. As more and more colonies sought independence, the founding fathers of these young democracies came to regard the Queen as a dependable friend and ally, rather than an aloof superior. She had already earmarked 'Granny's house' for the general use of the Commonwealth, making it clear that Marlborough House should retain its status as a royal palace, to give the organisation added royal kudos. So who was actually supposed to be administering this new Commonwealth? Despite the stuff about all members having 'equal status', the British government assumed that it was still in charge. After all, it was to London that the leaders came each year for their conferences, with a British minister in the chair. Britain, surely, was more equal than the rest?

By the mid-Sixties, however, the new members were having other thoughts. Arnold Smith, then an adviser to the Canadian Prime Minister, witnessed a telling moment at the 1964 meeting. The British Secretary of State for Commonwealth Relations, Duncan Sandys, launched into a speech presenting decolonisation as a British gift to the world. 'His speech was pure Britannia nutrix, the proud mother who had nursed her infants to strength and independence,' Smith wrote later. Suddenly an African voice interrupted. 'Now come, Mr Chairman, let's be frank with each other,' said Dr Hastings Banda of newly independent Malawi. 'You British have not been as pig-headed as other imperialists. You have recognised in time what is inevitable and accepted it gracefully. That is your greatness and we honour you for it. But it has not been all voluntary. There's been a significant element of persuasion and many of us here have been among the persuaders.' He then went around the table pointing out the number of prime ministers present – himself included – who had actually been imprisoned by the British in the not-too-distant past. Had Nehru, nine times a prisoner, not just passed away in May 1964, the list would have been even longer.

It was Kwame Nkrumah of Ghana who addressed that 1964 meeting with the idea of an independent Commonwealth management operation. Crucially, he argued that it should not be controlled by the British. Though the British government loathed the idea, the other heads agreed, and Arnold Smith was hired as the first Secretary-General in 1965. The British government did its best to put this upstart body in its place. At the 1965 meeting of Commonwealth finance ministers, Smith discovered that the British Commonwealth Office had taken it upon itself to organise the seating plan and had allocated him a place next to the shorthand typists. He swiftly relocated himself alongside the chairman. At the annual Buckingham Palace reception for the Diplomatic Corps, the Queen and the Duke were surprised to come across Smith at the bottom end of the greeting line, lurking in the sub-ambassadorial undergrowth, somewhere beneath the lowest-ranking chargé d'affaires. 'What are you doing down here?' the Duke asked him. 'It's your party, Sir,' Smith's wife, Eve, replied. 'Yes, but you know who organises these things!' said the Duke conspiratorially. 'The Commonwealth Relations Office.' Within a week, after some 'royal prodding' in Whitehall, Arnold Smith was informed that he had mysteriously been granted an extraordinary special status. In future he was to be placed ahead of even the most senior ambassador at the Court of St James.

The Smiths would often find themselves invited to dinner *à quatre* with the Queen and the Duke. The Palace, he wrote, showed 'a concerted effort to give us a welcome and to impress upon Whitehall officials that I was to be considered one of the Queen's advisers'. In the battle between the new Commonwealth administration and the British establishment, the Queen was not just ensuring fair play. She appeared to be siding with the Commonwealth.

Within weeks of Smith's arrival, he would be handling the first major Commonwealth schism, following the Unilateral Declaration of Independence (UDI) in the white-run colony of Rhodesia. The row would open a fault line between 'old' and 'new' members of the Commonwealth, as the former continued to misunderstand the depth of feeling among the latter when it came to colonisation and its legacy. As the former Commonwealth Secretary-General, Chief Emeka Anyaoku, later wrote: 'Only people who have lived through the dying days of colonial rule can fully appreciate how deeply the sense of racial inequality was embedded in people's consciousness at the time.' He has pointed out that Siaka Stevens, President of Sierra Leone in the Sixties, even wanted to create a new national honour; Stevens wanted to call it the Order of the Mosquito, in recognition of the insect that had sent so many would-be European settlers to an early grave in West Africa and had curtailed the colonial ambitions of so many others. As far as Stevens and some of his generation of West African leaders were concerned, the long delay in discovering quinine, as a treatment for malaria, was actually a blessing.

Rhodesia's unilateral declaration of independence – and Britain's dithering on the matter – had enraged the younger African nations. As a result, an important precedent was set. The Commonwealth no longer felt obliged to assemble in London, since it was no longer under the auspices of the British government. The growing faction of recently liberated ex-colonies wanted to have meetings on their own terms. Those 'fireside chat' gatherings of the past were very much at an end. In 1965, the African leaders demanded an emergency Commonwealth meeting to present a united front against Rhodesia's white rulers. They did not want the meeting in London, but in Nigeria. Britain, they argued, had been utterly hypocritical in failing to intervene against the white rebellion in Rhodesia when a colonial insurrection by black insurgents anywhere else would, surely, have been met with brute force. Patsy Robertson, a former Jamaican journalist who would run media operations at Marlborough House for many years, had just joined Arnold Smith's team. She well recalls how much the rest of the 'club' enjoyed ganging up on the British delegation, led by Harold Wilson. 'I remember, in Lagos, we had this all-night session confronting the British as never before,' she says. 'The next morning, at six or seven, the lift opened and out stepped Lester Pearson [Prime Minister of Canada] and he said: "What fun we had". And I realised how much people enjoyed this.' At one point, an exasperated Wilson had complained to Albert Margai, Prime Minister of Sierra Leone: 'Stop your caucusing!' Margai's swift riposte caused much mirth: 'Harold, we're not Caucasians.'

The UDI crisis also set an important precedent for the new-look Commonwealth. Two nations, Ghana and Tanzania, had been so enraged by Britain's response that they severed diplomatic relations with London. Crucially, though, they did not also sever relations with the Commonwealth. As the former Secretary-General Sonny Ramphal explains, this was a pivotal moment. No longer could anyone claim that the Commonwealth was 'British'. It might still have the Queen as symbolic Head and its headquarters in London, but it had now established its credentials as an independent body. Its Canadian Secretary-General, Arnold Smith, owed no loyalty to the British government, even if Britain was still expected to pay the lion's share of the bills, under a funding formula based on each nation's wealth. This new spirit of independence would make life increasingly difficult for the Queen.

By the end of the Sixties, the Commonwealth had risen in size to nearly thirty member states. Since all enjoyed equal status, the old guard could be outvoted with ease. Many leaders had rather enjoyed the experience of kicking the British at that emergency meeting in Lagos. Might these regular gatherings of 'the club' not move to a different location under a different chairman every other year instead? And might these events not have a new name? It seemed silly to keep calling them 'prime ministers' conferences' when so many republican leaders were now presidents. The idea of the 'Commonwealth Heads of Government Meeting' was born. As a result, one of the uglier words in the diplomatic lexicon was coined – the 'CHOGM' (pronounced: *cho-gum)*. Before today's busy calendar of peripatetic international talking shops – from the G7 and the G20 to APEC and OPEC – the CHOGM was the only truly global gathering outside the United Nations.

THE TALKING SHOP

It was agreed that the first CHOGM was to be held in 1971 in Singapore. The Queen, understandably, expected to be there. The idea of holding this summit outside Britain met with no opposition whatsoever from the recently elected British Prime Minister, Edward Heath. He was positively delighted. Like his predecessor, Harold Wilson, Heath was resigned to the fact that many leaders looked on Commonwealth meetings as primarily an opportunity to beat the old colonial power over the head. If he was to be spared the job of hosting the event, so much the better. What's more, he was preparing to implement a deeply unpopular policy, which threatened to split the Commonwealth down the middle. He was going to resume arms sales to the apartheid regime in South Africa. As a result, he had bad news for the Queen.

Knowing that his policy would create a poisonous atmosphere in Singapore, he formally advised her that she should not attend, explaining that she might be drawn into an embarrassing dispute. It was advice that she would always regret taking. It left her 'deeply unhappy', in the words of Heath's biographer, John Campbell, particularly because of the Prime Minister's 'undisguised disrespect' for the Commonwealth and many of its leaders. For a relatively new

Prime Minister to tell the Queen, in her twentieth year as Head of the Commonwealth, that she was not to attend an important assembly of her beloved organisation must have been a challenge, even for someone as thick-skinned as Heath. What we do know is that the Queen was determined not to miss another one.

Heath's decision to sell arms to South Africa led some countries to threaten an exit from the Commonwealth altogether. At the summit, there were heated exchanges about the evils of capitalism and Britain's collusion with racist South Africa. Heath loathed the entire exercise. To compound his bad mood, there was one further embarrassment. Long before the summit, officials from the Singapore government of Lee Kuan Yew had travelled to Britain in the hope of acquiring a fleet of forty Daimlers to carry the leaders around town. A Commonwealth summit, they explained, should be using Commonwealth-built vehicles. Daimler, however, was unable to guarantee delivery within the fifteen-month deadline. Singapore turned to Germany as India had ahead of the 1961 tour. Mercedes promised to deliver in less than half that time. Heath refused all offers of an official Mercedes and insisted on riding in the British High Commissioner's Rolls-Royce.

Yet compromise prevailed. In the end, the British government was persuaded to limit its arms sales to South Africa to a few naval helicopters. Of greater significance was a joint declaration signed by all the leaders, laying down a new set of shared principles regarding good governance and human rights. Not that some of the signatories would take much notice. In the very same week, one of these Commonwealth nations discovered it had a new leader. This was the occasion when President Obote of Uganda was deposed by Idi Amin.

Those who did make it to Singapore were all adamant that Heath had made a major mistake in excluding the Queen. His own Foreign Secretary, Sir Alec Douglas-Home, agreed. 'He was really quite annoyed with Heath,' says former Commonwealth Secretary-General Sonny Ramphal. If there was one thing that would have lifted the sour, bellicose mood, it was the Queen. 'It was a disservice to her and the Commonwealth that Ted Heath advised her not to go,' says Emeka Anyaoku, a future Secretary-General who, back then, was a rising star within the organisation. 'I believe had the Queen been there, the atmosphere and the tone of the discussions would have been a lot more even-tempered.'

A senior member of the Royal Household says that the Queen has always regretted missing Singapore, because it would mean she could never claim a '100 per cent' attendance record. As her former Private Secretary, Lord Charteris, told the royal biographer, Robert Lacey, 'If she's there, you see, they behave. It's like Nanny being there. It also works because she knows them all and they like her.'

By keeping the Queen at home, Heath had not merely left her determined to attend the next CHOGM, but had also, unwittingly, opened up a secret back-channel between the Queen and the Commonwealth Secretariat, one that would surely have infuriated him if he had ever known. The Commonwealth archives contain a memo from a senior official reporting on a lunch with Philip Moore, the Queen's deputy Private Secretary, in 1972. Moore had been complaining that the Queen's red boxes contained 'virtually nothing about the Commonwealth'. The official, Hunter Wade, agreed that the secretariat would begin sending papers 'of particular interest' to the Queen, adding that 'the problems faced by Commonwealth countries in the wake of British entry into the EEC was a case in point'. In other words, the Head of the Commonwealth was about to be fed potentially hostile reports on Heath's beloved European project behind his back.

Having detested Singapore, Heath informed Arnold Smith that another gathering would surely not be required until 1975 'at the earliest'. Smith was having none of it. The British government did not own the Commonwealth. The members would have a meeting in 1973, whether Heath liked it or not, and Smith had already drawn up plans for one in the Canadian capital, Ottawa. The monarch was definitely in favour of the idea. So an all-Canadian plot was hatched by the Canadian Commonwealth Secretary-General, involving the Canadian Prime Minister, Pierre Trudeau, and the Queen of Canada herself. First, Smith asked Trudeau if he would be the host, and Trudeau readily agreed. Then, in his capacity as her Canadian Prime Minister, Trudeau invited the Queen to come. She was under no obligation to seek the permission of her British Prime Minister and gladly accepted, without talking to Edward Heath. The summit now had the Head of the Commonwealth on board, leaving Heath with little option but to put it in his diary. He was much more interested in steering Britain into the new European Common Market than in being dragged to another stormy meeting with the ex-imperial club. 'The reluctant traveller was Edward Heath himself,' wrote Smith. 'Up to the last few days, he would not say whether he would come. It was the Queen's firmness in showing that she at any rate would be in Canada that ended his sulky attitude. He could hardly stay away if she were there. So he came.'

This time the Queen's presence would, indeed, have a conciliatory, calming effect on everyone. Despite some robust arguments about Rhodesia, nuclear weapons and Marxism, Heath had a much more congenial trip. He even agreed to sign up for another CHOGM two years later, although by then he would have been ejected from Downing Street in favour of Labour's Harold Wilson – but not before meddling with the Queen's travel plans, once more.

When Heath called an election for the end of February 1974, the Queen was already undertaking a major tour of her Pacific realms. It meant that she had to abandon her visit to Australia after just two days, without even wearing the new yellow chiffon 'wattle' dress that her designer, Ian Thomas, had created specially for the visit. This was certainly a far cry from the sort of treatment she had received from her earlier Conservative prime ministers. In 1959, Harold Macmillan had shelved the idea of a June election entirely, because he did not want to disrupt the Queen's summer tour of Canada. Since she would need to be at home for the result, he deferred the election until October. Heath had much more pressing concerns on his mind in 1974 than the Queen's travel arrangements. Britain was regularly being paralysed by strikes and industrial action. In forcing her early return from Australia, however, he further undermined the case for the Crown in a country that was already developing an appetite for republicanism. This was only a year after Britain's entry into the EEC, at the expense of the old Commonwealth cousins, and a year before an Australian prime minister would be sacked by the Queen's Governor-General. Thanks to Heath, the Queen's default position had been made very clear: all realms are equal, but one is more equal than others.

The Commonwealth, meanwhile, was in robust form after that unexpectedly happy Canadian gathering. Pierre Trudeau had come up with a number of clever innovations in Ottawa, which would help create a very different sort of summit atmosphere, one that endures to this day. There would be no reading of pre-prepared texts, as at the United Nations. That immediately spared everyone hours of pointless tedium. He came up with the idea of a Commonwealth flag and, more importantly, the idea of the 'retreat'. This was an informal break at a secluded location, where the leaders could relax without officials and any formal record-keeping. 'It was a place where leaders could share things they would not discuss with their own wives,' explains Patsy Robertson. 'Trudeau played a historic role in defining the culture of the Commonwealth,' says Kamalesh Sharma. These retreats could, in a matter of hours, reach conclusions that it might take years to extract from the UN. The leaders would emerge from the 1977 retreat at Gleneagles, for example, with the first concerted international plan to ostracise white South Africa from world sport. Some retreats were memorable for other reasons. Years later, at the 1989 CHOGM in Malaysia, the leaders 'retreated' to a spa resort at Langkawi, where the hosts introduced a karaoke session, to the horror of Mrs Thatcher. 'Various leaders came up and gave excruciating performances of well-known tunes,' Stuart Mole recalls. 'Mrs Thatcher sat there, clutching her handbag and hating every moment of it. I don't think she sang anything.'

After Trudeau's success in 1973, the next CHOGM was scheduled for Jamaica in 1975. The Jamaican Prime Minister, Michael Manley, was keen to present himself as a world statesman, but was strangely fearful of the Queen. According to his friend, Sir Sonny Ramphal, Manley was worried that a royal visit would damage his left-wing credentials. 'He was posturing as a Marxist,' Sir Sonny said later. 'Of course, she was a star. All his republicanism vanished.' Manley would not be the first – or last – radical politician to mellow under the influence of a little royal stardust. At the Queen's request, the 1977 meeting came to London to coincide with her Silver Jubilee celebrations. There were fears among some of the more radical Commonwealth leaders that holding that year's summit alongside her Jubilee might lead to a latter-day London 'durbar', an ostentatious homage to the ex-colonial matriarch in the old imperial capital. 'You have to remember that these guys were just out of their freedom struggle,' explains Sonny Ramphal. 'Their political intuition was focussed in that direction. But as they got to know the Queen, all that melted away.'

'HEATHEN' RITES

During those acutely sensitive early gatherings of her Commonwealth, the Queen rapidly realised that it was her role to keep the peace – discreetly but firmly. She made a series of subtle but important gestures, which, when viewed from a distance, make her views on the need to 'de-imperialise' the Commonwealth brand abundantly clear. In 1966, she approved a suggestion to rename Empire Day as Commonwealth Day and, just for good measure, she shifted the date from Queen Victoria's birthday to her own official birthday (the date would later move to March). At the same time the Queen also gave a very clear indication of the sort of Commonwealth that she favoured. It would embroil her in a controversy from which she made no attempt to extricate herself. It was also in 1966 that a London vicar, Austen Williams of St Martin-in-the-Fields, together with the Royal Commonwealth Society (RCS)* organised a multi-faith service for the eve of Commonwealth Day. They planned to include all the main religions and an invitation was issued to the Queen and the Duke of Edinburgh, who readily accepted. The presence of the Supreme Governor of the Church of England herself, however, was not enough to avert furious complaints afterwards. Some traditionalists objected to 'heathen' rites being observed in an Anglican church. The Bishop of London, supported by the secretary to the Archbishop of Canterbury, warned that such an overtly non-Christian event, particularly one calling itself a 'service', should not be permitted in a Christian church again.

Chastened by such senior clergy, the organisers backed down from holding another multi-faith church service. The Queen was plainly unhappy. In 1968 the organisers arranged something called an 'act of witness' in the secular setting of the Guildhall in the City of London.

* Originally established in 1868 as the Colonial Society, the Royal Commonwealth Society was one of the first chartered institutes to welcome women as both speakers and members. It promotes Commonwealth ideals around the world, even in non-Commonwealth nations like the USA and Ireland.

Though the Queen attended once again, to show her support for the idea, she disliked the compromise. 'The message came through that she would not come to it if it continued to be held in a secular location. She felt it was a faith occasion and should be organised like one,' says Stuart Mole, a former director-general of the RCS. It was the Queen who came up with a solution, too. Westminster Abbey, like St George's Chapel, Windsor, comes under the direct authority of the monarch rather than any bishop. As such, it is known as a 'royal peculiar'. As Mole recalls: 'The Queen said: "You can use my royal peculiar to do this and then you don't need the Church of England. You don't need bishops on your back". So they did.'

As a result, in 1972 the event was remodelled at Westminster Abbey under a new title. It was not a 'service' but an 'observance'. The Queen was delighted to attend, and much enjoyed tea with Arnold Smith at Marlborough House afterwards. 'She and the Duke of Edinburgh were extremely pleased that it was possible this year to hold the Commonwealth Day Observance at Westminster Abbey,' her assistant Private Secretary, Bill Heseltine, wrote to Smith, 'and the Queen felt the tea party made a most apt and pleasant sequel'. Both the Abbey service and the party would become immovable fixtures in the royal diary for decades to come.

The observance has since been rebranded once again and is now a 'celebration'. Yet the event remains as quirkily omnispiritual as ever and now frequently enjoys live television coverage on the BBC. Come Commonwealth Day 2018, for example, it featured a dozen faiths, a conch-blower, a Maori choir, a band of Ghanaian drummers, pop star Liam Payne and a prayer from a Sunni Muslim cleric: 'O magnificent Creator, enable us to respect and celebrate the diversity you have created.' The sermon came not from a clergyman but from Andrew Bastawrous, a young British eye doctor who left home to set up 100 eye clinics in Kenya and is now at the forefront of the royal campaign against blindness in the Commonwealth. The Queen listened attentively, but she knew the story already. A few weeks before, she had invited him to a private audience at the Palace.

The Queen sees no conflict between her role as Head of the Commonwealth and that of Supreme Governor of the Church of England. Indeed, she regards them as complementary. She is the first to acknowledge that the Commonwealth comprises all faiths and none, and that most of its citizens do not happen to share her own (there are more Muslims and Hindus than Christians among the 2.4 billion citizens of the fifty-three member states). She regards it as her duty to defend the religious freedoms of all of them. Stuart Mole recalls an illuminating conversation with her when she came to visit the Royal Commonwealth Society shortly after a church service to mark her 2002 Golden Jubilee. 'As I was escorting her, she stopped me as we were walking along and said to me: "I need to tell you something". I thought: "Oh my God, she's about to tell me I've got brown shoes on or something". And she said: "Do you know, at that service, there was no Hindu representative. Wasn't that bad?" There had been a multi-faith attendance and they'd missed out the Hindus for whatever reason. I was very interested that she should have said that. Obviously that was a point of connection between her and the Commonwealth.'

One of the Prince of Wales's most famous quotes is his 1994 remark that, as King, he intends to be a 'defender of faith' rather than Defender of *the* Faith – the monarch's subsidiary title since 1521. The Prince's words made banner headlines at the time and were interpreted by some senior Anglican clergy as bordering on the rebellious. In fact he was merely endorsing the status quo, for the Queen has been doing precisely the same all through her reign. She even said so in 2012, at a Lambeth Palace reception marking her Diamond Jubilee. It was just entirely overlooked at the time. 'The concept of our established Church is occasionally misunderstood and commonly under-appreciated. Its role is not to defend Anglicanism to the exclusion of other religions,' she told a room full of clergy from all the main religions. 'Instead, the Church has a duty to protect the free practice of all faiths in this country. Gently and assuredly, the Church of England has created an environment for other faith communities and indeed people of no faith to live freely.' She could very well have been summing up her own philosophy towards both her Church and her Commonwealth. She had no demands for action, no finger-wagging lectures on human rights but, rather, 'a duty to protect . . . gently and assuredly'.

It is the Commonwealth that has been the main driver of Britain's evolution from a monocultural to a multicultural society, a challenging process for any nation. As one faith leader after another has attested, however, the Queen has played a major part in smoothing that process. Whatever their religion, they have found it very reassuring to have a head of state who is entirely comfortable putting faith at the heart of national life. 'The fact that she is head of a diverse, worldwide association means that she's never felt any instinct to panic about multi-culturalism,' the former Archbishop of Canterbury, Dr Rowan Williams, has explained. 'That's part of the message her Christmas broadcasts have given almost subliminally over the years.' The Archbishop of York, Dr John Sentamu, puts it down to confidence. 'Because she's so secure in her faith as a believer in Christ, it actually gives her room to reach to anybody,' he says, pointing to her Christmas broadcasts. 'There is no way you hear them without her ever talking about the way of Christ.'

'THE QUEEN MATTERS'

While Commonwealth fortunes fluctuated around the world, there was no question that the organisation was declining in prominence and prestige, as far as the British government was concerned. Until 1966 there had been a Colonial Office to handle those parts of the old empire still under British control, and a Commonwealth Relations Office dealing with independent ex-colonies. In 1966, they merged into a single Commonwealth Office and, just two years later, that was itself absorbed into the new Foreign & Commonwealth Office, at the very moment it was wholly preoccupied elsewhere. By then the overarching foreign-policy objectives were Britain's entry into the European Common Market and the state of relations with Washington. 'The Foreign Office at that time was very much of the opinion that the Queen and Commonwealth was a load of nonsense,' says Sir Roger du Boulay, the diplomatic veteran who began his career in Africa, went on to serve in Washington and Paris and later became Vice-Marshal of the Diplomatic Corps – the link between the Foreign Office and the Palace. 'Those mandarins thought it was their right to run the country and what was important was America and Europe, not the Commonwealth.' He clearly remembers the words of the Queen's Private Secretary when he was appointed Vice-Marshal in 1975. 'The first thing Martin Charteris said to me was this: "Now look, I want you to understand. The Queen matters!" And she did.'

The Commonwealth still 'mattered', too, during the eleven years of Margaret Thatcher's tenure in Downing Street. It might have been at odds with her on many points, but she never forgot that it stood full-square behind Britain during the Falklands conflict of 1982. Even those with whom Mrs Thatcher quarrelled most vehemently, like Sonny Ramphal, would acknowledge that she took the Commonwealth seriously and commanded its respect, if not its affection. 'It is a remarkable institution. No one could ever have invented or designed it,' she said in her speech at her dinner to mark Ramphal's retirement as Secretary-General. 'We don't tell each other what to do. We listen and make up our own minds.' Her successor, John Major, also had a strong regard for the organisation, having lived in Nigeria before entering politics. 'He worked in the Commonwealth as a young man,' says Robin (now Lord) Butler,* the former Cabinet Secretary. 'And then there was cricket. He was someone who was naturally respectful of institutions anyway but cricket was a big thing with him. That gave him a natural affinity with some of the leaders.' To this day, Sir John Major says that one of his happiest Commonwealth memories is opening the batting against his Australian counterpart, Bob Hawke, at a cricket match during the 1991 CHOGM in Harare. Emeka Anyaoku and Stuart Mole point out that it was Major and his Chancellor of the Exchequer, Ken Clarke, who pioneered Commonwealth debt-relief strategies for poor nations, which would eventually be adopted by the World Bank and the International Monetary Fund.

It was also Major who invited the Commonwealth to meet in Edinburgh in 1997, though he would have been ejected from Downing Street by the time it happened. His successor, Tony Blair, would host the event. Stuart Mole, one of the senior organisers from the Commonwealth Secretariat, remembers that Blair and his team wanted the summit to promote his new 'Cool Britannia' agenda, right down to a 'funky' version of the national anthem played on dustbins and pieces of piping. 'It sounded as if they were playing a central heating system,' recalls Mole. 'Although this was Edinburgh, the word went out: "No kilts. We don't want lots of Scottishness".' More problematic was the retreat, at the home of golf in St Andrews. Never

* Cabinet Secretary 1988–98, he was Britain's senior civil servant under Margaret Thatcher, John Major and Tony Blair, before being elevated to the House of Lords as Lord Butler of Brockwell. The Queen made him a Knight of the Garter in 2004.

having attended a retreat before, Blair's officials decided to arrange it their way, with rows of chairs in front of a dais from which Blair would address all the other leaders. Stuart Mole remembers the heated row: 'We got in there and said: "We cannot have this arrangement. This is just not how it is." It was supposed to be informal and in the round. Their attitude was that it was a photo opportunity.'

Blair never warmed to the Commonwealth after that. According to Lord Howell, his staff once discussed removing the 'C' from the title of the 'FCO' altogether. Though he had retired by then, Sir Sonny Ramphal was surprised by Blair's indifference towards the Commonwealth. 'I expected better internationalist policies from him,' he says. 'He lacked the empathy for dealing with the developing world – something which Callaghan and Wilson [his Labour predecessors in Downing Street] had.'

At one summit, Blair left an executive session to watch football on television. In 2003, Nigeria were the hosts and had been meticulous in ensuring that everything was ready for the Abuja summit. 'There had been a certain amount of trepidation and unfair stereotyping about anything running on time in Nigeria,' recalls Stuart Mole, 'but the Nigerians did a brilliant job with the opening ceremony.' Everyone, including the Queen, had got there on time – with one exception. 'It was running perfectly until Tony Blair completely threw it. The whole opening ceremony was delayed by fifteen minutes.' The Secretary-General of the time, Don McKinnon, the no-nonsense former Foreign Minister of New Zealand, was distinctly unimpressed that Blair ended up arriving after the Head of the Commonwealth. As one of his team remarked: 'Of course Tony comes after the Queen. He's the Emperor.'

'FRUMPISH AND BANAL'

Blair provides a useful indication of his general opinion of the Commonwealth in his autobiography. He does not mention it at all. His lack of enthusiasm may have stemmed, in part, from the diplomatic disaster which befell the first two state visits of his new administration – to two of the largest nations in the Commonwealth. Though Blair might have enjoyed a large parliamentary majority and a fair wind at home, this could also lead to complacency and cockiness overseas. That was certainly the case when his government despatched the Queen to India and Pakistan to mark the fiftieth anniversary of independence. Any hopes of a rerun of that triumphal tour of 1961 would soon be dashed.

Since India had been the Queen's first port of call on her 1961 tour, Pakistan would be first on her itinerary this time, in October 1997. It was a nervous start to the tour as the Queen arrived in Islamabad. This was her first overseas trip since the death of Diana, Princess of Wales, who had been something of a local hero in Pakistan after her visit to a children's hospital there not long before her death. The Queen used her opening state banquet speech to pay tribute to the Princess and to thank Pakistan for sharing 'our grief at Diana's tragic early death'. Her words were well received and, thereafter, the trip followed the usual pattern. In her speech to parliament, the Queen contrasted her 1961 visit – when there had been no parliament at all, because of the military coup – with the 'vigour and self-assurance' of modern democratic Pakistan.* She and the Duke of Edinburgh were quartered in the same Lahore suite in which they had stayed in 1961, and rode in a horse-drawn carriage to a dinner at the Lahore Fort (no one was asked for a medical certificate this time). Later on, the Duke travelled to the wilds of Chitral to inspect aid work and hand out polo prizes. So far, so good.

But the beginnings of a diplomatic disaster were taking place on the High Commissioner's lawn. Robin Cook, accompanying the Queen on his first state visit as Foreign Secretary since Labour's return to power in May 1997, was accosted by members of Pakistan's media at a British reception. To their delight, he expressed Britain's willingness to act as a broker in any peace negotiations with India over the disputed territory of Kashmir. His words chimed with a passage in the Queen's banquet speech in which she had spoken of her hopes for 'reconciliation' on the issue. When Pakistani news reports announced a fresh breakthrough on the future of Kashmir, the Indian government was appalled. It wanted no external interference. The mood worsened when the British High Commissioner in India, Sir David Gore-Booth,† was

* This would be short-lived. There was another military coup two years later.

† Despite his nickname of 'Gore Blimey', Sir David was a diplomat of the old school, joining the Foreign Office after Eton and Oxford. Pre-Delhi, he served as Ambassador to Saudi Arabia. His father, Sir Paul (later Lord Gore-Booth), had been High Commissioner during the Queen's first state visit in 1961.

tackled on the subject at a press conference ahead of the Queen's arrival in Delhi. His dismissive retort that the Indians should 'stop tilting at windmills' brought simmering resentments to the boil.

As the Queen and the Duke spent a private weekend at a Pakistani hill station prior to the start of the Indian leg of the tour, Cook returned home for a couple of days 'on business'. When the royal party arrived in Delhi the following week, however, the mood was toxic. The Indian Prime Minister had been quoted in the media belittling Britain as a 'third rate power', while *The Times of India* printed the following on its front-page: 'Thought for the Day: "Frumpish and banal" – Malcolm Muggeridge, British writer, referring to Queen Elizabeth II'. Some guests found that their invitations to royal events were mysteriously rescinded. The Band of the Royal Marines, due to perform at a royal event at the National Museum, were suddenly told not to bother coming. The original itinerary included a slot for a speech by the Queen in Madras. Though the speech had already been drafted, her Indian hosts suddenly removed it from the official schedule.

The mood worsened when the royal party visited Amritsar, scene of the 1919 massacre of 379 unarmed protestors by British forces. There had already been demands by a small but vociferous protest group for the Queen to make a formal apology. When a television camera overheard the Duke of Edinburgh suggesting the official death toll had been exaggerated, the mood soured further. As the media pointed the blame at Robin Cook – who had not only stirred things up in Pakistan, but had approved every aspect of the Queen's programme – the Foreign Secretary was in no mood to take responsibility. He had only been in the job for a matter of months. A prickly but gifted parliamentary performer with a high regard for his own brilliance, he was not about to allow this tour to besmirch his reputation. Cook redirected all the blame towards the media, the Royal Household, junior staff – anyone, in fact, but himself. He even blamed the previous Conservative government for agreeing to the visit in the first place, arguing that the fiftieth anniversary of independence had been a silly time for a royal tour anyway. What Cook was less keen to discuss was the urgent 'business' that had called him back to the UK halfway through the state visit. It later emerged that he had not spent the weekend on pressing international affairs of state, but had been at home in his constituency with the new woman in his life – his diary secretary, Gaynor Regan for whom he had recently left his wife.

Officially, both sides maintained the niceties. In his speech at the state banquet in the Lutyens-designed Rashtrapati Bhavan – formerly the Viceroy's Residence – President Narayanan assured the Queen that 'the esteem and affection and depth of feeling for Your Majesty have only increased with each visit'. The Queen replied that 'a deep, real and durable friendship is the bedrock of our contemporary partnership'. The final straw came as the Queen went to fly home. The Indian authorities roughed up one member of the British High Commission team and tried to block her press secretary from boarding the plane. The visit, *The Times* pronounced, had been a 'disaster'. 'Conceived in error, botched at birth,' wrote the BBC's veteran India expert, Mark Tully.

Sir David Gore-Booth had a difficult task as he sat down to write his despatch on the tour for his boss, the Foreign Secretary (and now released after a Freedom of Information request). Showing an almost Olympian capacity for looking on the bright side, he painted the tour as a great result for all concerned. Gore-Booth opened with a quote from the Irish writer Brendan Behan: 'All publicity is good, except an obituary notice.' The tour had taken place on two levels, 'the real and the imagined', he explained. 'At the real level, the Visit was full of symbolism and redolent with success.' The speeches, he added, 'correctly pointed out that through thick and thin there are certain fundamental values which unite Britain and India in a relationship which, as much as if not more than any other, deserves the label of special'. He dismissed the 'imagined-level stories of missing invitations, bands and speeches that were seized on and masticated by a carnivorous British press only too eager to find fault'. Gore-Booth concluded with another reference to Brendan Behan: 'No obituary notices are being written here.'

The actual mood inside the British High Commission was less upbeat. One diplomat recalls 'a perfect storm of factors' and believes that blame resides across the board: 'The Palace were feeling bruised. They were fixated on getting over the Queen's first tour after Diana's death and ended up blaming the Foreign Office. Then you had the Foreign Office still working out how to get on with new Labour after the Tories had been in for so long. And in the middle of all this, Cook's marriage was falling apart. Everyone had taken their eye off the ball when it came to what Cook and the Queen said in Pakistan. The Indians were to blame, too. They were not happy that Labour had got in to power because Labour were more active on the Kashmir issue.' The British diplomats, according to one of those involved, were 'pretty devastated' by the diplomatic setback. It is an astonishing measure of the failure of the tour that the FCO personnel department even felt obliged to write to the relevant officials, assuring them that the visit would not be held against them on their records. Sir David, who died in 2004, had been tipped as a future British Ambassador to the United Nations. His staff, whom he stoutly defended from the internal fallout after the visit and who were very fond of him, believe that the royal debacle scuppered his UN prospects.

A senior Palace veteran agrees with Gore-Booth's thesis to a certain extent: 'India was the one you had to lock in and it was always very difficult. There was and is a special relationship there but the imperial dimension is love/hate. We have to try to get the love bit right and we can't do a lot about the hate. But we have to work with the superpower of the future.'

Following the departure of Tony Blair in 2007, it appeared that his successor, Gordon Brown, had no great interest in the Commonwealth either. As Secretary-General, Don McKinnon was invited to a dinner at Downing Street at which Brown referred to him as 'the head of the British Commonwealth'. 'Sorry, Gordon,' McKinnon replied. 'Wrong on two counts. The Queen is the head and the "British Commonwealth" died in 1949.'*

In fact, Brown would warm to the Commonwealth in due course, even persuading the French President, Nicolas Sarkozy, to attend the 2009 summit in Trinidad in order to add his support to a Commonwealth proposal for an international climate-change fund. Shortly afterwards, it was adopted at the UN's 2009 summit on

* The 'British' Commonwealth still had its adherents, as McKinnon discovered soon after his appointment in 2000. Having invited him to lunch, the Queen Mother implored him to 'look after the family'. Did she mean the Royal Family, he wondered, or his own? 'No, no, the *old* Commonwealth family,' she explained.

climate change in Copenhagen, one of very few things on which that much-hyped but largely inconsequential gathering agreed.

Like Brown, David Cameron treated the Commonwealth with a mixture of respect and exasperation after his arrival in Number Ten in 2010. He was, however, keen to show willing. When the proposed host of the 2017 summit, Vanuatu, was hit by a devastating cyclone, Cameron offered Britain as a new location and moved the date to 2018. It would be his successor, Theresa May, who ended up as the host.

THE ROYAL AUDIENCE

As so many leaders have testified over so many years, had it not been for the Queen, the CHOGMs might have finished years ago and the Commonwealth itself might well have imploded. 'The Queen is the personification, not just the Head, of the Commonwealth,' says Alex Downer, the longest-serving Foreign Minister in Australian history who went on to be High Commissioner to the UK. 'Hyperbole never does anybody much good but she is loved through the Commonwealth and no one knows what would have happened without her.' Former Prime Minister David Cameron is in little doubt. 'I suspect it would never have got off the ground the way it did without the Queen as its champion,' he says. 'I think she ensured its birth, its growth and development at every stage. Without her it wouldn't have happened.'

From the early days up until the 1990s, the Queen's relationship with the leaders was more personal. Her core business at every summit was an audience with every single head of government, however small the nation or disagreeable its representative. Her schedule for the 1981 CHOGM in Melbourne shows back-to-back audiences on board the Royal Yacht, starting on a Monday morning and continuing until Friday afternoon, plus a banquet for the leaders, a reception for ministers and another reception for senior officials in between. Sonny Ramphal remembers the routine very well: 'No matter what was being debated, when the allotted time came you would see a head of government slip away from the meeting because his or her twenty minutes were due. That, for many heads, was a priceless moment, an intimate moment, a moment when they discovered how much the Queen knew about their countries, about their problems. That stunned them.' 'You feel you're not being judged by her,' says the former Foreign Office minister, Baroness Amos. 'For many prime ministers and presidents, to have someone you can confide in is very important.'

Sir Robert Woodard, the former captain of the Royal Yacht, was astonished by the raucous informality at a Commonwealth dinner that the Queen held on board *Britannia* during the 1993 Heads of Government Meeting in Cyprus. 'The banquet was hysterical because a lot of the older leaders were old friends of the Queen,' he recalls. 'They were actually heckling her when she got up to speak. One of them joked: "I hope this isn't going to be long!" It was that sort of thing. And she'd wave her hands at them and say: "Now be quiet! I want to be serious just for a minute". There were roars of laughter and this wonderful atmosphere. Many of them were at each other's throats the rest of the time. Some of them were at war. But on the evening, it was just one big family.'

Over time, there has been a marked shift in the Queen's role at these summits. When the Commonwealth gathered in Edinburgh in 1997, the Secretary-General at that time, Chief Emeka Anyaoku, and his team felt that it was time she participated inside the summit, even if some of the more republican-minded leaders might not approve. For the first time she would attend the opening and make a speech. 'She'd previously been "offshore" as it were,' recalls Stuart Mole, Anyaoku's chief of staff. 'She'd have her audiences. And she'd have her parties and a banquet but she wouldn't actually be in the meeting. Even though a lot of people thought she was in the meeting, she wasn't!' This was the Nineties, the low point of the Queen's reign – that period of marriage breakdowns, media assaults on the state of the royal finances, the Windsor Castle fire and eventual tragedy. The Edinburgh summit came just weeks after the death of Diana, Princess of Wales. Anyaoku, a Nigerian chieftain and staunch royalist, understood the importance of symbolism in an organisation spread across so many faiths and backgrounds on every continent. He wanted to formalise the monarch's role even more. It had been his idea to create what are sometimes called the Commonwealth's 'crown jewels'. To mark the Queen's fortieth anniversary as Head in 1992, he had commissioned a gold mace to symbolise her authority at formal Commonwealth occasions, just like those in her parliaments. And there would be a set of silver-gilt goblets, each inscribed with the name of a member state, for use at Commonwealth banquets.

Anyaoku's plan would formalise what had previously been a more personal, less structured role for the Queen. There was no opposition. The Edinburgh summit also occurred just before the golden wedding anniversary of the Queen and the Duke of Edinburgh. Anyaoku organised a present from the Commonwealth, and suggested a contribution of £1,500 from the larger nations and £1,000 from the smaller. He was delighted when every nation insisted on the higher amount anyway. A large decorative panel, featuring the Commonwealth emblem, was commissioned for the Windsor Castle restoration, plus paintings of a peacock and a golden oriole for the couple's private collection of bird pictures.

After Edinburgh came a gradual increase in the royal presence. The Prince of Wales and the Duchess of Cornwall attended the fringes of the 2007 summit in Uganda. Come the 2015 Malta summit, they were on the stage with the Queen and the Duke of Edinburgh. This was not just about gently elevating the profile of the Prince of Wales within the organisation, but about boosting the profile of the organisation itself, with an enhanced role for the star of the show. One of the Commonwealth's inbuilt advantages is a lack of rules. Like Britain's unwritten constitution, it continuously evolves by consensus rather than by codified regulation. So as more and more international groupings and summits compete for space in the diaries of world leaders, the CHOGM format has adapted.

It is an irony that the founders of the modern Commonwealth were so keen to minimise the role of King George VI and his family, whereas today's leaders have no qualms at all about royal interference. Rather, it is one of the factors that helps attract the attention of both world leaders and the media. Remove the royal presence and many politicians and the press might find that they had other engagements when the next CHOGM came around. Today's Commonwealth is not the global powerhouse of yesteryear; it is a good place for networking, but not the great geopolitical circus it once was. Beef up the royal presence, on the other hand, and at least the calibre of the delegations will rise accordingly.

A 'BLOODY USEFUL NETWORK'

Commentators and critics routinely question 'the point of the Commonwealth'. They contrast its campaigns on behalf of women in the developing world with the fact that most of its fifty-three member states still criminalise homosexuality. Its supporters point out that, in an imperfect world, it is in the vanguard of reform. Kamalesh Sharma, Secretary-General for eight years, is proud that of the fifty-two nations in Africa, it is those that are members of the Commonwealth that show the highest standards in terms of democracy and the rule of law. He points to two globally respected monitors of good governance, the Mo Ibrahim Index and the Berlin-based Transparency International. 'Those guys don't take any nonsense,' he says. 'And every year seven or eight of the top ten will be Commonwealth members. What are the odds on that result, year after year, out of fifty-two nations? I always say to the heads of government: "This is what sets you apart".' Sharma argues that it was the Commonwealth that was the first intergovernmental group to introduce its own system of policing, penalties and punishments.

It may not have been enough to prevent corrupt dictators, like Zimbabwe's Robert Mugabe, from persecuting their opponents and robbing their people. No one likes to be suspended or thrown out of a club, though. Over the years, countries like Pakistan and Fiji may have been excluded from the fold for bad behaviour for a few years, but they have always been extremely keen to get back in again. Zimbabwe, the Maldives and Gambia all resigned as members, before they could be expelled for human-rights abuses. Gambia returned in 2018 after a change of regime and was formally welcomed back with a ceremony at Marlborough House. Its Ambassador formally became a High Commissioner once again and, a few days later, was delighted to find himself at Commonwealth Day drinks with the Prince of Wales and the Duke of Cambridge. Gambia's flag was brought out of the Marlborough House cupboard, where it had been stored for five years, and resumed its place alongside the flags of all the other Commonwealth nations that fly above the Mall. The same cupboard still contains the flags of Zimbabwe and the Maldives, both carefully wrapped up, waiting for the day when they fly once more. Like a family – and the

Queen insists that this *is* a family – you can have rows and feuds and door-slamming walkouts. Yet you never really leave.

It is why David Cameron has mixed views on the Commonwealth. 'It creates a normality of behaviour, expectations, rules. You just wish it did less shilly-shallying. It is a bit disappointing because it is by consensus and too wobbly. It is never as tough as you want it to be,' says the former Prime Minister. 'It's a great network. You get to know a bunch of people who you might never get to meet. You learn a lot about issues, spend quality time with important leaders from India and Pakistan and so on. But do you actually get things done as a Commonwealth? Only a bit.'

Sir Simon Fraser, head of the Diplomatic Service during the Cameron years, offers a frank assessment from the British diplomatic perspective: 'The Commonwealth is not an efficient diplomatic instrument because it is a very diverse group of countries. It is misplaced to think it is going to become a terribly important instrument of our foreign policy. But having said that, it's a hugely useful asset in this area of soft power linked to the monarchy and international relations in the broader sense ... I'm not a traditionalist by nature but if you've got valid traditions, you should maintain them.' Harvard's Professor Joseph Nye, creator of the concept of 'soft power', concurs: 'It's a mistake to think of the Commonwealth as an effective executive institution. It's not,' he says. 'But as a place where people can pull together, and where Britain is at the centre of a network, it's a very important aspect of British soft power.'

It is a long-standing Foreign Office complaint that Britain is in an impossible position within the Commonwealth anyway. If it pursues a policy with vigour, it is accused of rewinding the imperial clock and waving a big stick. If it stands back, it is accused of indifference. It was often said, during the Blair years, that the only reason Tony Blair attended any Commonwealth events was that he would be accused of snubbing the Queen if he did not. The considered view of many other nations, however, is that Britain is not nearly engaged enough. 'It is very very important for the UK to have that locomotive function,' says Kamalesh Sharma. 'There must be a sense of belief that we have a special organisation.'

For all its faults, though, there are two aspects of the Commonwealth that confound its critics. Once in the club, countries never want to leave. And there have been some pretty unusual applications for membership. Former Foreign Secretary Jack Straw says that he was always struck by the fact that all these outposts of the old empire were so attached to the ex-colonial club. 'There is this argument that the empire was wrong but no one would have signed up to the Commonwealth if the empire was as terrible as it is now being written up,' he comments. 'In fact, you now have additional countries trying to join.'

He recalls that in 2004, during a visit to Algeria, the President asked if his country might join. 'I thought "What?" So, I asked the interpreter and he said: "Yes, he wants to join the Commonwealth".' Since 1995 even countries that were not part of the former British Empire have been eligible to join, if they have a close connection to those that were, and are willing to convert to speaking English. Mozambique (formerly under Portuguese rule) and Rwanda (once a Belgian colony) are both enthusiastic recent recruits, the latter having been accepted as host for the 2020 summit.

A more recent application has been that of Togo, formerly part of imperial France. The former Secretary-General, Chief Emeka Anyaoku, says that he once received an application from the Palestinian leader, Yasser Arafat, during the mid-Nineties.

Lord Howell, the President of the Royal Commonwealth Society, even recalls an approach from Japan during his days in government. 'This minister said: "We would like to cooperate with you in India and we'd like to join the Commonwealth." I said it was not quite like that, that they had their Emperor and we have the Queen and so on. Then he said: "Joint venture? Joint venture?"' Lord Howell is in favour of some sort of associate membership that would give the wider world access to some of the Commonwealth's non-political activities – particularly in areas like education and business. Countries like Japan, he says, are 'mystified' that so many ex-colonies want to remain linked to the former imperial power, via the Queen. 'It is a huge compliment to the UK in historical terms,' says Sir Malcolm Rifkind. 'There is no nostalgia for empire whatsoever in those countries and a lot of criticism. Yet, there is also this feeling that this period of their history was not 100 per cent negative. We're talking about civil service, the rule of law, the English language and so on.'

Having spent most of its existence talking about human rights, the Commonwealth is now looking at new ways to harness its own commercial potential. In 2017, the Commonwealth Enterprise and Investment Council – a business-led organisation that tries to keep its distance from politicians and bureaucrats – organised its first trade summit. More than thirty trade ministers from around the world came to Lancaster House in London. They heard the Council's chairman, Lord Marland, outlining the prospects for intra-Commonwealth trade (predicted to exceed a trillion pounds in 2020) and the mathematics of the so-called 'Commonwealth advantage'. This asserts that a business deal conducted between two Commonwealth nations costs 19 per cent less than the equivalent deal between non-Commonwealth nations, thanks to a shared language, legal system and established business practice. A year later, the Council held its own business forum alongside the 2018 Commonwealth summit, attended by the Prince of Wales, Bill Gates and 800 businessmen, including non-Commonwealth delegations from China and Saudi Arabia. The event was so oversubscribed that it could have sold three times the available space.

In Britain, talk of Commonwealth trade would inevitably become embroiled in the debate about Brexit. Those in favour of leaving the European Union would point to the business potential in re-engaging with old Commonwealth allies following Britain's release from EU trade rules. Those opposed to Brexit would point out that Britain's trade with the Commonwealth is tiny compared to that with the EU – just 9 per cent of UK exports, compared to 44 per cent for the EU – and that it is deluded imperialist lunacy to suggest that the old empire will solve Britain's problems.

Even the most passionate Commonwealth fans have never claimed that, however. 'I try to damp that down. I don't see the Commonwealth as an alternative,' says Lord Howell. 'But it is dawning on people that the Indian Ocean is as important as the Atlantic; that this is a post-West era; that we have to network like hell in Asia, and the Commonwealth is a bloody useful network.' Both Britain's allies and rivals wonder why the UK does not make more of its Commonwealth connections. Lord Butler recalls a conversation between Margaret Thatcher and Ronald Reagan on the subject. 'President Reagan said: "You're very fortunate in having the Commonwealth because you meet, at one meeting, leaders of fifty-odd countries of the world that an American president doesn't have a chance to meet in the whole of their term of office".'

Britain's relationship with the Commonwealth, however, is very different from that which France enjoys with towards its own ex-imperial association. The Paris-based Francophonie has a very simple priority: the promotion of all things French. Chief Emeka Anyaoku says that the two organisations reflect two very different colonial philosophies. 'The French believed in assimilation so the Francophonie thrives on French culture. The British believed in letting you remain what you were. So the Commonwealth emphasises diversity.'

Kamalesh Sharma says that the two organisations get on well and frequently collaborate when dealing with global entities like the G20. 'The head of the Francophonie once said to me: "We only came in to existence because of you!"' Formed in 1970, the Francophonie maintains a more relaxed admissions policy and different tiers of membership. Countries need only the flimsiest French connection – if any – to join. Full members include Greece and Macedonia, while 'observer' members include Uruguay, Mexico and Ukraine, none of them known for speaking French. Since France is content to pay nearly all the bills, no one seems too bothered if the French President takes charge.

'The French President has the upper hand,' says Marc Roche, veteran London correspondent of *Le Monde* and French-language biographer of the Queen. 'Some of the members have been pretty stinky.' He cites Omar Bongo, ruler of Gabon for forty-two years, and Mobutu Sese Seko (of dog-smuggling repute), who plundered £10 billion during his thirty-two years in charge of Zaire. 'It can be a nasty business. You don't have that in the Commonwealth.'

The Head of the Commonwealth is also a *de facto* member of the Francophonie, since she is the Queen of Canada. With more than seven million French-speaking citizens, Canada is an active member of both organisations. Roche recalls comparing the rival organisations with the Queen at the Harare Commonwealth summit in 1991. 'I said to her: "We have the Francophonie which is the equivalent". And she said: "Yes, it's the same. But it's very different, you know." Those were her exact words. You can read what you like into that!'

As far as the Queen is concerned, however, the Commonwealth is about a great deal more than gatherings of argumentative politicians. Nor has she come to expect a great deal from a secretariat that, despite its palatial premises at Marlborough House, has a global budget of less than £50 million. That is less than one-fifth of the annual budget of a single London borough. 'We once worked out that we cost less than the canteen facilities at the United Nations,' says one Commonwealth staffer. Since a change of leadership in 2015 and the appointment of Baroness Scotland, the first woman, as Secretary-General, there have been a series of awkward leaks about internal finances and no sense of a grand new strategic vision. Fresh initiatives on cleaner oceans and the plight of small island states have made some headway, but the organisation is unlikely to regain anything like the clout it enjoyed during the war against apartheid.

However, the formal endorsement of the Prince of Wales as the Queen's successor provides a sense of long-term continuity at a leadership level. At the political level, there is a sense of stability. The return of a post-Mugabe Zimbabwe to the fold would add to the sense of a Commonwealth that, in the words of one British diplomat, has 'got its mojo back'.

As Jacinda Ardern, Prime Minister of New Zealand puts it: 'In today's environment, with this fractured approach to issues and this individualism within countries, to know that there is actually an organisation with common values and common goals feels more important now than it ever has.'

Few could recall a CHOGM as contented and even-tempered as the 2018 summit in London and Windsor. The host, Prime Minister Theresa May, puts a lot of that down to the Queen herself. She recalls the surprise on the faces of many leaders when the Queen suddenly walked in to a reception during the retreat element of the summit. 'People hadn't known that was going to happen,' she says. 'Seeing the Commonwealth leaders all queuing up to speak to Her Majesty really showed the family nature of it.'

One former Marlborough House veteran reiterates the allure of the Queen. 'At the end of the day, some of them might be a bit sniffy about Britain and the monarchy,' he says, 'but they all love a bit of royal jelly on their toast.'

FRIENDS AND FRIENDLY GAMES

The success of the 2018 Commonwealth Heads of Government Meeting underlined a resurgence in the other side of the organisation, the daily people-to-people operations that carry on in spite of (rather than because of) the politicians and bureaucrats. It is this work that the Queen and her family are particularly keen to support.

Since her Diamond Jubilee in 2012, she has been launching or promoting one very substantial Commonwealth initiative after another. All have followed that familiar pattern: they all involve young and dynamic individuals rather than governments.

On a miserable winter evening, Buckingham Palace is filling up again. The Duchess of Cambridge and the Countess of Wessex are the co-hosts of the Commonwealth Fashion Exchange, uniting designers and tiny artisan producers from all over the Commonwealth. All through the state apartments, famous fashion-industry figures study the results over champagne and canapés. One mannequin is draped in a joint creation between London-based Stella McCartney and a silk cooperative from southern India. New Zealand's Karen Walker has teamed up with a group of craftswomen in the Cook Islands. Among the up-and-coming designers is Euphemia Sydney-Davies, thirty-one, a true child of the Commonwealth. Having fled a Sierra Leone war zone at the age of five with her mother, she moved to Gambia, then Kenya and finally to Britain. Having teamed up with a weaver of high quality *kente* cloth from Ghana, Euphemia is standing in Buckingham Palace, discussing the finer points of her creation with, among others, the Duchess, the Countess and Anna Wintour, editor-in-chief of *Vogue*. No words, she says afterwards, can do justice to the occasion. It has been, quite simply, the most exciting night of her life. The following day, a few weeks short of her 92nd birthday, the Head of the Commonwealth herself will continue this theme by attending her first catwalk show at London Fashion Week. No model, no designer and no outfit will attract as much attention as the Queen.

Despite its meagre budget and its constant struggle for attention on a crowded world stage, the Commonwealth still has the ability to touch people in a way that other organisations cannot. For, aside from the Queen, it is best-known for two things: sport and sacrifice. 'Mention the Commonwealth to most people and they immediately think of the

Games,' says Sir John Key, former Prime Minister of New Zealand. The Commonwealth Games have become the second-largest multi-sport tournament in the world after the Olympics. The event has long been the most popular and high-profile manifestation of Commonwealth bonhomie. Falling exactly midway between summer Olympiads, and featuring some of the greatest athletes and keenest sporting nations in the world, it attracts a global television audience. World records are broken. Olympic champions strive for gold.

Yet there is a certain charm that the Olympics cannot replicate. This is an event in which nations and territories as small as the Isle of Man and Anguilla can compete against a sporting powerhouse like Australia. At one end of the sporting spectrum, the Games include world and Olympic champions; at the other, they give an international platform to tiny teams from tiny places – like, say, the middle-aged members of the Cook Islands lawn bowls team. 'The Commonwealth Games has a spirit and a friendliness which, if we're being honest, the Olympics doesn't have,' says Lord Coe. Praise indeed from the Olympian who ran the 2012 London Olympics. 'The athletes recognise the competition is important, but you are not entirely defined by standing on that rostrum.' Though they attract a global audience, the Commonwealth Games have never enjoyed anything like the same financial or media clout as the Olympics. The entire budget for the 2014 Glasgow Games was just 4 per cent of the cost of the 2012 London Olympics. Those arriving at the athletes' village in Glasgow might have found themselves in the breakfast queue with Olympic legends like Jamaica's Usain Bolt. Or they might have met Norfolk Island's badminton team. In 2014, there were only six competitive badminton players on the South Pacific island, and five of them competed at the Commonwealth Games. Back home, the only place they could train or compete was a single community hall, and even then they were required to remove their floor markings each time the hall was booked for a dance or wedding. Asked what they were most looking forward to at the Commonwealth Games, they had a charming reply: 'Opponents'.

Unlike the ultra-professional world of the modern Olympian, these are games that can still throw up the occasional fairytale. Marcus Stephen was a teenager on the tiny Pacific island of Nauru, the smallest independent nation in the Commonwealth, when he registered for the 1990 games with just three days to spare. When he won gold in the weightlifting, Nauru exploded with joy and a national holiday was declared. Stephen would go on to win multiple Commonwealth medals and a world championship silver medal and would compete at three Olympics. In 2003, he was elected to parliament and rose to be President of his country.

Even he could not quite match the sporting journey of a Commonwealth Games legend who would become one of the Queen's favourite athletes. As Britain's former sports minister, Denis Howell, put it: 'The story of Precious McKenzie is one of the most incredible in the history of sport.' Born in a 'coloured' ward in pre-war South Africa, McKenzie was a sickly infant who nearly died from a botched childhood operation. He never met his father, who was killed by a crocodile soon after his birth. His mother was a chronic alcoholic; and he would never grow taller than 4 feet 10 inches. At one stage, a sadistic foster mother claimed that he and his sister were possessed by devils and took them to a witch doctor, who scarred them for life with cuts all over their bodies. McKenzie excelled as a gymnast at a mission school, but his hopes of becoming a circus acrobat were thwarted by South Africa's apartheid laws. He turned to weightlifting and even set a new national record, but was barred from the South African Olympic squad because of the colour of his skin. Britain gave him citizenship in time for the 1966 Commonwealth Games in Jamaica, where he won the first of four Commonwealth gold medals (and danced a calypso with a teenage Princess Anne). Though Olympic success would elude him, he had a legion of fans, among them Prince Andrew and Prince Edward, and in 1975 the Queen invited him to Buckingham Palace. After winning gold yet again at the 1978 Edmonton Games, he was intercepted by a policeman, who steered him to a waiting squad car. The Queen was in the midst of a garden party nearby and wanted to know why McKenzie was not there. 'We got there just in time,' he told sports writer Brian Oliver. 'I was taken straight to the Queen and she said "Where have you been?" I said I hadn't been invited, and she said, "Well, you are now." I asked her if I could have a photo taken with her and she said "Of course". Later on I sent the photo to Buckingham Palace and asked if the Queen would autograph it for me, and she did. It is one of my proudest possessions.' McKenzie would retire to New Zealand, where he still has many fans, among them the former Prime Minister, Sir John Key.

Holding an Olympiad, says Key, is a 'pipe dream' for most of the world. However, staging 'the friendly games', is entirely possible for a medium-sized nation like his own. Key is proud that his wife, Bronagh, took part in the opening ceremony for the 1974 Christchurch games as a schoolgirl. The opening routine is similar to that of the Olympics, with a Commonwealth baton much like the Olympic torch. Unlike the torch, which is lit from the rays of the sun in Olympia, Greece and then carried afar by athletes (a 'tradition' invented for Hitler's 1936 Berlin Games), the baton contains a message from the Queen.

The first 'Empire Sports Meeting' took place in London in 1911, following the Coronation of George V, but it was in 1930 that the modern event took shape in Hamilton, Canada. From the start, the intention was that the Games should be 'merrier and less stern' than the Olympics. Indeed they were. When a sprinter from New Zealand was twice disqualified for a false start, the roar of the crowds persuaded the judges to allow him a third attempt. Great sporting moments – like Roger Bannister and John Landy both running a sub-four-minute mile at Vancouver in 1954 – were not without elements of farce. At the 1950 Auckland Games, the marathon winner was attacked by a dog three miles from the finish. By 1954 the event had become the British Empire and Commonwealth Games; and, after the 1966 Games, the word 'Empire' was dropped altogether. The 'British' would finally go, ahead of the first 'Commonwealth Games' in 1978 in Edmonton, to which the Queen and the Duke of Edinburgh brought Prince Andrew and Prince Edward.

With no language barrier, the closing ceremony would often descend into a sing-song. In Perth, the 1962 Games concluded with 700 athletes surrounding the Duke of Edinburgh's car, singing 'Waltzing Matilda'. The entire stadium serenaded the Queen with 'Auld Lang Syne' at the 1982 Games in Brisbane. Coming shortly after the Falklands War, it was a particularly emotional moment. Long before South Africa became a sporting pariah during the apartheid era, the Commonwealth was taking a stand against the country's racial policies on the field of play. Having been chosen to host the 1934 Games, South Africa had the honour taken away in

1932 because of its treatment of black athletes. The Commonwealth Games have a sense of humour, too. The opening ceremony for the 2014 Glasgow Games, held in front of the Queen at Celtic Park, had plenty of big-name entertainment, including Rod Stewart and the Pipes and Drums of the Scottish Regiments. It also lampooned the grandiose nature of Olympic opening ceremonies with a giant haggis, dancing Tunnock's teacakes and a team of Scottish terriers to lead in each national team. Four years later, the Prince of Wales would open the 2018 Gold Coast games in Queensland, Australia, in a ceremony featuring a Kombi van, a surf scene, an Aboriginal 'smoking' ceremony and a flying white whale.

THE FALLEN

Perhaps the ultimate symbol of the ties that bind the Commonwealth are those still, silent and impeccably maintained patches of sacred ground scattered all over the world under the banner of the Commonwealth War Graves Commission. It is often said that Australia was forged as a country on the beaches of Gallipoli in 1915. In the same way, Canada points to a staggering feat of arms in April 1917 as its coming-of-age as a modern nation. It was at Vimy Ridge, following two years of failed British and French attempts, that the four meticulously trained divisions of the Canadian Corps stormed a pivotal escarpment near Arras in northern France. They not only held it, but redrew the map of the Western Front, at the cost of 3,500 Canadian lives. In April 2017, the Prince of Wales and his sons joined the Canadian Prime Minister, Justin Trudeau, at Vimy Ridge to salute them all. 'This was, and remains, the single bloodiest day in Canadian military history. Yet Canadians displayed a strength of character and commitment to one another that is still evident today,' Prince Charles told a crowd of 25,000 Canadians. 'They did not waver. This was Canada at its best.' The Prime Minister echoed the sentiment. '*Canada est né ici*,' Trudeau declared. Canada was, indeed, born here.

Towering over them was the 6,000-ton double-pillared limestone memorial to the dead, unveiled in 1936 by King Edward VIII, shortly before the Second World War would see the Empire rallying to the Crown once again. Nearby, the final resting places of the dead are immaculately maintained in perpetuity by the Commonwealth War

Graves Commission. For many people, this organisation represents the very best of Commonwealth values. At the height of the Great War, Fabian Ware, a former schoolmaster-turned-journalist who had been rejected by the Army for being too old, was running an ambulance unit for the British Red Cross in northern France. He was deeply troubled by the lack of organisation when it came to burying the dead, and began lobbying the authorities. The result was the Imperial War Graves Commission (it switched to 'Commonwealth' in 1960). From the outset, it embraced several key, forward-thinking principles: the dead would be buried without regard to rank or faith; all would have a headstone of equal size; and all those with no known grave would be assured of a permanent memorial somewhere. Long before the formal creation of the modern Commonwealth or its Secretariat, this was the first Commonwealth institution in which all member nations enjoyed equal status. As its royal charter made clear, the Commission's role was not just to bury the dead. It was 'to strengthen the bonds of union between all classes and races in Our Dominions'.

Tone was all. The finest architects and gardeners of the day – including Sir Edwin Lutyens and Gertrude Jekyll – were charged with creating these sacred spaces, while the empire's pre-eminent man of letters, Rudyard Kipling, himself a bereaved father, established the language of commemoration: 'Known unto God'; 'Their name liveth for evermore', and so on. To this day, the care and attention that the Commission devotes to the graves and memorials commemorating 1.7 million men and women from all over the old Empire at 23,000 locations in more than 150 countries is unfailingly moving. The grass will always be mown before it gets too long. Every row of graves will contain pretty but sturdy plants chosen to minimise the splashback of rain against the headstones. Many of these places are still so full of unexploded ordnance that the Commission staff have to tread carefully. At Vimy, for example, some sections of the memorial area are still deemed too dangerous for the Commission's lawnmowers. Standards still have to be maintained, however. So they employ sheep.

Wherever members of the Royal Family travel in the world, a call on a Commonwealth cemetery will always be a priority. 'It's hugely impressive and very challenging,' says the Princess Royal, who has visited cemeteries in places as remote as Somalia and Madagascar. 'Often, you have no idea that British forces have been in those areas. A grave might be very isolated but it is never forgotten.' The Princess's husband, Vice Admiral Sir Timothy Laurence, is the Commission's vice-chairman and has helped to establish a foundation to encourage young people to become guides and volunteers at particularly important sites. When the Commission created a commemorative garden at the 2017 Chelsea Flower Show, to mark its centenary, most of the Royal Family turned up in support.

A commemoration of every notable British wartime anniversary inevitably becomes a Commonwealth affair, be it the Battle of Britain or the Allied invasion of Normandy. Stand at the very centre of London, on Hyde Park Corner, and there are substantial monuments to Commonwealth sacrifice in every direction: the Australian War Memorial; the New Zealand Memorial; the Commonwealth Memorial Gates honouring the fallen from across the Indian subcontinent, Africa and the Caribbean (with the inscription 'Our Future Is Greater Than Our Past'). Here, too, is the mighty memorial to those who had one of the most dangerous jobs of the Second World War. Of those who volunteered for Bomber Command, nearly half – more than 55,000 – would not survive. Their life expectancy was significantly lower than that of a First World War infantryman at the Somme. The shock was felt across the Commonwealth. Ten thousand aircrew from Canada alone were killed – nearly 60 per cent of Bomber Command's Canadian intake. Nonagenarian veterans from as far afield as Australia were present at the 2018 opening of the magnificent new International Bomber Command Centre in Lincoln.

Come Remembrance Sunday, the Queen invites all the High Commissioners of all the Commonwealth nations to lay a wreath at the Cenotaph. Across her realms, there is still one decoration that transcends all the rest – the Victoria Cross. Although countries like Australia, Canada and New Zealand would develop their own honours systems over time, all still retain the VC as the ultimate recognition of valour. No fewer than four VCs, for example, were awarded to Canadian soldiers for valour at Vimy Ridge. Only one of them lived to receive it in person. Today, all living recipients of the Victoria Cross and the George Cross (awarded for the highest gallantry away from the battlefield) come to London every two years – at no cost to themselves – for a series of reunion events and a party given by the Queen or the Prince of Wales.

It is the monarchy that acts as the bridge between all these different strands of the Commonwealth story, between past and present, between both military and civilian sacrifice. In the summer of 2017, the Queen and the Duke visited the East End of London to mark the centenary of a defining moment of the Great War. On 13th June 1917, a fleet of German Gotha bombers attacked London in the heaviest daylight raid of the war. One bomb landed on North Street primary school in Poplar, plunging through two floors before exploding in the infant class below, killing eighteen children aged between four and six and injuring many more. Many of the survivors, old and young, never recovered. Having found the body of his own five-year-old son in the wreckage, the school caretaker took his own life some months later. The battlefield had suddenly moved from the Western Front to home and hearth. Enormous crowds from across London turned out to honour the victims of an attack which caused such revulsion that it is said to have altered the course of royal history. The following month, the Royal Family changed their name from Saxe-Coburg-Gotha to the House of Windsor. The fact that they had shared their name with the bomber made it no longer tenable.

A century on, a diligent team of local historians managed to track down relatives of all but one of those killed at the school for a memorial service. Even a hundred years later, the events of that day reduced several of them to tears as they joined the Queen and the Duke of Edinburgh at All Saints Church, Poplar. 'There is something about the killing of young children that is profoundly disturbing: all that innocence, all those unwritten stories and all that unfulfilled potential,' said the Right Reverend Adrian Newman, Bishop of Stepney, before the names of the dead were read out.

But the day was not just about commemorating a tragic footnote to a war that killed millions. The Queen had also come to visit the replacement primary school built nearby after the war was over. Now called Mayflower Primary School, it serves one of the most multicultural areas in Britain. As a result, up to 96 per cent of Mayflower pupils do not speak English as their first language. Yet most have a Commonwealth connection thanks to a substantial local Bangladeshi community. Greeted with near-hysterical applause, the Queen and the Duke toured the school and learned that the centenary had helped to bring the whole community together. Projects based on the events of 1917 had actually helped to create a fresh sense of shared heritage among children of all backgrounds. Rather than presenting the First World War as a remote, whites-only conflict from another age, here was a connection. The Queen was even shown a spying game in which the children had to crack a code in order to bring a British special agent home from Berlin.

Escorting her was her local representative, the Lord-Lieutenant of Greater London, Sir Kenneth Olisa. An eminent businessman and banker, whose father was from Nigeria and whose mother was from Nottingham, Sir Kenneth sees it as his role to keep the monarchy in tune with every community and culture in the capital. 'An individual's identity is not about history. It's about heritage,' he said afterwards. 'The Commonwealth is a big family full of heritage and the job Her Majesty has done in keeping that family together is something of which we should all be very proud.'

TIP OF THE ICEBERG

All through her reign, it is her Christmas broadcast to the Commonwealth that has been perhaps the most familiar and popular aspect of that job. She is now so proficient that the production teams refer to her as 'one-take Windsor'. Back in 1952, delivering her first Christmas message by radio, she was still using imperial terminology. 'We belong, all of us, to the British Commonwealth and Empire, that immense union of nations, with their homes set in all the four corners of the Earth,' she said from her desk at Sandringham. By the time of her first televised broadcast five years later, the language had switched from imperial to fraternal. 'This year, Ghana and Malaya joined our brotherhood. Both these countries are now entirely self-governing. Both achieved their new status amicably and peacefully,' she said. Distancing herself from monarchs of old, she echoed her twenty-first birthday pledge from ten years before: 'I cannot lead you into battle, I do not give you laws or administer justice but I can do something else, I can give you my heart and my devotion to these old islands and to all the peoples of our brotherhood of nations.'

Sixty years further on, the Queen now talks of the Commonwealth simply as 'family'. In 2017, she dwelt on the theme of family as she reflected on the dark moments of that year – including terror attacks in Britain and hurricanes in the Caribbean. The tone became lighter, almost jaunty, as she looked forward to a new royal baby, a royal wedding and another family gathering, the 2018 CHOGM. Her wide-eyed, almost evangelical regard for the Commonwealth as a young woman has long since mellowed. In the early years of her reign the Queen had called it 'one of the most hopeful and imaginative experiments in international affairs that the world has ever seen'. Proclaiming the need to 'advance concord and understanding' among its members, she solemnly stated: 'No purpose comes nearer to my own desires.'

By 2017 she had lowered the volume considerably, describing the Commonwealth merely as 'vibrant'. It was also 'an inspiring way of bringing people together'. The Queen is a realist. The 'new conception, built on the highest qualities of the spirit of man', which she was describing in 1953, has become a more modest entity with more modest aspirations.

Just as the Prince of Wales has built his Prince's Trust and the Duke of Edinburgh has created his Duke of Edinburgh's Award, so this is the Queen's equivalent. Both those organisations have undergone sensible restructuring in recent years, so that they can look to a prosperous future with someone else at the helm. It is why the Queen was so keen to resolve the question of her own successor as Head of the Commonwealth when the leaders gathered in London in 2018 – and to appoint Prince Harry as Commonwealth Youth Ambassador. So much for the claims of Nehru and the other founders of the modern Commonwealth that the monarch would have no powers whatsoever. In his first speech as Youth Ambassador, at the summit's youth forum, Prince Harry repeated his grandmother's twenty-first birthday pledge and then announced 150 new Commonwealth Scholarships for low-and middle-income countries. They would, he explained, be called The Queen Elizabeth Commonwealth Scholarships, in her honour. Along with all the Queen's trusts, her Young Leaders, her Commonwealth Canopy and the rest, these are yet another example of the way in which she believes the Commonwealth does its best work – at the human level. A month later, as she watched Prince Harry and

Meghan Markle step out into the world as the Duke and Duchess of Sussex, there was one more accolade for the Queen. The Duchess had chosen to have the emblems of every Commonwealth nation sewn into her veil, a reprise of the Queen's own decision to do the same with her Coronation gown.

In the aftermath of the wedding and the 2018 CHOGM, the Queen could reflect that the royal/Commonwealth connection had seldom been stronger. 'The Commonwealth was one of the greatest acts of collective statesmanship of the last century,' says former Secretary-General Kamalesh Sharma. 'But it is a bit of a nonsense, frankly, without the King or Queen as the nominal head. It would unravel very speedily if it was just another grouping buffeting around the world.' Former Foreign Secretary David Owen has one word of caution for the Prince of Wales: 'He must act very slowly and deliberately. That word, "Head" of the Commonwealth, should be used as sparingly as possible.'

It remains the case that no one has such a comprehensive personal knowledge of the Commonwealth and its leaders as the Queen or her eldest son. At her Silver Jubilee, she cracked a rare Commonwealth joke. 'It is easy enough to define what the Commonwealth is not,' she said. 'Indeed, this is quite a popular pastime.' She went on to give her own definition of what it actually was. She compared it to an iceberg, with the politicians and summits operating above the surface and most of the activity going on, out of sight, below.

She was too modest to position herself on this iceberg, of course, but then she didn't need to. Without her at the top of it, the whole thing would long since have disappeared beneath the waterline.

Chapter 5

THE REALMS

'My peoples'

THE DIVISIBLE CROWN

The young trainees are lined up at the Garden Door of Buckingham Palace in their uniforms. Some are in their chefs' whites, some in housekeeping dresses. Three are in the scarlet-and-black livery of royal footmen. All are a little nervous. It looks like a very grand version of television's job-hunting show, *The Apprentice*, and they are about to meet the boss. Except that these nine enterprising young people are all accomplished in their chosen professions already. Nor is there a contest. The fact that they are here at all means they have already won. The boss in question could not be less like Lord Sugar, Donald Trump or any other TV pantomime boss-from-hell. She is the Queen. And she is on her way.

The monarch wants to meet the winners of her first Royal Household Hospitality Scholarships. It's a new scheme to provide on-the-job training in the hospitality industry at one of the world's best-known hospitality venues – Buckingham Palace. Over six weeks they will be involved in every aspect of Royal Household life, above and below stairs. Some will learn about looking after Old Master paintings or running a vacuum cleaner over 200-year-old rugs or how to lay a table for a royal lunch. Some will be involved in preparing food for the Royal Family. Others will serve it, when not pouring the drinks.

Once they have learned the ropes at the Palace, they will do the same at Windsor Castle during one of the busiest periods of the year – Royal Ascot week. This, though, is not a royal recruitment exercise. At the end of six weeks of intensive training, all of these star pupils will then return home with a certificate and a new entry on their curriculum vitae, which will stand them in good stead for life. And they all have one thing in common. They are all drawn from the Queen's Caribbean realms. In other words, she is their Queen, too.

It's one more human thread in the latticework of connections between the Queen and all those parts of the world that have long since ceased to be British territory, but have retained her as their head of state.

Today, there are sixteen independent nations that have the Queen as their head of state. Once they would have been called 'dominions' or 'kingdoms', but are now known as 'realms'. The Queen sometimes refers to them collectively as 'the monarchies'. They are – in theory, at least – all equal in her eyes. Just like cricket, she is post-imperial adhesive-cum-balm. Whatever the current tensions between her British government and any of her other governments on any given issue, the Queen has to defuse, evade or rise above them. Sometimes, it can be difficult. In 2018, a fresh political scandal would expose British ministers to legitimate attacks from their Caribbean counterparts, bring down a British Cabinet minister, threaten the Prime Minister and overshadow Theresa May's first – and possibly last – international summit on British soil. The 'Windrush scandal' – named after the ship that brought the first Caribbean migrants to Britain in 1948 – united both the left and right of British politics. It revealed that thousands of Commonwealth citizens who had been working and raising families in Britain for decades had suddenly been threatened with deportation, due to the cack-handed implementation of a new immigration strategy. Many had lost their jobs. Others had been denied healthcare, for which they had paid taxes all their lives. And the first response of the British government had been to ignore all this. Finally, when the issue threatened to dominate the 2018 Commonwealth summit at Buckingham Palace, ministers began to engage seriously. It would conclude with the resignation of Home

Secretary Amber Rudd. If it was a painful business for those on either side of the debate, it was particularly awkward for the one person inescapably caught in the middle: the Queen. The 'divisible' Crown* had not been this divided for a long time.

To many outsiders, it might seem incomprehensible that nations born out of the barbarism of the slave trade should want anything to do with the former oppressor, let alone retain the Crown as the ultimate authority. Why, for that matter, do the descendants of the convicts, exiles, migrants and pioneers who settled long ago in Australasia and Canada, along with the indigenous peoples whom they displaced, still embrace their connection with the Crown? That they do is, in no small part, down to its wearer. Yet for how much longer?

The Queen's international role is a source of endless confusion, which is understandable given that it falls into five categories. It is as Queen of the United Kingdom that she is best known and most usually observed. She is also the Head of the Commonwealth, in which capacity she has no formal position within its fifty-three member states. Countries like India, Ghana or Malaysia went to considerable trouble to extricate themselves from the British Empire and its Crown. They now enjoy the benefits of belonging to the Commonwealth, but have no obligation to Elizabeth II beyond recognising her as its titular head.

Thirdly, she is Queen of Britain's overseas territories (the modern term for colonies), which remain British sovereign territory. There are fourteen of these, ranging from Gibraltar and the Falkland Islands to more than 600,000 square miles of the British Antarctic Territory (a quarter of it in her name, following that 2012 decision to rename 170,000 square miles of snow 'Queen Elizabeth Land'). Additionally, she is Queen of the Crown dependencies, which consist of the Channel Islands and the Isle of Man. These are self-governing 'possessions' of the Crown. They don't belong to Britain, but 'depend' on Britain for their defence and international relations.

* Under the Statute of Westminster of 1931, each independent nation within the British Empire had the right to legislate for itself, without the say of the British Parliament. The monarch formally became a separate entity in each dominion – King of Canada, King of New Zealand and so on – enshrining the concept of a 'divisible' Crown.

Finally, there are the realms, all those independent nations that choose to retain her as sovereign. In addition to Britain, there are fifteen others, including Australia, Canada, New Zealand and much of the Caribbean. All told, it makes her head of state of between one eighth and one sixth of the Earth's surface, more than any other leader by some distance.

Viewed from afar, this might seem like an outdated relationship in a twenty-first-century world. Except, as one generation of politicians after another tends to discover, there is little public appetite to replace Elizabeth II with a retired politician.

She cannot be in sixteen nations at once, which is why she is represented by a Governor-General in the fifteen nations where she is not permanently resident. Her bonds with her realms are lasting and familial. Aside from language and law, they include any number of historical, military and charitable ties. Most important is the personal dimension. The Queen has always known that this is an ongoing relationship and, like all friendships, needs to be nurtured. As with her Commonwealth trusts and initiatives, she likes to support projects as far removed from the orbit of her politicians as possible. It is why those nine young hopefuls from the Caribbean hotel trade are here at the Palace to join the royal team. It is the Queen's small way of promoting the local economy in small island nations that are dependent on the tourist industry. She originally asked Prince Harry to announce the scheme when he was in the region a year earlier. He has been following its progress ever since and comes round to Buckingham Palace shortly before the scholars are due to be introduced to the Queen.

'Nice rooms? Not all bunked in one room together?' he asks them. 'Not like one of those TV shows?' They all laugh.

Some of these 'apprentices' are very well qualified already. Jared Forbes is chef to the Governor-General of the Bahamas and, when he's not doing that, he is a part-time policeman. Prince Harry is impressed, though he is a little worried how the Governor-General is managing to get by without his cook. 'He's probably eating baked beans from a tin now!' he jokes. The Prince is impressed by their tidiness: 'You all look immaculate. You all look as though you've been here for years.' And he gives them one word of advice that he learned in the Army: never be afraid to ask. 'There's no such thing as a stupid question,' he tells them.

Before he goes, Prince Harry assures them that they won't be the only ones a little in awe of his grandmother. 'Met the Queen yet?' he asks. 'If you suddenly bump into her in the corridor, don't panic!' Then, with a big smile, he adds: 'We all do.'

The big moment comes as the Queen returns to London after a weekend at Windsor. The scholars do their best to follow Prince Harry's advice, as she asks them all how they are getting on. Like Prince Harry, she is delighted to meet Jared Forbes. 'You're the Governor-General's chef, are you? And a policeman? That's an interesting mixture,' she says. As Queen of the Bahamas, she is well up to speed on news from Nassau. 'You've just had an election,' the Queen continues. 'Has it calmed down?' Talk turns to Jared's favourite dishes. 'You like cakes?' says the Queen. 'We're rather fond of that, so that's very good.'

Jonathan Alleyne, from Barbados, explains that he is learning hotel management at the Sandy Lane hotel resort on the island. It's a busy place, he tells the Queen, who seems to know all about it. 'I think Sandy Lane is always busy,' she says. 'A good place to start one's career.' Almost as good, perhaps, as Buckingham Palace. Wishing them all well, she heads inside, whereupon these scholars do what people so often do these days after they have met the Queen. They put their hand on their heart, open their mouth wide, take a sharp intake of breath and squeak: 'Oh my God!'

Michelle Montejo, who works at the San Ignacio Resort Hotel in Belize, has been transfixed by the Queen's face. 'She has such beautiful skin. I need to ask who does her makeup. Flawless,' she says. And she cannot wait to call her family back in Belize. 'It was really a proud moment to talk about my country and my resort and to finally meet Her Majesty,' she says dreamily. 'Best day of my life.'

Just up the Mall, another group of royal staff are packing their bags before heading off to the largest realm of the lot. Canada is about to celebrate the 150th anniversary of confederation – and the creation of Canada itself. The Queen, who has visited Canada more than any other nation outside Britain, was there to celebrate the 100th. She will not make it this time, though, for the simple reason that having reached her tenth decade, she has followed doctors' advice to avoid long-haul travel. The Duke of Edinburgh, five years her senior, has done the same. So the Prince of Wales will represent the Queen, accompanied by the Duchess of Cornwall, and will ride through Ottawa in a horse-drawn carriage. Nine months later, the Prince will be standing in for the Queen again in Australia, when he heads to Queensland to open those 2018 Gold Coast Commonwealth Games, before making his sixteenth tour of Australia, a place where he enjoyed some of his happiest school days and which he still regards as a home from home.

These visits will not command the sort of exuberance and downright hysteria that greeted the Queen in the early years of her reign – when two-thirds of the entire population of New Zealand and three-quarters of Australia turned out to see her in person. The crowds, which would continue to be immense for several decades, are no longer what they were. Commentators have attributed the decline to familiarity, to the fact that it is easier to watch these things on television and to the downturn in royal fortunes during the Nineties. So has royalty lost its allure? Has the spell been broken? Republicans would like to think so. Yet neither the opinion polls nor the indicators from the political mainstream suggest there is any great appetite for constitutional upheaval at present. It is perhaps one of the most significant, if understated achievements of the Queen that she still sits on sixteen thrones, even if she would probably bridle at the word 'achievement'. In her view it has not, in any sense, been a strategic or competitive process, but rather a simple case of doing one's duty. If having done so, she one day finds that a majority nonetheless prefer an alternative constitutional settlement, then she would be the first to wish her replacement well. For now, it is an issue that remains off the mainstream agenda in her sixteen capitals, not to mention all her other possessions and territories, from Guernsey to Tristan da Cunha.

Like royalist fervour, the appetite for republicanism has ebbed and flowed in different places at different stages of the reign. In parts of Canada, the Crown seemed doomed throughout the Sixties, until a change of heart during the Seventies. After the Watergate scandal across the border in the USA, many Canadians felt grateful to have an apolitical dynasty rather than a politician as head of state. In Australia, by contrast, the Seventies were just the start of the republican movement. By the early Eighties the new Labour leader and future Prime Minister of Australia, Bob Hawke, confidently predicted the end of the Crown there. 'The Queen is a decent hard-working lady doing a useful job,' he told journalists in Melbourne, 'but, by the end of the century, the monarchy will be phased out.' Just weeks before that deadline had expired, the Australian people were given a referendum on the issue and rejected the idea.

In April 1975, ahead of the Commonwealth meeting in Kingston, the British High Commissioner to Jamaica, John Hennings, predicted that the Queen's upcoming visit would be her 'last' as Queen of Jamaica. Evidently no one had informed the cheering crowds who greeted her again in 1983. Nearly twenty years after Hennings predicted the advent of a Jamaican republic, another British High Commissioner, Derek Milton, was reporting back to London on the mixed reaction to the Queen's 1994 visit. Foreign Office files, newly released under Freedom of Information rules, show that while the Jamaican public were happy enough to see the Queen, her Prime Minister, Percival 'P. J.' Patterson, had informed Milton that a constitutional referendum was imminent and that the Queen would be gone within four years. 'Mr Patterson may want to go down in history as the man who made Jamaica a Republic but I would not bet on that happening in the near future,' wrote Milton. Eight years later the Queen was still head of state, and Patterson was still Prime Minister when she arrived on her Golden Jubilee tour of 2002. Yet he was long gone by the time Prince Harry arrived to mark the Queen of Jamaica's Diamond Jubilee in 2012.

Though Jamaica had not (and still has not) found the appetite for that referendum on the monarchy, they have occurred elsewhere from time to time, always with the same result: a public preference for an unelected absentee royal head of state rather than yet another politician. Republicans sometimes talk of her 'clinging on'. After more than sixty-five years, it has been quite a cling. So how has she done it? The stories vary from realm to realm, but what is common to all of them is that this has never been about 'clinging'. It has been more a case of leading by example. And despite inevitable mistakes, a few upheavals and the best efforts of some of her politicians, it is an example of which the Queen's subjects seem to approve.

AUSTRALIA AND NEW ZEALAND

The round-the-world Coronation tour that began in 1953 remains the most ambitious royal expedition of all time. It would take the Queen more than 40,000 miles, most of them by sea, going from east to west. Along the way she would shake 13,213 hands and acknowledge 6,770 curtseys (the bows were not recorded). She would make 157 speeches herself and endure 276 by other people. The only recorded public display of irritation, according to the *News Chronicle*, was a rebuke to a member of her own entourage during a reception. 'Are you tired, General?' she asked. 'No, Ma'am.' 'Then take your hands out of your pockets and stand up straight.' Separated from her children for four months, and on a treadmill of repetitive formal occasions for days on end, the Queen certainly had private moments when her patience snapped. On the fifth week of the Australian leg of the tour, she and the Duke had been allocated a weekend to recuperate at a government chalet on the shores of the O'Shannassy Reservoir. Even so, there would still be a couple of public engagements in the form of a church service and an inspection of wildlife, for the benefit of the camera crew making an official film of the tour.

Evidently the royal couple had forgotten about their appointment with the film crew as they began arguing in the chalet. It concluded with the Duke charging out of the door, followed by a flying pair of tennis shoes plus tennis racket; followed, in turn, by a very angry Queen, shouting for him to return. The distinguished cameraman, Loch Townsend, and his deputy had been waiting, as instructed, and were already concerned about the fading light. When the door opened, Townsend and his team simply began filming. They were as astonished to find themselves watching a royal bust-up as the Queen and the Duke were to find themselves on-camera. Moments after the couple had retreated indoors (or, as Townsend recalled, the Queen had 'dragged' the Duke inside), the irascible royal press secretary, Commander Richard Colville, came striding over in a state of even greater indignation than usual. Townsend, who still had many days of filming ahead, knew when he was beaten. He opened the back of the camera, removed 300 feet of exposed film and told Colville: 'Commander, I have a present for you. You might like to give it to Her Majesty.' Shortly afterwards, an attendant appeared with a tray of beer and sandwiches by way of thanks. The Queen was not far behind. 'I'm sorry for that little interlude,' she told Townsend, 'but, as you know, it happens in every marriage. Now, what would you like me to do?'

If royal tempers had reached snapping point, it was not surprising. As Dr Jane Connors explains in *The Glittering Thread*, an excellent study of the tour's impact on Australian society, much of the southern hemisphere seemed in the grip of royalist hysteria. Hence the crowd that gathered outside the Hotel Gollan in Lismore, following a brief royal 'refreshment' stop. They were queuing up for a piece of unused royal toilet paper – one sheet per person – in much the same way that medieval pilgrims might once have queued to acquire a fragment of the Cross or a saintly nail clipping. The small mining town of Lithgow experienced the only traffic jam in its history as people from miles around descended for the Queen's twenty-five-minute stopover before re-boarding the Royal Train. At one point she walked along a length of red, white and blue carpet created by the staff of a local wool factory. What to do with the carpet? Afterwards, it was decided that the fairest solution was to cut it into tiny pieces, so that everyone had a souvenir. 'The adulation was extraordinary,' the Duke of Edinburgh said. Neither he nor the Queen would see anything quite like it again.

The almost messianic levels of excitement had been the same in New Zealand, where the royal couple landed first. The standard explanation for all this euphoria is that these loyal dominions were seeing a reigning monarch for the first time. This was true, but another factor was involved. The Queen was making up for years of bitter disappointment, at a time of mounting geopolitical uncertainty. For this tour had originally been discussed as far back as the Thirties.

In 1938, it was agreed that King George VI and Queen Elizabeth would visit Canada and the USA the following year. It would mean that Canada was the first dominion to receive a reigning monarch – quite a coup for Ottawa. The governments of Australia and New Zealand started bidding for a royal visit in 1940, plans that were promptly shelved with the declaration of war. After the end of the war, however, it was South Africa that was deemed the most pressing case for a visit from the King. India was already preparing to part company with the British Empire, and there were powerful Afrikaner voices in South Africa making similar arguments. There was no questioning the loyalty of Australia and New Zealand; they could wait a little longer. So it was, in 1947, that the King, the Queen and their daughters set off in HMS *Vanguard* for that tour of southern Africa, ahead of Princess Elizabeth's twenty-first-birthday speech.

Plans were then announced, in March 1948, for the King to visit Australia and New Zealand in early 1949. He would not merely be thanking them for their patience, but for their stalwart support from Day One of the war. This was a time when most people still regarded themselves as British. Up until the 1948 Nationality and Citizenship Act, all Australian citizens were considered to be British subjects anyway. In a 1947 poll, two-thirds of Australians said they wished to remain so. Their future Queen, however, would not be coming on the 1949 trip. By the spring of 1948 she was the newly married Duchess of Edinburgh and was already expecting Prince Charles. The King and Queen would head Down Under with Princess Margaret.

By the summer of 1948 the planning was well under way in Australia. Dr Connors has unearthed the story of one entrepreneurial woman who had cornered the entire market in ostrich feathers, ahead of all the hat-making that was likely to ensue. Plans were so far advanced that, in London, the King's equerry, Group Captain Peter Townsend, was asked to assemble a selection of films for the royal voyage. Commander Colville and his team in the press office were busy fielding media enquiries with their customary economy of detail. The Australian Consolidated Press submitted a lengthy list of questions about royal 'likes and dislikes' for a special royal supplement, to which the Palace replied: 'No information'. The nearest to a semblance of a story was the official response to a question about Princess Margaret's preferred choice of dances. Back came the reply: 'All kinds of dances, waltzes, reels and modern steps.'

In November 1948, however, the bunting had to go back in the box. The King had reported severe cramps in both legs. While he insisted on going about his duties, not least to avoid worrying Princess Elizabeth who was due to give birth at any minute, there could be no arguing with the great cardiovascular expert, Professor Sir James Learmonth. After seeing the King on 12th November, he diagnosed arteriosclerosis. Worse still, there was talk of a possible amputation. The tour planned for the start of 1949 was off.

The King responded well to treatment, buoyed by the arrival of Prince Charles, his first grandchild, but he was well aware of the inconvenience all this had caused. As he explained in his 1948 Christmas broadcast: 'By an unkind stroke of fate, it fell to me a month ago to make a decision that caused me much distress – to postpone the journey for which my peoples in Australia and New Zealand had been making such kindly preparations.' He had been greatly comforted, he added, by 'the wave of sympathy and concern which flowed back to me not only from the Australians and New Zealanders themselves but from friends known and unknown in this great brotherhood of nations'.

On the other side of the world, however, the public were crestfallen. One Australian supplier of street decorations stood to lose £20,000. We can only imagine the dismay of that speculator stranded with Australia's entire supply of ostrich feathers. Towards the end of 1949, the doctors decided that the King had recuperated so well that he could start drawing up new plans for the Antipodes. It was, by now, too late to think about 1950 and plans were well advanced for the Festival of Britain in 1951. So the Palace agreed a new date with Canberra and Wellington. The King, Queen and Princess Margaret would arrive in early 1952.

Once again, itineraries were prepared for the longest tour ever planned by a reigning British monarch. This time the King's newest realm would be bolted onto the schedule, too. Following the Partition of India into both India and Pakistan in 1947, Ceylon had become an independent nation in 1948, opting for dominion status with the King as head of state. Plans were so advanced that in the autumn of 1951, the King did something quite extraordinary. He manufactured a general election in Britain, ahead of his departure, in order to ensure that there wouldn't be one while he was away.

The 1950 general election had been won by Clement Attlee's Labour Party with a slender majority of eight. Parliamentary business soon ground to a halt. By today's standards, a majority of eight might seem a workable situation, but the post-war House of Commons was an older, frailer legislature than today's. The sight of elderly MPs being dragged from their hospital beds for a routine vote was commonplace. By the summer of 1951, the King was getting worried. Nine MPs had already died or retired through ill-health since the election the year before, and the King – who was in poor health himself – was planning to be away for many months. On 1st September, he wrote to the Prime Minister making his views clear. 'It would be very difficult for me to go away for five or six months unless it was reasonably certain that political stability would prevail,' the King explained. 'It would be disastrous if my visits to three of the self-governing countries of the British Commonwealth had to be postponed or even interrupted on account of political upheavals at home.'

The Prime Minister had been giving much thought to the issue himself, as he informed the King five days later. 'Among the factors to which I have given particular attention was the need for avoiding any political crises while Your Majesty was out of the country,' he wrote. So he agreed to meet the King later in the month to seek a formal dissolution of Parliament. Britain went to the polls in October 1951, Attlee duly lost and Winston Churchill returned to Downing Street with a Conservative majority of seventeen. Long before it had even started, the royal tour of 1952 had inadvertently made history.

Except that it would not be the King who would undertake the tour. No sooner had Clement Attlee decided to seek that dissolution than the King's doctors had bad news. X-rays had revealed a worrying patch on one of his lungs and they would need to conduct a bronchoscopy to remove a sample for examination. That took place on 16th September and promptly revealed the need to remove the King's entire left lung. There was no official mention of cancer. A blocked bronchial tube was given as the reason and, on 23rd September, the King went under the knife once more. Though the operation went according to plan, there were sufficient concerns about his recovery that Princess Elizabeth and the Duke of Edinburgh were asked to delay their long-planned tour of Canada and the USA by a week. When they did finally leave a week later, they carried a draft accession declaration, just in case. Two days later, the people of Australia and New Zealand received the news they were dreading, but expecting. For the third time, the King would have to cancel his plans to see them. His 1952 tour was off. However, the Palace was pleased to announce that Princess Elizabeth and the Duke of Edinburgh would take his place. Thousands of members of hundreds of welcoming committees from Perth to Auckland could breathe a sigh of relief.

They just needed to change the names and faces on the covers of all the souvenir programmes. By now the Empire had formally come to an end. Australia, New Zealand and all the other dominions had signed up to the new-look Commonwealth, too. They were no longer talked of as dominions, but as realms.

By the end of January 1952 the excitement was building all round the world. The crew of the BOAC Argonaut that would fly the Princess on the first leg of her tour became minor celebrities in their own right. Captain Robert Parker from Bracknell in Berkshire and his team of six men and one woman were presented to the British media ahead of the nineteen-hour flight, via Libya, to Kenya, where the Princess and the Duke would have a few days of official engagements and a short safari. In the Kenyan port of Mombasa they would then board the SS *Gothic*, a Shaw Savill cargo liner converted into a surrogate royal yacht, and sail across the Indian Ocean to Ceylon, where six RAF Shackleton seaplanes were preparing to escort the *Gothic* into Colombo. From there, the royal couple would arrive in Fremantle, Australia on 1st March to begin their tour Down Under. Having mapped it all out ahead of the cancelled 1949 tour, Australia's Lieutenant-General, Frank Berryman, the distinguished war hero placed in charge of the royal visit, knew every inch of the itinerary off by heart anyway. What could possibly go wrong?

The Princess and the Duke were among the last to learn of the King's death that epochal day in February 1952. By then the news had travelled around the world, and the Commonwealth was already in shock. Australia and New Zealand mournfully put the bunting away once more. Lt-Gen. Berryman folded up his plans again. Among the first announcements of the new reign, however, was that the Princess's tour of Australia and New Zealand was not cancelled, but postponed. By the time these two supremely patient and loyal realms would finally get to see their sovereign, there would have been one further catalyst for all this suppressed monarchist euphoria: the Coronation. As in Britain, so in most corners of the old empire, 2nd June 1953 was the cue for Coronation balls, Coronation fetes, street parties, receptions and carnivals across the Commonwealth and, especially, across the realms. Families and entire communities would gather around grainy black-and-white television screens in Britain and around wireless sets all over the world. The atmosphere was every bit as febrile and emotional in Australia and New Zealand – but with one important difference. As far as they were concerned, this Coronation business was all well and good but it was only a dress rehearsal. The real business would not begin until 23rd November 1953, when the Queen and the Duke finally boarded a plane and set off for the southern hemisphere. Unlike their previous attempt, the royal couple would travel in the other direction, from east to west, via Bermuda, Jamaica and the South Seas. Was it any wonder that, after so many years of waiting and three false starts, the Ozzies and the Kiwis momentarily took leave of their senses when the royal foot finally did touch home soil?

New Zealand would be the first to clap eyes on the Queen when the SS *Gothic* docked in Auckland on 23rd December. Every part of the country had been sprucing itself up in anticipation. For example, a maintenance team had been hard at work along the entire 25-mile stretch of road from Hokitika to Greymouth, in preparation for a single royal car journey. Because it would be a one-way journey, they had only resurfaced the left-hand side of the road along which the Queen would be travelling, leaving the opposite direction still full of potholes. Locals would forever after refer to the smooth half as 'Lizzie's side'. Most of the country turned out to see her, the royal presence not merely a matter of glamour and celebrity, but an important piece of economic symbolism. Two-thirds of all New Zealand's exports were destined for Britain in 1953. After all the uncertainty of wartime (New Zealand had played a gallant part in the recent Korean War, too), there was a sense that the good times really were back.

A day after the Queen's arrival, however, the country suffered one of its worst peacetime disasters when a landslide destroyed a bridge at Tangiwai. The Wellington–Auckland express train plunged into the Whangaehu River, killing 151 people. Yet it was the royal tour that would continue to dominate the headlines. The Queen would later meet survivors of the crash and quickly rewrote her Christmas broadcast – in the days when it was delivered live – to include her sorrow for 'a most grievous railway accident … which will have brought tragedy into many homes'.

Listening back in Britain, the young Prince Charles and Princess Anne also heard their mother issue a gentle rebuke to some of her more over-excited subjects at the end of this unrepeatable Coronation year. 'Some people have expressed the hope that my reign may mark a new Elizabethan age,' said the Queen. 'Frankly I do not myself feel at all like my great Tudor forebear, who was blessed with neither husband nor children, who ruled as a despot and was never able to leave her native shores.' And there was plenty of that extravagant praise for the Commonwealth which would begin to fade as the years went by. She was 'so proud' to be the head of 'the most effective and progressive association of peoples which history has yet seen'. A few days later, she would open the democratically elected parliament of one of the most egalitarian nations on Earth. Yet even here in modern New Zealand there were still glaring inequalities. And this non-despotic Queen Elizabeth was not averse to the odd moment of autocracy, when it came to meeting her less privileged subjects.

New Zealand's Maori community had wanted to give the Queen the grandest welcome. Waitangi is New Zealand's answer to Runnymede, the sacred spot on which the Crown and the indigenous Maori had signed their treaty in 1840. Yet the government had permitted only a brief, watered-down welcome. Another Maori welcome, amid the boiling mud springs of Rotorua, was grudgingly extended to 3,000 (it had originally been limited to 200). The government officials in charge of the royal programme had decided that there was no time at all for a visit to the 'marae' or meeting ground of the Maori King at Tūrangawaewae. More important, non-Maori civic worthies were waiting elsewhere, they argued. However, the Queen wanted to pay her respects nonetheless. On 30th December, the authorities finally agreed that she should pause outside the Maori royal compound for three minutes on her way to Hamilton. Once at the King's gates, however, enormous crowds swallowed up the royal party, who were escorted inside the King's hut for a chat. Maori warriors and maidens danced in tribute outside. 'It was the real thing, it really was,' the Queen's lady-in-waiting, the former Lady Pamela Mountbatten, recalled years later. The government minders were becoming increasingly restless and were looking at their watches. 'We were told that the official programme was awaiting, that there was no way we could stay, that we had to get back,' said Lady Pamela. Eventually the Queen had to yield to her advisers, but not before stretching her visit from three minutes to seventeen. 'We were so disappointed,' Lady Pamela added.

'Finally, as we drove away over the bridge, two enormous war canoes came down the river, each 100 ft long with 100 warriors. And we went off to the next boring official ceremony!'

All along the royal route, towns competed to erect the most impressive welcome-arch. Some went for a Scottish theme, reflecting the origins of many New Zealanders. The town of Papakura was decorated with depictions of Mount Everest, in case someone forgot to inform the Queen that she was in the home town of Sir Edmund Hillary, conqueror of Everest. Unsurprisingly, sheep were an ever-present feature of the itinerary. Some farmers decorated their flocks in red, white and blue. Only in New Zealand, perhaps, could the Queen and Duke meet celebrity sheep-shearers. In Waikato, the royal couple were introduced to the famous Bowen brothers, Ivan and Ken, as they demonstrated their prowess with the shears. Might the Duke like a go, they wondered? 'No thank you,' he laughed. 'I might nick it and we've had enough mutton on this tour!' Years later, newspapers would regularly include the remark in the list of supposed 'gaffes' by the Duke. The Kiwi public thought it was very funny indeed.

If the crowds were big in New Zealand, they were at times overwhelming in Australia, where the royal couple arrived on 3rd February 1954. First-aid stations were busy throughout the tour. In Cairns, 500 people needed medical treatment after a grandstand collapsed. The problem for the tour planners, as ever, was accommodating all the competing priorities. Every mayor wanted to resurrect the civic welcome that had been prepared for 1949, rearranged for 1952 and then cancelled on both occasions; every town had its extremely well-rehearsed cultural display. The Melbourne *Herald* awarded the premier of Queensland, Vince Gair, the Australian record for speed-introductions as he took the Queen through a greeting line of 260 people in forty-one minutes. As with the Maori elders in New Zealand, so Australia's Aboriginal community would play a peripheral role, though they were as keen as any to see the Queen. There were reports of groups of Aboriginal children making bus trips of many hundreds of miles for a glimpse of the royal party. The Queen would make a very specific point of referring to 'my peoples' in one speech after another but she incurred the wrath of one group of civic worthies in Queensland. It was felt she had spent much too long talking to a group of Torres Straits Islanders at the expense of the usual VIP herd.

Dr Jane Connors has unearthed many examples of eye-popping snobbery by officialdom. In the Tasmanian town of Devonport, a teacher called Gwen Dixon had spent months of her own time travelling all over her region teaching 2,000 children to sing 'Merrie England' to the royal couple at the local sports ground. Informed that she would be introduced to the Queen for her troubles, Gwen had even bought a special dress and gloves for the occasion. She was then told, at the very last minute, that other local dignitaries had pulled rank, insisting that they should take precedence over a mere teacher and housewife. Gwen was no longer in the greeting line. However, after a bravura performance by her choir, she would have her reward. As the royal Land Rover was driving round the sports ground for one last time, it suddenly stopped. The Duke of Edinburgh climbed out, walked up to Gwen, shook her hand and said: 'Her Majesty has wished me to express, on our behalf, our thanks for the children's beautiful singing. It was much appreciated.' Clearly the royal intelligence network had picked up word of Gwen's unsung efforts. Why else would she subsequently receive an invitation to a garden party at Buckingham Palace?

The crowds continued to defy modern comprehension. One million people lined the streets in Sydney, where the police were ordered to travel by train as the roads had become impassable. Another 120,000 children packed the Sydney cricket ground and 250,000 people simply waited to watch the royal car come back to Government House at the end of the evening. One million were seen lining the road from the aerodrome in Melbourne. Time and again, public-address systems failed when overhead wires snapped under the weight of people clinging on to them for a better view.

In one state after the next, the monarch was heralded as a fairytale come true, most famously when her adoring Prime Minister, Robert Menzies, presented her with what would amount to an Australian Crown Jewel. Made of yellow and white diamonds on platinum, the 'Wattle' brooch is not merely a stunning representation of the national flower, but of the national character, too. Here is an exquisite piece that exudes energy and colour, one that would be immortalised in that 1954 portrait by Sir William Dargie. The Duke, by contrast, was fondly portrayed as a bloke who, all things being equal, would rather be having a beer with his mates. While he seemed at his happiest inspecting new technology or military facilities, he was content to play along with the popular narrative. When the Queen went racing at Randwick, the Duke sneaked off to watch a match at Sydney Cricket Ground, where he spurned a royal box in favour of the pavilion. The media were thrilled.

As he explained years later, it was important to remember that this manic level of interest was never going to last. 'It could have been corroding,' he told Gyles Brandreth. 'It would have been very easy to play to the gallery but I took a conscious decision not to do that. Safer not to be too popular. You can't fall too far.'

It was a sensible approach. There was always going to be a next time. And it was never going to be quite the same. The explosion of evangelical royalist fervour in 1954 would sit a little uneasily with Australia's sense of itself as an unstuffy, can-do egalitarian sporting powerhouse. Many would look back with faint embarrassment to the fact that the greatest spectator event in Australian history was a royal and not a sporting one (the Australian government estimates that 75 per cent of the entire population saw the Queen in the flesh). Those epic scenes of 1954 have been well documented, in many books and films. Dargie's 'wattle' portrait has become a national treasure. So what happened next? The story behind the subsequent royal tour of Australia and New Zealand is less well known, but perhaps more instructive. For if 1954 was a relatively straightforward exercise in introducing the monarch to the people, then what was Round Two?

It would certainly be more challenging. By 1963 the novelty had worn off, television had come of age and the royal couple were nine years older. The royal gloss was fading in Britain, too. In the wake of the Suez fiasco, the monarchy had been attacked for being out of touch, not least in Lord Altrincham's famous broadside,* and the monarchy would be a rich seam for the satirists of the Sixties.

There was another issue of profound concern, particularly in New Zealand. Britain's new-found determination to join the EEC threatened economic collapse. New Zealand has often been regarded as the

* In 1957, the Tory peer Lord Altrincham used his little-known magazine, the *National and English Review*, to criticise the Queen for her 'priggish' demeanour and 'tweedy' court. A keen monarchist, he was concerned that the monarchy was losing touch with the public. The Duke of Argyll called for his execution, and Lord Altrincham was assaulted in the street. Years later he would be thanked by the Queen's Private Secretary. It had been a useful lesson.

most royalist of all the Queen's realms. So the fact that ministers in Wellington were not very enthusiastic about welcoming the monarch at this particular time reflects the depth of feeling. The European issue was also a source of concern in Australia, though not to quite the same extent. Around 18 per cent of Australian trade in the early Sixties was with Britain. A full decade before Britain's eventual entry into the Common Market, Europe was already colouring relations with historical allies whom most in Britain would regard as siblings.

The Queen's tour of 1963 was dreamed up by Australia's longest-serving Prime Minister, Robert Menzies, an ardent royalist. He had been keen for the Queen to make a return visit, ostensibly to mark the fiftieth anniversary of Canberra as the national capital. He had discussed it with her in person and she had agreed. At Buckingham Palace, officials started making plans in the summer of 1962. Surely, if the Queen was going all that way, should she not visit New Zealand, too? So strong were those concerns about Britain's flirtation with Europe that the Kiwis had yet to issue an invitation. As her Private Secretary, Sir Michael Adeane, wrote to a colleague: 'It is hoped that Mr Holyoake,* to whom a hint has been dropped, might suggest the Queen going to New Zealand beforehand.'

Holyoake finally took the hint and, once again, the Queen began a grand tour on the other side of the world, travelling, via Fiji, to New Zealand. On this occasion, however, her Maori subjects would enjoy much greater prominence than before. The Queen's visit coincided with the annual ceremonies to mark the 1840 Treaty of Waitangi between the Crown and the Maori. By the 1960s a Maori protest movement was gathering political momentum, with its claims that the treaty had not been fairly observed. The New Zealand government wanted to present the Queen as the guarantor of fair play. 'It was on this hallowed ground that pledges were given on behalf of Queen Victoria to the Maori chiefs when they ceded sovereignty to the Crown,' she told the Waitangi crowds. 'Today I want to renew those pledges and to assure my Maori people that the obligations entered into at Waitangi go far deeper than any legal provision.' It was her duty, she said, to ensure 'the trust of the Maori people is

* Keith Holyoake was the Prime Minister of New Zealand and latterly Governor-General, the only person to hold both posts.

never betrayed'. These were uncompromising words for a sovereign to deliver. The reference to 'my' Maori people did not go unnoticed. The Queen was also determined to make it clear that if there was any betrayal, it would not be her doing. 'I will do my part,' she continued. 'But remember that these pledges are given on behalf of the self-governing people of New Zealand and her democratically elected Government.' And in a final flourish that might almost have been scripted by Lord Altrincham, she concluded: '*He iwi Kotahi tatou*; we are all one people'.

It was a rare highlight during an eleven-day tour, which, by common consent, was not a patch on her five-week triumph in 1953–4. While large, excited crowds still greeted the Queen in Auckland and Christchurch, the turnout in Wellington was deeply disappointing. The British High Commissioner, Francis Cumming-Bruce, informed London that what passed for a crowd in the capital was 'mainly silent and there was little waving'. The mood was obviously rubbing off on the royal couple. 'It was on several occasions thought that the Queen looked drawn and very tired and this induced a sober mood amongst spectators, many of whom expressed disappointment,' Cumming-Bruce confided to Duncan Sandys, Secretary of State for Commonwealth Relations, in a confidential memo.

In Australia, there would be further mixed reviews and similar observations: the crowds were smaller, the displays less spectacular and the civic worthies as keen as ever on hogging the royal presence. The thirty-eight-day itinerary was considerably shorter than the two-month epic of 1954 and, on this occasion, the Royal Yacht would provide the odd breather at sea. It was still a punishing schedule, not least because every state had decided on its own programme, without paying much attention to the actual wishes of the visitor. For example, the Queen wanted to visit a migrant hostel. The request had been passed from the Palace to the immigration minister, Alick Downer, who had identified a suitable location during the Queensland leg of the tour. And yet nothing happened. As the British High Commissioner, Sir William Oliver, reported to his bosses: 'The Queensland government were approached but rejected the suggestion on the grounds that they could not waste any of Her Majesty's precious time in this state by asking her to visit a federal hostel. And so this project, despite Her Majesty's expressed interest, found no place in her programme.' Downer had also asked the states to make an effort to include 'new Australians' – non-British migrants who had only recently become royal subjects – in their civic functions. Once again, his requests fell on deaf ears.

The Australian press was largely upbeat in its coverage. By common consent, the jolliest part of the tour was in Darwin – the one part of Australia omitted from the great 1954 odyssey – where the Queen enjoyed a rodeo and the Duke of Edinburgh took part in a cattle round-up. The couple also made a point of visiting an Aboriginal family, Philip and Hannah Roberts and their six daughters, at their home, though it was an atypical one. A self-educated medical orderly, Mr Roberts had recently moved his family into a white suburb. As the royal visitors arrived, the neighbours serenaded them with the national anthem.

Back in London, however, the Commonwealth Office was becoming increasingly alarmed about the negative tone of the British press coverage. On 18th March, a telegram marked 'urgent' reached the British High Commissions in Canberra and Wellington. 'There have been reports suggesting that the Royal Tour has not been an outstanding success,' it said. 'Send urgently by bag a confidential report.'

In New Zealand, Cumming-Bruce did not hold back about the 'deflated mood' and placed much of the blame on British foreign policy. 'Eighteen months of negotiations of British membership of the EEC shook New Zealand opinion profoundly,' he warned. 'The suggestions in public discussion that Britain's relationship with the Commonwealth was likely to be progressively subordinated ... constituted a severe shock to that part of the New Zealand people that attach the highest value to retaining the closest possible links.' He pointed out that it was widely believed that the Queen had been sent to New Zealand by the British government as a sop to its old Kiwi allies. 'This story was much repeated and has been accepted by many who should know better,' said Cumming-Bruce. He was also scathing about the New Zealand government's 'air of casualness' and 'sloppiness', singling out the Prime Minister in particular. 'Holyoake appeared rather sloppy in some of his appearances. His addresses to the Queen singularly failed to do justice to the occasion; they lacked vital spark, the tone sounded rather patronising and he tended to address himself to the public rather than to the Queen.'

Cumming-Bruce tempered some of these remarks in his official despatch to London three weeks later, insisting that the tour had shown New Zealanders that 'their Queen can move about them without pomp and circumstance'. However, he repeated his point that 'the timing of the visit, coming as it did so shortly after the great debate on Britain joining the EEC, significantly affected its psychological impact.'

Over in Canberra, British diplomats were a little less downcast. Sir William Oliver insisted that the visit had been anything but a failure, and that a lot of British reporting was 'far-fetched and quite off the mark'. He attributed this to the fact that some British reporters were not 'the courtier type' but, rather, were 'looking for trouble'. He attributed the smaller crowds to the fact that most Australians had televisions. Those on the street were 'only a tithe of those who watched her progress with no less warmth on television screens at home'.

The main problem, he concluded, was striking the correct balance between 'informality' and 'royal spectacle.'

Touching on an eternal royal paradox, he added: 'It is not only children who want and expect a Queen to wear a crown.' *The Economist* put it another way: 'It is only against a background of regal magnificence that [Australians] love to read of the postman who entered a cottage in the Snowy Mountains and found the Queen eating an egg. But people do not want the Queen to be human all the time.'

Most people agreed that Australians had changed their attitude towards the monarch, and that this was no bad thing. 'They are beginning to think of her as the Queen of Australia,' said Sir William, adding that they had also 'grown out of the "Faerie Queen" attitude which is not in my opinion natural to Australians'. It was still natural to at least one very eminent Australian, however. Newly dubbed a Knight of the Thistle, Sir Robert Menzies perhaps marked the high point of Australian prime-ministerial chivalry with his oft-quoted line to his Queen at the state banquet in her honour: 'All I ask you to remember in this country of yours is that every man, woman and child who even sees you ... will remember it with joy – in the words of the old 17th century poet ... "I did but see her passing by and yet I love her till I die".' One senior Australian diplomat still looks back on this as 'peak cringe'.

One person well placed to judge the tour, from both the Palace and the Australian side, is Sir William Heseltine, the Australian civil servant who would go on to join the Palace and become Private Secretary to the Queen. Sir William was working in Canberra at the time. 'I would call the Sixties tour anti-climactic,' he says. 'There was a certain flatness to it. Television made it less essential to stand on the road. The attempt to replay '54 didn't really work.' Suddenly, Australian opinion-formers and public opinion itself began to look towards the USA as a more exciting and useful ally, especially if the erstwhile mother country was going to concentrate on Europe.

The affection for the Royal Family, however, still ran deeper than cosmetic appearances might suggest. When the Queen next returned Down Under in 1970, the old dominions had certainly recovered their enthusiasm. If it wasn't quite 1954 all over again, it wasn't far off. An important factor was the simple fact that the Queen and the Duke were accompanied by their two eldest children, both now young adults. 'We had Charles and Anne with us which generated a lot of excitement and there was nothing lacking in the warmth of the welcome,' says Sir William Heseltine, who was by then the Queen's press secretary. 'That and all the subsequent visits through the Seventies and Eighties went swimmingly.' By now the Palace and the realms had adopted a new strategy. Rather than try to cover the entire nation for the sake of it, the Queen would make shorter visits based around a specific event. In 1970, she was marking the bicentenary of Captain Cook's first landings in Australia (just as her next visit, in 1973, would be to open the Sydney Opera House).

The crowds that turned out to watch the Royal Yacht bring the Queen into Brisbane were the largest since 1954, with an estimated 250,000 on the waterfront. Thousands of small craft were kept at a distance, until a message was passed down from the Queen to the harbour authorities: 'let them come closer'. Though Britain was just two years away from entering the Common Market, the sense of shock had subsided. It was hardly news and, in any case, Australia's flirtation with the USA had started to wane. A recent visit by the US President, and the attendant macho security circus, had reminded people that their Queen was rather more human. And in 1970 the country was in the process of withdrawing from a terrible mistake – the Vietnam War. As Queen of Great Britain, the monarch had stayed out of the conflict. As Queen of Australia, though, she was in the thick of it. Over eight years, more than 50,000 of her Australian servicemen and women would serve alongside the Americans in Vietnam, and 520 would not return.

In Brisbane, the Queen held an investiture on the Royal Yacht and there was no question of who would be first in line. By tradition, the award of the Victoria or George Cross comes ahead of every other decoration, from a knighthood downwards. In May 1969, Warrant Officer Class II Keith Payne had been serving with a training unit in Vietnam when his company came under a sustained North Vietnamese attack on three sides. Though wounded himself and under constant fire, he would not withdraw until he had rescued more than forty wounded men and led them out of enemy territory. A year later he came to receive his VC from the Queen in person. The investiture was about to begin when the Queen's equerry, Lieutenant-Commander Jock Slater, had a problem as he lined up all the recipients. Number One in the queue was missing. 'I went dashing round the ship looking for him,' Slater recalls. Eventually, he found Payne alone on the Verandah Deck, grabbing a final smoke before his big moment. Being attacked by an overwhelming force of Viet Cong enemy troops was not nearly as daunting as meeting the Queen. 'Sir, I have never been so nervous in all my life,' explained the reluctant hero, stubbing out his cigarette.

Despite the size of the overwhelmingly friendly crowds, however, the first signs of a rebellious spirit could be detected here and there. Shortly before the Queen was due to come ashore at Botany Bay, to replicate Captain Cook's landing, a speedboat came tearing up to the beach and a young man leaped ashore to plant an Australian (not a British) flag firmly in the sand. When the Queen did arrive, no one could hear her words because vandals had disconnected the microphone.

But the royal couple themselves had been happy to cause a few upsets on this trip, too. Before the arrival in Australia, the Queen had, once again, visited New Zealand. In the capital, Wellington, which had proved so morose on her previous trip, the weather was doing the royal party no favours. 'The joys of windy Wellington!' says the

Princess Royal, at the mere mention of the tour. Here, the Queen agreed to try out a break with protocol. Before arriving at yet another greeting line in the capital, the royal car would stop short and the Queen would walk the last 50–60 yards, stopping to say 'Hello' to random members of the public. It might have alarmed the police, but it was a tremendous success with the public and the media. The *Daily Mail* journalist Vincent Mulchrone immediately gave this new experiment a name. He called it a 'walkabout'. Within a few days, it had gone from a trial run to a mandatory crowd-pleaser. When the Queen returned to the UK, her British subjects were clamouring for similar access to their monarch, and the first British walkabout was recorded in Coventry. New Zealanders, however, would always be proud that they saw it first. They were also particularly proud of one of the Queen's dinner guests on board the Royal Yacht during her visit. Only three people in history had won the Victoria Cross twice, and the last was Captain Charles Upham from Christchurch.

Famously contemptuous of fame ('I don't want to be treated differently from any other bastard,' he said in a rare interview), this taciturn farmer was typical of his breed and generation in his deep, visceral disapproval of Britain's ever-closer ties with Europe. A year after his dinner with the Queen, he made a brief foray into the political arena with an uncompromising letter to *The Daily Telegraph*. 'They'll cheat you yet, those Germans,' wrote Upham, whose enduring dislike for the old enemy extended to banning German cars from his property. The generations who had fought for King, country and Commonwealth had been increasingly hurt by the British policy of general disengagement 'East of Suez'. They had been hurt all the way back in 1940, when the British talked of fighting on 'alone' after the fall of France, despite the fact that Australia and New Zealand had loyally declared war on the same day as Britain. They felt nothing less than betrayed, as British MPs voted to join the new EEC in 1972.

Alick Downer, that frustrated Minister for Migration during the Queen's 1963 visit, had gone on to become Australia's High Commissioner in London. There he fought a losing battle with the British government to recognise the damage that accession to the EEC would do to the UK's old allies. Years later, his son, Alex, would be appointed to the same job, having been Foreign Minister longer than anyone in Australian political history. He can still recall standing with his father at the Menin Gate, that great memorial to the Commonwealth war dead in Flanders. Downer senior had tears in his eyes as he read the names of Australia's fallen, while denouncing the British Labour politician Roy Jenkins. During the European debate, Jenkins had called for Britain to abandon the politics of 'kith and kin' in favour of European integration. Downer senior returned to Australia 'a sad man' just three months before Britain's accession to the Common Market on 1st January 1973. Other Australians were even more upset as Britain started giving Europeans preferential treatment – not just in terms of trade, but even at passport control – to the detriment of the Commonwealth cousins. The Deputy Prime Minister, Doug Anthony, from the centre-right Liberal Party, renounced a lifetime's loyalty to the Queen and joined the republican movement.

Britain had not, actually, turned its back on 'kith and kin'. In negotiating its way into the Common Market, the British mandarins had been acutely aware of the need to remember the Commonwealth cousinhood. In his report, 'Britain's Entry Into the European Community', the UK's lead negotiator, Sir Con O'Neill, recorded that the British public felt a deep sense of debt and honour to a vulnerable ally like New Zealand. In early 1970, his delegation had received the following brief: 'The essential need is to provide New Zealand with a breathing space long enough for her to make the painful adjustments to her economy.' As he explained, failure could have had serious implications in Britain: 'The way the Community would treat her had become a touchstone, for millions of people, of their attitude towards our entry.' In 1971, the leader of the UK delegation to the Council of Europe, Duncan Sandys (himself a former Secretary of State for Commonwealth Relations), warned the French Prime Minister that he and many others would never support a deal 'which betrayed New Zealand's trust in Britain'.

The events of 1972 were a challenge for the Queen in all her realms. Here was Britain being demonised as a cheating lover walking out on the Commonwealth family and abandoning them for a sexy new paramour on the continent. The situation was especially challenging for the monarchy in Australia. There, the Liberals were kicked out and the country elected a Labour Prime Minister, Gough Whitlam, with a radical agenda and the slogan 'It's Time'. Though not actively seeking a republic at this stage, he launched a contest to find a new Australian national anthem instead of 'God Save the Queen'. In 1973, 'Advance Australia Fair' pipped 'Waltzing Matilda' to the top slot.

That same year the Queen invited Whitlam and his wife, Margaret, to Windsor and ordered the full treatment. Her Private Secretary, Martin Charteris, would later recall the almost girlish way in which the Queen fussed over Whitlam's gift, a sheepskin rug. 'She sat on that rug, stroked it and said how lovely it was,' Charteris told the writer Graham Turner. 'It was an arrant use of sexuality.' It obviously worked, as Whitlam later told Charteris, 'Well if she's like that, it's alright with me.' He would not be saying that two years later.

Many commentators like to point to Whitlam's dismissal in 1975 as the start of serious Australian republicanism. The two houses of the Australian parliament were locked in a Budget stalemate that was threatening the economy. Whitlam went to see the Queen's representative, the Governor-General Sir John Kerr, to seek a partial election in the upper house, the Senate. To his astonishment, Sir John, a retired judge, dismissed him. He then invited the leader of the opposition, Malcolm Fraser, to form a caretaker government ahead of a full election.

The Queen had known nothing about any of this, to her eternal relief. Nonetheless, Whitlam's supporters would paint the Crown – and, by extension, the Queen – as the villain, even though the electorate roundly rejected their man. Fraser won the subsequent election very comfortably, but many Australians, particularly those on the left, were still angered that a democratically elected government could be fired by the monarch's representative. Ahead of the Queen's Silver Jubilee tour of 1977, there were fears that the monarch could be in for a much unhappier tour than that of 1963. As he packed his bags for the trip, Sir William Heseltine received warnings from Down Under. 'I was told by all my friends and relations in Australia there would be demonstrations because of the dismissal,' he says. 'Everyone was expecting protests, though I was not.'

The global Silver Jubilee celebrations of 1977 would be one of the high points of the Queen's reign. While Britain was bogged down in economic crises, the monarchy offered something to cheer about and rally round. There were, though, republican elements within the Labour government of Jim Callaghan who regarded twenty-five years of a hereditary monarch as something to be overlooked rather than celebrated. When the London Celebrations Committee proposed floodlighting the buildings along the Thames during the summer, the Energy Minister, Tony Benn, vetoed the idea as a waste of electricity.

'Bloody nonsense,' Callaghan replied. 'I think this is pernickety bureaucracy.' The lights went on. All over Britain there would be the first big street parties and bonfires since the Coronation. And there was certainly no shortage of enthusiasm when the Queen set off to celebrate in her realms. Despite the upheavals that Britain's European entry had caused to its economy, New Zealanders were ecstatic to see their Queen again. Sir William Heseltine recalls that the chief problem was over-lengthy cultural displays, and persuading event organisers that the Queen neither wanted nor expected a five-course meal at every stop. In just over a fortnight she would cover the entire country, usually commuting by plane each day from wherever her beloved *Britannia* was berthed. As an Australian, Sir William would always discern the small but significant differences between a royal welcome in New Zealand and one in his native land. The Kiwis, he says, tended to be less chatty – like the mother and child who met the Queen on a walkabout in Wellington. Mother (to child, one inch from Queen's nose): 'Wyve y' fleg.'

The crunch, though, would come in Australia. Would the Whitlam affair sour the Jubilee mood, particularly since Sir John Kerr was still Governor-General? As such, he was the Queen's official host when she arrived in Canberra.*

In fact, there was no trouble in Canberra, or anywhere else. Sir William recalls 'a few mild protests up to this point, but nothing to justify the alarmist prophecies'. What was becoming increasingly clear was that the country had managed to compartmentalise the monarch, and detach the Queen of Great Britain from the Queen of Australia and the Head of the Commonwealth. She might have turned up in a yacht called *Britannia*, but she had not come as a Brit. It was summed up by an editorial in *The Sydney Morning Herald*:

* Sir John would resign later in the year, shortly after turning up, inebriated, to present the Melbourne Cup.

'She is by her presence certifying that the bond of the Commonwealth – the intangible link, so hard for others to understand, between independent nations of widely different outlooks – is still a reality. It is a changing reality, but it is proving a remarkably enduring one.'

Even when the royal party attended the last day of the Centenary Test between Australia and England at the Melbourne Cricket Ground, there was no sense that the Queen favoured one side over the other. The only tension was when Australian government officials tried to move the Duke of Edinburgh on to his next engagement, just as the match was reaching an enthralling climax. The Duke was said to be apoplectic.*

The royal weddings of the Eighties, along with the subsequent royal babies, would remove any mainstream appetite for republicanism. After successful visits by the Prince and Princess of Wales, who had wowed Australians by turning up with baby Prince William in 1983, there were renewed suggestions that the Prince should spend a few years as Governor-General. That was taking things too far, however, for the new Labour Prime Minister, Bob Hawke, and his party. In 1986, the Queen returned to Australia to abolish the last vestigial remnants of colonial interference. For complicated legal reasons, the British Privy Council was still, in theory, the ultimate Australian court of appeal and the British Parliament could, in theory, still interfere with state politics. All that was formally abolished at both ends. Having announced that her last official task in London had been to sign the Australia Act, while her first official engagement in Australia had been to do exactly the same thing, she went on: 'Anachronistic constitutional arrangements have disappeared but the friendship between two nations has been strengthened.'

By now, her hitherto sceptical Australian Prime Minister had become a firm fan. 'She has arguably got the most difficult job in the world,' said Bob Hawke, 'and she discharges it with an absolutely remarkable capacity and composure, relieved by a magnificent sense of humour.'

If there was anything to worry about, it was the situation in New Zealand, where the monarchy was increasingly seen as fair game for the more extreme elements of the Maori protest movement. In 1986,

* Australia won by forty-five runs.

the Queen was hit by an egg, which caught her coat. Though the incident alarmed her – Prime Minister David Lange called it 'deplorable' – she later made a joke that she preferred New Zealand eggs 'for breakfast'. Elsewhere, there was repeated baring of Maori bottoms and the occasional 'Go Home, Liz' banner. As ever, the hosts reacted indignantly to the slightest criticism from members of the British media, some of whom had accused New Zealand of failing to protect the Queen. 'I don't remember complaining when a man got into her bedroom at Buckingham Palace,'* an exasperated David Lange told ITN's Trevor McDonald. 'I wish you would look after her as well as we do in New Zealand.'

As in Britain, so in Australia, the warm sunshine that bathed the monarchy all through the Eighties was not to last. The 1991 election of an avowedly republican Australian Prime Minister, Paul Keating, coincided with the sharp decline in public support for the Royal Family, after its own domestic setbacks. The 1992 '*annus horribilis*' of collapsed royal marriages, bugged phones, a confessional Princess of Wales and the Windsor Castle fire caused deep and lasting damage to royal reputations in all the realms. 'It was the damage done to the monarchy by its own younger members in the early 1990s that set the wind behind the real push for a republic,' says one senior Palace figure from those years. Keating drew up plans for a referendum. There was added momentum in 1993, when Sydney was selected as the host city for the 2000 Olympics because the Olympic charter decreed that the Games should be opened by the 'head of state'. Keating even came to Balmoral to discuss his plans with the Queen that year. 'He was extremely courteous to the Queen, he couldn't have been more so,' says a member of the party (though one official later revealed that the Queen's first words after the encounter had been: 'I really do need a very large drink.')

The Queen was hardly going to engage Keating in a debate. Her twin concerns were to ensure that he was genuine and that whatever might happen should happen amicably. Given the political situation,

* In 1982, unemployed decorator Michael Fagan broke into the Queen's bedroom at Buckingham Palace. She kept him talking until help finally arrived. The incident revealed a series of police blunders.

it was deemed inappropriate for the Queen to set foot in Australia until the matter was settled. A tour in the meantime might be embarrassing and could smack of 'clinging on'. So in 1994, the Prince of Wales spoke on the Queen's behalf when he made a historic speech in Sydney. 'Some people will doubtless prefer the stability of a system that has been reasonably well tried and tested over the years, while others will see real advantages in doing things differently,' he said. 'Personally, I happen to think that it is a sign of a mature and self-confident nature to debate those issues and to use the democratic process.' In other words: your call.

The electorate would eject Keating before he could hold his referendum. His (monarchist) successor, John Howard, accepted that the issue could not now be set aside. He organised a constitutional convention in 1998 to devise an alternative to the Crown, which could then be put to the people. For the most part it would be a debate about process, not personalities, though the death of Diana, Princess of Wales in 1997 had, inevitably, coloured some attitudes towards the House of Windsor. The 55:45 result in favour of the status quo was certainly a surprise to most republicans, who were convinced that the nadir in royal fortunes would be enough to get them over the twin thresholds required: not merely an overall majority, but overall majorities in a majority of the six states.

At Buckingham Palace, less than two months short of the new millennium, there were no great celebrations. Some courtiers – and, it is said by some, the Duke of Edinburgh – were incredulous and less than thrilled. The inevitable had not been avoided, merely deferred. Others voiced a quiet contentment that the concept of constitutional monarchy still held firm in a progressive, modern democracy. Yet it had been a grim experience for an institution that is supposed to stand above political debate to be in the thick of it.

An ex-member of the royal team at the time says that they had explored and 'road-tested' every scenario. 'There was a fear of a run on the Crown. We expected the outcome would be OK, given the threshold, but the risk was that it would trigger something in a country like New Zealand where the result just needs to be fifty per cent plus one. So there was a concern about the domino effect. We did examine all options, including the thought that it might be better to say "let's go before we're pushed"; it was only speculative.'

One thing was not speculative, however. We now learn from a very senior Palace official that the Queen did come to one firm conclusion ahead of the Australian vote. In the event of this or any other realm opting to become a republic, it would then have to get on with it. 'It could not be tied to the death of the Queen,' says the source. 'That would be untenable for the Prince of Wales, untenable for the Queen and untenable for the country itself because, obviously, they'd be looking at their watches waiting for her to pass away. So if any realm was going to walk away from its sovereign relationship, the Palace view was: "You've got to name a date because we can't have this lingering 'deathwatch'."'

Because of the republican rumblings and the 1999 referendum, the Queen had not set foot in Australia for eight years. In 2000, it was time to return. As soon as the referendum had been announced, it was agreed that she would visit shortly afterwards, regardless of the result. Some Palace veterans regard this as one of the most challenging and sensitive tours of her reign – and one of her most underrated achievements.

Both the Palace and the Australian government were keen to avoid any suggestion of triumphalism. Her arrival at a Canberra air base took place at night with no guard of honour, no public access, no bouquet and not even a red carpet. The greeting party of four consisted of the Prime Minister and the Governor-General, plus their wives.

Predicting that a broadly republican-minded media would seek to compare the crowds with those that had greeted her first visit, John Howard had gone out of his way to play down expectations. He made a point of telling the media not to expect big crowds. 'Nobody should imagine that it will be anything like it was in 1954,' he told reporters. 'The world has moved on. It's very different.'

It was not that different, however, as around 10,000 people gathered to cheer the Queen as she arrived at Sydney Opera House. The main themes of the visit, according to the Palace, were unity and multiculturalism. In her main speech of the tour, the Queen struck a note of humility that won applause from both royalist and republican commentators. There was no skirting around the vote on the Crown or, as she called it, 'the proposal to amend the constitution'. She had followed it 'with the closest interest' and it had not made a jot of difference to her 'lasting respect and deep affection' for the place. 'I shall continue faithfully to serve as Queen of Australia under the Constitution to the very best of my ability, as I have tried to do for the past forty-eight years,' she told guests at a state lunch in the Sydney Convention Centre. 'That is my duty. It is also my privilege and pleasure.'

She had been heading for this 'rugged, honest, creative land' when her father died in 1952. 'I have shared the joys and the sorrows, the challenges and the changes that have shaped this country's history over these past fifty years,' she added. Some were in tears at the end. The following day, several prominent republicans, including former Olympic gold medallist Dawn Fraser, said that they would still like the Queen to open the Olympics later in the year. It had already been decided, however, that this duty should fall to an Australian and that the Queen's representative, the Governor-General, Sir William Deane, would have the honour. The Queen, however, would formally open the new Olympic stadium during her visit. In one of the oddest and saddest moments of the tour, she did so watched by no one at all, bar a handful of construction workers, a few reporters and the Governor-General. All 110,000 seats remained empty, for 'security reasons'. Elsewhere, though, the crowds continued to defy expectations. When the Queen ventured to the remote town of Bourke, 'gateway to the Outback', she met a delirious contingent from the even more remote town of Coolabah, 80 miles further on. Coolabah had the distinction of recording the highest vote for the monarchy in the whole of Australia. Of its fifty voters, forty-six had supported the Crown. So all forty-six had chartered a bus to see the Queen in Bourke, leaving the four republicans to keep an eye on Coolabah.

Two years later, the Queen was back again to mark her Golden Jubilee, and republicanism was firmly off the agenda. By the time she returned for her sixteenth visit in 2011, to attend the Commonwealth summit in Perth, the conversation had moved on from removing the Crown to securing its future. The impetus was coming from the British Prime Minister, David Cameron, who was keen to amend the rules on royal succession before they could blow up into a political issue. The Duke and Duchess of Cambridge had been married six months earlier and it was reasonable to assume the couple would soon want children. Under existing rules, any first-born girl would be superseded by any subsequent younger brother. David Cameron wanted to head off all charges of twenty-first-century institutional sexism before they might arise. So he asked the leaders of all the other fifteen realms to attend a mini-summit in Perth. 'I initiated it – and the Crown was fully supportive,' he says. 'The thinking was that we had better get on with it, better to have the thing sorted out.' While they were at it, this prime ministerial gathering could also discuss two other pieces of ancient and oppressive legislation. In addition to the law excluding Roman Catholics from the line of succession, Cameron wanted to overturn the law ordering all lineal descendants of George II to seek the sovereign's permission before marrying.

Over the years, many British MPs and peers had argued for changing these laws of succession, but had been rebuffed by successive governments citing the same arguments: 'too complicated', 'a Pandora's Box', 'impossible to get all the realms to agree', 'waste of parliamentary time', and so on. Given all the issues facing the world, some would argue that it was absurd for sixteen modern democracies to spend even one minute discussing the dynastic arrangements of one family.

Cameron could see its symbolic importance, however. So he and his Foreign Secretary, William Hague, were pleasantly surprised at the enthusiasm with which the other fifteen prime ministers – including Australia's republican premier, Julia Gillard – approached the subject. Lord Hague says that, until he saw all the realms sitting down at the table together, he had never fully appreciated the extent of the Queen's authority. 'They all liked having this role,' he says. 'They liked the fact that a little parliament in somewhere like Tuvalu was going to have a veto on the future of the British monarchy. And even though someone like Julia Gillard might have been on the other side of the argument, she took it very seriously.'

Tom Fletcher, foreign policy adviser at Number Ten Downing Street, remembers the quietly pivotal role of the Queen's Private Secretary, Sir Christopher Geidt, as he calmly guided sixteen prime ministers through the constitutional elephant-grass. 'It was handled very closely by the Palace,' says Fletcher. 'It was very interesting because they wouldn't normally lean in on policy issues.'

Hague still marvels at the speed of the outcome. 'In the space of forty-five minutes, they had all agreed the principles for equal succession,' he says. All their efforts would be rendered largely redundant on 22nd July 2013, when two footmen walked across the gravel at Buckingham Palace to place the traditional announcement before the railings: it was a boy. None the less, the sixteen realms had all rather enjoyed their modest part in the latest chapter of a thousand-year-old story.

By now Australian support for a presidential model had dwindled to around one-third and the once-mighty Australian Republic Movement was down to a single, part-time employee. In New Zealand, as younger royal visitors continued to come and go, the issue was dormant, if not comatose. Any campaign to replace the monarch with a president would always be easier in New Zealand, given that it is a unitary state rather than a federation. Yet republican-leaning prime ministers had been and gone without seeking to put the issue to the test. One of them had been Jim Bolger, the Queen's host at the 1995 Commonwealth summit in Auckland.

It is a general rule that when the Queen travels to one of the old dominions, they foot the bill. In 1995, as the Queen prepared to head for New Zealand, Bolger's government suggested that she might like to fly on a scheduled flight. Officials at the Foreign Office in London tried to scupper the idea, arguing that the Queen does not take scheduled flights, 'for security reasons'. However, as the Queen's staff at the Palace had to remind the British government, all things relating to a tour of New Zealand were a matter for her New Zealand government. On 30th October 1995, she duly boarded Air New Zealand Flight NZ1 for the long journey from London to Auckland via Los Angeles. The Queen had First Class to herself (Prince Philip was flying in separately from South Africa), undisturbed by the duty-free trolley, and watched a Sam Neill film called *Cinema of Unease*. The Business Class cabin was occupied by twenty-six members of the Royal Household, and 384 ordinary passengers filled economy, safe in the knowledge that their flight was not going to be delayed. Each received a commemorative pen.

Though that visit would see another small Maori protest, it also marked a change in Maori attitudes towards the monarchy. The old days of bottom-baring would give way to respect when the Queen, dressed in her kiwi-feather coat, acted once again as ceremonial guarantor of Maori rights. She signed an Act granting historic compensation of nearly 40,000 acres of land and £26 million to a federation of Maori tribes in the North Island. She did so on the advice of her government, of course, but giving her Royal Assent to it in public, in front of a deputation of Maori elders, was a reminder that their forebears had done a deal with Queen Victoria in 1840, not with the government of a nation that did not exist at the time. Since then, many Maori have come to view the Crown as an ally in the quest for justice, rather than as a symbol of oppression.

'If the Government in Wellington ever decided to set up a republic, we would want our own sovereign state,' said Rick Rakihia Tau, chief of the Ngai Tahu tribe, during the Queen's Golden Jubilee tour in 2002. 'We signed a treaty with the Crown in 1840, not with the white settlers.' By then, New Zealand had another republican in charge, Labour's Helen Clark, who received what Palace officials sometimes refer to as 'the look' when she arrived at the Queen's state banquet in a trouser suit. Nothing was said, however. Indeed, many Palace staff speak very highly of Clark, who would later stand (unsuccessfully) to be Secretary-General of the United Nations.

Come the Queen's Diamond Jubilee in 2012, the Queen's future in both her Australasian realms seemed settled for the foreseeable future. Republicanism was neither a burning issue nor a taboo subject, and that is how it would remain – something deemed inevitable at some point, but just not now. The 2018 wedding of the Duke and Duchess of Sussex, just weeks after the birth of Prince Louis, third child of the Duke and Duchess of Cambridge, would certainly not bring that day any closer.

The British government has sought to re-engage with the region, too, and is poised to do so again once the UK has settled on a post-Brexit direction. 'When we were elected in 2010, we thought there were various things we could do overseas that were worthwhile and one was to pivot to Australasia,' says former Prime Minister David Cameron. 'The Foreign Secretary hadn't been to Australia for seventeen years and obviously there is a great relationship with the Crown there.' Britain's lack of interest in the region had not gone unnoticed. Alex Downer, former High Commissioner for Australia, points out that it was the Queen, rather than the British Foreign Office, who kept that relationship strong and secure during the years of neglect. 'I don't think there's a country in the world – not even New Zealand – where Australians feel more loved than Britain,' he explains. 'In all those years when the British Foreign Secretary never came to Australia, it didn't really matter so much because the Queen came.'

Over the subsequent years the republican pendulum would swing in both directions in Canberra and Wellington. The former Prime Minister of New Zealand, Sir John Key, whose centre-right administration broadly overlapped with that of David Cameron, cannot now envisage a republic in his own lifetime. 'There was a time, to be blunt, when the monarchy was under a lot more pressure. I used to think it [a republic] was inevitable,' says Sir John, a staunch monarchist. Even with a change of reign, he believes that there would be 'no appetite'.

As Britain seeks new trade deals post-Brexit, Sir John says that he senses no residual bitterness towards the way Britain turned its back on its old allies, on the way into Europe. 'In 1984, New Zealand went bankrupt. Did Britain have an impact? Absolutely. But the truth is that if we'd started to do some modern economic thinking, we could have taken control of the situation. People have moved on and think Britain is a market we want to be in.' Like Australia's Alex Downer, he puts it down to the Queen.

By the time of the 2018 Commonwealth summit, a committed republican was at the helm in Australia. Malcolm Turnbull had been the leader of the campaign to remove the Crown back in 1999. His belief in the need for an Australian-born head of state remains undimmed. Yet he is entirely happy having a royal Head of the Commonwealth, and robustly endorsed the Prince of Wales as the next head when the subject arose at the London summit. So, too, did the new, republican-minded Prime Minister of New Zealand, Jacinda Ardern. Having travelled halfway around the world while seven months pregnant to attend her first Commonwealth gathering, Ardern enjoyed long private audiences with both the Prince of Wales and the Queen and was invited to make one of the toasts at the Queen's banquet. The experience had merely reinforced her personal respect for the 'hugely impressive' monarch. 'I have to say, I admire the stamina of Her Majesty because my feet are killing me and she's been working all day,' Ardern reflected as she left Buckingham Palace.

The arguments for and against the monarchy have not changed, but there has been an important shift in the tone of the debate. The awkwardness has gone, even when discussing the future of the Crown in royal company. As Malcolm Turnbull is among the first to admit, however, it is just not a pressing issue for the moment. 'There needs to be very strong popular momentum,' he has said. 'There has to be a sense that the time is right. There are many more urgent issues confronting Australia than the desire for Australia to become a republic.'

The first approximation of a twenty-first-century vote on the subject would come in 2016, as New Zealand held a referendum on the adoption of a new flag. Voters could choose a new design – championed by the Prime Minister, John Key, his royalist credentials notwithstanding – that featured the silver fern, sacred emblem of the revered All Blacks rugby team. Or they could stick with the existing flag, featuring the British Union flag in the top-left corner. 'I wasn't trying to dump the Union Jack. It was a branding exercise,' says Sir John. 'The Canadians have done it with the maple leaf. But some people feared a reduction in our ties with the UK and a republic.' In the end, it boiled down to a simple choice: modernity versus Empire, Queen and tradition. Nearly 57 per cent of Kiwis voted for the latter.

CANADA

If the British connection coloured the Queen's fortunes Down Under, it was the French connection that would play the most significant part in the royal story in her largest realm. Roughly one-fifth of Canada speaks French as a first language, a legacy of the days when a lot of the territory belonged to pre-revolutionary France. It would all become British in the eighteenth century and, 100 years later, would become a nation, with the confederation of three colonies under one name approved by Queen Victoria: Canada. It was the first self-governing dominion and the first to receive a visit from a reigning monarch, when King George VI and the Queen arrived in 1939. That trip went so well that, as Queen Mother, she would return to Canada more than to any other part of the Commonwealth. Her last visit, at the age of eighty-nine, would conclude, appropriately, with a day at the races. The crowds on that first visit were not just enormous – the turnout of half a million people in Windsor, Ontario was greater than Windsor, Berkshire had ever produced – but also very respectful. More than 20,000 people in Sudbury turned out to watch the Royal Train come through at 1 a.m., but did so in silence so as not to wake the King. To the relief of the royal party, the welcomes in French Canadian areas were every bit as enthusiastic as anywhere else.

After the Second World War, during which tens of thousands from all parts of Canada gave their lives, the King was keen to visit once more. With his health failing, he would send Princess Elizabeth with the Duke of Edinburgh in his place in October 1951, with a few days in Washington with President Truman added on. Even then, the trip was delayed by a week while the Princess awaited that all-clear after the King's lung operation. When the Princess and the Duke finally climbed aboard their BOAC Stratocruiser plane, she had that draft accession declaration with her, just in case. The first port of call was the French-speaking heartland of Quebec, where the crowds were as excited as any. From the outset, the Princess made a point of wearing the Maple Leaf brooch that the King had given the Queen ahead of the 1939 tour, a gesture warmly applauded by the media. It was a hugely ambitious tour, designed to carry the royal couple all across Canada and then back again. Much of the journey would be by special Royal Train decorated in the Princess's favourite 'surf green', along with green damask and taffeta curtains and a light-brown carpet. If it was snug and well insulated against the increasingly bracing weather, the Duke found it faintly claustrophobic. 'I feel like a poached egg. I just can't breathe on trains,' he announced as he disembarked in Vancouver.

To this day, says the Countess of Wessex, a favourite Royal Family story concerns the occasion when the couple returned to the Royal Train in a remote town to find a band, as usual, waiting on the platform: 'Instead of getting on the train,' she says, 'the Duke of Edinburgh went up to the bandmaster and said: "Look, we never get to hear the band because whenever the band strike up the train always pulls out of the station. So it'd be really nice to actually hear you play." So they started playing. And the train pulled out of the station with the Queen and the Duke of Edinburgh still standing on the platform!'

Wreath-layings and military engagements took pride of place. In Ottawa, where the royal couple were greeted by 13,000 children singing 'O Canada', they were also entertained to an evening of square-dancing by the Governor-General, Viscount Alexander. The Princess was photographed in a 'peasant blouse' and dirndl skirt, but it was the sight of a beaming Duke in turned-up jeans, suede loafers and checked shirt (with the price ticket still attached) that is perhaps the most striking. Sixty years later, the Duke and Duchess of Cambridge would be photographed in something similar during their first overseas tour.

Canada's indigenous Indians were included, although the Princess's tour of a wigwam took place at a 'model' wigwam village in Calgary. The press were delighted to see the future monarch making small talk with characters like Chief Heavyshield, Chief Crowchild, Maurice Many-Fingers and Two Ton Young Man. She appeared especially touched when Mrs Heavyshield suddenly produced a hand-stitched doeskin suit for Princess Anne. All through the tour there were informal moments that would be simply unthinkable at home: a 'Grub Pile' lunch of barbecued buffalo and 'sinkers' (doughnuts) at the Calgary Corral; a horse-drawn sleigh ride *à deux* in front of the cameras (with the Duke at the helm); the students of McGill University in Montreal chanting, 'Yea, Betty! Yea, Windsor! Yea, Betty Windsor!' It was French-speaking Montreal that attracted a crowd of one million people, the largest of the tour. The sight of them singing 'God Save the King' in French would surely have assured any doubters that French Canada was every bit as royalist as Windsor, Ontario. Or was it?

Back in Britain, the King was so thrilled by the success of the visit that he sent the Royal Train to collect the couple when their liner docked in Liverpool, and promptly made them both Privy Councillors on their return. At a 'welcome home' luncheon in the City of London, the Princess was seated next to Winston Churchill. Her speech saluted North America as an inspirational example in a divided world: 'On this visit, we passed across what is surely one of the miracles of the world today, that vast 4,000-mile frontier without a single gun pointed in fear on either side.' Canada's ties with both Britain and the USA were a central theme of her early years as Queen. During her 1957 state visit to the USA, she visited Canada to open parliament wearing what would become known as Norman Hartnell's 'Maple Leaf of Canada' dress. On her 1959 visit to Canada, she would welcome both the Canadian Prime Minister, John Diefenbaker, and the US President, Dwight Eisenhower, on board the Royal Yacht for the opening of the St Lawrence seaway and, with it, a new era in US–Canadian trade. Yet it was another demanding tour, all the more so as the Princess had a secret, which she confided to a handful of people, among them Mrs Eisenhower. She was pregnant. These vast trans-continental tours of Canada could not be repeated. Better, surely, to make shorter, more regular visits to a few provinces at a time.

By the time she embarked on her next full Canadian tour, the Queen would not only have given birth to Prince Andrew but to Prince Edward, too. Her 1964 trip, ostensibly to mark the centenary of the conferences that led to the creation of the Dominion of Canada, was taking place against an alarmingly different backdrop. A vocal French Canadian separatist movement had threatened demonstrations and violence, so much so that there were calls in Britain for the visit to be cancelled, just as there had been ahead of that 1961 tour of Ghana. In this case, there were the makings of a constitutional crisis. As Queen of Canada, her Canadian Prime Minister, Lester Pearson, was advising her to come. Her British Prime Minister, Sir Alec Douglas-Home, had his doubts. He was sufficiently concerned that he asked the Cabinet Secretary for advice on who would trump whom in the matter. In the end, the two leaders agreed to keep in touch as the tour progressed.

It would be one of the most uncomfortable visits of the Queen's reign, with tensions already heightened by events over the border in the United States, notably the advent of the civil-rights movement and the recent assassination of President John F. Kennedy. In Montreal, over-zealous policing merely stoked up local resentment towards the royal visitor, particularly after thirty-four arrests on a day of protest that became known as 'Truncheon Sunday'. The Queen had done her best to foster a spirit of national unity. Two years earlier, she had formally adopted her own Canadian coat of arms, featuring both the maple leaf and the French fleur-de-lys. Now, addressing the provincial parliament in Quebec – in fluent French – she declared: 'I am pleased to think that there exists in our Commonwealth a country where I can express myself officially in French.' But the separatists were not listening. The final straw was when *Britannia*'s gangplank collapsed moments before the Queen was due to walk up it. It was a tour to forget. As Professor Philip Murphy has pointed out, both Lester Pearson and the British Foreign Office began to start contemplating the demise of the Crown in Canada within the next five years. Neither thought that would necessarily be a bad thing, either.

Three years later, however, the Queen received a rather warmer welcome when she returned to mark both the Expo 67 World Fair in Montreal and the centenary of Canada as a confederation. The latter was clearly an event of pan-Canadian importance, and the Queen sent members of the family to all the provinces that she could not get to herself. At Expo 67, she also turned a potential public relations disaster into a triumph. Sir William Heseltine was the Queen's press secretary at the time and remembers the long queues of people being kept outside so as not to disturb the royal visitors. 'The Prime Minister came to have lunch and Prince Philip got at him and said "This is monstrous, all these people queueing up and you won't let them in. We're going to go back after lunch and they must be allowed in".' The royal couple duly returned and took an unscheduled ride on the new airborne 'minirail', receiving a roar of approval from the crowds flooding in below, as word spread of what had happened.

Canada had always been an enthusiastic founder member of the Commonwealth, pushing for India to stay in back in 1949, producing the first Secretary-General, Arnold Smith, and instigating Commonwealth Day around the world. It was a Canadian prime minister, Pierre Trudeau, who volunteered to host the make-or-break Commonwealth Heads of Government Meeting in 1973, following the disastrous slanging match which had occurred in Singapore. Trudeau had not taken the organisation very seriously in his early days, famously sliding down the bannister at Lancaster House during a prime ministers' meeting in London in 1969. Sonny Ramphal thinks he liked to play the fool in public to show his French-speaking power base that he was unimpressed by the trappings of British royalty. 'Trudeau was a slow starter,' says Ramphal, 'but he became one of the great Commonwealth leaders.' Among his contributions was the creation of the 'retreat' at Commonwealth summits, in order to achieve quiet consensus. He also had the bright idea of allowing leaders just one adviser each in the conference room – rather than a posse of bruisers – to keep things intimate.

For all his bluster and charisma in front of the cameras, Trudeau was less of a showman in the presence of the Queen. Indeed, it seems he was as nervous of her as anyone else. We know that, because he is perhaps the only Prime Minister in history who has gone through an entire private royal audience with a third person in the room. It happened during the filming of *Royal Family*, the original royal documentary, in 1968. BBC technician Dave Gorringe was present to record a few snippets of conversation as Trudeau came for his first audience. 'I vividly remember, he was a Robert Redford type and a lovely man,' Gorringe told William Shawcross years later. 'The Queen was making all the going and his answers were not very good and it lasted about ten minutes. She eventually pushed a buzzer for the door to open. He walked out and the doors closed and she said: 'Well, he didn't have much to say for himself, did he?"'

It was not a charge that could ever be levelled at the Duke of Edinburgh. In 1969, he famously told an Ottawa press conference that 'we don't come here for our health'. As he put it: 'The monarchy exists in Canada for historical reasons . . . I think the important thing about it is that if at any stage people think that it has no further part to play, then for goodness' sake, let's end the thing on amicable grounds without having a row about it.' By now, however, the Canadian republicanism seemed to be on the wane.

A fiery French Canadian lawyer, Trudeau had never been a monarchist, but neither would he turn out to be avowedly republican. 'He was probably a republican, or at least started as one,' says a former royal Private Secretary. 'But I think he was beguiled by the Queen. He was a very shrewd politician and he knew there was not much in it for him. He was a class act, too. I remember he made a speech at a state banquet at the Ottawa national hall. It was white tie – the Queen in her white fur which we don't mention any more, given to her by the Hudson Bay Company – and it was a dazzling evening. He made the most perfect speech, a mixture of French and English without looking at a note at all.'

Trudeau preferred to make the monarch, and the trappings of monarchy, more Canadian rather than seek a replacement. Over the years he developed a good rapport with the Queen, who was happy to indulge what Ramphal calls Trudeau's 'boyish antics'. There was one potentially tricky evening when Trudeau invited a local (republican) student leader called 'King Steve' to join a dinner on board the Royal Yacht in Vancouver. Some members of the Royal Household were nervous, even more so when a van screeched to a halt on the quayside to deposit the young man, amid chants of 'Steve for King'. The Duke of Edinburgh, however, was adamant that if the student had been invited to dinner, then 'to dinner he must come'. Jock Slater, the Queen's equerry at the time, remembers that Steve was late and 'oddly attired' but he escorted him into the Drawing Room to be presented to the Queen. It later emerged that 'King Steve' had come prepared to deliver a republican speech but had lost his nerve. 'He was overawed and subdued,' says Slater, 'and what he planned to say never happened.' Slater recalls the evening for another reason. Trudeau's wife of a few weeks, Margaret, was already pregnant with the future Prime Minister of Canada.

All through the Seventies, Canada would see plenty of the Royal Family. Prince Andrew was despatched to spend six months at a Canadian school, just as Prince Charles had enjoyed part of his education in Australia (Prince Edward would do the same in New Zealand). In 1976, the Queen came to open the Montreal Olympics, where Princess Anne was part of the British equestrian team. And the Queen Mother was never parted from her beloved Canada for long.

In 1982, Trudeau invited the Queen on a short visit with a very profound purpose. She was to sign the Canada Act, as publicly as possible, in front of the cameras and the people. In doing so, she severed the very last constitutional ties with Britain. 'The constitution of Canada has come home,' declared the ever-theatrical Trudeau. The Queen was privately said to be delighted that there was now less chance of being dragged into a constitutional row.

As the future of the monarchy became more uncertain in the southern hemisphere, it became sedate and settled in the Queen's great North American realm. Opinion polls would dip during the dark years of the Nineties and nudge upwards alongside the Jubilees that followed.

The Queen would endure one excruciating episode in 1995, just as Quebec was preparing to vote in a referendum on independence. A prankster from a French-speaking Montreal radio show called the Palace posing as Jean Chrétien, the former Justice Minister and the architect of the Canada Act, who had gone on to become Prime Minister. The radio hoaxer had managed to get through to the Queen herself. For seventeen minutes, the semi-serious conversation meandered, mainly in French, even touching on royal plans for Hallowe'en. Much of it was then broadcast across Quebec a few hours later. No great harm was done, however, except perhaps to the separatist cause. The pro-independence campaign failed, by just 1 per cent. Some have suggested that the Queen's fluency in French, and her ready knowledge of all things Québécois, might have persuaded some voters that the Canadian Crown was not such a remote institution after all.

The Queen would look back on it with a certain degree of amusement. As she reportedly told (the real) Chrétien years later: 'I didn't think you sounded quite like yourself. But I thought, given all the duress you were under, you might have been drunk.'

Returning for her Golden Jubilee in 2002, not long after the death of the Queen Mother, the Queen told banquet guests one of her mother's favourite stories about that first visit by a reigning monarch in 1939. Queen Elizabeth had met two Boer War veterans who had been debating whether she was actually English or Scottish. 'My mother paused, and then replied: "Since I have landed in Quebec, I think we can say that I am a Canadian". Ladies and Gentlemen, my mother, like most mothers, often had the last word. But in this case I know exactly how she felt.' The Queen added: 'I treasure my place in the life of Canada and my bond with Canadians everywhere.'

By 2015, the Queen would be having audiences with another member of the Trudeau family when Justin Trudeau, eldest son of Pierre (who had died in 2000) led the Liberal party to victory in the general election. Later that year, as one of the new boys at the 2015 Commonwealth summit in Malta, Trudeau junior was invited to make the banquet toast in honour of the Queen. After he pointed out that she had performed her first official Canadian duty in 1935 – appearing on a postage stamp at the age of nine – he reminded the assembled heads that his father had been the Queen's fourth Prime Minister while he was her twelfth. Rising to respond, the Queen joked: 'Thank you, Mr Prime Minister of Canada, for making me feel so old!'

Though the Queen met him several times as a baby, Justin Trudeau's earliest memory of her comes a little later. 'I remember one day having to rush home from school because she was going to stop by for lunch and we had to be there to receive her,' he says. 'I was terribly worried because although I was going to get changed into better clothes, I was going to have to wear the same shoes and I needed to keep them clean all morning. And I don't think I was able to.'

Later in life, it would be his brightly-coloured socks rather than his shoes which would attract royal attention. Heading for his audience with the Queen ahead of the 2018 Commonwealth summit in London, he revealed that he had chosen a pair of grey socks covered in pink moose. 'They match the suit,' he explained.

Having attended the 100th anniversary of Canada in person, the Queen had given up long-distance by the time that 150th anniversary came round in 2017. So, she asked the Prince of Wales to represent her. 'Each time he comes he feels a bit more of Canada seeping in to his bloodstream,' explained the Governor-General David Johnston, as he prepared his residence, Rideau Hall, for the Prince and the Duchess of Cornwall. 'I try to make it as homely as possible; to make it their home.'

After travelling to Parliament Hill, Ottawa, in the royal horse-drawn carriage, the Prince spoke on the Queen's behalf, praising Canada as 'a champion of human rights; as a peace-keeper; a responsible steward of the environment; and as a powerful and consistent example of diversity and the power of inclusion'. Mr Johnston then flew over to London to celebrate with the Queen at Canada House. A broad cross-section of UK-based Canadians were gathered in one room and a broad cross-section of royal Canadian treasures were in another. The exhibition ranged from the letter confirming Queen Victoria's approval of the name 'Canada' to the puck that the Queen threw at a Vancouver ice-hockey game on her Golden Jubilee tour. Ahead of this visit, the Queen had given much thought as to how she might mark the 150th. She had asked the Royal Librarian, Oliver

Urquhart Irvine, to assemble facsimiles of all the key documents and images from Canadian history and create a one-off commemorative book at the Windsor book bindery. This was to be her present to the people of Canada. They, in turn, had one for her: a brooch in the shape of a Northern Star snowflake, crafted with diamonds and sapphires (it was the year of her Sapphire Jubilee). It would be a companion piece to that Maple Leaf brooch, which King George VI gave to his Queen in 1939. 'We are blessed that you are our Queen,' the Governor-General told her. 'Thank you for your selfless service to our country.'

THE CARIBBEAN

Most of the Queen's realms, like much of her Commonwealth, consist of smaller island nations. These former colonies or protectorates have only achieved independence from Britain during her reign. As such, their ties with the Crown tend to be more practical and less sentimental than those of the 'old' realms, although their affection for the Queen herself is genuine and straightforward. She is religious, above politics, inexpensive, very famous and someone whom other countries do not, on the whole, want to offend. There is also the fact that having her as head of state affords them a degree of extra influence over the former colonial power. As that Windrush scandal exploded days before Theresa May's Commonwealth summit in London in 2018, many aggrieved Caribbean leaders were about to have one-on-one audiences with the Queen and members of her family. The British Prime Minister was well aware that they would bend royal ears.

The British public might like the idea of the Queen being embraced as head of state elsewhere, but, as Philip Murphy has pointed out, the Foreign Office has regarded these multiple monarchies as a potential conflict of interest. He has shown that it was covert British government policy to dissuade some soon-to-be-independent states from becoming realms. One or two, like Trinidad and Tobago, duly obliged, seeking independence in 1962 and then becoming a republic fourteen years later.

But most of the Caribbean ex-colonies – formerly known as the British West Indies – have chosen to retain the sovereign. The most significant of them, Jamaica, was still a colony when the Queen first visited at the start of her great post-Coronation tour. Within five years it would be at the heart of moves to turn the West Indies into an independent federal nation, a move followed closely by the Queen herself. Patsy Robertson, who would go on to become head of Commonwealth communications, was a young Jamaican diplomat working on the discussions. She remembers that the delegates were most impressed when the Queen invited the negotiating teams round to the Palace for drinks. 'She was lovely,' says Robertson.'She had been to Jamaica already and they had a love affair with her.'

When plans for a federation foundered, Jamaica wasted no time in seeking independence for itself, but there was no great appetite for a republican constitution. The country preferred to keep the Queen as head of state and guarantor of this fledgling democracy. Because she had never presided over an independence ceremony, Princess Margaret was despatched to lower the flag and open the new parliament. Plans to send her on a scheduled flight were dropped, in favour of a special BOAC aircraft – not to spare the Princess's blushes, the Palace insisted, but Jamaica's. From the outset, most Jamaicans drew a clear distinction between Britain and its Queen, and continue to do so, despite routine calls for a republic.

Most of the smaller Caribbean colonies would take a similar view, working on the basis that if the British government was not going to pay them the attention they deserved, they would rather have back-door access to the most important person in Britain.

Jamaica was keen to emphasise its status as a front-rank Commonwealth nation and launched a bid to host the 1966 British Empire and Commonwealth Games. These had never taken place outside the old white dominions, but Jamaica easily beat rival bids from Scotland and Rhodesia. In 1973, the Jamaican Prime Minister, Michael Manley, reiterated the point when he agreed to host the 1975 Commonwealth Heads of Government Meeting in Kingston, the first in the Caribbean. In the same year that he was hosting the Queen and her Commonwealth, Manley would also set up a constitutional commission to explore the creation of a Jamaican republic. His radicalism only went so far, however. As Sir Sonny Ramphal notes in his memoirs: ' I think he rather enjoyed escorting the Queen about Kingston to rapturous crowds.'

One newly elected Jamaican prime minister after another would voice a desire for a locally born head of state, only to find that the public had more pressing issues. As the Queen arrived during a Caribbean tour in 1994, a parliamentary constitutional reform committee had just recommended her replacement with a president. 'Government ministers took no interest at all in the preparations for the visit,' the British High Commissioner, Derek Milton, wrote to his superiors in London. 'Many Jamaicans were virtually unaware of the visit.' Yet police reinforcements were needed to hold back the crowds trying to welcome the Queen to National Heroes Park. 'As people realised that Her Majesty was on the island,' Milton wrote, 'she once again captured the public imagination and proved to be a crowd puller (even though information about the programme remained sketchy) ... People were genuinely glad to see "Missis Queen" again.'

Opinion polls, he noted, were evenly divided on the idea of a republic. 'Some may see Her Majesty as an anachronism (a white, faraway figure who visits only infrequently) but many black Jamaicans have had a special affection for the British Crown ever since Queen Victoria abolished slavery.' He added that many still regarded the Crown as a 'final court of appeal against their local leaders'. The latest proposal for a presidency was shelved, with all the others.

In 2012, Portia Simpson Miller became the next Prime Minister to make the near-mandatory pledge to usher in a republic. Later in the year, she was hosting Prince Harry as he came to Jamaica as the Queen's emissary during her Diamond Jubilee. On the eve of the visit, she told the BBC that Britain should consider apologising for its role in the slave trade and that she was seeking a referendum on the Crown. The following day, a very public and genuine hug with Prince Harry highlighted the difficulties in separating the constitutional from the personal. She was out of office before she could hold her referendum. Her successor duly made the same pledge to deliver a republic, and duly found that the electorate had other priorities.

Other Caribbean leaders would find themselves in a similar situation, torn between a largely middle-class preoccupation with replacing the Queen and genuine popular support for a monarchy that was regarded as an old-fashioned but unbribable roadblock against parliamentary wrongdoing. Some republicans have argued that the monarchy is not a bulwark against anything, pointing to the Queen's impotence in preventing the American invasion of Grenada, one of her independent Commonwealth realms. In October 1983, President Ronald Reagan had ordered US forces to seize control of the island, citing fears for several hundred US nationals after a coup by revolutionary forces and the execution of the (pro-Marxist) Prime Minister. The British Government was not given prior warning and the US had not informed Grenada's head of state either. However, it later emerged that the Queen's representative, her Governor-General, was being kept in the loop. A locally-born ex-teacher who had been appointed on the advice of the country's Prime Minister, he had been quietly supporting the US plan all along. He just hadn't mentioned it to the Queen, who was said to be furious with everyone involved. At least it showed Grenadans that she cared. Besides, in the aftermath of the short-lived revolution that had led to the invasion, people yearned for stability and had no desire to sever links with the Crown.

Talk of republicanism is irrelevant among the British overseas territories in the region. As long as they remain attached to Britain, the Queen is non-negotiable. To periodic accusations of 'colonialism', the British government will merely point out that these are places that have chosen to remain colonies, albeit with their own legislatures for local matters. The Foreign Office view is that they are welcome to seek independence at any time. For now, Westminster serves a useful multiple role as cash-cow, dartboard and seal of approval for offshore financial services. The royal connection confers added prestige and a lucrative line in commemorative stamps and coins. The run of independence ceremonies across the region during the Sixties and Seventies petered out in the early Eighties. In places like the Turks and Caicos or the British Virgin Islands, there is little popular appetite for independence and all the uncertainty that would come with it. Yet, the Queen of all people knows that nothing can be taken for granted.

During her 1994 tour of the region, she arrived in Anguilla for the first time and visited its tiny parliament, the House of Assembly. Departing from the general carnival atmosphere, the leader of the opposition, Hubert Hughes, used his speech of welcome to attack the 'discriminatory' British Nationality Act, accusing the UK of reducing Caribbean migrants to the status of 'indigents'. The ruling party was furious. In his subsequent despatch to London, the Governor, Alan Shave, castigated Hughes for his 'ill-considered remarks about FCO meddling which will have cost him future election support.' Not quite. The following month, he was elected Chief Minister, a post he would occupy for eleven years. His remarks about the British Nationality Act were merely a foretaste of the Windrush scandal a generation later.

As the Queen's tour moved on to Bermuda, there was a similar incident in Hamilton. The Governor, Lord Waddington, informed London of an awkward moment during the social centrepiece of the trip: 'The Speaker's dinner went without a hitch but the Premier could not resist the opportunity to make a speech which ruffled some feathers by its indirect reference to the independence issue. Many Bermudians felt that it was an inappropriate speech for such an occasion.' It might have 'ruffled feathers', but it was not wholly inappropriate, given that the premier, Sir John Swan, would indeed hold a referendum on independence the following year. He resigned when the proposal was defeated by three to one.

Separatist noises could be heard across the region again two decades later as a series of grievances coalesced. Britain was accused of a slow and inadequate response in helping those islands hit by Hurricane Irma in 2017. Locals would point to the disparity between UK spending on 'white' overseas territories like the Falkland Islands and St Helena (recent recipient of £250 million for a failed airport scheme) versus 'black' territories in the Caribbean (which received a combined pot of £32 million to deal with the devastation from Irma). The Windrush scandal of 2018 had coincided with proposals to impose strict new disclosure rules on Caribbean tax havens. Westminster insisted it was in the interests of transparency and financial probity. The islands called it a 'colonial' threat to their chief source of income. A few politicians have since revived the case for independence. Even so, it seems likely to be some time before another member of the Royal Family has to watch a Union flag coming down at midnight.

Creating a new country is much harder than creating a new head of state. For now, another Caribbean republic is more feasible than a new independent Caribbean nation. The most active standard-bearer for republicanism in the region has been the long-serving socialist Prime Minister of St Vincent and the Grenadines, 'Comrade' Ralph Gonsalves. Although his nation includes the famous royal holiday destination of Mustique, he decided to hold a referendum on the Crown in 2009. There was more than a whiff of attention-seeking about the timing. The Queen was due in the Caribbean that very week to attend the Commonwealth summit in Port of Spain, Trinidad. It would certainly have been a story if she had arrived in the region to find herself minus a throne. Her subjects had other ideas, however, and rejected the idea by that same 55:45 margin as the Australians had done a decade before. Since it would have required a two-thirds majority to amend the constitution, the referendum was barely discussed at the summit. Mr Gonsalves was all smiles at the Queen's banquet later in the week and gladly accepted an invitation to Prince William's wedding eighteen months later. Around the Caribbean the view seemed to be that Comrade Ralph was simply being Comrade Ralph. 'He's a good friend,' says Sir Sonny Ramphal, 'but he's always been a Marxist undergraduate!'

Ramphal points out that one left-wing Caribbean leader – he will not say which one – told him of an intriguing meeting with the Cuban communist dictator, Fidel Castro. 'It was very important to be in the good graces of Fidel at that time,' Ramphal recalls. 'In the course of the conversation, this prime minister explained: "I was thinking we ought to become a republic". He thought it would go down well with Fidel. But Fidel said: "Why? Does the Queen interfere?"

Prime Minister: "No."

Castro: "Then why would you do that? You want to be a big tourist island and she's good for showing off your stability. Why are you doing that?"'

So, those who still find it hard to understand why so many young nations born from colonial oppression and imperial bondage should still want the British sovereign as head of state might care to ponder this unlikely fact: Fidel Castro was a fan.

'Fidel was a pragmatist,' says Ramphal. 'That's why he lasted.' Pragmatism is probably why Elizabeth II – Queen of Antigua & Barbuda, the Bahamas, Barbados, Grenada, Jamaica, St Kitts & Nevis, St Lucia and St Vincent & the Grenadines, plus mainland Belize – has lasted even longer.

THE PACIFIC

If the loyalty of the Caribbean realms can be baffling for republican rationalists, then the island realms of the Pacific must seem even more confusing. The Queen did not become Queen of Papua New Guinea (PNG) because its people decided to retain her. She is their sovereign because they actually invited her to become their head of state. As such, it is the one part of the world where the Queen is, effectively, an elected monarch.

Nearly twice the size of Britain and with more than 800 languages, PNG is one of the most diverse nations on Earth. Following periods of German and British control, it was administered by Australia until becoming self-governing in 1973. Full independence would follow shortly, and Australia's Labour government, led by Gough Whitlam, was pushing PNG in the direction of a republican constitution. The new government of PNG had another idea, though. The Queen's Private Secretary, Martin Charteris, recalled a visit from the Australian High Commissioner in London, Sir John Bunting. 'You're not going to believe this but they want the Queen to be their Queen,' he told the startled Charteris. The reasons were threefold: the Queen had visited PNG and the people liked her; they wanted someone 'above the fight' who could remain impeccably neutral; and they wanted to retain all the traditional knighthoods and decorations. There was vague talk about the possibility of reviewing the situation after ten years, but the main thing was that they did not want a president. They wanted a monarch – and not just any monarch.

Charteris informed the Queen who was both 'tickled' and touched. 'She accepted straight away,' he said. In September 1975, the Prince of Wales was present for the independence celebrations as the new nation of PNG became the Queen's latest crown. He has returned several times, most recently for the Queen's Diamond Jubilee, and speaks a smattering of PNG's unique pidgin English, Tok Pisin. Its official term for the Prince of Wales is 'Number One Piccaninny Belong Missus Queen'. If any thought had been given to removing the Queen after those ten years were up, it was soon forgotten when the time came. More than forty years after independence, a car pulls up at the Grand Entrance to Buckingham Palace. Sir Robert Dadae, the Queen's tenth Governor-General of Papua New Guinea, has come to see her and receive his knighthood. 'It was necessary to have the Queen as head of state,' he explains on the way out. 'She has a very special place in our system of government.' It is quite a special system.

At the other end of the spectrum are the Solomon Islands, a Pacific archipelago of 900 islands east of Papua New Guinea, and perhaps the Queen's most amorphous realm. Several uninhabited islands have already been swallowed up by rising sea levels during the course of her reign, and a few of the inhabited ones have been evacuated before they follow suit. At the same time, one or two new islets have sprouted above the waves, due to volcanic eruptions in the area.

Though remote, the Solomons are not as lonely as the Queen's smallest realm. Midway between Australia and Hawaii sits Tuvalu, the fourth-smallest nation in the world. According to the United Nations World Tourism Organisation, it also has the distinction of being the least-visited. On average, just 2,000 tourists arrive in any given year. One might imagine Tuvalu would want all the friends and influence it could get and yet, even here, there have been republican murmurings. In 2008, this cluster of Pacific reefs and atolls held a referendum on dispensing with the Queen, at the behest of a former prime minister with presidential ambitions. Most people did not bother to vote in a plebiscite which showed that less than one-tenth of Tuvalu's 9,000-strong electorate supported the idea of a republic.

Given the lack of visitors, it was not surprising that the Queen and the Duke of Edinburgh received an exuberant welcome when the Royal Yacht dropped anchor there in 1982. Indeed, it turned out to be one of the most memorable arrivals in royal history. The visitors were ferried ashore in a pair of war canoes, which were then lifted out of the water and carried up the main street by teams of 'warriors' with the Queen and Duke still aboard. It was, perhaps, the only time the monarch has been held aloft by one of her own Cabinet ministers, in the form of Henry Naisali, Tuvalu's Finance Minister. Dressed in a ceremonial grass skirt, he was among those carrying the Queen's canoe. When introduced to him later, she joked that it was the first time she had seen a haystack wearing dark glasses.

A less happy royal 'first' occurred in this part of the Pacific in 1987 – the Queen's one and only abdication. Fiji had become part of the British Empire in 1874 at its own request (it actually asked twice before being accepted) and became independent in 1970, while retaining the Queen as head of state. Her visits – six in all – are remembered with great fondness both by the Fijians and by the Queen's staff. Sir William Heseltine says that the only people who were less than enthusiastic were the crew of the Royal Yacht. It was an important ritual, before each arrival, for the Fijian chiefs to come aboard to present the Queen with a *tabua*, a whale tooth, as a sign of peace, respect and permission to land. However, the chiefs would always come drenched in coconut oil, which left terrible marks on the royal deck. Sir William remembers that the programme would always involve a rich blend of British ceremony and Fijian tradition, most memorably when torch-bearing warriors would run alongside the royal car all through the capital, Suva, to the state banquet.

All of that was forgotten in 1987 when a Fijian soldier, Colonel Sitiveni Rabuka, staged two military coups and went on to proclaim himself acting head of state. It soon became clear that the position of the Queen's representative, the Governor-General, was untenable. When Commonwealth leaders met in Vancouver, Heseltine discussed the situation with the Queen. 'I thought there was no point in getting the poor man to keep on going as Governor-General without any local support,' he recalls. 'And the Queen agreed with this. I got hold of him on the phone and suggested the time had come for him to retire.' He agreed and the Queen instructed her Fijian self to resign from the throne of Fiji – which was duly kicked out of the Commonwealth.

Sir William says that Mrs Thatcher was bitterly opposed to the resignation, and that he caught 'a swing of handbag' as a result. The British Prime Minister regarded it as nothing less than an abdication. 'Which it was – that is a reasonable description,' says Sir William. 'But Mrs Thatcher thought that was an awful thing to have done.' However, the Queen was acting as Queen of Fiji, and Mrs Thatcher had no right to intervene – yet another reminder of the constitutional difficulties that can arise when a 'divisible' Crown finds it is at odds with itself.

To this day, Fiji and its former monarch have never entirely recognised the divorce. Until recently, the Queen's official birthday was a public holiday, and she only came off the banknotes in 2012 – long after her 'abdication'. The Union flag remains part of the Fijian flag (there was talk of dropping it, but no great public appetite); St Edward's Crown remains on military badges; the Queen's portraits still hang in many public buildings; and the Queen herself has never formally dropped the title conferred on Queen Victoria – Tui Viti, Monarch of the Fijians.

Thirty years on from that abdication, a large crowd gathers in Norwich outside the University of East Anglia's Sainsbury Centre for Visual Arts. It is staging a major exhibition called 'Fiji: Art & Life in the Pacific' and the Queen wants to look round it. Though it is a freezing January morning, four barefoot, bare-chested Fijian men in grass skirts (led by a Fijian Lance Corporal from the Household Cavalry) have formed a guard of honour.

She is reunited with the *tabua* that she received on her first visit in 1953 and chats knowledgeably with the academics about exhibits like kava bowls, war clubs and baskets. When shown a Fijian bark-cloth wedding dress, the Queen nonchalantly mentions that she knew the bride's father. She enjoys herself so much that the visit runs on far longer than planned. Also present is the Fijian High Commissioner, Jitoko Tikolevu, dressed in the traditional *sulu*, a black Pacific version of a kilt. When he is introduced to the Queen, he performs an accolade still reserved only for royalty. He goes down on one knee and claps three times. 'We still think of her as Queen of Fiji,' says Mr Tikolevu. 'We can't wait for her next visit.'

Chapter 6

THE SPECIAL RELATIONSHIP

'A ten-gallon tiara'

Diplomats and politicians have long talked up the 'special relationship' between Britain and the United States, even if the phrase is much more common on the eastern side of the Atlantic. Equally, there are commentators in both Britain and the USA who regard any notion of a 'special relationship' as sentimental, subservient wishful thinking on the part of the British establishment. There have certainly been some strong individual pairings between Number Ten and the White House, notably Churchill and Roosevelt, Thatcher and Reagan and, latterly, Blair and George W. Bush. However, historians will note that there has been a more subtle, yet more consistent 'special relationship' operating between the White House and Buckingham Palace throughout the reign of Elizabeth II. It is not one forged in late-night crisis talks or the heat of battle. Rather, it is an enduring bond that is equally strong, but built on familiarity and the personal touch – be it the decision to play the 'Star-Spangled Banner' outside the Palace the morning after 9/11 or a simple invitation to tea, on learning that a nonagenarian Henry Kissinger was passing through London. Unlike the Queen's dealings with most countries, which have followed a well-established pattern, this is a friendship that has broken the bilateral mould. There can be few people in the USA, let alone the rest of the world, who have lived through the administrations of sixteen presidents – more than one-third of the total – and met twelve of them. Monarch Number Forty (since 1066) has met Presidents Thirty Three to Forty Five (with one exception, Number Thirty Six, Lyndon B Johnson).

Of the handful of private foreign holidays that the Queen has enjoyed in her life (all horse-related), five have been spent in the USA. In 2018, the Royal Family welcomed their first American Princess. Yet, the Queen's own 'special relationship' goes back to the nursery.

American influences were making an indelible mark on Princess Elizabeth as a little girl. By far the most important foreign tour that her parents undertook was their 1939 trip to Canada and the USA, just before the Second World War. No reigning British monarch had set foot in the United States before and the US leg of the tour was, in part, to bolster popular support for Britain ahead of any forthcoming hostilities in Europe. It was also designed to boost the profile of King George VI in a country where his elder brother had been very popular. That Edward VIII's love for an American had cost him his throne had made him a sympathetic, even heroic, figure to many. The ticker-tape welcome from a crowd of between three and four million in New York was proof that the new King and Queen had made their mark. It would, though, be an extremely stressful challenge for a naturally shy monarch of a nation on the cusp of war. Writing home after being knighted on the Royal Train somewhere near Buffalo – 'the first Englishman to be so treated by his Sovereign on American soil' – the King's private secretary, Sir Alan 'Tommy' Lascelles, complained of the hosts' 'monstrous' lack of organisation. 'The President's happy-go-lucky temperament is largely to blame,' he told his wife, Joan. However, the royal couple were rather enjoying the informality. The Queen wrote an excited letter to her daughters about a memorable picnic lunch: 'All our food on one plate – a little salmon, some turkey, some ham, lettuce beans & HOT DOGS too!' While some Americans were appalled at the idea of serving hot dogs to a king, the Royal Family would never forget it.

Growing up in wartime Windsor, the future Queen was acutely aware of the strain on her father as he tried to buoy the morale of a nation facing invasion at any moment. As such, she could sense the redemptive significance of America's entry into the war. Come victory and the drab, near-bankrupt years of austerity that followed, it was America that represented fun and glamour. Like so many others, the Princesses were entranced by the explosive arrival of the first American musical after the war, *Oklahoma!* (Princess Margaret reportedly went to see it more than thirty times). Princess Elizabeth and Prince Philip watched it together as a courting couple in 1947; 'People Will Say We're in Love' has been one of 'their' songs ever since.

***

Her first experience of the US came not long after the birth of Princess Anne when she flew over the border during her 1951 tour of Canada, to visit President Harry Truman at the White House. Britain and the USA were fighting side by side yet again, this time in Korea. Truman was enchanted by his visitor, famously remarking: 'When I was a little boy, I read about a fairy princess – and there she is.' Washington turned out in force. At a single British Embassy reception, the Princess was required to shake 1,574 hands. It was just a foretaste.

Her next visit – as Queen – was of an entirely different magnitude. Britain was just recovering from the embarrassment of its Suez adventure. The bilateral relationship had suffered and it fell to the Royal Family to help the British government patch things up in the autumn of 1957, starting with a trip to mark the 350th anniversary of the first English colony at Jamestown. The pace was relentless. During a fifteen-hour visit to New York, the Queen managed to address the United Nations, attend a mayoral lunch for 1,500, an English Speaking Union dinner for 4,500 and a separate Commonwealth ball for 4,500. An estimated one million people turned out to welcome her to Washington DC, where the Queen got on famously with the Eisenhowers. The President had even laid on the celebrated Fred Waring and his band for the state banquet at the White House. Come the allotted moment, the Queen and the first lady simply carried on talking, engrossed in their conversation. The President eventually had to turn to his master of ceremonies, actor Ted Hartley, and tell him: 'Ted, please tell Mrs Eisenhower and Her Majesty to cut it short. We can't keep Fred Waring waiting.'

As well as the usual formalities, the Queen and the Duke paid their first visit to a supermarket. 'How nice you can bring your children along,' she told shoppers as she marvelled at the sight of a frozen-food section. One day was also set aside for some serious horse talk at the estate of the Anglophile philanthropist Paul Mellon, in the aptly named Upperville. The visit was an unqualified success and 'buried George III for good and all' according to the Prime Minister, Harold Macmillan.

It was in 1959 that the Queen first entertained a US president at home, when President Eisenhower spent two days with the monarch at Balmoral. Eisenhower found the experience so agreeable that he asked the Queen for 'her' scone recipe (though not her own, she duly transcribed it in her own hand). Two years later she welcomed President John F. Kennedy and his wife, Jackie, to dinner at Buckingham Palace, following the President's meeting with the Soviet leader, Nikita Khrushchev. The television series, *The Crown*, would portray a jealous Queen and a miserable first lady (the latter injecting drugs in order to get through the evening). Both storylines were invention. Jackie Kennedy and her sister came back for lunch the following year, though the Queen would never see John F. Kennedy again. His assassination would touch her deeply at a time when she was heavily pregnant with Prince Edward. Doctors advised her against attending the national memorial service at St Paul's Cathedral, so she held her own at Windsor instead and invited 400 US servicemen. She would take a close personal interest in the Kennedy memorial, erected nearby at Runnymede, and made a stirring speech at its inauguration, saluting a man who 'championed liberty in an age when its very foundations were being threatened on a universal scale'. Prince Philip held the hand of John Junior, the little boy who had moved the whole world by saluting his father's coffin at the funeral. Hence the added poignancy when that same four-year-old performed a respectful bow to the Queen.

Britain's decision to stay out of the Vietnam War meant that the paths of the Queen and President Lyndon B. Johnson never crossed. The President had little time for Prime Minister Harold Wilson, whom he called a 'creep' for his pacifism over Vietnam, but Johnson had been extremely keen to meet the Queen at the funeral of Sir Winston Churchill. In the end, bronchitis and strict orders from his doctors ruled out a trip to London.

Yet again it was the Queen who helped soothe any bilateral bruising when she invited Johnson's successor, Richard Nixon, to lunch with the family in 1969. 'Both my daughters follow you very closely,' the President joked with Prince Charles.

The moment was captured in the very first royal documentary, *Royal Family*, as was the arrival of the new American Ambassador, Walter Annenberg, to present his credentials. It would become a famous moment, after the Queen asked him how he was settling in. Overcome with nerves, the Ambassador dissolved into incoherent babbling about 'the discomfiture as a result of a need for elements of refurbishment and rehabilitation'. He was much mocked in the press as a result, though the Queen's Marshal of the Diplomatic Corps, Alistair Harrison who looks after royal relations with all the diplomatic missions, says it happens to the most distinguished envoys: 'It's a very colourful and potentially very enjoyable ceremony but it does happen that some ambassadors get quite nervous about it. It's important to know what you're going to say to Her Majesty. Be relaxed, be ready for quite a wide ranging conversation and don't worry if you make a mistake. Everybody does.'* At least Annenberg was spared the fate that befell one more recent arrival. 'I did have an ambassador whose mobile phone went off very loudly during the audience,' says Harrison. 'The Queen took it totally in her stride and, if anything, was slightly amused. The Ambassador was very embarrassed.' A fervent Anglophile, Annenberg has been remembered with gratitude by prime ministers ever since, having paid for the indoor swimming pool at Chequers.

It was at Chequers that the Queen met Nixon once again, when he dropped in for lunch during his brief stopover for talks with Edward Heath in 1971. Heath's preoccupation with Europe, to the exclusion of all else, was starting to worry Henry Kissinger at the State Department in Washington. It was the Royal Family who would keep the flame of the 'special relationship' aglow, with visits to the Nixon White House by the Duke of Edinburgh, Prince Charles and Princess Anne. Gerald Ford was in the White House by the time of the Queen's next presidential encounter, when she crossed the Atlantic for her sensational 1976 state visit.

* In recent years, the Queen has dispensed with some of the more arcane rituals for presenting credentials. Ambassadors are still driven to the Palace in a horse-drawn carriage, but these days they wear morning dress rather than evening dress. Nor are they expected to walk backwards out of the audience room. As the Marshal, Alistair Harrison, explains: 'There are two priceless vases on either side of the door. I always say: "The Queen would much rather see your back than see you back into those".' He himself must double-check the badge of office that he wears on a chain. One side shows an olive branch, the other a sword. 'I make sure that the olive branch is outwards which is the signal to the Queen that the ambassador comes in peace.'

***

Having 'buried' George III during her previous tour, the Queen would find that her ancestor was anything but forgotten this time as the USA marked its 200th birthday and the 1776 American Declaration of Independence. Despite the passage of time and all those familial bonds between the USA and the UK, it was an anniversary that had still required a degree of delicacy. After the idea of a royal visit had been suggested by President Nixon as far back as 1973, the Prime Minister's private secretary, Robert Armstrong, wrote to his opposite number at the Palace wondering 'whether it was right for The Queen to be associated with the celebration of a rebellion from the British Crown'.

By 1976, post-Watergate, there was a new President in the White House and a new Prime Minister in Downing Street. The Queen was delighted to take part in America's celebrations. Even so, the British side felt it was probably best to allow the USA to let off Independence Day steam before despatching the Queen to join the party. She would not be there for 4th July. 'Forgiveness can only go so far,' as a British Embassy spokesman explained to *The New York Times*. So plans were made for the Queen to sail in from Bermuda in the Royal Yacht on 6th July. Having endured a Force Nine gale, which laid low most of the royal party, though not the Queen herself, George III's great-great-great-great-granddaughter stepped ashore in Philadelphia, where the founding fathers had issued their world-changing statement of defiance. There she presented a 6.5-ton bicentennial bell cast by the same London foundry that had made the original Liberty Bell in Independence Hall, and went on to deliver a well-remembered speech. Bearing the unmistakeable imprimatur of her Private Secretary, Martin Charteris, it managed to paint the American Revolution as a triumph on both sides of the Atlantic.

'It seems to me that Independence Day should be celebrated as much in Britain as in America,' she told thousands of Pennsylvanians. 'Not in rejoicing at the separation of the American colonies from the British Crown but in sincere gratitude to the Founding Fathers of this great Republic for having taught Britain a very valuable lesson. We lost the American colonies because we lacked that statesmanship "to know the right time, and the manner of yielding what is impossible to keep".' Placing the blame not on her ancestor, but firmly on his quarrelsome ministers, she went on: 'We learnt to respect the right of others to govern themselves in their own ways. Without that great act in the cause of liberty, performed in Independence Hall two hundred years ago, we could never have transformed an Empire into a Commonwealth!' It was, she said, the beginning of one of history's great partnerships, through war and peace: 'Together, as friends and allies, we can face the uncertainties of the future, and this is something for which we in Britain can also celebrate the Fourth of July.'

For this state visit, the Queen would be accompanied by her new Foreign Secretary, Anthony Crosland, and his American-born journalist wife. She wrote a famous account of the tour, in which she recalled the Queen's advice on how to get through arduous tours like these. 'One plants one's feet like this,' the Queen told her. 'Always keep them parallel. Make sure your weight is evenly distributed. That's all there is to it.'

The advice would be invaluable, with a punishing itinerary in 100-degree heat up the eastern seaboard of the USA. At the White House, President Gerald Ford welcomed the Queen to a state banquet for more than 200 guests – including Hollywood stars Cary Grant, Telly Savalas and Merle Oberon, plus corporate A-listers such as J. Willard Marriott of the Marriott Corporation and Henry Heinz II. Ford did his best to emphasise the positive side of Britain's colonial exploits on this side of the Atlantic. 'Nearly four centuries ago, the British came to a wilderness and built a new civilisation on British custom, British fortitude, British law and British government,' he told the Queen. Thereafter, the United States 'established a nation that adapted the best of British traditions to the American climate and to the American character'.

The Queen quoted George III's famous words about being the last man to want separation but the first to seek the 'friendship of the United States as an independent power'. She also spoke of how the British Empire had been transformed into the Commonwealth 'with imagination and good will'. There was some amusement when the after-dinner cabaret, pop duo The Captain & Tennille, launched into their moderately risqué hit 'Muskrat Love'. That turned to considerable un-amusement when the President invited the Queen to dance. The band chose that very moment to strike up a different tune: 'The Lady Is a Tramp'. The press, however, were thrilled.

The royal couple arrived by Royal Yacht in New York, where the Queen went shopping at Bloomingdale's. *Britannia*'s future captain,

Anthony Morrow, remembers the drama and attention: 'It was massive – floodlights and flags. We did a Sunset ceremony and an opera singer on board broke into the national anthems as they were being played. It was wonderful.'

There would be a state banquet for the Fords on board, in Rhode Island, during which US security officials insisted that a special telephone had to be installed to ensure permanent communication with the President. When the Chief Petty Officer attempted to make a call from the ship, he was surprised to hear a mysterious voice saying: 'We are never off this line.' There would also be a small but deeply symbolic tweaking of protocol, in honour of the USA. Though Royal Navy rules did not normally permit the piping aboard of a non-royal dignitary dressed in plain clothes, the Queen insisted that an exception should be made for President Ford.

The royal party sailed on to Boston and thence crossed the border to Montreal in time to open the 1976 Olympics. Britain may have been an international laughing stock. One month before, the pound had reached a new low against the dollar and two months later, the Chancellor of the Exchequer would go on bended knee to the International Monetary Fund in search of a bail-out. For a jaded British public, the Queen's North American tour at least provided a comforting sense that the country still carried some sort of clout.

In her Christmas broadcast, the Queen returned to the theme of reconciliation embraced so vividly on her US tour. 'Who would have thought, 200 years ago, that a descendant of King George III could have taken part in these celebrations?' she asked. 'The United States was born in bitter conflict with Britain but we didn't remain enemies for long. From our reconciliation came incalculable benefits to mankind and a partnership which, together with many countries of the Commonwealth, was proved in two world wars and ensured that the light of liberty was not extinguished.'

The visit marked the revival of a relationship that would reach new heights during the Ronald Reagan years.

***

The next President to be her guest in Britain was Jimmy Carter. She had met him during the bicentenary but his trip to London in 1977, for a G7 summit and a NATO meeting, was memorable for two reasons. First, he surprised his hosts by announcing that it was the first time he had ever set foot outside the USA. Second, he became a little over-familiar with the Queen Mother. As William Shawcross notes in her official biography, the Queen Mother hated being told that she reminded people of their own mothers. Having informed her that she did, indeed, remind him of his own mother – 'Miz Lillian' – Carter kissed the Queen Mother on the lips. As she later remarked, no one had done that since the death of George VI. 'I took a sharp step backwards,' she recalled, 'not far enough.'

If Carter was the most awkward presidential visitor to the Palace, he would be succeeded by perhaps the most charming. Under Ronald Reagan, the transatlantic relationship would be as 'special' as it had been at any stage since D-Day. Not only would he get on famously with the occupants of both Downing Street and Buckingham Palace, but he was also extremely comfortable on a horse, a skill that would lead to one of the most celebrated photographs of the Queen's reign.

It was the Prince of Wales who first got to know the Reagans, when on shore leave while serving in the Royal Navy. He was entertained by Nancy Reagan in both California and Washington. She made such an impression on the Heir to the Throne that he insisted she come to his wedding in 1981. It was no mere diplomatic invitation. At the family party afterwards, the first lady joined Princess Grace of Monaco at the Queen's table.

The following year, when Britain embarked on that bold and precarious mission to the other end of the world to liberate the Falkland Islands, Reagan would be a staunch ally. Just like the UK's Commonwealth allies, America came down firmly on Britain's side. For the Queen, as both a proud head of the Armed Forces and the mother of a serving Royal Navy officer,* America's support was deeply felt. So both the Queen and her Prime Minister were keen to make a great fuss of Reagan when they invited him to Britain during his European tour of June 1982. Reagan was trying to juggle a G7 summit in France with state visits to Italy and Germany, plus an

* Prince Andrew sailed to the South Atlantic in HMS *Invincible*. He was on deck when it came under attack from an Exocet missile. Serving with 802 Naval Air Squadron, his missions included anti-submarine work, anti-surface warfare, inter-ship delivery, search and rescue and casualty evacuation. 'I definitely went there a boy and came back a man,' he said later.

audience with the Pope. His staff did not want the elaborate hoopla of a state visit to Britain as well.

So it was agreed that the Reagans would come to Windsor Castle for a semi-private stay – and a spot of riding – with the Queen, in between more formal visits on the continent. They arrived by helicopter in time for a small black-tie dinner with the Royal Family on the first night. The next morning, the world's press had arrived for a prearranged photo opportunity, with the two heads of state on horseback. Reagan enjoyed some cheerful banter with the photographers. 'If you stand still, I'll take it over the top,' he yelled astride Centennial, one of the Queen's stallions. The Queen, who had no wish for a press conference, set off on Burmese, her Canadian mare, with Reagan in hot pursuit, followed by teams of bodyguards on both four legs and four wheels. It was a proper ride, lasting a good hour and covering much of the park. It included a stop to talk to the farmworkers responsible for the two royal dairy herds, precisely the sort of encounter enjoyed by George III – 'Farmer George' – when he rode out there each day two centuries before.

The King who lost America would be a theme of the speeches that followed later in the day. Reagan became the first US President to address both Houses of Parliament. The White House had wanted him to address MPs and peers in Westminster Hall, the great hammer-beamed medieval chamber where deceased monarchs lie in state. However, use of the hall would require cross-party support, and the Labour leader, Michael Foot, would not agree. Margaret Thatcher duly arranged for the Royal Gallery to be used, but Reagan's officials told the British that the deal was off. It fell to the British Ambassador, Sir Nico Henderson, to calm things down by pointing out that both the French and Soviet leaders had spoken in the same place and 'it would look petty' for the President to refuse.

It was a tour de force by the former Hollywood actor with the common touch. Reagan joked that when he had dined beneath a portrait of George III at the British Embassy in Washington, Mrs Thatcher had urged him to let 'bygones be bygones'. His visit to Europe, he said, was very simple: to combat totalitarianism. In a foretaste of perhaps his most famous quote,* he declared: 'From here I will go to Berlin, where

* Visiting West Berlin in June 1987, Reagan declared: 'Mr Gorbachev, tear down this wall'. It fell in November 1989.

there stands a grim symbol of power untamed. The Berlin Wall, that dreadful gray gash across the city.' He was applauded as he linked liberation struggles through history to the battle for the Falklands and Britain's Blitz spirit during the war. Reagan particularly enjoyed retelling the story of the London woman pulled from the wreckage of her own home after an air raid: 'The rescuers found a bottle of brandy. And since she was barely conscious, one of the workers pulled the cork to give her a taste of it. She came around immediately and said, "Here now – put it back. That's for emergencies".'

He was on equally gregarious form later as 158 guests gathered for dinner in St George's Hall, Windsor. Here, the Queen had laid on exactly the same display of priceless china, crystal and silver gilt that she would produce for a state visit, even though this did not technically qualify as one. She, too, had a George III joke, as she recalled the warmth of the reception she had received during the bicentenary: 'Had King George III been able to foresee the long-term consequences of his actions, he might not have felt so grieved about the loss of his colonies.'

She saluted Reagan's 'honesty, patience, and skill' as both an ally and intermediary. He, in turn, talked of royal 'tradition and renewal', and his excitement at an imminent royal arrival. The most obvious absentee from the dinner was just about to give birth to Prince William. 'We in America share your excitement about the impending birth of a child to the Prince and the Princess of Wales,' said Reagan. 'We pray that God will continue to bless your family with health, happiness, and wisdom.' The two heads of state had not merely hit it off. This was a friendship that would endure long after Reagan had done the one thing the Queen would not do – retire.

Following that hugely successful Windsor visit by the Reagans in 1982, the Queen made a return trip to the USA early in 1983, fulfilling a lifetime's ambition to tour the West Coast. Since the President was a former governor of California, she was in good hands. Not wanting to mire the trip in extra layers of protocol and the full Washington rigmarole, the two governments never billed this as a 'state visit', but as a 'royal visit', bolting it on to a tour of Mexico that took place immediately beforehand. That way, the Royal Yacht was already perfectly positioned on the Pacific coast.

As with her previous visit, the tour began with atrocious weather, so much so that the Queen had to be transported around San Diego in a US Navy bus. In Hollywood, Ronald Reagan laid on a star-packed lunch for 500. The entertainment included Frank Sinatra, Bob Hope and Perry Como, but the arrangements left some of the local talent rather peeved. 'Ronald Reagan was asked who should be at the top table,' recalls Sir Brian Fall, then serving as Private Secretary to the British Foreign Secretary, Francis Pym. 'Should it be actor friends or political friends? He couldn't sort it out so he said: "Why don't we pack it out with Brits in Hollywood?" '

The result was a top table full of British-born stars like Julie Andrews and Dudley Moore. For some status-obsessed Hollywood egos, it was all too much. The Palace press office, which had played no part in the planning, was left fending off accusations that the Queen was only interested in sitting with fellow Brits. 'I was on the table next door with Julie Andrews's husband,*' Sir Brian recalls. 'He was so pissed off at not being on the right table that he walked off and left a gap.' Others, like Jack Valenti, President of the Motion Picture Association, were less prickly. 'Valenti thought he was big enough to host his own table,' says Sir Brian.

The dreadful weather continued, to the point that even the Queen's journey from the Yacht's berth at Long Beach to the nearest airport was in doubt. At the last minute, an off-duty (unshaven) school bus driver and his (unwashed) vehicle were commandeered to get the royal party to the airport in time to fly to Santa Barbara. They were due for lunch at the Reagans' ranch. On landing, more heavy-duty off-road vehicles were needed to get them up the hill, where fog and rain precluded the two things the Queen had most been looking forward to: the view and an excursion with the President on horseback. She did her best to boost the morale of some very disappointed hosts. 'I've never seen such rain, never. Our ranch was way up at the top of a hill up these windy roads; and we were sure the Queen wouldn't come,' Nancy Reagan told William Shawcross. 'When they got there, we were full of apologies; she kept saying "No, this is an adventure! This is an adventure!" '

* Blake Edwards, director of *Breakfast at Tiffany's* and *10*.

The Reagans had prepared an intimate Tex-Mex lunch with tacos and refried beans (according to Sally Bedell Smith, the Queen later said how much she had enjoyed the 'used beans'). Sir Brian Fall says that while the Queen had been hoping for some interesting conversation about politics, the President turned out to be very much in ranch mode. 'Here she was having her tête-à-tête with the leader of the Western world. And yet he refused to talk politics. It was all about being on the farm and chopping wood! I think she'd have enjoyed some serious politics.'

Back in Long Beach, the first lady dined with the royal couple aboard *Britannia* and stayed the night on board. It was another highly unusual and personal touch, a reminder of the way in which tours of the USA might often depart from the usual script.

The next stop was San Francisco, though there was a further change of plan. 'The idea was for *Britannia* to chunter up and go through the Golden Gate Bridge but the weather was so foul, she couldn't get there,' says Sir Brian. 'I'm flying to San Francisco,' the Queen told her officials. 'I'm not going on this boat.'

The Reagans put Air Force Two at the Queen's disposal instead. Staff recall her excitedly pressing her face against the aircraft's window to enjoy an aerial view of the Golden Gate Bridge. Now there was a fresh problem. Where to stay? There was no Yacht in San Francisco and there was an urgent need to find accommodation for a monarch, a consort and both royal and presidential entourages. In no time, the combined power of the White House, the Palace and the personal contacts of the former state governor soon sorted things out. The Queen and the Duke were installed in the Presidential Suite at the St Francis Hotel. Nancy Reagan even arranged for works of art from local museums to be rounded up and hung on the walls. 'The next question was: where to go for dinner?' says Sir Brian. The President's well-connected deputy chief of staff came to the rescue. 'Mike Deaver managed to empty Trader Vic's so we went there.' For the Queen, who had not eaten in a restaurant for fifteen years, it was a novel experience, right down to being given a fortune cookie at the end (she read the message and then put it in her handbag).

Britannia finally caught up and, two days later, the Queen and the Duke organised a return dinner for the President on board. It also happened to be the Reagans' thirty-first wedding anniversary. 'They were so nice, so sweet and the crew made us a huge anniversary card and a cake,' the former first lady recalled. 'They toasted us and after all of this, Ronnie got up and said: "I know I promised Nancy everything in the world when we got married but I don't know how I can top this." And then after dinner, I sang: "Our love is here to stay".'

Not since the war had the 'special relationship' been quite this tender, though it would be tested seven months later, following that American invasion of one of the Queen's realms, Grenada, without any word of warning to the head of state.

The Queen's affection for America, and for her many friends there, was such that she returned for private tours of ranches and studs in 1984, 1986 and 1989. It was during her 1984 tour – while visiting her mare, Round Tower, then stabled at the Kentucky ranch of Will and Sarah Farish – that she received news of the attempted assassination of Margaret Thatcher at the Conservative Party conference in Brighton.

***

Following the first Gulf War of 1990, and Britain's support for the US-led liberation of Kuwait, however, it was time for another very public journey across the Atlantic. George H. W. Bush was now in the White House and, with his wife Barbara, would become firm royal friends. Of all the US presidents, Bush was closest to the Queen in age. Like her (and Prince Philip), he had served in the Second World War. At one point the youngest aviator in the US Navy, he was shot down over the Pacific in 1944, but went on to complete fifty-eight combat missions. Two years in to his administration, he had invited the Queen to pay a state visit and to enjoy a very great accolade. She would be the first British monarch in history to address a joint session of Congress. By now, much of the US media was more interested in the cracks in the royal fairytale that were starting to filter through from the British press, although it would be another two years before the Queen's '*annus horribilis*'. The *Washington Post* heralded the visit with a less-than-reverential piece that would have been unthinkable during her previous state visit. It began: 'The Queen's a frump, Chuck's a chump, Fergie's plump and her Dad's a cad. Anne's spouse is a louse, her brother's a fop, and Di's fancy marriage is clearly a flop.'

Yet once the Queen had landed on US soil, America soon rediscovered its appetite for royal razzmatazz. There was an inauspicious start, following President Bush's formal welcome on the White House lawn. He stepped aside from the lectern and invited the Queen to respond. She began with a joke of sorts – 'It is fifteen years since our last visit to Washington, when, with a gallant disregard for history, we shared wholeheartedly in the celebrations of the 200th anniversary of the founding of this great nation.' Although her audience laughed at the joke, the problem was that no one could see her. The British Ambassador at the time, Sir Antony Acland, says it was a simple oversight: 'After his speech of welcome President Bush, who wasn't very well at the time, was supposed to press a pedal which lifted the platform on which the Queen was going to speak. He forgot to do it. And the Queen being half his size, was mostly invisible to a lot of people.' The moment was encapsulated in the words of NBC's Jim Miklaszeski: 'She's gone! All I got is a talking hat!' To this day, Palace officials and diplomats still refer to the state visit as 'the talking hat tour'.

Two days later, 16th May 1991, the Queen came to make her address to Congress. As Acland reported back to London, 'the atmosphere in the Chamber was one of genuine and unusually well-behaved anticipation'. They were not to be disappointed. 'Her Private Secretary and I said it would be excellent if she could start her speech with a very simple joke,' says Acland. 'She was somewhat reluctant to do this. She said she wasn't in the habit of making jokes in her speeches. So I didn't know if she was going to do it but she came in and looked around and smiled and said: "I do hope you can see me today". And she got a standing ovation.'

Dressed in pale orange, the Queen went on to receive several standing ovations from a packed chamber, during what would be the speech of the tour. 'Some people believe that power grows from the barrel of a gun,' she said. 'So it can, but history shows that it never grows well nor for very long. Force, in the end, is sterile. We have gone a better way: our societies rest on mutual agreement, on contract and on consensus.'

The White House staff were taking no chances with the arrangements for this state banquet. The US Marines Band played the Queen into the State Dining Room to the reassuringly familiar sounds of William Walton. Col. John Bourgeois was under strict orders not to repeat the error of 1976. Asked if he would be playing 'The Lady Is a Tramp', he replied: 'It's long been removed from the repertoire.' Instead of a pop duo, the after-dinner entertainment was the soprano, Jessye Norman. Following the Maine lobster and roast lamb, President Bush saluted a relationship 'which has never been more special' and the Queen's resilience. 'Rain or shine, your long walks have left even the Secret Service agents panting away,' he told her. 'I'm glad that my fibrillating heart was not taxed by a competitive walk-off today.' The Queen praised the President for his 'quiet courage' during the Gulf War – 'what Thoreau described as "three-o'clock-in-the-morning courage",' she said – and recalled her father's visit to President Roosevelt: 'No wonder I cannot feel a stranger here. The British have never felt America to be a foreign land.'

During her stay in Washington, the Queen also had her first encounter with the President's son, George W. Bush, then in charge of the Texas Rangers baseball team. He had been forewarned by his mother not to talk to the Queen, as he could be 'mercurial'. The Queen herself was rather intrigued, particularly since he had cowboy boots etched with the words 'God Save the Queen'. At one point she asked him if he was the black sheep of the family. 'I guess so,' replied Bush Junior. 'All families have them,' observed the Queen. 'Who's yours?' Bush Junior replied, at which point the first lady intervened with a cry of 'Don't answer that!'

A highlight of the Washington leg occurred during the Queen's visit to a new housing project. She was due to visit the home of Alice Frazier, sixty-seven, an African American grandmother of considerably greater physical stature than the Queen. The visit became world news when Alice engulfed her in a bear hug, before offering her chicken wings, iced tea and potato salad. 'They said I wasn't supposed to do it but I just couldn't stop myself,' she told reporters. 'Shoot, she's a woman just like I am. If she didn't have that crown on, she'd be just like me.' Ms Frazier had been particularly excited, she explained, because her fifteen-year-old granddaughter, Laverne, had just made her a great-grandmother for the third time. 'That's tremendous to have three great-grandchildren,' the Queen said brightly, by way of congratulation. Though the media were desperate to paint the bear hug as a great faux pas, the Palace and the Foreign Office were not worried. 'It's not something that often happens but the

Queen took it in good spirit,' says Sir Antony Acland. 'One didn't want to make a fuss about it or make it a breach of protocol.'

After four days in Washington, the Queen climbed back aboard Concorde for the next leg of the tour, her mission accomplished in the capital. As the *New York Times* put it, the Queen had 'created a fuss in Washington this week that no other national leader could match, not even Mr Gorbachev at the height of Gorbomania'.

The visit moved on to Florida, a state which the Queen had never visited before. The Royal Yacht had sailed in to meet her in Miami, though a diplomatic incident nearly curtailed the entire programme. As *Britannia*'s crew waited for the royal party to arrive, they flushed through all the royal baths and heads (ship's lavatories) as a precaution. Whereupon *Britannia*'s captain, Rear Admiral Robert Woodard, suddenly had a furious official from the Miami port authority thumping on his door. 'He said we had polluted his harbour, that we were fined ten thousand dollars and that we had to leave in two hours,' he recalls. The fact that *Britannia* was due to host a state banquet a few hours later made no difference whatsoever. Rules were rules. It would require the intervention of the White House to allow *Britannia* to remain alongside.

In Miami, the press heard Uriah Goldfinger, a twelve-year-old pupil at Coconut Grove Elementary School, ask the royal guest how long she had been Queen. 'Too long,' she replied. 'Wait and read about it in your history book.' It prompted some commentators to ask whether Britain was asking too much of a grandmother who had just turned sixty-five. Even then, a year before the fortieth anniversary of her accession to the Throne, there was the same retirement speculation that would surface at subsequent key stages of her life – and promptly vanish, when it became quite clear that she had no intention of retiring. Later on, the Queen was reunited with two ex-heads of state now comfortably into their own retirement, and showing a few signs of it, too. The Queen had invited the hosts of both her previous state visits, the Reagans and the Fords, to her banquet in the Royal Yacht. Ronald Reagan, delighted to be back on board, had an animated chat with the Queen about the state of the economy, much of it captured by film-maker Edward Mirzoeff, making an award-winning BBC documentary to mark the fortieth anniversary of her accession. Both the Queen and Reagan were concerned about the spiralling cost of spending – 'the next generation are going to have a very difficult time,' she observed – but viewers would be captivated by Reagan's preoccupation with finding decaffeinated coffee. This, it transpires, had become something of an obsession. Sir Robert Woodard remembers Reagan's confusion as the port came round after dinner. 'Decaf, Ma'am?' he asked. 'That'll come later,' she replied, nodding at the port. 'Just pass it on.' Much to the Queen's amusement, the next evening one of the ship's stewards produced a decanter labelled 'Decaffeinated Port'.

The main purpose of the Florida leg was to visit the Tampa headquarters of General 'Stormin' Norman' Schwarzkopf, the architect of the Gulf War victory, who was to receive an honorary knighthood. Travelling by sea over the weekend also gave the Queen a bit of breathing space. 'The plan was to go round the bottom of Florida and pull in to Tampa so she could knight Stormin' Norman,' says Woodard. What should have been a relaxing weekend became rather dramatic. At Loggerhead Key, *Britannia* dropped anchor for a picnic, with the Duke of Edinburgh in charge. 'He very much liked organising the barbecue and didn't thank you if you tried to help,' says Sir Antony Acland. 'It was his act and it was a mistake to interfere.' While the Duke was cooking, Woodard received a call from Britain. East Midlands Police had just received a warning that a bomb had been planted four feet below *Britannia*'s waterline and would explode within an hour. Woodard quietly asked his senior officer to carry out the standard checking procedure with a minimum of fuss. The Queen, sensing that something was up, asked for an explanation. Woodard hid nothing from her and found her as stoical as ever. 'She said it was hard to know when to take these things seriously,' he recalls. Besides, as he pointed out to the Queen, *Britannia* was currently anchored just four feet above the seabed anyway. 'If it had gone off, we'd just have sat there like a rather grand hotel.' The picnic continued without a murmur.

In Tampa, the Queen duly invested General Schwarzkopf with his knighthood and invited him on a tour of the Yacht. What impressed him most was not the state apartments, but the engine room. At first he assumed that all the gleaming boilers and pipework must be some sort of museum display and asked to see the 'real' engine room. On being told that he was already in it, he was dumbfounded. 'You could eat your lunch off that,' he told Woodard. 'I'd rather you didn't,' the Rear Admiral replied. 'It would make rather a mess.'

The official tour concluded with a tour of Texas, including a visit to the Johnson Space Center and Mission Control, Houston. The Queen was particularly keen to ask astronaut Mike Foale why certain food would not float in space – surface tension, came the answer – while Prince Philip put on space gloves to handle moving objects in a vacuum. This final leg of the tour included a trip to the Alamo in San Antonio and a visit to the Antioch Baptist Church in downtown Houston. Even the Queen's Private Secretary, Sir Robert Fellowes, was caught up in the gospel-singing swing of things, according to the Ambassador. In his despatch to the FCO, Sir Antony noted that one of the highlights of the three days in Texas had been 'the sight of the Queen's Private Secretary jabbing his finger in the air and crying "Amen" and "awl rayte".'

For the locals, the high point was the Queen's speech on the lawn of the state Capitol in Austin. 'No state commands such fierce pride and loyalty,' the Queen told her hosts. 'Lesser mortals are pitied for their misfortune in not being born Texans.' This prompted euphoric applause from the thousands who had waited for hours in scorching sunshine to see the monarch. As *USA Today* put it: 'Texas was taking to the Queen like ticks to a hound dog'. The *Chicago Tribune* observed that the Lone Star State had 'donned a ten-gallon tiara'.

The calibre of the speeches – and the warmth with which they were received – was a notable feature of this tour. No one was calling the Queen a 'frump' any more. Nor did anyone begrudge her four days of private horse-watching in Kentucky, ahead of her return to Britain.

***

Relations between London and Washington cooled to a business-like level during the Clinton years, largely because of politics. The fact that John Major's Conservatives had provided active support for George H. W. Bush's 1992 election campaign angered Clinton. There would be heated disagreements over the Western response to war in Bosnia, and Major stopped taking Clinton's calls after the USA granted a visa to Sinn Fein leader Gerry Adams in 1994. There would be no state visit in either direction in that sort of climate. In the same year, however, the Queen fulfilled her now-familiar role as keeper of the 'special relationship'. Clinton might not have had the full royal treatment at Windsor or Buckingham Palace, but he would get it elsewhere. The fiftieth anniversary of D-Day was looming. There would be major events in Britain ahead of the 6th June commemorations, followed by a spectacular re-invasion of Normandy. The leaders of all the Allied nations would board the Royal Yacht at Portsmouth for the day, review a fleet of international warships and then sail for France, accompanied by ocean liners full of veterans. Only one ally, however, would be invited to stay overnight in *Britannia*. Bill and Hillary Clinton, who had just flown in from commemorations at Second World War battlefields in Italy, were given cabins nine and eleven, the best suite apart from the Queen's. A presidential bodyguard took up position at the door and refused to let anyone inside, including the steward bringing the Clintons' morning coffee.

The commemorations began with a banquet for the leaders at Portsmouth Guildhall on the night of 4th June. As John Major would recall, the Queen averted an awkward situation when she was shown the seating plan. The Foreign Office had followed protocol by seating the Queen next to the King of Norway and Prince Bernhard of the Netherlands, while the presidents of France and the USA were to be placed some way down the table. Since D-Day involved the Americans, British and Canadians liberating France, it would be very odd to put the Queen of Britain and Canada at the head of the table and the presidents of America and France somewhere else. The Queen changed the placement. 'Of course, people will expect President Clinton and President Mitterrand to sit beside me,' she told her Private Secretary, 'and, in any event, I see my cousins all the time.'

Clinton would later recall the 'clever manner in which she discussed public issues, probing me for information and insights without venturing too far into her own political views'. He was up early the following day for his exercise routine. No one could fail to spot him. 'He put on these DayGlo neoprene things and asked me where he could find a two kilometre run,' says Sir Robert Woodard, *Britannia*'s captain. 'I said: "Mr President, run round the dockyard because if you run outside into Portsmouth, you'll be swamped." He set off and didn't really run anywhere. He stopped to talk to every dock worker, every crane driver. He came back and the whole Yacht came to attention for the president in his strange clinging garb.' The crew would remain at attention for some time.

'He walked half way across the gangway and stopped,' laughs Woodard. 'He did his post-running press-ups and hip jerks for quite literally five minutes with the whole Yacht standing to attention. Then he went down and was politely late for breakfast.'

Only a handful of senior members of the Royal Household were at the breakfast table, along with the Duke of Edinburgh. One recalls the extraordinary moment when Clinton began to describe his visit to Italy the previous day: 'He was talking about visiting the US graves at Anzio and suddenly he burst into tears – which was unexpected.'

There would be many emotional moments during the course of one of the great days in *Britannia*'s history. With crowds packing every yard of shoreline and the sides of countless ships out in the Solent, the world leaders were overwhelmed. Poland's tearful President, Lech Walesa, was left speechless, raising clasped hands aloft to the crowds. Surveying the scene, Clinton admitted that what stuck in his mind were the words of a predecessor. 'The one thing that encapsulates it all for me,' he said, 'is Eisenhower's phrase that D-Day represented the fury of an aroused democracy.'

American national pride, understandably, dictated that he could not be seen to re-invade France in the Queen's Yacht. He and the first lady had to transfer to a launch that would carry them to an adjacent American warship. They would arrive in France aboard the aircraft carrier *George Washington*, then the world's largest warship. Jumping off *Britannia* onto a ship's launch for the transfer several miles out in a choppy English Channel was not for the faint-hearted. 'Transfers at sea can be rather amusing,' remarked the Princess Royal as the Queen waved off her American guests. Fortunately for UK–US relations, there was nothing amusing about this one.

***

It would be George W. Bush who became the first US President to pay a full state visit to the United Kingdom when he arrived with his wife, Laura, in 2003. By now, two seismic events had intervened. On a personal level, the Royal Family had been through the maelstrom of the Nineties, culminating in the death of Diana, Princess of Wales in 1997. There were few places where Diana's star had shone brighter than in the USA. And four years later, the US endured the worst terrorist attack in its history when nearly 3,000 people were killed in four co-ordinated attacks on American soil involving hijacked airliners. Though the vast majority of the dead were US citizens, 371 of them were from abroad, sixty-seven of them British. No foreign nation lost more. The events of 11th September 2001 had drawn Britain and America as close together as they had been at any time during the Queen's reign. Tony Blair had been the first world leader to arrive in Washington after the attacks, to show solidarity with Britain's wounded ally. 'Tony rose to the occasion,' says the then Foreign Secretary, Jack Straw. 'Bush required a lot of emotional support. Anybody would in that situation and he received it from Tony.'

The television images of the attacks on the twin towers of New York's World Trade Center shocked the Queen as she watched at Balmoral. Years later, when visiting Ground Zero, she would tell the widow of a New York fire chief: 'I don't think I've ever seen anything in my life as bad as that.'

The morning after the attacks, she ordered the Union flag on Buckingham Palace to be lowered to half-mast and asked the band to play the 'Star-Spangled Banner' during Changing the Guard. For grieving expatriate Americans, as well as tourists marooned in London by the sudden ban on all aircraft movements, it was both comforting and profoundly moving. Nor were US citizens the only ones weeping openly in front of the Palace.

As Bill Clinton told William Shawcross later: 'I knew her well enough to know that she thought of it herself. It took my breath away. It was wonderful. It was something I will never forget for as long as I live.' He would be equally moved by her letter to the American people which was read out by the British Ambassador, Sir Christopher Meyer, at a New York memorial service for the Britons killed in the attacks. It included a line that is destined to go down in history as one of the Queen's most-quoted sayings: 'Grief is the price we pay for love.' 'It was a perfectly fine letter until that stunning sentence,' Bill Clinton said later. 'I don't know how to explain the impact it had on the audience. It was so wise and so true that it somehow made people feel better. It was a healing statement. It was just so pointed and eloquent.'

Against this emotional backdrop, the 2003 state visit of George W. Bush was always going to be a congenial affair, regardless of the (smaller-than-expected) anti-war protests outside the Palace. There would be no carriage procession, though that was nothing to do with the protestors. US security officials were never going to allow any president to travel through a major capital city in a horse-drawn vehicle made of wood and leather. Security imperatives led to a somewhat comical welcome. The Bushes, who had already arrived the night before, drove in the US presidential limousine from one side of the Palace to the other for the official ceremony. The visitors were bowled over by the hospitality. Unlike the dreadful Ceausescus, who had been paranoid about anyone touching their clothes, the Secretary of State, General Colin Powell, was delighted by the royal treatment. 'I went to see Colin Powell at the Palace,' says Jack Straw, 'and he was joking how he was getting even better service than when he was a senior officer in the Army having his bags unpacked and clothes hung up.'

That evening, as she served halibut, chicken and praline ice cream at her state banquet, the Queen deployed the S-word in her state-banquet speech. Noting that it had been Winston Churchill who had coined the term 'special relationship', she went on: 'Despite occasional criticism of the term, I believe it admirably describes our friendship. Like all special friends, we can talk frankly and we can disagree from time to time – even sometimes fall out over a particular issue. But the depth and breadth of our partnership means that disputes can be quickly overcome and forgiven.'

The following night, Bush arranged a return dinner at the US Ambassador's residence, Winfield House, with tortillas, lamb and fudge brownies. Lord Lloyd Webber,* no less, had agreed to provide the musical entertainment. It was an intimate affair for around sixty guests, says Jack Straw, adding that his wife, Alice, found herself

* The creator of Evita, Jesus Christ Superstar and Cats, among many other theatrical hits, London-born Andrew Lloyd Webber has been described by Forbes magazine as 'the most successful composer of musicals in history'.

having one of those 'I'm sure we've met before' conversations with a strangely familiar guest. 'I'm Michael Caine,' he replied.

Looking back on the first US state visit, Straw says it was 'brilliant', not least because the visitor was 'flattered and pleased' but also extremely relaxed. 'Bush had less of an ego than most leaders I encountered,' he says. 'He didn't feel the need for it.'

George W. Bush was determined to reciprocate the gesture before the end of his second presidential term. Half a century after her first state visit to the USA, the Queen was on her way back and heading for Richmond, Virginia. It would be a subdued start, however. A month earlier, the state had suffered the worst campus shooting in US history, the killing of 32 students at Virginia Tech University. The Queen had made the same journey during her 1957 tour when she had attended that 350th anniversary of the foundation of the English colony of Jamestown. Now she was heading back for the 400th. There would be very few other guests who attended both. 'We decided to work it around the fiftieth anniversary of her first state visit which was a wonderful peg,' says Sir David Manning, the British Ambassador to Washington, who would go on to become a senior adviser to Prince William and Prince Harry. 'When we had a party at the Embassy with pictures of her with so many former Presidents, Americans were amazed. You saw the images of this very glamorous young woman fifty years earlier. She's living history and there aren't many people on the planet like that.'

Her arrival in Richmond, Virginia was something of a comedy of errors. The wrong stairs were wheeled out to her chartered British Airways flight and the red carpet was in the wrong place. Huge crowds – boosted by the governor's declaration of a public holiday – waited in the rain to see her arrival at the state Capitol, where her speech was relayed on loudspeakers. The Queen spoke of the way good friends can disagree from time to time, 'safe in the knowledge that the bonds that draw us together are far stronger than any temporary differences of opinion. The people of the United Kingdom have such a relationship with the people of this great nation.' It was a tacit acknowledgement that Britain's support for the US-led war in Iraq remained as contentious as ever in the United Kingdom – not that it would make any difference to the strength of the transatlantic bond. 'It is one of the most durable international collaborations anywhere in the world at any time in history,' she declared, 'a friendship for which I certainly in my lifetime have had good cause to be thankful.'

The scene she found in Jamestown had changed dramatically since her previous visit, not least because of the discovery of the original settlers' fort in a different place. In Williamsburg, she visited pre-revolutionary William and Mary College, the second-oldest university in the USA, founded by her Stuart forebears. In recognition of the Queen's eighty-one years – she was about to overtake Queen Victoria as the longest-lived monarch in British history – the schedule was very different from previous tours. Ten years had passed since the decommissioning of *Britannia*, so there would be no unwinding at sea. Before heading for Washington and the main part of the tour, the Queen returned to her favourite stomping ground in the bluegrass state of Kentucky. It was not entirely accidental that the visit should coincide with the Kentucky Derby. Among those in the crowd was local resident Matthew Barzun, who would go on to become US Ambassador to Britain under a later administration. It was the first time he had seen her with his own eyes, although the Queen's presence had not been publicised, since it was a private visit. 'It was so neat,' he remembers. 'She was coming through the hallway, like normal people but with state police. Nothing special. And then people were saying: "Oh my gosh! Look who's here." It was lovely when the word got out to see 150,000 Americans atwitter with her presence.' It was also the Queen's first Trump encounter, though not with the future President. Among those on her VIP balcony was Ivana Trump, ex-wife of the future premier.

Though the White House has welcomed almost every international leader of any significance in living memory, there was still a palpable buzz about the place as staff prepared for the monarch the following week. Admiral Steve Rochon, the Chief Usher of the White House, had all his household staff chanting a new mantra: 'Pristine for the Queen!' He had decreed that on the night of the state banquet, even the White House electrician would have to be in white tie. 'It's not just another head of state. There are not many queens left in this world,' the Admiral explained to a BBC documentary crew. 'She's always been viewed as very special to this country. For God's sake

– that's royalty!' After a distinguished career in the US Coast Guard, Rochon had suddenly become an expert in gardening. 'I lose sleep over the flowers,' he admitted. 'One of my biggest concerns is the wisteria that drape the south portico. I'm hoping we don't get a strong wind that will blow those beautiful flowers away.'

On the eve of their formal welcome at the White House, the Queen and the Duke made a low-key arrival in Washington. Foreign Secretary (now Dame) Margaret Beckett, the minister in attendance for the state visit, remembers the Queen fondly telling her the story of the President's royalist cowboy boots at her first meeting with him all those years before.

Bush wanted to make this visit a highlight of his presidency. 'One of the things which impressed Bush's people was they'd never ever been able to get him into white tie for anything. He hated that kind of formality,' says Dame Margaret. 'But he was prepared to do it because it was the Queen. He was very charming to us.'

As with the arrival ceremony arranged by Bush Senior, there would be an amusing, unscripted moment with Bush Junior. In his speech of welcome, the President recalled the Queen's earlier visits to the USA. 'You helped us celebrate our bicentennial in 17...,' he announced, before correcting himself: 'Er, 1976'. A roar of laughter spread across the lawn. The Queen, greatly amused, gave him a mock-reproachful glance as Bush came back with an elegant aside: 'she gave me a look only a mother could give a child.'

The American media enjoyed studying the protocol in forensic detail, noting that all President Bush's previous state banquets had been four-course black-tie affairs. This one was five courses – pea soup, Dover sole, lamb, cheese and 'rose blossom' pudding – and white tie to boot. 'How does George W. Bush, a towel-snapping Texan who puts his feet on the coffee table, drinks water straight from the bottle, and was once caught on tape talking with food in his mouth, prepare for a state dinner with the Queen?' asked *The New York Times*. 'With tips from an etiquette guide, of course – and a little gentle prodding from his wife.' Not only had the President agreed to a new dress code, but he would be staying up well beyond his regular 9.00 p.m. bedtime, too.

Before the pea soup arrived, the President used his banquet speech to return to themes raised earlier on the White House lawn:

'Friendships remain strong when they are continually renewed, and the American people appreciate Your Majesty's commitment to our friendship.' Wearing the Queen Mary Tiara and her blue Garter sash and star, the Queen was not reciting a Foreign Office script, but speaking from the heart. 'Those of us who have witnessed the peace and stability and prosperity enjoyed in the United Kingdom and the rest of Europe over these post-war years have every reason to remember that this has been founded on the bedrock of the Atlantic Alliance.' All the good things in life, she said, continued to flourish 'safe in the knowledge of this simple truth'.

As in the past, British and American officials had included a NASA-related element to the state visit, mindful of keen royal interest in space travel. At the Goddard Space Flight Center, near Washington, they watched a live link to the International Space Station, where three astronauts were performing weightless somersaults. With his unerring eye for the practical, the Duke had some direct questions. 'What do you do about natural functions?' he asked one astronaut. 'A very good question,' came the reply.

In scale and dramatic content, this might have been a more modest tour than those grand adventures of yesteryear. It still maintained a ferocious pace for two octogenarians, incorporating up to six engagements per day, though the walkabouts had been gently scaled back and the guest lists somewhat reduced (down to a mere 700 guests at the Queen's Embassy garden party). The media impact seemed much the same as on previous tours. 'Capital Goes Gaga Over The Queen for a Day,' declared *The Washington Post*. There was also a particular warmth and familiarity, almost a cosiness, about this tour.

The guests at the state banquet included the Queen's old friend Nancy Reagan, former Secretary of State George Shultz and his wife, Charlotte (who had organised so much of the Queen's 1983 tour), and some racing chums. A last-minute invitation had been extended to Calvin Borel, winning jockey in the Kentucky Derby. Later in the visit, the Queen and the Duke would join veterans of the Second World War to view a new memorial. Generously, the President decided not to attend. Instead, 'Bush 43' (as the forty-third president was known in the family) asked 'Bush 41' and former first lady, Barbara Bush, to accompany the royal couple. 'Bush president gave way to Bush *père* on their visit to the new memorial and it was very special,' says Sir David Manning. 'Bush 41 had a fine war record as a pilot. And there they all were, walking around like old friends. Those occasions touch people in a way that is very hard to measure but it matters.'

For the Queen, it was a delightful reprise of her previous state visit. 'She was very comfortable with Bush 41. It was a very warm relationship,' adds Sir David. 'She had an easy rapport with Bush 43, too, which was very evident at the less formal return dinner that she gave at the Embassy after his white tie banquet.' For that event, there was a marginally less onerous dress code of black tie. Rather than a hierarchical seating plan, there were round tables – and no numbers. Each table was named after a Derby-winning horse. When the formal photographs were taken before dinner, the Queen insisted on dragging a reluctant Bush 41 plus Barbara into the official line-up alongside Bush 43 and Laura.

The speeches were kept to a minimum. 'Mr President,' the Queen began, 'I wondered whether I should start this toast saying: "When I was here in 1776" . . .' The room guffawed. Saluting the 'strength and vitality' of the old alliance, she raised a glass to the Bushes and to 'enduring friendship'. In his equally brief reply, the President thanked the Queen for 'the love and affection you have shown the American people over many years', before raising a toast 'to our closest of friends, the British people'.

***

Within a couple of years, however, the gloss appeared to be fading on the 'special relationship' as a new tenant moved in to the White House. Given Britain's closeness to the previous Republican regime, Barack Obama was hardly predisposed to be very friendly, even if Gordon Brown's Labour Party was a more natural fit with Obama's Democrats than Bush's Republicans. There were reports that Obama had evicted the bust of Winston Churchill from the White House (not entirely true; there had been two busts – one had been on loan from the British government and was simply returned, while Obama left another untouched in pride of place in a hallway). Obama had also written about his Kenyan grandfather being tortured by the British during the Mau Mau rebellion (a claim later disputed by members of Obama's family), at the same time as the Queen was acceding to the Throne in that Kenyan treehouse.

David Cameron has an alternative theory. 'I think that he started out as not particularly warm towards the UK,' Cameron admits. 'Someone said that the only thing Britain had ever done for Obama was we lost his luggage. He flew from America to Kenya via the UK and we lost it. But he ended up in a very good place in the end.' That he did was in no small part down to the Queen.

The Obamas enjoyed their first royal encounter when they arrived in London for the 2009 G20 summit and had a private meeting with the Queen and Prince Philip ahead of a summit reception. 'I know they connected then,' says Matthew Barzun, former US Ambassador. As Obama told an interviewer beforehand: 'I think in the imagination of people throughout America, what the Queen stands for, her decency and her civility and what she represents, is very important.' After the meeting, he gave the monarch an iPod containing footage of her 2007 state visit to America. The royal couple gave him silver-framed signed photographs. During the reception that followed, cameras picked up an age-old 'faux pas' story, when Michelle Obama was seen to put her arm around the Queen. In fact the Queen has never been bothered by an occasional gentle steer, when it is merely a question of good manners. It was not a faux pas at all. Indeed, the most interesting aspect of the encounter was the fact that the Queen simultaneously put her arm around the US first lady too. It turned out that the two of them had been swapping heel sizes. Later that summer, when Michelle Obama and her daughters paid a private visit to London, the Queen gave them a private tour of the Palace.

Obama's White House, with its sunny mantra of 'hope' and 'change', did not click with Gordon Brown's rather dour Downing Street operation, still feeling battered from the financial crash of 2008. Yet the White House–Palace relationship remained a warm one. Brown's departure in 2010 was followed by a mood change at Number Ten and by the first coalition government of the Queen's reign. British and American diplomats started to discuss the idea of a state visit in earnest with great enthusiasm from both heads of state. A date was fixed which would crown four of the most historic and happy weeks of the reign. In the space of a month in the spring of 2011, the Queen would host Prince William's wedding, make her first state visit to

Ireland and, finally, welcome the Obamas to stay. Unlike the visit of George W. Bush in 2003, there were no protests this time. Even so, US security chiefs ruled out a carriage procession once again. As with the Bushes, the Obamas were welcomed inside the Palace grounds rather than on Horse Guards. After lunch, the exchange of gifts went far beyond iPods and photos. The Queen gave Obama a specially bound selection of facsimile letters from Queen Victoria to presidents of the USA. The Queen was particularly touched when Obama gave her a specially bound selection of photographs and documents of that first state visit by her parents to the United States in 1939.

That visit would also surface in the special Royal Collection exhibition that the Queen had laid on for her visitors. The Obamas were greatly amused to see her mother's famous letter about 'HOT DOGS too!' Here also was a rather weightier item from the Royal Archives, George III's handwritten lament after the loss of the American colonies: 'America is lost! Must we fall beneath the blow?' Mr Obama laughed and exclaimed: 'That was just a temporary blip in the relationship!' There was no question that this state visit was going swimmingly. The mood was infectious. Sir Simon Fraser, former head of the Diplomatic Service, describes it as 'the most fun state visit' of his career. 'It was such an attractive event and the state banquet had such interesting people.' The most in-demand couple of the moment, the newly-wed Duke and Duchess of Cambridge, loyally found an alternative engagement on the night of the banquet so as not to deflect the focus from the two heads of state (the Cambridges had a private meeting with the Obamas earlier). However, there was no shortage of glamour at a white-tie banquet that included a number of Hollywood stars. The then Foreign Secretary, William Hague, recalls that his wife, Ffion, was placed next to Tom Hanks and helped the actor through the bewildering assortment of cutlery and crystal at his place. 'Ffion coached Tom Hanks through the whole meal. After that, he called her "coach"!' What sticks in Lord Hague's mind most of all, however, was the impact of the visit on both sides. 'Even for the most powerful man in the world, this is still going to be one of the things on his wall in perpetuity,' he says. Ahead of a dinner of sole and new-season lamb (with a Chablis Grand Cru Les Clos 2004 and Echézeaux Grand Cru 1990 Romanée-Conti), the Queen told her guests: 'We are here to celebrate the tried, tested and, yes, special relationship between our two countries.'

The only 'blip' in this entire visit would come as the President was reaching his own conclusion. He picked up his glass for the toast, which the orchestra of the Scots Guards took as its cue to start playing the national anthem. Obama had not finished talking. As British diplomats gritted their teeth and curled their toes, Obama's homage to the S-word was drowned out by the strings. Yet on he went: 'To Her Majesty the Queen, to the vitality of the special relationship between our peoples, and in the words of Shakespeare, "to this blessed plot, this Earth, this realm, this England".' The Queen pretended not to notice. 'That was very kind,' she told him as the footmen started serving the sole, the sunny ambience swiftly restored.

'What was really striking to me was when it came to the timetable, Obama would do what the Queen told him to,' Hague recalls. 'So when the Queen said it was time for the whole thing to be over – it was only teatime for Obama, being jet-lagged – he said: "Is she serious?" But off they all went. The President of the United States would probably not defer to anyone else in the world!'

The following day, Obama would receive an honour denied to all his predecessors, when he was invited to address both Houses of Parliament. David Cameron had arranged for the speech to be made in Westminster Hall, the great chamber denied to Ronald Reagan in 1982 by the Labour opposition. There were no objections to Obama. 'It gave him a brilliant platform,' says Cameron, though he believes the real magic of the trip for the President was 'the kudos of doing things with her Majesty'. He is in no doubt that it was the Queen, rather than her ministers, who laid the foundations for the transatlantic relationship, which continued through the Obama years. 'It wasn't certain that the US president and the UK prime minister, or America and Britain, would be as close under Obama as it turned out to be. And I think that the state visit played a big role in that because actually he really enjoyed it and he really liked her. And it benefitted me because when I visited him in 2012, it was like I was getting the benefit of the state visit, which I felt rather guilty about. What Buckingham Palace and the Queen give is extra heft. So state visits are worth doing.'

***

When Obama took office for his second term, he gave some thought to returning the compliment. In 2013, he appointed a new Ambassador to London, Matthew Barzun, a Harvard-educated campaign supporter who was familiar with royal etiquette, having previously served as US Ambassador to Sweden. Barzun had the rare extra honour of being invited to a small dinner party, known as a 'dine and sleep', at Windsor Castle. As he recalls: 'It was really special, getting to spend a night at Windsor Castle and sixteen of us sitting round a dining room table and corgis running around. And the Queen's feeding them under the table.' Among the other guests were the Archbishop of Canterbury and actress Dame Maggie Smith, star of one of the Queen's favourite programmes, *Downton Abbey*. Every guest had a special mini-exhibition prepared in their honour in the Royal Library, featuring suitable items from the Royal Collection. Barzun still recalls that his display included letters from George VI's state visit to the USA – 'the little handwritten note about how unbelievably hot it is in America and he had to change his shirt six times in one day' – and a British military map from the American Revolution. He was so impressed by the royal attention to detail that he decided to replicate it when he got back to the US Embassy. 'Little gestures like that make such a difference. When people came to Winfield House I'd try to do the same. So if someone came from Newcastle, say, I'd try to put on Dire Straits or some great music from their neck of the woods – as a conversation starter.'

Barzun was honoured to find himself seated next to the Queen at dinner. 'It was a long dinner where you're talking about all sorts of things. I know it's a cliché but there's this twinkle in her eye when she's talking about President and Mrs Obama. It's real.'

Barzun was on a mission that night, however. 'I had a little bit of business I was trying to do,' he says. He had received a request from Washington – to explore the idea of another state visit to the USA. Although it had been announced that the Queen's days of long-distance flying were over, might she at least consider a trip to Washington? The request had come from the President himself. 'He really wanted her to come to Washington one more time. She had just publicly said she was not doing the long-haul stuff anymore but we were trying to figure out a way. I said: "Well, what if we did this ... and that?" I didn't want it to turn into a business meeting.' The Queen had another idea for a meeting with the President, says the Ambassador. 'It was: "Why doesn't he come here?' And I said: "OK, well ..." You could just tell that she was going to make it happen one way or the other.'

Sure enough, almost exactly a year later, in the final months of the Obama administration, the presidential helicopter touched down on the lawns outside Windsor Castle. There was no guard of honour or motorcade waiting for the Obamas, just the Queen, the Duke and his Land Rover. He would drive the four of them the short distance up to the Castle for lunch. And this was not just any lunch. The previous day, the Queen had celebrated her ninetieth birthday – the first monarch in history to do so. 'She is truly one of my favourite people,' the President said later, after giving her an album of photographs of her meetings with all those presidents going back to Harry Truman. 'Should we be fortunate enough to reach ninety, may we be as vibrant as she is.'

This would be a tricky political visit, coming just weeks after that curt presidential attack on Britain's foreign-policy 'shit show', and just weeks before the UK's referendum on whether to leave the European Union. These would be sensitive matters for discussion the following day in Downing Street.

Yet nothing would illustrate the dual axis of the 'special relationship' as eloquently as the scene later that evening, when the President and first lady dropped in for dinner with the Duke and Duchess of Cambridge and Prince Harry. Cameras captured the President being introduced to two-year-old Prince George in his dressing gown – and clutching the toy Portuguese water dog that the Obamas had sent him as a baby. The scene was on front pages around the world the next day.*

The following day, after talks with David Cameron, the two leaders faced a press conference to discuss Brexit, terrorism and much else. Inevitably Obama was also asked about the state of the special relationship. He replied with the story of an unnamed senior member of the White House team responsible for organising his overseas trips. 'She

* A week later, President Obama would get one of the loudest laughs at his final White House correspondents' dinner when he observed how people were already losing interest in him as they looked ahead to the next presidency. 'Last week, Prince George showed up to our meeting in his bathrobe,' he joked. 'That was a slap in the face!'

has had one request the entire time that I have been President,' he said. Though this globe-trotting White House pro had seen every world leader come and go over the years, all she really wanted was a proper 'peek' at the Queen. So, after lunch with the President, the Queen ensured that his trusty aide got more than a glimpse. She arranged a proper introduction. 'That,' said Obama, 'is the special relationship.'

***

Once again, the relationship would be tested by the arrival of a new incumbent in the White House. Just weeks after the inauguration of Donald Trump in 2017, Theresa May travelled to Washington to meet him. She duly issued an invitation, on behalf of the Queen, for Trump to make a state visit in the near future. The plan stalled, however, due to the threat of protests from activists and Left-wing pressure groups who announced their intention to disrupt the visit, citing Trump's remarks about immigration, women, Brexit and assorted grievances besides. The Liberal Democrat leader, Sir Vince Cable, said that such a state visit would 'embarrass' the Queen and the country while the Labour Mayor of London, Sadiq Khan, declared that Trump was 'not welcome' in the capital.

There had been no protests of any note against recent state visits from nations such as Saudi Arabia, China and Indonesia, nor against official visitors from other countries demonstrably less liberal, less multi-cultural and less pro-British than the USA. Over the years, the British government has foisted the most dreadful guests on the Queen, not least the Romanian dictator to whom Sir Vince Cable's predecessor, David Steel, gave that Labrador puppy. Yet, as far as some were concerned, Donald Trump was in a category all of his own. Little wonder that, in his first year in office, the US President preferred to make a state visit to Paris – where President Emmanuel Macron laid on dinner at the Eiffel Tower and obligingly confined demonstrators to a different part of the city – rather than come to London.

There was not, in fact, the faintest possibility that the Queen would be 'embarrassed' to meet Trump. According to one former member of staff, she was intrigued to meet a head of state who, like her, had a Scottish mother and who, like her, happens to own a large area of Scottish countryside (the Balmoral estate in her case and a pair of famous golf courses in Trump's). Furthermore, some of Trump's relatives have stayed close to their Scottish roots and local community projects on the Hebridean Isle of Lewis where Trump's mother, Mary, was born.

Having downgraded his trip from a state visit to an official one, President Trump arrived in Britain on July 12th, 2018.

The following day, while tens of thousands of protestors marched through London, Mr Trump flew by helicopter to talks with Theresa May at Chequers. There was an awkward atmosphere thanks to an interview in that morning's *Sun* newspaper in which he had criticised her handling of the Brexit negotiations. Despite Mr Trump's subsequent insistence that the bilateral relationship was at 'the highest level of special', it neither felt nor looked like it.

Yet there was no such *froideur* two hours later as the President, accompanied by the first lady, arrived at Windsor for tea with the Queen. The smiles appeared warm and uncomplicated. The Coldstream Guards had formed a Guard of Honour on the Quadrangle and the Queen invited the President to join her to inspect them. It was a novel experience for both them, since she had usually delegated this role to the Duke of Edinburgh (recently retired from such occasions). Some Trump critics accused the President of breaching protocol by walking both the wrong side and in front of the Queen but Palace insiders said that she hadn't been remotely bothered. 'People are always nervous on these occasions. I think he was just focussing hard on not touching her and not tripping,' said one.

After introducing the Trumps to her small entourage, including her US-born lady-in-waiting, the Countess of Airlie, the Queen led them in to her private quarters and tea in the Oak Room, her inner sanctum. Mindful of American tastes, she had ordered fresh coffee, too. It was just the three of them as the rest of the White House team were entertained to tea (plus coffee, sandwiches – minus crust – and cakes) in the more formal Crimson Drawing Room. Clearly, the two heads of state got on well as the meeting overran by nearly twenty minutes (an age at this end of the protocol spectrum).

Afterwards, the President was almost taciturn by his standards. 'It was a very easy talk,' he told ITV's Piers Morgan. 'We had a great feeling.' Did she like him? He was almost coy. 'Well I don't want to speak for her but I can tell you I liked her. I liked her a lot.'

The nearest to a revelation was his disclosure that the Queen had said of Brexit that 'it's a very complex problem ... nobody had any idea how complex that was going to be'. No one could argue with that. Then the President corrected himself: 'I've heard very strongly from a lot of people, you just don't talk about that conversation with the Queen, right?' The serial Tweeter was suddenly watching his words. 'Let me tell you what I can talk about. She is an incredible woman, she is so sharp, she is so beautiful, when I say beautiful – inside and out. That is a beautiful woman.'

However much the 'special relationship' may fluctuate at the political level, it has always been underpinned by that mutual respect between the Queen and the American people. Sir Antony Acland's conclusion to his despatch to the Foreign Secretary on that 1991 tour rings as true today as it did then: 'Our two countries are and remain the best of friends and that friendship is well symbolised by the extraordinary respect which the American people have for the latest representative of a monarchy to whose real and imagined abuses the US owes its existence.'

Chapter 7

EUROPE

'Vive la reine!'

ZIZETTE

By any standards, it was a demanding schedule for a twenty-two-year-old Princess. She had been overseas just once before, to southern Africa the previous year. That tour had been with her parents and sister. Now, six months after her marriage to Prince Philip, Princess Elizabeth, Duchess of Edinburgh was to be the principal focus of attention on her first overseas tour as Number One – to France.

What was ostensibly a springtime weekend break to Paris had rapidly become the continental spectacle of the year. There were also ambitious diplomatic expectations, too. The last royal visit to Paris, by the King and Queen in 1938, had been a great success. Since then the Second World War, the fall of France and the British retreat from Dunkirk, had left the public on either side of the Channel less sure of each other. The Princess's task was to help rebuild the bonhomie. And the French were more than enthusiastic about the visit.

The authorities had made plans for up to one million spectators descending on the royal route. Tour operators from as far afield as Belgium, Holland and Scandinavia had organised 'royal visit excursions'. Though the Duke and Duchess of Edinburgh had specifically said that they wanted no presents, the British Embassy had been inundated with gifts, ranging from a sports car and silk stockings, to a case of Camembert cheese and a gold model of the Eiffel Tower. Someone had also sent a perambulator.

Of all the gifts, this was actually the most appropriate. For the Princess was already three months pregnant with Prince Charles. Not that anyone outside the immediate family had the faintest idea. Once again, it is a sign of how much the world has changed that such news was not only withheld until the last possible minute, but was, even then, wreathed in obfuscation. The only indication that the future sovereign was expecting came after her return from Paris, when it was announced that the Princess would 'undertake no public engagements after the end of June'.

Undeterred, she launched herself into her four-day tour on the hottest Whitsun weekend in record. It is hard to imagine a pregnant Princess being subjected to anything comparable today. This was a tour that would involve alcoholic toasts, five-course lunches and dinners, several late nights, plenty of unpasteurised food, a stomach bug, a nightclub and what came close to a plane crash. Just three years after the end of the Second World War, though, Britain was a more stoical place than it is today. A princess raised on wartime notions of duty was not about to let her own medical condition upset months of planning.

Tens of thousands lined the streets of Paris just to see the royal car on its way through the city – a reception that reportedly moved the Princess 'to tears'. The official purpose of the visit was the opening of a new exhibition called 'Eight Centuries of British Life in Paris' at the Galliera Museum, where the organisers included one Georges Pompidou. Almost quarter of a century later, he would be her host for one of the most important visits of her entire reign. On this occasion he was a member of the local commission for tourism.

The Princess's host in 1948 was President Vincent Auriol. At the Elysée Palace he conferred the *Légion d'honneur* on his guest, whereupon protocol would normally have dictated a kiss on both cheeks for the recipient. 'I delegate my powers to your illustrious husband,' the President announced theatrically, before awarding Prince Philip the Croix de Guerre for his war service.

The following day, the royal couple went up the Eiffel Tower by *ascenseur* while the crowds tried to follow suit using the stairs. It is estimated that half a million people lined the banks of the Seine to watch the Princess and the Duke enjoying a sightseeing trip by motor launch. The numbers were so great on the Avenue Foch that the royal car took half an hour to crawl through the crowds.

The media attention was relentless, causing the Duke to become increasingly agitated, particularly as he had succumbed to a stomach bug. Still clinging vainly to their original 'quiet weekend' idea, the Edinburghs switched to an anonymous car one evening and vanished for a private dinner at the Tour d'Argent, overlooking the Seine. Within five minutes of their arrival a crowd of at least a thousand had congregated on the street outside, while the Princess, in a blue dress with white fur cape, and the Duke, with a jaunty red carnation in the buttonhole of his dinner jacket, found that most of the restaurant had been cleared out. As they dined on tomato soup, fillet of sole, breast and leg of duck and finally chocolate-vanilla soufflé, the Duke was furious to discover a hidden camera lens in an adjacent table.

Then it was on to the nightclub of the moment, the Chez Carrere Cabaret. Once again the place had been emptied of anything resembling the public. The pregnant Princess and the ailing Duke still managed to dance until 1.35 a.m., before being driven back to the British Embassy residence. 'One of the most appalling evenings I have ever spent,' the Princess's Private Secretary, Jock Colville, later told biographer Elizabeth Longford. 'Everybody dressed up to the nines, nobody in either place – except the lens.'

The crowds were out in force again on the final evening to watch 'Zizette', as many French liked to call the Princess, arrive at the Opéra in what was described as a 'white silk gown, very tight at the waist, with billowing crinoline effect skirt'. Her wardrobe had not only given no clue to her condition, but had made a lasting impression on this most demanding of audiences. 'She is wearing the "New Look". *Mais oui!*' announced Christian Dior, no less. 'The Princess's style is just right. Her hemline is only a little shorter than some of our new frocks.'

On her first visit to a racecourse that she would come to know very well over the years, the Princess was welcomed by some of the largest crowds ever seen at Longchamp. Even France's communist papers hailed the visit a success. For criticism, one had to turn to Scotland, where church organisations complained that a princess who should be offering 'guidance' to the young had gone racing on a Sunday. Yet there was no doubt the trip had been a diplomatic triumph. British papers likened it all to a reverse Norman Conquest, a view shared by Jock Colville, who said: 'In four hectic days the Princess conquered Paris.' In his report to the Foreign Office, the British Ambassador, Sir Oliver Harvey, noted that 'it was an unusual experience to see the townsfolk of Paris cheer an English Princess from the Place de la Bastille'.

It was soon back to Britain with a bump, in more ways than one. As the Vickers Viking of the King's Flight came into London Airport, there was a sudden explosion of emergency Very lights, to alert the pilot that he was on course for the wrong runway. Within hours the Duke would be back at work at the Royal Naval Staff College, while the pregnant Princess caught up with the King and Queen. Although she had not returned with the perambulator or the case of Camembert, she had accepted a bottle of Grande Reserve 1798 brandy from the Tour d'Argent, for the King.

And so began a French connection that would see the Queen visit France more than any other non-Commonwealth nation. And it would be in France, years later, that she helped lead Britain into a turbulent adventure that would result in one of the greatest political crises of her lifetime.

FRENCH LESSONS

The Queen has been known to reflect ruefully that she would have liked a more rounded education than the one she received in her Windsor Castle schoolroom. There was certainly a difference of opinion between her grandmother, Queen Mary, who argued for a more disciplined educational programme, and Queen Elizabeth, the future Queen Mother, who believed that lessons should be interspersed with breaks for ponies and games of racing demon.

But the Queen evidently had excellent tuition in two areas. One was constitutional history thanks to Henry Marten, Vice-Provost of nearby Eton. Himself an Old Etonian, he had returned to the school as a 'beak', or master, in the reign of Queen Victoria. Having spent his entire adult life teaching classrooms full of boys, Marten would absent-mindedly chew his handkerchief and address the solitary

Princess as 'gentlemen'. She would prove a model pupil, however, and Marten's reward was a knighthood, conferred by the King, in front of the whole school, in 1945.

The Princess's other strong subject was French. Not only was it still the lingua franca of the royal houses and embassies of Europe, but it was essential for any future sovereign of Canada, with its substantial French-speaking population. The Princess's main tutor was Vicomtesse de Bellaigue, who had escaped to Britain at the outbreak of the Second World War with her husband and two young sons. While her husband joined General de Gaulle's Free French forces, 'Toni' de Bellaigue began teaching French to the daughters of the King's Private Secretary, Lord Hardinge of Penshurst. In 1941, he recommended her to the King and Queen as a tutor for Princess Elizabeth and her younger sister, Princess Margaret. Both girls would end up speaking excellent French. Years later, Toni de Bellaigue recalled that her elder charge was '*très naturelle* ... a strong sense of duty mixed with *joie de vivre*'.

It was Queen Elizabeth, rather than King George VI, who was the great royal Francophile. Wartime relations between General de Gaulle and both the King and Prime Minister Winston Churchill could be prickly at the best of times. Queen Elizabeth, though, would enjoy a lifelong rapport with the General. As Duchess of York, she had been both entranced and shocked during her own early visits to Paris. 'Too disgusting,' she wrote home from her first visit. 'Women with no pants.' As Queen, her love for the place was sealed in 1938 when she accompanied the King on his state visit to France. The largest Union flag ever seen was flown from the Eiffel Tower, while the French government had invited the Queen to select coverings for the royal quarters in advance. There was even a nod to her Scottish ancestry, in the form of a Loch Ness monster floating in the Seine.

Two years later, after the fall of France and the retreat from Dunkirk, much of Britain – the King included – subscribed to the view that 'we're better off alone'. Not so the Queen who, on the fall of Paris, broadcast to the women of France, in French. Come the end of the war, de Gaulle would be effusive in his thanks to her. As Queen Mother, she would enjoy regular summer holidays in France, touring the Loire Valley and Provence to cries of '*Vive la reine*', reducing sentimental mayors to tears and, on one occasion, playing the Marseillaise on a mouth organ.

Her toasts were famous – a glass raised high in homage to all that she admired and then plunged down in disapproval of the villain of the moment. 'Up with de Gaulle,' was a regular refrain at the Clarence House dinner table. Marc Roche, London-based correspondent of *Le Monde* for many years and the Queen's French-language biographer, says that de Gaulle always felt it was Queen Elizabeth who had made wartime London 'bearable'. Roche was also reliably informed that the Queen Mother, never known for her love of football, had insisted on a toast to the French after learning of their 1998 World Cup triumph over Brazil.

'She just clicked with the French – and it's the same with the Queen. She just clicked, too,' explains Roche. He points to the fact that France is one of a tiny handful of places where the Queen has gone 'on holiday', albeit to inspect horses in Normandy. 'It's the country she has been to more through her heart than reason,' he says. The feeling is entirely mutual, he adds. He goes so far as to suggest that the Queen Mother and the Queen have actually helped salvage France's own post-war sense of honour. For Roche believes that the royal friendship with de Gaulle and the Free French went a long way to bolstering the wartime narrative that France would prefer to remember, as opposed to the collaborationist Vichy regime of Marshal Pétain.

'The record of France was bad. It is such a raw issue,' says Roche. 'The deportation of Jews by the French without the Germans asking; the Gestapo being swamped with denunciations. It was a terrible episode. But the Queen and the Queen Mother knew de Gaulle, and de Gaulle is what saved the honour of France. The Queen has helped to legitimise the record of wartime France. She may have done it subconsciously but I believe it is why the older generation, in particular, love her so much.'

By choosing France as her first European destination, Roche argues, and by returning so often, both in a public and private capacity, the Queen has earned herself a unique place in the French collective memory.

Her appeal extends to the younger generations, too, he adds. It is normally a strict in-house rule (and a source of national pride) at the French offices of *Vanity Fair* that the French edition of the magazine never copies its English-language namesakes. That rule was cheerfully torn up when the July 2017 edition appeared on the news-stands with the same Annie Leibovitz portrait of the Queen that had already appeared in the British and US editions. The headline, however, was thoroughly French: '*La reine du cool*'.

British commentators routinely make the point that, having decommissioned their own monarchy so forcefully, the French have been trying to add a certain royal lustre to their presidents ever since. The former British Ambassador to France, Sir Christopher Mallaby, has likened the sentiment to those who wish to impose something on others, but 'Not In My Back Yard'. 'The French think that monarchy is a splendid arrangement for other people, but not for themselves,' he told a Foreign Office seminar on UK–French relations in 2014. 'They are NIMBY monarchists.'

1957

Following that first visit as a Princess in 1948, the Queen's return to Paris in 1957, for her first state visit as monarch, was an even more exuberant affair. The authorities estimated that the crowds that gathered along the river to watch another '*promenade sur la Seine*' were the largest to view the Queen since her coronation four years before. Once again, her fluent French was a factor. 'There is a quality in Her Majesty's voice which the French as a whole find profoundly moving,' the British Ambassador, Sir Gladwyn Jebb, wrote in his confidential despatch to the Foreign Secretary afterwards. When she visited the Opéra, the crowds grew so big and disobedient that mounted police drew their swords.

The most striking aspect of the visit, Jebb went on, was the reaction in the '*faubourgs rouges*' – the left-leaning areas on her itinerary. In Lille, then 'an overwhelmingly working-class town', the warmth of the welcome at a Renault factory was only soured by the way the workers 'were kept in the distance by the management'. It was a similar story at a textile factory in Roubaix. 'The most remarkable aspect of the visit was the tremendous ovation that the Queen received from the workers,' Jebb reported.

These were the dying days of the short-lived Fourth Republic when the French head of state was still a relatively ceremonial figure.

Her host, President René Coty, would soon give way to the Fifth Republic and its first executive head of state, General de Gaulle. During his 1960 state visit to London, the General would be charmed by the Queen (and, as ever, by her mother). He would later describe the House of Windsor as the world's 'only legitimate monarchy'. Yet if he loved Britain's Royal Family, the same did not apply to her government. Britain's relations with France would remain distinctly cool for a decade, during which the General would twice veto British membership of the new EEC. France and Germany were the two dominant powers in the early common market (as, indeed, they remain today) and Britain was not joining as long as France had a president determined to blackball his neighbour across the Channel. Much as he liked the Queen personally, de Gaulle would do her no favours in Canada, either, as he stirred up the crowds in French-speaking Quebec, addressing separatist rallies with cries of '*Vive le Québec libre!*' All that would change in dramatic style, in 1972.

BRENTRY

Following the resignation of the General in 1969, France would quickly come round to the idea of Britain in the EEC, thanks to that former civil servant who had welcomed the Queen to his exhibition in 1948. Georges Pompidou had been elected President of France in 1969 and was setting France on a new path. He wanted British involvement in the new European project and he had both a strong ally and a kindred spirit in Downing Street – the passionately pro-European Edward Heath. By 1971, provisional terms for Britain's membership had been agreed. Heath not only needed to get it through Parliament. He wanted Britain's entry to be marked in triumphalist style with a spectacular and grandiose celebration of shared values, while also reassuring sceptics that Britain's national identity was not about to be lost in the European mix. There could surely be no better illustration than a state visit to France by the Queen. And whereas her previous visits had been largely remembered for the spectacle, this one, both governments agreed, should go down in history for its substance, too.

The man in the middle was a diplomat of great stature and style, who also happened to be married to Sir Winston Churchill's daughter, Mary. Sir Christopher Soames had been appointed British Ambassador to Paris while General de Gaulle was still in charge of France (and while Harold Wilson was Prime Minister of Britain). British Embassy staff of the period have fond memories of a charismatic figure described by one of his team as 'the Great Pachyderm, winning support and affection everywhere with tremendous trumpetings, brushing aside opposition with a genial sweep of the trunk and occasionally a savage prod from the tusk'.

Soames had found himself ostracised by de Gaulle when a confidential report to London, accurately detailing his lunch conversation with the President about Britain's European prospects, was leaked by Wilson to other European leaders. Following the arrival of Pompidou, however, Soames was back in favour at the Elysée. In October 1971, his Foreign Office masters asked him to sound out French thoughts on a state visit by the Queen. He went directly to Pompidou, who welcomed the idea '*avec tout coeur*' – so much so that he already had a date in mind. He hoped the Queen would come in May 1972. Having already booked in the Queen of the Netherlands for June, Pompidou wanted the British visit to have star billing.

The excitement on the French side was in danger of spiralling out of control, as the Foreign Office archives reveal. Soon afterwards, at a party in honour of the Russian premier, Leonid Brezhnev, the French Foreign Minister, Maurice Schumann, had been heard boasting that France had forced the Queen to tear up her own rules. It had always been British policy that there should be just one state visit to a country in each reign. Monarchs would, of course, make multiple tours of the Empire, but no more than one official visit to a 'foreign' land. Since the Queen had already paid a state visit to France in 1957, so Schumann noisily proclaimed, France was clearly a very special object of royal favouritism. Earwigging furiously at the same party, Soames was quick to report back to London. 'I know the Queen is understandably anxious not to give the impression that we are running after the French,' he wrote to Sir Denis Greenhill, head of the Foreign Office. 'Too much of this sort of stuff in the French press may well quite reasonably infuriate her – and a lot of others beside.'

In his response, Greenhill admitted that the one-country-per-reign rule did, indeed, exist, but would now be abolished. After all, the Queen was still only in her forties. As Greenhill pointed out to Soames, if the Queen could only go to a country once, then she would soon be reduced to state visits to 'relatively unimportant countries'. Eventually there would be nowhere left to visit at all.

A spot of French bragging at grand diplomatic receptions was a relatively minor concern. Britain's entry in to the EEC was far from complete. Embracing the Common Market, as most knew it in Britain, had serious implications for British farming and fishing as well as for all those Commonwealth cousins and allies whose economies had long depended on exports to the mother country. There was anti-EEC feeling at both ends of the British political spectrum.

In the very week that Soames was sounding out Pompidou, the House of Commons was in the midst of a furious debate on Britain's European future. And yet the government were already attempting to embroil the Queen in it. It prompted a stern warning from her Private Secretary, Sir Michael Adeane, that there should be no further discussion of a state visit until Parliament had voted on the matter. On 28th October 1971, MPs voted by 356:244 that Britain should move towards membership of the EEC. Even this was not the end of the matter. It was merely the start of months of further parliamentary debate on the terms of the deal. The issue remained a deeply divisive – even toxic – one. Yet Heath and his ministers had no compunction about getting the Queen on board already. Britain was on its way into Europe, and planning for the great state visit could begin in earnest.

The following day the Foreign Secretary, Sir Alec Douglas-Home, met the French Ambassador, cheerfully assuring him privately that 'there should not be too much trouble' getting all the relevant legislation through the House of Commons before the visit. The FCO's main worry was the Germans. If Britain was about to send the Queen on a headline-grabbing tour of France, it would surely infuriate the other main power. 'The Germans are likely therefore to think that the balance has swung heavily in favour of France,' Lees Mayall, Vice-Marshal of the Diplomatic Corps, warned Adeane at the Palace. The FCO had a crafty solution. Before announcing the French visit, it wanted the Queen to issue an invitation to the President of Germany, asking him to pay a state visit to Britain. German honour was duly salvaged. Gustav Heinemann would, indeed, be welcomed by the Queen a year later.

News of the Queen's proposed visit to Paris went down extremely well in the media. *The Times* applauded the end of the one-state-visit-per-country rule while *The Sunday Telegraph* (then a staunchly pro-European publication) proclaimed it would stop 'the antis' complaining. The excitement seemed to have got the better of the Prime Minister, too. There was mild panic at both the Palace and the FCO when it appeared that Edward Heath was thinking of coming along, too. By tradition, the Queen would always be accompanied by a Foreign Office minister on her travels, on the understanding that he or she would keep a low profile. The whole point of such visits was that they were above politics. A Prime Minister was certainly neither expected nor welcome. In later years the rule was relaxed on a handful of special occasions, such as brief appearances by David Cameron at state banquets in Dublin and Berlin. In 1971 however, there was no royal or diplomatic appetite to have Heath in the royal entourage, however much this *grand projet* had been his handiwork. In a Foreign Office memo on 29th October 1971, Lees Mayall warned his colleagues of a 'difficulty'. After his weekly audience with the Queen, Heath had intimated to her Private Secretary 'that he might like to accompany her'. Could anyone offer a precedent for this?

The Queen's opinion on her British prime ministers (thirteen of them, up to the point of Theresa May) has always been as well guarded as her thoughts on so much else. It is, though, safe to say that Heath would never feature in her top five, and probably not in her top ten. Though only Margaret Thatcher was closer to the Queen in terms of age, Heath was never very comfortable in her company. 'He was a bachelor whose only passions were sailing and classical music. I don't think there was a lot of small talk,' says one former member of the Royal Household.

Not long before, Heath had also banned the Queen from that 1971 Commonwealth Heads of Government Meeting in Singapore, an instruction that would grate with her for evermore. So, having scuppered her own travel plans in 1971, Heath was certainly not going to receive any encouragement from the Queen to be part of her next adventure. A few weeks later, the Foreign Office's Charles Wiggin wrote to Lees Mayall confirming that there was no precedent for a prime minister to join a monarch on a state visit. Heath, he hoped, had been 'three-quarters joking about the idea'. The Prime Minister was determined not to be omitted entirely from the bilateral razzmatazz of the state visit. He would choose the very week of the state visit to take his first flight in Concorde, the great UK–French collaboration, although, when it happened, the British public would have to study their newspapers closely to find any mention of it.

REQUESTS AND REFUSALS

The Queen had been dropping some heavy hints of her own. In November, the Foreign Office received a letter from Heath's Private Secretary, Robert Armstrong, following the weekly audience. The Queen had told the Prime Minister that she hoped her visit might take her beyond Paris and the industrial north, where she had been on her previous visits. In short, she wanted to see real France. She would dearly like to visit Bordeaux, the Loire Valley and, if possible, the lands of her forebear, William the Conqueror, in Normandy (or at least see the great Bayeux Tapestry). All this would be passed on to the Embassy in Paris. The Queen was not under any illusions about the true purpose of the visit, however. This was business, not pleasure, as a letter from her deputy Private Secretary, Martin Charteris, to the FCO illustrates. Despite her already excellent grasp of French, the Queen wanted to become even more fluent. She wished to embrace the new fashion for do-it-yourself learning and would like some Linguaphone teaching tapes. 'Not just a lot of stuff about food and architecture,' Charteris added firmly. The Queen, he explained, wanted to discuss the finer points of EEC membership with President Pompidou and needed 'modern business phrases and economic language'. Time was of the essence, as the Queen was hoping to start brushing up on her business French during the upcoming state visit to Thailand and beyond. 'I should like to ship these in HMY [the Royal Yacht] so she could listen to them during quiet periods of the South East Asia tour,' Charteris explained, thereby raising a glorious image of *Britannia* sailing serenely through the South China Sea, with the Queen on the Verandah Deck, headphones on, talking to herself in French about European farm subsidies.

No sooner had the visit been announced than all manner of requests started pouring in to the British Embassy. Besides the usual heavy-handed reminders from people seeking invitations to royal receptions, there were plenty of business propositions, too. An executive from a French food manufacturer wondered if he might be permitted to put the Queen's face on some commemorative yoghurt pots. The response from the Palace was firm. 'There is, in this country, a standing rule that the Queen's portrait may not appear on any packets, cartons, or containers and this specifically includes such refined packages as chocolate boxes,' wrote R. F. Hill in the Lord Chamberlain's Office, adding that 'a genuine souvenir' would be 'quite acceptable.'

Much of the organisation had been left to Roger du Boulay, then Head of Chancery at the British Embassy in Paris. On him had fallen tasks great and small, not least organising the presentation of an honorary knighthood to President Pompidou. The Queen would be making him a Knight Grand Commander of the Order of the Bath. Although the Most Honourable Order of the Bath might be an illustrious and ancient order of chivalry, originating from medieval forms of purification, it did not translate well. '"*L'Ordre du Bain*" sounds very uncouth in French,' he warned Bill Heseltine at the Palace. 'Should we not stick to the English?'.

Du Boulay was also negotiating with the French about the royal itinerary. The Queen might have set her heart on Bordeaux, but the French had other ideas. It would mean her being introduced to some of M. Pompidou's opponents. 'The President does not want to invite the Queen to the Bordeaux area for political reasons,' du Boulay told the Palace. However, both sides had agreed that southern France should be included, with Arles and Avignon on the schedule, along with a day-trip to the wilds of the Camargue for the Duke of Edinburgh. Whereupon a storm appeared that threatened to wreck the entire state visit. It had nothing to do with politics or economics, let alone the Common Market. It concerned Gallic *amour propre*.

At issue was the question of royal transport. The French were adamant that the Queen should travel across France in a French aeroplane. Buckingham Palace, however, was insistent that she should not. The issue for the Queen was not so much one of safety, but of precedent. The French might be proposing the presidential Caravelle and it might be a perfectly proper aircraft, but if the Queen accepted a flight from one president, then how could she turn down a flight from another without causing offence? As Martin Charteris explained in a letter to Sir Christopher Soames, the Palace had rejected all offers of flights from other hosts during recent visits. To fly in a French plane would deeply hurt the Turks, the Brazilians, the Chileans and the Thais, among others. As a result, the Palace was standing firm. The Captain of the Queen's Flight was Air Commodore Archie Winskill, who had twice won the Distinguished Flying Cross for his gallantry. Yet he was not going to risk his sovereign in a French plane. The Queen would fly in a VC10 of the Royal Air Force, and Winskill had already ordered one. The French, it transpired, were not budging, either. It was their show, the Queen was their guest and she would fly in their plane. Caught in the middle, with weightier matters to attend to, Sir Christopher was clearly exasperated. He informed the Foreign Secretary that 'it could be necessary to take it up with Pompidou himself'. The President was shortly due to meet Edward Heath at Chequers.

Cue panic at the Foreign Office as officials looked for urgent solutions. The British side tried a compromise: why not send the Queen by train? It turned out that this had been overruled by the French. Lees Mayall reported – intriguingly – that President Pompidou 'has a strong personal dislike of trains and railway stations'.

Sir Alec Douglas-Home, in turn, raised the matter in a confidential memo to the Defence Secretary, Lord Carrington, and the Prime Minister himself. As well as not wanting to offend other countries, there was also the question of culpability. 'An accident in a foreign aircraft would be blamed on us for permitting the flight but also, however unreasonably, on the foreign authorities.' However, the wily Sir Alec believed that he might have found a possible way through the impasse. For the Palace had broken its own precedent once before, during a visit to North America. 'I am advised that the Queen flew in an aircraft of the [United States] Presidential Flight,' the Foreign Secretary noted. The Ministry of Defence had also done its homework, sending the British Defence Attaché in Paris to fly with the President's personal pilot, a Lt-Col Dezier, who had already clocked up 970 hours on the Caravelle alone. When all this was presented to Edward Heath, his mind was made up. On 17th March, the Palace was informed that the Prime Minister would be formally advising the Queen to fly in M. Pompidou's plane. Therefore, she could not refuse. The French and the Foreign Office had outwitted the Palace.

If there was relief at the British Embassy, there were still plenty of other matters to be resolved. With just two months to go before the visit, President Pompidou suddenly announced that France would hold a referendum on whether it wanted Britain to join the Common Market after all. Staff at the Foreign Office were astonished. It was certainly unorthodox, if not extremely rude, to vote on the reliability of a close ally just weeks before a state visit. But the President explained that if a 'new Europe' was to embrace the 'oldest democracy in the world', then the decision should be 'ratified by every French man and woman.' It was pure showmanship by M. Pompidou. Neither he nor anyone else had any doubt about the result. The latest French polls showed that 61 per cent of people believed Britain would be a 'loyal partner' in Europe, while just 5 per cent thought Britain would 'torpedo the market'. In the event, M. Pompidou's referendum duly endorsed Britain's entry, but on such a poor turnout that the whole exercise backfired. The President had shown poor political judgement – and rather poor manners, too.

FAMILY BUSINESS

At the British Embassy, Sir Christopher Soames had something else to worry about. He had received a message from the Palace that the Queen wanted to set aside some time to visit her uncle, the exiled Duke of Windsor, at his home outside Paris. But she did 'not wish anything to be said or done about it for the time being'. This was one aspect of the visit beyond the control of either government. Relations between the Palace and the former King Edward VIII were a matter of great delicacy for the Royal Family themselves. His abdication in 1936, in order to marry the American divorcee Wallis Simpson, had created the gravest royal crisis of modern times. The Duke's subsequent arguments with his younger brother, King George VI, over money, status and the King's refusal to make the Duchess 'Her Royal Highness' had been neither forgotten nor forgiven by the Queen Mother. She still held the Duke responsible for the strains that, in her view, had led to the King's early death at the age of fifty-six. The

Queen, however, had always sought to keep relations correct, and maintained regular contact via Sir Christopher Soames. His son, Sir Nicholas Soames, MP, recalls the evening when he and his father accompanied the Prince of Wales on his first visit to the Duke's house in the Bois de Boulogne in 1971. 'It had to be arranged with the Foreign Office and the Queen had to give her permission. It was diplomatically very complicated for all sorts of reasons,' he says. 'But it was a quite extraordinary moment to see the two of them together – two Prince of Waleses. I'll never forget it. It was rather touching. We all sat away from them and they had a great pow-wow.'

Prince Charles would record that 'tragic' and peculiar evening in his diary. He observed that the Duke was 'in very good form' as he lamented his strict upbringing and 'talked about how difficult my family made it for him for the past thirty-three years'. The Duchess, meanwhile, 'kept flitting to and fro like a strange bat ... a hard woman – totally unsympathetic and somewhat superficial'.

The following year, as the Queen's visit drew closer, the Duke's health was declining rapidly and he was virtually confined to bed. This would almost certainly be the Queen's last opportunity to see her uncle. President Pompidou, however, was terrified that the Duke might die before or during the state visit, and wanted assurances that this would not curtail the royal tour. Another urgent telegram was despatched from Soames to the Foreign Secretary, reporting the President's concerns and making it clear that 'cancellation would rankle'. There was little that anyone, except the Duke's doctor, Dr Jean Thin, could do about it, however. So Soames called him. Warning of the grave threat to 'the outcome of the Queen's mission', he dropped some heavy hints. As Thin would later recall to the biographer Michael Bloch: 'The Ambassador came to the point and told me bluntly that it was alright for the Duke to die before or after the visit but that it would be politically disastrous if he were to expire in the course of it. Was there anything I could do to reassure him about the timing of the Duke's end?' The doctor, who by all accounts was somewhat appalled by this line of questioning, replied that there was not.

The episode not only illustrates the fragility of diplomatic nerves in the run-up to Britain's entry into Europe, but is also eerily reminiscent of the death of the Duke's father. On the night of 20th

January 1936, George V's doctor, Lord Dawson of Penn, gave the King a lethal dose of morphine and cocaine. It meant that his passing could be formally announced by *The Times* the following morning, and not by the less respectable evening newspapers later in the day. It must go down as the most extreme example of royal news management in history (when the details were finally revealed in 1986, one historian called it 'murder'). Was the British government seriously suggesting that the Duke might care to perform one final service to his country? That might be going too far. However, the diligent Soames arranged for the doctor to give him a nightly bulletin throughout the visit.

PRICKLY PORTRAITS

In those final weeks, the Foreign Office began drawing up its briefing papers for the Queen. Whether they told her anything she did not know already, the confidential policy briefs sent to the Palace offer a very useful sense of British government thinking at the time. Looking back on the era of General de Gaulle, the FCO's considered view was that his 'grandiose vision showed itself to be an illusion', but 'its afterglow lingers on'. By contrast, de Gaulle's successor was more of a realist. 'President Pompidou's eye is not focussed on the far horizon,' continued the FCO summary, adding that the current occupant of the Elysée was notably more pro-British than his predecessor. 'The Anglophobia which was so fashionable in French official circles is on the wane.' There could be no complacency, though. Just four years earlier, anti-capitalist student riots had led to general strikes and such serious civil upheaval that President de Gaulle had briefly fled the country, fearing revolution. The FCO paper – approved by Sir Christopher himself – became positively poetic: 'The danger remains of an explosion like that of 1968. Frenchmen glance apprehensively over their shoulders from time to time, especially in May when ghosts walk.'

Even more colourful were the confidential FCO pen portraits of the main players on the French side. Had some of them leaked out ahead of the visit, the Queen might never have made it across the Channel while Britain's application to join the Common Market could have been torn to shreds there and then. The Foreign

Office did not hold back. The French Prime Minister, Jacques Chaban-Delmas, received a vitriolic review: 'His charm and panache (cultivated almost as a fetish) are offset by his vanity and touchiness in the face of criticism. Age and hard work are combining to diminish his notoriety as a womaniser but he still has a keenly roving eye. He was divorced from his first wife. His second was killed in a car accident. Nothing daunted, he is expected to remarry the lady with whom he is currently in love, the wife of an elderly doctor.'

Even Maurice Schumann, France's Anglophile Foreign Minister and a good friend of Edward Heath, was not spared. The FCO briefing of the time noted that he had been 'deeply marked' by his wartime experience in London alongside General de Gaulle. 'His belief that Europe is incomplete without Britain dates from this time.' However, he suffered from a 'reputation for political weakness and time-serving ... He likes to be liked and it is easier to like him than respect him.' Madame Schumann, it added, was 'attractively quiet and unassuming but has a lively intelligence and is a pleasant companion'.

There was a double-edged compliment for Roger Frey, Minister of Administrative Reform. While he might be 'too carefully dressed and presented', he also had a certain James Bond quality: 'There is something about the softness of his manner and the cold blue of his eyes which inevitably recalls the more sinister visions of the Ian Fleming novels. He does not inspire trust.'

Of the French Cabinet line-up, however, one stood above all the rest – Finance Minister Valéry Giscard d'Estaing. Known as 'the cactus', his 'cold and calculating character' and 'large measure of social arrogance' had made him 'insensitive to other people'. The report continued: 'He is capable, as his career well shows, of serious errors of political judgement, in particular of timing. With these handicaps it is remarkable that he now occupies one of the key positions in French politics. This is almost entirely due to his combination of quick intelligence, energy and practical ability.' In terms of Giscard's clear ambitions for the presidency, it seemed that he had little competition. 'On the intellectual level, he has no peers and few rivals,' the authors noted, praising his capacity to deliver the most complex budget speech without notes. The FCO summary concluded icily: 'Married to a rich and pretty wife to whom he is not always very kind'. Four years later, Giscard and his wife, Anne-Amoyne, would be guests of the Queen, making a state visit of their own to Buckingham Palace.

But what of the Queen's hosts on this occasion? The Foreign Office papers reveal an equally clinical analysis of the French President and his wife. 'M. Pompidou's father was the son of a peasant who became a village schoolmaster,' began a profile dripping with old-style FCO snobbery. 'He mixes the cunning and mistrust of the Auvergnat countryman with the suavity of the Rothschild director.' Of his wife, Claude, apparently happier in the company of contemporary artists than politicians or when restoring old farmhouses, the document noted that her life had been plagued by 'gossip and innuendo'. 'Mme Pompidou is shy with somewhat bohemian tastes,' it went on. 'In recent years, her life has diverged from that of her husband. She has loyally supported him in his new role, living perhaps not very happily in the confines of a gilded cage.'

BIENVENUE

If her Parisian debut back in 1948 had been in sweltering heat, the Queen was almost underdressed as she arrived in the French capital at noon on 15th May 1972. Chilly intermittent rain made her grateful for the brown belted coat over her sleeveless brown-and-white Hardy Amies dress. The public lining the streets to see her pass by in her state limousine – a Citroën-Maserati hybrid – would not get a decent look until the convoy reached Les Invalides, whereupon the rain had eased enough for the roof to be pulled back. The crowds were neither as large nor as chaotic as those that had greeted her on her previous visits. That was of little concern to commentators like Charles Hargrove of *The Times*. This state visit would not only be a 'historic milestone' for President Pompidou, but would also 'swing the British people firmly behind the new Europe and jog them out of their concern for the price of butter'. As far as *The Times* was concerned, it made the Queen's 1957 state visit almost incidental, even if the crowds had been larger. 'The context is quite different,' declared *The Times*, 'and the significance immeasurably greater.'

Most of the press, British and French, echoed the sense that this state visit was history in the making, rather than a mere exercise in elegant bilateral back-scratching.

The British Embassy in the rue du Faubourg Saint-Honoré had seldom, if ever, looked more regal. Following his victory at Waterloo in 1815, the Duke of Wellington had actually turned down what would become the Elysée Palace in favour of this stupendously grand residence, for use as his Paris headquarters. To this day, it still contains a throne room – complete with throne.

The Ambassador was determined to exceed all expectations. 'He played a blinder,' recalls his son, Sir Nicholas Soames. 'And so did my mother and so did Nanny.' Although the Soames children had long since left the nursery, their much-loved nanny, Hilda King, would stay with the family for fifty-five years. When the Soameses moved to Paris, nanny came too, happily volunteering for the role of Embassy florist. Come the royal visit, she excelled herself. 'Nanny did all the flowers for the state visit and I don't think I have ever seen anything so beautiful in my life,' Sir Nicholas recalls. 'She couldn't speak a word of French but she would negotiate in the French flower market and beat them into submission. It just looked unbelievably beautiful and it was all done by Nanny. At the end, she was presented to the Queen who gave her a signed photograph. She treasured it for the rest of her life.'

It wasn't just the wishes of the Queen which had to be considered but those of the royal entourage. For example, there had to be 'special arrangements' (otherwise known as large gin and tonics) for Bobo MacDonald, the Queen's dresser. The principal concern of Sir Christopher and his team, however, was to equal, if not outshine, the French in terms of food, drink and elegance.

Round One, however, would go to President Pompidou, with an Elysée Palace welcome lunch of grilled turbot, roast duck, asparagus, cheeses and 'Trianon' ice cream, with Meursault 1969 to accompany the fish and Château Lafite Rothschild 1961 for the duck. Before sitting down, the two heads of state had gifts to exchange. Mindful, perhaps, of her first meeting with M. Pompidou at that 1948 art exhibition, and of Madame Pompidou's interest in contemporary art, the Queen had chosen an abstract painting by Graham Sutherland, called 'Form in an Estuary'.

Though Sutherland's technique had so displeased the Ambassador's mother-in-law, Clementine Churchill, that she had consigned his portrait of Sir Winston to a bonfire, the former war artist was a great favourite of the Queen Mother and had been awarded the Order of Merit in 1960. For Madame Pompidou there was an equally contemporary piece, a brooch with 'E II R' in polished gold, shining 'through the facets of a citrine surrounded by eighteen-carat gold textured wires with pavé diamond darts and scattered diamonds'. Laid out on a table was the badge and ribbon of the GCB for M. Pompidou. As per Roger du Boulay's suggestion, it was formally presented as 'of the Bath', not '*du Bain*'. There would be no decoration for the Queen, since she had received the *Légion d'honneur* on her previous visit. However, the Pompidous had commissioned a hand-made tablecloth and bedspread for the monarch. For Prince Philip, there was a Sèvres porcelain grasshopper.

After lunch, the couple were driven to a residence as palatial as Buckingham Palace, the Grand Trianon at Versailles, which had been renovated at great expense by General de Gaulle to flatter foreign visitors. The first beneficiary after that had been British, too – former Prime Minister Harold Wilson. If all the replica eighteenth-century gilt and velvet had amused the Huddersfield-born chemist's son, one can only wonder how it went down with the man who occupied it ahead of the Queen, Leonid Brezhnev. The curators had been thrilled at the prospect of finally having real royalty in France's grandest royal palace. They were, however, a little disappointed when the recce party from Buckingham Palace had ruled out use of the almost parodically opulent royal bedroom suite, with its vast gilt bed. The Queen and the Duke had, instead, opted for the simpler, quieter 'Consort's Bedroom'.

There was no time to explore, though. Within fifteen minutes of her arrival, the Queen was due to hold a reception for the entire Paris Diplomatic Corps. Every detail would be scrutinised by these gimlet-eyed followers of protocol. In Britain, and around what some still called 'the old Empire', there was continued alarm – if not fury – about Britain's embrace of Europe at the expense of old allies.

WAR OF WORDS

Back in Westminster, the Shadow Europe Minister, Peter Shore, would denounce the royal trip as 'ill-advised and mistimed'. It was certainly unusual for a former Cabinet minister to attack a state visit while it was actually in progress, but Shore was adamant that a constitutional line had been crossed. There was nothing wrong with promoting friendship with France, but it was quite wrong 'for the Crown to be used, as it has been used this week, to give authority to a particular treaty'.

The need to placate the Commonwealth nations, and particularly the Queen's realms, had not escaped Soames and his masters. There would also be a series of small but significant gestures towards the Commonwealth members of the Diplomatic Corps. They would be welcomed at Versailles ahead of all the other ambassadors and would also have their own photograph taken with the Queen.

At the same moment the final touches were being applied to the centrepiece of the whole visit: the speech to be delivered at that evening's state banquet. It would be the definitive statement on Britain's relations not just with France, but with the new European political edifice. The Queen would deliver it on live television beamed across the continent. Any sovereign's speech during a state visit is always the result of three-way collaboration involving the embassy, the Foreign & Commonwealth Office and the Palace – plus occasional input from the Prime Minister's office in Downing Street. On this occasion the process would be far from straightforward and offers a fascinating insight into the competing priorities at the Palace and the FCO. It shows that, far from merely parroting a set text written by her officials, the Queen has had considerably greater involvement in some of her major pronouncements over the years. On the issue of the UK's entry into Europe, the British government view in 1972 can be summed up simply as 'full steam ahead'. At the Palace, the view was unquestionably 'steady as she goes'.

Stored in the National Archives at Kew are successive drafts of the Queen's speech that night. First crafted by Sir Christopher Soames, it began as a stylish and occasionally Churchillian piece of oratory, which would not have sounded out of place if the Queen were a politician addressing a party conference or pouring treacle over some trade summit. The text hailed France as a 'treasure house of the human spirit, a gallery of all that is creative ... I rejoice that I shall be able to see what survives of our common past and what is being fashioned for our common future.' A recurring complaint from Eurosceptics over the years is that the British public were never told the whole story when Britain joined the Common Market, that they were merely led to believe it would be a latter-day version of the Hanseatic League – the alliance of cities and merchants of the Middle Ages. Yet it is hard to fault the Foreign Office's candour in this attempt. 'This is not simply a mercantile league designed to bring about certain profitable adjustments in our national economies, important though that may be,' wrote Soames and his team. 'It is much more. It is a beginning, a point of departure, a turning point in the history of Europe. The destinies of the peoples living on either side of [the Channel] have permanently and irrevocably been joined. This is the size of the change we are seeking to bring about. This is the ultimate meaning of our accession. That is the measure of our faith in the European future.'

Alongside this rich encomium of all things European, there was also an acknowledgement that the Commonwealth – or what the text called 'traditional interests' – had to be 'considered and safeguarded'. However, some things were already beyond the point of no return. 'Some longstanding ideas have been re-shaped by circumstance.'

This was going too far. The European debate was certainly not settled in Britain. For the Queen to 'rejoice' and proclaim her 'faith' in a 'European future' would be difficult territory, with Parliament still sharply divided on the issue. Back at the Foreign Office, senior diplomats started suggesting their own amendments to Soames's draft. C. M. James of the Western European department ran a line through the section on 'permanent and irrevocable' change. 'Too strong when Parliamentary assent still in the balance,' he wrote in the margin. 'Brings the Queen too much into the political arena.'

The next FCO draft would still include a ringing endorsement of European integration. This was to be a 'partnership speaking on great matters with one voice and gathering the genius of many'.

No sooner had this text reached Buckingham Palace in April 1972 than the Queen's Private Secretary, Martin Charteris, started pruning. Out came any lines that might have seemed arrogant and antagonistic to a Commonwealth audience. They included the phrase 'Europe – with its predominant share in the world's commerce, its unique sophistication'.

Any words which suggested that the Queen might personally share the Europhile passions of her senior diplomats and her Prime Minister were chopped. The FCO wanted her to say: 'It gives me great satisfaction to know that the ties between our two countries are being multiplied.' With a judicious stroke of the Charteris pen, this was reduced to: 'Every day, the ties between our two countries are being multiplied.' Thus was sentiment deftly transformed into mere fact. On 28th April, Charteris sent his provisional draft back to the Foreign Office, with a covering letter that made it quite clear there might well be further royal editing. 'The Queen may, of course, make massive alterations to the text.' So much for that received wisdom that the Queen would read out a telephone directory, if her Prime Minister placed one in her hands. Here was her most senior official stating that she would have no hesitation in making 'massive' changes to her government's words. And she did.

On 4th May, Charteris sent back the Queen's own revised version. As Soames would observe later in his despatch, the Queen had indeed been choosing her words carefully. Gone was the reference to 'a common enterprise, dominated by no single focus of national power'. Gone was 'a partnership speaking on great matters with one voice and gathering the genius of many'. More importantly, there was no mention whatsoever of a 'turning point in history'.

And there was one further vintage example of royal editing, in the closing section. The earlier versions had contained the line: 'I delight that our two countries have found this common sense of purpose.' This came back from the Queen as: 'I hope that our two countries will find a common sense of purpose.' In other words, they hadn't found it, and she was not delighted.

If the Foreign Office mandarins were unhappy with this watered-down version of their hymn of praise for Europe, the Foreign Secretary was not going to rock the boat. Sir Alec Douglas-Home professed himself perfectly happy. 'Another splendid speech,' he scribbled on his copy of the text a few days before the visit began. His only query concerned another speech that the Queen was due to give on the second day of her tour, to the city council of Paris at the Hôtel de Ville. It included the line: 'Much of the destiny of Europe has flowed through London and Paris like their rivers.' 'It's very good,' Sir Alec noted politely. 'But does destiny flow like a river? I can't make up my mind!'

VERSAILLES

The refurbished Palace of Versailles had seldom looked quite like this since the days of Marie-Antoinette. As Sir Christopher Soames would write to the Foreign Secretary when it was all over: 'Versailles that evening seemed restored to the purposes for which it had been built, a dream of vanished royal splendour.' President Pompidou had arranged a ballet performance – a truncated version of the ghostly *Giselle* – before leading the Queen through to the Galerie des Cotelle and dinner for 150 at a table lit by 480 candelabra.

It would still be many years before state banquet etiquette permitted speeches before food, however. In 1972, etiquette still demanded after-dinner oratory. The Queen and President Pompidou would have to work their way through a dinner of Périgord foie gras (served with a 1949 Château d'Yquem), lobster pie, leg of St-Florentin lamb, iced gateau and strawberries, before this crowning moment. In as much as Britain's entry to the European Union ever had a coronation, this was probably it. Thanks to the enduring influence of Toni de Bellaigue (and, possibly, a little help from Linguaphone, too), the evening would be conducted almost entirely in French.

President Pompidou began the speeches by assuring the Queen of the 'unanimous reactions of friendship and respect' of the French people – feelings based on 'deep sympathy for the person who bears the weight of the Crown with such grace and dignity'.

Describing Britain and France as 'the two oldest European nations' (a claim with which many might legitimately quarrel), he recalled how they had both been 'at daggers drawn and yet passionately attracted to one another'. The members of the Foreign Office speech-vetting committee had been so nervous about the subject of General de Gaulle that they had even advised the Queen not to utter his name, unless President Pompidou should bring him up first. Christopher

Ewart-Biggs, then minister at the British Embassy,* had warned that it would be 'untactful'. Yet President Pompidou had no such reservations about bringing up his predecessor. 'We shall not forget that in 1940, when France was literally submerged by Hitler's might, Britain alone refused to yield and saved the freedom of the world,' he declared. 'We shall not forget that by welcoming General de Gaulle on your soil, you enabled first Free France, then the whole of France to keep on fighting.'

And there was some eloquent straight-talking, too: 'Not so long ago, your country seemed to consider the Economic Community as one of those continental conditions which, for more than three centuries, Britain had been set stubbornly and successfully to destroy. On her part, France saw in Britain a country determinedly turned toward the ocean, that is to say on the fringe of Europe. We have now convinced each other of the contrary. For the first time in more than ten centuries, from the Sea of Norway to the Mediterranean, the peoples of western Europe are definitely committed to follow the path of economic integration and political co-operation.' There could be 'no afterthoughts', he said firmly. Just over four decades later he would be proved spectacularly wrong. On a night like this, however, Brexit must have seemed as implausible as a last-minute appearance from Louis XVI.

Finally the Queen rose to address the guests with a speech that had, by now, been distilled more carefully than a five-star brandy. Some – though not all – of her amendments had been accepted. The Foreign Office had succeeded in putting some of its preferred options back. In her draft, the Queen had written: 'There is now the prospect that this ancient relationship may be given a new dimension.' On the night, the 'may' had been altered to 'will'. And the Foreign Office had significantly upgraded what would today be called the 'big vision': it was 'a turning point in history', after all. Who had insisted on re-inserting this line? Might it have been the Prime Minister himself? Downing Street always has the last say on such matters. At

* A popular Foreign Office figure, Ewart-Biggs wore a smoked monocle over his glass eye, the result of a war wound at El Alamein. After a good lunch, he would transfer the monocle to his good eye and enjoy a furtive snooze. Soon after arriving as British Ambassador to Dublin in 1976, he was assassinated, along with a young civil servant, by the IRA.

the end of the battle of the speech drafts, between the most Europhile British government in history and the innately cautious Queen and her courtiers, it would appear that the honours were even. There was one section of her speech that had sailed through every draft from beginning to end without a problem. It was one that brought a welcome note of levity on the night. 'We may drive on different sides of the road,' said the Queen, 'but we are going the same way.'

Though the speeches were over, the evening certainly was not. The two heads of state emerged for an after-dinner reception in Versailles's Hall of Mirrors for 2,000 people. 'Only the television lights and the crush of prominent French men and women using their elbows to get near The Queen and the Duke of Edinburgh marred the great reception in the Galerie des Glaces,' wrote Sir Christopher Soames in his despatch afterwards. The French media were entranced by it all. In the words of *Le Figaro*, the Queen's speech and her presence represented nothing less than the 'consecration' of a new era.

VIVE LA DIFFERENCE

The tone of the visit had been firmly established. Now it was time for both sides to enjoy the ambience and the mutual admiration. The following day, the Queen was feted at the Hôtel de Ville as she addressed the municipal council of Paris. In the same rooms where Edward VII had proclaimed the Entente Cordiale in 1904, the Queen saluted Paris with some of the more flowery language that she and her advisers had expunged from the state-banquet speech the night before. 'For us, she is like no other city; rather, she is a light that shines in the imagination,' she noted, once more in fluent French. 'She is timeless, yet she moves with the times.' Despite the Foreign Secretary's misgivings about whether destiny could 'flow' like a river, the Queen rather thought it could: 'Much of the destiny of Europe has flowed through London and Paris like the Seine and the Thames . . .'

Once again, the French media commended the Queen's sense of style – particularly her turquoise beret – and were equally impressed by her choice of guests for a small lunch party that followed at the British Embassy. Rather than inviting the usual civic worthies, the Queen had replicated the 'informal' luncheons that she and the

Duke of Edinburgh had already introduced at Buckingham Palace. At home, every few months, a dozen eminent people at the top of their trades – a theatre director, perhaps, plus a bishop, a chief constable, a professor, and so on – would receive a call from the Deputy Master of the Royal Household asking if they might like to have lunch with the Queen. After the initial guffaws and replies of 'pull the other one', they would be invited to ring the Palace switchboard, ask for the Deputy Master and establish that the invitation was, indeed, genuine. Few have ever declined. The Queen decided to do exactly the same in Paris, mixing together a leading physician, a television executive, the novelist Jean d'Ormesson, and the couturier Pierre Balmain.

For the embassy kitchens, this was just the first challenge of the day. That evening, it was the Queen's turn to host the President to dinner. The Ambassador was in his element – food was always a central plank of British diplomacy during the Soames years. 'The first thing Soames did each day was have a meeting with the cooks to decide what was going to be eaten,' says Sir Roger du Boulay, who served as his Head of Chancery and well remembers his boss's attention to detail. 'He would say: "We haven't thought about the colour. We need some colour – tomatoes or carrots!" And even his house wine would be a fine claret.'

Ahead of the visit, the Ambassador and his chef had carefully plotted how the Queen's return banquet might outdo anything the French could produce. Consommé Madrilène was followed by poached salmon with mousseline sauce, fillet of beef with 'pearls of Périgord' and Sherbet Pauline Borghese. Even the greatest French wine snobs could not fault a selection that included Château Laville Haut-Brion 1962, Château Latour 1949 and Pol Roger 1955 champagne. The Queen had assisted in all this gastronomic one-upmanship by despatching boxes of her finest tableware from home. 'The Palace sent the accoutrements. I remember the unpacking and out came this enormous golden candelabra,' says du Boulay. 'There was a footman who had this wonderful title – Yeoman of the something or other – and I said to him: "I bet there isn't another one like that anywhere in the world". And he said: "There are fifty more like that at home".'

Du Boulay remembers that the Ambassador took such pride in the occasion that he insisted on decanting all the claret himself, including the bottles that would be served at the 'reserve' banquet in another part of the embassy for middle-ranking officials. Since Sir Christopher had enough on his mind, du Boulay did not trouble him with an extra drama. As the Queen, in her silk silver-lamé dress embroidered in gold and silver and overlaid with the sash of the *Légion d'honneur*, awaited the arrival of the President, du Boulay received a telephone call. An Irish voice on the other end of the phone informed him that a bomb was due to explode inside the Embassy in five minutes. 'I was lucky enough to have Perkins* at my side at the time,' du Boulay wrote in his memoir of the period. 'We almost agreed without speaking that there was no time to do anything effective. It was quite a long five minutes. The ambassador never knew.'

The next morning, the presidential Caravelle was waiting to fly the royal party south to the sunshine of Provence. A flight that had threatened to become such a disastrous diplomatic bone of contention passed almost without comment in the media. The press had much more fun when the radiator hose of the royal car exploded in a cloud of steam in the heat of Avignon. According to Sir Christopher Soames, this was the day when 'the psychology of the visit changed'. As he wrote later: 'The sun shone and people shouted. It was rediscovered with delight that, in the British monarchy, majesty can subsist with human warmth and simplicity, as it has never done in France, whether under the flummery of the Bourbons or the Olympian austerity of General de Gaulle.' Even the cantankerous communist Mayor of Arles, it was noted, was charmed. While the Queen inspected the papal palaces and the famous Pont d'Avignon, the Duke of Edinburgh took a helicopter to enjoy a few hours of birdwatching with conservationists in the Camargue. 'The Duke astonished his hosts in the Camargue by successfully identifying a Little Stint, the smallest of the British waders,' the Ambassador noted proudly.

Though all eyes had been on the Queen, the Duke was attracting quite a following of his own among the French public. After yet

* Albert Perkins joined the Metropolitan Police in 1927 and served as protection officer to both the Queen Mother and the Queen. Those who addressed him as 'Perkins' would be gently taken aside and informed that it was '*Mr* Perkins'. They would have to go one step further shortly before his retirement. In 1973, the Queen gave him a knighthood.

another chorus of '*Vive la reine!*', an Avignon man caused cheers when he shouted, '*Vive le duc!*' The Duke ignored him. '*Vive le prince!*' he shouted. Still no response. Undeterred, the man yelled: '*Vive le roi!*' At which point, the Duke burst out laughing and threw up his hands.

It had been arranged that the Prince of Wales, then serving as a junior officer in the Royal Navy, should land in nearby Toulon and join his parents. Together, they spent the evening privately at the celebrated Hotel Baumanière near Les Baux-de-Provence, ahead of one of the most unusual days of any state visit before or since – one that covered hundreds of miles, a factory floor, a day's racing, the Duke of Windsor and a very grand disco.

The morning started with a royal tour of Les Baux, during which the mayor, Raymond Thuillier, placed a firm hand on the Queen's shoulder to stop her straying too close to the edge of a 700-foot precipice. Throughout her reign, dignitaries and VIPs have been scolded in the media for that faux pas of 'touching' the monarch. On this occasion, though, the media did not castigate M. Thuillier for his over-protective impulse. It was a long drop.

Prince Charles, meanwhile, made mildly flirtatious small talk – in French – to a group of local girls dressed in traditional and voluminous Provençal dresses. 'A miniskirt would be more practical,' he said, much to their delight. After inspecting the Aérospatiale factory in Marseilles, the royal party were then ushered back on board the Caravelle and left the South of France for a chilly Paris, just in time for the racing at Longchamp. The fifth race had been billed as the Queen Elizabeth II Cup, after which the Queen departed quietly for what would be her last encounter with the former King Edward VIII.

Though the Duke had nobly declined to die during one of the most important visits of his niece's reign, he was, by now, bedridden and fading fast. Yet he was adamant that he was not going to receive the Queen in either his bedclothes or his bed. Having asked Dr Thin to hide the intravenous drip beneath his shirt, the Duke put on a blue blazer and moved to an armchair in an adjacent sitting room.

As the Queen entered the room with Prince Philip and the Prince of Wales, the Duke summoned all his strength to rise to his feet and then bow, much to the consternation of his doctor. The Queen urged him to sit down and the two of them sat talking for around quarter of an hour, mainly, it was said, about her visit. One of those present informed the biographer Sarah Bradford that the Queen had tears in her eyes as she left the room. She had been moved not just by her uncle's pained chivalry, but by the way in which the Duke had reminded her of her beloved father. Downstairs, the royal party were given tea by the Duchess of Windsor, who was almost overcome with nerves, her hands shaking so badly that she dropped a cup. Just nine days later the Duke was dead, his body flown home to Britain for burial.

DANCING QUEEN

At the British Embassy there were just a few hours to go before one of the grandest occasions in its history, an evening considerably more glamorous even than the Queen's banquet for President Pompidou earlier in the week. To conclude the visit, Sir Christopher Soames and his team had decided to invite President and Madame Pompidou to a white-tie Embassy ball for 1,200, including both the older and younger generations. In addition to the great and good of France, at least 300 'young' would also be included, with the Prince of Wales acting as host to the *jeunesse dorée.*

A giant marquee had been erected over much of the handsome embassy garden. Though the embassy already had its own ballroom, a substantial temporary dance floor was added for the festivities. There would need to be a proper band, of course, but also a disco for 'the young'. Few British ambassadors would have had the confidence and clout to propose something on quite such a scale. The bill for the evening was estimated at £25,000, a sum equivalent to the annual salaries of two Cabinet ministers in 1972. Even the biggest event in the embassy calendar, the annual garden party for the Queen's birthday, was run on a budget of £2,000. Little wonder that memos had been flying all over Whitehall, finally reaching ministerial level. Edward Youde, a future Governor of Hong Kong then running the Foreign Office's personnel department, warned that the cost was ten times that of the dance to mark the Queen's state visit to Brazil three years earlier. Soames would end up footing some of the bill from his own pocket.

Few of those present would forget the spectacle of that evening, or the moment when the Queen entered the ball. 'She walked in to absolute silence and she looked amazing,' says Sir Nicholas Soames. 'It was the least vulgar occasion I've ever seen. Everyone was in their absolute finest.' By now the Queen was on the home straight, but it would still be a long evening of introductions. 'My father's greatest problem was moving her down the line because everyone wanted to touch the hem,' says Sir Nicholas.

While he has fond memories of strutting his stuff to disco hits in full military uniform, one guest who was less keen on dancing was President Pompidou. According to John Ellison of the *Daily Express*, shortly after midnight the Queen suggested that the two of them might lead the dancing. 'It would have been the final definitive gesture of this triumphant visit,' wrote Ellison, 'and it is to be regretted that a man as cultured as M. Pompidou has this small chink in his social armour. He blushingly declined.'

In truth, by this stage no dancing was required to set the seal on a phenomenally successful visit. The *Express* was typical of all the British press when it observed that, despite the 'undoubted friendship' between the French President and the British Prime Minister, 'it needed the Royal Family to clinch the new European deal'. It added: 'Historians may find it amusing to note that in this Twentieth Century, such momentous issues can still turn around an evening of laughter and an invitation to dance in the home of the British Ambassador.'

The next day, the French Prime Minister, Jacques Chaban-Delmas, escorted the royal party to Rouen, where the Royal Yacht *Britannia* was waiting to carry the Queen home. Despite the passage of more than 500 years, the royal convoy sped straight past the spot where Joan of Arc had been burned to death by English troops in 1431. The authorities were adamant that the final focus should be a forward-looking one, not headlines about the Maid of Orléans.

As she entertained M. Chaban-Delmas to a valedictory cup of tea and a ham sandwich on board the Royal Yacht, the Queen despatched a farewell message to M. Pompidou and the French people. In it, she expressed a 'sincere hope that my visit may have helped to affirm the new and hopeful chapter that is opening in the long history of the relationship between our two countries'.

Reflecting on the success of the visit, *The Economist* gave full marks to the visitor. 'She remains a symbol in Europe, in a way Britons barely appreciate, of the good things Britain protected in a European war,' it declared. 'Britain has a particular part to play in the making of Europe and its French-speaking Queen has symbolised it well.'

MONSIEUR LE PRESIDENT

The Queen's relationships with her subsequent French counterparts appear to have been a more mixed affair. She is said to have been fond of socialist President François Mitterrand, whom she met many times and with whom she would open the Channel Tunnel in 1994. There was an easy rapport, too, with the urbane Jacques Chirac. Both presidents would be hosts and guests of the Queen during reciprocal state visits. As London bureau chief for *Le Monde*, Marc Roche was attending the Queen's Golden Jubilee media reception in the very week of the French presidential election in 2002. Chirac was about to take on the neo-fascist Jean-Marie Le Pen, in the second round, and Roche raised the subject with the Queen. 'We were three French journalists standing there and she came to us. I said: "The situation in France, Ma'am, is terrible". And she said: "I hope the French will vote well". So my headline in *Le Monde* was "*La Reine* Votes Chirac"!'

There seems to have been less of a rapport with the quasi-aristocratic Valéry Giscard d'Estaing. Among other things, there was what the French press referred to as '*l'incident de la fenêtre*' at the return banquet during Giscard's 1976 state visit to London. During dinner at the French Embassy, the Queen wanted a window opened to bring in some fresh air. Giscard ordered it shut again. In later life, his romantic novel, *The President and the Princess*, featured an affair between a French leader and a British princess, inviting much speculation (which he denied) that he had harboured a *tendresse* for the late Diana, Princess of Wales. Nonetheless, he would always remain inordinately proud of the Queen's gift to him during his state visit – Sandringham Samba, a Labrador puppy from her own kennels.

The pattern of such visits, of course, is dictated entirely by the government, not the Palace. Soon after his election in 2007, Nicolas Sarkozy received an invitation to pay a state visit to Britain. With weeks to go before his arrival, he had married the singer Carla Bruni, ensuring that he would not be coming on his own. The 2008 visit, held at Windsor Castle, was not quite the success that both sides had hoped for. Marc Roche, by now forgiven for divulging the Queen's remarks about Le Pen six years earlier, was among the guests. 'After the dinner, there were drinks and cigars,' he recalls. 'The Queen was there and I remember talking to Prince Charles. People were saying: "Where are Sarko and Madame?" They weren't there.' The president and his new wife, it transpired, had gone off to bed. 'It was a real faux-pas,' says Roche. 'I don't think he really appreciated it but then he was devoid of charm.'

Sarkozy had left office before any return fixture could be arranged. The Queen was, once again, back on French soil in 2014, for the seventieth anniversary of the D-Day landings in Normandy. In recognition of her personal connection with the war, President Hollande had not only chosen to hold his international ceremony in the former British sector, but had invited the Queen to pay a state visit afterwards. In blazing sunshine, the last head of state to wear uniform in the Second World War was greeted on the same Ouistreham sand where so many men – her father's men – had stormed ashore on 6th June 1944 to liberate France and create a free Europe. As the band struck up 'It's a long way to Tipperary', the VIP grandstand – filled with world leaders, including Presidents Putin and Obama – rose as one to applaud her arrival. So, too, did the adjacent grandstand, filled with the people of Normandy and with French veterans. Whereupon the familiar refrain could be heard once again: '*Vive la reine!*'

Above: Princess Elizabeth (centre) with Princess Margaret, sounding the whistle of the royal train, South Africa, 1947.

Below: Princess Elizabeth, aged 20, during that 1947 tour of southern Africa, her first experience of overseas travel.

Right: Princess Elizabeth during her first visit to Paris in 1948. Vast crowds turned out to welcome 'Zizette', who had yet to tell the world that she was expecting Prince Charles.

Above: Farewell to Empire. Buckingham Palace, April 1949. King George VI and the Prime Ministers of the eight founder members of the modern Commonwealth.

Below: Nairobi, Kenya 1952. Princess Elizabeth is greeted by Prince Selim, a three-year-old boy born the same day as Prince Charles and named after him. He was not easily parted from his bouquet.

Right: With Prince Philip in the grounds of Sagana Lodge, a wedding present from the Kenyan government. Within hours, she would be Queen.

Left: The round-the-world 'Coronation' tour of 1953–4 was the longest in royal history. An early destination was Tonga where the guests sat cross-legged at Queen Salote's state banquet.

Below: In early 1954, the tour reached Australia. Most of the country turned out to see the first visit by a reigning monarch. The Queen and Prince Philip arrive in Hobart, Tasmania.

Below: The Queen returned via Africa and was finally reunited with her children on board *Britannia* in Libya. Before going aboard, she visited the Commonwealth Cemetery at Tobruk to honour the thousands of Allied troops killed there in 1941–2.

Above: The Queen with Germaine Coty, the wife of the French President, René Coty, during her first state visit to France in 1957. The Paris crowds grew so large that mounted police drew their swords at L'Opéra.

Below: The Queen visits her first supermarket – the Giant Food Shopping Center in Maryland – during the 1957 state visit to the USA. Prince Philip was particularly interested in the frozen food section.

Above: The Queen on Broadway. A ticker-tape welcome from New York City as the royal couple travel to City Hall, October 1957.

Left: President John F Kennedy and the First Lady, Jacqueline Kennedy, dine at Buckingham Palace, June 1961.

Above: An elephant called Beauty carries the Queen in to Jaipur, alongside the Maharajah of Jaipur, early on in the six-week tour of India, Pakistan and Nepal in 1961. The government of Jawaharlal Nehru wanted the tour to focus on industry and progress in modern, independent India. The Maharajah had other ideas.

Above: Kathmandu, 1961. A visit to the palatial Hanuman Dhoka. The Duke of Edinburgh has his 'infected' trigger finger wrapped in a bandage, conveniently ruling him out of the King of Nepal's tiger hunt. Weeks later, he would be a co-founder of the World Wildlife Fund.

Below: There had been parliamentary calls for the Queen to abandon her 1961 tour of newly-independent Ghana following a spate of bombings in the capital, Accra. The Queen was having none of it, to the delight of President Kwame Nkrumah who drove her through Accra in an open Rolls-Royce.

Above: For the first banquet of her first state visit to West Germany in 1965, the Queen asked Hardy Amies to design an evening gown matching the rococo swirls of the Augustusburg Palace. Her host was President Heinrich Lübke.

Below: Children in Household Cavalry costumes welcome the Queen to Chile in 1968.

Above: The Queen leaves the official greeting line to meet random members of the public in Launceston, Tasmania, during her 1970 tour of Australia. Days earlier she had done the same in New Zealand. The press had christened it a 'walkabout'. A royal tradition was born.

Below: Emperor Hirohito of Japan is welcomed to London by the Queen in 1971. War veterans demonstrated in silence, though one man threw his coat at the royal carriage.

Left: Brentry. May 1972. The French President, Georges Pompidou, welcomes the Queen to the Palace of Versailles. Her state visit was a celebration of Britain's forthcoming membership of the European Economic Community.

Below: Reviewing the Republican Guard with President Pompidou. The state visit would include racing at Longchamp, a tour of Provence, fierce gastronomic competition between the Élysée Palace and the British Embassy – and the Queen's last encounter with the dying Duke of Windsor.

Left: Canadian Prime Minister Pierre Trudeau welcomes the Queen to Toronto in June 1973. He was her fourth Canadian Prime Minister. His son, Justin, would be her twelfth.

Below: Mobutu Sese Seko, ruler of Zaire, arrives on a state visit in 1973. Few of her staff had ever seen the Queen as angry as when she learned that Mrs Mobutu had smuggled a dog in to Buckingham Palace.

Below: The Queen opens the 1976 Olympics in Montreal. She would do the same in London 36 years later – with James Bond.

Right: The Royal Family and Commonwealth leaders gather at St Paul's Cathedral to mark the Queen's Silver Jubilee in June 1977. Fears of a late appearance by Uganda's despotic Idi Amin proved unfounded.

Below: Marking twenty five years. A Silver Jubilee walkabout in Barbados, November 1977.

Left: 'That frightful little man.' The Queen lays on a full state welcome for the Romanian dictator, Nicolae Ceausescu, in 1978.

Left: A day at the races with the Emir of Bahrain during the Gulf tour of 1979.

Below: The 1979 Commonwealth Heads of Government Meeting (CHOGM) in Lusaka, Zambia. The Queen welcomes the leaders – including the new British Prime Minister, Margaret Thatcher – to an historic summit which led to the creation of Zimbabwe.

Left: April 1980. Lord Soames, Governor of Rhodesia, and his military liaison officer, Lt-Col Andrew Parker Bowles (left) join the Prince of Wales as the Union flag is lowered at Government House, Salisbury. Come midnight, Rhodesia would become Zimbabwe and Salisbury would be Harare.

Right: Lady-in-waiting. In Marrakesh, the Queen is left wondering what has happened to her host, King Hassan, during her chaotic state visit to Morocco. October 1980.

Below: Welcome to Windsor, Mr President. The Queen takes Ronald Reagan on an equestrian tour of the Great Park. June 1982.

Above: 'It's an adventure!' Torrential rain fails to dampen the Queen's enthusiasm as she visits Ronald and Nancy Reagan at Rancho Del Cielo, California in March 1983.

Below: The Prince and Princess of Wales meet Pope John Paul II at the Vatican during their 1985 tour of Italy. A plan for the Prince to 'attend' a Mass was curtailed by Buckingham Palace.

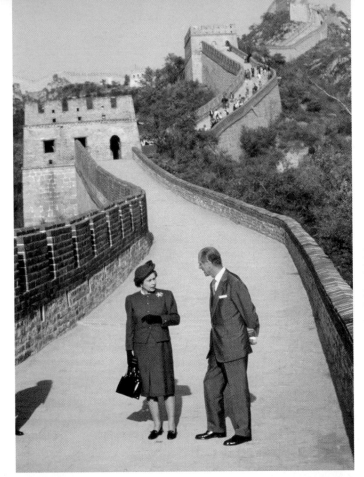

Left: The Queen and Prince Philip on the Great Wall of China during their groundbreaking 1986 state visit. The American media called it 'one of the most symbolic turnabouts in 20th Century history'.

Below: Soviet leader Mikhail Gorbachev comes to lunch with the Queen at Windsor Castle, April 1989. He invited her to visit the Soviet Union. It had collapsed by the time she got to Moscow.

Above: 'All I got is a talking hat!' – NBC commentator after President George Bush fails to lower the lectern at the start of the 1991 state visit to the USA.

Left: The Queen and Duke in Bugac, Hungary, May 1993.

Below: The Princess of Wales with Crown Prince Dipendra of Nepal (1971–2001) at a banquet at the Royal Palace in Kathmandu, March 1993.

Above: The Queen and the French President, François Mitterrand, open the Channel Tunnel in May 1994. Having cut a ribbon on French soil, they travelled through the 31-mile, £10 billion rail link and cut another one in Kent.

Below: June 1994. Britannia leaves Portsmouth for Normandy ahead of the 50th anniversary of D-Day.

Above: 'You and I have spent most of our lives believing that this evening could never happen' – the Queen to President Boris Yeltsin at the Kremlin, October 1994.

Left: President Nelson Mandela welcomes the Queen to South Africa in 1995. A year later (*below*), the roles are reversed during his state visit to London. He would become one of the only (non-royal) world leaders to address her as 'Elizabeth'.

Above: Making an exit. After handing Hong Kong to China on June 30, 1997, the Prince of Wales sails away in Britannia shortly after midnight.

Below: The Queen visits the Golden Temple in Amritsar during her 1997 state visit to India.

Above: 'She gave me a look only a mother could give a child.' President George W. Bush welcomes the Queen to the White House, May 2007.

Below left: The Duke and Duchess of Cambridge at the 2011 Calgary Stampede.

Right: Prince Harry receives a hug from Jamaica's republican Prime Minister, Portia Simpson Miller, 2012.

Left: So near, so far. The 2011 state visit to Ireland, the first since independence, was one of the most important of the reign. The Queen visits Croke Park, sacred nationalist landmark and home of the Gaelic Athletic Association. She is welcomed by Irish President Mary McAleese and the GAA's Christy Cooney.

Right: The Prince of Wales and the Duchess of Cornwall take the Queen's 2012 Diamond Jubilee message to Australia and meet the crowds in Adelaide.

Above: April 2016. Barack and Michelle Obama fly in to Windsor to wish the Queen a happy birthday. She had entered her tenth decade the previous day.

Left: President Obama meets Prince George at Kensington Palace.

Left: King Felipe VI of Spain at the Queen's state banquet, Buckingham Palace, July 2017.

Above: Succession success. The Prince of Wales was unanimously endorsed as future Head of the Commonwealth at the 2018 London CHOGM. It was hosted by the Queen, together with the Secretary-General, Baroness Scotland, and Prime Minister Theresa May.

Below: June 2018. A month after the wedding of Prince Harry to the American actress, Meghan Markle, the Queen invited the new Duchess of Sussex to join her for a day of engagements in Cheshire.

Chapter 8

AFRICAN QUEEN

'There is cause for real concern at the possibility
of an attack on the Queen's aircraft'

DANGER ZONE

The press, the security services and the Prime Minister were as one: the Queen was in danger. Her upcoming overseas tour was not merely ambitious, but fraught with risks. And those risks went far beyond the possibility of her being dragged into an embarrassing political confrontation. That was a foregone conclusion anyway. What was worrying the authorities was the possibility of the Queen being killed. That, at least, was the conclusion of several leading intelligence experts in the early summer of 1979, as the monarch prepared to attend the Commonwealth summit in Zambia, an event that several world leaders were rather keen to avoid. Not since her 1961 state visit to Ghana – when a spate of bombings had led to parliamentary demands for cancellation of the tour – had the Queen been urged to cancel her travel plans for fear of assassination. Once again, the destination was Africa. This time, however, dozens of nations were looking forward to a chance to vent their anger against British foreign policy. As the Foreign Secretary, Lord Carrington, would admit later: 'It had all the hallmarks, that meeting, of being very unpleasant, not to say a disaster.'

In the end, as she had done in Ghana all those years before, it would be the Queen herself who would calm jittery politicians, showing some backbone and pulling off a remarkable piece of international peacekeeping. But in the run-up to the visit, things were not looking good at all. According to several credible reports, the monarch might not even make it to the Zambian capital, Lusaka, alive. The city was on the fringes of a war zone. A senior official at the Ministry of Defence had already warned that her Royal Air Force aircraft risked being blasted out of the sky by guerrillas armed with shoulder-fired Soviet-designed SA-7 missiles, capable of hitting anything within a two-mile range at up to 12,000 feet.* Two Air Rhodesia civilian airliners had been shot down this way in the same region just months before. One disappeared with all on board. Another managed a crash landing that killed most of the passengers, although some escaped. Of the eighteen survivors, ten were rounded up as they staggered from the wreckage and were executed by guerrillas.

The right wing of the Conservative Party was working itself into a fever of anxiety, thanks to reports like the one which reached the desk of the British Prime Minister on 18th July 1979. Margaret Thatcher, newly installed in Downing Street two months earlier, had been alerted to the possibility of a Cuban-backed assassination attempt on the Queen's life. Dotty as it might seem today, Fidel Castro – that closet fan of Her Majesty – was said to be behind a plot to attack the summit, murder the Head of the Commonwealth and create mayhem across the continent.

On top of all that, Mrs Thatcher had been alerted to threats to her own life at the summit. Days before she was due to head for Zambia, Bill Deedes, family friend and editor of *The Daily Telegraph*, sent her a personal note reporting the conversation that he had just had with a leading African politician passing through London. Dark forces, he had been warned, 'would be waiting in the wings for Mrs Thatcher' in Zambia. Not wishing to sound too alarmist, Deedes added cheerily: 'In such matters I would rather be superfluous now than sorry later. So I pass it on.'

All the arrangements for the summit were in disarray, too. The bedrooms for the visiting heads of government were unfinished. One hotel still lacked a boiler, having had no hot water for two months. A fleet of 100 new cars had been ordered to transport all the VIPs

* According to America's Federal Bureau of Investigation, the SA-7 was responsible for bringing down twenty-nine civilian aircraft between 1978 and 1998, accounting for 550 lives.

around Lusaka, but the whole lot were still impounded in neighbouring Botswana. The summit's host, President Kenneth Kaunda, was becoming more prickly by the day and was already picking fights with Mrs Thatcher. Other leaders, including the Prime Minister of Singapore, Lee Kuan Yew, were so worried about the security arrangements that they were looking for excuses to stay away altogether. And all the while, thousands of Marxist 'freedom-fighters' waging guerrilla war in neighbouring Rhodesia were camped around the city, taking potshots at anything they regarded as remotely suspicious.

In London, it was not just Conservative MPs who were alarmed. At the Ministry of Defence in London, senior members of the Armed Forces were also expressing serious reservations about the wisdom of despatching the Queen to a maelstrom of African violence. Sir Douglas Bader, the heroic and much-decorated wartime fighter pilot, had joined the public appeal for her to stay at home. Most significantly, this was a view shared not only by the Prime Minister of the United Kingdom, but by the Prime Minister of New Zealand, too. There was, however, one compelling argument in favour of this ostensibly suicidal royal tour: the Queen was very much looking forward to it.

As Head of the Commonwealth, she was not merely determined to join the rest of the 'club' in Lusaka, with the Duke of Edinburgh at her side. The couple were even going to bring one of their children, too. With such palpable royal enthusiasm on one side, and such grave reservations from two governments on the other, here were the makings of a full-scale constitutional crisis. Yet it would turn out to be among the most important decisions of the Queen's reign. For, as we now discover, she would play a pivotal executive role at a key moment in the history not just of modern Africa, but of the Commonwealth, too. We are often told 'the Queen does not do politics' – and indeed she does not. But over nearly seven decades on the Throne, there have been moments when she has strayed close to the line. On this occasion, she was willing to cross it.

DECLARATIONS OF INDEPENDENCE

Like so many African nations in the late Seventies, Zambia was a fledgling republic adjusting to the concept of parliamentary democracy. On gaining independence from Britain in 1964, the former colony of Northern Rhodesia had opted for a Soviet-style model of government, a one-party state under President Kenneth Kaunda, a former teacher and the youngest of eight children of a Church of Scotland missionary. He would remain in charge for the next twenty-seven years. Though blessed with some of the richest copper deposits in the world, Zambia faced the familiar problems of corruption, food shortages and poor education. For 'KK', however, the overarching issue was bringing an end to white minority rule in neighbouring Rhodesia. Here, a bloody civil war was raging, one that frequently spilled over onto Zambian soil. As well as ending the violence on his doorstep, Kaunda hoped to bolster his position as the elder statesman of African politics. Hence his determination to bring the Commonwealth – and above all the Queen – to his capital for a grand summit. The problem was Lusaka's proximity to the fighting. It was only 70 miles from the Rhodesian border.

Prior to independence in 1964, Northern Rhodesia had met Britain's key preconditions for independent nation status, notably free elections and majority rule. This did not happen in the neighbouring colony of Southern Rhodesia, which renamed itself plain 'Rhodesia'. There, the white minority in charge of the colonial government argued that the country was not yet ready for black majority rule and issued its 'Unilateral Declaration of Independence' from Britain in November 1965. Their new leader, Ian Smith, declared: 'The mantle of the pioneers has fallen on our shoulders to sustain civilisation in a primitive country.' Though this was still British territory, the Labour government of Harold Wilson was reluctant to intervene by force in a colony that had been such a loyal part of Britain's war effort just two decades earlier, and was now being led by a former RAF Spitfire pilot with many friends in Britain. So Wilson ordered the Governor, the symbol of Crown authority in the capital, Salisbury, to sack the colonial government. The Rhodesian authorities ignored the edict. When the Governor accused them of treason, they ignored that, too. The Crown had ceased to command any authority and, in due course, this staunchly royalist colony proclaimed itself a republic.

Rhodesia, like its white supremacist neighbour, South Africa, was now a pariah state. At the same time, colonies all over the former British Empire were heading in the opposite direction, embracing majority rule, gaining independence and joining the Commonwealth. The old, white dominions were now in the minority, and the younger nations had just voted to create the new Commonwealth Secretariat, based in that former royal palace, Marlborough House. No sooner had the Canadian diplomat Arnold Smith started his new job as Secretary-General in 1965, than he was plunged straight into the Rhodesian crisis. The majority of the Commonwealth nations warned Smith that they were very unhappy with Britain's feeble response to Rhodesia's illegal, white supremacist independence. So the Secretary-General drew up a plan of action and submitted it to Harold Wilson. He suggested that the British government should send troops to Rhodesia and that the Queen should broadcast to its people. Wilson refused. Undaunted, Smith raised his plan with the Queen herself at an audience at Buckingham Palace shortly afterwards.

'I never felt inhibited from raising sensitive subjects with her on which my views differed from the British,' he wrote in his memoirs. 'She did not comment directly but I had the impression that she would have willingly taken a more active role in the Rhodesian crisis had Wilson asked her to do so,' said Smith. Perhaps he was being naïve. Yet if he was overstepping the mark in trying to involve the Queen in the dispute, he would have received some sort of signal from the Palace. He did not.

Like the rest of the world, Britain refused to recognise Rhodesia's new rebel administration and helped impose international sanctions. Yet Ian Smith's whites-only regime in Rhodesia could still depend on the support of the whites-only regime in neighbouring South Africa. It also managed to circumvent most sanctions. By the mid-Seventies, however, two black nationalist guerrilla movements were operational in the Rhodesian countryside. One was led by the Marxist ex-schoolteacher Robert Mugabe, from his base over the border in communist Mozambique. Newly independent from Portugal after a bloody struggle, Mozambique became the only country in the world to incorporate the Kalashnikov AK-47 rifle in its national flag. The other guerrilla army was led by former trade unionist Joshua Nkomo, from his base in Lusaka in neighbouring Zambia. Whereas Mugabe was largely supplied by China, Nkomo enjoyed military support from the Soviet Union.

Rhodesia's 'bush war' would last for years, with massacres and executions on both sides. It was both a vicious interracial war and a proxy version of the Cold War. Those white 'settlers' – who had rallied to Britain's side in two world wars – still enjoyed support and sympathy from relatives abroad, from the Conservative benches at Westminster and throughout the 'old' Commonwealth. That sympathy would grow with each new report of missionaries or white families being raped and murdered in their homes. The black 'freedom-fighters', on the other hand, were avenging years of colonial oppression and capitalist exploitation – heroes to socialists everywhere, and to the worldwide movement of non-aligned states. If apartheid was ever to be dismantled in South Africa, then white Rhodesia would have to be toppled first. As the war intensified, the USA attempted to help broker a peace deal, without success. It was now an issue that threatened to split the Commonwealth on both ideological and racial lines: majority black communists versus minority white capitalists. And as the Commonwealth approached its next summit, the time had come to resolve it.

This was the backdrop to a meeting that, decades later, many people still regard as the Queen's finest hour. But why on earth did it have to be held on the edge of a war zone?

It has long been part of British – and Commonwealth – political folklore that it was Margaret Thatcher who endeavoured to scupper the 1979 Lusaka summit, using security fears as an excuse to undermine the unity of the organisation. Given all the battles that she would have with the Commonwealth over southern Africa during her years in office, it is a convenient narrative. But in fact those same fears were already causing deep concern at the highest level, long before she first planted that famous handbag on the desk at Number Ten.

It was not renegade white Rhodesian forces the Foreign Office was worried about so much as poorly trained, undisciplined guerrilla movements. With every fresh atrocity in the bush war came renewed appeals to keep the Queen away. In October 1978, Jim Callaghan received a letter from the Conservative MP Ian Lloyd, reminding the Prime Minister of the fate of passengers on Air Rhodesia Flight 825, just weeks earlier. 'Terrorists who consider it legitimate to butcher the survivors of an air disaster, missionaries and countless thousands of their own people could not be expected to have many inhibitions about their targets, particularly if they happen to be Europeans,' wrote Lloyd, before circulating his letter to the press. Downing Street received many similar letters.

There were more practical worries, too. In the same month the British High Commissioner, Len Allinson, sent a telegram to London warning about standards of hospitality. 'Violent crime is rampant and the problem of ensuring security will be exacerbated by scattered accommodation,' he wrote. 'A German colleague has given us a horrific account of the official visit of the German Chancellor last July.' While the German entourage lost most of their luggage, the recent visit by the British Minister of Overseas Development, Judith Hart, had not been without incident. 'We even had to chivvy the hotel to make Mrs Hart's bed!' Allinson reported.

A month later, he had much more alarming news to report. The new Commonwealth Secretary-General, Sonny Ramphal, had just been to inspect Lusaka and had given Allinson a very frank appraisal. 'Ramphal told me that, in his view, Zambia was on the verge of collapse. Even the smallest things were not working. He believes Kaunda to be worried about the possibility of an Army coup.'

By January 1979, a note of gentle panic was starting to permeate Foreign Office correspondence. Roger Barltrop, head of the Foreign Office's Commonwealth Coordination department, wrote to his colleagues asking what advice they should be giving the Foreign Secretary to pass on to the Queen. Balancing the deteriorating security situation with a desire not to alienate African members of the Commonwealth, Barltrop's considered view was that 'the right decision would appear to be to advise the Queen to accept President Kaunda's invitation, at the same time informing her that her Ministers would keep the security situation under constant review'. He continued: 'The Zambians have made it clear that they expect the Queen to be present; and they and other Africans might well take it as a slight if she did not attend the first regular CHOGM to be held in Africa.' To compound the problem, the Queen was not simply planning to visit Zambia. There were three other important African nations – all former British colonies – on her itinerary, too. They would all be furious if the British government spoiled their big moment.

Barltrop also reminded his colleagues about the damage caused by the Queen's no-show when the Commonwealth had met in Singapore in 1971. 'Non-attendance at Lusaka,' he wrote, 'could affect invitations to future Commonwealth Heads of Government Meetings in some countries, especially republics.' No one needed to be reminded what the Queen would think about that. On top of that was the possibility that some of her other prime ministers might offer conflicting advice on the subject. 'It would seem best not to stimulate the governments of the Queen's other Realms on this point,' Barltrop warned. But one of those other realms was getting ready to cause trouble.

DIVISIONS

Britain was a matter of weeks away from a political milestone: the election of its first female Prime Minister. For now, however, Margaret Thatcher was still in opposition and Jim Callaghan, successor to Harold Wilson, was in Downing Street. His young and energetic Foreign Secretary, David Owen, planned to use the Lusaka summit to engineer a Rhodesian peace deal and had discussed his plans in some detail with the Queen. To this day, he remains in no doubt about her determination to attend. Indeed, he goes so far as to say that the Queen was looking forward to seeing the Rhodesian problem resolved once and for all, as was he. 'That was going to be a very important conference and we had engineered it,' he says. 'She knew what I wanted to do. She understood.'

Owen had devoted a great deal of effort to brokering a deal between the warring factions in Rhodesia. He had travelled around Africa, meeting white Rhodesia's Ian Smith – 'a difficult bastard' – and many of the key African leaders. He had watched one attempted peace conference, involving all the main players in Geneva in 1976, collapse in bitter disagreement. Owen hoped to organise another one in London in 1978, but had been warned by his ablest advisers on the subject that it was too soon; that the Rhodesians would play for time, in the hope of a Conservative victory in the forthcoming British election. With a heavy heart he concluded: 'No more Genevas.' So he had deferred the idea of fresh negotiations until after the 1979 election. Rhodesia would soon be holding an election itself and, this time, the black majority would be allowed a vote of sorts. Given that the white minority would still retain control of all key state apparatus, including the judiciary, the leaders of the black liberation movements called for a boycott. Most of the world denounced the election as a sham.

But white Rhodesians still hoped that if Mrs Thatcher was elected in Britain, she might be more sympathetic to their cause. Knowing that he could achieve nothing until after the election, David Owen could merely pin his hopes on a Labour win. In the meantime, he accompanied the Queen to the Persian Gulf for the start of her first major tour of the Middle East. During quiet moments aboard the Royal Yacht, he talked her through his Rhodesia strategy. 'In February 1979, when we were in Kuwait and Saudi, I really filled her in,' he recalls. 'I told her: "Everything was geared to the Commonwealth meeting. There'll be an election by then, and obviously we think we'll win it. That's the time when we've got to get Zambia and Kenneth Kaunda to step up to the plate". She was fascinated by it.'

As for her personal relations with the summit host, Kenneth Kaunda, and the other black African leaders, Owen is clear: 'There's no question. They were very good, very warm.'

If David Owen still had high hopes for the summit, some of Whitehall's most important figures were becoming seriously concerned. Over the years, historians and commentators have asserted that there were no serious threats to the Queen's safety. In fact there were. Government papers, newly released under Freedom of Information legislation, reflect the level of genuine concern. On 19th March, the Cabinet Secretary, Sir John Hunt, wrote to the head of the Foreign Office, Sir Michael Palliser, with serious worries. Sir John began by quoting the latest Joint Intelligence Committee Report, which warned: 'In Zambia, the concentration of air-defence equipment at Lusaka International Airport and the proximity of trigger-happy ZAPU [Nkomo's guerrilla force] personnel whom the Zambian authorities are unable to control will continue to make the use of the airport hazardous. There is a considerable risk of further mistaken attacks on civil (or Zambian military) aircraft.' Sir John continued: 'If this assessment is accepted, it looks as though we may have to give rather careful thought to The Queen going to Lusaka. I know you are keeping it under review but wondered if you could tell me when you expect it to have to come to the crunch.'

Most white Rhodesians did not want the Lusaka summit to happen, knowing that it would only result in greater Commonwealth pressure to end white rule. They also had considerable support in New Zealand, where many had family connections. The Prime Minister of

New Zealand, Robert Muldoon, had recently alienated many black African leaders with sympathetic remarks towards both Rhodesia and South Africa. Memories were still fresh of the 1976 Montreal Olympics, where twenty-five African countries had announced a last-minute boycott in response to a South African tour by the New Zealand rugby team, the All Blacks. Muldoon was already voicing public fears about the safety of the monarch in Zambia. After all, she was Queen of New Zealand, too. 'He will almost certainly raise the subject with the UK Government,' Britain's High Commissioner to New Zealand warned his bosses on 6th April. Other prime ministers were starting to worry about their own safety. According to the Foreign Office, Singapore's Prime Minister Lee Kuan Yew was beginning to wobble. He had just asked the British High Commissioner for a frank security assessment, purporting to be concerned about the possible assassination of Muldoon.

'He asked whether the Zambians really thought they could prevent an attack on Mr Muldoon,' the High Commissioner, John Hennings, told Sir Anthony Duff. 'What were we doing? Were we offering Zambia an SAS regiment?' Hennings added: 'Lee has a high concern for his own security.' Like a growing number of other people, both Muldoon and Lee Kuan Yew wanted the Commonwealth summit moved to the relative safety of the Kenyan capital, Nairobi.

Things were getting worse. On 12th April, the Foreign Office's Central Africa department received an urgent call from the Ministry of Defence. A crew from the Queen's Flight were about to undertake a 'proving' flight – a trial run – to Lusaka. The Ministry of Defence official, a Mr Perry, insisted that the flight should be cancelled. He warned that there was 'a serious risk of the aircraft, which is conspicuous in colour and markings, being shot down'. By now, however, the Ministry of Defence's increasingly alarmist talk was starting to annoy Foreign Office officials like Assistant Under-Secretary Derek Day. A former Olympic hockey player, who had recently served as Ambassador to Ethiopia, Day knew Africa well and sensed that the Chiefs of Staff were trying to scupper the whole royal tour: 'The action that is being taken in respect of the proving flight seems to be the first shot in their campaign to get the visit called off.' While the Queen herself had no such qualms, she was now worried that all the nervousness about Zambia might affect her proposed tours of the three other African nations on her schedule. She certainly did not want those to be curtailed and her Private Secretary, Philip Moore, made her views clear to the Foreign Office.

GUINEA PIGS

Over at Buckingham Palace, there was certainly no appetite for cancelling the 'proving' flight, let alone the Queen's visit. Indeed, many of her staff – from her chef and her personal detective to her most senior officials – were about to head for Lusaka. Zambia would be her fourth nation during this, the most wide-ranging African tour of a reign that had started in a Kenyan treehouse in 1952. And she was so looking forward to it that nineteen-year-old Prince Andrew would be coming along, too.

As with every royal tour, a 'recce' team would go out in advance to check everything from the bedding arrangements to the state banquet, via every stretch of red carpet in between. Leading this particular recce would be William Heseltine, the Queen's deputy Private Secretary. Known for being calm under fire, it appeared that he might need to display that quality in its most literal sense, as he assembled a party that included the Queen's personal protection officer and her chef, Peter Page.

As the Royal Household team were preparing to depart, the Cabinet Secretary himself, Sir John Hunt, asked all the main players to a meeting in his office on St George's Day, 23rd April. Those present included Heseltine as well as the Queen's principal Private Secretary, Sir Philip Moore; the British High Commissioner to Zambia, Len Allinson; the Prime Minister's Private Secretary for foreign affairs, Bryan Cartledge; and the Captain of the Queen's Flight, Air Commodore Archie Winskill.* It was finally agreed that the 'proving' flight should go ahead. Having twice been shot down over enemy territory during the Second World War (and having twice escaped capture), Winskill was perfectly happy to act as a guinea pig. Heseltine, however, would have to be 'very careful' not to upset the Zambians by overstating British safety concerns. Rather, he was to ask subtle questions and pass the answers back to London for further scrutiny by the Joint Intelligence Committee. Only favoured allies would be privy to the results: 'The JIC assessment

* Within a few years, all of them, like Sir Philip, would be knighted.

could be sent to the Americans and Old Commonwealth countries but external distribution should be considered on a case by case basis.' In other words, the nations of the 'new' Commonwealth were not to be trusted.

Even after more than twenty-five years on the Throne, this was exciting new ground for the Queen. All four nations on her itinerary had been British colonies at the start of her reign and all were now republics, led by authoritarian founding fathers. They had all had bitter quarrels with the former colonial power, but all these leaders had forged a close personal rapport with the Queen herself. The Foreign Office started to prepare its briefing notes for the Queen and her team. First to welcome her would be Julius Nyerere, the ex-schoolmaster in charge of Tanzania and known by all as 'Mwalimu' – a term of address for an important teacher. As the British High Commissioner, Peter Moon, wrote to his masters in London, Nyerere might have had endless fights with the British government – even breaking off diplomatic relations at one point – but he had nothing but the deepest respect for the Queen. To him, the Queen was an emissary of Britain's people, not of its government. 'For the mass of village people in Tanzania, there is still only one Queen in the world, the British Queen,' Moon assured the Foreign Office. 'The sight of the Queen being welcomed in Tanzania will serve to demonstrate to a world audience that whatever differences there may be over the grave problems of southern Africa, both countries attach the highest importance to their bilateral relations'.

The personal connection ran deep. 'The Queen had a particularly good relationship with Julius Nyerere,' says Frank (now Lord) Judd, the former Foreign Office minister who went on to be director of Oxfam. Having known Nyerere well enough to be at his deathbed, Judd sees many similarities between the two leaders. 'He was a serious guy and that was one basis of his friendship with the Queen. He was a very sincere Catholic which was another. And one of his pastimes was translating Shakespeare into Swahili!' Looking back, Sonny Ramphal reiterates that the reason men like Nyerere got on so well with the Queen was that she had been finding her way as a new monarch in parallel with their own struggles for independence. 'She was a young woman when the Nyereres and Kaundas were young men,' says Ramphal. 'She understood their aspirations in the way an old grandee never would.'

The tour would also include Malawi. The Queen had grown very fond of Dr Hastings Banda, its 'Life President', though in his case there was a considerable age gap. Officially born in 1906, and therefore twenty years older than her, he was believed by some to have been born in 1898, making him a Victorian. Having led the former colony of Nyasaland to independence, Banda had been dreaming of a visit from the Queen since it was reborn as Malawi in 1964. After having worked as a medical doctor in Scotland for many years, he was something of an expert on British history. He was also fiercely anti-communist, anti-pop culture, pro-Commonwealth and one of the few black African leaders to maintain diplomatic relations with South Africa and Israel. Seldom seen without his black homburg hat, sunglasses and fly-whisk, he was rigorous in balancing the economy and repaying international loans. Though in favour of technological progress, he disliked other facets of modernisation. Journalists covering the royal tour would be warned that a jacket and tie were expected at all times, and that flared trousers were not permitted 'if the bottom of the trouser is one-sixth more than the narrowest part of the leg'. As for political opposition, Banda liked to describe any would-be opponents as 'food for crocodiles'. In his personality notes for the royal party, the British High Commissioner Mike Scott summed him up thus: 'One of the most remarkable figures in Africa. In some ways he is like an African chief and draws on the respect due to his age ... With advancing years, he shows increasingly an old man's weakness for rambling on about the heroic past but his grip and ruthlessness have in no way diminished.' The Queen's decision to visit Malawi, said Scott, had given Banda 'the greatest pleasure.' Indeed, the President's Private Secretary admitted that on giving the President the news, he 'could at that moment have asked for anything and got it'.

The welcome would be no less effusive in Botswana, where the President, Sir Seretse Khama, was an Anglophile with a British wife and two sons enjoying a British education. Years later, Botswana would become a much-loved destination for both Prince William and Prince Harry; the latter would woo the future Duchess of Sussex there, and even chose a Botswanan diamond for her engagement ring. The Foreign Office, however, had wanted to omit this leg of the tour altogether, in order to free up more time elsewhere. That idea was scrapped when word reached the Foreign Secretary, David Owen, a great admirer of Sir Seretse Khama. 'Outwardly easygoing, he is shrewd and level headed,' Britain's High Commissioner, Wilfred Turner, wrote from the capital, Gabarone. Khama, he went on, was 'devoid of personal vanity' and 'believes firmly that multi-party democracy of the Westminster model is the right system for Botswana. A firm believer in the Commonwealth connection.'

The Queen should also expect to be grilled about the royal farms, however. 'Cattle is an unfailingly successful topic of conversation,' Turner added. 'The President is probably the largest owner in the country and all Ministers own cattle. It is not polite to ask how many cattle are owned but almost any other aspect of a beast can be discussed.' So far, so good. It would be the fourth and final destination, Zambia, that would be the problem.

At the end of April 1979, William Heseltine and his Palace colleagues set off for Africa. In Tanzania, they were warmly received by President Nyerere in person. He was thrilled to learn that the Queen and Prince Philip would be bringing Prince Andrew, too. In Malawi, the 'recce' party were astonished by the opulence of the Life President's palatial residences. They were also charmed by the two sisters who seemed to control every aspect of the unmarried Banda's life. Tall and stately, Miss Kadzamira rejoiced in the title of 'Official Hostess'. Her sister, Miss Mary – 'short and full of giggles', in the words of one member of the British party – was Dr Banda's Private Secretary. Tanzania and Malawi were clearly well prepared for the Queen. Ditto Botswana. Zambia was a very different story.

Back in Britain, the Conservatives had just won the general election and Margaret Thatcher's era as Prime Minister had begun. At the very moment her new government was being sworn in before the Queen at Buckingham Palace, the Palace guinea pigs were arriving in Lusaka. The omens were not encouraging. Though no one had fired any missiles at his RAF Andover of the Queen's Flight, Air Commodore Archie Winskill was formally detained by the military on arrival, on the grounds that he had lacked official clearance to land. This was a novel experience for the double DFC-winning Battle of Britain veteran. The Palace team found a city in chaos, with a nightly curfew imposed, due to recent raids from Rhodesian special forces. As Heseltine reported back to London: 'Everyone has to be indoors by 8.00 p.m. and as the stories of shootings, lootings and general misbehaviour of the troops mounting the road blocks multiply, you are not disposed to quibble.' To make matters worse, half the people he needed to talk to were not in the country.

Soon after landing in Zambia, Winskill received a secret telex from the office of the Assistant Chief of the Air Staff in London. It warned him that British intelligence had just learned of three new SA-7 missile attacks on aircraft in the area, though none had hit its target. It read: 'Although risk has marginally increased since you departed UK, consider flight can continue; nevertheless, believe threat from SA-7 would be reduced if aircraft remained above 15,000 feet in controlled airspace whenever possible.' Whether Winskill chose to share that alarming piece of news with the rest of the Palace team is unclear. The following day, as the party flew to inspect the Queen's itinerary through Zambia's copper belt, he deployed the same Spitfire-style evasion tactics he had learned during the war, approaching the runway in what Sir William Heseltine remembers as a 'perpendicular dive'.

Though the plane landed safely, Winskill then found himself under arrest once more, along with his entire crew. Again he was accused of landing without permission – a ludicrous situation, given that the entire mission had been arranged with the President's office. What was most alarming was not the general level of incompetence, but the fact that the Zambian government and the Zambian Defence Force did not appear to be talking to each other. The next day, Heseltine and the High Commissioner, Len Allinson, had a meeting with President Kaunda, who 'immediately expressed his regrets' that the Queen's personal pilot had twice been arrested for landing his plane where he had been supposed to land it. However, there was one upside to this embarrassing shambles. Knowing how sensitive Kaunda could be to criticisms from the British side, London was still reluctant to voice the true extent of its security concerns. Yet when Heseltine gently suggested that the British would like to send a senior military official to 'check everything over' just before the Queen's arrival, Kaunda positively welcomed the idea. By now, Heseltine had other things to worry about, not least the Queen's accommodation. She was due to stay at State Lodge, a government guest house. 'Considerable work is in progress on extending the kitchens and bedrooms,' he noted. 'I found it incredibly pongy, but I hope this will not be noticeable when the workmen have left. It is in a most attractive setting.'

ENTER THE IRON LADY

Now that Mrs Thatcher had been elected, white Rhodesia and its network of allies wasted no time in trying to persuade the Prime Minister and her new Foreign Secretary, Lord Carrington, to be more sympathetic. With any luck, they thought, they might still be able to scupper the Queen's visit to Zambia, and thus undermine a Commonwealth summit that would not play well for white Rhodesian interests. The Rhodesian leader, Ian Smith, wrote to the new British Prime Minister declaring: 'All Rhodesians thank God for your magnificent victory.' Within days, Carrington had received a 'secret memo' from Harry Grenfell, a well-known British businessman with influence and connections all over Africa. His mother had known Cecil Rhodes, the colonial founder of Rhodesia, and he himself was friendly with Malawi's President Banda; Grenfell was now urging the British government to get the Commonwealth summit moved from Zambia to the relative safety of Kenya. Lusaka, he warned, was now at the mercy of rogue Zimbabwean nationalist guerrillas, and Zambia's President, Kenneth Kaunda, could do nothing about it. 'Kaunda does not have the forces to control Joshua Nkomo's undisciplined forces,' wrote Grenfell. Playing on Western fears of Soviet influence, he reported 'Joshua Nkomo is virtually under the control of the KGB in Lusaka.' He included a graphic account of Nkomo's reprisals against white civilians living in Zambia not far from the Queen's guest house. Grenfell reported that, just two weeks earlier, Nkomo's guerrillas had attacked a white family a mere 12 miles outside Lusaka. 'The mother was raped in front of the family, the father and mother were tortured in front of the children, then all murdered,' wrote Grenfell. 'It would be unthinkable to hold [CHOGM] in Zambia or Zimbabwe/Rhodesia whilst they are at war.'

While FCO officials had been all in favour of sending the Queen to Lusaka while Labour had been in power, they were now less enthusiastic under the new Tory leadership. James Paterson of the Commonwealth Coordination department concluded that Grenfell had made some 'good points'. However, Britain could not be seen to be demanding a change of summit venue when so many African nations were adamant that the summit should take place in Lusaka. It would be better for the British to lie low and leave it to others to make trouble.

New Zealand's Robert Muldoon was more than happy to step forward. On 22nd May, he told his Cabinet that 'there are a lot of surface to air missiles in the area. If we do fly into Lusaka, I will certainly be on the edge of my seat.' With so much else to deal with during her first month in office, the subject was still not uppermost in Mrs Thatcher's mind. That changed on 1st June after she received a long secret memo from the Cabinet Secretary, Sir John Hunt, laying out the situation. He was certainly not glossing over the dangers: 'There is cause for real concern at the possibility of an attack on the Queen's aircraft as it approaches or leaves Lusaka from anti-aircraft missiles held by the Zambian forces and, more particularly, from those held by ZAPU [Nkomo's Zimbabwe African People's Union]. There have been several instances of missiles being fired within Zambia on civilian or Zambian airforce aircraft in the nervous belief that they were Rhodesian. There can be no great confidence that the risk of similar inadvertent attack on The Queen's aircraft would be removed by the issuing of official Zambian instructions.'

Presented with this bleak report from her most senior civil servant about the potential assassination of the Queen during her first few months in office, it is not entirely surprising that Mrs Thatcher began to have reservations about Lusaka. A staunch monarchist representing an avowedly royalist party, she would be appalled at any suggestion that she might be endangering the Queen. Should the visit go ahead and anything go wrong, it would be the instant end of her prime-ministerial career. For Sir John was clear about the options. The Queen was going to Lusaka wearing two hats. For the first few days she would be paying a state visit to Zambia as Queen of the UK and would, therefore, be 'solely dependent' on Mrs Thatcher's advice for that part of the trip. However, others were entitled to advise her when it came to the Commonwealth summit: 'It would be open to Prime Ministers of her other realms to give their views on the advisability of her presence in Lusaka as head of the Commonwealth.' Ultimately, he asserted, the final call was Mrs Thatcher's: 'In the last resort, the UK Prime Minister must have the ultimate duty (as Prime Minister of the country where the Queen resides) to tender advice on the matter.' This was a bold constitutional claim by the British government – namely, that its own advice outweighs that of the Queen's other realms. To this day it is one with which constitutional lawyers in Canberra or Ottawa, or any of the Queen's other realms, might well disagree. For it challenges the sacred notion of the divisibility of the Crown. And that claim was about to be put to the test.

On the very same day, the Foreign Office sent all its central African missions an alarming new report about another VIP flight that had recently come under attack in Zambian air space. In gripping minute-by-minute detail – which reads more like a film script than an official report – it detailed the fate of a Falcon jet from Gabon, which had been flying an official delegation, including a senior Gabonese minister, from Botswana to Lusaka a few weeks earlier. The report was written by the captain of an Air Botswana aircraft who witnessed the entire episode from above. The pilot of the VIP Falcon jet had reported fuel trouble and had requested emergency permission to land at Livingstone, a Zambian town close to the Rhodesian border. The Zambian air-traffic controller insisted that, emergency or not, he would still have to get diplomatic clearance first. After a frantic few minutes, the pilot was told that although diplomatic clearance had been granted, the air-traffic controller was still unable to contact the ground troops surrounding the airport. 'The pilot was now extremely agitated and expressed fear for the safety of his passengers and demanded permission to land,' said the report. 'It was ten seconds after the Falcon was cleared to land that the next transmission came from Livingstone. In the background could clearly be heard rapid fire of heavy guns and a very distressed controller shouted: "For God's sake climb quickly, quickly! You are being shot at by the ground troops, steer on 057 radial and continue to Lusaka, I cannot give you permission to land. I have no communication with these soldiers. Climb, quickly climb." '

Panic had broken out on board the ministerial jet, as a 'very distressed' female voice came on the airwaves shrieking that the President of Gabon, no less, was on board the aircraft. Seconds later the pilot reported that his plane had been hit and could not possibly make it to Lusaka. Whereupon the captain of Air Botswana flight A2-ABY, who knew the area well and had been listening in, saved the day. He quickly contacted air-traffic control at nearby Victoria Falls, just over the border in Rhodesia, obtained emergency clearance for the Gabonese jet and directed the Falcon to safety. 'Is this not in

Rhodesia?' the Falcon pilot asked as his bullet-scarred plane descended towards the hated pariah state. 'In your position,' his saviour from Air Botswana replied, 'you cannot be choosy.'

By early June, the Queen's safety had become a major talking point in the British press. Now the 'will she?/ won't she?' debate was joined by Sir Douglas Bader. Writing in the *Daily Express*, the great fighter ace, famous for his wartime heroics despite losing both legs in a pre-war accident, declared that the Queen should not travel to Zambia. A week later, the New Zealand Prime Minister, Robert Muldoon, was in London for a lunch meeting with Mrs Thatcher and held a press conference reiterating his worries about the Lusaka summit. 'If it's held, I'll go. No question about that. The concern is for the safety of the Queen,' he said, adding that Mrs Thatcher was of the same view.

Previously classified minutes of the lunch meeting reveal how the politicians were a great deal more worried than the Queen herself. Lord Carrington, it was noted, feared that ZAPU guerrillas 'might resort to some act of desperation' against the Queen. As the Prime Minister noted: 'The Queen is determined to go to Lusaka and Kenneth Kaunda is determined to have her.'

Though two of her prime ministers had grave doubts, neither the Queen nor her officials were giving any thought to cancellation. Rather, they were already planning their packing. The British High Commission was bombarded with questions. What would Prince Andrew need for his safari? Back came the reply: 'Normal bush wear and stout shoes. Mosquito nets will be provided.' The Master of the Royal Household wanted to know the precise dimensions of the plates that he hoped to use at his state banquet. He would also require twelve dozen bottles of tonic water and six dozen of soda (the Queen would bring her own spirits to go with it). Like the Queen, the Commonwealth Secretary-General, Sonny Ramphal, was extremely anxious to see the summit go ahead. If it was derailed, he feared that the entire Commonwealth might fall apart. Looking back, he believes that the Queen felt much the same. He knew that winning round Mrs Thatcher was essential.

Ramphal feared that Mrs Thatcher might be about to recognise the result of the recent Rhodesian election, following which the rebel colony had renamed itself 'Zimbabwe-Rhodesia'. A black prime minister had been installed, Bishop Abel Muzorewa, but all state controls were still in the hands of the white minority. The two Zimbabwean liberation movements had boycotted the election entirely. The United Nations, the USA and most of the world had refused to recognise the result. If Britain endorsed the vote and granted independence to this regime, there might be full-scale war in a country where up to 500 people were already being killed each week. Ramphal went to see Mrs Thatcher a week after her lunch with Robert Muldoon – whom he still refers to by the nickname that his opponents liked to use. 'Piggy Muldoon was poking the fire,' he says. 'He was trying to sabotage the meeting.' In his memoirs, Ramphal recalled that he was expecting trouble. He found that Mrs Thatcher was a 'good listener to well-marshalled argument', though she would not be swayed when he urged her to stop referring to the two liberation movements as 'terrorists'. Could she not acknowledge that they were just like Tito's partisans fighting the Nazis in the Second World War? Might she, he begged, call them 'freedom-fighters'? Not a chance. 'Of course they are terrorists,' Mrs Thatcher replied. 'They are just like the IRA'. However, Ramphal was also able to remind her of one crucial factor that was not lost on the new Prime Minister. Oil-rich Nigeria had just announced that it would refuse all future trade with British companies until Britain 'clarified' its position on Rhodesia. As a result, British firms had just been prevented from bidding for a £100 million port development. Ramphal assured her that if she came to Lusaka in a positive frame of mind, there would be 'no ganging up on her'. Her mind was still not made up, however, on what advice she would be giving the Queen.

The summit was now six weeks away. With each passing day, the tension mounted. On 21st June, Len Allinson reported from Lusaka that another plane – from Mozambique – had been shot at by Robert Mugabe's guerrillas. In the same week a plane carrying Lord Harlech, Mrs Thatcher's special envoy to the region, had been detained by the Zambian authorities, just like Archie Winskill's RAF Andover the previous month. By now, Britain had appointed its senior military expert to travel there to inspect royal security arrangements, under the agreement that President Kaunda had reached with William Heseltine. Except that when Air Vice-Marshal Henry Reed-Purvis arrived to see Kaunda on 25th June, the President was not available. Reed-Purvis was informed by an assistant that the President had no recollection of any such agreement about security. As it happened, on the same day Rhodesian special forces decided to launch an audacious assault on a guerrilla base in Lusaka itself, just a mile from the Commonwealth conference venue. With a battle raging on his doorstep – literally – President Kaunda quickly changed his attitude. The next day he agreed to meet the Air Vice-Marshal after all.

In the British media, the mood swung between concern for the Queen and praise for her *sangfroid*, for it remained abundantly clear that she was not wavering in her enthusiasm. On 28th June, *The Daily Telegraph* quoted an 'informed source' saying that 'the Queen is accustomed to visiting countries where there is some danger', adding: 'It is not in the Queen's nature to shirk responsibility.' The *Daily Mail*, on the other hand, was reporting fresh security warnings under the headline 'Queen's Life in Danger'. It called for cancellation. A few years later the Queen's relationship with Mrs Thatcher would reach crisis point over allegations of disagreements on both social and Commonwealth policy. Even in those early days of the new Tory government, however, there were signs of friction. One guest at a Palace garden party in the run-up to the summit was struck by the almost theatrical way in which the Queen and her officials would say: '*When* we go to Lusaka ...' He adds: 'There was no question of "if".'

It was not just the fact that the Queen felt a duty to attend any gathering of 'her' Commonwealth. She was also, no doubt, mindful of an argument echoed by that wise old Africa hand, Sir Anthony Duff, in a recent memo to Foreign Office ministers. He warned that if the Queen abandoned Lusaka, it could even jeopardise Prince Charles's prospects of being Head of the Commonwealth in the future. As he put it: 'If a feeling developed that the Queen, when acting as Head of the Commonwealth, was too much subject to the control of the British government, it might increase the numbers who argued, when the time for the succession came, that the next head of the Commonwealth should not be the Queen's successor.'

The tensions between the Palace and Downing Street would come to a head on 2nd July. During a visit to Australia, Mrs Thatcher was asked whether she would finally confirm that the Queen would be going to Lusaka. She would say only that she 'hoped' this was the case, but could not yet offer 'final advice'. Commonwealth officials were dismayed by her negative tone, echoing Robert Muldoon's 'serious concern'. 'I was shocked at her ineptness,' former Secretary-General, Arnold Smith, wrote in his memoirs. 'It was, after all, not the job of the British Prime Minister to advise the Head of the Commonwealth on this matter. It was the responsibility of Sonny Ramphal as Secretary-General or of all the Heads of Government collectively.' He was wrong on both counts. The Queen would be travelling to Africa in her capacity as the head of state of the United Kingdom. It was only once she arrived at the summit in Lusaka that, with a wave of the constitutional magic wand, she would be transformed from Queen of the UK into Head of the Commonwealth. Even then, its leaders had no right to give her formal advice, and vice versa.

But the Queen's thoughts were abundantly clear a few hours later, when the Palace took the extraordinary step of issuing a statement. It was a terse message, but one that wrong-footed Mrs Thatcher and the Rhodesian lobby. The statement said simply that it was the Queen's 'firm intention' to travel to all four African nations, including Zambia, the following month. It was now abundantly clear to Mrs Thatcher that nothing was going to stop the Queen. It was a question of minimising the risks as far as possible.

Deals had to be struck – and fast. Sonny Ramphal was well aware that one more rogue missile could scupper everything. So the Commonwealth Secretary-General had managed to persuade Joshua Nkomo and his guerrilla army to offer a ceasefire for the duration of the Queen's African tour. Nkomo then downgraded his ceasefire to a mealy-mouthed offer of a 'standstill'. But it was enough to extract an assurance from the new Muzorewa government of 'Zimbabwe-Rhodesia' that it would take 'no action which would endanger Queen Elizabeth or anyone attending the Commonwealth conference'. Now Mrs Thatcher had one further demand for President Kaunda, if she was not going to make things more difficult. She wanted a senior British military expert to be allowed to supervise patrols around the airport for the duration of the summit. The President agreed at once.

And so, on 9th July, the relevant Cabinet ministers, civil servants, diplomats, intelligence services and military chiefs trooped into the Prime Minister's office in Downing Street for a final conference. Their conclusion was a masterpiece of Whitehall-speak: 'In the light of the very thorough precautions, there was no need for the Queen to be advised not to leave the country.' It was now down to Mrs Thatcher to make the formal decision. The following week, on 17th July, she informed the House of Commons that her mind was made up: she was *not* going to tell the Queen not to go to Zambia. It was just as well, because two days later the monarch was on her way.

'LONGA-LIVA-QUEEEEN'

The royal tour set off at a familiar pace in Tanzania, with the usual blend of military parades and cultural displays. William Heseltine can still recall the smell of cloves in Zanzibar, and the royal trip to a model village on the slopes of Mount Kilimanjaro, built on the principles of President Nyerere's doomed '*ujama*' vision of collective farming. Conditions were basic in a country that had only just emerged from its own local conflict, ousting the deranged Idi Amin from neighbouring Uganda. Much to the amusement of the royal party, the Queen's press secretary, Michael Shea, was in something of a state. A rat, he reported, had walked across his bed. At head-of-state level, however, the mutual admiration between the monarch and the Shakespeare-loving president grew ever stronger.

From Tanzania, the royal party flew on to Malawi, starting in the old capital, Blantyre. The League of Malawi Women could always be expected to turn out on such occasions wearing the *Chirundu*, a form of ceremonial national dress featuring the Life President's face. But no one could ever recall seeing them in such numbers. Together with crowds of schoolchildren, they lined the entire eight-mile route from the airport to Banda's Sanjika Palace, with chants of 'Longa-liva-Queeeeen' all the way. An exchange of decorations – an honorary knighthood for President Banda, and the Order of the Lion of Malawi (First Class) for the Queen – was followed by a reception for 350 and a state banquet. The evident rapport between the two leaders manifested itself in several ways. The African media regarded it as highly significant that Banda had removed his sunglasses in the presence of the Queen. British royal observers were struck by the unusual sight of the Queen with her elbows on the table for much of the state banquet, deep in conversation with her host. An entire roasted ox was carried aloft by six warriors, after which the President rose to speak at length. His speech was largely a homage to his own economic policies and to Scotland. He reminded his guests that Blantyre was named after the birthplace of the Scottish missionary, David Livingstone. Banda explained that he himself had been educated at a Scottish mission school and that he had enjoyed his years working there. In reply, the Queen assured him that he was still fondly remembered at Edinburgh Royal Infirmary. But she also used the occasion to lay down a clear marker for the forthcoming summit in Lusaka, 'when everyone will have opportunities for that consultation and cooperation which is the essential fabric of the Commonwealth'. In a relatively short speech, she mentioned Commonwealth 'cooperation' three times. The Head was laying down an early demand for unity.

The next day, the royal party moved on to the new capital, Lilongwe. A walkabout and wreath-laying were followed by a meeting with war veterans from the King's African Rifles. They included one old soldier who had served the Crown in both world wars and could remember his regimental number, but not his age. Dr Banda and the 'Official Hostess' produced a private lunch for the royal party at another presidential palace, where the Queen planted one of twenty-four English roses that had come with her. They were a personal gift for President Banda. Now one week into her tour, she was to have a rest day. She had chosen to spend twenty-four hours on Malawi's Zomba Plateau, taking in Queen's View, a famous vantage point named after her mother, who had visited in 1957.

If the Queen was greatly enjoying herself, the same could not be said of Margaret Thatcher, as she prepared to fly out to join her monarch and her fellow Commonwealth leaders in Lusaka. She was still uneasy about the idea. A senior member of the Commonwealth team (and future Secretary-General), Emeka Anyaoku, believes that her earlier reluctance to let the Queen go to Lusaka was, in part, due to self-interest. 'She didn't want to go herself,' he says. 'The Queen not going would have been a possible excuse for her.' The fact that Mrs Thatcher would eventually arrive in Lusaka wearing dark glasses reflects the strains on the new Prime Minister. Her Foreign Secretary, Lord Carrington, later described an exchange, after seeing her produce the sunglasses during the flight to Zambia. 'Margaret answered very clearly: "I am absolutely certain that when I land at Lusaka they are going to throw acid in my face." I laughed. "You totally misunderstand Africans! They're more likely to cheer you." Margaret stared at me. "I don't believe you." '

We might laugh at this melodramatic moment in the prime-ministerial VC10, but Mrs Thatcher's fears were more understandable in the light of newly unearthed correspondence. In the very week the Queen left for Africa, she received a letter from the former Foreign Office minister, Julian Amery. The son-in-law of the former Prime Minister Harold Macmillan, Amery was firmly on the right of the party and someone whom Mrs Thatcher would come to regard as an authority on African matters. Downing Street papers show that Amery had obtained a report from an American academic who had been monitoring the recent Rhodesian elections and claimed to have uncovered a Cuba-based international communist plot to kill the Queen in Lusaka. The assassination would then be blamed on the Rhodesians. Professor John Hutchinson of the University of California in Los Angeles added that he had heard similar rumours from anti-Castro Cuban exiles in the United States. He wanted to discuss his findings with both the British and South African governments. 'The great fear in Salisbury is that someone will kill the Queen and blame it on Zimbabwe Rhodesia,' he wrote. 'The Cuban representatives I have met with believe that the Queen and other participants in the conference are in grave danger. They believe Castro intends to invade Zimbabwe if security deteriorates sufficiently and that he may well intend to disrupt the Commonwealth conference.' With hindsight, it is a Cold War conspiracy theory at the far end of the bonkers spectrum. How could Castro possibly hope to invade one, if not two, landlocked African countries? Though Israeli commandos had launched an astonishingly successful raid on Uganda's Entebbe Airport to rescue more than 100 hijacked hostages three years earlier, Hutchinson's scenario was preposterous. Cuba was no Israel. The fact that this report reached the desk of the Prime Minister a fortnight before the summit illustrates the febrile international backdrop to Lusaka. However, the need for a deal on Rhodesia had now become even more pressing. On the eve of the summit came news from Lagos. Nigeria had just announced it was nationalising British Petroleum as a punishment for Britain's policy on Rhodesia.

After a final day with Dr Banda and the 'Official Hostess' at the Sanjika Palace in Lilongwe, the Queen, Prince Philip and Prince Andrew departed for their third African state visit. Over two days they were shown the best of Botswana's two chief industries – diamond mining and cattle – and attended Sir Seretse Khama's somewhat chaotic state banquet in their honour at the Holiday Inn in Gabarone. While the President saluted the Queen's 'great personal courage and commitment', the police patrolled the premises ordering all the other hotel guests to 'stay in your rooms'. It was the calm before the storm. The Foreign Office had just sent a telex to the Queen's Private Secretary containing a draft copy of the speech that President Kaunda was intending to deliver at his state banquet for the Queen in Lusaka. And it made for excruciating reading. Kaunda was going to begin by congratulating the Queen on making a 'personal' decision to come to Zambia, when it was manifestly a visit on behalf of both her nation and her Commonwealth. In the very next sentence, he went off the scale: 'You made it amidst and despite intensified psychological warfare by our arch-enemies aimed at maligning our country and destroying the Commonwealth.' Here was a clear dig at Mrs Thatcher's earlier reluctance towards the idea, one which would be deeply embarrassing for the Queen to sit through and was guaranteed to alienate Mrs Thatcher. Kaunda could hardly have been more flattering about the Queen herself: 'You are an all-weather friend ... The entire world became a board of examiners assessing Buckingham Palace's performance in a "test" on Commonwealth leadership. We are glad Your Majesty passed with distinction.' Never entirely comfortable hearing herself being praised to the skies, the Queen would cringe at being told: 'People like you strengthen the positive forces that make universal brotherhood and love instruments of true and durable peace.' Most problematic, however, were Kaunda's attacks on the 'tottering rebel regime in Rhodesia' and their sympathisers. 'We hope that the small lunatic fringe in Rhodesia will not lead to the break-up of the Commonwealth.' In tone and substance, it could hardly have been further from the Queen's unifying call for 'cooperation' a few days earlier.

As if that was not enough of a headache for the British High Commissioner, Len Allinson, he had just been informed that Kaunda was going to introduce the Queen to the anti-Rhodesian guerrilla leader, Joshua Nkomo, when she landed at the airport. While this was, presumably, one way of ensuring that Nkomo's jumpy militiamen did not fire any SA-7 missiles at the royal plane on its way in, it could hardly be more likely to enrage the white leadership of

Zimbabwe-Rhodesia and create a hostile mood. Still, at least it took everyone's minds off the fact that, the very same day, Rhodesian commandos had just launched another raid into Zambia, possibly in revenge for the abduction of a group of white missionaries three days earlier. The Queen was now less than twenty-four hours away.

Allinson immediately went in search of the author of this dreadful speech that President Kaunda was about to deliver. The same man had also been behind the royal invitation for Nkomo. He was Mark Chona, the President's political adviser and a man whom Foreign Office notes describe as 'quite unscrupulous'. Allinson accused Chona and his boss of 'dragging the Queen into politics'. For good measure, he also asked the Commonwealth Secretary-General, Sonny Ramphal, to lean on Kaunda, too. President Kaunda let it be known that he was 'gravely shocked' to be told whom he could and could not invite on to his red carpet. Yet, eventually, Allinson was informed that Nkomo would be asked to stay away. Mightily relieved, the High Commissioner immediately sent a telex to the royal party, now preparing to leave Botswana, reassuring them that the Queen would not face any awkward introductions at the end of her three-and-a-half-hour flight. However, there was a thinly veiled threat to the British government, delivered to Allinson by Chona. While the Queen would be 'respected' in Lusaka, said Chona, 'Mrs Thatcher must bear in mind that Zambian lives had been lost at the hands of the rebel regime. Zambia had its public opinion and the Prime Minister must expect it to be felt.' As Allinson noted: 'A sinister note which I was not able to explore further.' Nor was there any indication whether Kaunda would be altering his hysterical speech. If he persisted with his anti-Thatcher, anti-Rhodesia, anti-consensus rant, the Commonwealth would be in serious trouble.

TWO LADIES

Shortly after 4 p.m. on Friday 27th July 1979, unmolested by gunfire or stray missiles, the Queen finally arrived in Lusaka, her first visit to independent Zambia. As Patsy Robertson, then running the press operation for the Commonwealth, recalls, the excitement had been building all day. 'I remember the morning when it started. The Zambian news said: 'Two ladies are coming from Britain. One we love – and then another one later".' In fact, by arriving first, the Queen had helped to dampen much of the pent-up hostility towards Mrs Thatcher. Everyone wanted to see the Queen. As Len Allinson recorded in his despatch on the visit: 'Members of the Central Committee (the Zambian Politburo) were, as usual, unable to refrain from intervening at the eleventh hour to produce their inimitable masterly touch of chaos. When the Queen arrived at Lusaka Airport, the invited British children were swamped by councillors and party militants and saw nothing of the Queen. The prize for the worst offender undoubtedly went to Mr Mainza Chona.' Brother of the difficult Mark Chona, Mainza Chona was the Secretary-General of Zambia's only political party, UNIP, and the second most important figure in the country, after the President. He would soon come to annoy British diplomats even more than his brother.

Accompanied by the President, the Queen was then driven to the royal quarters at State Lodge, where William Heseltine was relieved to find that the overwhelming 'pong' he had encountered on his recce was no more. After tea with the Kaundas, the Queen and Prince Philip hosted a reception for all the press covering her visit. Throughout the visit, the media would be struck by the passionate public response on every leg of the royal route. 'These were no mere "sent" crowds on the instruction of the party,' wrote Len Allinson. 'The reason cannot be explained quite so simply. There was gratitude that the Queen had come to Zambia in its time of trouble. There was undoubtedly also an aura of mystery and respect about the person of the Queen.' The following day, the Central Committee Commissar of Lusaka Province, Fines Bulawayo, was visited by a delegation of local elders with an urgent request. The public, they insisted, wanted the monarch's police escort removed because it was obstructing their view. 'The people wanted to see the Queen,' Bulawayo explained. 'She had no need for police protection. The people were her safeguard.'

Even so, Air Commodore Archie Winskill was taking no chances as he flew the royal party up to view Zambia's copper belt near Kitwe. As he approached the runway, the ex-fighter pilot decided against a leisurely regal approach and put the royal Andover into another 'perpendicular dive' on approach, just in case a stray freedom-fighter with a missile launcher and poor communications had failed to receive the 'ceasefire' message. Once again, the crowds were historic. The head of Roan Consolidated Mines reported a 'dramatic' drop in production that day because most of his miners wanted to line the route. Len Allinson watched the branch of a large tree give way under the weight of spectators outside a clinic in Kitwe. 'It was a heart-warming sight to see the big smiles on the faces of the grown-ups and children alike watching the royal vehicles disappearing down the road and still chanting "KK, Queenie. KK, Queenie!" '

As 'KK' was fast learning, having 'Queenie' around was extremely good for the Kaunda brand. That evening, however, as he rose to address the state banquet at the Intercontinental Hotel, there was considerable nervousness on the British side when the President began to speak. With much waving of the white handkerchief that he always carried in his right hand, he proceeded to deliver a rambling address on the Queen's 'humanity', on the 'dignity, freedom and equality' embodied in the Commonwealth and on his hopes for peace and democracy in Rhodesia. However, all the incendiary passages from his original text had miraculously disappeared. The Queen, in reply, saluted Zambia's position and influence in the world as 'a tremendous tribute both to your leadership and to the people of Zambia'. In wishing President Kaunda well in his chairmanship of the Commonwealth summit, there was a clear message to the (still predominantly white) Rhodesian leadership over the border: 'Never has it been so forcibly impressed on us that we all belong to one human race.'

Both sides would regard the evening as a great success, although Prince Philip was later heard to remark of Kaunda's meanderings that he had a 'ragbag' for a mind. Instead of the pan-continental meltdown that would have occurred if Kaunda had said what he was originally planning to say, the scene was now set for a harmonious Commonwealth summit.

So what had happened to bring about this dramatic change of mood? Allinson's official despatch to London once the visit was over would record simply that President Kaunda had been planning to 'include some highly unacceptable passages' in his speech but, after being 'confronted', he had 'backed down'. This provoked an extraordinary response from the Queen's Private Secretary, Philip Moore. It is one that reveals exactly what did take place. Writing to Roger du Boulay at the Foreign Office from Balmoral, Moore insisted that Allinson's despatch should be rewritten to make it very clear that the Queen had actually pulled off a political triumph of her own. There was no question in his mind (and therefore the Queen's) that this was 'the most important and successful overseas tour from a political point of view that the Queen has made for many years'. And key to its success had been one factor that was being overlooked: 'The Queen intervened personally with the President.' Moore outlined what had gone on between the two heads of state. 'When we arrived at Lusaka, Len Allinson reported to me that he thought that the only way in which he could get the offending passages removed from Kaunda's speech was for the Queen to speak to him personally. This the Queen did in the motor car and later that evening Mark Chona came to see me to say that the President had agreed to make all the amendments for which we asked.' As a result, Moore formally requested that the despatch should state that the Queen had made 'a personal intervention'. In fact, she had saved the day. It seems unthinkable that Moore would have made this intervention on his own without the authority of the Queen herself. Perhaps, in this instance, she wanted future diplomats to know that if they ever found themselves confronted with some impending diplomatic disaster of this sort in the future, she might be the person to sort it out.

The official Foreign Despatch, newly-released after an FOI request, states: 'The Zambians backed down, although the necessary amendments to the speech were only made as a result of a personal intervention by The Queen with President Kaunda.' What it was that she actually said to him is anyone's guess.

DING DONG

By now, all the other Commonwealth leaders were on their way to Lusaka. Having finished the first part of her tour of Zambia, the Queen had now morphed from UK head of state into Head of the Commonwealth. After a twenty-four-hour break at the Luangwa Game Park, she returned to Lusaka to begin her audiences with all the politicians, while Prince Philip took Prince Andrew to visit copper mines, schools and wildlife conservation projects. Such was the size of the Commonwealth by 1979 that the Queen's audiences would take four full days. One leader after another would quietly break away from the summit chamber for that precious one-on-one meeting. Rather than drag them all across Lusaka to her State Lodge quarters, the Queen had taken over a small villa in the summit complex, just like those occupied by the leaders. Sir William Heseltine recalls that the Queen's page, Ernest Bennett, had done his best to give the place a regal feel, though the ambience was more suburban than palatial. The buzzer installed for the beginning and end of the Queen's audiences turned out to be a standard 'ding-dong' house doorbell. A lucky few would be invited to lunch in the villa next door, and the Queen insisted that the guest list should include the leaders of some of the Commonwealth's smallest nations as well as the biggest. Day One saw the Solomon Islands, Sri Lanka and Tonga come to lunch. 'She saw everyone,' Lord Carrington said afterwards. 'They all had a hut and she had a grand hut and it was quite clear how they felt about her.'

Back in the conference chamber, tension was building ahead of the crunch debate on Rhodesia. Right up to the last moment, President Kaunda could not resist antagonising Mrs Thatcher. On the eve of her arrival, he gave a newspaper interview in which he accused her of being so obsessed with Russian influence in the region that she was losing her 'reason'. As Len Allinson later recorded, Kaunda was still suffering from 'paranoia' that the British would try to 'sidestep' the issue of Rhodesia at the very last moment. There was added drama when Mrs Thatcher attempted a discreet arrival shortly before midnight on 30th July– wearing her protective sunglasses – only to find herself ambushed by an unscheduled press conference orchestrated by the Chona brothers. Kaunda's tactics were still in danger of scuppering the summit. However, the wily Sonny Ramphal was doing his best to soothe tempers in the conference room. The Queen was doing the same in her audiences at her little villa. Nigeria, she suggested, might like to tone down the combative language; Australia's Malcolm Fraser was encouraged to help Zambia find a solution, and so on. There were more royal manoeuvres at the Queen's banquet for all the heads of government on opening night. She was on fine form with all the leaders, of course. 'You're the same generation as my mother,' she teased Hastings Banda at one point. 'And there's no stopping her!'

Chief Emeka Anyaoku well remembers her broader strategy. The Queen ensured that she did not just make time for the leaders, but for all the ministers, officials and fixers, too. 'Usually, the Queen would give a banquet for heads and, after the banquet, she'd have a reception for foreign ministers and leave by 10.30. But on this occasion, she was there until midnight making sure she talked to everyone,' Anyaoku recalls. 'Her calming and restraining influence was very much at work. That was what encouraged them to agree how they should work out their formula for dealing with the Rhodesian crisis.' The Queen could not be in the conference chamber. But she could still set the tone.

Two days later, in the first discussion of Rhodesia, there was no 'ganging up' on Mrs Thatcher, as the British had feared, and no ranting by Kaunda either. Instead, the President invited 'Mwalimu', the revered Julius Nyerere, to speak on the subject of Rhodesia. The donnish Tanzanian leader carefully outlined his belief that only Britain had the 'responsibility, the experience and the political will' to create a lasting constitution for its war-torn colony, one that could command unanimous Commonwealth support. His words were supported by the Kenyan President, Daniel arap Moi, whereupon it was Mrs Thatcher's turn. Would she seek a new start for Rhodesia or would she insist on endorsing white rule and the status quo? The entire future of the Commonwealth hung in the balance at this point. If she argued that Rhodesia and the puppet regime of Bishop Muzorewa constituted a legitimate example of majority rule, then many African leaders would have stood up and walked out. But if the British Prime Minister declared that it was time for constitutional change, Rhodesia would know the game was up.

Mrs Thatcher began by arguing that so much had changed in Rhodesia, that Bishop Muzorewa was an African president who had been elected by an 'African majority', that there was no further need to use 'the bomb and the gun to kill and maim men, women and children'. The Commonwealth held its breath. Her own consultations, she went on, had nonetheless convinced her that the existing Rhodesian constitution was 'defective'. On hearing that one word, Ramphal and all the other leaders realised that history had been made. Mrs Thatcher was not going to recognise the Smith/Muzorewa regime. Old Rhodesia was doomed. 'The debate was over,' he wrote in his memoirs. Mrs Thatcher had more. It would be Britain, she said, that would now get all the parties together as quickly as possible to deliver 'genuine black majority rule'.

As the leaders set off on their 'retreat' – a day-trip to the Victoria Falls – the following day, six key players, including Mrs Thatcher, Kaunda and Nyerere, stayed behind to iron out the final details. The whole deal nearly came unstuck when the Australian Prime Minister, Malcolm Fraser, leaked everything to the Australian press before the key conditions could be formally agreed and signed. Disaster loomed. The whole deal might be off, if the British press and the right wing of the Conservative Party urged Mrs Thatcher to think again before doing a deal with people whom she herself had called 'terrorists'. Knowing that a lot of Conservatives – including her husband, Denis – had deep sympathy for and personal ties with white Rhodesia, she had made sure to invite an influential member of that very section of the party to accompany her. However, Ian Gow, her parliamentary Private Secretary, was of little use at the crucial moment. As Mrs Thatcher's biographer, Charles Moore, has revealed, Gow had taken what he thought were anti-malaria pills with a glass of alcohol over lunch. They were in fact sleeping pills and he had passed out.

Given the urgency of securing the deal before news could break in the UK, Ramphal hauled all the leaders back from their retreat and, in a matter of hours, a final agreement was hurriedly signed by every Commonwealth nation. At that very moment, the Head of the Commonwealth was on her way home, perhaps raising a glass to her own handiwork on board her chartered British Caledonian Boeing 707. Back in Lusaka, Mrs Thatcher was in reflective mood as she discussed the future of Rhodesia with Sonny Ramphal. 'You realise, of course, that we have given it to the communist,' she told him over lunch.

Before it was all over, there would be one more extraordinary moment. On the advice of her officials, Mrs Thatcher had accepted President Kaunda's invitation to address the annual dinner of the Zambian Press Club. She had much to say on journalistic integrity and on the 'perilously thin' line 'between honest revelation and disingenuous sensationalism'. But she began on a personal note. Turning to Kaunda, she said: 'You may not know, Mr President, you and I have something in common which is a mark of good fortune. We are both the parents of twins.' At the end of her speech, she received an ovation, a chorus of 'For she's a jolly good fellow' and an invitation from President Kaunda to join him on the dance floor. The band had even composed a new tune in their honour: 'Now come and dance, nice Maggie, You have nothing to fear. Maggie's a good lady. KK's a good man …' The moment would be captured in one of the most famous photographs of the Iron Lady's premiership. What it does not reveal is that Mrs Thatcher was suffering from a violent stomach bug and had not eaten for the previous twenty-four hours.

The Lusaka Commonwealth conference had, indeed, made history. It would lead to the Lancaster House peace conference in London, which would ensure the end of the long and brutal Rhodesian bush war, free elections and the creation of Zimbabwe – all in less than a year. That would, in turn, give the Commonwealth the impetus to seek the greatest prize within its grasp – the end of apartheid in South Africa. 'At the crucial time, the Queen exercised her stabilising influence,' Ramphal reflected afterwards. 'She was diplomatically brilliant. The Queen brought to Lusaka a healing touch of rather special significance.'

She had also done her British Prime Minister a great favour. Having arrived in fear of an acid attack, Mrs Thatcher had departed on a high. Her official biographer, Charles Moore, is in no doubt that, despite earlier tensions with the Palace, the Queen's presence had 'actually made life easier for Mrs Thatcher'. As the Iron Lady later reflected in an interview with William Shawcross: 'If the Queen wanted to go, then the Queen had to go and all the necessary security had to be put in place. It was a very successful conference and I was glad she was there. She knew everyone.' Less than three months into the new job, the Prime Minister had made a good impression, too.

The banner headline in the state-controlled *Zambian Weekend World* summed it all up as follows: 'Queen like Jesus – Visit like Second Coming.' Not, perhaps, a sentiment with which the modest Supreme Governor of the Church of England would agree. Even the Queen might concede though, that after all the doom and gloom just weeks earlier, something miraculous had occurred. Her Commonwealth was not just in one piece, but reinvigorated and as strong as ever. She would never experience another meeting quite like that at Lusaka.

Chapter 9

THE YACHT

'I had to be carried off kicking and screaming'

HOME AT LAST

On the evening of 11th December 1997, the Prince of Wales rose to make the shortest after-dinner speech of his life. 'I just want to get blindly, madly drunk,' he declared and sat down again, to thunderous applause. His audience knew exactly how he felt. Having been the very first royal passenger in the Royal Yacht in 1954, it was appropriate that the Prince should be the principal guest of honour at *Britannia*'s farewell dinner more than four decades and more than one million miles later. Hours earlier, *Britannia* had been decommissioned in front of the Queen and the Royal Family at a ceremony on the Portsmouth quayside. It had been faultless, just like all those parades and displays that *Britannia* had produced on royal duty all over the world. On that final day, however, the Band of the Royal Marines had one surprise that was not on the order of service. As they marched off parade, they burst into 'Auld Lang Syne'. For many old salts in the windswept grandstands it was the moment when even the tungsten reserve of the Senior Service finally gave way.

The Queen was seen to shed a tear that day, as was the Princess Royal. They were not alone. As former Chief Petty Officer Dick Field told *Britannia*'s official biographer, Richard Johnstone-Bryden: 'If the press had swung their cameras around, they would have caught another 2,000 former Royal Yacht officers and Yachtsmen doing exactly the same thing. It was the worst day of our lives.'

No study of the international role of the Queen and the Royal Family is complete without looking at how they got there and back. During a reign that began with seaplanes and steam trains, the Queen has far surpassed the travel records of all previous monarchs combined. She has reigned right through the age of civilian supersonic travel, from beginning to end, trying it a few times herself along the way. Concorde was never a favourite, although she used it occasionally and it did make a spectacular appearance at landmark royal occasions, such as the 2002 Golden Jubilee. Helicopters, as we know, are not greatly loved. There have been a few notable workhorses during the reign, particularly that Vickers VC10 for longer flights, and both the Hawker Siddeley Andover and the British Aerospace BAe 146 for shorter hops. On the ground, the Royal Train has barely changed in decades, the decor of its rolling stock still firmly and fondly rooted in the 1970s, with its plastic avocado-coloured baths, Formica surfaces and brown furniture. Much overseas travel was also undertaken by train in the early years. For most of the 1947 tour of southern Africa, the 1951 tour of Canada and the 1965 tour of West Germany, the Queen lived aboard a train. When a lack of suitable airfields prohibited air travel for the long-distance part of the 1981 state visit to Sri Lanka, the Queen's hosts decided to rebuild the royal train in which she had travelled during her 1954 visit. While many enjoyed the nostalgic sight of the monarch's stately progress in the original royal rolling stock, it was a much longer journey than in 1954. The top speed had been reduced to 25 mph.

At home, the Royal Mews maintains the State Bentley plus a fleet of Rolls-Royces of varying vintages, assorted saloons and various models of the Land Rover Discovery. For state occasions there are coaches, carriages and landaus, ranging from the famously slow and uncomfortable Gold State Coach, built for George III, to the Diamond Jubilee State Coach, incorporating twenty-first-century hydraulic stabilisers.

Yet there has never been the slightest doubt about the favourite mode of royal travel. Over more than forty years the Royal Yacht *Britannia* would be so much more than a dignified means of transporting the head of state of a famous maritime nation overseas. It would serve as a secure, ocean-going palace-cum-embassy-cum-trade-platform. Above and beyond that, *Britannia* was the nearest the Queen has ever had to her 'own' home. All the other palaces and castles were inherited. All had been furnished and equipped by her predecessors over forty reigns. It was in *Britannia* that the Queen and the Duke of Edinburgh could experiment with their own ideas and, choose everything from the light fittings to the carpet. It was in *Britannia* that the monarch could get as near to being off-duty as a head of sixteen states could be. All the Royal Family would feel much the same way. When Princess Anne was asked whether she wanted her twenty-first-birthday party in London, Windsor or Scotland, she replied that she wanted none of the above. She would like it in Portsmouth, please, on board the Yacht. As a result, for the first (and last time) in *Britannia*'s history, the royal carpet was rolled up to make way for a dance floor.

First conceived in pre-war Britain under the government of Neville Chamberlain, *Britannia* would still be showing the world how to make an entrance – and exit – up to the threshold of the twenty-first century. The arrival of the Queen in Cape Town harbour in 1995, with Table Mountain in the distance and Nelson Mandela on the quayside, will be in school history books many generations from now. The sight of the Royal Yacht sailing serenely out of Hong Kong a little after midnight on 1st July 1997, carrying the Prince of Wales and the colony's last Governor, Lord Patten, was the ultimate in dignified departures. And when *Britannia* was in town, everybody knew it. Commodore Anthony Morrow, *Britannia*'s last captain, was serving as Signal Officer in 1977 when the Yacht berthed in Melbourne and he was able to acquire a ticket for the Centenary Test match at the mighty Melbourne Cricket Ground. An important message was received from London requiring his attention, and *Britannia*'s wireless operator contacted the stadium. To Morrow's horror, he suddenly heard the public address system announce: 'Would Lieutenant Commander Morrow please contact the Royal Yacht.' He will never forget what happened next: 'As I got up to leave, the entire stadium stood up and clapped!'

Just as it has often been said that the Commonwealth would not have lasted all these years without the support of the Queen, it might also be argued that the Queen would not have managed all that she has without *Britannia*. On one level, there was a practical point. For it was only thanks to the Yacht, particularly in the early part of the reign, that the Queen or a member of the Royal Family could actually visit parts of the Commonwealth that had seldom (if ever) seen a royal visitor. Then there was the diplomatic dimension. On occasions fraught with sensitivity and security issues, the Yacht could provide a detached platform for more restrained and harmonious discussions. Those present at fractious Commonwealth meetings like the 1985 Nassau summit, where the issue of South Africa was threatening an irreparable split within the organisation, recall that it was not just the Queen who held things together. So did *Britannia*. With both Greek and Turkish elements protesting against the Crown at the 1993 summit in Limassol, Cyprus, *Britannia* provided a dignified base in which the Head of the Commonwealth could meet every leader individually and hold her banquet.

Above all, whatever the destination or event, the Yacht would simply make it so much easier for the Queen to get on with being Queen. Ask those close to the monarch for the secret of her indefatigability and they will usually cite the winning combination of good health, a strong faith and Prince Philip. Her former Private Secretary, Lord Charteris, was once asked the same question and memorably replied: 'The Queen is as strong as a yak.' He went on: 'She sleeps well, she's got very good legs and she can stand for a long time.' He might also have added that, for most of her reign, she also had her Yacht.

Rear Admiral Sir Robert Woodard well remembers the day in 1990 when he went to see the Queen on being appointed Flag Officer Royal Yachts, as Britannia's captain was known. Would it be helpful, she asked him, if she were to offer her own thoughts on the role of the Yacht? He said it would. 'People who know us at all know that Buckingham Palace is the office,' she began, 'Windsor Castle is for weekends and the occasional state thing and Sandringham and Balmoral are for holidays. Well, they aren't what I would call holidays. For example, there are ninety people coming to stay with us at Balmoral this summer. The only holiday I get every year is from Portsmouth the long way round to Aberdeen on the Royal Yacht when I can get up when I like and wear what I like and be completely free. And if you, as Flag Officer Royal Yachts, can produce the Royal Yacht for my summer holidays, that's all I ask.'

For the person with surely the most abnormal position in British national life, the Yacht offered the one thing the Queen craved – a spot of normality. *Britannia* would be a place for fun, for mischief and – in a world governed by ritual and tradition – for the spur-of-the-moment.

Commander John Prichard would recall a Western Isles cruise during the Eighties when *Britannia* found itself on the same course as the square-rigged sailing giants of the Tall Ships Race. The Queen was listening to a jazz recital by her Band of the Royal Marines when she spotted the Soviet ship *Kruzenshtern*. 'Shall we give them some music? What can you play?' she asked the bandmaster. Moments later, a crew of weather-beaten Soviet seamen suddenly found themselves being slowly overtaken by the Royal Yacht with the band playing 'Tiger Rag' and the Queen of the United Kingdom waving at them. As Prichard recalled: 'The Russians looked absolutely astounded with what was going on.'

The diplomat, Roger du Boulay, and his wife joined the Yacht for a week in 1974 during his years as Resident Commissioner of the New Hebrides in the Pacific. Like those Russian sailors aboard the *Kruzenshtern*, the du Boulays were similarly astounded one night when dinner was followed by the ship's entertainment – 'an elaborate pantomime' – in front of the Royal Family and the crew, with the Queen acting as wardrobe assistant. 'It involved the equerry taking the part of a Polynesian beauty,' says du Boulay. 'I remember him sitting on the floor and I remember seeing the Queen kneeling on the floor. He was stripped to the waist and she was fitting a brassiere on to him. It was an extraordinary sight!' On board, informality would go a long way – but it had its limits. John Gorton, former Prime Minister of Australia, later recalled one beach barbecue with the family during a 1970 tour of Australia, when the royal party decided it was time for a swim. 'Princess Anne was thrown in and then Prince Philip,' he said. 'I was sitting next to Her Majesty and I was just about to throw her in but I looked at her and something about the way she looked at me told me that perhaps I shouldn't. In the end, the Queen was the only one who stayed dry.'

SHIP NUMBER 691

As both a ship and a royal residence, *Britannia* was unique. There was no other palace in which the Royal Family would seat their guests on cheap wicker chairs (purchased by Prince Philip during a Hong Kong stopover in 1959), just as there was no other Royal Navy ship in which orders were delivered in complete silence and by hand. The Yacht was certainly not a new idea (nor would it even be a new design). There was an unbroken line of 83 Royal Yachts dating back to the reign of King Charles II. Some were built as a statement of authority, others for recreation or racing. *Britannia*'s immediate predecessor was the *Victoria and Albert*, launched in 1899. Queen Victoria never set foot on board, having learned of early stability problems before it had even gone to sea. It spent its years in northern Europe, seldom venturing out of British waters. Perhaps the *V&A*'s most famous voyage was one of its last, taking King George VI and his family on a visit to the Britannia Royal Naval College, Dartmouth in 1939. It was there that Princess Elizabeth had her first proper introduction to a promising young naval cadet, Prince Philip of Greece and Denmark. By now, the King had already discussed the idea of a new Yacht with the Prime Minister of the day, Neville Chamberlain, and the Admiralty had settled on a budget of £900,000. Dockyards were invited to submit preliminary suggestions by 12th September 1939. Nine days before that deadline, Britain declared war on Germany. It would be many years before anyone gave the idea of a Yacht much thought again.

After the war, a suitably regal vessel was required to carry the King and his family to the Cape for their 1947 tour of southern Africa. The choice of the Royal Navy's new battleship, HMS *Vanguard*, helped to focus minds on the need for a new Yacht. There was not only the need to ferry members of the Royal Family to more exotic destinations than the old *V&A* (which had spent the war as an accommodation unit in Portsmouth and would soon be heading for the scrapyard). If there was to be a new Royal Yacht, it would be a good idea to get on with it, while there were still a few old salts who remembered how things were done in the old one. What's more, with the King's health in decline, many felt that a spell at sea might have a restorative effect. It was a Labour Prime Minister, Clement Attlee, who announced plans for a new Royal Yacht in October 1951, just before the general election. Wisely and very correctly, he had cleared the announcement with the leader of the opposition, Winston Churchill. There was not the faintest chance that Churchill would have any problem with the idea. However, it was important to ensure that the new ship did not become an issue during the election campaign, a precaution ignored by John Major's government many years later, with disastrous results.

From the outset, the Admiralty announced that a medium-sized hospital ship would be included in the nation's rearmament programme, with a dual role as a Royal Yacht in peacetime. The Glasgow shipbuilders, John Brown & Co., were selected, on the understanding that they would move quickly, in light of the King's health. The contract was signed at the start of February 1952. As with those original bids back in 1939, weightier matters intervened. By the morning of 6th February, the King had died in his sleep at Sandringham. There would, though,be no delay in getting this ship afloat. One of the Queen's very first audiences in the same month she succeeded to the Throne was with the Controller of Navy Construction, in order to discuss the new Yacht. By June, the keel was laid, with an absolute minimum of fuss or fanfare. For now, this new vessel was simply Ship Number 691. With an eye on both time and price, it was decided to base the new vessel on an existing design, a pair of North Sea ferries already serving the route between Harwich and the Hook of Holland. There would be a few modifications to the new model – a sleeker bow and stern, to make the hull look more royal, and a reduced draught (the amount of ship below the waterline). If the Yacht was going to enter some of the shallower harbours and rivers of the Commonwealth, then it would need to clear the bottom. Nor was the Yacht's alter ego as a hospital ship a fabrication. The Royal Navy's medical Director-General drew up detailed plans for medical use – including 200 beds in the royal apartments and an open-air ward for tuberculosis sufferers on the Verandah Deck (which would also be strengthened to accommodate helicopter landings). A full operating theatre and X-ray facility were incorporated and a clear deadline was established. The new ship would be able to switch from a royal role to a medical one in twenty-four hours.

Senior figures at the Admiralty were not the only ones keeping a close eye on developments. So was the Duke of Edinburgh. He was still creating a new role for himself, in the face of a Palace establishment resolutely determined to keep him away from affairs of state. The new Yacht would be a perfect distraction, when he wasn't busy chairing the committee in charge of the Coronation or taking charge of the royal estates. 'You had to be on your toes when Prince Philip was on board,' explained Dr John Brown, chief architect and later managing director of the shipyard. On one occasion, the Duke was on board when a new winch mechanism was being tested. The Duke was unimpressed. 'He promptly ordered it out,' Brown told the authors of a private anthology of *Britannia* memories compiled by ex-Yachtsmen. 'That was typical of him.'

It was also the Duke who chose *Britannia*'s famous colour scheme, based on the livery of his own Dragon-class sailing boat, *Bluebottle*. 'She was dark blue with a red boot topping which I thought looked rather smart,' the Duke told Richard Johnstone-Bryden. It was decided to complement the blue hull with a thin gold band around the top, for an extra £90. While the use of gold leaf would be more expensive than gold paint, it would need replacing less often and thus save money on the long-term maintenance bill. Everyone was acutely aware of likely public attitudes to the costs, although parliamentary questions on the subject never escalated into the media storm that some had anticipated. The original estimate of £1.6 million would finally reach £2.1 million, but, as with plans for the Coronation, the public consensus was that the new Queen should have something to be proud of, not something done on the cheap. Even so, she took issue with the extravagant designs for the interior. John Brown & Co. had built the *Queen Mary* and the *Queen Elizabeth* and the original proposals for the new Yacht involved the sort of grandeur to be found in the smartest sections of an ocean liner. The Queen wanted none of it, and commissioned Sir Hugh Casson to come up with something more homely. 'The Queen is a meticulous observer with very strong views; there was no question of showing her a drawing room and her saying "All right, that will do",' he wrote later. 'She had definite views on everything from the door handles to the shape of the lampshades.'

On 8th April 1953, two months before her Coronation, the Queen was in Scotland to launch 'Ship 691'. The name would remain a closely guarded secret up to the very moment the Queen announced it. A crowd of 30,000 – including 7,000 children and 300 striking steel-platers, who had voted to abandon their three-week strike for an hour to see the Queen launch their handiwork – had assembled inside the John Brown shipyard. Its owner, Lord Aberconway, welcomed her by recalling her first visit, aged twelve, to the launch of the liner *Queen Elizabeth* in 1938 and her return, as an eighteen-year-old Princess, to launch HMS *Vanguard*. The new ship, he assured her, would bring happiness to the 'far portions of the Empire', but was also equipped to do a fine job as a hospital ship. 'If such a time does arise, she will be well fitted for it, and the occupants will rejoice that it is your ship,' he told her.

Dressed in black, for the court was still mourning the recent death of Queen Mary, the Queen departed from the usual ship-launching script. 'I name this ship *Britannia*. I wish success to her and to all who sail in her.' No one is entirely sure why she did not invoke the Almighty with the customary words 'May God bless all who sail in her'. Perhaps the Queen felt it was inappropriate to exhort God to bless herself. Another break with tradition was the smashing of a bottle of Empire wine, rather than champagne, over *Britannia*'s bows. Though the Admiralty had been unenthusiastic about a name that, in their view, was too Anglocentric and not worldly enough, *Britannia* was the favoured choice of the Queen and the Duke. It was also hugely popular with the public.

Among those in the crowd that day was Jock Slater, a teenage schoolboy who would one day serve in the Yacht, would later become the Queen's Equerry and finally end up as First Sea Lord in charge of the entire Royal Navy. He had been taken along to watch by a family friend who lived nearby. 'The cheering was so loud that we couldn't hear what the Queen said and had no idea what the Yacht was called until we got home and heard it on the news,' he laughs.

One person who saw and heard everything very clearly was the eight-year-old girl chosen to present the flowers to the Queen. Robin Bullard was the step-granddaughter of the shipyard's chairman, Lord Aberconway. Now Robin, Countess of Onslow, she remembers having lessons in how to curtsey, and the roar of the crowd as the name was announced. She also remembers the family presenting the Queen with a set of 'absolutely beautiful' glass goblets engraved by Laurence Whistler, brother of Rex Whistler (the artist and 'Bright Young Thing' who had been killed in action in Normandy). The Queen made a short speech in which she paid a warm tribute to her late father. The King, she said, had been the guiding hand behind this great new royal undertaking: 'He felt most strongly, as I do, that a Yacht was a necessity not a luxury for the Head of our great British Commonwealth, between whose countries the sea is no barrier but the natural and indestructible highway.'

Like the Coronation, the Yacht would help make the country feel a little prouder of itself once more. Prince Philip touched on that in his foreword to the anthology of *Britannia*'s years at sea. 'During the almost fifty years of her service, she played a very special part in Britain's recovery after the war,' he wrote. 'She managed to project all that was best in British life.'

To emphasise that recovery, and to revitalise the new-look Commonwealth still taking shape after the London Declaration of 1949, the Queen and the Duke were already preparing for what remains the most ambitious royal tour in history. *Britannia* would not be ready in time for the start of that great Coronation tour of 1953–4 in which the royal couple circumnavigated the world via the South Seas, New Zealand and Australia. Most of that journey would be spent in the converted cargo-liner, the SS *Gothic*, which had been specially chartered and repainted for the trip. Since the charter fee for this one trip would equate to 10 per cent of the entire cost of building *Britannia*, the Yacht was already proving its worth. However, by the time the royal couple were on the latter stages of their tour, *Britannia* was ready to meet them en route. The Yacht had done well in all its sea trials, including a testing encounter with a 97mph wind off Scotland, and an entire ship's company had been recruited and trained up. The Royal Yacht Service – an entirely separate arm of the Royal Navy – was up and running once again.

On 14th April 1954, the Queen Mother travelled to Portsmouth to entrust the Yacht's first two royal passengers to the crew. Prince Charles, aged five, and Princess Anne, aged three, were welcomed aboard, along with Miss Lightbody and Miss Peebles, their nannies. Two Yachtsmen were given additional duties as lifeguards, a role that would come to be known by a new name throughout *Britannia*'s years of service – 'Sea Daddy'. Leading Stoker Mechanics Rutter and McKeown were among the first in a job with one overarching rule: never, ever let your charge out of your sight.

The Yacht set sail, via Malta, to the Libyan port of Tobruk to meet the Queen. Such were the formalities of international diplomacy that the Queen and the Duke were expected to visit the main Commonwealth cemetery and to have tea with King Idris of Libya before being reunited with the children they had not seen for five months. Not that the young passengers were unduly troubled. Both had been given plenty of duties on board and were having the time of their lives. 'We were kept very busy,' the Princess recalls. There were lots of things to do, all sorts of places to go and things to keep clean, scrubbing and polishing.'

The Princess can remember enjoying a pedal car in the shape of the Yacht and a rubber swimming pool, while, even now, the Prince of Wales can still recollect the smell as the rum ration* was issued. He was also mesmerised by the sight of all the rusting wrecks still littering the port of Tobruk, after some of the worst fighting of the North African campaign. War still loomed fresh in so many minds. Finally, at 11.46 on 1st May 1954, the Queen was piped aboard for the first time. For her, as for the officers and crew, it was a rather nerve-racking moment. After all, the story of Queen Victoria and her new yacht had not been a happy one. From the outset, however, it was clear that *Britannia* would have a very special atmosphere. The following day, a Sunday morning service was held in the Royal Dining Room. With no ship's chaplain – the Queen had decided that would be an unnecessary luxury - the service was taken by the Flag Officer Royal Yachts, *Britannia*'s captain, Vice Admiral Conolly Abel Smith. He duly recited the traditional prayer for the Queen, the Queen Mother, the Duke, Prince Charles and 'all the Royal Family' – at the end of which, a small voice broke the silence. 'He hasn't prayed for me, Mummy,' said Princess Anne, at which point the entire congregation burst out laughing. Here was a moment that would set the tone for *Britannia*'s next one million miles.

PLOTTING A COURSE

As the great Coronation tour was nearing its end in May 1954, most of Britain was looking forward to seeing the Queen sail up the Thames,

* Dating back to the eighteenth century, the rum ration or 'tot' was the daily measure of rum given to all non-officers at noon. Equivalent to 70 ml of alcohol at 95.5% proof, it was easily enough to put anyone over the modern driving limit. By the Sixties, the Admiralty had decided it was positively dangerous in an age of hair-trigger missile technology. The Navy Minister at the time, David Owen tested it on himself: 'I drank the tot at noon and I couldn't make a decision after 2.30,' he says. To avoid a mutiny, the tot was replaced by three daily cans of beer.

through Tower Bridge and back to London. It was due to be the most spectacular display of royal pageantry since the Coronation. The Prime Minister, Winston Churchill, had been ferried out the day before to join the Yacht off the Isle of Wight for the final leg. The Queen had also invited another guest to join this select party, Sir Hugh Casson, the designer of the Yacht's royal apartments. This might have been the eve of a triumphal homecoming but the minds of the Queen and the Duke were clearly on home furnishings and colour schemes. Following dinner and a film on the ship's projector, the Duke of Edinburgh steered Sir Hugh away from the other guests to talk through a list of proposed alterations. As the architect recalled in his diary, the Queen then also sneaked away to be part of this interior designers' pow-wow. 'The Queen joined us, explaining that Winston was the centre of attraction and she could safely leave him,' Sir Hugh said later. 'We all three sat on the main stairs and discussed various suggestions for improvements.' The Queen, he noted, was especially keen to give the Verandah Deck 'a more domestic character'.

London turned out in huge numbers to watch the end of the first circumnavigation of the globe by a reigning monarch. As *Britannia* cruised up the Thames Estuary and the river gradually started to narrow, the rest of the royal entourage were gently encouraged to stand back, so that the public would have a clear view of the Queen and her family on the Royal Bridge. Vehicles on both sides of the river honked their horns. As the Yacht passed beneath Tower Bridge, the Band of the Royal Marines struck up 'Rule, Britannia!' and the quayside cranes lowered their jibs in salute – a powerful act of homage, memorably repeated in 1965 on the day of Sir Winston Churchill's funeral. 'The whole experience was at once deeply moving and yet I felt completely detached and dreamlike,' wrote Sir Hugh Casson. *Britannia* had got off to the best possible start. Before stepping ashore, Vice Admiral Abel Smith was knighted in the Royal Dining Room – with his own sword.

The Yacht returned to its home port of Portsmouth for initial alterations. The *V&A* would now head for the scrapyard and the Duke of Edinburgh was keen to move some of the contents across, including silver, glass and the binnacle.* The Queen wanted some

* The binnacle was the ornate pillar block housing the ship's compass. Carved from a single piece of oak, it had been in every Royal Yacht since 1817.

reminders of her previous voyages. She asked to have her sofa and armchair from *Vanguard* and the Neptune-style mirror and wheat-sheaf-shaped sconces from the *Gothic* installed in her new sitting room in *Britannia*. While she wanted a light, homely atmosphere, the Duke wanted his sitting room to be more of a study, with darker wood, a leather-topped writing desk, plenty of book space and a display case housing a model of his first command, HMS *Magpie*. They had already choosen different layouts for their connecting bedrooms on the Shelter Deck above. The Queen preferred a bright floral decor and lace-embroidered bed linen, while the Duke had selected a darker finish. He had also given specific instructions about his own linen. There were to be no lace borders on anything.

True to the Queen's speech on the day of the launch, *Britannia*'s early priorities were the Commonwealth. Later that summer, the crew set sail for Canada, the first transatlantic voyage by a Royal Yacht. There they picked up the Duke of Edinburgh, who had been despatched to open the Commonwealth Games in Vancouver, and brought him home. The following year, the Yacht was in the Caribbean, before embarking on its first summer cruise to Scotland via the west coast of Britain. There would be picnics in the sand dunes of Wales – where a local harbourmaster, helping to lift the children ashore, was reduced to tears on being informed that he was carrying the future Prince of Wales onto Welsh soil for the first time. The Prince could test the patience of some of the crew, however. En route to the Isle of Man, he kicked his football over the side and asked his 'Sea Daddy' if he could get it back. The request was passed up to Vice Admiral Abel Smith, who agreed that it might be a useful exercise in seamanship to lower a boat to retrieve it. The Prince regarded this as enormous fun and, soon afterwards, cheekily kicked his ball over the side once more. He never saw it again.

The cruise was such a success that it quickly established the template for the next four decades. The Royal Family simply adored cruising the west coast of Britain. The main thing was being able to stop anywhere on a whim and go ashore with a minimum of fuss. As Johnstone-Bryden records, the Queen was enjoying an evening stroll alone on the shores of Loch Torridon when a shepherd appeared. He simply raised his hat, observed that it was 'a grand evening for a walk,

Your Majesty' and walked on. Prince Philip, meanwhile, would relish the prospect of setting up his barbecue in the unlikeliest spots – and cooking anything that took his fancy. 'He'd lead ashore with all the barbecue kit and the Queen would come later with the salad supplies and all the side dishes,' says Sir Robert Woodard. 'He's a brilliant and very innovative cook. If you produced any strange animal out of the sea, he'd prepare it and cook it. You shouldn't be surprised if you ate an octopus.'

A pre-dinner ritual was soon established, which was still going strong in *Britannia*'s final years. 'I always briefed the family every evening in the Drawing Room on the piano. The top of a grand piano makes a good chart table,' explains Commodore Anthony Morrow, *Britannia*'s last captain. His predecessor, Sir Robert Woodard, also fondly recalls the nightly debate. 'We'd gather round the piano with a big chart and all the Royal Family would be there saying "Can we do this or that?" The Queen would listen and say: "I rather fancy going to so and so". Then she would look at me and I might have to explain that the tide or wind was wrong and there would be more deliberation. Then the Queen would say: "That's what we're going to do".'

On that first cruise there was also a stop at the Castle of Mey, the Queen Mother's sixteenth-century fortress at the top right-hand corner of the British mainland, not far from John o' Groats. She had bought it soon after the death of the King, as a place of solace and escape, but always looked forward to the annual sighting of *Britannia* on the horizon. A day of family fun would always conclude with much light-hearted radio banter between Yacht and castle, plus the odd firework as *Britannia* sailed off again. From those earliest voyages, regardless of the weather – and it could be atrocious – there was a magical quality to *Britannia* that would lift the mood on the most demanding diplomatic missions. According to the Princess Royal, when *Britannia* finally did reach Aberdeen at the end of that first summer cruise, she did not want to leave: 'I had to be carried off kicking and screaming.'

EXPLORATION

The new monarch had already circumnavigated the globe, but her Yacht had not. On her 1953–4 tour, the Queen and Duke had gone in a westerly direction. In 1956, *Britannia* would head in the opposite direction. The plan was to take the Duke of Edinburgh to open the Melbourne Games and then head for Antarctica to link up with the Commonwealth Trans-Antarctic Expedition. Organised by the British explorer Vivian Fuchs and New Zealand's Sir Edmund Hillary, the conqueror of Everest, it would involve two teams making the first overland trek to the South Pole since Amundsen and Scott. When it became clear that royal punctuality and the vagaries of polar exploration were not compatible – the expedition would not start in earnest for another year – the Duke decided it would be an ideal opportunity to pay a royal visit to parts of the world that had never enjoyed one before. Among all the extra equipment loaded on board for the voyage were additional fridges, large quantities of long-life milk and a Land Rover. There were several changes of plan due to factors beyond royal control. Egypt's nationalisation of the Suez Canal in 1956 forced the Yacht to sail round Africa via the Cape of Good Hope and pick up the Duke in East Africa. When he reached Singapore, rioting diverted *Britannia* to Malaysia. After visits to Ceylon and Papua New Guinea, the Yacht arrived in Melbourne in time for the Games.

Contrary to the fictitious depiction of the tour in the television series, *The Crown*, *Britannia* did not then set sail for fun and games in the South Seas. Instead the Duke was joined by two distinguished, elderly companions. One was the artist Edward Seago and the other was the explorer Sir Raymond Priestley MC, who, in his youth, had been to Antarctica with Britain's two most celebrated polar adventurers, Sir Ernest Shackleton and Robert Scott.

The Crown also includes a fabricated argument between *Britannia*'s captain, Vice Admiral Sir Conolly Abel Smith, and the Duke in which the latter orders the Yacht to sail thousands of miles off-course to repatriate an injured fisherman to Tonga. Not only did it never happen but former Royal Yachtsmen are even more incredulous that the fictional Duke should be shown mocking Sir Conolly for spending the Second World War on 'shore duty'. Throughout *Britannia*'s years at sea, the Duke was acutely conscious that it was the Flag Officer Royal Yachts who was in charge of the ship, not he. Nor would he have traduced anyone's war record, least of all that of an admiral who could hardly have been further from the shirker depicted in *The*

Crown. The grandson of a VC, Abel Smith had fought in the Great War, was one of the first pilots in the history of the Fleet Air Arm and, like the Duke, was mentioned in despatches during the Second World War.

The Yacht sailed via New Zealand and the Chatham Islands ('not unlike the Shetlands,' according to the Duke), before reaching Antarctica in time for Christmas. There the Duke was scheduled to broadcast a message to the Commonwealth via the BBC, ahead of the Queen's traditional Christmas Day wireless broadcast.* This was not simply a spot of Christmas fun for the benefit of the Royal Family. Like the Queen's speech at the launch of *Britannia* and again, on her great Coronation tour, there was a subtext to it: the lack of Commonwealth boundaries. It was reminding the world that the Royal Family was a Commonwealth family. It was also reassuring the British people, whose post-war self-esteem had taken a hefty kick during the 1956 Suez crisis, that Britain still had a few things to be proud of. Parallel royal broadcasts from Antarctica and Sandringham on Christmas Day – whatever next?

'We are absent, most of us, because there is a Commonwealth,' declared a crackly Duke. 'I hope all of you at Sandringham are enjoying a very happy Christmas and I hope you children are having a lot of fun. I am sorry I am not with you,' he told his family, before concluding with a prayer 'that the Lord watch between me and thee when we are absent from each other'. Moments later, listeners heard the Queen. 'Of all the voices we have heard this afternoon, none has given my children and myself greater joy than that of my husband,' she said.

After sending a message of 'hope and encouragement' to the sick, to those on duty and to those 'whose destiny it is to walk through life alone', she returned to the Duke. 'If my husband cannot be at home on Christmas Day, I could not wish for a better reason than that he should be travelling in other parts of the Commonwealth.' The following day, *Britannia*'s crew saw their first iceberg. They would go on to visit the scientific research stations dotted around the Antarctic Circle and to have an uncomfortably close encounter with a whaling

* She would deliver her first Christmas broadcast by television the following year, four months after Lord Altrincham's appeal for a more modern monarchy.

ship, the stench of which 'cannot be described', according to the Duke.

The Yacht pressed on via some of the loneliest spots on Earth, including Tristan da Cunha and St Helena, before finally meeting up with the Queen in Lisbon for the 1957 state visit to Portugal. By then, the tour had attracted international media attention because the Duke's Private Secretary, Lieutenant Commander Mike Parker, had become embroiled in divorce proceedings. Parker flew home early to calm the story down (though he was still working for the Duke months later). Back in the Fifties, any mention of divorce in royal circles was a news story, and the foreign media began to speculate on the state of the royal marriage itself, so much so that the Palace went as far as issuing a statement denying any 'rift'. Unlike the recent dramatisation, it was, in fact, a comedy moment when the Queen and Duke were finally reunited. Knowing that he had grown a beard on his travels, the Queen had arranged for everyone in the royal entourage – herself included – to put on fake whiskers just before the Duke walked in.

His round-the-world Commonwealth tour had been such a success that he and *Britannia* would complete another one, two years later in 1959. That same year, the Yacht would then take the Queen and the Duke to Canada for that opening of the St Lawrence Seaway linking the Atlantic to the Great Lakes of North America. Accompanied by the President of the United States, Dwight D. Eisenhower, and the Prime Minister of Canada, John Diefenbaker, the royal couple were on deck as *Britannia* sailed through a specially constructed 'gate' between the American and Canadian banks of the St Lawrence River. There had, inevitably, been some complex questions of protocol. US security officials were uneasy about the possibility of a bomb being dropped from a seaway bridge. The crew of *Britannia* were more concerned about the prospect of actually hitting a bridge. Two of the Yacht's three masts were taller than six of the bridges along the way. Special hinge mechanisms had been attached to ensure that the tops could be folded down just far enough to squeeze underneath. Older 'Yotties' would remember the consternation when a loud explosion was heard as the Yacht sailed through one lock. It turned out to be the sound of a bursting fender, squeezed beyond endurance between *Britannia* and the wall of the lock. One of the officers on duty, Captain

North Dalrymple-Hamilton, would never forget the sight of the Queen, the Duke and the President all joining in the collective effort to spare *Britannia*'s paintwork by heaving the Yacht away from the wall.

Britannia's official history records the night during that 1959 tour when Dalrymple-Hamilton received an agitated call from the Queen's formidable dresser, Bobo MacDonald. One can only imagine the reaction of *Britannia*'s duty officer as 'Miss MacDonald' came on the line with the words 'There is a bat in the Queen's bedroom and Her Majesty does not like bats.' There was not a moment to lose. The Queen was at a dinner ashore, but would soon be returning. With a fellow officer and a pair of tennis rackets, Dalrymple-Hamilton managed to 'down' the unfortunate bat with minutes to spare, only to spot another one flapping around in the Royal Drawing Room.

Britannia would come to know the St Lawrence Seaway well, completing several trips through it over the years. One of the problems of such a famous vessel, with such a famous cargo, sailing through such a confined space was that large crowds would always gather for miles on end. One of *Britannia*'s longest-serving yachtsmen, Warrant Officer Albert 'Dixie' Deane, remembers that off-duty Yachtsmen would be asked to form 'waving parties' on the upper decks. 'It was exhausting for the people on the bridge to wave all the way through but they didn't want to upset the locals,' he recalls. 'So we had a party whose job was just to wave.' It was a very *Britannia* solution to a very *Britannia* problem.

SHIP'S COMPANY

During that first decade at sea, *Britannia* crossed the Atlantic seventeen times and visited every continent. Yet there were just a handful of trips to non-Commonwealth countries, most of them to neighbouring monarchies, including Norway (1955), Sweden (1956), Denmark (1957) and Holland (1958). The Swedish visit got off to an inauspicious start when *Britannia*'s arrival was delayed by bad weather and fog. In a letter to the Queen on the latest political situation, the Prime Minister, Anthony Eden, began by offering 'warmest sympathy for Your Majesty's rough journey'. This was especially unfortunate as the King of Sweden had laid on a welcome flypast of 300 aircraft to coincide with the Queen's arrival. In their determination to make up for lost time, *Britannia* and its escort of Royal Navy destroyers went full steam ahead as soon the fog cleared. 'In trying to make up time, the ships produced a wash which destroyed a certain number of boat houses and jetties in the Stockholm Archipelago,' the British Ambassador to Stockholm, Sir Robert Hankey, informed the Foreign Office, 'but the matter has been settled and compensation is being paid.' In fact, the Ambassador had to go on Swedish television to apologise, and the final bill for the mini-tsunami created by *Britannia* cost the British taxpayer £100,000. The Queen was still an hour late.

Throughout those early years, *Britannia* and its crew largely divided their time between tours of the British Isles and trips to the ends of the old Empire, with shore leave in between. While the Yacht's officers would come on secondment from the Royal Navy, spending a year or two in the Yacht before returning to what they called 'the grey Navy', the other ranks could stay for life if they elected to join the Permanent Royal Yacht Service (PRYS). Known as Royal Yachtsmen or Yotties, they would be away from home for considerably longer than their contemporaries in conventional ships. The only promotion ladder in this one-ship navy was known as 'dead man's shoes'. Until the man in the next job up from you moved on, you remained where you were. This proved no great deterrent for men like Able Seaman Ellis 'Norrie' Norrell, who served in *Britannia* right from the start. Having begun at the bottom, doing jobs like painting the hull while dangling over the side in a bosun's chair, he rose via the laundry to one of the most exalted positions in the Yacht, coxswain of the Royal Barge (the Queen's launch). 'I'd only been in the job five minutes when we were at Cowes and I hit a gangway and broke the windscreen,' he recalls. His immediate concern was how he would break the news to his father, a veteran of the previous Royal Yacht, the *V&A*. 'I thought: "Dad's not going to be pleased I've been sacked".' Norrell said his farewells to his crew and waited for the summons. But when it came, he was in for a surprise. 'The commander poured me a drink and said: "Don't worry about it. Accidents happen."' 'Norrie', as he is still known to generations of Yachtsmen, would go on to notch up a record thirty-four years in *Britannia*.

All who served in the Yacht would recall a sense of almost familial camaraderie, which came down from the very top. 'If the Queen saw a yachtsman working over the side without a lifejacket on, I was the first to know,' says Sir Robert Woodard. 'Anything that risked life or limb would need immediate sorting out. She wouldn't remonstrate. She'd just say: "Quick, quick, there's someone without a lifejacket". She got to know them extremely well.'

Stalwarts like 'Dixie' Deane and 'Norrie' Norrell are still invited to royal receptions, long into their retirement. At a recent one, Norrell needed no introduction. 'The Queen said to me: "Hello, Norrie. Where's Dixie?" I explained that he was actually on holiday and she said: "Oh good. I was worried he might be unwell".'

It was a challenge for any outsider to drop into this well-oiled machine, with all its quirks and unusual rules, no matter how senior you might be. Sir Robert Woodard recalls taking command in 1990. By then he had flown both jets and helicopters from aircraft carriers, had commanded a frigate and a destroyer and had taught both the Prince of Wales and the Duke of York along the way. He was running the Royal Navy's submarine base at Faslane when he received a call about the *Britannia* job (he was dressed as Father Christmas at the time). Even he had to adapt. 'When you are in command of a warship, you fall in the ship's company and you say: "This is the way this ship is going to run." If you went on board the Royal Yacht, it really was their home. They'd train you in their ways pretty quickly.'

The officers were not averse to a few pranks, either. Sir Robert's predecessor had left him strict instructions that the Queen insisted on her Flag Officer wearing his best uniform at all times on family cruises. 'Complete rubbish,' chuckles Sir Robert. 'It was Hawaiian shirts and sandals!' The Queen was greatly amused on the first occasion that Woodard appeared in full uniform. 'Wool? …' she ribbed him. 'Over the eyes? … Being pulled? …'

There was much to learn. When members of the Royal Family were on board, for example, the crew were to stay forward of the mainmast after 8 a.m., unless requested otherwise. There was a clear dividing line between the Royal Household quarters and the rest of the Yacht. Like all ships, this one had a framework of steel ribs. The green baize door or 'below stairs' section began at 'Rib Number 100'. Even at the royal end of the ship, there were further gradations. A cabin with a dark mahogany door was a royal cabin. A light-brown door denoted a Private Secretary, equerry or lady-in-waiting. But come the weekly ship's quiz, conducted over the Yacht's internal radio, there was no hierarchy. The team to beat was always the Chief Petty Officers' Mess. If the Wardroom (the officers' mess) ever managed it, there would be a ritual stamping of feet on the floor of the Wardroom, which sat immediately above the Chief Petty Officers' Mess. The Queen could be very competitive, too, although the questions might be gently skewed when she was on board. 'You might get a question about a steeplechase at Wetherby,' laughs one former member of the Royal Household. He recalls seeing the Foreign Secretary, Douglas Hurd, accompanying a state visit, being ordered off the phone and out of his cabin to add some extra brainpower to the royal team.

Whenever the Queen was on board, so too were the Band of the Royal Marines. They might perform at a small dinner for six or a floodlit shore display for thousands. In 1971, *Britannia* stopped at tiny Pitcairn Island in the Pacific, with Prince Philip and his uncle, Lord Mountbatten, on board. The Yacht's task was, in part, to conduct a Hydrographic Office survey of an area that had last been surveyed by Captain Cook. It was also to pay a royal visit to one of the Commonwealth's loneliest communities, established by Fletcher Christian and his collaborators after the 1789 mutiny on HMS *Bounty*.* Though the crew of *Britannia* outnumbered the entire population by more than two to one, the Band of the Royal Marines still insisted on going ashore in full uniform to perform their Beating Retreat ceremony on Pitcairn's only patch of flat open ground.

Into this unusual world, albeit briefly, stepped a young Lieutenant, Jock Slater. Having watched the launch of the Yacht as a schoolboy, the future First Sea Lord found himself appointed as a young 'season officer' for a year in 1961. He looks back on it with great fondness as an excellent test of initiative. He might be making up the numbers during the Duke of Gloucester's lunch for the King of Greece, at which he found himself seated next to Princess Sophia (the future Queen of Spain). Or he might be the duty officer as the Yacht arrived

* Dixie Deane recalls being given a guided tour of the island on the back of a motorbike driven by one Tom Christian, a direct descendant.

in Ghana for that famously challenging state visit to woo the temperamental father of Ghanaian independence, Kwame Nkrumah. Slater had a tricky task of his own. All the food for the Queen's state banquet had been flown in from London and transferred to a lorry. However, the lorry was not refrigerated and had gone missing, along with the driver. Slater finally tracked the man down to his home, where he had decided to stop off for lunch. Against the odds, the banquet, like the visit itself, would be a great success. The tour moved on to Liberia, where Slater's abiding memory is of the local military leaders stuffing their pockets with the Queen's cigars.

On the voyage home, Slater found himself deputed to organise a music competition. A former flautist with the National Youth Orchestra, his talent had been unearthed earlier in the year by the Queen Mother during her Mediterranean cruise. After being invited to dine at the royal table one evening, the Queen Mother later asked him to join her on the sofa. 'I gather that you were in the National Youth Orchestra,' she told him, having somehow received word of his musical ability. 'We thought it would be nice if you entertained us this evening.' Slater's polite protestation that he had no one to accompany him was instantly quashed when the Queen Mother pointed out that her lady-in-waiting, Lady Fermoy (grandmother of Lady Diana Spencer), had been a concert pianist. Young Slater went to retrieve his flute from his cabin and the pair then performed into the night as *Britannia* sailed for Tunis. Every Flag Officer was on the lookout for such hidden talents when recruiting. 'I always had a qualified yachtsman as one of my officers in case the royal family wanted to go sailing,' says Sir Robert Woodard. 'In the same way, I might pick someone because he was a pianist. You needed to cover every eventuality.'

Entertainment was a key part of life in the Yacht, particularly when the Royal Family were on board. There might be deck tennis or 'horse racing', involving model horses progressing across the deck according to the roll of giant dice. Films were always popular, if a little stressful for the young officer appointed as ship's projectionist. Anthony Morrow, who had three spells in *Britannia*, first arrived as a junior officer in 1965. He has vivid memories of screening the first James Bond film, *Dr No*, for the Queen and Duke, together with a cross-section of the ship's company, drawn by ballot. Fortunately, film selection was not his task. That was a job for the Queen's Equerry, with a proviso that there should not be 'too many writhing sheets'.

Every voyage would include a concert party (or 'sod's opera' as some called it) just like the one that Roger du Boulay had watched in the Pacific. The different sections of the ship would go to a great deal of trouble with their costumes and routines. 'That was naval life at that time in every ship,' says Anthony Morrow. 'We didn't have all the modern stuff like iPads. We had to ad-lib it and provide entertainment to keep the troops happy.' All guests were expected to take part, including royal ones. During a visit to New Zealand, a bare-chested Earl Mountbatten of Burma performed his own version of the Maori *haka*. *Britannia* veterans can even recall one occasion when the Queen was reluctantly persuaded to appear in a sketch as herself, at the behest of the medical officer. As she remarked afterwards: 'The Surgeon Commander got me to do that. If he does it again, he won't be a Surgeon Commander much longer.' One of the more memorable routines during *Britannia*'s later years was a clod-hopping display of Irish dancing, as the ship's Petty Officers attempted a version of the musical, *Riverdance*, wearing gumboots.

Former MP Frank Judd (now Lord Judd) was surprised to end up as part of the entertainment during his time as the Foreign Office minister 'in attendance' for part of the Queen's 1979 tour of the Persian Gulf. 'There was a lot of fun,' he recalls. 'They said: "Frank, you are part of the Household now and it's the custom on the ship to put on an entertainment and we'd rather like you to be part of it". I have a treasured photograph of me leading the chorus with Prince Philip and the Queen there.' He remembers leading his group, including the Queen's press secretary, in a fancy-dress variation of an old Forces number, with a chorus of 'Bum, titty, bum, titty, bum'. As far as he can remember, it went down well. 'The message we got was that the Queen thoroughly enjoyed it.'

After his debut performance for the Queen Mother in 1961, Jock Slater was always in demand with his flute. Years later he found himself back in *Britannia*, this time as Equerry to the Queen, and ended up writing a comedy sketch called 'The Musical Fairy Tale' during which he had to play the flute (in a helmet) while the Prince of Wales hit him on the head with a mallet. While these happy, village-hall-style rituals continued all over the world, from one continent to the next, the Royal Yacht was about to embark on a new career – as a television star and trade envoy.

SALE POWER

No reigning British monarch had ever visited South America until the Queen's dazzling arrival in Brazil in 1968. This was a very different affair from *Britannia*'s usual diet of long-distance Commonwealth tours and short hops around Europe. It is thought that half a million people turned out to watch the Queen join the Yacht, after she flew into the north-eastern city of Recife. More than 100,000 people came out to observe her three-hour stop in Salvador a few days later. Yet it was the royal arrival in Rio de Janeiro that showed how the Queen and her Yacht really could make a grand entrance. The marine cavalcade that greeted *Britannia* beneath Sugarloaf Mountain and the ticker-tape welcome for the Queen ashore offered high drama. And it was all captured by Richard Cawston's crew making that first television documentary. Now, more than ever, the British public could see the Yacht earning its keep overseas. But they were also privy to life on board, to the sense of *Britannia* as a relatively unostentatious sanctuary for the Queen during the happy mayhem of a state visit.

There was another important innovation once the royal party had moved on, by air, to Chile. The Yacht was then handed over to British industry for a series of trade-promotion events known as 'sea days'. The most senior figures in the Brazilian defence and industrial establishments were invited to lunch and to watch a display of seamanship and weaponry by the frigate HMS *Naiad*. The British Ambassador, Sir John Russell, reported back to his superiors on the 'unique advertising value' of the exercise: 'This was a most welcome filip for us in our efforts to break into the field of Brazilian naval and mercantile procurement, and I am in good hopes of seeing immediate returns here in the shape of orders for submarines and frigates.' The figures seem to support Sir John's optimism. Over the next ten years, Brazil would buy more British military hardware than any other Latin American country, by a margin of three to one. The shopping list would include Oberon-class submarines, Niterói-and Broadsword-class frigates, several helicopters and 400 Sea Cat missiles. The most surprising result, perhaps, was that it would be several years before

Britannia was called upon once again to act as a trade-promotion platform. When it did happen, it was a very similar sort of occasion during the Queen's 1975 state visit to Mexico. On that occasion, a combination of *Britannia*'s hospitality and a display of British firepower and naval technology by HMS *Tartar* in the waters off Veracruz led directly to the purchase of a number of patrol boats from Vosper Thorneycroft.

The following year, during the Queen's transatlantic tour to mark the bicentenary of American independence and open the 1976 Montreal Olympics, another sea day was sandwiched into the royal programme while the Yacht was in New York. The heads of thirty American corporations, with a combined value of $66 billion, trooped aboard to spend a day being wooed by the British Overseas Trade Board. The guests also included top financiers like Paul Volcker, future chairman of the Federal Reserve. Given that this was the mid-Seventies, a time when Britain's moribund economy was an international laughing stock, it was some achievement. Anthony Morrow was *Britannia*'s Signal Officer at the time. 'The Queen disappeared to go to Washington so we went to sea for a day from New York with a very strong crowd of business people,' he says. 'The main thing was just having them there. You would never refuse an invitation to go to the Royal Yacht. You might refuse some boring hotel or an embassy do but not a do in the Yacht. It was a particularly good event.'

It was only in the final quarter of *Britannia*'s operational life that the British government really woke up to the Yacht's potential as a trade platform. That was ironic, given that this was the period when funding of the Yacht was more politically divisive than ever. By the Nineties, *Britannia*'s annual running costs were averaging £9 million a year, comparable to those of a mid-ranking British embassy. Gaye Murdoch of British Invisibles, then the promotional arm of the UK financial services industry, has always maintained that the Yacht 'earned millions for Britain and was the envy of all our competitors'. It was hard to put a precise value on the '*Britannia* factor', but its existence was never questioned. In 1986, during a sea day in Shanghai, one British executive seeking a slice of a £4 billion steel contract expressed his thanks to *Britannia*'s then captain, Rear Admiral John Garnier. He had met all the key Chinese state officials he needed to see at lunch in the royal dining room. Under any other circumstances, he explained, it would have taken him six months to make contact with exactly the same people.

In 1993, during one stopover in Bombay, the Yacht was offered as a venue to sign new UK–Indian contracts. Deals that had been mired in legal haggling for months, if not years, were suddenly – and miraculously – resolved. In just four days, contracts worth a total of £1.5 billion were signed. And so it continued to the very end. On *Britannia*'s final trip, to the Middle and Far East in 1997, Commodore Anthony Morrow staged no fewer than eighty-eight commercial events on board, more than the combined total for the previous decade. The Yacht that had been designed for service as a hospital ship had found a perfect métier as a national conference centre. 'The crew were astonishingly helpful in every way and there weren't that many of them to do all the things that they were expected to do,' says the Princess Royal. 'You had boats to go ashore, gangways up and down, dining room tables in, dining room tables out, receptions – all of that was largely done by the crew.' Unfortunately it was just too late.

LOVE BOAT

One break in *Britannia*'s regular royal routine would occur after a royal wedding. There were four honeymoon cruises in the Yacht's forty-four-year-history, the only occasions when a double bed was installed on board. The first newly-weds were Princess Margaret and the Earl of Snowdon, who toured the West Indies in 1960. The Yacht was in the same location, bound for New Zealand, when Princess Anne and Captain Mark Phillips came aboard after their wedding in 1973. Though their Caribbean honeymoon coincided with stormy weather, they enjoyed more privacy than the Prince and Princess of Wales eight years later. Their honeymoon caused a diplomatic row before it had even started, when Spain objected to the couple sailing out of Gibraltar. The Spanish had always claimed the British overseas territory as their own and the Spanish King and Queen declined their wedding invitations as a result of the honeymoon plan. There were also a few less-than-romantic official engagements for the newly-weds, including that dinner for the President of Egypt. After their wedding in July 1986, the Duke and Duchess of York spent ten days sailing around the Azores.

By the time the Queen's youngest child, Prince Edward, Earl of Wessex was married to Sophie Rhys-Jones in 1999, the Yacht had been decommissioned. However, *Britannia* played an important role in the earlier years of their courtship. The Prince invited his future wife, to join him for the annual sailing regatta at Cowes on the Isle of Wight, much to the delight of the photographers covering the event. After a few days, though, the media attention was starting to grate. Sir Robert Woodard, the Yacht's captain, is still proud of his diversionary tactics. 'The paparazzi were being appalling, so I dressed up one Yachtsman as Miss Rhys-Jones and another as Prince Edward and put them in the Royal Barge and sent them off to Osborne House,' he chuckles. 'All the paparazzi went off behind them in pursuit. When they'd gone, Prince Edward and his girlfriend went down the other side, got into my barge and went off to spend the day alone at Beaulieu. They were very appreciative of that – and they still are.'

The Yacht's presence during Cowes Week was entirely down to the Duke of Edinburgh who greatly enjoyed taking part in the racing and the camaraderie at Britain's busiest annual sailing regatta. The Queen, for whom competitive sailing held as much appeal as algebra, would stay away. When Cowes Week was over and the time came to set sail for the Western Isles, she would ask the Yacht to pick her up in Portsmouth or Southampton rather than travel across to the Isle of Wight. 'She avoided Cowes like the plague,' says one former *Britannia* officer. 'It was Prince Philip's time and she let him get on with it.' For the Duke, *Britannia* represented an enduring connection with the Royal Navy career he had been forced to relinquish as a Commander when the Queen came to the Throne. Few dispute that he would have risen to the top of the Service, had he been given the chance.

'Don't forget he's an incredibly clever man who holds the record for being the youngest peacetime commander of a ship,' says Sir Robert Woodard. All of which might have made the Duke of Edinburgh a pretty daunting passenger for a captain of the Royal Yacht. Not so, says Woodard, who can recall just two occasions when the Duke took a 'particular interest' in the handling of the ship. One was when Woodard was attempting to deliver the Duke on time to an important charity engagement in West Palm Beach. *Britannia* had been allocated a small space in a busy harbour. The Yacht's one weakness was that its steering ceased to be effective at speeds of less than six knots (seven miles per hour) and a 20-knot cross-wind was threatening to pin it side-on against a corner of the quayside. Eventually, *Britannia* docked with the paintwork intact. 'My navigating officer was a sweaty wreck. The Duke looked up and said: "I think you can throw away your L-Plates now". And I'd been in command for two years!' Woodard's other hairy moment came as he took *Britannia* on one of the Yacht's greatest voyages – that reinvasion of Normandy ahead of the fiftieth anniversary of D-Day. The high point would be sailing up the Caen Ship Canal past Pegasus Bridge, the first piece of Nazi-occupied Europe to be liberated in 1944. There were just inches to spare on either side of the spot where British airborne forces had pulled off this heroic feat of arms. With the Queen and the Duke on the Royal Bridge, thousands of veterans lining both sides of the canal, crowds gathered for miles in either direction and live television cameras filming it all, Woodard and his crew were nervously steaming at cruising speed towards this tightest of squeezes. At which point, a familiar voice could be heard from the Royal Bridge. 'Keep your eyes on the road!' shouted the Duke, followed by a roar of laughter. As ever, he had every faith in the crew. Once again, it would prove well placed.

The Queen would prove equally unflappable. Even in a storm, says Commodore Anthony Morrow, *Britannia*'s last captain, she was a stoical sailor. During the 1969 review of the Western Fleet the weather got so bad that when the Queen returned to the Yacht, it was deemed too dangerous to make the leap from the Royal Barge back to *Britannia*. The entire Barge had to be hoisted up the side of the Yacht, with her inside it. When she was finally extricated, she remarked: 'Well, that was fun, wasn't it?' Sir Robert Woodard remembers a particularly wobbly moment while the Yacht was tied up in Bordeaux during the 1992 state visit to France. After the Queen's state banquet on board for President François Mitterrand, several hundred extra guests were invited to an after-dinner reception to watch the traditional quayside display by the Band of the Royal Marines. The Yacht's officers would ensure that everyone was evenly spread along the decks to ensure a good vantage point for another faultless performance of 'Highland Cathedral', 'Sunset' and all the other much-loved tunes. At the same time it was the task of the duty officer on the bridge to keep a close eye on the inclinometer, the gadget for monitoring the ship's angle. With several tons of well-fed French VIPs leaning over one side, the officer lowered a reciprocal amount of weight over the other, using the ship's barges as a counterbalance. However, President Mitterrand had neglected to tell the Queen that he had a surprise for her. Once the Royal Marines had finished their display on the quayside, the French set off a huge fireworks display in the opposite direction. At which point, all the guests charged across to the other side of the Yacht. Since it was already weighed down by the barges, *Britannia* lurched like the *Titanic*. 'The whole Yacht went right over to the point that the Queen asked me: "Are we going to be alright?",' recalls Woodard. 'I said: "Of course, we are." Because there was no point in both of us panicking.'

FAREWELL

All the Royal Family have their special memories of *Britannia*. All took part in the Yacht's final farewell tour around the United Kingdom in 1997. And all were there, with one notable exception, for the honourable but painful ceremony to mark the decommissioning of *Britannia* on 11th December 1997. The Queen Mother preferred not to take part. This was where the Queen had enjoyed so many family moments – not just with her own family, but with her 'family of nations'. What's more, her children had grown up with the Yachtsmen, a band of brothers who had spent more time attached to a single ship than the crew of any other ship in the Royal Navy. As a naval wife, mother and daughter herself, it is not surprising the Queen was upset that day. More than twenty years later, it is said that the Princess Royal dislikes hearing 'Highland Cathedral' because of its associations with *Britannia*. The little girl who proudly presented the bouquet on Clydeside that day in 1953, as the Queen launched her beloved *Britannia*, recalls saying farewell when the Yacht made its last appearance in London. 'She came down the Thames for a final goodbye and I remember weeping copiously seeing her for the last time,' says Robin, Countess of Onslow. She then watched the decommissioning ceremony on the news. 'It may well have been perhaps the only time that the Queen was close to welling up in public. But it was cruel of the television cameras to pan in on her. The vessel was almost another member of the Royal Family when you think of all the places that she's safely conveyed the family.'

In a world that increasingly appreciates the value of 'soft power' – the triumph of influence over coercion – many still find it bizarre that a leading maritime nation like Britain could have disposed of an asset as valuable as the Royal Yacht. Chief Emeka Anyaoku, the Nigerian former Secretary-General of the Commonwealth, remains baffled: '*Britannia* should have been replaced. Some latter day Prime Ministers of Britain have tended to underestimate the extent and the value of British soft power. If I were Prime Minister, I would pay greater attention to sustaining it.'

During his many years at Marlborough House, Chief Anyaoku would visit almost as many Commonwealth countries as the Queen. 'I didn't have *Britannia* so I never made it to Tuvalu,' he laughs, recalling the Queen's famous 1982 arrival in a war canoe. Yet he saw *Britannia* in action all over the world. And he has no doubt that the Queen could not have achieved all that she has without her Yacht.

Ultimately, *Britannia*'s demise was down to bad timing and political incompetence. At the moment when a substantial refit was required, in the mid-Nineties, the fortunes of the Royal Family were at a low ebb. In 1994, John Major's government announced that *Britannia* would be taken out of service in 1997, while ministers would retain an open mind on the possibility of a replacement. Shortly before the 1997 election, the same Conservative government announced that it would build a new yacht after all, with a budget of £60 million. But it had failed to follow the golden rule – observed when *Britannia* was ordered in 1951 – that major undertakings involving the monarchy require cross-party agreement. Tony Blair's Labour Party was not consulted and duly opposed the idea, which thus became an election issue. Unsurprisingly, on being elected a few months later, the new government declined to commission a new Yacht. Blair would later admit to the author that it had been a mistake to get rid of *Britannia* in the first place and that he would have retained it, if he had been elected sooner. Even within the Palace, however, there were those who felt, with a heavy heart, that the age of Royal Yachts was over. '*Britannia* ran out of road,' says one senior ex-member of the Royal Household. 'Visits were getting shorter and it was getting to the point that we would be doing some things simply because we could get the Yacht there, not because we needed to do them.'

A former Private Secretary agrees: 'The yacht is a sad departure but, for me, an unlamented one. It was, as someone said, "all kicks and no ha'pence". Every time the Queen did her Western Isles cruise, the press would work out to the nearest drop how much fuel they'd used, how much it cost and so on. Those days are over. Yes, lovely to go to Copenhagen or Stockholm by yacht but it was two days on the way there and two days on the way back and diaries are just busier. The Queen's a realist. She knew the time was up.'

The Royal Family themselves were determined to avoid becoming involved in any of the arguments. Whatever their personal attachment to the Yacht and its crew, this was very clearly a political matter and was thus strictly off-limits. Hence the brevity of that mournful speech by the Prince of Wales on the night of *Britannia*'s retirement. There were plenty in Parliament, the press and the general public keen to keep up the pressure for a new Yacht. There was support, too, from right across the Commonwealth. Chief Anyaoku, for example, joined one of several consortia that have campaigned for a new Yacht over the years. With no government willing to devote public money, along with inevitable sensitivities about sponsorship, each attempt has foundered. Of necessity, members of the Royal Family have stayed firmly detached from all debate. However, one consortium including senior ex-Royal Navy figures, a famous naval architect and leading maritime industry figures has drawn up advanced designs for a national sailing ship, with both a university and sail-training role when not on royal or scientific duty. The fully costed plans for the 'University of the Oceans' emphasise that it would be a 'UK flagship', most definitely not a 'yacht' and not dependent on public money.

One of *Britannia*'s inherent shortcomings was the word 'yacht' – with its connotations of luxury and idle pleasure. It actually derives from the seventeenth-century Dutch word for a racing boat or pilot launch. 'Some people will always associate "yacht" with gold taps, I'm afraid,' says one former officer. Perhaps if, at the very outset, *Britannia* had been designated the 'National Flagship' instead of the 'Royal Yacht', things might have taken a different turn.

Once there was no prospect of a reprieve for *Britannia*, some people, including the Princess Royal, argued that the Yacht should be scrapped or scuttled. Ministers thought otherwise, to the delight of the millions of visitors who have been to see it berthed in its new home in Leith, on the outskirts of Edinburgh. Now carefully maintained by a charity, the Royal Yacht *Britannia* Trust, the Yacht is one of Scotland's most popular attractions and an award-winning member of the 'Core Collection' of Britain's National Register of Historic Vessels. Visitors can look through the royal apartments and absorb that same airy, unostentatious, 'domestic' atmosphere that, between them, the Queen, the Duke and Sir Hugh Casson had wanted to create. It is the first and only place in Britain that anyone can view the bedroom of a living monarch. Aside from some minor alterations (the ladies-in-waiting's sitting room, for example, is now a gents lavatory), the only notable omissions are the original dining-room furniture and tableware. Prince Philip moved most of this to Frogmore House, Windsor to create a '*Britannia* Room' as a memorial to the Yacht and prevent the collection being broken up. Back in Edinburgh, the crowds on board the real *Britannia* are equally interested in the crew's old quarters. All like to look inside the Yachtsmen's bar, officially called the Unwinding Room and known to all as Ye Olde Honk Inn (the Princess of Wales dropped in there during her honeymoon and ended up playing the piano). Through a glass screen, the public can inspect the captain's cabin, faithfully laid out for breakfast exactly as it would have been, complete with plastic replica fry-up and morning newspaper (though ex-Yotties are always a little puzzled that the newspaper in question is the *Guardian*).

It is a reflection of the lasting bond between the Yacht, the officers, the crew and the passengers that there are still regular reunions of the Association of Royal Yachtsmen, many of them attended by a member of the Royal Family. A few years ago, the Queen invited all those attending a reunion to come for a reception first at Windsor Castle. She will always send a special message to be read out at the association's gatherings. Even more striking is the sight, each spring, of dozens of former Yotties dressed in their overalls as they return to perform a week's unpaid maintenance work on board. A former Marine Engineer Mechanic sets to work in the engine room, polishing the pipework. Former Able Seamen can be found on the staircase, sanding and varnishing the woodwork. Two former Leading Cooks get cracking in the Ship's Galley to produce meals for their old comrades. On the final day, the old Yachtsmen line up on the Verandah Deck to hear the time-honoured command for a naval celebration: 'Splice the mainbrace.' At which point, everyone receives a 'tot' of rum for their work. Before they drink it, they raise their glasses in a toast to someone who is not just a remote symbolic figure, but someone they are all very proud to know: 'The Queen'.

Chapter 10

ELIZABETH, MARGARET AND NELSON

'He needs a show'

HUMBLE AND OBEDIENT SERVANT

No other foreign country can claim to have had such an impact on the Queen as the one that she studiously avoided for the best part of half a century. Addressing the people of South Africa at the end of her 1995 state visit, she did not mince her words. It had been, she said, 'one of the outstanding experiences of my life'. Her life has been a catalogue of extraordinary experiences, so when she described this one as 'outstanding', it was praise of the highest order.

South Africa had been the first foreign country she visited, arriving with her parents back in 1947 ahead of that momentous twenty-first birthday pledge. And it was the future of South Africa that would bedevil her beloved Commonwealth for a large part of her reign. This was the issue that would bring her as close to a constitutional crisis as anything during the longest reign in history. There were moments when it threatened to cause a terminal schism and bring down the Commonwealth, too. Now, here she was, toasting South Africa's freedom and saluting perhaps the Commonwealth's greatest achievement. 'Outstanding' was no exaggeration.

For two decades, while the domestic royal story veered from the royal-wedding euphoria of the Eighties to the smoke-flecked matrimonial misery and tragedy of the Nineties, there was an entirely separate chain of events to preoccupy the Head of the Commonwealth. Fortunately for the Queen, her international fortunes were a royal story running entirely counter to her domestic ones. Though these were historically awful years at home, the monarchy could at least derive enormous solace and reaffirmation overseas. And dominating this chapter of her life were two titanic figures for whom the Queen would retain the highest regard. She would get to know them both very well, though the pair themselves would meet only fleetingly. One would fade from public view at the very moment the other emerged into the sunlight. They had passionately contrasting views on nearly all the issues of the day. If they were united on one point, it was in their respect for the Queen. She, in turn, bestowed on them arguably her most illustrious personal honour. Even by the exalted standards of the Order of Merit, there could be few more distinctive recipients than Margaret Thatcher and Nelson Mandela.

The relationship between the Queen and her first female Prime Minister will preoccupy historians for years to come. Her rapport with Nelson Mandela can be summed up by a series of letters stored in the Royal Archives. They are perhaps the only regular correspondence the Queen has ever received from anyone except family (or schoolchildren) that begin: 'Dear Elizabeth …' One thing we can be sure of is that Mrs Thatcher would not have started any letter to the Queen like that. According to her former principal Private Secretary, Robin Butler, the Conservative leader was always meticulous in observing the correct form, after an early brush with the Queen's private office. 'When she was still Leader of the Opposition, she went to some event at Buckingham Palace and she wrote a thank-you letter afterwards that started informally,' says Butler. 'I don't think she quite started it "Dear Elizabeth" but the Palace rang up Caroline* and said: "The Queen expects her Prime Minister or her Leader of the Opposition to observe the formalities".' According to Charles Moore, Mrs Thatcher's biographer, the Queen's Private Secretary had gently pointed out that 'Yours sincerely' was not quite the way to

* Caroline Stephens (later Lady Ryder) was Mrs Thatcher's diary secretary.

conclude a letter to the Sovereign. The 'correct' form would have been something along the lines of 'I have the honour, Ma'am, to remain Your Majesty's humble and obedient servant'.

This seems much more likely to have been the intervention of a courtier than an edict from the Queen. She has been famously forgiving of those negotiating royal protocol for the first time, whether it is the dinner guest drinking the contents of his finger-bowl or the nervous man who drops into a curtsey at an investiture. Mrs Thatcher, according to Charles Moore, 'wanted to observe the proprieties and had no desire to turn everything upside down.' He went on: 'Those who worked for her noticed how worried she always was by all matters of dress and protocol.'

From the moment Mrs Thatcher took office, she would be scrupulous in not keeping the Queen waiting, frequently turning up early for her weekly audience. On October 12th 1984, after that IRA bomb had destroyed the Conservative Party's conference hotel in Brighton, the Queen was in the USA and was desperately concerned to speak to her Prime Minister. On finally making contact with Mrs Thatcher's emergency headquarters by telephone, it is said that it was the Prime Minister who opened the conversation with a cheery: 'Are you having a wonderful time?'

Mrs Thatcher would certainly find it hard when the roles were reversed at the annual prime-ministerial visit to Balmoral. It is a tradition that the Royal Family like to do the cooking and cleaning, whenever there is a barbecue. The Prime Minister was almost goaded beyond endurance watching the Queen washing up after dinner. After yet another prime-ministerial offer of well-meaning but unwanted assistance, the Queen was heard to tell her lady-in-waiting: 'Could someone tell that woman to sit down.' When Mrs Thatcher wrote her thank-you letter afterwards, she included a pair of washing-up gloves.

According to the Queen's former Private Secretary, Sir William Heseltine, both monarch and Prime Minister enjoyed a strong mutual respect rather than a great rapport. 'It was a very correct relationship. There were other prime ministers with whom relations seemed warmer,' he says, pointing to the Labour leaders of the Seventies, Harold Wilson and Jim Callaghan. 'It was my observation that she was more at ease with these two. With Mrs Thatcher, relationships were always very proper but not perhaps as relaxed as with these two Labour PMs.'

As Moore has pointed out, Mrs Thatcher was extremely nervous at these meetings, arriving with a lengthy list of pressing matters. Since it was not in the Queen's nature to interrupt, the audiences could easily descend into a monologue. Robin Butler, who would accompany his boss to the Palace, suspects that they may not have been the most fruitful exchanges. 'I had a sense she had this list on her lap and worked her way conscientiously through it, which is probably not what the Queen wanted.' Contrary to the stereotypical Mrs Thatcher portrayed in cartoons and satirical dramas, the real one was not nearly as imperious as her detractors have suggested. 'She was not over-confident,' says Robin Butler. 'She was assertive because she was lacking in confidence. I got used to the fact she could listen while she talked and take it on board but you had to talk against her.' That was hardly the Queen's style.

Early tensions between the new Tory government, the Commonwealth and the Palace would subside after that triumph at the Lusaka Heads of Government Meeting in 1979. Just weeks into her premiership, Mrs Thatcher had helped devise a strategy that would bring peace to war-ravaged Rhodesia and would lead to black majority rule in a newly independent Zimbabwe. Many politicians have subsequently shared the credit for that achievement, although, as we now discover, the sudden outbreak of harmony owed so much to the discreet but determined interventions of the Queen herself. However, the leaders of the 'family of nations' would not stay united for long. And the Queen's powers of reconciliation would be even more important as a new Commonwealth fault line opened up during the 1980s, which would leave Mrs Thatcher on one side and everyone else on the other.

APARTHEID AND SANCTIONS

To begin with, the post-Lusaka consensus held firm. Things continued to go surprisingly well between the right-wing occupant of Number Ten and the predominantly left-leaning members of the Commonwealth. In 1982, Mrs Thatcher realised what a positive asset the Commonwealth could be, when Argentinian forces invaded the Falkland Islands. As Britain prepared to recapture sovereign territory and liberate the Queen's 1,800 British subjects living there, the post-colonial cousinhood rallied round. There was united Commonwealth support for Britain at the United Nations and, in some cases, military assistance, too. New Zealand offered to take over the Royal Navy's duties in the Caribbean, freeing up an extra warship for the Falklands task force. The Queen could certainly see ways in which the Commonwealth might help, according to one senior member of her staff. 'She wasn't actually ringing round but she might say in a conversation with the Prime Minister: "You might find that so and so has got a frigate".'

A year later, however, as the Commonwealth heads were meeting in Delhi, that Falklands consensus was already fading. New divisions were opening up on either side of that eternal question: what should be done about South Africa? The Queen had witnessed the racial divisions herself during that 1947 tour with her parents. The fact that King George VI had not even been allowed to pin medals on black South African war veterans lingered long in royal minds. The British Royal Family had been seen as a sympathetic ally among the black community, so much so that a prominent law student called Nelson Mandela had urged members of the African National Congress to give the King a respectful welcome.

But a year later, the election of the Afrikaner-dominated Nationalist Party had set the country on the path to apartheid – the system of dividing the nation on racial lines, with the whites in charge. Over the next decade, during which the Princess was crowned Queen of South Africa along with all her other realms, the government would bring in laws forbidding black Africans from entering certain parts of the country and a ban on mixed marriages. These were all laws passed in the Queen's name. However, her position was becoming increasingly untenable. How could she remain Queen of the United Kingdom, which was embarking on a post-imperial policy of granting independence and majority rule to its former colonies, and, at the same time, be Queen of South Africa, which was doing the complete opposite?

Matters would come to a head in 1960, when the South African Prime Minister, Dr Hendrik Verwoerd, announced his referendum on creating a South African republic. A month later, the British Prime Minister, Harold Macmillan, came to deliver his 'wind of change' speech to the South African parliament. One month after that, global condemnation followed a police attack on an unarmed crowd in Sharpeville. Several thousand blacks had gathered to protest against laws requiring them to carry passbooks. Sixty-nine of them were killed, in what would always be known as the Sharpeville Massacre. There were instant calls for South Africa to be expelled from the Commonwealth – though there was no need, following Verwoerd's successful referendum campaign to replace the Queen with a President (though the black majority had no vote). As has been shown, Commonwealth rules at the time required any nation that did not have the Queen as head of state to apply for membership. Having just become a republic, South Africa would therefore have to reapply. The fury voiced at the meeting of Commonwealth prime ministers in London in March 1961 made it very clear how that would end. So Verwoerd tore up his application before it was submitted. Thus began South Africa's three decades in the wilderness.

The country turned in on itself, as groups like the African National Congress (ANC) began to advocate resistance and sabotage. In 1962, Nelson Mandela, a leader of the ANC's armed wing, was arrested and in 1964, along with several others, was sentenced to life imprisonment (the prosecution had called for the death penalty). The struggle would continue from afar, thanks to the British-based Anti-Apartheid Movement. Over the years, a series of political, economic and sporting international boycotts would extend South Africa's isolation, though it was not until the mid-1980s that the pressure for change reached a new level. With Mikhail Gorbachev now in charge of the Soviet Union, East-West relations began to thaw. South Africa increasingly became the dominant foreign-policy issue of the day. By the 1980s, newly independent Zimbabwe had shown how black majority rule could be achieved. For the Commonwealth – and particularly for the younger African ex-colonies of the 'new' Commonwealth – there was no more important matter on the world stage. Here was a country where a white man could still beat a black worker to death and be fined £700; where infant mortality rates were 2.7 per cent for a white baby and 40 per cent for a black baby.

How best to bring about change though? The chief stumbling block was economic sanctions. Most Commonwealth states felt that these were critical in pushing South Africa's apartheid regime to the brink. Not so Mrs Thatcher, who believed that sanctions were harmful, both to the poorest in South Africa and to British trade interests. The Commonwealth Secretary-General of the period, Sir Sonny Ramphal, remains a stern critic of her stance. In his memoirs he goes as far as blaming Mrs Thatcher for keeping Mandela in prison. Had she not blocked sanctions so forcefully, he wrote, South Africa 'might not have been offered the lifeline it was given and Nelson Mandela might not have been robbed of a further decade of his freedom'. A major part of his memoirs is a section called, simply, 'The Thatcher Years'.

During the first few months of her premiership, Ramphal had gone to considerable efforts to prevent the African members of the Commonwealth from 'ganging up' on Mrs Thatcher, notably at that Commonwealth summit in Lusaka. It had been a shrewd move at the time, but now he would become more combative in his dealings. Mrs Thatcher, for her part, was finding the Commonwealth increasingly exasperating. As Charles Moore has pointed out, she particularly loathed being harangued about South Africa by countries that were, themselves, conducting secret trade deals with South Africa. She was also instinctively wary of nations that did not share her enthusiasm for the battle against international communism, something that a number of Commonwealth nations positively embraced. Mrs Thatcher would spend much of the Delhi summit defending America from a lot of vociferous anti-American rhetoric. The USA was in the Commonwealth doghouse, not least for its invasion of Grenada earlier in the year. Mrs Thatcher had her own reasons to be angry about Grenada. The US President, Ronald Reagan, her friend and ally, had attacked one of the Queen's Commonwealth realms without having had the courtesy to inform either the Queen or her British Prime Minister. At the Delhi summit, however, Mrs Thatcher ended up defending Reagan vigorously – so much so that there was virtually no mention of the USA in the final communiqué, beyond a call for fresh dialogue with the Soviet Union. Writing to Reagan about it, Mrs Thatcher added: 'It is by no means an ideal document but you should have seen the earlier versions!'

It did not help that the arrangements for the Delhi summit bordered on the chaotic. At one point during the retreat to Goa, Denis

Thatcher's patience finally snapped during yet another power cut. He stormed out onto the couple's hotel balcony and proclaimed to anyone within earshot: 'This place is very high on the buggeration factor!' Denis Thatcher was not the only one infuriated by some of the arrangements at the 1983 Commonwealth summit. The Queen and her staff were equally frustrated by a series of pointless confrontations with the Indian government. Though Lord Butler recalls the Queen's high regard for the veteran Prime Minister, Indira Gandhi, the same did not apply to her officials. Before the Queen had even landed, her arrival plans had to bend to the demands of Hindu astrologers, who warned that the scheduled touchdown at noon was inauspicious. The Queen's VC10 was duly delayed until 12.05. The most absurd quarrel occurred when the Queen was preparing to welcome Mother Teresa of Calcutta to her guest quarters at the presidential palace. The monarch was planning to salute the Nobel Prize-winning charity worker, nun and future saint by presenting her with the Order of Merit, the same honour that her great-grandfather had awarded to Florence Nightingale. What was supposed to be one of the highlights of the royal visit turned to farce when the Indian government intervened, saying it was 'impossible'. 'They said: "There's no way the Queen can possibly give any order to anybody in the presidential palace." It was forbidden,' says Sir William Heseltine. 'They were bent on putting obstacles in the way.' The Queen circumvented the problem by giving Mother Teresa her OM in the garden. As it turned out, it was a prettier and more appropriate location – and made for a better photograph, too.

The Queen's Indian visit had left a mark on her, however – one that would cause a certain amount of discomfort at Downing Street. In her 1983 Christmas broadcast she dwelt at length on the poverty she had witnessed. Before arriving in India, the Queen had visited Bangladesh, where she was visibly moved by an encounter with a tiny, starving child called Jamal. She promised his carers that she would raise his case with Princess Anne, who was due to visit the capital city, Dhaka, a few months later as President of Save the Children.* In her

* The Princess did, indeed, meet Jamal and made subsequent visits to the orphanage that was looking after him. 'There were places which we really felt were doing a particularly good job,' she says.

broadcast, the Queen departed from the usual Christmas script to include a short economics lesson: 'In spite of all the progress that has been made, the greatest problem in the world today remains the gap between rich and poor countries, and we shall not begin to close this gap until we hear less about nationalism and more about interdependence. One of the main aims of the Commonwealth is to make an effective contribution towards redressing the economic balance between nations.'

The Head of the Commonwealth went even further with a few suggestions: 'What we want to see is still more modern technology being used by poorer countries to provide employment and to produce primary products and components, which will be bought in turn by the richer countries at competitive prices.' Noting various technical advances, she also pointed up their shortcomings. 'Perhaps even more serious is the risk that this mastery of technology may blind us to the more fundamental needs of people. Electronics cannot create comradeship; computers cannot generate compassion; satellites cannot transmit tolerance.' In tone and substance, this was an astonishing address

The broadcast was also a major news story. The Queen was being 'political', said the right-of-centre press, adding that she clearly had an agenda. It was not one shared by her Prime Minister, either. Was the Queen now 'ganging up' on Mrs Thatcher like everyone else?

The suspicion was that the Commonwealth Secretariat of Sonny Ramphal had been bending the royal ear. Into this debate stepped the ferociously anti-Commonwealth Ulster Unionist MP, Enoch Powell. He did not want to see the Queen putting the 'interests and affairs of other countries' ahead of the best interests of the British. The Queen's press secretary, Michael Shea, stoked things further. Instead of a 'no comment', he issued a statement. 'The Christmas broadcast is a personal message to her Commonwealth,' it said. 'The Queen has all her people at heart, irrespective of race, creed or colour.' The Christmas broadcast is, indeed, the one official royal utterance that is not delivered on ministerial advice. *The Times*, historically the paragon of establishment thinking and firmly supportive of Mrs Thatcher, went further than Powell. The Rupert Murdoch-owned paper published a stern editorial. The warning that the Queen had been duped by fashionable 'global egalitarianism' and her 'questionable' economic theory was a legitimate topic of debate. It was but a foretaste of rows to come.

BRITANNIA CALMS THE WAVES

The next Commonwealth summit, in 1985, was even more ill-tempered. The 'club' was convening in the capital of the Bahamas, Nassau, and the issue of South African sanctions had reached a critical moment. Unless the Commonwealth agreed to specific measures against apartheid, some of its members would resign from the organisation altogether. The obstacle to such measures would, inevitably, be Mrs Thatcher. As in Lusaka, the Queen would have her work cut out keeping the peace.

More than three decades later, some find it baffling that Mrs Thatcher should have been so stout in her defence of the South African regime. Many – including David Cameron – detect the hand of Denis. 'Mrs Thatcher was on the wrong side of that argument. It was so unnecessary but there was Denis,' says Cameron. He sums up the Denis Thatcher world view as: "You can say what you like about South Africa but with the whites in charge, at least it's working ..." As the former Foreign Office Permanent Under-Secretary, Patrick Wright, noted in his diary in 1986: 'All her (and Denis's) instincts are in favour of the South African Whites.'

In his biography of Lady Thatcher, Charles Moore reveals how Denis Thatcher's fondness for South Africa went deep. He had relatives there, and it was to South Africa that he went in 1964 to recover from a nervous breakdown. Mrs Thatcher was more sceptical, regarding apartheid as a form of 'racial socialism'. She was friendly with anti-apartheid campaigners like Helen Suzman (whom she nominated for an honorary GCMG, Dame Grand Cross of the Order of St Michael and St George, the highest honour for a diplomat). Mrs Thatcher's primary goal was a non-violent transition rather than a revolution. Much as it may surprise the left-wing critics who have demonised her ever since, she also did something that neither of her Labour predecessors had done. She was the first British Prime Minister to seek the release of Nelson Mandela.

The stakes could hardly have been higher ahead of the 1985 Commonwealth summit. Addressing journalists in London, Sonny Ramphal announced that the Nassau meeting might well be as historically significant as the abolition of slavery. Mrs Thatcher had no such expectations. According to Charles Moore, when the British Airways chairman, Lord King, offered her a seat on a special Commonwealth Concorde flight to Nassau, she declined. 'Stick to VC10s,' she wrote on a memo. She had no wish to be accused of upstaging the Queen. With the Royal Yacht *Britannia* in pride of place in the harbour, there was little chance of that.

The Queen was not sitting idly by on the margins. Well aware of the threat to her organisation, the Head of the Commonwealth was doing some discreet pre-emptive peacemaking. The Canadian Prime Minister, Brian Mulroney, would later admit that she had been leaning on him. 'The Queen personally asked me to work with other leaders to prevent a major split within the group,' he wrote. Other leaders – including Zambia's Kenneth Kaunda and Australia's Bob Hawke – did the same. The Iron Lady, however, was in truly ferrous form. When battle commenced, it was fierce and uncompromising. First to speak on South Africa was Mahathir Mohamed of Malaysia. 'If the Commonwealth refuses to do something definite then the club should cease to pretend,' he declared. 'It should admit that it really cannot contribute to solving the problems faced by its members, if not the world.'

Then things became more personal. When she was accused of putting pennies ahead of 'black lives', Mrs Thatcher accused others around the table of rank hypocrisy for their own dealings with South Africa. 'I had never been so insulted as I had by the people in that room,' she wrote in her memoirs. As with any heated argument in which people say something they instantly regret, so the Commonwealth leaders realised that perhaps the ganging up had gone too far. Wrath gave way to a search for some sort of consensus. Sonny Ramphal eventually stitched up a deal to which everyone could sign up. It was agreed that the Commonwealth would implement a series of minor sanctions, such as a ban on krugerrand coins and trade promotions. More importantly, Bob Hawke secured an agreement that the Commonwealth would send an 'eminent persons group' to South Africa. Though some African nations disliked the idea of any dialogue with the apartheid regime, it would turn out to be both a vital and an inspired proposal. Unity had been maintained, although Mrs Thatcher would not go home without upsetting everyone once more. When a journalist suggested that she had finally come round to the idea of sanctions, she replied witheringly that they were little more than a 'tiny' gesture. Her Foreign Secretary, Geoffrey Howe, was appalled. The Commonwealth had given a large amount of ground to meet her, and now she had undone all that goodwill by belittling the deal. His boss, he later recalled, had 'humiliated three dozen other heads of government, devalued the policy which they just agreed, and demeaned herself'.

The Queen, meanwhile, could content herself that another potential Commonwealth disaster had been narrowly averted. The summit had not been without its dramas for her. As she waited for guests to arrive at her banquet on board *Britannia*, there was no sign of the summit host, Sir Lynden Pindling.* A proud but prickly soul, he had been upset by local anti-corruption demonstrations against him and had learned that protestors were waiting on the road to the port. So he decided to travel to the banquet by boat and invited other leaders to join him. Unfortunately, the Royal Navy patrols guarding the Royal Yacht had not been informed and ordered the boat to remain outside the security cordon. The Queen was left pacing her deck and looking at her watch. 'Pindling and the others, including Kenneth Kaunda, were stopped by this security boat, which said "Go out to sea and identify yourself",' says Patsy Robertson. 'There was poor KK waiting to be identified while the Queen was waiting and tapping her fingers on the rail because she couldn't start without the PM. As they traipsed up the gangway, Sonny Ramphal said: "Ma'am, the boat people have arrived!" It was very funny.'

When an embarrassed Pindling tried to explain his decision to come by sea and avoid the protestors, the Queen was greatly amused. 'Whatever for?' she said. 'We've all seen those demonstrations and

* In 1967, Pindling formed the first black Bahamian administration, led the islands to independence in 1973 – when Prince Charles had a famous dance with Mrs Pindling – and served as Prime Minister for more than two decades. He was knighted in 1983 and had the national airport named after him, following his death in 2000.

the banners. They say "The Chief's a thief".' As in Lusaka, she did her best to make the evening as jolly as possible, making sure she had a friendly conversation with everyone. Stuart Mole, a senior member of Sonny Ramphal's team, vividly remembers the after-dinner reception on board the Royal Yacht. 'The Queen had a drinks party on the deck at the end of the evening. We looked down on the dock and there was a Beating Retreat from the Band of the Royal Marines and also the Royal Bahamian Police Band. They almost competed against each other in different styles. It was magical.'

Nassau might not have achieved a great deal, but a break-up had been averted and, crucially, it had come up with a process and a strategy. The Commonwealth delegation would head to Pretoria with a proposal: if the ANC would suspend violence and start talking, would South Africa release political prisoners, including Nelson Mandela?

EMINENT PERSONS

Predictably, the idea of the seven-strong 'Eminent Persons Group' – including the former Nigerian leader General Olusegun Obasanjo, ex-Australian Prime Minister Malcolm Fraser, and Lord Barber, former Chancellor of the Exchequer – was strongly opposed by the South African government. P. W. Botha, who had recently upgraded his position from Prime Minister to 'State President', initially refused to talk to them. It was Mrs Thatcher who told him not to be so stupid and, for good measure, got President Reagan to tell him the same thing. Even those critical of the British Prime Minister (Sonny Ramphal among them) give her credit for opening the necessary doors to the group.

One of the most important doors of all, however, was the one to the cell of Nelson Mandela at Pollsmoor Prison. There, they found Prisoner 466/64, dressed in a suit with an ANC belt, in high spirits. Emeka Anyaoku, the Commonwealth Deputy Secretary-General who was accompanying the mission, remembers the respect that Mandela was accorded by his captors. At one point the members of the group remonstrated when the South African Justice Minister, Kobie Coetsee, and his officials insisted on joining the meeting. 'Let them come,' Mandela joked, adding that they would hear it all anyway. There was a comedy of manners when, having done the introductions, the minister duly retreated. 'Please stay,' said Mandela. 'No, this is your occasion,' said Coetsee. 'I insist,' said Mandela. 'I really think this is your day,' the minister replied, leaving one of his officials to sit in on the meeting. Chief Anyaoku was struck by the fact that the official insisted on calling Mandela 'Sir'.

Mandela would tell the Commonwealth delegation that their visits – there would be three in all – were the most important in his twenty-four years of captivity. On being introduced to Lord Barber, the prisoner replied: 'I am told Mrs Thatcher says President Gorbachev is a man with whom she can do business. Will you please tell her that it would be far far easier and very much safer to do business with Nelson Mandela.' It was certainly a historic moment as the group outlined the proposed deal to their host. Mandela immediately accepted the need to call a halt to all violence, in exchange for an end to the ban on the ANC. There would be no such accommodation from President Botha, during a glacial meeting in which he briskly dismissed the ANC as 'communists'. Yet the mere fact that the South African President received a delegation who had just met Mandela was a start. Whereupon the South African government did something extraordinary.

On the very morning the Commonwealth visitors were preparing to meet a top-level government delegation, South African jets suddenly invaded the air space of three neighbours, bombing suspected ANC bases in Zambia, Zimbabwe and Botswana – all of them Commonwealth countries. As Chief Anyaoku recalls, the 'Eminent Persons Group' duly stormed out of the country so quickly that he left some of his clothes in the hotel laundry.

International outrage was immediate and across the board. Mrs Thatcher was appalled, telling Botha that the attacks were a 'watershed' and shattered the 'trust and confidence which I had thought we had established'. South Africa had just alienated the one key figure whose goodwill it needed most. Mrs Thatcher had realised that P. W. Botha was a dud after all. She was equally convinced, however, that the release of Nelson Mandela was central to any solution.

The Commonwealth was certainly not giving up now. It had been agreed in Nassau that there could be a special conference to discuss the findings of the eminent fact-finders. It would not be a full gathering of the Commonwealth but an emergency meeting of seven key leaders. And there was a great deal to discuss. A date was fixed for a meeting in London at Marlborough House in early August 1986 and the Queen was informed. She was in no doubt about the gravity of the situation. Among those pressing her to intervene directly was Desmond Tutu. The newly installed Archbishop of Cape Town had just written her an anguished personal letter, begging for her help in suppressing the 'most vicious system since Nazism'. The special Commonwealth conference might clash with her holiday at Balmoral, but she was certainly not going to miss it. Once again the Head of the Commonwealth would prove crucial to proceedings. The Queen was not to know that the conference would crown one of the most challenging fortnights of her reign.

BOYCOTTS AND BAD NEWS

When the 'Eminent Persons Group' published their report, *Mission to South Africa*, in June 1986, it did something that few official reports have done, before or since. It became an overnight international best-seller. Penguin Books rushed it out as an emergency paperback and its conclusion proved bleak and uncompromising. The world could 'stand by and allow the cycle of violence to spiral', it said, or take 'concerted action' of an effective kind. 'Such action may offer the last opportunity to avert what could be the worst bloodbath since the Second World War.' That certainly set the scene for the Marlborough House mini-summit. Surely now, the Commonwealth leaders thought, Mrs Thatcher would come round to the idea of sanctions? No she would not, they were told. Out of deference to her European partners (not a concern that usually troubled her), she would wait to see the EEC's view, following its own mission to South Africa. If that was not enough to upset most of the Commonwealth, they were enraged by an interview she gave to the *Guardian* in early July. The sanctions lobby, she said, were simply high-minded liberals polishing their halos to salve their consciences. Her concern, she told Hugo Young, was for the poor: 'South Africa runs the best economy in the whole of Africa. You wish all of the people of South Africa to inherit that economy and not to ruin it. Have you looked at the three million people who could be turned back – who come into South Africa to work, who remit their earnings to other people? I do not know where it would end. Please, I am not going to be the one who causes fantastic starvation, unemployment and misery in South Africa.'

In short, it was a 'No'. And on the very same day, two countries announced that they would be boycotting the upcoming Commonwealth Games in Edinburgh as a result. Edinburgh had ended up hosting the 1986 Games as a goodwill gesture as much as anything else, since nowhere else had offered to host them. The city had staged them in 1970 and the facilities were still there. So why not? All that was needed was a new logo and a new mascot – a cheeky Scottie dog called 'Mac', as it turned out. Money was already tight, long before the sudden news that Nigeria and Ghana would not be turning up, thanks to Mrs Thatcher's position on sanctions. In the words of a Nigerian government spokesman, they wished to 'dramatise to the British government how strongly we feel about the matter'.

Over the coming weeks more African nations would follow suit, along with most of the Caribbean. The Games would not only be diminished; they would also be overwhelmingly white. It was an alarming prospect, not just for the organisers, but for the Head of the Commonwealth herself. Sir Malcolm Rifkind was both an Edinburgh MP and Secretary of State for Scotland at the time. As such, he regularly accompanied the Queen and the Royal Family to Scottish events and well remembers the nervous mood. 'They'd have been very upset,' he says. 'If people boycott the Commonwealth Games, it's only a matter of time before they could boycott the Commonwealth.'

The Queen was not only concerned about the Games, but about the emergency conference at Marlborough House the following week. On the day after the first boycotts of the Games were announced, she let it be known that she was planning to break her holiday and head back to London ahead of the conference. She wished to give a dinner for the Commonwealth leaders at Buckingham Palace ahead of their deliberations. It was, the Palace explained, traditional for her to entertain the leaders at Commonwealth summits. It was also her understanding that the British government was keen on the idea – because Ramphal had said as much. In fact, the government was not. This was no ordinary summit. Downing Street was worried and more than a little suspicious about the Queen's insistence on a royal banquet. It was not hard to spot the fingerprints of the

Secretary-General. As Ramphal and his successor, Chief Anyaoku, would later make clear, they badly needed the Queen's involvement.

Mrs Thatcher and her staff would feel a great deal more worried on the morning of 20th July. There, on the front page of *The Sunday Times*, was the headline 'Queen dismayed by "uncaring" Thatcher'. It was not just an unwelcome distraction, a mere three days before the wedding of Prince Andrew to Sarah Ferguson. It was, if true, a bona-fide constitutional crisis. For the article stated that the Queen 'considers her prime minister's approach often to be uncaring, confrontational and socially divisive'. As well as highlighting deep divisions over the Commonwealth, it reported an even broader chasm between Downing Street and the Palace. The Queen's 'dismay' extended to the recent strike by Britain's coal miners and American bombing raids on Libya. The Queen was said to believe that Mrs Thatcher's unyielding confrontation with the miners had caused 'long-term damage' to the social fabric of Britain. What's more, she was said to have 'misgivings' about Britain's decision to let US bombers conduct their Libyan raids from British bases. The monarch was thus not only at odds with her Prime Minister but with Mrs Thatcher's friend and ally, Ronald Reagan. As *The Sunday Times* editor, Andrew Neil, would later claim, here was 'an unprecedented insight into a ruling monarch's political views'.

Inside the Palace, the royal wedding suddenly felt like a sideshow. Senior officials had been vaguely aware that *The Sunday Times* would be running a 'think piece' about the monarchy. The Queen's press secretary, Michael Shea, had let it be known that he had been talking to the paper, ahead of what would be a very favourable article on his boss. One senior member of the Royal Household recalls Shea saying: 'I've just had a rather good chat to so-and-so and I think there might be quite a good story in *The Sunday Times*.' On the evening before the story broke, Shea was saying much the same to a gathering of European courtiers at Windsor. The unofficial trade union of continental royal aides was in town en masse ahead of the royal wedding and had gathered at Windsor for drinks with the Queen. Those present even remember Shea being 'boastful' about the impending results of his deft news management.

Mrs Thatcher's press secretary, Bernard Ingham, was getting a very different read-out from his own sources concerning the story.

When he heard the true nature of the article, Sir William Heseltine, the Queen's Private Secretary, was thunderstruck. He instantly contacted his opposite number at Number Ten, Nigel Wicks, and the pair of them agreed on a course of action. Sir William would head straight to Windsor, where the Queen was about to join the European courtiers for drinks, and would advise her to call Mrs Thatcher and make it very clear that this had nothing to do with her. The Queen duly contacted her Prime Minister and had what Heseltine later described as 'a very amicable conversation'.

It was Mrs Thatcher's view that there should be no response until both sides knew exactly what they were dealing with. When they did, the Palace issued a statement saying the story was 'entirely without foundation'. Andrew Neil was so annoyed by this that he refused to publish it. As far as he was concerned, the story had come from unimpeachable 'sources' deep within the Palace, who had spoken to his reporter, Simon Freeman. At the Palace, Michael Shea assured his colleagues – and thus the Queen – that none of the explosive assertions in the story were his. The paper had talked of 'sources' in the plural, not 'a source'. Someone else must have been involved.

Meanwhile, the rest of the media and the wider world were left to judge for themselves. It did seem unlikely that, after more than three decades of wholly impartial dedication to duty, the Queen would suddenly deliver a broadside against a Conservative government via any newspaper. On the other hand, there had been a run of recent reports of tensions between Queen and Prime Minister. In June, the same newspaper had reported that the Queen had been 'sickened' by television footage of police violence in the South African townships and that she was 'concerned' about the Commonwealth rift over sanctions. Other papers had been exploring the constitutional conflict of interest between a queen of several realms that happened to be in sharp disagreement with one another at the same time. 'Can she blow the whistle if divisions within the Commonwealth get out of hand?' asked a *Financial Times* columnist.

So *The Sunday Times*'s scoop had not come entirely out of the blue. The phrase 'no smoke without fire' was much in use that week. Was the article true? 'I think everyone in Commonwealth circles felt it was right,' says Stuart Mole, then special assistant to Ramphal. No one at the Palace or at Downing Street, however, seriously believed that the Queen had authorised, or even nudged, anyone to speak in those terms about her government. While the origins of the story seemed most peculiar, the sentiments attributed to the Queen did not. Many wanted to believe that she did harbour grave doubts about Thatcherism. That is why the story was so damaging.

To her credit, Mrs Thatcher made no attempt to offer any counter-spin. She made it clear to her officials that there was to be no briefing or subterfuge in her defence. That she was upset, however, was beyond doubt. 'Very hurt' is how Lord Butler remembers it. 'She was in awe of the Queen and at the same time she had a certain political sense about the Queen which took one of two forms,' he says. 'First, she didn't want to be on the wrong side of the Queen or for people to think that she was on the wrong side of the Queen, as it would damage her politically. But personally, she was deeply in awe of the Queen and would be deeply hurt if she felt the Queen was not approving of what she was doing.'

Mrs Thatcher's sense of deference towards the Queen even extended to invitations and clothes. 'In general, she had a policy of not appearing at occasions with the Queen unless she absolutely had to,' says Lord Butler. 'As a woman, she was extremely conscious of how they were dressed, relative to each other. Mrs Thatcher would not have wanted to out-dress the Queen. Similarly, she would not have wanted to wear the same thing.' On one occasion when she did, a Palace spokeswoman attempted to head off the inevitable news story with a line that merely amplified it: 'The Queen never notices what other people are wearing.'

For her part, those close to the Queen say that her view of Mrs Thatcher was a mixture of profound respect for her achievements and a mild fascination in learning what made her tick, something she was keen to discover in all world leaders*. Both women were born within seven months of each other, and shared many essential character traits. As Kenneth Harris, biographer of both, observed: 'Neither of them is intellectual, introspective or philosophical; both are direct, matter-of-fact, down-to-earth, practical and

* During her 2007 state visit to the USA, the Queen was most intrigued by President George W. Bush's 9 p.m. bedtime. 'Does he get up very early?' she asked her Ambassador.

perceptive.' There was even, at times, a vaguely competitive streak. When the Queen was holding her annual Diplomatic Reception, she noticed that Margaret Thatcher was feeling faint and required a seat. 'Oh, look, she's keeled over again,' the monarch remarked, without any great sympathy, as she continued glad-handing her way through more than a thousand diplomats and their spouses.

But no one in the inner royal circle has admitted to hearing the Queen express any sort of unease, let alone criticism, about Mrs Thatcher. 'It's just so *not* her,' says one who knows her well. Inside Buckingham Palace, the Private Secretary Sir William Heseltine was trying to find out why *The Sunday Times* was so confident in putting words into the Queen's mouth. It gradually emerged that the 'sources' were just one 'source', namely Michael Shea. Despite his protestations that he was not to blame, he was named the following weekend by *The Observer*, on the same day that *The Sunday Times* made further accusations against the Palace. If the Royal Household objected so strongly to the story, it asked, why had they not intervened when they learned that it was about to appear?

The following day, Sir William had a letter published in *The Sunday Times*'s stablemate, *The Times*. In it, he acknowledged that Shea had spoken to Freeman of *The Sunday Times*. He also accepted that Freeman had read some of the material back to him, but said that none of it bore any relation to the thrust of the article. This, in turn, prompted the paper's editor, Andrew Neil, to reveal that Shea had been informed of the whole lot. He added witheringly: 'Those at the Palace who knew about *The Sunday Times* articles before their publication were playing with fire and did not have the wit to blow it out before it burned them.'

The big mystery was over. Shea had taken it upon himself to discuss, hypothetically and with no basis in fact, what the monarch might or might not feel on some particularly sensitive contemporary issues. The lesser mystery was: why? Shea died in 2009, but those who knew him well say that he was of a liberal, centre-left persuasion and had overstepped the mark while talking up his employer's neutrality during a period of political turmoil; that in trying to present the Queen merely as someone who was not pro-Thatcher (or pro-anyone else), he had ended up painting her as being anti-Thatcher. 'He was a victim of hubris,' says Sir William Heseltine. 'He got a bit carried away with himself.' The former Foreign Secretary, David Owen, knew Shea well. 'People say he was put up to it by the Queen but I don't believe a word of it,' says Owen. 'I'm certain she didn't like a lot of the flak she was having to grapple with over the Commonwealth. I'm sure she was critical of it, too, but I don't believe she put Shea up to that story. He may have felt something needed to be done. I think it was clear she would drop him – and she did drop him.'

The timing of this entire episode was no coincidence, as *The Sunday Times* editor gleefully admitted later on. Not only was there a wedding on, but those troubled Commonwealth Games were about to begin, followed swiftly by the special Commonwealth summit on South Africa. It was a perfect media storm. The Queen, the Commonwealth and Mrs Thatcher would be lumped together in the spotlight for days on end. On the same weekend that Shea was named as the source of *The Sunday Times* stories, the Queen was at her Edinburgh residence, the Palace of Holyroodhouse, for the Commonwealth Games. Among the guests was the Prime Minister. As they all sat down for dinner, Michael Shea's appetite can hardly have been helped by the discovery that he was being seated between the Queen and Mrs Thatcher. The press secretary offered the Prime Minister an apology, to which she replied: 'Don't worry, dear.' The damage had been done, however. Later that evening, Denis Thatcher admitted to one of the Queen's ladies-in-waiting that his wife was 'very upset' by it all.

One person who was not upset was the Secretary-General of the Commonwealth. As far as Sonny Ramphal was concerned, the whole episode had reinforced Mrs Thatcher's isolation from the Commonwealth consensus. To this day, he believes that *The Sunday Times* story was a true reflection of the Queen's inner thoughts at the time. 'I thought it was genuine, I knew it was genuine,' he says. 'I wouldn't have wanted it to go any further because if it got out of hand then the Queen's role would be diminished.' The story might have helped neither the Palace nor the British government, but Sir Sonny is in no doubt: 'It helped the Commonwealth.'

It did not, however, help the Commonwealth Games, the organisers of which were up against mounting debts and ever-dwindling competitors. The Games actually involve more nations than the Commonwealth has members, since they include Crown dependencies and overseas territories like Jersey and Gibraltar. Yet by the opening ceremony in 1986, more than thirty of the fifty-nine original teams had announced they were boycotting the event because of Mrs Thatcher's policies. Things had reached the point that British diplomats in some of the Commonwealth capitals were warning their Foreign Office masters that countries such as Zimbabwe were on the brink of cutting off diplomatic relations with Britain altogether. The daily bulletins – always included in the Queen's red box – must have made excruciating reading for the Head of the Commonwealth.

The situation was so chaotic that Bermuda's team took part in the opening ceremony, complete with their flag, panama hats and Bermuda shorts, only to be informed the very next day that they were, in fact, boycotting the event. The Bermudian athletes protested, hanging sheets out of their windows with the message 'Bermuda wants to stay'. It was to no avail. Sonny Ramphal was very sorry for the Scottish hosts. 'The Edinburgh folk were staunchly with the Commonwealth and I did everything I could but I did not have from Mrs Thatcher the help I needed,' he wrote in his memoirs. Shortly before the opening, he had appealed for her assistance in finding a solution that might rescue the Games. He well recalls her 'sharp' response. 'They're not my Games,' she told him. 'They're yours.' To make matters worse, the owner of the Labour-supporting *Mirror* and *Daily Record* newspapers, Robert Maxwell, had stepped in as self-styled saviour of the Games. As with so many of his other financial pledges, his promised rescue package would prove to be a bare-faced lie, but he greatly enjoyed the adulation of the moment. It was one more low moment for the Head of the Commonwealth as the leaders prepared for yet another showdown over South Africa. 'It wasn't just rather embarrassing for the Queen. It was a hundred per cent embarrassing,' Sir Malcolm Rifkind reflects. 'Much as I admired Margaret Thatcher, that could all have been avoided if she'd been more emollient without conceding on basic principles. Someone else would have done it in a much more emollient way.'

'WORKING' DINNER

Now all eyes were on the Marlborough House summit. Would Mrs Thatcher feel more conciliatory after *The Sunday Times* affair and the boycott of the Games in Edinburgh? An interview with Graham Turner for *The Sunday Telegraph*, shortly before the summit, provided the answer. Asked if she was not threatening the break-up of the Commonwealth with her intransigence on sanctions, she replied sternly: 'It is their Commonwealth. If they wish to break it up, I think it is absurd. What sort of relationship is it that ... this thing that we have created is not strong enough to take a difference of opinion? Good Heavens, look what it has had to withstand to date!'

Taking things as far as she could, the Queen fixed her get-together for the eve of the summit. Furthermore, it would not be called a banquet or even a dinner, but a 'working dinner', perhaps the first in Palace history. This showed that the Queen meant business. The dress code would be lounge suits, not black tie (let alone the white-tie rig expected at a state banquet) and she would not even be accompanied by the Duke of Edinburgh. As Sonny Ramphal argues, it was not a question of offering hospitality to the Commonwealth leaders. It was a cool, calculated move by the Queen to stop Mrs Thatcher and the rest of the Commonwealth from retreating to their bunkers. 'Mrs Thatcher was alone and the danger always was that if she remained isolated, damage to the Commonwealth could have ensued,' he says. 'The Queen was recognised by everybody to be of a different hue.'

Shortly before the dinner, Mrs Thatcher's press secretary, Bernard Ingham, wrote a memo to his boss distilling the general view: 'The media's interest can be summarised: is the Lady for turning? If not will the Commonwealth crack up?' He warned that the other leaders 'will play everything for TV kicks' and told her not to stop and talk to stray television cameras: 'Decline to be doorstepped. The media are seldom, if ever, in the business of helpful quotes. Their business is conflict.'

As the six other chosen leaders arrived in London, they came for one-on-one meetings with Mrs Thatcher ahead of the main meeting. The Cabinet files show that Canada's Brian Mulroney was perhaps even more cynical about the Commonwealth than Mrs Thatcher. 'He shared her view that a lot of cant was talked by some of its members,' says a Number Ten minute of the meeting. 'His impression was that "no one would jump off the bridge if the Commonwealth took a walk" in either Canada or the UK. The Prime Minister interjected that she would, in fact, be very upset if that happened.'

There was a less cordial meeting with the Zambian President, Kenneth Kaunda, emotional as ever as he tearfully waved his white handkerchief. The files note that he warned that South Africa would 'explode' without sanctions and that 'God would not forgive us' if there was no action on that front. Mrs Thatcher said they had better leave that debate for the summit. By now, she would have received the latest Foreign Office personality notes on the visitors. Of Kaunda, it was noted: 'He sets the tone of the government and the country and is better for it ... His weaknesses are that he is emotional, impressionable and a confused thinker ... His feelings for Britain might be described as a mixture of love and pain. He admires the Queen. His threat to withdraw Zambia from the Commonwealth may be more emotional outburst than real intent.'

The Cabinet briefing notes, as candid as ever, show that the Queen was in for a lively dinner, not that she needed any notes on these guests. She knew them all very well of old. Of Bob Hawke, the Australian prime minister, the FCO remarked: 'Intelligent, industrious, shrewd and articulate ... charming in private and very rude in public when it suits him. Not very well disposed towards Britain ... Increasingly doubtful of the relevance of the monarch to Australia ... A well-known drinker and womaniser in his ACTU [Australian Council of Trade Unions] days but is now a reformed character.'

Canada's Brian Mulroney was a 'shrewd politician, though he can give the impression of being glib and superficial. Easy to underestimate ... Good looking with a great deal of Irish charm.'*

British ministers were advised to tread warily when discussing the education of the Indian Prime Minister, Rajiv Gandhi, who was still 'very sensitive' about his failure to complete his degree at Cambridge. Sir Lynden Pindling, host of that Nassau summit was 'an extremely active and intelligent man.' But it was hardly surprising he had attracted demonstrations. 'He has acquired a Rolls-Royce and a

* More than thirty years later, the Mulroney family would have a delightful and very different royal encounter when the former Prime Minister's twin grandsons, Brian and Ben, were pages at the wedding of the Duke and Duchess of Sussex. Granddaughter Ivy, four, was a bridesmaid. The children's mother, Jessica, is a close friend of the Duchess.

mansion on Millionaires' Row and has become as guilty as the rest of the PLP leadership of the sins of arrogance and intolerance.' The final member of the mini-summit group was Robert Mugabe of Zimbabwe, by now regarded as a wise and mellowing presence in a Commonwealth from which he would later be ostracised. 'A Marxist Leninist but concedes that his philosophy needs to be adapted ... Not anti-white as such but prone to making ill-considered statements. Devoted to his wife Sally who is the only person with any real influence over him.'

Such was the guest list for the Queen's first 'working dinner'. Brian Mulroney later recorded in his journal that the monarch arrived 'in excellent cheer', full of anecdotes about the Edinburgh Games, and 'chatted easily with all'. The Queen was evidently concerned about Kenneth Kaunda, at one point asking Rajiv Gandhi: 'How is the emotional one?' Despite his awkward meeting with Mrs Thatcher earlier, Mulroney noted that 'KK' seemed in good spirits, not least since he 'adores the royal family'. The Zambian leader even interrupted the proceedings at one point to raise a toast to the Queen Mother, who was about to celebrate her eighty-sixth birthday.

Sir William Heseltine was one of a handful of officials present and remembers sitting next to Mugabe. 'I have to say I found him quite charming,' he says. 'However, I did note that the atmosphere was quite tense. It wasn't an easy time for Mrs Thatcher, who found herself at odds with virtually all the other members.'

There were no speeches and no agenda. All were acutely aware that the mere fact that the Queen had come down from Scotland to host this strange, one-off evening – a kitchen supper, by royal standards – was a statement in itself. Sonny Ramphal wrote in his memoirs that it had been entirely the Queen's idea and was designed to 'break the ice' before the hard bargaining over South Africa: 'The Queen's message was simple: the Commonwealth must not be in discord on this matter. It was a call for unity at a critical moment.' Geoffrey Howe, then Foreign Secretary, later described it as a 'deliberate act by the Queen to remind us all of our commitment to get on with each other.'

Summing up the Palace position, Sir William Heseltine explains: 'I don't think we were trying to get involved in the nuts and bolts. But the Queen wanted an atmosphere in which some solution might be reached. And I thought that, in her exemplary fashion, she managed to send them off in a much better mood than when they arrived. The atmosphere at the end of dinner seemed much better than at the beginning.' As Sir William would tell the BBC many years later: 'In terms of political initiatives, it was perhaps the boldest initiative of the decade – and a successful one.'

Sonny Ramphal recalls the subtle way in which the Queen steered the discussion on to the theme of unity. 'This was the conversation that she led around the table and the promise she drew from everyone there,' he says. The entire exercise, in his view, was a coded exhortation aimed at a single guest: 'It was a plea to Mrs Thatcher, in the company of everyone else, to fall in line. It was a plea for unity. It was a message to her Prime Minister which might have been harder to deliver privately.'

Brian Mulroney, however, recalls that the royal warning extended to everyone around the table. 'There was no doubt that Her Majesty sided with the Commonwealth,' he told biographer Sally Bedell Smith. 'But she couldn't speak out. You had to understand the nuances and body language. At the dinner, she was a great moderating influence on everyone. She led us through an elevated discussion of human rights.' Perhaps she had been rereading Desmond Tutu's letter to her. Mulroney's personal journal also includes an intriguing footnote to the evening. 'We left, all except Mrs T. and Sir Geoffrey [Howe], whom I spotted in confidential conversation with Her Majesty as the rest of us were escorted out.'

By the time the leaders signed their communiqué on 5th August, there had been progress of sorts. Six of the seven leaders had agreed a range of sanctions against South Africa, including a ban on air links, investment and food. What's more, all had agreed to set an important precedent. From now on, the Commonwealth could have a less consensual consensus; it could move forward on a key issue without unanimity, stating that it had agreed to proceed without Britain. Crucially, it had not broken up. For that, as Sonny Ramphal has said, credit should again go to the Queen. Echoing Nehru's original words about the foundation of the Commonwealth, he praised her for 'a much-needed touch of healing.'

Brian Mulroney was in no doubt that the Head of the Commonwealth had been pivotal. 'What saved the day was that Margaret was aware Her Majesty certainly wanted some kind of resolution,' he told Sally Bedell Smith. 'So we were able to put in there three or four financial things that Margaret accepted'.

'It could have gone much worse,' says Chief Emeka Anyaoku, the Commonwealth's future Secretary-General, imagining what would have happened had the Queen not played her part. 'Mrs Thatcher would have said she wanted nothing to do with it and the consensus in the Commonwealth would have broken down.' He is in no doubt that here, and in Lusaka, the Commonwealth had never been closer to self-destruction. In both cases, the Queen had come to the rescue. 'Her message was crystal clear: you mustn't allow the Commonwealth to fail,' he says without hesitation. 'This was what saved the organisation.'

GOODBYE, MARGARET. HELLO, NELSON

Having established that the Commonwealth and the British government could be at odds without terminal consequences, the last two Commonwealth summits of Mrs Thatcher's period in office were less combative. Sonny Ramphal has written that they were 'just as unpleasant but mattered less'. Yet the traditional left-wing vilification of Mrs Thatcher as a 'heartless' apologist for the status quo in South Africa seems both simplistic and misleading. If she was exasperated by many Commonwealth nations and by what she regarded as posturing hypocrisy, she was still determined to help secure change in South Africa, in her own way. Though she would continue to describe the ANC and their ilk as 'typical terrorists' and 'communists', she was equally convinced that the release of Nelson Mandela was central to a solution. She would also draw a distinction between the ANC's brand of terrorism and that of Irish republican groups like the IRA, pointing out that the IRA were in the business of attacking a democratic nation, whereas black South Africans were fighting a state that denied them their basic human rights.

As Professor Chris Richards of the University of Cape Town and President of the South African Historical Society has pointed out, Mrs Thatcher's role in Mandela's eventual release has often been overlooked. It was only thanks to her that the 'Eminent Persons Group' was able to enter South Africa and develop the negotiating strategy through which Mandela was eventually freed. Richards reiterates the point that no international organisations had actually been calling for Mandela's release until the Eighties. Even Amnesty International had refused to classify him as a 'prisoner of conscience' in the early years of his captivity, because of his refusal to renounce violence. In the December 2017 issue of the Commonwealth's very own in-house journal, *The Round Table*, Professor Richards delivered a fascinating verdict on Mrs Thatcher's role throughout that turbulent decade. It is one that many on the left and old Commonwealth hands like Sonny Ramphal would, doubtless, regard as heretical: 'On the specific question of the release of Mandela it may indeed be said that Thatcher, with her own firm ideas of how best to try to end apartheid, did do more than any other Commonwealth leader in the 1980s to try to get him released.'

So what did the Queen – in her much-conflicted roles as sovereign of Britain, sovereign of fifteen other countries and Head of the Commonwealth – really think of her Prime Minister? Despite the presumptions and conjecture of her press secretary and so many others, we still do not know. The Queen Mother's admiration for Mrs Thatcher was hardly a secret (one of her 'favourite politicians', according to her biographer, William Shawcross). There was, though, a patrician 'wet' Tory element within the aristocracy who sneered at the shopkeeper's daughter. The Queen remained predictably, steadfastly, unreadable on the subject of the Prime Minister. It is, perhaps, easier to imagine what the Queen might have thought of her Prime Minister's modus operandi. 'What she'd have been most upset about was not British government policy but Margaret Thatcher's tone, her personal aggression,' says Sir Malcolm Rifkind, who served all through the Thatcher years and went on to become Foreign Secretary himself. 'You can't separate Margaret Thatcher from her style.'

In 1990, just a few months before she left office, to be replaced by John Major, Mrs Thatcher did finally meet the man whose future had shaped so much of her foreign policy. Nelson Mandela had walked out of prison on 11th February 1990, instantly becoming one of the most influential statesmen on Earth, albeit as yet an unelected, unappointed one. His party, the ANC, ceased to be outlawed, and multiparty talks the following year would lead to an interim constitution. After some internecine tribal violence costing thousands of lives, elections would follow in 1994. Mandela could, though, already count on the Commonwealth as a *de facto* powerbase.

Within days of his release from prison, he made his first international flight to the Zambian capital, Lusaka, seat of the exiled ANC leadership. It was there that he met Commonwealth Secretary-General Sonny Ramphal and his deputy, Emeka Anyaoku. When Commonwealth foreign ministers met in Nigeria shortly afterwards, Mandela was invited to speak. He travelled briefly to London in April, to attend a Wembley stadium concert in his honour, and attended a reception at Sonny Ramphal's flat, where he thanked Commonwealth staff and key British supporters. He had also wanted to meet Mrs Thatcher, who had invited him to Downing Street, but the ANC leadership blocked the idea. He kept a promise to return to London in July, however, to attend Anyaoku's inaugural dinner as the new Commonwealth Secretary-General. There were already signs of the new, forward-looking, hatchet-burying Mandela mindset. Asked for a list of dinner companions, he did not want yet another gathering of stalwarts from the old anti-apartheid organisations. He specifically asked Anyaoku to round up a room full of senior British executives and financiers, to whom he could sell the long-term prospects of a future, democratic South Africa. There was another invitation from Mrs Thatcher to visit Downing Street, and this time Mandela was adamant that he would go.

The British Ambassador to South Africa, Sir Robin Renwick, who had come to know Mandela well, briefed Mrs Thatcher ahead of the meeting and implored her to listen. 'Please remember, he's waited 27 years to tell you his side of the story,' he told her. Neither side was ever going to agree on the sanctions issue, but there was much else to discuss and Mrs Thatcher was not short of advice on how Mandela might rebuild the South African economy. The conversation dragged on for so long that the bored media contingent outside ended up chanting the anti-apartheid hit 'Free Nelson Mandela'. Eventually, he emerged with gracious words for his host. 'There is no doubt that she is an enemy of apartheid,' he said. 'We've taken different positions, but there was never any enmity or quarrel whatsoever.'

How Mrs Thatcher must have wished for this sort of dialogue at all those Commonwealth gatherings during the preceding decade. These two giants of post-war politics declared that they could 'do business' with each other. There would be no time for that, however. Four months later, after what had by any measure been an exceptional eleven-year premiership, Mrs Thatcher would tender her resignation to the Queen. Following a Conservative leadership challenge by her old foe, Michael Heseltine, she had not won enough votes in the first round of voting to preclude a further vote and decided to stand down, rather than put her MPs' loyalty to the test. The Queen's regard for Britain's first female Prime Minister was reflected in her decision to award her the Order of Merit almost instantly. As Mrs Thatcher bade a tearful farewell to Downing Street, Mandela had not even got started.

'LET'S HAVE HIM'

For the rest of his life, Mandela would retain a special affection for the Commonwealth, always mindful of its key part – and the role of the Queen herself – in the story of modern South Africa. Her first meeting with Mandela would take place the following year, when the Commonwealth leaders gathered in the capital of Zimbabwe, Harare. This would be another important African tour, full of poignant personal memories for her. The last time she had been in Harare, it was called Salisbury and she had been there with her parents in 1947. Now she would be seeing how Zimbabwe had progressed since that turbulent independence process in which she had played such an important role.

But there was a significant stop along the way. During the excitement surrounding Mandela's release from jail in February 1990, much of the world had overlooked a historic occasion days later in neighbouring Namibia. The former German colony of South-West Africa had been controlled by South Africa since the First World War. As a sparsely populated appendage to one of the most ostracised nations in the world, it had led a lonely existence for many years. In March 1990, after a long and nasty guerrilla war on its northern border, it finally secured full independence. On the very same day, it joined the Commonwealth. The membership had now reached fifty. Though the Queen has never been competitive about numbers (unlike the French-speaking Francophonie), it was still a landmark moment for the Commonwealth and its Head. When the Queen came to the Throne, the Commonwealth had eight members. Now it could celebrate its half-century.

Though Namibia had not formally been part of the British Empire and had rubbed along with a variety of languages for years, its new leadership had been determined to join the English-speaking, Westminster-style 'club', and the 'club' was happy to oblige. Here, in effect, was a dry run for what might happen shortly in South Africa. The local experience of colonialism under the Germans, and latterly the South Africans, had been brutal at times. As one former diplomat puts it: 'Namibia became a dumping ground for the worst sort of Afrikaaner.' If majority black rule could work there, it would send a strong signal to South Africa next door. Britain, in particular, was keen to express its confidence in the Commonwealth's newest member in time-honoured fashion – with a state visit by the Queen. There was the added advantage of not having any colonial baggage in this former colony. Whereas other Commonwealth countries might still have a historical gripe with the former colonial power, this one looked upon the UK as a beacon of progress. All the bad stuff could be blamed on the Germans.

If Namibia had little knowledge of the Commonwealth, it knew even less about royal visits, but it was keen to learn. Former High Commissioner Sir Francis Richards has fond memories of a no-nonsense solution to the problem of finding a suitable open-topped vehicle from which the Queen could wave to the crowds. 'They found a Land Rover, took the top off and stuck a sofa on the back,' he recalls. It did the job perfectly. There was similar presence of mind when the desert wind at Windhoek International Airport threatened to blow away the red carpet, as the Queen's VC10 was approaching. The Namibians ordered a 25-stone policeman to stand on the far end of it. While that solved the carpet problem, the same wind would cause alarming problems with the royal hemline as the Queen descended the aircraft steps. The German population had been rather bemused by the arrival of the British Queen. The main local paper featured a cartoon showing an Afrikaaner, a German and a Namibian African being greeted by the Queen as she declared – John F. Kennedy-style – '*Ich bin ein Namibian.*'

The overarching theme of the visit was reconciliation. The royal itinerary would include both the former independence battlegrounds in the north – the revolutionary heartland – and the national agricultural show, focal point of the country's predominantly white farming community. As Richards recalls, the Germans and Afrikaners were no royalists. 'They were resentful that Britain was taking such a prominent role in their country but, at the same time, in terms of their safety in Namibia, this was seen as a very helpful development.' Any lingering doubts about the royal visitor were dispelled when she met the opposition leader, wearing his full cowboy kit, and presented him with the prize for best heifer. Without batting an eyelid, she later picked him out of a reception for 300 people at which he was wearing a suit. 'It was very impressive,' says Richards. 'He was certainly pleased.'

The Queen's speech at the state banquet was a surprisingly punchy one, her words aimed far beyond Namibia's borders. Africa, she said, could no longer use apartheid as an excuse for all its problems and had to recognise that 'autocracy and economic stagnation' were the greater threat. One year into independence, however, her visit had left an impression that is remembered to this day. 'It was a boost to Namibia's sense of identity as it tried to become a proper nation. It meant it was not a duckling being thrown out of the nest,' says Richards. 'There were high hopes.'

There were certainly high hopes on board the royal VC10 as it flew on to Harare, where large crowds welcomed the Queen and the Duke of Edinburgh as they drove through the city centre in an open car. Ahead of the Commonwealth summit, the Queen was formally paying a state visit to Zimbabwe itself. At President Mugabe's state banquet, she praised him for his 'wisdom and good judgment' in the way he had steered his country through to democratic prosperity. These were the days when she and so many others still regarded Mugabe as an exemplary firebrand-turned-founding-father, a man whom other Commonwealth leaders should emulate. 'Contemporary history is showing us daily that good government and equality of opportunity can overcome differences of race, culture or religion,' she told her audience.

Among the leaders gathering for the summit, however, there was a strange sense of uncertainty. With Nelson Mandela out of prison, Namibia running free, apartheid in terminal decline, the Berlin Wall dismantled and Mrs Thatcher off the scene – all developments that most of the Commonwealth would surely welcome – these were testing times, nonetheless. If no one was in the Commonwealth spotlight at that moment, where might it fall next? No one wanted to be the new *persona non grata*. The new Secretary-General, Chief Emeka Anyaoku, wanted this to be the summit where the Commonwealth reaffirmed its democratic principles, even if that might sound uncomfortable to some of its more dubious regimes.

For the first time in living memory, a British Prime Minister appeared to be looking forward to a Commonwealth summit. John Major had attended the previous one, in Malaysia, as Foreign Secretary. Now he was delighted to learn that Robert Mugabe – a fellow cricket enthusiast – had decided to bolt on a charity match for cricketing leaders and Major would even face a few balls himself. He was also looking forward to discussing the subject with the leader of a delegation of summit observers from South Africa's ANC – Nelson Mandela. The Prime Minister was keen to get South Africa back into the international sporting fold as an important step on the journey to majority rule. Since the ANC was still an exiled non-organisation from a non-Commonwealth nation, Mandela could hardly have a seat at the summit. Yet everyone could see the direction of travel in South Africa. Mandela was a very welcome observer.

As usual, the Queen would hold her audiences and then host the traditional black-tie banquet to get the leaders in a convivial frame of mind, before leaving them to their political hardball. She had brought the Royal Household team, and the marquee on the lawn of State House had been laid out with round tables of ten, thus ensuring that there was no 'top table' one-upmanship. As the guests started arriving for the pre-dinner drinks, Chief Anyaoku was informed that Mandela had been spotted at the entrance. 'He just turned up and got out of this old car,' recalls Charles Anson, the Queen's press secretary at the time. Anyaoku immediately tracked down the Queen's Private Secretary, Robert Fellowes. Mandela was not on the official guest list, as this was simply a dinner for heads of government and their spouses. Nor was he dressed in black tie, but a lounge suit. Yet he was clearly under the impression that he was expected. It was inconceivable that a man of such stature and humility would have decided to gatecrash. So there had obviously either been some confusion or some mischief. It would send out a terrible message if some 'jobsworth' official decided to bar entry to the most famous ex-political prisoner of modern times. On the other hand, might not the other major players in the South African story – not least the country's President, F. W. de Klerk, and the Zulus' Chief Buthelezi – feel snubbed? A decision was required instantly and only one person could make it.

The Queen had no doubts. 'Let's have him,' she said and deputed Sir Robert Fellowes to find Mandela and bring him into dinner, while quickly rearranging her banquet. As one senior ex-Household figure points out: 'There is no such thing as protocol. There is only common sense.' Rearranging an ordinary dinner party can be tricky enough. Rearranging a banquet for fifty prime ministers and presidents, while simultaneously trying to entertain them all to pre-dinner drinks, was an interesting challenge. 'The Queen really grabbed the situation,' says Charles Anson. 'She said that Mandela should be on a table near her, where he could see her and certainly not on the outside of the room. He couldn't be on her table but had to feel a part of it. Someone – I forget who – simply got kicked off a table in the inner orbit. Then the Queen had a chat with Mandela before and after, over drinks and then coffee.'

'Your Majesty, you're looking well, taking account of your tight schedule,' he told her at one point.

'Tomorrow, I'm going to see sixteen people. I may not look so good tomorrow!' the Queen replied. According to those present, their conversations were largely devoted to the healing power of sport. There was no question that they got along famously. 'There was a very agreeable chemistry between the two of them, absolutely no doubt about that,' says Anyaoku.

'He had a big presence,' says a member of the royal party. 'There was a sort of stateliness about him. He had beautiful manners. You knew you were in the presence of someone – and he had a great sense of humour.' Even now, no one is entirely sure who told Mandela to turn up, though many suspect it was the Zimbabwean leader and summit host, Robert Mugabe. While the Queen is never normally keen on unexpected guests, she was delighted by this one. It would be the start of a remarkable friendship.

BACK TO THE CAPE

On 9th May 1994, Nelson Mandela became the first President of a new, democratic South Africa. Within a month, to the delight of the Queen, one of his first executive acts was to return his country to the place it had vacated back in the early days of apartheid. 'South Africa coming back into the Commonwealth was, for me, but, more importantly, for the Queen, a moment of supreme joy,' says Sir Sonny Ramphal. Nor had it always been a foregone conclusion, as the former Secretary-General explains: 'I confess that I had harboured concerns at an earlier stage. I had asked myself whether after this terrible struggle, after this horrible experience of apartheid, black South Africa would want anything to do with the Commonwealth. I talked to Oliver Tambo, who held the ANC [presidency] for Nelson Mandela while he was in prison. I asked him: "Oliver, when this is all over, will South Africa be in the Commonwealth?" He looked at me quizzically and he said: "Sonny, black South Africa never left the Commonwealth". For me it was a tremendous relief. That would have been the kind of relief that the Queen would have felt when she heard it from Mandela.'

In Mandela's view, it had been the apartheid regime that had cut the Commonwealth link after the 1960 vote to abolish the South African Crown. While South Africans were certainly not about to reinstate the Queen, they were very happy to be back in the 'club'. After all, the Commonwealth Games were coming up in a matter of weeks. The web of Commonwealth connections had already been growing by the day. In anticipation of his victory, Mandela had been asking for Commonwealth assistance with everything from re-training the police to tax inspectors. The elections had been monitored by the largest team of Commonwealth observers ever assembled. Technically, the other member states had to be consulted to approve any new membership, but Emeka Anyaoku did not have to try very hard. On 1st June, he went to give the result to the Queen. 'She was delighted,' he recalls, 'but she'd already heard the news.' The Commonwealth had beaten the UN, too. It would be another three weeks before South Africa was readmitted to the General Assembly of the United Nations.

The following month there was a service of thanksgiving at Westminster Abbey – at which Archbishop Tutu danced for joy – and a big party at Marlborough House, where a shebeen band was playing in the garden. The Queen and the Prince of Wales were among the guests, as talk turned to her future travel plans. The time had come, surely, for her to make her first return to South Africa since her twenty-first birthday. Mandela was delighted. As he wrote – formally – to the Queen on 8th August 1994: 'Madam, I was delighted to hear that You are considering visiting South Africa in March 1995. You will be most welcome.' On that occasion, he signed it with a modest: 'N. R. Mandela.'

As with her trip to Namibia in 1991, this was fast work by royal standards. The new South Africa would be less than a year old and yet it was already getting a state visit. Indeed, it turns out that it might not have happened until much later, were it not for the Queen herself. Here was a fledgling democracy that had seen terrible violence in the run-up to the 1994 elections. According to Emeka Anyaoku, 14,000 South Africans were killed between 1990 and 1994, more than twice the number who were killed in the apartheid era. Sir Robert Woodard, the former Flag Officer Royal Yachts and captain of *Britannia* at that time, recalls that Douglas Hurd had serious reservations about the Queen travelling to South Africa so soon. 'The Foreign Secretary was worried and the Queen overruled him,' says Woodard. 'She said: "Mr Mandela is getting advice from lots of people but no one's actually giving him any help. He needs physical assistance and he needs a show". She was going to give him one.'

The Queen was not flattering herself. She was channelling her inner Bagehot. As the great Victorian constitutionalist had observed, the 'efficient' part of the state might get things done, but it is the 'dignified' elements that actually excite people. The new South African President had already seen a few foreign politicians and plenty of business leaders beating a path to his door. President Mitterrand and John Major were among the early visitors, though the French President's advance team had reportedly irritated their hosts by wanting Mandela to be at the airport an hour before their man was due to arrive. The idea was that Mandela would be filmed anxiously awaiting his French visitor. The idea was rejected, as were French requests for Mandela to appear at Mitterrand's side throughout his stay. Mandela's team were not going to let their man appear subordinate to the Frenchman. Though Mitterrand would make a lot of noise about France's revolutionary tradition and its opposition to apartheid, it had escaped no one that France had cheerfully sold fighter jets, helicopters and submarines to the apartheid regime. Furthermore, even a statesman of the stature of François Mitterrand simply could not generate the same razzmatazz as a state visit by the Queen. However, she had already foreseen a problem, as Woodard recalls: 'Her Majesty turned to me and said: "Sadly, we can't take the Yacht".'

According to Royal Household staff of that time, the Queen was concerned that there might be further media hostilities if it was announced that *Britannia* was sailing all the way to South Africa for a single state visit. Years later, that might seem an unlikely concern, particularly given the importance of the visit, but this was late 1994, with royal marital rifts and royal finances dominating the headlines as never before. The Queen felt battered and was in no mood to invite a further battering.

However, Woodard knew that there could be nothing quite as magnificent or as historically symbolic as the Queen arriving in Cape Town by sea, just as she had done in 1947. He also knew that any criticism could be offset if *Britannia* was seen to be earning its keep with commercial 'sea days' for British trade and industry. 'I said: "Ma'am, would you reconsider if I can get commercial stuff which would cover it?" She said: "Yes, you've got twenty-four hours". And in twenty-four hours, with the Master of the Household and his team, we sorted out five days of trade activity.'

The next issue was where to get the Queen on board. There was no question of her spending weeks at sea sailing to the Cape of Good Hope, as she had done in 1947. She would need to fly to the region, embark and then make her grand entrance. One thing was off-limits. As Woodard explains, she told the Rear Admiral that she had no wish to sail round the Cape itself. 'She said: "I'm not going round the Cape." I said: "Ma'am?" She said: "When I was twenty-one, I was there and I shared a cabin with Princess Margaret and we opened the scuttle [porthole] and we immediately got a wave in." She was a very good sailor but, like all sensible human beings, she hated being flung all over the place.' So, a plan was drawn up whereby the Queen would make a discreet night-time flight into Cape Town, fly by helicopter to the naval base at Simonstown and then join the Royal Yacht. It would be a short voyage of a few hours from there to Cape Town. It was only afterwards that Woodard would dare to point out that the journey from Simonstown did, in fact, involve going round the Cape of Good Hope after all.

Brilliant sunshine and a smattering of cloud around Table Mountain, along with a flotilla of horn-honking ships and small craft, greeted the Royal Yacht on the morning of 20th March 1995. It sailed in past Robben Island, the first prison where Mandela spent so many years, and came smartly alongside the quay. There stood not just the sober-suited symbol of free South Africa but the inspiration for an entire continent alongside his niece, Rochelle Mtirara. Following Mandela's recent split with his wife, Winnie, various members of his family would share the role of consort. Dressed in a sky-blue linen coat, one hand protecting her sky-blue hat from a breeze known as the 'Cape Doctor', even the Queen – veteran of so many grand entrances – must have felt the proverbial hand of history as, for the first time in nearly fifty years, she stepped ashore at Cape Town. 'Oh, Your Majesty, welcome to South Africa,' proclaimed the President. Unlike the 1947 arrival, when guns had been ruled out for fear of scaring the horses, there was not only a twenty-one-gun salute, but a flypast of six fighters trailing red, white and blue smoke. After working her way through a modest greeting line, including an ecstatic Archbishop Tutu, the Queen embarked on her first walkabout. Here, amid a predominantly white crowd, there was a vaguely surreal encounter. Having come halfway around the world to salute the new South Africa, one of the first groups whom the Queen met were the members of the West Cape Welsh Corgi Club. They had arrived at first light with their dogs, to grab the best spot.

At the President's residence, Tuynhuis, the Queen had a rare honour for Mandela. She would dispense with the usual state-visit ritual of giving her host the GCB (Knight or Dame Grand Cross of the Order of the Bath). For Mandela, she had reserved the same decoration that she had bestowed on Mother Teresa in India in 1983 – the Order of Merit. There were no footling protocol issues, as there had been in India. He, in turn, gave her the Order of Good Hope and a brooch in the colour of the new South African flag. The Queen had arrived with the twenty-first-birthday present she had received from the people of South Africa in 1947 – twenty-one exceptional diamonds. She made a point of wearing them later at the state banquet in Cape Town. Soon after walking into the room, to her great amusement, she twigged that some older South Africans were quite clearly counting them. Their reactions were not very subtle, either. 'They couldn't get it right,' she told a member of the Royal Household afterwards. 'That's because there are only seventeen of them around my neck.' Whereupon she lifted her wrist and shook it, explaining: 'The others are in a bracelet!'

Parliament was packed to hear the Queen deliver a speech that seemed to move her as much as her audience. 'Forty-eight years ago I watched my father opening parliament here,' she said, her voice betraying the odd crack of emotion. 'Of course, I come in very different circumstances.' Quoting George VI's reference to a 'peace which must be based on freedom and justice', she went on: 'Your struggle has shown that the only way to true peace is through those principles of which so many throughout this country have been doughty champions.'

Mandela's fondness for his visitor was clear from the official programme. Normal state-visit rules dictate that the host welcomes the visitor, lays on a spot of ceremony and a banquet and then leaves the guest to get on with it – as Mandela had done with the French President some months earlier. For the Queen, however, it was very different. Mandela kept popping up throughout her stay. It was much appreciated, as were the continuous references by Mandela and his team to the importance of the Commonwealth. He had been so keen to get everything spot-on that the public-works department had even spent £20,000 on new tablecloths and napkins for the Tuynhuis presidential residence, ahead of the visit. For President Mitterrand, they had used the old ones.

Two recurring features of the visit would be the size of the crowds and the absence of the hostility that members of the British party had feared. Douglas Hurd has admitted that he expected some residual resentment, as a result of Mrs Thatcher's long-standing opposition to sanctions. It never materialised, however, as the tour progressed from the poor districts of Cape Town to Port Elizabeth. In the shanty town of Missionvale, the Queen met an Irish nun called Sister Ethel, whose work would so impress her that she included her in that year's Christmas broadcast. On the next day of the tour, the Queen visited the most famous township of all. Soweto had long been synonymous with violence as well as injustice. The Foreign Office was particularly nervous about the royal engagements here. Once again the Queen had indicated that she had no such qualms, joking to one member of her team: 'As long as I don't have to sail round the Cape of Good Hope, I will do a walkabout in Soweto.'

There, in the much-troubled but defiant Johannesburg township, the Queen inspected a British-backed scheme to get more young people playing cricket (a pet project started by her cricket-mad Prime Minister, John Major, the previous year). With Mandela at her side, she unveiled a memorial to 607 members of the South African Native Labour Corps who had died aboard the troopship, SS *Mendi*, in February 1917. Bound for the Western Front, it went down after a collision in a foggy English Channel, with many tales of heroism among its black South African passengers. The joint attraction of the Queen and Nelson Mandela had brought much of Soweto on to the streets. 'They are all here for her not me,' the President told reporters, generously adding that the occasion had been 'one of the most unforgettable moments in our history'. There was another important factor, too. Whereas the British government had been in contact – often close contact – with its South African counterpart all through the years of apartheid, the Royal Family had not had any dealings with the country at all. As the Queen would find on her travels through the former Soviet Bloc during the same period, there were many nations with the same message for her: 'Thank you for *not* coming.'

The visit concluded in KwaZulu-Natal. Even when continuing unseasonal rain washed out a day at the races at Greyville, thousands braved the elements just to watch the Queen arrive for tea at the racecourse. By now she had been given the honorary title of '*Motlalepula*' – 'Rain Queen'. In Durban she was welcomed by King Goodwill of the Zulus, who presented her with a stuffed lioness. Too large for the royal flight, it would return to Britain in the Royal Yacht. Even *Britannia* could not accommodate another parting gift from South Africa, presented to her at a farewell ceremony in front of Durban City Hall. A very large bull – very much alive, too – was promptly donated to a Zululand agricultural research college. Before leaving, the Queen made her speech about 'one of the outstanding experiences of my life'. In bidding her farewell, Nelson Mandela remarked: 'It is one of the most extraordinary experiences of my life too.'

By now, the Queen had already invited Mandela to make a reciprocal state visit to the UK. 'You are well-versed in making history,' she had told him, 'but I hope that even for you that will be an important milestone.' He agreed instantly. Just a year later, the new South African flag would be draped the full length of the Mall.

'DEAR ELIZABETH'

Those who have worked closely with the Queen say that this was not merely a cordial friendship between two heads of state. It was more a meeting of minds between two people used to well-meaning but unhelpful flattery; both well aware of the pitfalls of being a 'national treasure'. 'It's very hard to say what creates personal chemistry but they both had an enormous weight of responsibility, a great weight of expectation,' says a senior member of the Royal Household of that era. 'They were both extremely emotionally intelligent people and those similarities sort of made them a natural fit. It's that ability to carry your authority with real lightness of touch.' Both had a keen sense of the importance of the past. Radical lawyer he might have been, but the true Mandela was shaped by his own royal lineage – he was descended from the princely rulers of the Thembu tribe – along with his traditional mission-schooling and early love of British history. As the South African journalist John Battersby put it: 'He had a particular affinity with Queen Elizabeth. Having his own royal tribal lineage, he was completely at ease with her.'

The Queen's thank-you letter to Mandela on 31st March 2005 went far beyond the sort of official bilateral platitudes that might be drafted and typed up by a Private Secretary. It was handwritten and from the heart. 'Dear Mr President,' she wrote, 'It was lovely to return after such a long time to a place which was my first overseas visit and is therefore still very clear and special in my memory.' As a leader with more years than most in office, she advised him to take the long view. 'I hope that the projects we saw and the many others that will follow will help the complex problems which will take time to solve and I am sure, given the marvellous atmosphere collectively which is so striking, will be overcome. Your own influence is so very important to this end and we wish you well.' She concluded: 'We look forward to welcoming you here next year. Your sincere friend, Elizabeth R.'

The two heads of state would meet sooner than that, when the Commonwealth assembled for its next summit in Auckland later that year. It would be Mandela's first Heads of Government Meeting as a leader. And while, predictably, he received plenty of adulation from the host nation and the other delegations, he was soon rolling up his sleeves and even trying to enlist the help of the Queen.

There were two issues hanging over the summit. First, a recent round of French nuclear tests on two French-owned atolls in the South Pacific had greatly upset all the Commonwealth nations in the region, including the summit hosts, New Zealand. Since France was not part of the Commonwealth, all the anger and protests were aimed at John Major instead, on the grounds that the British Prime Minister was an ally of France. The other issue was the death sentence which Nigeria had imposed on Ken Saro-Wiwa, a television producer and environmentalist, along with several others. Their crime had been to expose a lucrative oil-exploration deal between the country's corrupt military dictator, General Sani Abacha, and oil companies including Royal Dutch Shell. Though Abacha had not come to the summit, he had sent his abrasive and bombastic Foreign Minister, Tom Ikimi. A buffet for delegates and the media descended into farce as journalists attempted to interview Ikimi. 'Go away, I am having my lunch,' he told them. 'Is your lunch more important than a man's life?' asked one British journalist. 'Yes,' he replied.

During the summit, several leaders, including Canada's Jean Chrétien, voiced their concerns but the blue-robed Ikimi refused to engage in dialogue. 'You've all got blood on your hands!' he declared. Mandela was appalled and became so exasperated that he decided to seek out the Queen and ask her to intervene. Baroness Chalker, then Foreign Office Minister for Africa, remembers Mandela seeking advice on how best to go about it. 'He wanted the Queen to haul Abacha over the coals,' says Lady Chalker. 'I did explain it was not something she did, to which he said: "Well, she tells me what she thinks!"'

As the leaders prepared to head for their 'retreat' at a resort hotel in Queenstown, word came through that Saro-Wiwa and his fellow activists had been hanged in a Nigerian prison. It was a clear two-fingered rebuke to the authority of the Commonwealth. Mandela was so furious that he wanted Nigeria kicked out of the organisation there and then. Instead, the leaders settled on a more practical response, creating a new body called the Commonwealth Ministerial Action

Group (CMAG) to monitor violations of Commonwealth principles and pile the pressure on rogue members. As the future Secretary-General Don McKinnon would explain, CMAG was effectively placing a placard around the neck of badly behaved countries, 'advertising their deficiencies'. Nigeria would now be subject to repeated human-rights investigations. Previously, when countries like Britain had suggested such ideas, they would be dismissed as the old 'white' Commonwealth bossing younger nations around. With Mandela's wholehearted support, though, no one could claim there was anything 'colonial' about it. The presence of this new moral authority would certainly make life more awkward for the less progressive members of the Queen's favourite organisation.

No state visitor in years had drawn the sort of crowds that turned out to watch the Queen welcome Mandela to London in July 1996. Since the advent of television had made these things easier to watch at home, they had tended to attract modest crowds. Yet Horse Guards and the Mall were packed as if for a royal wedding. The President had arrived the previous evening and stayed at the Dorchester Hotel, from where he emerged in a tracksuit at 5 a.m. for his customary dawn stroll, a legacy of twenty-seven years in prison. By lunchtime, he was in a dark suit and was driven to Horse Guards for the formal greeting, accompanied by his daughter, Princess Zenani Mandela-Dlamini, in electric-blue. Dressed in a yellow silk dress and floral hat, the Queen was waiting with the Duke of Edinburgh, as they had done for so many state visitors over the years. The ritual would be exactly the same, but no previous visitor had provoked the sort of whooping and cheering that erupted as Mandela stepped out of his car to shake the Queen's hand. Chants of 'Nelson! Nelson!' rang round the old state parade ground behind Downing Street. 'Your Majesty!' beamed Mandela.

The two leaders climbed into the 1902 state landau for the procession to Buckingham Palace, flanked by the clanking, gleaming might of the Household Cavalry and cheered on their way by people like John Gevisser, twenty-seven. A London-based South African and ANC member, he had attended so many protests over the years outside nearby South Africa House, demanding Mandela's release. Now his leader was riding with the Queen – 'the biggest compliment we South Africans can have from Britain'. London-based singer Joe Mogotsi had sung at Mandela's inauguration in 1994. 'Madiba! Madiba!' he yelled at full pitch. Hearing his famous nickname, Mandela waved back.

Inside the Palace the Queen entertained her guests to a light lunch of asparagus mousse, salmon and summer pudding. As ever, considerable thought had gone into her gifts. Knowing that Mandela had spent much of his captivity reading a hidden copy of the works of Shakespeare, she presented him with an eight-volume set of Dr Johnson's edition. In return, Mandela presented her with a set of commemorative gold coins, plus a chess set for Prince Philip.

While the usual formalities were observed – tea with the Queen Mother, a wreath-laying at the Grave of the Unknown Warrior – the details were very much tailored to suit this special guest. Mindful of Mandela's body-clock, the Queen brought forward the start of her state banquet by half an hour, to ensure that her guest was in his bed in the Palace's Belgian Suite by 10 p.m. Though the dress code was the customary white tie, it was made clear that Mandela was very welcome to wear his own variation – no tie at all, but with the Order of Merit around his neck. The visit came at a time when every official visitor to the UK was automatically served British beef, in solidarity with the farming industry following an international ban on British beef. Mandela, however, did not like red meat. So the Queen produced a menu of sole, curried turkey and strawberry-and-lemon meringue, served with Louis Roederer champagne and a 1993 South African chardonnay.

Unusually, the state visitor found himself with a queen on either side of him at dinner, since the Queen Mother was determined to be there, three weeks short of her ninety-sixth birthday. The Queen herself had made a little-noticed but important concession to the forward-looking tone of the visit. Although she had worn her twenty-first-birthday diamonds in Cape Town the year before, she had decided not to wear any South African jewellery on this occasion. There was a lot to choose from, but she did not want to provoke discussions about bygone eras, let alone a debate over whether jewels should be handed back. Instead, she wore her Russian tiara from Queen Mary's collection. In her speech, she again saluted her guest's personal example: 'You have provided the leadership and, by your willingness to embrace your former captors, have set the course for national reconciliation.' Mandela in turn made no mention of either colonialism or sanctions, sticking to a short script proclaiming that 'the antagonisms of past centuries are no more'.

Mandela's popularity would lead to good-natured chaos everywhere. When the Prince of Wales took him to Brixton in south London, the visit had to be curtailed after thousands swamped the route of the walkabout. As Princess Zenani became detached from the main entourage, a rescue party had to wade in to extract her. When Mandela addressed both Houses of Parliament, several MPs and staff brought their children along to hear the first foreigner in more than thirty-five years invited to speak in Westminster Hall, Parliament's grandest chamber. Presidents Clinton and Reagan had been expected to make do with the Royal Gallery.

The adulation continued wherever Mandela went. When he visited John Major in Downing Street, the entire staff lined up, unprompted, to applaud him. Major was as moved as his guest. 'Mr President,' he told him, 'I want you to know this is the first time in six years all my staff have wanted to show their admiration like that.'

The most entertaining display of affection was that of a collection of fiercely competitive British academics. So many universities wanted to confer honorary degrees on Mandela that he could have spent all summer being feted in a range of different gowns and mortar boards on campuses all over Britain. Time was short, however, and he felt that he could not accept one institution without offending another. Prince Philip, Chancellor of the University of Cambridge, had the solution: a mass investiture in the garden at Buckingham Palace. The seats of learning would come to Mandela, not the other way round. Even then there was trouble, as Sonny Ramphal, then Chancellor of Warwick University, recorded in his memoirs. Oxford University, under the chancellorship of Lord Jenkins of Hillhead, conveyed a fabulously pompous message to the Queen's Private Secretary, explaining that it was quite impossible for Oxford to award anyone an honorary degree outside the precincts of the university. President Mandela would therefore have to come to Oxford. The Queen let it be known, in reply, that this was clearly Oxford's problem, not hers, and that everyone else would understand if Oxford chose not to turn up. At which point Roy Jenkins's panic-stricken staff suddenly unearthed a reason why he could actually confer the honorary degree after all. There was then the vexed question of a running order. It was decided that each university would have five minutes to perform its ceremony in order of the date of foundation. Oxford's 'Woy' Jenkins thus had the honour of leading the way – and the pleasure of being the first dignitary to attempt the public pronunciation of Mandela's second name, Rolihlahla.

Another break with tradition was the scrapping of the state visitor's 'return' banquet for the host. Mandela wondered if he might give the Queen lunch and an evening concert instead. Delighted not to have to find another non-African tiara, she joined him for a South African-style spread of scallops and asparagus tart, breast of chicken with 'bobotie', 'mealies' and beans and fruit with ice cream. Later on, the two heads of state attended a sell-out evening of South African-inspired music at the Royal Albert Hall or, as Mandela called it, 'that great round building'.

As the performance by Phil Collins, Hugh Masekela and Quincy Jones got going, the state visitor felt the urge to dance. According to Sally Bedell Smith, he discreetly turned to Sir Robin Renwick for advice. Would such a thing be allowed in the Royal Box? 'You should do it,' Renwick replied. 'Don't worry.' So, as the Ladysmith Black Mambazo chorus, who had performed at his Nobel Prize ceremony, began to sing, Mandela stood up and started to clap along. Other members of the Royal Family quickly followed suit, until the Queen herself was joining in. No one could recall the last time the monarch had been seen to boogie in public, least of all during a state visit. However, this had been the week when the rulebook had long since been consigned to a Palace waste-paper basket. Hence a poignant moment at the Dorchester earlier in the day. Abandoning the convention of no speeches at return banquets, Mandela had decided he would still say something, and delivered a personal tribute to 'this gracious lady' over lunch. The Queen, who usually avoids off-the-cuff speeches much as she avoids shellfish and cats, cheerfully broke her own rule. With no notes, she rose to praise 'this wonderful man'.

Mandela concluded his visit with two engagements that could hardly have been more different. In Trafalgar Square he appeared on the balcony of South Africa House, to the sort of scenes usually reserved for a homecoming cup-winning football team. 'I would like to put each and every one of you in my pocket and return with you to South Africa,' he told them. Before that, however, he had an entirely private meeting at Buckingham Palace with his fellow member of the Order of Merit, Margaret Thatcher. Neither would reveal the contents of the meeting though, when asked later, Mandela replied: 'let bygones be bygones'.

For both heads of state, it had been an intoxicating week. Though Mandela could usually be relied upon to say something nice about the most tedious event, he spoke from the heart before his departure when he told reporters that his welcome in 'one of the pastures of democracy' had been 'beyond my wildest expectations'. For the Queen, it would be another outstanding experience – an unforgettable highlight of the bleakest decade of her reign.

With outgoing and incoming state visits completed, it also meant that her friendship with Mandela would now become more 'normal'. When he was passing through Britain, as he often did on official or private business, he would drop in to say 'hello', without it being newsworthy. He was back the following year for the Commonwealth summit in Edinburgh, where he met the Queen several times. A year later, en route to addressing an EU summit in Wales, he dropped in at Windsor for tea. By now the conversation was more that of family friends than two world leaders, as they discussed the Queen Mother's birthday and news of Prince Harry's success at the common-entrance exams for Eton. 'Some are very difficult,' she told him. The President said he'd just looked at some of the exam papers and couldn't agree more.

By 1999, as he was preparing to step down from the presidency, he was addressing her by her first name, albeit applying certain formalities at the same time. 'Dear Elizabeth,' he began his letter to her in April 1999, as he invited her to pay another state visit to South Africa ahead of the Commonwealth summit in Durban later in the year. He signed off: 'Please accept, Your Majesty, the assurances of our highest esteem, Nelson.' By the time she came to that summit, he met her as an ex-President. Having made way for his ANC successor, Thabo Mbeki, in June 1999, he would become even more relaxed with the Queen, while never for a moment forgetting the dignity of her position. On being appointed an honorary Queen's Counsel in 2000, he insisted on making a twenty-four-hour round trip to London for the presentation, even though the Queen would not be at the ceremony. He felt it would be disrespectful to the monarch if he did not attend. 'We really tried to convince him not to travel to London for one day but he insisted,' his executive assistant, Zelda la Grange, wrote in her memoir. 'He wanted to honour his warm friendship with the Queen.' As soon as the Queen and Duke of Edinburgh learned that he was coming to London, they invited him to pop round to Buckingham Palace for tea afterwards.

Zelda la Grange was always amused by her boss's familiarity with the monarch. 'I think he was one of very few people who called her by her first name and she seemed to be amused by it,' she wrote, adding that Mandela's second wife, Graça Machel, would often try to correct him. 'When he was questioned one day by Mrs Machel and told that it was not proper to call the Queen by her first name, he responded: "But she calls me Nelson". On one occasion when he saw her he said: "Oh, Elizabeth, you've lost weight!" ' Mandela's friendship extended to the Prince of Wales and other members of the Royal Family, all of whom would make a point of dropping in to see him when in South Africa.

In December 2013, the Queen was 'deeply saddened' to learn of the death of her friend, at the age of ninety-five. 'Her Majesty remembers with great warmth her meetings with Mr Mandela,' she said in a statement, as she despatched the Prince of Wales to South Africa to represent her at his funeral. South Africa continues to command a special place in her affections. When South Africa's new President, Cyril Ramaphosa, paid his first official visit to Buckingham Palace ahead of the 2018 Commonwealth summit, officials were left looking at their watches as the audience ran on and on, to more than twice the allotted time. The Queen had wanted to show the new President – a protégé of Mandela – some of her correspondence with him. She had even had facsimile copies of it framed as a gift. The previous month, she had welcomed Thembi Tambo, daughter of former ANC president, Oliver Tambo, as the new South African High Commissioner to London. Her memories of those 'outstanding' experiences are as strong as ever.

Mandela's death came just nine months after that of Margaret Thatcher, his great foe in the eyes of most people – except those of

Mandela himself. In the space of a year, the Queen mourned two of the most important political figures of her reign, giants who would dominate their times.

It was a sign of the Queen's regard for her first female Prime Minister that she attended Margaret Thatcher's funeral in person. With the exception of close family and very close friends, the Queen normally stays away from funerals, for fear of intruding and of upstaging the other mourners. Her presence at St Paul's Cathedral elevated the event to a proper national occasion – a state funeral in all but name. At the end, the Queen spoke warmly to the Thatcher family on the steps of the cathedral. If there were any lingering doubts about her enduring respect for her former Prime Minister, they could be laid to rest alongside her. Margaret Thatcher might not have been garlanded with an honorary degree from her old university, Oxford, as Mandela had been. She might not have been honoured with a statue in Parliament Square, as Mandela had been. However, in simply being there as sovereign, the Queen had paid her a compliment granted to just one other politician of modern times: Winston Churchill.

Chapter 11

BREAKING THE ICE

'We have played a card which only Britain can play'

Garlanded with prizes and plaudits (and now the ultimate posthumous accolade of modern times – an international airport bearing his name), Václav Havel stands in the front rank of twentieth-century statesmen. As such, he could spot a class act when he saw one. Having become the first President of the Czech Republic, he had only a few things left on his bucket list. One of them was a visit from the Queen. Her arrival in 1996 would be an occasion for casting precedent and protocol aside, as he made this a more spectacular and personal affair than any previous state visit in his nation's short history. After she had left, the poet/playwright/ex-prisoner/president used his weekly broadcast to the nation to paint a portrait of his guest. It wasn't saccharine stuff about a nice woman in smart clothes who had been very gracious. Rather, he explained that the visit had been a lesson in political manners. He had been struck by the way in which the Queen had combined 'the dignity of the throne' with 'an ability to take things for what they are, curiosity, a sense of humour, a sense of perspective, an informal attitude'. In short, she had shown the 'real charisma of someone who has found the proper measure of playing the part'.

For Havel and his countrymen, the Queen's visit had been a genuinely historic moment in the modern story of a democratic nation born out of totalitarianism. And there has been the same sense of occasion – of a national turning point – in so many countries over the years. Take the Queen's 1979 visit to the United Arab Emirates, where her host was Sheikh Zayed, founding father of the nation. That visit went on to become part of the school history syllabus, for 'history' is what it was – and is – to a proud young country. Trips like these were not mere diplomatic pleasantries, but landmarks. The fact that the Queen continues to reign long after these events only gives them added resonance and poignancy. So any attempt to pick out the Queen's 'greatest' tours is an entirely subjective exercise. She would probably hope that they have all been 'great', in the eye of the beholder.

She has been the first reigning monarch to visit many countries, including Japan, Brazil and Tuvalu. She has visited countries that did not even exist when she came to the Throne – including Havel's Czech Republic. She has visited countries that do not exist any more, from Yugoslavia to Northern Rhodesia. Until the Royal Archives yield the answer many years hence, we will not know which have been her favourite (and her least favourite) tours. As Britain's Number One diplomat, she is far too diplomatic to say. What we can do, however, is listen to those who have travelled with her or have welcomed her. They will point to a handful of her more than 260 visits to more than 125 nations and territories and single out some of those which have not just been historic in the eyes of the Queen or her hosts but in the eyes of the whole world.

GERMANY, 1965

To this day, many Germans look back on two moments that have come to define Germany's post-war readmission to the international fold. The first was the visit of US President John F. Kennedy in 1963, just after the erection of the Berlin Wall, and his famous '*Ich bin ein Berliner*' speech.* The second was the arrival of the Queen in 1965. Thomas Kielinger, doyen of the German media in London and the Queen's German-language biographer, keeps an album of commemorative stamps from the period. The presence of the President and

* It has become received wisdom that Kennedy's grammar was incorrect and that he should have said '*Ich bin Berliner*'. As a result, he was describing himself as a jam doughnut, known as '*ein Berliner*'. Pure pedantry, say German linguists, pointing out that everyone in the 450,000-strong crowd knew exactly what he meant.

the monarch were the stand-out moments of the age, he says. If Kennedy provided morale-boosting political reassurance at the height of Cold War tensions, the Queen conveyed the same message, but with added glamour and mystique.

'There was a frenzy,' says Kielinger. 'The Queen and her sister were beautiful and charming and the tabloids had always had a field day with them. As Princesses, they boosted circulation for a long time. There was all this Anglophilia. Britain's soft power was huge.'

Germany had been eager for a royal visit for years. The stumbling block had been British nervousness. It was a reluctance that had baffled the German people, given that other old wartime foes had been ready to build new friendships. In his post-mortem of the visit, Sir Frank Roberts, the British Ambassador to Bonn (then the German capital), explained the dilemma: 'In Germany, there was a widespread feeling that Britain was reserved towards Europe and especially towards Germany and it was not understood why British memories should be longer than in other European countries which had suffered even more from Hitler's Reich.'

Sir Frank noted that the political relationship between the two countries was sound and sensible. Britain and Germany both agreed on the need for European unity, on the importance of transatlantic collaboration and on the significance of free trade. Both nations had been drawn further together by their mutual exasperation with the egotistical posturing of the French President, General de Gaulle. In 1963, de Gaulle had vetoed Britain's application to join the new EEC, on the grounds that the UK was 'insular' and 'maritime' (he would, of course, veto it again in 1967). In short, he was driving both London and Bonn up the wall in equal measure.

If Anglo-German relations were on an ever-upward trajectory at the political level, however, they lacked a key component. As Sir Frank observed bluntly: 'Warmth was missing from the relationship.' And there was only one person who could resolve that.

So why British nervousness about a state visit from the Queen? Within government, there were concerns about the response of the British public and press. Twenty years after the end of the Second World War, there were many – in working men's clubs, in Parliament and in Fleet Street – who were in no hurry to forgive or forget the events of two world wars. There had already been a state visit to

Britain by the first President of West Germany, Theodor Heuss, in 1958. It had not been deemed a great success, particularly after Heuss's visit to Oxford University. The German press were full of reports that he had been snubbed by students, who pointedly kept their hands in their pockets. This was certainly mild stuff compared to subsequent forms of student protest in Britain, but it had rankled in Germany, where the public still regarded the UK as the world leader in good manners. 'German Press treatment of the "undergraduates with hands in their pockets" story did more than anything else to mar the atmosphere,' the British Ambassador noted.

The government could not delay a state visit indefinitely, however, particularly since the Queen had already made state visits to both France and Italy. It was beginning to look rude. Now, with France thwarting Britain's European ambitions, the British government looked at Germany again and decided the time had come to play the royal trump card.

There was a marked lack of enthusiasm at the Palace, however. It was not because the Queen disliked the idea of visiting the land of some of her forefathers. Rather, the Royal Family were acutely conscious of their German roots and extremely sensitive to any charge of giving special treatment to the ex-enemy, as a result. Even after changing their family name from Saxe-Coburg-Gotha during the First World War and leading the Empire through the Second, the family had still not entirely shaken off saloon-bar gossip about the Windsors being a bunch of closet Germans. The fact that Prince Philip's sisters had all been on the other side, having married Germans, did not help.*

Furthermore, the Queen was well aware of the increasingly hostile feeling across her old Commonwealth realms towards Britain's quest for closer European integration. Britain's 'kith and kin' in the old dominions of Australia and New Zealand had lost blood and loved ones helping Britain fend off German invasion. How could it be that Britain was now seeking closer dealings with the old enemy, at their expense?

* The Duke's three surviving sisters were all married to German aristocrats who had served in German uniform during the war. Another sister, Cecile, had been killed in a 1937 plane crash, while the Duke's father had died in exile in Monte Carlo in 1944. His mother, Princess Andrew of Greece, had been the only immediate member of the family at his wedding in 1947.

So when the Foreign Secretary, Rab Butler, finally proposed a state visit in 1964, the Queen's Private Secretary, Sir Michael Adeane, was surprisingly cool in return. She would only go, he said, 'on advice' and 'at the request of the British Government'. Otherwise she would be accused of pursuing 'private ties and relationships', a charge that was 'all wrong and untrue'. Undeterred, the Conservative government formally issued that advice. It would be Harold Wilson's new Labour administration that was in charge by the time the Queen and Prince Philip took off for Bonn on 18th May 1965.

As with all the Queen's pioneering early tours, the level of interest was phenomenal from the outset. More than a thousand media from all over the world had travelled to Germany to chronicle this royal exercise in fence-mending. It was a bracing task for a young Australian civil servant who had recently arrived at the Palace. William Heseltine had just been appointed assistant to the press secretary, Commander Richard Colville, when the commander was laid low by ill health. Heseltine suddenly found himself dealing with one of the largest royal media operations ever seen. 'I was thrown in at the last minute,' he says. 'I had enough German to stagger through a dinner sitting next to a non-speaking burgermeister's wife but not to speak to 1,200 press.' He can still remember the photo-opportunity arranged after the Queen's lunch with Chancellor Ludwig Erhard. 'The programme said that after the lunch they were meant to go outside to "view the Rhine". All they could see was 1,200 press completely obliterating any view of the Rhine.'

This would be the first state visit to command live television coverage – and in exhaustive detail about every member of the entourage, too. Sir William still recalls a breathless commentator declaring: '*Hier kommt Lord Plunket* . . .'* To the delight of British diplomats, that coverage did not fade after the opening stages of the ten-day tour, but remained similarly breathless to the end. Knowing the importance of setting the pace and tone of a visit from the start, the Queen had made a particular effort ahead of the opening state banquet. It was to be held at the (then) presidential palace, the Augustusburg in

* Patrick Plunket, 7th Baron, was the Queen's Deputy Master of the Household, an unflappable source of courtierly common sense and one of her closest confidants until his early death from cancer in 1975.

Brühl, near Bonn. Given that the palace was celebrated for its swirling pale-blue rococo interiors, the Queen had already alerted her dress designer, Hardy Amies, who designed a sleeveless evening gown to match her surroundings. It was such a sensation that the photographer, Cecil Beaton, asked the Queen to wear it for a series of official portraits three years later. The sight of the Queen in her Brühl-inspired dress, her pearls shimmering inside the diamond-studded loops of the Vladimir Tiara, was precisely what the German public had been hoping for. Dreary egalitarianism might be what Germans sought and expected of their own leaders, but not of '*die Queen*'.

'What the Germans loved in 1965 was that the Queen did not make any compromise. There was no populist accommodation for modern Britain. She was majestic,' says Thomas Kielinger. 'She waved from on high. There was still that deference in Germany, even if it was in decline in Britain. In Germany, we admire the stylistic expression of grandeur. This was a great theatrical event. And Britain is the great country of the stage.'

In his speech of welcome, President Heinrich Lübke saluted Britain as 'the teacher of other nations', a nation that had made 'a decisive contribution to the spread of civilisation' and world trade. Taking the long view, he remarked that 'until the First World War, there was hardly any serious conflict of interest between our two countries'. He quoted Winston Churchill's dream of a 'United States of Europe', adding Germany's wish to see Britain 'included in the future unification of Europe'. In the meantime, Lübke hoped the Queen enjoyed her visit as much as Queen Victoria had enjoyed her own homecoming down the Rhine with Prince Albert 120 years before. There would be no glossing over the family roots on this tour.

While her dress had wowed the public, it was the Queen's words that would ensure glowing reviews from Germany's political class and the media. One phrase, in particular, was much quoted the following day: 'This tragic period in our relations is now happily over.'

Across Germany, six-figure crowds turned out in one region after another, as the Queen travelled in the royal train, which would be her home for eight of her ten nights on German soil. Sir Frank Roberts was informed by the German government that more television sets had been sold in the weeks immediately prior to the visit than in the whole of the previous year – happy echoes of Coronation Britain.

The Germans were thrilled when the Queen appeared in a foundry worker's helmet at the Mannesmann steel mill at Duisburg, but only because she had looked suitably regal a few hours earlier at the state lunch at the Schloss Benrath. Children and horses were a prominent feature of the programme. The Queen's soundbites might not match those of JFK but, in terms of public impact, post-war Germany had seen nothing quite like it.

On the British side, immense care had been taken to ensure that the Queen and the Duke were not filmed with any embarrassing German in-laws or cousins, despite the wishes of the German government to include them at major events. Ahead of the visit, the British Ambassador had written to the Queen's deputy Private Secretary, Martin Charteris, warning that her hosts were very unhappy about royal attempts to freeze out the German relatives. Sir Frank Roberts relayed his discussion with the President, who had pointed out that it would be very bad manners. 'The federal republic was basically a bourgeois country,' the President had explained, 'and public relations were bourgeois. It was universal practice that when a visitor from overseas with relatives was being entertained, the close relatives would as a matter of course be invited to dinner.' No matter that some of them had sported a swastika two decades earlier. If the Queen's German relations were blackballed from the royal guest list, President Lübke would get 'very severe criticism'.

In the end, little-known figures like the Duke of Brunswick and Prince Georg of Hanover were quietly slotted into dinners and receptions with a minimum of fuss. The Queen and Duke also spent the middle weekend in complete privacy with some of the Duke's relatives, not least so that he could show the Queen some of the places he had known as a boy. These included Salem Castle, former seat of the Duke's uncle, Prince Max of Baden, and a place where the young Prince Philip had spent part of his education. 'It was a private weekend and the press didn't bother them,' recalls Sir William Heseltine. 'I remember trying to get in past huge doors and guard dogs.'

The British press, for the most part, gave the visit very favourable coverage, although the royal photographer, Reginald Davis, remembers that this was out of deference to the Queen, not the hosts. He recalls that some of the British press party would always recoil at the sound of the German national anthem and conspicuously refused to stand to attention. 'When they played their national anthem, we made a point of walking around,' he says.

The only episode approaching a diplomatic incident, however, involved neither the British nor German media, but the French. They had taken magnificent Gallic umbrage at the Queen's speech in Koblenz on 20th May, in which she had referred obliquely to the most famous Anglo-German victory in history. This state visit was taking place just days before the 150th anniversary of the Battle of Waterloo and the Queen alluded to the Prussian Field Marshal, the Prince von Blücher, whose late arrival had helped the Duke of Wellington defeat Napoleon in 1815. The Queen did not actually talk about Waterloo. She was merely using it as a metaphor. 'For fifty years, we heard too much about the things which have divided us,' she said. 'Let us now make a great effort to remember the things which unite us.'

The French, perhaps prodded by their President, made a terrible fuss. 'The monstrous gaffe of Queen Elizabeth,' declared the headline in *Paris-Presse*. Even the normally sober *Le Figaro* called for an end to the 'celebration of victories' (though it stopped short of demanding the renaming of the Arc de Triomphe, the Gare d'Austerlitz and all of France's own victory-themed landmarks). The Foreign Office circulated an amused memo about French 'tantrums' and the German press poured scorn on their thin-skinned neighbours.

For many German commentators, the high point of the tour was the Queen's visit to Berlin and its grimly spectacular barrier with the communist East. The decision to include Berlin had been a delicate one, since it was not technically part of West Germany but Allied territory administered by Britain, France, the USA and the Soviets. Both the British and German governments had been determined to give the USSR 'no ground for claiming that the Allied status in Berlin had been tacitly undermined'. With that in mind, comic discussions took place between London and Bonn about how much of the wall the Queen might actually see without provoking a diplomatic incident with the Soviets. In the end, it was agreed that the Queen would look *at* the wall but not officially look *over* it. On the other hand, no one would mind very much if she had a quick peek across to the other side.

As far as the German media were concerned, she definitely had a very good gawp. The Frankfurt *Abendpost* reported the Queen's 'almost shocked expression', while the *Süddeutsche Zeitung* spoke of her being 'obviously moved'. There was no doubt that she got a good look, because she talked about it to the head of the Foreign Office, Sir Paul Gore-Booth, during ambassadorial presentations a few weeks later. He made a confidential note of the conversation, now lodged in the National Archives, noting that the Wall had made a 'considerable impression' on her. She admitted that she had previously doubted the need for quite so many troops on the border with Eastern Europe. 'One look at and over the Berlin Wall' had made her think again.

For the people of Berlin, still coming to terms with their isolation, it was a badly needed morale-booster. 'My uncle was the first post-war attorney general of Berlin,' says Thomas Kielinger. 'Being a beleaguered city, the Berliners felt particularly happy at being singled out for this special treatment.'

As it turned out, the Russians had not been greatly troubled by the royal presence at all and let it pass. Foreign Office files show that the communist East German government, on the other hand, was duly outraged. It set to work churning out some vintage propaganda. The state-controlled *Berliner Zeitung* ran a lengthy report on the punitive cost of all the Queen's castles, adding gravely: 'The dresses of the Queen, which are burnt after being worn once, are paid for by British workers.' Nonetheless, large numbers of East Germans had been seen straining for a look across no-man's-land for a glimpse of the Queen. A British intelligence official, M. P. Buxton, reported that the Soviet officer in charge of the Marienborn border crossing had asked a British interpreter if he could procure any Western periodicals. The Russian was most disappointed not to be able to see a good picture of the Queen.

As *Britannia* set sail for home after the Queen's farewell dinner in Hamburg, the West German press was heaping praise on what had been a landmark for both nations.* *Welt am Sonntag* noted that Britain

* Though the Queen is seldom accused of 'spin', she had done her prospects of positive coverage no harm by holding a reception for the media at the start of the tour. 'The most exciting party,' declared *Bild*. It was the first time any head of state had done such a thing in Germany. 'I do not think that they had ever been shaken hands with before, certainly not by their President,' the Queen's Private Secretary, Sir Michael Adeane, wrote afterwards.

had seen a new side of Germany. It also thanked the Queen for coming to the Berlin Wall. The paper noted tersely that when General de Gaulle had visited Germany three years earlier, he had not even set foot in Berlin, for fear of upsetting the Russians. One former state secretary from Hanover had gone as far as describing the crowds filling trains and buses to see the Queen as a '*Völkerwanderung*' – a phrase usually applied to the great European migrations that followed the decline of the Roman Empire.

In his despatch to London, the British Ambassador noted the way in which the German press had been studying the British coverage with a toothcomb – and had been pleasantly surprised by the results. 'The British public has, for the first time since mass media of communication came into their own, been exposed to a concentrated diet of unprejudiced reporting on Germany and the Germans,' said Sir Frank.

It had also been something of a novel experience for the Queen's first Labour administration. The new Foreign Secretary, a few months into his job, had been bowled over. 'I believe you had planned to be at Chequers for the weekend,' Michael Stewart wrote to the Prime Minister, Harold Wilson, on 26th May. 'If you could get back to greet Her Majesty, I think it would be well worth doing. The tour has been something of a personal triumph as well as a test of endurance.' Wilson did not need to be asked twice.

Clearly the Queen enjoyed herself. There are few non-Commonwealth nations she has toured more, having made five state visits to Germany and several more official ones. The rest of the family are regulars. Here is a G7, European and NATO partner with which Britain has so much in common, so many historical (and royal) ties and yet so much baggage. Reconciliation would be a theme of all her subsequent tours. On her next state visit, in 1978, the Queen was back at the Berlin Wall and won tearful applause for her speech to Berliners in which she declared: 'My people stand behind you.' There was more grumbling from the communist side of the wall and more complaints from the French, too. This time, they were upset that the Queen had obliquely alluded to French persecution of the Huguenots in one of her speeches. This was a period of heightened terrorist activity in Europe. The German media were bowled over by the fact that whereas the Soviet leader, Leonid Brezhnev, had recently visited Germany with hundreds of security men, the royal visitors had not. 'The Queen and Prince Consort brought with them one security officer each,' noted *Welt am Sonntag*, 'fewer than many a Bonn state secretary. Impressive indeed, this woman'. At a political level, the relationship was closer than ever (even if the Queen had not quite forgiven Chancellor Helmut Schmidt for stubbing out his cigarettes on the royal china the year before at a Palace dinner for the NATO summit in London). The chiefs of the German armed forces were thrilled to be invited to spend a day at sea in *Britannia*. 'Our Queen For Five Days,' the front page of *Bild* had declared. And so she was.

There would be more reconciling in 1992, as the Queen marked the reunification of Germany. She also honoured the civilian victims of the Allied bombing of Dresden at a service involving the choir of Coventry Cathedral and a lesson read (in German) by the Duke of Edinburgh. In 2015, she was still reconciling past and present as she visited a concentration camp for the first time, meeting survivors and liberators of Bergen-Belsen. 'She is so loved in Germany,' says former Prime Minister David Cameron, who was in Berlin for part of her 2015 visit. 'The crowds were off the charts. I was really struck by how many times she had been and how hard she worked on this relationship.'

So much has changed over the years, not least Germany's shape, size, borders and capital city. Yet this is a relationship that has fundamentally changed not one jot. Nor have the headlines. 'Your Majesty, You were wonderful,' declared the front page of Germany's largest newspaper, *Bild*, at the end of her 1965 tour. Half a century later, on 25th June 2015, the Queen could have been forgiven a vague feeling of déjà vu as she picked up *Bild* once again to see the headline: 'We Love You, Ma'am.'

CHINA, 1986

It is still remembered by the media for the single phrase: 'slitty eyed'. No profile of the Duke of Edinburgh ever since has been complete without a mandatory reference to his alleged remark to a group of Edinburgh students during the 1986 state visit to China. The precise wording has never been exact, because no recording of the conversation exists. It was based on the account that a student, Simon Kirby, twenty-one, gave to a reporter at the time, detonating a media explosion. More than three decades later, it is still the first thing that many people recall about this game-changing royal mission – though not those who perhaps matter most: the Chinese themselves.

This was, and remains, one of the most significant tours in royal history. It was only the second state visit to a communist country, following the Queen's 1972 trip to Tito's Yugoslavia, but on a completely different scale. If it was not quite up there with US President Richard Nixon's 1972 trip to China (which went on to be the subject of an opera), it was still a global diplomatic breakthrough closely observed not just in Britain but around the world. In the words of the *Los Angeles Times*, it was 'one of the most symbolic turnabouts in 20th century history'. The omens were certainly very promising ahead of the visit. Pedantic world-class sticklers for protocol they might be, but the Chinese would be very happy to break all their own rules for this trip. Nothing would be too much trouble for the honoured guests, Queen Elizabeth II, *Yilishabai Nuwang* (or '*Bixia*' – 'Your Majesty') and her consort, *Feilipu Qinwang*. The invitation to make a state visit had been issued two years earlier by the elderly Chinese leader Deng Xiaoping.* It would set the seal on the historic Joint Declaration on Hong Kong, signed by Deng and Margaret Thatcher in 1984. This agreed that the colony would revert to Chinese rule in 1997, but with a fifty-year transition period known as 'One Country. Two Systems'. The compromise deal would avert both a collapse in the markets and an exodus of millions of Hong Kong Chinese to Britain. The decision to send the Queen to China would not only show faith in the Chinese, but would reassure both Hong Kong's people and its stock market. On top of that, it would herald a new era in UK–Chinese relations.

The Queen was bringing her Royal Yacht, too, and the Chinese were determined to keep it unblemished. Special tiles were ordered from Holland to line the sides of Chinese ports in order to protect the Royal Yacht's paintwork. The plans for the Queen's banquet were a

* One of five members of the Chinese politburo, Deng was not officially head of state, but 'Chairman of the Central Advisory Commission of the Chinese Communist Party'. Although by now semi-retired, he still remained the *de facto* head of 1.4 billion people.

further indication of Chinese esteem. She was keen to host it on board *Britannia* in Shanghai, a clear breach of the Chinese rule that all state banquets should be in Peking (as the Foreign Office still called Beijing). Not only was this breaking protocol but the Chinese President and official head of state, Li Xiannian, was unwell. According to a confidential Foreign Office memo marked 'Gossip', he had recently suffered a series of 'heart attacks'. Li's officials were therefore most reluctant to let him fly to Shanghai for the Queen's dinner. However, on being informed of the plan, Li himself had replied: 'Why not?'

Shanghai was being given an extensive makeover in the Queen's honour. China's largest clock, on top of the Shanghai customs building, had just been repaired, so that it would chime once again for the first time since the Cultural Revolution. The Chinese wanted its 'Big Ben' chimes to make the Queen 'feel at home'.

The standard plan for any normal state visitor to China was to spend three days in Peking and then visit two other cities. The Queen, however, would visit five. With two weeks to go, the Ambassador, Richard Evans, had run out of embossed invitations and was ordering more from London. As usual, every business in the land was itching for a royal introduction. 'I appreciate that the royal party will have a very busy timetable but since our company has traded with China since 1898, I do feel that a fund of goodwill built up over many years by companies such as ours will do much to make the royal visit a happy and memorable occasion,' a Mr E. J. Dickson of Bethell Brothers wrote to the Foreign Office. His begging letter did the trick.

On 12th October 1986, the Queen emerged from her chartered British Airways Tristar in a white hat and lemon-yellow dress, telling the welcoming party: 'I'm very glad to come to China.' As we know from the minutes of the Royal Visits Committee in Whitehall earlier, this was entirely true. She had been wanting to come for years. Even royal aides, numbed by years of watching the precision marching of the Household Division, were impressed by the drill at the welcome ceremony in Tiananmen Square.*

* Just three years later, the world would see a very different side of Chinese military discipline, as democratic protests were brutally suppressed on the same spot.

One of the first engagements was the Queen's meeting with Deng Xiaoping. 'It was a memorable lunch, just eight of us,' says former Private Secretary, Sir William Heseltine. 'Deng greeted the Queen by saying what an honour it was that Her Majesty should have taken the trouble to come to lunch with an old man like him. To which she responded with one of her favourite lines: "Why, you're the same age as my mother, and she doesn't think of herself as being old at all".'

As lunch began, it was soon clear to the Queen that her host was uncomfortable. 'We'd been sitting at the table for about ten minutes and the Queen was sitting opposite Deng,' former Foreign Secretary Lord (Geoffrey) Howe told William Shawcross. 'She noticed he was fretting uneasily and she remembered he was a chain smoker. She leant across to me and said: "I think Mr Deng would be rather happier if he was allowed to smoke". I told him that and I have never seen a man light up more cheerfully than that. It was a very human touch and he appreciated it.' Feeling somewhat liberated, Deng didn't hold back on the spittoon either, firing off a volley into a receptacle a yard from his chair. 'She did not move a muscle,' her press secretary, Michael Shea, recalled later. 'He spat, as is Chinese custom, and the Duke of Edinburgh let out a guffaw. We all looked around and the Queen just didn't move.' Mrs Thatcher had been less phlegmatic on her first meeting with Deng in 1982. As Lord Butler told her biographer, Charles Moore, she was taken aback when the ageing premier started hawking in front of her. 'She moved her legs,' he told Moore. 'It threw her.'

'Deng was full of good humour during the luncheon,' the British Ambassador, Richard Evans, reported back to London. It was the same with Hu Yaobang, General Secretary of the Chinese Communist Party, who 'was at his most lively when conducting the Queen and Duke on a guided tour of some of the older buildings in the former Imperial City'. Both sides were delighted by the other's words at Li Xiannian's opening state banquet. 'We have made great achievements but have not yet totally freed our country from economic and technological backwardness,' said Li in an unexpectedly frank address. 'The British people, a great people full of wisdom and creativeness, have made outstanding contributions to human civilisation and social progress.'

The Queen voiced Britain's admiration for Chinese progress and its readiness to 'contribute to the realisation of China's plans for the future'. There was a joke about the first British emissary to China, lost at sea along with Elizabeth I's letter to the Emperor of Cathay – 'fortunately postal services have improved since 1602' – plus a clever reference to Deng's 'One Country. Two Systems' mantra. 'The future lies with the young,' said the Queen. 'From such contacts come a growing recognition that we have two traditions but one hope for the future.'

The Chinese leadership had been 'quite exceptionally friendly' to the Queen and the Duke, the Ambassador noted, and he was struck by the genuinely animated atmosphere at all the social events. 'It is often the case in China that conversation never really gets going at formal dinner parties,' he wrote in his post-tour telegram. 'It certainly did in Shanghai.'

There the crowds were of a magnitude seldom seen since the early years of the reign. 'The State Visit stirred considerable emotion among the Chinese,' Sir Richard reported. He was informed by the Chinese authorities that two million people had lined the streets from the old city to *Britannia*'s berth, to watch the Queen arrive at her state banquet for Li Xiannian. A million of them were still there at midnight to see her drive from the Royal Yacht to the State Guest House, where protocol required that the royal couple should sleep while in Shanghai. For the first time anyone could remember, the Bund – Shanghai's waterfront – was illuminated from end-to-end all night. The Queen provided another first for the colossal crowds lining the streets. Whereas it was the norm for Chinese leaders to travel everywhere at speed in blacked-out cars, she insisted on travelling slowly with the lights on in her limousine to give everyone a good look.

It was all going magnificently. The Foreign Secretary was also hitting it off with the premier (China's equivalent of Prime Minister), Zhao Ziyang. The British Embassy eagerly telexed London to report Geoffrey Howe's fruitful dinner discussion with Zhao, noting that he had 'paid tribute to privatisation and contracting out' and 'suggested that most countries were currently thinking on these lines'. Mrs Thatcher would be pleased, even more so when she learned of *Britannia*'s commercial activity.

While the Queen was not on board, *Britannia* had been touting for trade with trips up and down the Huangpu and Yangtze Rivers. A number of contracts had been signed. 'If the business foreshadowed were all to come to maturity, exports worth several tens of millions of pounds will have been generated,' the British Ambassador told his masters.

And so, having dealt with the political and commercial imperatives of the tour, the Queen and Duke could relax a little. The Ambassador would single out three unforgettable sights from the tour in his confidential despatch: the Queen and the Duke at the Great Wall of China, her voyage across the Dianchi Lake near Kunming and the Terracotta Warriors of Xian. One of the great archaeological discoveries of the age, this army of thousands of clay figures was buried with a great Chinese emperor in 209 BC and was rediscovered in 1974. Surrounded, as ever, by a similar army of officials in suits, the Queen and Duke stood at the edge of the airport-sized pit, staring down at the earthenware battalions stretching into the distance. 'There was this great hush,' one of those present later recalled. At which point one of the British reporters present could be heard muttering a passable imitation of the Duke in walkabout mode: 'And how long have you been a terracotta warrior?' Several members of the British party, including it is said the Queen, found themselves biting back the giggles.

The Queen and the senior members of the royal party were then given special permission to descend. 'We were allowed to step in to the pit and walk amongst them as though we were part of the army,' said Geoffrey Howe. 'One felt a tremendous sense of privilege and she was as enthusiastic and struck by it as I was.'

The mood of levity and wonder would not last very long afterwards. A group of British undergraduates on a student exchange from Edinburgh University were then introduced to the Duke, in his capacity as Chancellor of the University. It was, by all accounts, a light-hearted chat, during which the Duke asked them about their studies. Jollying the conversation along, he is supposed to have joked: 'If you stay here much longer you'll all be slitty-eyed.' When they, in turn, asked him about his own trip, he let slip that he found the pollution of Peking 'ghastly'. Moments later, the royal convoy was on its way, while a couple of members of the British press stayed behind, wandering among the crowd asking people for their impressions and recollections of the event. On a royal tour, with minimal time and space at many events, it is normal for the press to divide up different engagements and then swap notes afterwards, a system known as 'pooling'. Back on the media coach, heading for the airport, one reporter started reading back his quotes from the Edinburgh student, Simon Kirby. At which point one veteran tabloid reporter yelled out: 'Stop the bus!' In the days before mobile phones, a public phone box was still the best means of reporting a story. And this one was clearly destined for the front page.

The headlines are well known. 'Philip Gets It All Wong' screeched *The Sun* the next day, applying Fu Manchu-style touch-ups to a photo of the Duke. The paper's headline was much the same the following day: 'Queen Velly Velly Angry'. The Duke's friends have always pointed out that his supposed 'gaffes' were only ever a good-natured way of helping along a sticky conversation.

British diplomats did their best to play down the story. Reporting his 'principal impressions' of the tour to the Far Eastern department in London, Richard Evans reported that 'The Chinese pulled out all the stops.' After a fairly lengthy summary of the tour, he came to the unavoidable crux: 'It was, of course, unfortunate that the Duke of Edinburgh spoke as he did to the students from Edinburgh. I was out of earshot and so do not know precisely what he said (I have heard many versions). It was equally unfortunate that Kirby and the others were so ready to speak to the journalists who besieged them immediately after HRH had moved on (I do not think that they had any idea of the likely consequences). The handling of the incident by the Chinese was well-judged.' That was one way of describing the Chinese response. They had, in fact, instructed the media not to mention it at all.

In his subsequent official despatch, Sir Richard (as he had become following his knighthood from the departing Queen) devoted many pages to the success of the tour, before alluding to 'one incident which will have given people outside China the impression that the State Visit was less than a perfect success'. Avoiding any use of the Duke's alleged words, the Ambassador accused several British papers of being 'thoroughly offensive' and pinned all blame for the incident squarely on the press themselves. 'The Chinese Government is in no way disturbed by what the Duke of Edinburgh is alleged to have said, but is angry about the way in which a section of the British press published reports offensive to HRH at a time when he was a guest of the Chinese president.'

The incident, however, would not be brushed off so easily at the Foreign Office. On 21st November, a month after the tour, Thorold Masefield of the Far Eastern department circulated a blunt report attacking the FCO's entire approach to state visits and its lack of clear objectives. The Queen's tours, he insisted, should receive the same sort of preparation as the Prime Minister's. 'There is at present no process for writing up objectives for State Visits,' he warned. Advice was being 'fed piece-meal into the Palace' and briefings for the Queen seemed to consist of 'rather bland generalised background information'. He added: 'Much of this must already be known to the Queen. Interesting points, particularly those to get across to the Queen's hosts, are largely omitted.'

While television had provided some good coverage and scenic shots, he pointed out that the press had been given little fresh material. 'Perhaps, inevitably, their reports concentrated on trivia (sea slugs, spittoons, slitty eyes). Fuller daily briefing of the press corps, not on the details of the Queen's dress but on the relevance of the day's events to Sino/British relations, could have given them something else to write about.'

The embassy had a few other challenges, too. Before leaving China for Hong Kong, the Governor of Guangdong presented the Queen with an unusual bonsai jasmine tree in a bamboo cage for her garden at Windsor. The cage was too large to fit through the door of the small plane flying the Queen to Hong Kong, and the tree was too fragile to go in the hold, so the Chinese gave it a first-class train ticket to Hong Kong where it could be reunited with the Queen. By now, Foreign Office staff had given it a name – Jack – and arranged a police escort to Hong Kong airport, where it was placed in the Queen's plane for the journey home. Back in Britain, it had to enter the Ministry of Agriculture quarantine station at Harpenden. Philip Rouse of the FCO was sent to pick it up in his car. When it wouldn't fit in to that either, he had to borrow a British Airways truck. It finally reached the quarantine station at midnight, where the manager had been staying up to greet it. Rouse reported back to the embassy in Peking that the Ministry official was a 'Bonsai buff' who 'went down on his knees in ecstasy and delight'. Eventually, the tree passed quarantine and was last seen in a greenhouse in Windsor Great Park.

Over at the Foreign Office, officials found themselves fielding the usual complaints about the Queen's transport arrangements. Once again, there had been grumbles from British executives that she had flown to China in a US-built Tristar and had been driven around Peking in a Mercedes. 'De Gaulle would always use French manufacturers on foreign tours,' British businessman Tom Lyon wrote to Sir James Cleminson of the British Overseas Trade Board. 'If I came to your home and was not served Coleman's Mustard, I'd sell my shares!' The letter was one of many circulated around different Whitehall departments. Eric Beston of the Department of Trade and Industry offered a succinct defence: 'Departure from China on board HM Yacht can hardly be faulted.'

For all the glitches, the visit had achieved its overall aim of pushing open the door to the greatest closed society on Earth. It had reassured the millions of people living in Hong Kong and British businesses and diplomats had derived great benefits, too. The Chinese had certainly regarded it as a great success and were keen to discuss future royal visits. Princess Margaret would be in Peking in a matter of months. As ever, all this new-found goodwill would remain at the mercy of political events. The suppression of protests in Tiananmen Square three years later would put a halt to further royal visits for the time being, as would tensions in the run-up to the Hong Kong handover in 1997.

Thereafter, though, the royal connection would flourish once again. Chinese leaders enjoyed no fewer than three state visits to Britain between 1999 and 2015. No other nation has been a more regular guest at the Palace in recent times. So much for the 'gaffe'.

RUSSIA, 1994

The crew of *Britannia* had seen some strange sights over the years – icebergs, whales, a revolution,* the Queen Mother cooking bacon and

* In 1986, en route to meet the Queen in Australia, Rear Admiral John Garnier was taking *Britannia* through the Red Sea when civil war erupted in Aden. As the nearest Royal Navy vessel, the Yacht was diverted to pick up British nationals. Amid shooting and shelling between government and rebel forces, Lieutenant Robert Easson's rescue party ended up evacuating 1,082 people of fifty-five nationalities, plus one French dog.

eggs, and members of the Royal Family in fancy dress performing cabaret turns. Yet they had never seen anything quite like the sights that greeted them as they approached the Russian city of St Petersburg. All along the banks of the River Neva, there were rusting hulks everywhere. 'The Cold War had only just come to an end and I had spent my whole grown-up naval life with Cold War rules,' says *Britannia*'s former captain, Sir Robert Woodard. 'There were these amazing ships covered in rust with clothes lines all over the guns. They hadn't paid their sailors for weeks. They'd been chucked out of lodgings and were living on board with their families, which was extraordinary. Then there were redundant submarines filling up and emptying with the tide on one side and completely derelict merchant ships on the other, which quite narrowed the river.' It would be the only time that *Britannia*'s navigation officer was reduced to taking bearings from advertising billboards since the local nautical charts were of little use. Such was the state of post-Soviet Russia in 1994.

The Russians, for their part, had never seen anything quite like *Britannia*. Nor had they ever seen a reigning monarch. Now, all that was about to change. Like her visit to China eight years earlier, the Queen's 1994 state visit to meet President Boris Yeltsin was one of the great post-war diplomatic breakthroughs, upending more than seventy years of rigid communist protocol in the process – from flypasts to dress codes. For the first time since the reign of the last Tsar, dinner jackets would be worn at the Kremlin. The sense of happy amazement would be summed up by the Queen in her state banquet address to a beaming Yeltsin: 'You and I have spent most of our lives believing that this evening could never happen. I hope that you are as delighted as I am to be proved wrong.' He was indeed.

This state visit had been under discussion ever since the former Soviet leader, Mikhail Gorbachev, had invited the Queen five years earlier. Gorbachev's programme of *perestroika* ('restructuring') and *glasnost* ('openness') had led to the end of the Cold War and the collapse of the Iron Curtain around communist Eastern Europe. During the Gorbachev years, Yeltsin had risen to be Mayor of Moscow and the first democratically elected president of Russia, while Gorbachev remained in overall charge of the Soviet Union. Following the attempted coup of 1991, during which Gorbachev was held under house arrest, Yeltsin's defiance in the face of the plotters won the day. He emerged as the victor. The Soviet Union was formally dissolved within weeks, leaving Yeltsin at the helm in Russia. While speculators, entrepreneurs and criminal gangs embarked on a Wild West-style gold rush among the wreckage of all the old communist state enterprises, Britain was keen to bolster Yeltsin's democratic reforms. The President, in turn, was keen to show the people that his administration commanded international respect. It was time for the Queen to make that state visit.

'There were plenty of people in the Foreign Office saying that we should wait until they had a "proper" democracy,' says Sir Brian Fall, Britain's Ambassador to Moscow at the time. 'And the bean counters were saying: "No, let's wait and see if they've got a proper economy. Then let's put them in the royal visits programme." But that would have been too late. The right decision was to go right then, when it could do some good because people would appreciate it more.' Sir Brian believes that the Queen and her advisers were of the same view. For this was the period when she has putting forward exactly the same arguments for making a prompt visit to Nelson Mandela's newly-democratic South Africa – as she would a few months later – regardless of all those advising a more cautious approach. The Nineties might have been pretty miserable for the monarchy on the domestic front. On the world stage, however, the Queen was at the top of her game.

Before taking over in Moscow, Sir Brian Fall had already been Private Secretary to three Foreign Secretaries, later serving as number two in Washington, before becoming Britain's High Commissioner to Canada (and receiving the first of his two knighthoods). Having found himself *de facto* ambassador to ten other countries, following the collapse of the Soviet Union, he was determined to present the UK as a reliable partner. He could see how important it was to show support for Yeltsin's shaky free-market democracy in the face of so much turmoil and uncertainty. There was already something of a diplomatic vacuum in Moscow and everything to play for. The Queen and the rest of the Royal Family would be keen to play. Fall would have the rare distinction of organising separate visits for the Queen, the Duke of Edinburgh, the Prince of Wales, the Princess of Wales and the Princess Royal during his three years in Moscow.

'It was a very exciting time. You really couldn't see more than two weeks ahead,' recalls Sir Francis Richards, then number two at the British Embassy. As a result, this would be a seat-of-the-pants state visit, in comparison to the usual planning process for the Queen's tours. One year before the Queen's arrival, the Prince of Wales had acted as an advance party to establish the appetite for a full state visit. The Duke of Edinburgh had also visited in a semi-private sporting capacity, as President of the International Equestrian Federation. However, the decision to send the Queen was not made until the summer of 1994. She would be arriving that very autumn. There really was no time to lose.

In July, Sir Ken Scott, the Queen's deputy Private Secretary (an old Eastern European hand, having been Ambassador to Yugoslavia) arrived on the customary recce mission.

The visit would begin with the usual formalities in Moscow and then move on to the great imperial city of St Petersburg, where the Queen would repay President Yeltsin's hospitality aboard the Royal Yacht. Sir Ken went to see the newly-elected Mayor of St Petersburg, Anatoly Sobchak, and his deputy, a former Lieutenant Colonel in the KGB called Vladimir Putin. Much of the discussion revolved around arrangements for *Britannia*. Sir Ken was delighted to be told that the Yacht would be berthed on the illustrious Embankment of the Red Fleet, on exactly the same spot where the Russian cruiser, *Aurora*, had fired the first shot of the Russian Revolution. He decided to keep pushing his luck. 'Before the revolution, of course, it was called the English Embankment,' he told Messrs Sobchak and Putin. 'Wouldn't it be nice to call it that again?' The mayor agreed that it was an excellent idea.

Getting *Britannia* to St Petersburg was relatively easy. Getting President Yeltsin on board for the Queen's return banquet was another matter. Under Soviet-era rules, Russian leaders did not attend return banquets or, indeed, accept foreign hospitality outside the Kremlin. Yet here were the British expecting the President to come all the way to St Petersburg to be fed by the Queen. 'Getting the top man out of the Kremlin for a return dinner? That hadn't happened for thirty years,' says Sir Brian Fall. 'Getting him to St Petersburg? Unheard of.' Yet the Russians agreed to it all. Yeltsin might not do it for anyone else, but he would do it for the Queen.

There would be one or two stumbling blocks. For a visit of this calibre, the Queen had requested that royal Rolls-Royces be sent ahead to both Moscow and St Petersburg (there would be no complaints about the monarch being ferried around in a Mercedes on this trip). The British Embassy arranged for the Moscow model to be displayed in the local Rolls-Royce showroom, until Sir Brian received a complaint from the royal chauffeur. 'He was wondering if the Ambassador could help him sweep the scantily clad girls off the bonnet,' he recalls. 'They were trying to put Miss Moscow on the front!'

The only notable irritant, as far as the Palace and the FCO were concerned, would occur back in Britain. Jonathan Dimbleby's new biography of the Prince of Wales, written with the Prince's help, was being serialised in the days before the visit. As a result, the Prince's complaints about an unhappy childhood were dominating the front pages of the papers, at a time when both Buckingham Palace and the British government had been hoping to focus on the historic state visit. With that in mind, the Duke of Edinburgh gave an interview to the author for the *Daily Telegraph* on the eve of the visit. In it, he delivered a thinly veiled message to the Prince – 'I've never discussed private matters and I don't think the Queen has, either' – before offering an intriguing family perspective on the forthcoming visit.

For there was an important personal dimension to this trip. When the Bolsheviks executed the Russian imperial family, the Romanovs, in 1918, they were executing the cousins of King George V, the Queen's grandfather. Many years later it would emerge that it had been the King himself, rather than his ministers, who had refused to offer sanctuary to Tsar Nicholas II. George V had been afraid of risking the contamination of Britain with the Bolshevism that was sweeping the continent.

The Queen could not possibly visit St Petersburg without visiting the tombs of the tsars at the Peter and Paul Fortress. A space had been reserved there for the imminent interment of the newly identified remains of Nicholas II. Yet this aspect of the visit would be even more personal for the Duke of Edinburgh, whose own family had been intimately connected with the Russian Revolution. The Duke was the great-great-grandson of Tsar Nicholas I and a great-nephew of Tsar Alexander III. The last Russian sovereign,

Tsar Nicholas II had been a guest at the wedding of the Duke's own parents in 1903 and his boorish behaviour had entered family legend. The Duke's mother had called Nicholas a 'stupid donkey' after he threw a white slipper at her carriage and accidentally hit her in the face. So closely related is the Duke to the tsars that he provided one of the DNA samples that enabled scientists to identify the Romanov remains. Hence he had given this visit a great deal of thought.

The contrasting fates of the British and Russian monarchies in the early part of the twentieth century, the Duke explained, were down to constitutional evolution. 'We got over the industrial revolution and the development of an urban industrial intelligentsia reasonably easily. We did because we had a constitutional monarchy,' he said. 'He [Nicholas II] was, by constitution, the autocrat.'

The Duke's primary interest was in the fate of his great-aunt, the Grand Duchess Elizabeth Feodorovna, who had founded an order of nuns in Moscow before being arrested by the Bolsheviks. 'She was eventually taken and thrown down a mineshaft in Siberia,' he said. 'They lobbed some hand grenades on top of her.'* Her heroism had a profound impact on the Duke's own mother, Princess Andrew of Greece, who founded her own order of nuns in 1949. As a result, the Duke was keen to visit not only the royal tombs in St Petersburg, but the original site of Elizabeth's convent in Moscow. He was at pains to stress that he bore no grudges. 'It was part of family folklore,' he explained. 'But I don't look at this as a family occasion. You can't condemn a whole nation for what a few extremists do or did.' He was as keen as his hosts to take a positive, forward-looking approach. 'We went through this whole drama of the collapse of the Marxist state and now we see the gradual recombining of countries that had been

* Following the 1905 assassination of her husband, Grand Duke Sergei (Tsar Nicholas II's uncle), Elizabeth Feodorovna founded Moscow's Convent of St Martha and St Mary in 1909. She was among a group of royal relatives arrested in 1918 and pushed down a mineshaft near Alapaevsk. Simon Sebag Montefiore's *The Romanovs* describes her final moments as she led a chorus of 'Lord Save Your People' while a Chekist death squad rained grenades and burning wood on her. Lenin welcomed her death, saying that 'virtue with the crown on it' was a 'greater enemy' than 'a hundred tyrant tsars'.

in contact with each other for three or four hundred years on a fairly open basis. There is tremendous potential.'

That potential was clear the moment the Queen's BAe 146* touched down at Moscow's Vnukovo Airport at 4.30 p.m. on Monday 17th October 1994. The BAe 146 might be a modest thirty-seat runaround compared to some presidential airliners, but it was escorted into Moscow by Russian SU-27 jets, which then performed a brilliant display of aerobatics overhead, an honour that had not been given to any visiting head of state since the 1970s.

The Queen was driven straight to the Kremlin where President Yeltsin and his wife, Naina, had arranged a carefully choreographed handshake in the middle of St George's Hall, the largest room in the Kremlin. The two couples entered at opposite ends of the 300-foot chamber and met for bracing handshakes halfway, beneath six 400-bulb chandeliers. Much as the British press had been relishing the prospect of a presidential bear hug, Mr Yeltsin appeared to offer a small but respectful bow, before handing the Queen a large bouquet of roses. She seemed more than usually pleased to receive them.

Those close to the Queen say that she has always had a deep respect for Boris Yeltsin. 'The Queen took a real shine to Yeltsin. She admired him,' says Sir Robert Woodard. 'I think she thought that a man who can control a country this size has to be very special.'

Less than two hours later, the Queen was expected at the Bolshoi Theatre with the Yeltsins for a performance of *Giselle*. It is a ballet that has featured more often than most on her travel (not least at Versailles, on her epic 1972 state visit to France). Sir Brian Fall reveals the reason: '*Giselle* is what you put on if you have VIPs – because it's short.' More than seventy years of communism had certainly not eroded the Russian appetite for some royal grandeur (or 'Queen bling', as one former Private Secretary calls it). Indeed, Embassy staff had pointed out to the Palace that the Russian public were very much expecting a monarch who looked like a monarch at this particular occasion, even if Mr Yeltsin would be attending the

* There are still two BAe 146 aircraft operated by the RAF's 32 (The Royal) Squadron. Despite the squadron's name, they spend most of their time flying government ministers and senior military personnel.

ballet in a lounge suit. Every gaze was fixed on what was still known as the 'Tsar's Box', as the Queen made her entry in a silk floral jacket over a long green evening dress, with white gloves, diamonds and tiara. All six tiers of the theatre rose to applaud her and carried on doing so all through the British national anthem. There would be much wearing of mink throughout this visit, too. The animal-rights lobby might have ensured that royal furs were pushed to the back of the cupboard at home, but Russia was expecting nothing less.

The first evening concluded with a British Embassy reception for a cross-section of Russian life that would have been inconceivable just a few years earlier. 'There were a lot of unreconstructed people and a lot of liberal ones,' says Sir Francis Richards, who helped prepare the guest list. 'But we never encountered any resistance.' The cellist Mstislav Rostropovich, and Yelena Bonner, widow of the dissident Andrei Sakharov, were among those invited.

The following morning, though, would present the Queen with a vivid illustration of the chaos and infighting that bedevilled Russian public life. The plan had been for her to walk across Red Square to visit the mighty onion-domed St Basil's Cathedral, hear a choir and meet the Russian public. However, one of several competing security forces claiming jurisdiction over the Queen had decided to clear the square of ordinary people in order to ensure her safety. As a result, the only people the Queen and the Duke encountered were the international media and a handful of tourists.

To make matters worse, the Mayor of Moscow, Yury Luzhkov, intervened to redirect the Queen away from St Basil's to a less interesting part of Red Square. She was shown the decidedly unimpressive Kazan Cathedral, a replica of an old Orthodox church that the mayor had recently rebuilt. 'There were moments when the whole thing went off-script,' says one member of the party. 'The Queen and Yeltsin came down the great staircase while the Great Bell of the Kremlin tolled and immediately this thug, Luzhkov, grabbed her by the arm and took her across Red Square. She was meant to be going to St Basil's to hear these wonderful singers and Luzhkov had ruined it. She never got to hear the singers.' Palace officials were incandescent. 'A complete cock-up,' one of the press team shouted at his Russian opposite number. 'She's here to meet the people, not thin air.'

The Queen and her host were getting on extremely well, regardless. Before that evening's state banquet (caviar, salmon in champagne, asparagus soup, chicken supreme and, finally, strawberry parfait) in the Kremlin's fifteenth-century Faceted Hall, the two leaders exchanged gifts. The Queen gave the president a Spode dinner service decorated with Russian double eagles in gold, and a pair of gold cufflinks. There was also a miniature walnut chest full of seeds for Mrs Yeltsin's garden. In return, Yeltsin gave the Queen a samovar (still in regular Palace use at teatime) and a bejewelled clock.

Officials glanced nervously at the President's glass. It was only three weeks since an excruciating episode during a transatlantic stopover in Ireland. Yeltsin had been supposed to have bilateral talks with the Irish Prime Minister, Albert Reynolds. Having circled inexplicably for an hour, the presidential jet had finally landed at Shannon Airport only for Yeltsin's deputy to come down the steps. His boss, he explained, would not be getting off the plane as he was 'very tired'. Yeltsin, on his first outing in a dinner jacket, was determined to be on his best behaviour for the Queen, refusing all drinks at the pre-banquet reception. He confined himself to a vodka at the start, red wine for the toasts and a little Georgian brandy at the end. The President used his speech to salute the Queen as a beacon of stability in an unstable world. 'In Russia, the Queen is seen as the personification of state wisdom, continuity of history, greatness of the nation,' he told his guests. 'Bearing your mission with dignity, Your Majesty, you confirm an important idea: monarchy can be an integral part of a democratic system of government, an embodiment of the spiritual and historic unity of a nation.'

Yeltsin appeared visibly touched by the Queen's reply. 'Times of change are not times of comfort,' she acknowledged, but she had every faith in his mission. 'The process of change has brought uncertainty and not all are convinced that this great effort will be rewarded with the success it deserves. I firmly believe it will be.'

The programme was unusually brisk, with good reason. 'You had to see a lot but not spend too long in any one place or someone would discover that some awful thing had happened there,' says Sir Brian Fall. 'There were skeletons everywhere.' One direct result of the state visit was the return of the former St Andrew's Anglican Church in Moscow to the Church of England. Shut down by the Bolsheviks, it had ended up as a communist recording studio. The Duke of Edinburgh also finally made it to the convent that his heroic great-aunt had founded before her grisly death.

The Ambassador's wife, Delmar Fall, had been closely involved in every step of the programme. For the Queen's lunch at the British Embassy, she decided to set aside protocol and avoid seating everyone according to their embassy rank. Instead, she sat the Queen next to the embassy doctor, Hugh Carpenter, a popular character among Moscow's British community. 'He was certainly not someone to be intimidated by who he was sitting next to,' she recalls. 'I remember his wife sitting across the room making hand gestures as if to say: "Stop talking so much". The Queen was very amused and said: "I must try that on Philip some time". She certainly enjoyed it.'

Once the royal tour moved on to St Petersburg, there was a marked change in atmosphere. Not only had the main political imperatives been addressed, but the crowds were larger and much more enthusiastic, a reminder of the more European character of the city. At the immense blue-and-white Catherine Palace – the Romanovs' answer to Versailles, with its Hall of Mirrors and Amber Room – the old imperial flag was flying for the first time anyone could remember. The challenge for the staff of the Hermitage was how best to show off one of the world's greatest museums in the space of an hour and a quarter. The Queen sidestepped a special exhibition on Tsar Nicholas II and Tsarina Alexandra. Diplomats – and the Queen herself – were determined that what was primarily a forward-looking tour should not become a Nicholas II memorial roadshow.

Yet the sight of *Britannia*'s Royal Barge carrying the Queen and Duke up the River Neva to the tombs of the tsars, bells ringing out along the shoreline and the sun bouncing off St Petersburg's domes and spires, was a powerful reminder of old dynastic ties. Inside the cathedral-fortress – where the future Kings Edward VII and George V attended the funeral of Tsar Alexander III a century earlier – the Queen studiously avoided either comment or expression, beyond polite interest at being informed about some building work. She could have been viewing a moderately interesting library extension in the West Midlands.

The Mayor and his protégé, Vladimir Putin, had laid on a royal lunch at another former imperial palace. There was a minor drama when the Queen's lady-in-waiting, Lady Dugdale, fell and broke her hip. The Master of the Household, Sir Simon Cooper, and *Britannia*'s captain, Robert Woodard, carried her in an oak chair to a waiting car and thence to the Royal Yacht, where she would remain in her cabin until being flown home from Helsinki three days later. Afterwards the Queen and President Yeltsin shifted the focus on to shared sacrifice at the Piskarevskoye Memorial Cemetery, the resting place of many of the estimated 1.5 million Russians killed in the three-year siege of Leningrad, one of the most destructive in history.

Woodard was struck by the sight of the two leaders paying their respects in front of a group of Royal Navy veterans, survivors of the hellish Arctic convoys: 'The Queen marched with Boris Yeltsin who was about seven feet tall – with these Russian guards who are taller than that. They marched together about 300 yards while the Funeral March from Saul was coming out of loudspeakers in the trees. And they were marching over a million dead bodies. Then they got up to the Memorial and there were some of our sailors in white berets. It was very moving.'

Britannia was about to provide the climax to the visit, though not before hosting a noisy pirate-themed children's party for the residents of a local orphanage. In the kitchens, the royal chefs were already working on a Scottish-themed state-banquet menu of medallions of salmon Glamis, roast saddle of Balmoral venison and a chocolate marquise.

As night fell on the newly renamed English Embankment, President Yeltsin, his senior ministers and the speakers of both houses of parliament came aboard for a very convivial evening. Though it has always been the convention that there are no speeches at return state banquets, the Queen decided to make a rare exception (as would happen with Nelson Mandela two years later). She had clearly talked it through with the Duke of Edinburgh. 'I could see Prince Philip looking at her very amused, holding his chin and with a twinkle in his eye,' says Delmar Fall. 'And she called for a gavel and she went "tap", "tap", "tap" – and she got up and she made a little speech. No notes!'

Sir Robert Woodard, at the far end of the table, remembers standing as the Queen raised a glass to the Russians, and then sitting down again. 'Suddenly a stun grenade went off – or so I thought! There was this huge explosion from the top of the table. And it was Boris Yeltsin bringing his fist down.' Lady Fall saw exactly what happened. 'The Queen offered the gavel to Yeltsin, through an interpreter, and he said: "Russian men don't need gavels!" And he took his fist and he thumped the table and all the glassware went everywhere. Suddenly there was this deadly silence when we all wondered "What the hell?" and then we laughed.'

It was not the drink talking. By all accounts, Yeltsin had once again been abstemious with the royal wine. He was just feeling very emotional and very Russian. With no interpreter, he proceeded to hold forth passionately (in Russian) for several minutes. Sir Robert Woodard says that the President was clearly speaking from the heart. 'I certainly felt the drink reports were over-exaggerated. In the main, you were dealing with a really brilliant character, a man full of enthusiasm,' he says. 'Yeltsin admired Her Majesty hugely. There were tears in his eyes when he left.'

There was one final piece of theatre, the traditional quayside Beating Retreat by the Band of the Royal Marines. The Queen was going to wrap up in style against the cold. 'She came downstairs and I was standing next to Prince Philip. And she was in the most gorgeous full-length fur cape,' says Lady Fall. 'I looked at him and said: "Oooh!" And he said: "Canadian!" '

The Band of the Royal Marines did not disappoint. To the Ambassador's delight, Yeltsin turned to the Queen and proclaimed: "That's the way the Russian national anthem ought to be played!" As Fall observes: 'It really was an enormous compliment.'

A Russian guard of honour returned the compliment from the quayside as *Britannia* made a floodlit departure beneath a fireworks display. There could be no grander or more dramatic exit, though it could easily have ended in embarrassment, if not disaster. Woodard was having to guide *Britannia* out of a strange harbour in darkness using out-of-date charts for navigation and with a strong tide running against him. On board was a Russian pilot, hired for his local expertise, though not his language skills. 'We went into the first corner,' says Sir Robert. 'I turned to the pilot and said: "Can I cut the corner to port?" and he said: "Da! Da!" We cut the corner. But as we did so, an officer came running up and said: "Sir, you do know that the pilot has come up to me and asked: "Which side is port?" It became a famous remark!'

Fortunately, earlier in the day, Woodard had been informed that the Russians could no longer afford to illuminate their navigation buoys at night. He had taken the precaution of sending his navigation officer down the river before to plot a route for just such an eventuality. 'I had sent him off in my barge to take back-bearings on any lights that would help us navigate. And thank goodness he did because we were navigating our way out using bus shelters and Coca-Cola hoardings!'

'We have played a card which only Britain can play,' Sir Brian wrote in his official despatch to the Foreign Secretary, Douglas Hurd. The timing, he added, had proved ideal. 'All of this happened at exactly the right time: when Russia was still in the throes of an incomplete revolution and the democrats and reformers much in need of encouragement.' The visit would resonate particularly, he said, with those Russians who neither wanted a return to old-style communism nor were impressed by the 'pushy young men in BMWs'. The winner had been Yeltsin. 'The Queen's visit gave him a rare opportunity to emphasise and celebrate the continuity of the new Russia and the old.'

Although Britain's relations with Russia might enter a downward spiral a decade later, culminating in chemical assassinations and diplomatic expulsions, the course was set fair for the next few years. 'It was enormously important. All sorts of things had gone wrong but it was very important in persuading senior Russian figures that the world had changed,' says Sir Francis Richards. 'They hadn't yet worked out what it was like to be a proper country with proper politicians. It had a catalytic role.'

It had also made Britain the envy of the other diplomatic missions. 'They just realised this was a league we played in and nobody else did,' says Sir Brian. The Ambassador and his wife would certainly notice a change. 'The Russians were very much warmer afterwards,' says Lady Fall. 'We'd go into the Kremlin and we'd always be hugged by Mrs Yeltsin.'

IRELAND, 2011

Whatever their period of office, all the officials and politicians who have worked with the Queen single out the 2011 state visit to Ireland as the work of a stateswoman. The former head of the Foreign Office, Sir

Simon Fraser, remembers it as 'the most interesting and dramatic visit' of recent years. As far as the Queen was concerned, it was also one of the most enjoyable. 'She was so excited about it and really looking forward to it. It was quite sweet,' the Duke of Cambridge said afterwards.

Having visited more countries than all her predecessors put together, the Queen had to wait until after her eighty-fifth birthday before visiting the country closest to home. The United Kingdom has just one land border, and no British monarch had crossed it in the century since her grandfather's visit in 1911. Indeed, when George V had last visited Dublin, there was no border to cross, as the Republic of Ireland did not yet exist. Ireland had been as much a part of the United Kingdom as Surrey.

The subsequent hundred years had seen partition, separation, independence and a chaotic, tempestuous, often bloody love–hate relationship. It was one characterised by ancestral bitterness – stretching back past the Potato Famine and Oliver Cromwell to the Tudors – as well as sectarian conflict and profound political distrust. At the same time, at another level, there were deep, unbreakable human bonds between the two peoples: ties of marriage, literature, sport, horses, music and even saving lives at sea. When the Irish Free State was established in 1922, the volunteers manning all the Royal National Lifeboat Institution stations around the island of Ireland saw no need to change their organisation. They had a higher calling than politics. As a result, it is still the RNLI that rescues those in peril, from Cork in the South to Portrush in the North. Similarly, there is still just the one Irish rugby team.

In a culture more fixated with symbols than most, it was the Crown that had been the ultimate emblem of Irish misery, as far as the South was concerned, its wearer the personification of one nation's injustice to another. Conversely, in the North, the Crown was not far below the Almighty, in the Unionist pantheon. Through the worst of 'the Troubles' – the thirty-year paramilitary conflict that left more than 3,500 dead (more than half of them civilians) – the Queen must have despaired of ever setting foot in a country that she had so often glimpsed from a distance. The conflict had been deeply personal at times. Prince Philip's uncle, Earl Mountbatten, and members of his family had been killed by the IRA on holiday in Ireland in 1979. As Head of the Armed Forces and of the Royal Ulster Constabulary, the

Queen was fully attuned to the risks and sacrifices made by those serving in her name. She had endured more bomb scares and threats on her own life than she cared to remember. On one occasion, she was advised to move out of Buckingham Palace because of credible threats of a mortar attack (she refused). In 1982, the IRA had blown up her Household Cavalry as they processed from their barracks in Hyde Park for their daily Guard Change. 'It was a nice, sunny day and suddenly one heard this explosion one heard all the time in Northern Ireland,' recalls the man who was in command that day, Brigadier (then Lt-Col) Andrew Parker Bowles.* 'One of the barriers opened and someone said "They've blown up the Guard". So we all set off – all the farriers were wearing their leather aprons, naked to the waist – and we all ran down to where the smoke was rising. The first horse I saw was Sefton. He had a bloody great hole in him and I made a mental note I'd never see Sefton again. But he managed to pull through.' Later on that day, Parker Bowles spoke to the Queen who did not mince her words. She told him it was 'the most ghastly day of my life'.

The Good Friday Agreement of 1998 would change all that. In bringing together the British and Irish governments and all the main political parties of Northern Ireland, it laid the foundations for a peaceful power-sharing future and secured an end to the worst of the violence. Yet it would still take a further decade before all sides felt confident that they could lead what might be termed a 'normal' life. If the island of Ireland really was going to draw a line under the past, however, nothing would say so with quite the same impact as a state visit by the Queen.

There had been a long series of stepping stones, starting all the way back in 1993, when the President of the Republic, Mary Robinson, had met the monarch during an official visit to London. There had been no issue whatsoever about the Irish head of state travelling to the UK. Yet the converse was still unthinkable. In 1998, the Queen and the new President, Mary McAleese, met near Ypres in Belgium for the unveiling of a memorial to the nearly 50,000 Irishmen who died in Flanders fighting for King and country in the First World War.

* On July 20, 1982, twin bombs in Hyde Park and Regents Park killed a total of 11 men and seven horses. Parker Bowles sought to erect a memorial to his dead men but came up against ministerial opposition. 'The politicians didn't want another memorial. So I went to the Queen Mother – who went to the Queen,' he says. 'If you stop in Hyde Park, it's there.'

Other members of the family would make visits in connection with their various patronages and charities. For now, the Queen knew she was still at the back of the queue. But she had made it very clear indeed to her ministers that she was ready and willing. Unlike her first visit to Germany, there was no nervousness at the Palace about this idea. On being despatched to Dublin as Britain's new ambassador in 2009, Julian King* was informed that the Palace and the British government were keen to push for a state visit. The timing was in the hands of the Irish. 'There were one or two very outline ideas for a programme,' says King, 'but there was no guarantee it was going to happen.'

Britain was doing its best to be a good neighbour. At the end of 2010, as Ireland struggled to recover from the financial crash, Dublin was finding it increasingly hard to get a loan from the usual lenders, when the British Chancellor, George Osborne, offered to lend £3.2 billion. It was snapped up. Even so, the Irish government was still stalling on that invitation at the start of 2011. The crumbling Fianna Fáil government of Brian Cowen was voicing reservations about a royal visit until certain judicial reforms had been completed in the North. Fortunately for the monarch, she had an important ally in the Republic: President McAleese. The former university academic only had a matter of months to go before the end of her second term as President and she was not going to let her successor have the pleasure of welcoming the Queen if she could possibly help it. This did the trick. The invitation was eventually issued and accepted just days before a change of Irish government and the arrival of Enda Kenny as the new Prime Minister.

Planning could begin in earnest, and it was clear that the Queen had her own ideas. 'Up until that stage, outline ideas had focussed on a short visit of around one and a half days in Dublin,' says Sir Julian King. That was certainly not what the Queen had in mind. For most of the time, Palace officials spend their days trying to protect the royal timetable and to limit demands on the Queen's time. On this occasion, says the former Ambassador, the Queen was keen to extend the arrangements. 'It became very clear to me very early on that the Palace were interested in a longer and bigger visit if the Irish were open to that. Not everybody on the Irish side had been thinking on that kind of scale!'

* Knighted before his fiftieth birthday, Sir Julian went on to become Ambassador to Paris. In 2016, after the Brexit vote, he was appointed Britain's last European Commissioner.

In the heated debate that followed the announcement, some commentators argued that a state visit was a case of going too far too soon. Surely, it was argued, the Queen should make a private visit first, to test the waters? At the Palace, however, there was a very clear desire to get on with it and to do this properly. That meant that one of the Queen's first engagements would be a wreath-laying at the Garden of Remembrance, the memorial to all those who had perished in the heroic struggles against the British Crown. This was an integral part of the itinerary for any state visitor to Ireland. Some hardline nationalists were appalled at the idea of the old enemy paying respects, yet it would surely have offended republican sentiment very much more if the Queen did not go there. It would be like a state visitor to London boycotting the Grave of the Unknown Warrior at Westminster Abbey. Both sides agreed it was essential.

Then the discussions threw up a more original suggestion: a royal visit to Croke Park. The home of the Gaelic Athletic Association had been the scene of the original Bloody Sunday. In November 1920, the killing of fourteen British agents in Dublin had been swiftly followed by a savage revenge attack on the crowd at the Gaelic football match at Croke Park. British 'Black and Tan' auxiliaries opened fire on the crowd, killing fourteen civilians and injuring many more. There are few sites more sacred to Irish nationalism, and yet the Irish were keen for the Queen to go there.

More than a thousand international press had been accredited ahead of the Queen's arrival on 17th May 2011. The monarchy, like much of Britain,was still on a high, following the wedding of the Duke and Duchess of Cambridge a month before. Ahead of his marriage, the Duke had been mulling over what to wear, given his various military appointments. As a serving officer in the Royal Air Force, he would be expected to wear his RAF uniform. The Queen, however, had other ideas. She had just appointed him Colonel of the Irish Guards. 'I was given a categorical: "No, you'll wear this!"' as the Duke explained afterwards. Whether her upcoming visit to Ireland had influenced the Queen is unclear, but it was an Irish Guards officer standing at the altar of Westminster Abbey on 29th April 2011.

Three weeks later, the bookmakers were offering bets on the Queen's choice of clothes as the royal BAe 146 flew into Baldonnel's

Casement Aerodrome, named after Sir Roger Casement, the Irish republican hero executed for treason in the midst of the First World War. Even the most blasé old pros on the press grandstand could not resist a cheer as the cabin door opened. The Queen was wearing emerald-green (or 'jade' as a Palace official described it). Though it had understandably been the bookies' favourite, it underlined the drama of the moment. As one reporter remarked, the monarch could almost have got back on the plane there and then: 'Job done.'

Accompanied by the Presidential Motorcycle Squadron of the Irish Cavalry Corps, the Queen and Prince Philip were driven 10 miles to Áras an Uachtaráin, the presidential residence on the outskirts of Dublin. The Queen's first glimpse of Ireland was a strange one. The route was lined with crowd barriers, behind which stood no crowds because it had been declared a sterile zone. The government had laid on the largest security operation in living memory, involving 10,000 troops and police (1,000 more than the total strength of the Irish Defence Forces). It had been decided that the best place for the public to catch a glimpse of the Queen was on television. At the front door of the former viceregal residence, it was hard to tell who was more elated as President McAleese (in fuchsia) welcomed her opposite number, inviting the Queen to plant an Irish oak, before a lunch of smoked chicken, turbot and buttermilk ice cream.

The Queen had chosen an appropriately neutral white dress made by her own dresser, Angela Kelly, for the engagement that was to follow. The public had been kept at least 300 yards away from Dublin's Garden of Remembrance, for the most meaningful moment of a tour already laden with symbolism. The distant protests of a small republican demonstration in O'Connell Street and the clatter of news and security helicopters were briefly drowned out by a sound that would have kick-started civil disorder just a few years earlier: 'God Save the Queen' ringing out over Ireland's answer to the Cenotaph. The Queen then placed her wreath against the memorial to 'all those who gave their lives in the cause of Irish freedom', took three steps back and bowed. It was no perfunctory nod of the head – as might be expected from a courtier at the Palace. This was a very clear and pronounced leaning forward from the waist up. The monarch who bows to no one was bowing to the heroes of Irish nationalism. She had still not been heard to utter a word. Few people had actually seen her in the flesh. Yet a bumper daytime television audience had been glued to it all, and the papers had their story. 'Job done,' once more.

The small republican demonstrations had dwindled to nothing the following day as the royal convoy made for Croke Park. This equally momentous engagement had been so thoroughly trailed and dissected that it almost felt scripted. It is hard to convey a grand sense of occasion – indeed of genuine history – in an empty stadium; all the harder when the stadium is one of the largest in Europe. The Queen emerged from the players' tunnel to be greeted by a group of children and was shown a video about Gaelic football. The president of the sport's governing body made a dignified speech, which did not gloss over the atrocity of 1920 but did not labour the point, either. Everyone knew why the Queen was here, and it was not through a love of Irish football. 'In our shared history, there have been many tragic events that have hurt us all – including those who died in this place,' said Christy Cooney. But there was magnanimity, too: 'Your Majesty, your presence does honour to our association, to its special place in Irish life, and to its hundreds of thousands of members. Today will go down in the history of the GAA.'

The big surprise of the day would come not at the football stadium, but later. The superior power of a stateswoman's wardrobe over that of any statesman was amply demonstrated as the Queen arrived at the state banquet at Dublin Castle. Angela Kelly, something of a specialist in diplomatic embroidery, had designed her a dress hand-stitched with 2,091 shamrocks. Unlike those grand entrances in Germany or Russia, it was not a night to bring out the grandest specimens in the jewellery box but, rather, the most appropriate ones. Along with a new Irish harp brooch, designed specially for the occasion, the Queen wore the Girls of Great Britain and Ireland Tiara. It had been a wedding present to Queen Mary in 1893 who, in turn, had made it a wedding present to Princess Elizabeth.

As the Queen rose to address the guests in the onetime citadel of British power in Ireland, there was intense interest in the content and tone of one of the most important banquet speeches of her reign. Any overseas speech by the monarch is delivered on government advice, usually with her Foreign Secretary in attendance. For this one, very unusually, her Prime Minister had come along, too.

The Ambassador had done some extensive homework. 'We spoke to some well-known Irish writers and historians about what images it might mean for them,' says Sir Julian King. Ultimately, though, it had to be personal for it to work. 'It was done very closely with the Household and with the Queen. Not a lot of time was spent with bureaucrats in the Foreign Office.'

Very few knew what was coming next. '*A Uachtaráin agus a chairde*,' the Queen began. Her words – 'President and friends' – were properly pronounced and greeted with an instant round of applause. Pop-eyed President McAleese's repeated mouthing of 'Wow!' would become as much a part of the story as the Queen's debut in Gaelic. The gesture almost – though not quite – upstaged the definitive statement of the tour. After a pointed reference to the 'importance of being able to bow to the past, but not be bound by it', the Queen was frank: 'It is a sad and regrettable reality that, through history, our islands have experienced more than their fair share of heartache, turbulence and loss. These events have touched us all, many of us personally, and are a painful legacy.' That would be as close as she came to mentioning Lord Mountbatten.

'To all those who have suffered as a consequence of our troubled past, I extend my sincere thoughts and deep sympathy. With the benefit of historical hindsight, we can all see things which we would wish had been done differently or not at all.' For a sovereign who is so often called upon to apologise for things she hasn't done – and for which she cannot apologise without ministerial instruction – this was, nonetheless, the closest to an apology that anyone was expecting. There was praise for her speech across the Irish media. Perhaps the most notable reaction was a single word from the Sinn Fein President, Gerry Adams. Amid a predictable demand for a full apology from the British monarch, he managed to acknowledge that her words had been 'genuine'. Praise indeed.

From then on, the rest of the tour would be a stroll, a wholly good-natured celebration of those same human connections that the Queen regards as the greatest strength of her Commonwealth. Ireland's love of Guinness and horseracing were saluted with a visit to the original Guinness factory and a trip to the Irish National Stud. Instead of a return banquet for the President, which could not have been anything other than an anticlimax, the Queen laid on a concert. Among the star turns was local boy-band, Westlife. Sir Julian King acknowledges that a dinner would have been considerably cheaper for the taxpayer, but insists that the effect was worth it. After the sterile security arrangements up to that point, it was, he says, electrifying when the Queen escorted the President onto the concert stage: 'I don't think anybody quite anticipated the roar of approval that came from the crowd. That was almost a heart-stopping moment.'

As so often happens on a state visit, the atmosphere and tempo changed completely outside the capital. Security was significantly less paranoid in the second city of Cork, where large crowds were finally allowed near the royal visitors as they toured the English Market. The Queen struck up such a rapport with garrulous fishmonger Pat O'Connell* that he later received an invitation to a royal reception in London.

When she passed through the ancient town of Cashel, its Sinn Fein mayor, Michael Browne, was in the greeting line and became the first member of his party to shake the monarch's hand. 'I just said to her: "Welcome to Cashel, Your Majesty and I hope you enjoy your stay",' he said afterwards. 'No more, no less.' Browne was terminally ill with just a few weeks to live, yet his party hierarchy were furious. In a sorry footnote to the tour, he was later suspended from the party for his courtesy. It would prove to be a serious misjudgement. 'Sinn Fein recognised that they hadn't caught the mood because there were some huge approval ratings for the visit – 80 or 90 per cent,' says Sir Julian King. 'Among Sinn Fein supporters there was a massive majority too.'

The visit would resonate at many levels, its impact felt long after the Queen's departure. From the opening of the first British Irish Chamber of Commerce to the invitation to the Irish Ambassador to Britain to lay a wreath at the Cenotaph on each Remembrance Sunday, that green dress, that bow and those few words of Gaelic had been a catalyst for so many fresh initiatives, large and small, on either side of the Irish Sea. Once again, it had been at a human level that the tour had its greatest effect. 'Some people can be cynical about large staged state occasions but this definitely caught a moment' says Sir Julian. 'An Irish friend said to me that it was "OK to feel good about the Brits".'

* The Queen much enjoyed O'Connell's reference to the unlovely monkfish as a 'mother-in-law fish'.

Even after a life spent making and being history, it had been a genuine thrill for the Queen. 'This was like a big door opening up to her that had been locked for so long,' said the Duke of Cambridge. 'And now she has been able to see what's behind the door.'

The following year, King would find himself on the other side of the border as Director-General of the Northern Ireland Office. He was there to welcome the Queen yet again, this time as her Diamond Jubilee tour of the United Kingdom took her to Northern Ireland. There were many more happy landmarks during the visit, including the Queen's first big Northern Irish walkabout. Held in the grounds of Stormont, it involved such a large crowd – more than 20,000 people, plus picnics – that she eventually had to meet them in an open car. Shortly before the visit, says Sir Julian, he received an extraordinary call. Sinn Fein, it transpired, would not be so hostile to this visit. Having punished the late Mayor of Cashel for having the temerity to meet the Queen, the Sinn Fein leaders were now wondering if there might be any chance of a royal introduction after all. 'They realised they had misread the public mood,' says Sir Julian. 'Gerry Adams and Martin McGuinness reached out – to say would it be possible to meet the Queen at some point?'

In 2012, one of the defining moments in Irish history took place as McGuinness, the former terrorist and IRA capo-turned-politician, finally shook the Queen's hand. Many people who have been introduced to the Queen at some point in their lives will keep a framed photograph of that moment in pride of place. On his own desk, Sir Julian King keeps a photo of the Queen meeting Martin McGuinness instead.

In this isle of sometimes fratricidal symbolism, it was the Queen's handshake with McGuinness that was the definitive illustration of the new normal. And it was all because of that state visit the year before. This harmonious mood could not continue indefinitely at a political level, of course. There would be plenty of bilateral setbacks, not least the issue of the UK-Irish border in a post-Brexit era. Even so, the Queen's visit has recalibrated the relationship permanently. There will always be rows but henceforth, they will be conducted at a different pitch.

'I think it was the most transformative bit of diplomacy I have seen. It was amazing,' says David Cameron. Tellingly, he adds that the Queen was faintly embarrassed by the adulation. 'She was, as ever, not sure what all the fuss was about.' Cameron remembers talking to the Queen about her historic handshake with the leader of an organisation that had once been hell-bent on exterminating her entire family. The Prime Minister remarked that her encounter with McGuinness had been a very great milestone of modern diplomacy.

The Queen's reply sums up her modest, no-nonsense approach to a job she has been doing longer than most people can remember. 'What was I meant to do?' she replied. 'Of course I shook his hand. It would be awkward not to.'

Chapter 12

THE PRINCE OF WALES

'Man-eating spiders and acid-squirting caterpillars'

KING IN WAITING

Years of delicate diplomacy and hard graft have led up to this moment. All those meetings and receptions and dinners that the Prince of Wales has had with thousands of politicians and tens of thousands of officials in dozens of countries over half a century are about to be put to the test. All the walkabouts, the interminable speeches, the voyages, the long flights, the reluctant photocalls, the funny hats, the remorseless menus and the considerable dangers (including near-misses with both elephant and buffalo) have all, ultimately, been aimed at this morning's meeting. No one is taking anything for granted as the leaders of the fifty-three nations of the Commonwealth gather for their 'retreat' at Windsor Castle. It comes the day after the Queen's frank, heartfelt appeal to the heads of government to endorse her son and heir as the next Head of the Commonwealth. She has given the politicians the run of both Buckingham Palace and Windsor Castle for their summit. Yet she knows, from long experience, that there can be no complacency in matters involving a querulous organisation with opaque, imprecise rules.

A few hours later the issue is resolved in gloriously anticlimactic fashion. There is no puff of white smoke, no Oscars-style ceremonial opening of an envelope. Instead, a two-sided 'Leaders' Statement' is handed out to the media. Paragraph three states simply: 'The next Head of the Commonwealth shall be His Royal Highness The Prince of Wales.' It is hardly a surprise that his name is there. There was never any other candidate anyway. The key word, though, is 'shall'. There is no ambiguity. An organisation that is usually much happier voicing nebulous aspirations, rather than concrete results, could not be clearer on the issue. This has been a topic so delicate that royal officials have refused to discuss it in public for decades. Now it has just been resolved in a sentence. Whenever the time comes, King Charles III will be the first monarch to be automatically proclaimed Head of the Commonwealth. It is a very big deal – a landmark in the modern royal story. Yet the eventual official Commonwealth communiqué on the 2018 summit would actually devote more words to a modest new funding initiative for small island economies than any mention of the future Head.

Almost any other international organisation – be it sporting, political or economic – can expect plenty of infighting each time it goes through a change of leadership, particularly if there has not actually been any change at the top for more than sixty-five years. Yet here is the future leadership of an organisation comprising 2.4 billion people and it has apparently been resolved with the sort of 100 per cent agreement that we might expect from a people's congress in North Korea. At the prime-ministerial press conference that follows, there is only one line of questioning from the media: surely there must have been some sort of argument? This is the Commonwealth, after all. But no. Theresa May describes the decision as 'unanimous'.

It is by far the most significant step to date in the Prince's gradual evolution from Heir to the Throne to King-in-waiting. It is also a very robust validation of all that the Queen has done for this organisation over the years. In recent years Palace officials have talked of the 'Team Windsor' strategy, of the Queen's desire to have a synchronised royal operation across the generations. The monarchy has not worked like this since the reign of Victoria. It has always been designed to run as a two-tier organisation, with the sovereign running the main show and the Heir to the Throne running a self-sufficient support act.* In recent years it has been run as a three-tier operation, with a gradual transfer of duties – though not of powers – from the Queen to the Prince of Wales. Royal commentators, inevitably, look for differences between the respective modus operandi of mother and son. The two unquestionably have different tastes, different styles and different outlooks shaped by different childhoods. The Queen likes her menus in French, her horses on the flat and her papers in red boxes. The Prince prefers food in English and horses that jump, while his boxes are green. However, to view them as an either/or is to miss the point. While the Queen is comfortably the longest-reigning monarch in British history, the Prince is easily the longest-serving Heir to the Throne. He has been a full-time figure in public life since leaving the Royal Navy in 1976 – longer than almost any British politician. Between the two of them, they have well over a century of experience on which to draw. That the Queen has made such an impact on the world is in no small part down to the Duke of Edinburgh, their children and now their grandchildren, along with her mother, her sister and her cousins. That the Queen views the Commonwealth as her 'family of nations' is because her dealings with it – and with the rest of the planet – have so often been conducted through her own family.

PRINCE CHARMING

Ahead of that 2018 summit, some political commentators and critics of the Prince of Wales had warned that the Commonwealth nations would not take kindly to the British Crown interfering in its future leadership arrangements. One newspaper claimed that the Prince of Wales had not shown enough interest in the job; that he had not done

* The monarchy, with the exception of the Prince of Wales and his family, is funded primarily by the Sovereign Grant. This consists of 15 per cent of the surplus of the Crown Estate (increased to 25 per cent for ten years from 2017 to cover the refurbishment of Buckingham Palace – yielding £76.1 million in 2017-18). The monarch also receives the surplus from the thirteenth-century, 46,000-acre Duchy of Lancaster (£20.1 million in 2017–2018) and income from private investments. The Prince of Wales, his wife, his sons plus dependants are funded by the surplus of the fourteenth-century, 130,000-acre Duchy of Cornwall (£22 million in 2017-18).

enough to deserve it. Yet, those making these arguments, like generals fighting the previous war, had not noticed that the world takes a different view of the Prince of Wales these days. The old narratives – that he is either a restless royal meddler or half of the most famous marriage breakdown in history – are both well out of date as the Prince enters his eighth decade. He is as busy as ever, but contented and, increasingly, seen as an extension of the Queen, a *de facto* head of state without in any way being a replacement. He can stand in for his mother without encroaching on her dignity or treading on her toes. That is because all this has happened with her blessing.

A few months before the London summit, a distinctive new type of royal tour unfolds in Asia – the semi-state visit. In the space of a fortnight, the Prince and the Duchess of Cornwall will undertake more than fifty different engagements in four Commonwealth countries. The idea has been to create extra momentum ahead of the summit and to secure the enthusiastic involvement of the most important Commonwealth nation of all – India.

Day One kicks off in a sweltering Singapore, with the Prince and the Duchess setting the pace from the outset. In the first few hours the Prince meets the President and Prime Minister of Singapore, pays his respects at the country's Cenotaph, attends an inter-faith event at a local mosque. He then visits a nature reserve which is going to provide the photo of the day, but the Prince wisely keeps his distance when a game warden plucks a snake from a nearby tree. It looks suspiciously as if it might have been put there for his benefit and is a harmless bronzeback. Even so, the Prince is content just to look. As the royal tour doctor, Professor Charles Deakin, later explains: 'On the whole, it's best not to touch snakes on tour.' The Duchess peels off for a separate engagement devoted to one of her key concerns, improving child literacy.

Every day of this tour, and every other tour, will involve this blend of bilateral schmoozing, princely passions, a couple of photo-opportunities (seldom enjoyed) and a small element of sightseeing, plus the occasional grand set-piece event. Whenever possible, lunch will be omitted from the schedule. The Prince takes a dim view of lunch. 'I'm like a camel,' he is fond of saying, often to the chagrin of those in the entourage who do not feel very camel-like by the time they get to lunchtime. The Duchess of Cornwall clearly disagrees, too, having become the proud patron of a charity dedicated to food and friendship that calls itself The Big Lunch. The Prince prefers a very small lunch, if there must be lunch at all, usually a quick egg sandwich in the back of the royal car.

Day One concludes with a presidential dinner of wagyu beef and fried lobster, at which the Prince talks at length about Singapore's part in the Commonwealth story. He points out that the very first Commonwealth Heads of Government Meeting was held here and talks of old links with Britain. He also recalls being entertained on one of his first visits to the country, in the days of Lee Kuan Yew, the father of the current Prime Minister. 'I seem to recall it was described as "a small lunch" in the programme, but it turned out to include over twenty courses!' he says. Therein, perhaps, lies the key to the princely dislike of big meals in the middle of the day. It's an engaging speech, gently reminding the audience that the Prince's local connections go right back to the man revered as the founder of modern Singapore.

The following day includes a visit to a wet-fish market, inner-city gardening projects and a tour of a major research centre established by the British entrepreneur, James Dyson, who employs more than a thousand people here. The Prince poses for the photographers as he brandishes a Dyson vacuum cleaner, and is taken into an acoustic test centre lined with rather alarming sound insulation. 'Oh Lord,' he jokes. 'The eggbox treatment!' There's a lunchtime visit to a restaurant that employs young people from troubled backgrounds (mineral water only for the guest of honour) and then a tour of the grand old buildings that used to house Singapore's Supreme Court and its government. These have been converted into a civic centre and the country's new National Gallery. Unlike its namesake in London, this one has no 'monstrous carbuncle' – as the Prince famously described the proposed extension of London's National Gallery in 1984 – and its French architect turns out to be a fan of the Prince's views on architecture. To cap it all, he is shown the room where his favourite uncle, Lord Mountbatten, took the Japanese surrender in 1945. It would be hard to contrive an engagement that ticks more princely boxes. The Duchess, meanwhile, is touring a community centre where she turns her hand to art, flower-arranging and cookery and drops in on a yoga class for senior citizens. They all obediently freeze in position as she walks in. She spots a 'back brick' and tells her guide that she never travels without one. 'Healthy ageing – that's what we all need!' she says cheerfully.

The British High Commissioner's residence is packed on two floors for an evening reception of several hundred people, all of whom will get a royal handshake and a chat. Again there is a big Queen-and-Commonwealth dimension to the evening. The royal couple meet a local Queen's Young Leader, a winner of the Queen's Commonwealth Essay Prize and Dr Anthony Yee, chairman of the local branch of the Royal Commonwealth Society. His organisation virtually disappeared, he says, when British foreign policy switched its focus from the Commonwealth to Europe. Now, after Britain's Brexit referendum, it is thriving again.

From Singapore, the Prince's RAF Voyager (the newish fuel tanker that doubles up as a VIP aircraft for British government use) flies on to Brunei, home of the staunchly Anglophile Sultan of Brunei. This is home to 750 members of the British Armed Forces – many of them Gurkhas – who help protect the Sultan's borders. After a parade and a trip to the British High Commission, the couple are due at the Sultan of Brunei's Palace, the gold-domed Istana Nurul Iman. Visitors walk through a series of fountain-filled courtyards into a densely carpeted cross between a luxury hotel and a university campus. Unseen is the Sultan's famous car collection in the voluminous underground garages below. The two royal families are old friends. 'You don't look a day older,' snorts the Prince as he is greeted by the Sultan. The Duchess disappears for separate talks with the Raja Isteri, the Queen consort. Later, they all meet up with the extended Royal Family for what is on the itinerary as 'tea', but is closer to a state banquet. In the octagonal dining room, beneath an eclectic art collection including a Picasso, the fifty guests sit at round tables. The royal staff have just been through with a ruler, measuring a gap of precisely 10 inches between the armrests of every royal chair. Umpteen courses, including lobster dumplings, beef floss and banana in coconut cream, are served on gold plates. The Sultan has arranged a similarly extensive spread in an adjacent courtyard for the rest of the British entourage, right down to the bag-carriers and camera crews. There are few takers for the RAF's Dundee cake as everyone climbs back on board the Voyager to fly on to Kuala Lumpur.

Malaysia is a major Commonwealth economy – and a monarchy to boot – which has never been visited by the Prince before, partly because of the country's mercurial bilateral relationship with Britain. However, the Prince's reputation has preceded him at the Islamic Arts Museum. Everyone is well aware of his long track record in promoting links between Islam and the West, and he has even brought along a senior academic, Dr Afifi al-Akiti, from his Oxford Centre for Islamic Studies. There is big applause when the Prince unveils his own signature in Arabic (he was practising it the night before) and then makes a speech about the contribution of Islamic scholars to geometric understanding. From eternal truths about cosmic patterns, he moves swiftly on to drains and road-building at a conference on town planning. He is equally in his element here, too, and has brought along Jeremy Cross from his Prince's Foundation for Building Community, although the Prince does most of the talking. 'I've been trying for years to persuade the utility companies to put their cables and everything else in one trench so that they don't keep digging up the road,' he tells one group of town planners as he goes on to outline his philosophy. 'We should always start by putting the human being – the pedestrian – at the centre of things so that you have a walkable, liveable area that's attractive.'

He is soon out of the capital, Kuala Lumpur, and on his way to a university campus run by the University of Nottingham. It is staging the first ever Commonwealth Youth Summit, and the Prince is welcomed like a rock star as he appears on the balcony of the main building and then works his way through to the main hall. On to a research centre and another engagement that could hardly be more him. The research centre runs the 'Forgotten Foods Network', dedicated to creating new food sources from neglected crops that were used by the Mayans, Aztecs and other ancient cultures. The Prince, who has signs banning genetically modified crops at his Highgrove home, is thrilled. He tastes experimental dishes such as dragonfruit tortellini with turmeric yogurt and a curry-flavoured crisp made from desert weed. 'I'm waiting for an explosion,' he says excitedly.

Next stop is tea at the Agong's Palace with the King of Malaysia, Sultan Muhammad V (the throne rotates between the country's nine royal houses). They have plenty to discuss. They last met in 2015 when the King visited the Prince's Islamic centre in Oxford, a side of his life that is becoming quite a theme on this tour. Few Western VIPs come here with this depth of knowledge about Islamic and Malaysian culture. It helps to explain why there is such a big turnout for the main event of the tour. The UK has organised a series of events around the sixtieth anniversary of independence for the former Federation of Malaya. It has been a turbulent six decades – at one point Malaysia had a 'Buy British last' trade boycott – but now relations are thriving. The Prince is the host at a black-tie UK banquet for 550 leading national figures, among them Jimmy Choo, the Malaysian-born shoe legend who moved to Britain as a struggling student. He has never forgotten that he was only able to start his shoe empire thanks to a £40-a-week grant from the Prince's Trust. No wonder he remains eternally grateful to the Prince, whom he proudly refers to as his 'godbrother'.

Most unusually, to the delight of British diplomats, all nine of the country's extremely competitive royal houses are in the same room tonight, along with the Prime Minister and most of the government. The turnout far exceeds a recent dinner for President Hollande of France. The Malaysian press are drawing comparisons with the last visit of a similar magnitude – that of President Obama. It is clear that, as far as Malaysia is concerned, the Prince is a state visitor in all but name.

The British High Commissioner, Malaysian-born Victoria Treadell, has organised a suitably bilateral menu of Scottish smoked salmon with Malaysian lime and 'Rendang beef Wellington'. Two Irish Guardsmen have just been extracted from a jungle training exercise in Thailand and flown up here in ceremonial uniform and bearskins to lend an extra royal flourish to the proceedings.

In his speech, the Prince hails Malaysia as a 'powerful model' to the region and talks up its close ties with Britain in defence, education and business, as well as its importance to the Commonwealth. He reminds his audience of what can be achieved by motivated young people, pointing to the example of a beaming Jimmy Choo. Many in the room had no idea of the key role that the Prince has played in helping one of Malaysia's most famous brand names get off the ground. The evening has exceeded Foreign Office expectations.

There will be several trips into the depths of this large nation of states and sultanates. The Prince flies north to extend birthday greetings to the Sultan of Perak, an Oxford-and Harvard-educated ex-banker who lives in another gold-domed palace, and thence to a wildlife conference in Royal Belum State Park. Afterwards he is taken for a boat ride to look for wildlife in the rainforest around the lake. Thanks to the armed guards combing the forest for anything resembling a security threat, there isn't a creature to be seen.

There is also a visit to a Commonwealth cemetery in Taiping. Wherever they go in the world, the Royal Family will first consult the Commonwealth War Graves Commission, which honours 1.7 million Commonwealth war dead in 23,000 locations across more than 150 nations and territories. In this one cemetery alone lie 864 Commonwealth troops who died fighting the Japanese in the Second World War. A lone piper, in Malaysian uniform, plays a faultless lament. The Prince pauses at the grave of Squadron Leader Arthur Scarf, VC, who died in 1941 as the Japanese were advancing on Singapore. Having taken to the skies in the RAF's only airworthy Blenheim bomber, he was mortally wounded but managed to get his crew home unscathed. Among the medical team working on him was his pregnant wife, who gave blood in a desperate but hopeless attempt to save him and then lost her baby soon afterwards. His headstone reads: 'His love of life was only exceeded by the courage encompassing his death.' The cemetery is beautifully maintained, as these places always are, a source of profound solace to loved ones far away. As the nearby headstone of Warrant Officer Class 1 James Ednie of the Black Watch puts it: 'Unforgotten. A little plot for ever Scotland.' The Prince is momentarily speechless, as moved as everyone else as he walks down the rows of those who fell in the service of King and country.

This tour should also have included Burma, but that has fallen off the schedule following the recent persecution of its Rohingya Muslim minority. So the Prince and the Duchess fly home via India and a meeting with the most powerful man in the Commonwealth, Indian Prime Minister Narendra Modi. Of the thousands of handshakes on this tour, this is the most important. It was India that led to the creation of the modern Commonwealth and that today accounts for half its population. Delhi has rather lost interest of late, seeing the Commonwealth as a diminished entity with some awkward colonial baggage. It has been nearly a decade since an Indian Prime Minister last attended a Commonwealth summit. On behalf of the Queen, the

Prince formally invites Modi to London – an invitation that would not have been offered unless the Prince was expecting a 'Yes'. It is a coup for both the British government, as hosts, and for the Commonwealth.

The Prince and the Duchess return home in time for Remembrance Sunday at the Cenotaph, where the Prince will stand in for the Queen once more. There has been no diminution of the Queen's immense global stature. Yet the aura around the Prince has unquestionably changed in recent years. He is no longer regarded as an understudy, a substitute, a probationer. World leaders now see him as one of their own.

APPRENTICE

The Prince's first overseas tour would come at the age of five, when he and three-year-old Princess Anne sailed off in the brand-new Royal Yacht *Britannia* to meet the Queen and the Duke of Edinburgh on the homebound stage of their great Coronation tour of the Commonwealth. Thereafter there was little travelling further than Scotland or the Isle of Wight until the Prince reached the age of seventeen. He was then despatched to spend two terms at Timbertop, the Outward Bound arm of Australia's prestigious Geelong Grammar School. Though it involved a lot of rough living under canvas and some memorably unpleasant insects, the Prince would look back on it as the happiest part of his education. Compared to the spartan conditions at his Scottish public school, Gordonstoun, it was delightful, as he informed family and friends – including the Prime Minister's wife. Lord (Robin) Butler, who served as Private Secretary to Harold Wilson, says there was some confusion in Downing Street when Mary Wilson received a letter from Australia with no address, but clearly from someone who knew her well enough to sign off as 'Yours, Charles'. 'The staff went to Mary and she at once realised it was from Prince Charles,' says Lord Butler. 'The very fact he felt warm enough to write to her says something.'

The Prince would retain a lifelong bond with Australia, and returned in 1967 on his first official overseas visit in order to represent the Queen at the funeral of former Prime Minister Harold Holt. Having been invested as Prince of Wales at Caernarfon Castle in

1969, he would now begin travelling in earnest. Although his finals were fast approaching at Cambridge University in May 1970, the Prince was still expected to accompany his parents and sister to Australia and New Zealand on that lively tour during which the 'walkabout' entered the English language. He would return alone, via Japan, to attend Expo 70 in Tokyo and have dinner with Emperor Hirohito and the Imperial Family. No sooner had he graduated from Cambridge than the process of moulding a future Head of the Commonwealth began in earnest.

On 23rd June 1970, the Prince was invited to spend a day at Marlborough House, the home of the Commonwealth Secretariat. Files in the Commonwealth archives show that it was no mere courtesy visit. 'The Prince does <u>not</u> particularly need to meet young people during his visit,' said an internal memo. He had clearly been well briefed in advance – perhaps even by the Queen – because no sooner had he sat down for lunch than the Prince began grilling the Secretary-General, Arnold Smith, on the upcoming Commonwealth summit in Singapore the following year. He was especially keen to find out whether a decision had been made on the Queen's attendance. Given the Queen's eternal displeasure at not being asked, it is more than tempting to regard this as a planted question. Smith diplomatically replied that 'no decision had been taken'.

The Prince voiced his concern (one he would be voicing for the next fifty years) that young people seemed 'pretty indifferent' to the Commonwealth and that it was receiving hostile treatment in the British media. He was also keen to find out more about India's views on the organisation.

This was certainly not small talk. During his visit to the economics department of Marlborough House, a lively discussion ensued when the Prince asked whether some countries had been given independence too soon. One official, a Mr Kellock, firmly rejected that idea, saying that 'the timing was right; it was the preparation that had been wrong'.

Clearly Smith and his team wanted the Prince onside as a high-profile youth ambassador – exactly the same sort of role that the Queen would have in mind for both Prince William and Prince Harry a generation later. Smith later wrote that the Prince, 'in his individualistic way', was 'every bit as good a public educator as his mother'.

Later that year, he addressed 5,000 members of the Institute of Directors at the Albert Hall on the subject of 'Youth and the Commonwealth'. It was one of Prince Charles's first major public speeches and he did not hold back. Why, he asked, were people not 'almost ecstatic' about the opportunities presented by the Commonwealth? He went on to attack the airline industry for the lack of cheap flights. The Prince wanted more people to be able to have some of the life-enhancing experiences that he had enjoyed in Australia – 'the country where I became a man'. He was even nostalgic for the 'man-eating spiders and acid-squirting caterpillars' that he had encountered on a school outing to Papua New Guinea.

What comes through very clearly is that this earnest twenty-one-year-old was already giving much thought to the direction of international politics and his likely place in them. A month after his day at Commonwealth headquarters, he was off to the White House. President Richard Nixon had laid on an eventful visit for the Heir to the Throne and Princess Anne, including a cookout at Camp David, a dinner dance for 700 and a trip to the top of the Washington Monument, from where the Prince raced the President's son-in-law back down the 898 stairs to the bottom (and won). A half-hour chat on leadership in the Oval Office turned into a ninety-minute discussion on the world, during which the President discussed Vietnam, the threat of communism in India and his view that the Prince should be 'a presence'. It soon emerged that the President was also trying to pair off the young Prince with his unmarried elder daughter, Tricia, twenty-four. The two found themselves seated next to each other at one meal after another, while the President and first lady told the Prince: 'We hope we can get out of sight so you will feel completely at home.' Had there been any mutual attraction – which it seems there was not – it would surely have been quashed by clunking press headlines suggesting that the pair were already an item. Many years later, the Prince would relay the story to President George W. Bush, with a light-hearted promise that he would not try to set up his two sons with his girls, Jenna and Barbara. But the Prince and his sister had clearly been touched by Nixon's efforts to make them welcome. The Prince later wrote to the Foreign Secretary, Sir Alec Douglas-Home, saying that the President had been 'extremely hospitable' and 'overflowing with kind remarks' about the 'special relationship'.

When the Prince sought to repay the compliment a few months later in a speech to the UK/US friendship society, the Pilgrims of Great Britain, there was an extraordinary intervention from the government. Heath's officials did not want the Prince to talk about the 'special relationship' at all. In December 1970, the Prince's Private Secretary, Edward Smith, alerted his young master to the Foreign Office view that 'whereas there once was such a relationship, there no longer is'. Any mention of it would 'annoy all the Europeans'. Once again the FCO was showing that it was much more concerned about not upsetting new EEC partners than about alienating old allies. Just as Heath would infuriate the Queen the following year by standing between her and her Commonwealth, so he was testing the patience of her son.

A few weeks earlier, the Prince had personally discussed the impact upon the Commonwealth of Britain's EEC entry with the Prime Minister, when they both attended the funeral of former French President Charles de Gaulle. Afterwards, the Prince wrote that Heath had assured him that any economic impact would be minimal. Heath could not resist a dig at the Commonwealth, too, adding that 'there was one thing he could not stand and that was being told what to do by African countries'.

As a future monarch and therefore obliged to listen to ministerial advice, the Prince amended his speech to the Pilgrims. However, he did so grudgingly. He omitted the word 'special', but continued to talk of a 'close relationship' between Britain and the USA, one forged in 'historical bonds of culture and language'. As the Prince's official biographer, Jonathan Dimbleby, has observed: 'The issue was the first but very far from the last potential casus belli between the Prince and the mandarins.'

It was also in 1970 that the Prince was sent to Fiji for his first experience of a ceremony that his mother, on government advice, could never undertake herself – handing independence to a former colony. All through the Sixties, as one colony after another sought to go its own way, the Queen had despatched Prince Philip, Princess Margaret or one of her cousins to lower the flag. Now it was the turn of the younger generation. The Prince was particularly struck by the good humour of the Fijians, along with the complete absence of ill will towards the outgoing colonial power.

He was becoming fascinated by the Commonwealth and its vastly different cultures and power struggles. The following year, he accompanied Princess Anne on a joint visit to Kenya, the key African state that would for ever be associated with the Queen's accession to the Throne. Here the Prince conducted his first investiture, as he dubbed the President of the East African Court of Appeal a Knight Bachelor. While Princess Anne learned about the work of Save the Children, her elder brother disappeared for several days on a walking safari through what the British High Commissioner, Sir Eric Norris, called 'Kenya's harshest country'. The only transport consisted of a few camels to carry the baggage. It was, said Norris, a very unusual safari for a VIP – 'not one of the plush kind organised for wealthy tourists but a simple one'. Not only were there no refrigerated drinks, there were not even any tents. 'The Prince regarded this safari as the highlight of his visit and one of the most interesting things he has ever done,' Norris informed his masters at the Foreign Office, adding: 'HRH was such a congenial travelling companion that all others from the hard-boiled escort to the camel men much enjoyed the expedition.' Royal photographer Reg Davis remembers that the Prince also reappeared with his first beard.

The Kenyans were delighted at what amounted to a vote of confidence in the region, particularly given the turmoil in so many neighbouring states. 'With revolution next door,' wrote Norris, 'the Heir to the Throne was calmly wandering around the wildest parts of Kenya guarded only against the possibility of attack by elephant, lion or rhino. Kenyan chests were well out.'

BACHELOR DAYS

The Prince would see a great deal of the world during his subsequent five years in the Royal Navy. He did not take to the Navy with quite the enthusiasm his father had shown. 'Poor Charles,' the Queen remarked to one dinner guest not long afterwards. 'Hopeless at maths and they made him a navigation officer!' Yet the Prince went on to qualify as a helicopter pilot, encouraged by his Dartmouth tutor, Robert Woodard, the future captain of the Royal Yacht. 'I was responsible for his welfare. I took him to pubs and learned how he was dreading his future because nothing was private,' says Woodard.

'But he did well. He flew the Wessex 5 off HMS *Hermes* carrying commandos.' After taking command of the minesweeper HMS *Bronington*, the Prince left the Royal Navy in 1976. From then on, as a full-time member of the royal team, his foreign assignments on behalf of the Queen would become more serious. He was also starting to test the boundaries of what was, and was not, politically and constitutionally acceptable. The then Foreign Secretary, David Owen, was astonished and impressed to receive a five-page handwritten letter from the Prince reporting his impressions from a recent visit to Brazil, so much so that he was unsure how to respond. 'I didn't reply for weeks which was very bad so in the end I went to see him.'

By far the most challenging mission for the Prince, however, would come in 1980. Following the success of that hot-tempered, touch-and-go Commonwealth meeting in Lusaka the year before, Rhodesia was now finally about to become Zimbabwe. Unlike so many previous independence ceremonies, this one came fraught with danger, not least the disarming of two trigger-happy guerrilla armies and a very angry buffalo. Even the ceremony itself would result in riots, tear gas and a furious diplomatic incident involving the Secretary-General of the United Nations, no less. And there, as a spectator in the midst of it all, was the Prince's future wife.

HANDOVER NUMBER ONE

The bloody Rhodesian civil war was over. Following that speedy Lancaster House agreement between all sides in the Rhodesian civil war, Britain had re-established the position of Governor of Rhodesia to organise elections and independence. Margaret Thatcher had selected Christopher (now Lord) Soames – that charismatic former Ambassador to France – for the job.

The election would be won by Robert Mugabe's ZANU Patriotic Front, ahead of rival guerrilla leader Joshua Nkomo and white leader Ian Smith. Independence could now go ahead and the Prince of Wales would do the honours. However, the Governor, the Palace and the Foreign Office had a problem: there wasn't much time.

The Foreign Office sent a telegram to Soames suggesting a reliable ex-army ceremonial expert called Colonel Eric Hefford, who would put together a decent handover parade for £1,300. Soames replied that the government could save itself £1,300. Colonel Hefford was not required, 'as we have the services of an Army officer, Lt Col Parker Bowles, Assistant Adjutant General (London District) who is experienced in ceremonial matters'.

Andrew Parker Bowles had joined the Royal Horse Guards (The Blues) fresh from school at Ampleforth and knew the Royal Family of old. His parents had been racing friends of the Queen Mother, whom he credits with persuading him to stay in the Army when he was about to leave it, fed up with endless ceremonial duties. 'My father was horrified,' he says. 'Before I knew it, I was having lunch with the Queen Mother. She said: "I've got just the job for you. The Governor-General of New Zealand is looking for a new ADC. Go and see him tomorrow afternoon." And I did.'

Parker Bowles would go on to thrive in the Army, rising to Brigadier, and would command the Household Cavalry during two very different episodes, both of which remain engraved in regimental history: the 1981 royal wedding procession of the Prince and Princess of Wales and the 1982 IRA bomb attack in Hyde Park. In 1973, he had married Camilla Shand, the former girlfriend of the Prince of Wales, who was said to have been heartbroken on hearing the news of her engagement while serving in the Caribbean with the Royal Navy. By 1979, Andrew Parker Bowles was a major 'doing a pretty ordinary Army job in London' when Major-General John Acland, whom he knew and greatly admired, was sent to run the Commonwealth Monitoring Force keeping the peace in Rhodesia ahead of the elections.* Parker Bowles offered his services and, days later, he was in the African bush trying to persuade thousands of heavily armed guerrillas to withdraw from the battlefield and let democracy take its course.

'My job was to work with the returning armies of Mugabe and Nkomo and put them in assembly areas. The white Rhodesians were looking for a reason to lure them out and kill them. So I had to keep them in these camps which were pretty rough,' he recalls. He grew to know and rather like Robert Mugabe, who once gave him a book for his young son, Tom.

* Acland's ADC in Rhodesia, a young Scots Guards Officer called Iain Duncan Smith, would later become leader of the Conservative Party.

With a tiny British unit of half a dozen men at his disposal, Parker Bowles – by now an acting Lieutenant Colonel – had a dangerous job. In the first week of 1979, he earned a Queen's Commendation for Brave Conduct. He had set off into the bush around Bindura to negotiate with a renegade force of 400 Zimbabwe African National Liberation Army (ZANLA) guerrillas, who were still operational and were warning they would fight anyone in their path. The citation – for 'exceptional courage' – notes that 'Lieutenant Colonel Parker Bowles covered miles searching for them and on a number of occasions had weapons pointed at him. Entirely unprotected, without thought for his own safety but fully conscious of the tremendous risk, he was ultimately responsible for bringing the group into the Assembly Area without casualties to either side.'

Even that paled before his encounter with an altogether more aggressive adversary. Once the elections were over and it became clear that all sides were going to accept the result, Parker Bowles could turn his attention to the handover arrangements. As the Governor's chief military liaison officer and a friend of the Soames family, he had a room at his disposal at Government House. So he invited his wife, Camilla, to join him for the week of the independence celebrations, before it had been decided that the Prince was coming. 'It became a feast for the press,' he laughs. 'I just said to Camilla: "Come out and stay with the Soameses".' The *Daily Mail*'s Nigel Dempster reported: 'Charles's old flame lights up darkest Zimbabwe'.

It was Andrew Parker Bowles, however, whom the Prince should have been most grateful to see. For in advance of the royal visit, the thirty-year-old officer took it upon himself to double-check every section of the itinerary that the Foreign Office had proposed for the Prince. This included a trip to the Henderson Veterinary Research Station at Mazowe, where staff had developed an experimental programme to domesticate the notoriously irascible African buffalo. Known as the Cape buffalo, it remains one of the most dangerous animals on Earth. Yet the vets at Mazowe were so convinced they had found a way to tame a creature responsible for at least 200 deaths each year that they were going to invite the Prince to ride one.

Parker Bowles was not convinced: 'I went to this agricultural college and they said: "We'll show the Prince this and that and then we'll get him to ride this tame buffalo." And I said I wanted to see someone else ride it. There was no saddle and it had only been half-tamed. They said it was fine to ride and they put this little local boy on it to show me. It was pointless putting him on because on the day there would be a mass of press and a strange adult white man riding it.' There was nothing for it. The gallant Lieutenant Colonel decided to climb aboard and test the plan himself. 'After a few minutes, I was thrown off and before I knew where I was, the other so-called "tame" buffalo came along and gored me. I've still got a hole in my leg.' He points to where the horn went through his right thigh, noting that a difference of a few inches would have killed him.

Everyone made light of the incident. According to *The Daily Telegraph*, the director of the college, Dr John Cundy, said that the animal – called Ziggy – was 'extremely tame' and had merely reacted to 'the Colonel's Blues & Royals style'. Had the Prince followed the Foreign Office plan, though, he would have been in grave danger. 'I always remind him that if it hadn't gored me and had gored him, things might be very different these days,' laughs Parker Bowles. 'He gives me a wry smile and, rightly, takes it quite lightly.' It had been a serious incident, though. Parker Bowles had been badly hurt and only left hospital with three days to go before the handover. 'I tried to stand up the next day and collapsed,' he recalls. 'They'd found a piece of my corduroy trouser with the artery.' He still managed to be back on duty in time to greet the Prince.

And there would still be further dramas. During a tour of Salisbury (which would be Harare within a couple of days) the Prince was taken on a tour of the Glen Norah township, having expressed an interest in looking at urban housing. The royal convoy promptly stopped outside a two-room shack owned by Ransford Makwara, a twenty-two-year-old unemployed man who immediately assumed that he was about to be arrested and ran for it. 'The poor man thought it was the police so he locked himself in the loo at the bottom of the garden and wouldn't come out,' says Parker Bowles. Eventually, Makwara was persuaded to emerge from the lavatory and show the Prince the pot of beans he had stewing on his fire.

The Prince had been well briefed on the leaders of both the old Rhodesia and the new Zimbabwe. Foreign Office notes show he was warned that Joshua Nkomo remained 'bitter and wary ... left with a feeling that his present position does not reflect his past as "father" of Rhodesian African nationalism' (Nkomo had won twenty of the 100 seats available, while Mugabe won fifty-seven). The Prince was warned to be particularly wary of Rex Nhongo, the commander of the ZANLA forces. 'Drinks heavily' according to his FCO biography. 'His wife (still known by her nom de guerre as "Spill Blood") is Minister for Youth and Sport in the new Government.' The notes added that Nhongo 'was something of a trial to Col Parker Bowles's patience'. Parker Bowles puts it more succinctly: 'Rex Nhongho threatened to kill me at one stage.' It was Nhongho himself, however, who would be murdered in mysterious circumstances some time later.

Despite reports that Camilla Parker Bowles would act as the Prince's official companion at the eve-of-independence dinner, the honour was actually given to Barbara Travers, twenty-eight, a nurse and a farmer's daughter, who described herself 'the luckiest girl in Rhodesia'.

As dusk fell the following day, the flag was finally lowered at Government House with Governor Soames standing alongside the Prince. Just behind them, running the show with military precision and a keen eye on his watch, was Parker Bowles. The atmosphere was positively jovial. Lord Soames and Mugabe had by now built up such a rapport that, seven years later, the latter would travel all the way to a Hampshire country village to attend Soames's funeral. Shortly before the handover, the outgoing Governor had felt able to offer Mugabe an immortal piece of advice from one political operator to another. Leaning through the window of Mugabe's departing car, he told him: 'Now, don't f*** it up!'

At least ninety nations had sent delegations of one sort or another to witness the historic moment. Beforehand, they were invited to a state banquet of kingclip fillets and chicken supreme, given by President-elect Canaan Banana. Among those present was the UN Secretary-General, Kurt Waldheim. He was in a dreadful mood long before he arrived, having been subjected to a 'disrespectful' security search during his flight connection in London. He was equally furious that he and his wife had been given an 'intolerable' dinner placement (ie., not on the top table with the Prince of Wales). Waldheim duly lodged a formal complaint with the British mission at the UN.

The VIPs arrived at Salisbury's Rufaro Stadium in time for the midnight ceremony. Pumped up by the pre-handover entertainment – led by the god of reggae himself, Bob Marley – some sections of the crowd were already out of control. While Andrew Parker Bowles monitored the ceremonial, his wife sat with the Governor's daughter, Emma Soames. 'Emma said to Camilla: "Look at all these people crying",' says Parker Bowles. 'And it was tear gas!' He was still keeping a close eye on his watch to ensure that, on the stroke of midnight, the Union flag came down for the last time and the Zimbabwean flag was hoisted for the first.

'The people of this country have shown great courage, determination and adaptability,' the Prince told the crowds, even trying a little Shona, before reading out the message he had brought from the Queen: 'It is a moment for people of all races and all political persuasions to forget the bitterness of the past.' In the same spirit, Robert Mugabe urged his compatriots to move on: 'The wrongs of the past must now stand forgiven and forgotten.'

The global response was overwhelmingly favourable. 'Rhodesia may now become another Kenya. It almost became another Angola,' wrote the *Chicago Tribune*. 'The world owes thanks to the British that it did not.' Still in her first year in office, Mrs Thatcher was delighted by this early diplomatic coup and was on the runway to welcome the handover team back to London. It was certainly a more joyous occasion than the Prince's final flag-lowering experience, which would take place seventeen years later in a Hong Kong downpour.

MARRIAGE

The following year (with Parker Bowles and his Household Cavalry Escort riding alongside their carriage), the Prince and Princess of Wales were married in a wedding ceremony beamed around the world to what was then the largest live television audience for a royal event. They were the most celebrated and closely studied young couple on Earth and every nation – even closed, authoritarian ones – wanted to see them. The couple had yet to undertake any official international tours when the Princess learned that she was expecting Prince William in the summer of 1982. The next spring, all three of them travelled to Australia and New Zealand, the first time that a royal baby had joined a royal tour. For the Prince of Wales, who had by now undertaken more than fifty international tours, it was a familiar ordeal. For the Princess it was exhilarating but, at times, bewildering to be the focus of so much attention from the press and the public. Countries all over the world were keen to extend invitations.

One royal ritual that involves the whole family is the Queen's annual Diplomatic Reception. Known as 'The Dip', it is the largest indoor event in the Palace calendar, with high commissioners, ambassadors and senior embassy staff, plus spouses from every legation in London, invited to a buffet dinner followed by dancing. First, they all line up for a handshake and a brief chat with the Royal Family. Understandably, everyone wanted a word with the Princess when she made her debut. Malcolm Rifkind, then a junior minister, met her at an event the next day and asked if she had enjoyed her first 'Dip'. 'I made a terrible mistake,' she told him. 'I was making small talk and all these ambassadors said "You must visit". I said "I'd love to". Then, this morning, my office got six calls from embassies saying "The Princess of Wales wants to come. Can we discuss dates?" I won't do that again!'

Not long after the Australian triumph and a subsequent Canadian tour, the Princess was expecting Prince Harry, and it would be 1985 before the Prince and Princess toured together again, this time to Italy. The trip included a meeting with the Pope and the embarrassing cancellation of a plan for the Prince and Princess to attend (but not celebrate) Mass at the Vatican. Their staff had neglected to consult the Queen until the last minute. It emerged that she had grave concerns about the constitutional implications for a future Supreme Governor of the Church of England. Here was a reminder that all official foreign tours are 'on behalf of the Queen', and there could be no question of representing her at an event that she would not have attended herself.

The Italian tour established a template for the couple's tours over the next few years. There would be manic interest in the Princess, her every piece of clothing, her every item of jewellery, her every utterance. As for the Prince, there would be polite curiosity. The Italian tour would also introduce an engagingly eccentric, old-world dimension to princely tours for many years to come. The Prince had invited the portrait painter John Ward to make an artistic record of the Venice leg of the tour, and to give him some lessons in sketching. It was such a success that for many years afterwards, the Prince's tours would include a travelling artist in the entourage.*

As far as the Foreign Office was concerned, the couple were diplomatic gold dust of the highest calibre. The grandest US publications and their high-minded commentators found themselves devoting pages to the Waleses' 1985 tour of America. Arriving directly from a tour of Australia, the Prince himself could barely think straight, confiding to his diary: 'We arrived feeling very jet-lagged indeed.' Even in his befuddled state, however, he retained his sharp eye for the absurdity of these situations. His official biography includes his original take on a very familiar scene, as he described the couple's arrival on US soil: 'Great batteries of photographers and TV people rose up like the Philharmonia Chorus mounted on white-painted scaffolds and made a noise like a giant sneezing as all the apertures went off in union.' It was as eloquent a summary as anything written by the armies of reporters that day.

The tour is remembered chiefly for two moments: President Ronald Reagan's absent-minded after-dinner toast to 'Princess David' at the White House banquet, and the Princess being spun around the White House dance floor by John Travolta. In fact the President was not the only one being forgetful. As the Prince noted in his journal, he had been so sleep-deprived that he delivered a speech of 'unutterable nonsense', forgot to toast the President, sat down and then had to stand up again and raise his glass. As for his own dancing companion, he ended up with a 'very good American ballerina whose name I forget'. He was sorry not to see an old friend from his bachelor days. 'I had been rather hoping that Diana Ross would be there,' he admitted.

The Prince was, increasingly, beginning to stamp his own mark on these tours. There would be the standard formalities – all these trips were on behalf of the Queen and at the behest of the Foreign Office – but there would be a greater emphasis on princely passions,

* Artists including Emma Sargent, Susannah Fiennes and James Hart Dyke have been among those invited to join royal tours. The Prince would always pay their costs himself. In return, artists would offer him one or two pieces of their work from the tour – plus tuition, if there was enough time for the Prince to escape with his easel.

particularly the environment. In the Eighties he was mocked for talking to plants and for speaking in alarming detail about sewage systems. By the early Nineties, as green issues had evolved from the crankier fringes of political discourse to the cross-party mainstream, the Prince was regarded as a significant international figure in this field, pulling together key players in places like Brazil and Eastern Europe. Most of the media were preoccupied with what the Princess was doing and wearing – and with any signs of strain on the royal marriage. The Foreign Office, meanwhile, would cheerfully have had both of them touring the world non-stop.

'The Prince and Princess of Wales came together in May 1990 and there was terrific excitement because they were a real glamour couple,' Sir John Birch, former Ambassador to Hungary, told the British Diplomatic Oral History Programme. 'Everyone took a shine to them. Although at that time things were really on the rocks for them, I didn't spot it at all. They spent a lot of time with us. We were entranced with her.'

A royal tour can be both a magnifying glass and an amplifier for the central cast, for better or worse. There is an intensity of interest that is seldom experienced at home. It is certainly the worst place to endure a personal crisis. Surrounded by strangers in an unfamiliar setting, on permanent display in front of a travelling media circus, it can be a lonely place. No plane will leave without you, no bag is going to go astray and there will seldom be a traffic jam. Nonetheless, the stresses of the Waleses' 1992 visits to India and South Korea meant that these would be their last tours together.

It has now entered public mythology that, during the couple's tour of India, the Princess made her famous solo trip to the Taj Mahal as some sort of cry for help, a signal to the world that her marriage was in crisis. In fact it was standard practice for the couple to pursue different programmes on a non-ceremonial day. The Taj Mahal had long been in the diary for the Princess. Lynda Chalker, then the Foreign Office Minister for Overseas Development, was accompanying the Prince that day. She sensed that he knew what was coming but was determined to stick to the FCO schedule. 'The Princess went off and sat in front of the Taj Mahal,' she recalls. 'I was with the Prince in the back of the old white Rolls Royce touring health projects that day and he was quite nervous I think. But he was remarkable – mind over matter.'

Baroness Chalker recalls that there was a certain atmosphere later on, back at the High Commission, after the media impact of the Princess's visit to the Taj Mahal became apparent. The Princess, she says, was 'quite silent' while, as the minister in attendance, she found herself intervening between the Prince and the diplomats. 'The High Commissioner wanted to give him some advice and I thought it inappropriate,' says the Baroness, herself a former diplomat. 'In that world you have to make a very subtle judgement.'

Even though the royal couple were delivering major dividends for British business, the media narrative was beyond redemption. The publication of Andrew Morton's portrait of a broken marriage, written with the Princess's assistance, had made any semblance of normality impossible. The Korea tour was the last straw. When the couple appeared side-by-side looking sad, British papers talked about 'The Glums'. The fact that they happened to be at a wreath-laying ceremony for those who had died in the Korean War made no difference. 'They were in a cemetery,' one exasperated member of the entourage told an accompanying reporter. 'What did you expect? Cartwheels?' Soon afterwards, Prime Minister John Major told Parliament that the couple were separating.

A NEW DIRECTION

From then on, the Prince and Princess would travel the world apart. While they would no longer deliver quite the same diplomatic impact as they had when together, they would end up covering twice the territory. The following year, before embarking on a trip to Saudi Arabia and the Gulf, the Prince made a speech in Oxford's Sheldonian Theatre, which would become a major plank of his foreign policy objectives for decades thereafter. Called 'Islam and the West', it was a plea for greater understanding and mutual appreciation between both cultural traditions. He acknowledged the cruelty of the Western invasions of the Crusades and the Napoleonic Wars and the vital contribution of Islam to Western society and science. Western views of Islam, he warned, had been 'hijacked by the extreme and the superficial'. When he arrived in the Gulf some days later, he was embraced as both bridge-builder and friend. His speech was played and replayed on television networks – as would still be the case when he returned on future tours. There would be many visits to this part of the world.

'Charles is very good in the Arab world,' says one senior Foreign Office figure who worked with the Prince in the Middle East. 'It is mainly the continuity thing. They are always complaining to ministers: "But I only just got to know your predecessor". They like continuity. That is the number one draw with the Prince.'

The Prince's track record as a patron of Islamic foundations – even having lessons in Arabic – gives him an added eminence in the region. 'I don't think he's given the credit he deserves,' says Jack Straw, the former Foreign Secretary, who sits on the strategy advisory committee of the Prince's Oxford Centre for Islamic Studies. 'There is that unsung side of Prince Charles which is very important in helping to give British Muslims and those around the world the sense that people understand their religion and respect it.' Tom Fletcher, author of *The Naked Diplomat* and a former British Ambassador to Lebanon, says that the Prince was very much an asset in the region, even in postings – like his own – which were deemed too dangerous for a royal visit. 'I popped in to see the Prince a couple of times at Clarence House. He was stunning on the interfaith stuff,' says Fletcher. 'To see him debate the obscure aspects of Islam with a Sunni cleric was extraordinary.'

For many years, the Prince would be something of a royal pathfinder. Before the Queen's historic state visits to places like Poland, Hungary and Russia, the Prince went first, acting as a test pilot for the monarch. Sir Brian Fall, British Ambassador to Russia, entertained the Prince when he became the most senior member of the Royal Family since the Russian Revolution to visit St Petersburg. As Fall soon discovered, the Prince could be surprisingly outspoken, as when he was shown a new development in the city. 'He went around saying "What an ugly building" and "How could it be allowed in a great city like St Petersburg?" and it then turned out that the main people like the quantity surveyor and the engineers involved were Brits. So it wasn't the best trade promotion.'

As ever, the pace of the Prince's visit was frantic. Delmar Fall, the Ambassador's wife, recalls a familiar hiccup in the arrangements. 'We had a problem when Prince Charles suddenly cancelled lunch!' she recalls. Her remonstrations with the Prince's Private Secretary about the needs of the rest of the entourage fell on deaf ears. 'I said: "But you've got thirty people here who aren't going to get lunch. You can't just expect them to go to McDonald's".'

'He's not the most enthusiastic traveller and he likes to travel in some style so his visits are quite serious events when they happen. He has quite strong views,' says a senior Foreign Office mandarin. 'But he can be very good in difficult situations. At a time when we were having a problem with the Saudis in the early years of the Cameron government, the relationship with the King of Saudi Arabia was not in a good state. There was a problem over arms deals and a kind of misunderstanding. Prince Charles did a very good job of picking up the pieces there.'

The Prince does not travel light. He is a firm believer that if there is to be a royal visit somewhere, it must be done to an appropriate standard. His critics ask why he needs to travel with a team that includes two valets, two typists and a chef; his supporters point out that he and the rest of the Royal Family are fairly modest compared to many world leaders. The French President, for example, flies around in a customised presidential airliner purchased by former premier Nicolas Sarkozy and equipped with a bespoke £65,000 baguette oven. In 2017, it emerged that President Emmanuel Macron's administration was looking to replace the President's Airbus A330 with a new Airbus A319 (though the baking arrangements have yet to be finalised). The Queen, by contrast, is the only head of state of a G7 nation without her own designated plane. She, the Prince of Wales and the rest of the Royal Family share a range of aircraft with the chiefs of the Armed Forces, the Prime Minister and other government ministers.

One senior ex-member of the Prince's team says that diplomats would often be surprised by the size of his entourage. 'The first thing every embassy would ask was the size of the royal party – which could be around twenty people – and then they would always say: "Why does he need so many people?" I would say: "Let's defer that conversation until after the visit and see if you still think it's a problem." And we would never have any complaints because he always delivered. There was always a charisma when he arrived. He never underperformed. No one was dissatisfied.'

All the Prince's visits are orchestrated via the Royal Visits Committee at the Foreign Office, which includes the most senior civil servants and royal Private Secretaries. Its members know to expect a certain amount of haggling from the Prince's team. Like the Queen, he must follow ministerial advice. Yet, he still enjoys some leeway in arranging the itinerary. Before one visit to Japan, for example, the Prince was keen to explore parts of the country he had not seen before. As he told one of his Private Secretaries: 'I'll do it if I can spend 70 per cent of the time outside Tokyo.'

There was some similar bartering in 1996 when the Prince was despatched on a tour of Central Asian republics which had been part of the old Soviet Union. Though some of his hosts had a deeply suspect record on human rights, there were important commercial opportunities for British companies in this newly emerging market. The Prince's staff proposed a schedule that seemed closely aligned to the old Silk Road between China and the West. 'I suspect it was his own determination to see Samarkand,' says the Foreign Secretary of that time, Malcolm Rifkind, with a knowing smile. Sure enough, the ancient Uzbek cities of Samarkand and Bukhara featured prominently on the final itinerary.

What some of his office called 'The Stans Tour' was another groundbreaking royal mission to places like Kazakhstan and Kyrgyzstan, nations that had never seen a royal visitor before. Perhaps the most challenging leg of the visit was in Turkmenistan, where the Prince was invited to spend the evening at the pink palace of the country's horse-obsessed dictator, President Saparmurat Niyazov. As well as banning dogs and pop music, he was in the habit of presenting visiting dignitaries with horses, a source of repeated diplomatic problems. Sir Brian Fall, the acting Ambassador, and his staff were left to sort out the mess after Niyazov gave a horse to the British Prime Minister during a stopover in 1993. John Major then flew home, leaving his gift in Turkmenistan. The French Embassy was in the same position as it wondered what do with the horse given to President Mitterrand. Fall arranged for both animals to be taken by train to Moscow (their grooms were robbed of all their money and tickets en route) and then flown to Britain. 'The French horse bit the British horse, of course,' he recalls. Even then, there was no obvious role for Major's highly-strung stallion.* 'Typical bloody military,' laughs Fall. 'We knew perfectly well these horses were not fit for military duty and we told London. There was a big to-do.'

* Named Maksat, the horse had an unhappy spell with the Household Cavalry, was obviously unsuitable for army life and ended up living happily on a Welsh farm.

So when the Prince of Wales arrived in Turkmenistan in 1996, the Foreign Office had one very clear instruction for the new British Ambassador, Neil Hook, and the Prince's officials: no more horses. It was a tense evening as the royal convoy pulled up at the President's floodlit pink palace. Niyazov was in expansive form. 'Look at my house,' he told the Prince. 'Isn't it beautiful?' 'Yes,' the Prince replied, reaching for the tactful *mot juste.* 'We call it strawberries and cream.' Niyazov then took the Prince firmly by the arm and led him down to a vast equestrian arena, where an energetic display of Turkmen horsemanship was laid on for the Prince's benefit. As the two men walked through the stables, Niyazov sang the praises of one horse after another. It looked increasingly likely that the Prince was about to be offered one at any minute. The Prince, however, was managing to hold his own, dodging every presidential blandishment. 'We were always told you were very active in racing,' the President remarked. 'I did a bit of steeplechasing but I never made myself look very respectable,' came the reply. Niyazov asked the Prince which horse he most admired. Prince Charles craftily observed how impressed he was that the President could manage so many horses, when he himself had too many to look after. Frequently rubbing his back, the Prince lamented that a bad back made riding very painful these days. Time and again, very genially and diplomatically, he made it quite clear that the last thing he actually wanted was a horse. At the end of a twenty-two-course banquet, the Prince left Niyazov's pink palace with nothing more awkward than a pom-pom hat and a carpet.

DANGER

There was more haggling ahead of an even more challenging trip two years later. It was one that highlighted an aspect of royal travel which, with a few exceptions – like the Lusaka Commonwealth meeting of 1979 or the 1994 attack on the Prince in a Sydney park by a man armed with a starting pistol* – tends to go unreported: the

* Australia-born David Kang, twenty-three, fired two blank shots at the Prince on Australia Day 1994. The Prince, who barely flinched, was widely praised for his sangfroid and later likened it to standing his ground when he was charged by an elephant in Kenya. Lucky not to have been shot, Kang was spared jail, sentenced to community service, later studied law and has since qualified as a barrister.

element of danger on a royal visit. In 1998, the Foreign Office asked the Prince to visit Sri Lanka to mark the sixtieth anniversary of independence. The country was involved in a long and bitter civil war between Tamil separatists and the Sinhalese-majority government, with regular explosions and suicide attacks all over the country. The Prince did not shrink from visiting a war zone, but if he was to go there, then he would jolly well include a visit to somewhere else he genuinely wanted to see – the mysterious mountain kingdom of Bhutan. A former member of staff remembers the discussions with the Foreign Office: 'Sri Lanka was very dangerous so we said: "Well if he's doing that, you'll have to let him do Bhutan too." Diplomatically, it was a pointless trip. We had no embassy there. But he wanted to go.'

The result was an extremely high-risk tour of Sri Lanka, followed by a scenic visit to the Gurkha heartlands of Nepal, from where the Prince could enter Bhutan for three days of Himalayan hiking. During the pre-tour 'recce' his staff had tried to include a spot of walking in Sri Lanka, but encountered stern resistance from the Sri Lankan security chiefs. It was too risky, they said. When the Prince's staff asked why, they would be given the same catch-all excuse: 'Snakes'.

As the chartered royal flight approached the Sri Lankan capital, Colombo, the Prince tried to lighten the mood. 'Have you got your bullet-proof vests?' he joked to the accompanying press pack (some of whom actually had). No sooner had the flight touched down than the dramas – and comedy – began on the Colombo tarmac. The Sri Lankan artillery unit performing the twenty-one-gun salute to welcome the Prince inadvertently managed to set fire to the grass beside the runway with red-hot shell casings. As fire engines raced past the royal dais, the Prince was invited to inspect the guard of honour, whereupon a stray dog appeared from nowhere and joined him. At this precise moment the military band struck up 'The Liberty Bell', better known as the theme tune to *Monty Python*. As the Prince remarked later, he was biting his tongue so hard to retain his composure that he nearly drew blood. His first engagement was originally supposed to have been a visit to the Buddhist holy of holies, the Temple of the Tooth, but terrorists had blown up part of it earlier in the week. So he was taken, instead, to a Courtaulds factory producing men's Y-front underpants for Marks & Spencer. Doing his level best to keep the mood upbeat, the Prince made a speech thanking the workforce for 'providing hidden support to substantial parts of the UK population'.

The following day was the moment his team were dreading. The security risk was now so high that the independence anniversary celebrations could no longer be held in public, but had been relocated to the grounds of the presidential compound. 'People kept on blowing things up,' says a member of the entourage. 'There was the Prince sitting alongside this very unpopular president and we all felt as if we were on borrowed time, that we might get mown down at any minute – like the assassination of Sadat.* It only needs one soldier to turn round with a gun. But the Prince is brave – and he is stoical.' Even as he was flying out of Colombo, nine people were blown up at a checkpoint through which the Prince had passed just a few hours earlier. No one was going to begrudge him three days in the Himalayas after all that.

In the years following their separation, both the Prince and Princess of Wales had each worked out a new modus operandi for their international work. Although the breakdown of any marriage is an intensely sad and personal matter, much of the world felt entitled to have an opinion on the failings of this one. To their credit, both sides had adopted Churchill's old maxim of 'KBO',† continuing to represent the Queen and their various charities all over the globe, taking some solace from the impact their work might have on others. For the Prince, however, the subsequent dip in his own popularity coincided with concerns inside the Commonwealth. Was he starting to lose interest in the Commonwealth? If he took foreign holidays, they would be spent on alpine ski slopes or in the Mediterranean sun. His well-publicised outreach work in the Islamic world was all well and good, but other parts of the world were feeling neglected.

'He was seeing too many emirs and not enough Commonwealth leaders,' says one former Marlborough House insider. The Commonwealth Secretariat had made periodic attempts at giving

* On 6th October 1981, the Egyptian President, Anwar Sadat, was viewing a military parade in Cairo when a handful of soldiers taking part in the march-past attacked the presidential box with grenades and AK-47 rifles, killing Sadat and ten others.

† 'Keep Buggering On.'

the Prince a more hands-on role. Stuart Mole, former chief of staff at Marlborough House during the 1980s and 1990s, remembers the familiar debate. 'Every secretary-general I have known was thinking about the future relationship. Back then, there was a feeling that Prince Charles wasn't very interested in the Commonwealth. There was also a counter-argument that he didn't want to tread on his mother's toes, that he didn't like being seen as a walking dummy and wanted a proper job'.

The Prince's separation from the Princess coincided with the rise of a new Commonwealth superstar, one who was even being discussed as a potential future head of the organisation. Having been elected President of a new, democratic South Africa in 1994, Nelson Mandela had sought his country's immediate return to the organisation. With the monarchy at a low ebb, some commentators began to argue that he might one day be the ideal person to lead it, rather than the British monarch – not that Mandela himself ever expressed the faintest desire to do so. 'With Mandela in his prime, there was a sudden realisation of the lack of automaticity,' says one of the Prince's staff. 'It was being suggested that Mandela would be a good Head of the Commonwealth and we had to consider how to deal with it if it gathered momentum. It wasn't serious but it was on the radar. The Prince was at rock bottom and at his world-weariest.'

HANDOVER NUMBER TWO

The nadir would come in 1997. In July, the Prince was despatched to Hong Kong to lower the Union flag. This was not like the previous independence ceremonies he had conducted, for the simple reason that Hong Kong was not about to become independent. After 150 years under the British Crown, it was to be absorbed into mainland China. This plot did not follow the usual simplistic British Empire narrative of imperialist, racist baddies being kicked out to make way for plucky, democratic good guys. Most of the residents emphatically wanted to remain under British rule. They had not merely prospered under the Crown, but had grown into one of the world's pre-eminent financial centres. Nor, having been decolonised, could they even take their place at the Commonwealth table. Quite the opposite: having been part of the family of nations via Britain ever since the creation of the Commonwealth – even fielding its own team at the Commonwealth Games and winning a total of five gold medals – Hong Kong would now be removed from the organisation. This might well be a moment for unalloyed celebration in Beijing. In Hong Kong, however, it felt distinctly unpromising, a step, if not into the dark, into uncertainty.

Around the world, third-party commentators billed it as the end of the British Empire. No matter that other dependent territories, from Bermuda to Gibraltar and the Caymans, still remained firmly wedded to the Crown and had no intention of letting go. Britain was just a few weeks into a dynamic new Labour administration, embracing a mantra of 'Cool Britannia'. The handover of Hong Kong was the perfect emblem of the decline of the old order, a deliciously convenient manifestation of millennial change. And here was the personification of that old world order, the Prince of Wales, complete with the ultimate symbol of the ancient regime – the soon-to-be-redundant *Britannia*.

Little wonder the Prince was in melancholy mood as he presided over the last days of post-imperial rule from his base on board the Royal Yacht. What made him sadder still was that this was *Britannia*'s last cruise. The new Labour government of Tony Blair had confirmed that *Britannia* would be decommissioned later in the year. Blair had never actually been on board before, let alone seen *Britannia* doing what it did best – promoting Britain overseas. When the Prime Minister and his wife, Cherie, arrived in Hong Kong, the Prince invited them round to the Royal Yacht. A member of the royal party recalls the excruciating moment when, at the Prince's suggestion, the ship's captain, Commodore Anthony Morrow, offered to give them a guided tour of the ship. Suddenly there was heckling from the back of the room. 'Lobbying!' shouted Blair's spin doctor, Alastair Campbell. 'I suppose he thought he was being funny,' says one of those present. 'But it was just embarrassing.'

What would have been even more embarrassing was the near-disaster at the British handover ceremony on the night of 30th June. Grandstands for thousands of spectators and VIPs had been erected around the parade ground at HMS *Tamar*, the main British base. At the stroke of midnight this famous old complex – dominated by the high-rise Prince of Wales Building – would become the headquarters of the Chinese People's Liberation Army. It was essential for British prestige and national pride that this last hurrah should be conducted without a hitch. On arrival, the Prince's equerry, Lieutenant Commander John Lavery, placed the Prince's speech safely on his own seat and then went about his duties, ensuring that his boss was introduced to the right VIPs in the right order. The proceedings were not helped by a tropical downpour, which, in the absence of covered grandstands, drenched all those without an umbrella – including the Prince himself. Dressed in full Royal Navy uniform, he at least had the luxury of a peaked cap. The outgoing governor, Chris Patten, looked as if he had gone swimming fully clothed.

As the Pipes and Drums of the Black Watch ushered all the military detachments into the centre of the parade square, Lavery reached for the Prince's speech. It was not there. A frantic search ensured. This could not only turn into a career-ending moment for the equerry. If the Prince failed to read out the Queen's farewell message of thanks and best wishes to her four million soon-to-be ex-subjects, the embarrassment to both the nation and the monarchy – captured on live television around the world – did not bear thinking about. Suddenly Lavery spotted a diligent cleaner emptying the contents of a dustpan into a bin off to one side. With moments to spare, he found the royal speech in the bin, extracted it and returned to the VIP grandstand, where he handed it to the Prince.

The events of that evening, historic as they were, would be eclipsed by the thunderbolt that struck two months later. The death of Diana, Princess of Wales in a Paris car crash in the early hours of 31st August 1997 reverberates to this day, as her sons ensure that her place in their lives and the life of the nation is enshrined and honoured. Though the Princess had been divorced for a year, her death was the single gravest blow to the monarchy since the abdication of Edward VIII. While most people would see it for what it was – the premature death of a globally adored young mother, and a tragedy for all concerned – it would, inevitably, polarise those who had taken sides in the 'war of the Waleses'. Even the Prince's harshest critics could not fault his love for, or devotion to, his sons. Those qualities would now be more important than ever as he restructured his life to fit around them.

Diana's death would certainly accelerate the pace of change that had been under way inside the Royal Household for several years.

Conventional wisdom holds that the monarchy was grudgingly pushed into reforming itself after the '*annus horribilis*' of 1992 – a dismal run of royal separations and scandals, culminating in the Windsor Castle fire. In fact the Queen had initiated a wholesale overhaul of royal management and finances as far back as 1986. The events of 1992 had simply hastened the process, speeding up a royal plan for the Queen to pay income tax (although John Major's government had told her there was no need). In 1994, the Prince had taken part in a documentary, primarily about his public life, in which he had talked about the 'irretrievable' breakdown of his marriage. A year later, the Princess of Wales responded in kind with a surprise interview for the BBC's *Panorama*, primarily about her private life, in which she cast doubts on the Prince's fitness to be King. The *Panorama* film had two instant results. First, the Queen asked the couple to seek a divorce. Next, she set up an internal family committee called the Way Ahead Group, to examine every aspect of royal life, even those issues beyond its control, such as male primogeniture. So changes to the machinery of monarchy were already in hand by the time tearful crowds were piling up their flowers against the gates of Kensington Palace in the first week of September 1997.

The effect of the death of the Princess was to precipitate a change of tone, a fresh mindset. There was a greater willingness to look at new ways of doing the same old things, as opposed to new things to replace the old. For example, there would be more young people and fewer civic worthies at an away-day to the shires. Buckingham Palace would start holding more receptions for different strands of public life. It wasn't a case of reducing support for old favourites like the Scouts or the Not Forgotten Association. Yet the Queen would hold additional events recognising other elements of British life – from the retail industry to education. A new department called the 'Co-Ordination and Research Unit' was established to help the monarchy become more proactive. Instead of waiting to be invited to the centenary of an important milestone, the Palace would seek out appropriate commemorations. Instead of waiting to be asked to different parts of the country, royal officials would look for those places that were not issuing invitations to find out why.

The British public would not see an overnight transformation. This would be reform by stealth. Royal change has always been incremental, for good reason. 'We were future-proofing,' says a member of the Royal Household during that period. The monarchy does not move at the pace of a political party, let alone a commercial brand. You cannot 'relaunch' the Crown or subject it to a 'makeover'. However following the death of the Princess, the Prince of Wales had to reassess his priorities both at home and overseas.

SUCCESSION

The Prince already had a long-standing tour in the diary, to southern Africa. Since it coincided with his younger son's half-term from school, thirteen-year-old Prince Harry would come along, too. The schedule included meetings with President Nelson Mandela and a charity concert in Johannesburg featuring the Spice Girls. Throughout it all, there was the vexed issue of how the Prince should honour the memory of his late ex-wife, in a part of the world where she had been an active charity campaigner. There was palpable nervousness within the royal camp about hitting the right note, ahead of the Prince's big speech at Mandela's banquet in Cape Town. As his officials offered up various drafts, the Prince grew increasingly angry, adamant that he would find his own form of words.

In the end, he thanked all South Africans for their sorrow, praised Diana's work in the fields of Aids and landmines, and saluted the way she 'brought a real difference to the lives of very many people on this continent and elsewhere'. He received a standing ovation. Among those on his feet was a grieving Cape Town resident, the Princess's brother. Two months earlier, Earl Spencer's address at her funeral had been seen as a thinly veiled critique of the monarchy. Now there was a rapprochement.

The Prince's position vis-à-vis the Commonwealth remained unclear, however. There were still influential voices among certain member governments who felt that he was insufficiently interested in the organisation; there were those who felt that the Prince should steer well clear of what was his mother's territory; and there were those who wanted to sever the link with the monarchy altogether. When Australia announced that it would hold its referendum on the monarchy just weeks before the new millennium, the Royal Family would not be looking forward to the twenty-first century with great confidence. Yet as some republicans sought to personalise the referendum campaign, the surprise result in favour of the status quo would show that most people still had more faith in the system of monarchy, rather than in an ex-politician, to safeguard their constitutional rights.

Less than three months later, on a tour of the Caribbean, the Prince delivered his most forthright eulogy to the Commonwealth in many years, calling it 'a wonderful resource' embodying 'a particular kind of decency and humanity'. That same year, a new Commonwealth Secretary-General arrived at Marlborough House. Don McKinnon was the experienced ex-Foreign Minister of New Zealand, a straight-talking, horse-riding ex-farmer who was keen to engage with the Prince and 'pull him closer into the fold'. McKinnon had created provocative headlines by publicly stating (correctly) that the position of Head of the Commonwealth was not hereditary. Some at the Palace took it as barely concealed criticism. In fact McKinnon says he was simply keen to raise the Prince's profile. 'There was a need for people to get to know him,' says McKinnon. 'He could not just get away with saying "I was there in 1965 . . ." '

McKinnon found that the succession kept surfacing during his time in office from 2000 to 2008. At one point, he says that the British Foreign Office demanded a detailed plan of action on succession arrangements. He refused, saying it was premature and irrelevant. He believed Prince Charles was the right man for the job and should not worry about 'treading on the Queen's toes'. As he puts it: 'I think there were feelings in the earlier days that this was his mother's territory. But I raised this with the Queen and she said: "The Commonwealth is big enough for all of us".' He likes to quote the former Nigerian President, Olusegun Obasanjo, on the subject: 'We don't feel so small that we have to reject the monarchy to feel big.' That, says McKinnon, was the view shared by all the heads he spoke to, though he still believes the succession should not be automatic. 'You may get a monarch in the future who does two or three amazingly stupid things so we don't want to give automaticity to this. But we don't want to look as if we are being pedantic either.'

One of the problems was that there were also influential figures in the Prince's circle urging him to forget about the Commonwealth altogether and focus on shoring up his position at home. Tony Blair's view of the organisation as an irritating anachronism was shared by some of the modernising forces in the Prince's camp. It was a battle for the Prince's ear.

Much of the Prince's core charity work – from the environment to youth opportunities – was a natural fit with the work of the twenty-first-century Commonwealth. The glory days of nation-building and beating apartheid were now giving way to the less glamorous promotion of human rights and sustainability. In the new era of spin and 'eye-catching initiatives', the Commonwealth, like a good deal of the Prince's work, was seen as worthy but dull.

However, the Prince was now much more contented in his private life. There had been a renaissance of his romance with Camilla Parker Bowles. She was, by now, divorced from the Brigadier (who says that most of the fault for the breakdown of their marriage was his own, even though 'Camilla took the wrap' in the press). The couple, who have two children and five grandchildren, would remain on very good terms.

In 2005, the Prince and Mrs Parker Bowles were married in a civil ceremony in Windsor Town Hall, followed by a blessing in St George's Chapel. Thereafter, she would become the Duchess of Cornwall. Don McKinnon was among the guests and remembers 'an upswell of goodwill towards a man who had gone through years of lurid headlines . . . a palpable sense of relief among guests, family and the couple themselves.' There were some surreal moments, too. He remembers receiving a friendly wave from the Queen at the wedding reception. He walked over, to find her deep in conversation with her Windsor farming staff. 'Don used to farm in New Zealand,' she told them. 'He'll understand your problems with the heifers.'

With the Duchess at his side, the Prince now had a soulmate and, on his travels, someone with whom he could share the stresses and hilarities of royal touring. McKinnon had plans to ease the Prince into a more elevated Commonwealth role, inviting the couple to take part on the periphery of the 2007 summit in Kampala. 'I wanted him to contribute at the foreign ministers' meeting and made sure he met lots of young people,' says McKinnon. 'The Prince thoroughly enjoyed it all as I knew he would.'

In the next few years the Prince's profile would begin to shift, almost imperceptibly, towards the role of King-in-waiting, with the full support of the Queen and her new Private Secretary, Christopher Geidt, a powerful advocate of greater Commonwealth engagement. The Prince would stand in for the Queen at the opening of the 2010 Commonwealth Games in Delhi, a far-from-straightforward substitution. In the absence of the monarch, the hosts wanted the Indian President to open the Games. The Games federation and the Palace were adamant that it should be the Prince. In a classic diplomatic fudge, the Prince declared the Games open while President Patil then proclaimed: 'Let the Games begin.'

During the Queen's 2012 Diamond Jubilee celebrations, it was the Prince who took on most of the long-distance travel to ensure that her Jubilee message was trumpeted through her realms. By now the Prince had been touring the Commonwealth so extensively for so long that the only people who knew it better than he did were his own parents.

A year later, in 2013, he was at that Commonwealth summit in Sri Lanka and standing in for the Queen following her recent self-imposed ban on long-haul travel. It coincided with the Prince's 65th birthday. 'The Colombo summit was a very delicate one,' says one Secretariat insider. Many heads of government had stayed away in protest against President Rajapaksa's crackdown on the Tamil minority, although the President argued that he had managed to bring the years of carnage to an end. The British Prime Minister, David Cameron, had arrived with major concerns about human rights in the north of the country. Cameron concedes that he was not making things easy for the Prince's position. 'It was obviously difficult for him as I was lashing the Sri Lankan President in bilateral meetings really quite toughly and there was this blinding row going on about Rajapaksa's behaviour,' he says.

While human rights were the headline issue, there was also a tentative attempt to raise the delicate issue of Commonwealth succession. Both Buckingham Palace and the Commonwealth Secretariat were pushing for the heads of government to reach a settled position on the next Head of the organisation. At the 2013 Commonwealth Day reception in London, the Queen had come to Marlborough House to sign the Commonwealth's new charter. McKinnon's successor as Secretary-General, Kamalesh Sharma, made a speech saluting her stewardship of the organisation, before adding pointedly: 'The support given to you in this endeavour by the Prince of Wales deepens the Commonwealth's links to the Crown.' The Queen, in turn, thanked Sharma for his 'thoughtful words about the link between the Crown and the Commonwealth and its enduring value'. To old Commonwealth hands, the message was clear: it was time for the Commonwealth to endorse the Prince as Head-in-waiting. 'The view here was that he'd earned it,' says a senior Buckingham Palace adviser. 'So, that was the opportunity for anyone to stand up and say they didn't want Charles. And they didn't say anything!'

A plan was hatched at the Palace. Since there had not been so much as a murmur of disapproval, royal officials were keen to move forward at the summit in Colombo, given that the Prince would be there himself. The idea of addressing the succession issue would have to be raised by one of the leaders, but preferably not by the British government, for fear of raising republican or anti-imperial hackles. Instead, the Queen's officials talked to the Prime Minister of New Zealand, John Key.

'The Palace came to us and asked if we would push that issue,' says Key. 'We formally wrote that we were going to support that proposition and progress it. The Commonwealth wouldn't exist without the monarchy and I was very supportive of the Queen and of the family.' In the end, however, it was the Prince and his officials who applied the brakes. They felt it was too soon and did not want the matter raised while the Prince was at the summit. 'Clarence House was keen not to be seen to be pushing it,' says Key. So apart from a cursory discussion, during which it seemed everyone was entirely happy with the idea of the Prince taking over, nothing was resolved.

None the less, all the politicians present were left in no doubt about the Prince's feelings towards the organisation. At the summit banquet, which he hosted on behalf of the Queen, the Prince was expected to say the customary few words of thanks and let dinner commence. Except that, on this evening, the Prince said rather more than that. Speaking from a few notes rather than a script, he reflected that having made more than 150 visits to more than forty Commonwealth nations, the institution was 'in the blood'. He reminisced about representing the Queen at handover ceremonies in places like Fiji and the Bahamas – where he had been expected to dance the night away -and a challenging waterskiing trip with Dom

Mintoff, Prime Minister of Malta. His abiding memory was of Mintoff's bath hat and of the wax plugs in his ears.

He talked of his childhood memories of Australia's Sir Robert Menzies; of Ghana's Kwame Nkrumah (who had given him a bow and arrows as a boy); and of being greeted by one million people on the streets of Malawi, courtesy of Dr Hastings Banda. By the end of this whistlestop tour of Commonwealth greats – concluding with Canada's Pierre Trudeau – and his tribute to Commonwealth 'family values', the Prince's audience could be in no doubt. There was no one else in the room with a remotely comparable grasp of this organisation. David Cameron says that the Heir to the Throne handled this ill-tempered summit very skilfully, particularly when it came to entertaining all the heads. 'I remember being very impressed at how well he knew everyone,' says Cameron. 'He had something to say to all of them. His speech was very well-judged.'

It was Cameron's offer to rescue the 2017 Commonwealth summit from cyclone-battered Vanuatu and stage it in London in 2018 that would be a game-changer for the Prince. The fact that this would almost certainly be the Queen's last Commonwealth summit meant that there would be a record turnout of heads of government, and also that the issue of the headship could be addressed without any awkwardness.

In the run-up to the summit, the Prince joined the Queen to host a Palace reception for every strand of the Commonwealth diaspora in Britain, many of them people whom the Prince had nominated himself. The guests included Pakistan-born Carlisle spice-shop owner Saj Ghafoor, England rugby players Billy and Mako Vunipola (whose parents are from Tonga), and Jude Kereama, the New Zealand-born masterchef with an award-winning restaurant in the Cornish village of Porthleven. The Prince talked to them all.

So the scene is set as the summit begins. While fifty-three leaders converge on London, countless similar, multi-layered, people-to-people Commonwealth connections emerge. The Prince is in his element as he tours the various conferences alongside the main summit, like the Youth Forum and the People's Forum. 'The Youth Forum's getting older,' he jokes as he bumps into the Duchess of Cornwall in a room full of youth activists. He has something to say to all of them. When one young man explains that he is from Cameroon, the Prince excitedly recalls his visit there in the Royal Yacht and the saga of the ship's cooling system being blocked by jellyfish: 'I've never been so hot in my life!' Jonathan Barcant, twenty-nine, talks about using climate-resilient plants to build hurricane defences in Trinidad. The Prince is thrilled: 'I've thought for years that Nature holds all of the answers!' He is equally excited to meet a young economist from the Seychelles who has successfully campaigned for a ban on plastic bags. They are soon deep in conversation about raw sewage.

The following day he is holding audiences for individual visiting heads of government – the Queen cannot meet all of them – and entertaining delegates to an al-fresco tea party at Clarence House in honour of the international arm of his Prince's Trust. Speakers include a police officer from Barbados, who has slashed youth offending with the help of the Trust, and Roland Vella, fourteen, a Maltese schoolboy who says the Trust has turned his life around. Just more human layers in the tangle of global connections that make up the modern Commonwealth. At the summit's opening ceremony, the Prince is centre stage as the Queen voices her wish for him to continue the 'important work started by my father' and the Maltese Prime Minister, the outgoing 'chair in office', announces that this is the consensus position anyway. Later on, the Prince helps the Queen host a reception for those leaders attending their first summit. Before the evening banquet, as the ninety-two-year-old Queen is on her feet for over an hour meeting and greeting all the delegations, the Prince is at her side doing the same. He is entirely at home with this lot, just as they are with him. The next day, his endorsement as future head is actually little more than a formality. 'It was very clear that people wanted the Prince of Wales to be the next head of the Commonwealth,' says the summit host, Theresa May, afterwards. 'There was a tremendous feeling of coming together -the family of the Commonwealth – and also of continuity.'

'He continues that link between what has gone before and what will be with his own dedication to climate change, to the Prince's Trust and to all those other charities strongly embedded in the Commonwealth,' says the Secretary-General, Baroness Scotland. 'He's been there.'

Those who have been with him on Commonwealth duty have no doubt the Prince is the man for the part. 'He's travelled God knows how many miles to meet and greet and talk to these people. He's knowledgeable. I think he'll be a great success,' says Brig Andrew Parker Bowles. And he firmly believes that the Duchess of Cornwall will be an asset, too. 'She'll do a good job, do her best. That's her usual form.'

The Prince who has presided over so many handovers in his time will eventually find that the Commonwealth handover is going to be somewhat easier than most dared imagine a few years before. It is a slightly different picture when it comes to the realms, where the monarch automatically becomes head of state. Some officials expect a change of reign to hasten moves towards a republican model in some of them, but time and again, the public has shown itself to be stubbornly resistant to constitutional change. And how long before the Prince himself decides to curtail his own long-haul travel plans and delegate them to his sons?

As for the rest of the world beyond the Commonwealth, most people have now known the Prince, just as they have known the Queen, for so long that they have a settled view that is unlikely to move much. 'Once the Prince is on the Throne, he is the ticket,' says the German commentator and royal biographer, Thomas Kielinger. 'The monarchy is older than any given person and you've lived with some very funny characters on the Throne. The Queen's high age has given Charles an umbrella. Our first chancellor after the war was seventy-three so age is not an issue.'

Continuity in a turbulent, changing world is one of the Prince's strongest suits. His familiar and outspoken views on well-known subjects – which once alarmed diplomats and senior civil servants – have lost their novelty value and, in many cases, have become received wisdom. His tours have taken on a more serious, more statesmanlike feel. Instead of artists, his entourage now includes senior government representatives. Suggestions of unconstitutional interference in political matters, through his famous handwritten 'black spider' memos to ministers, have turned out to be earnest missives on non-political issues – subjects such as badgers or the Patagonian toothfish – rather than hard-nosed lobbying. Former ministers have no complaints. In fact, they have welcomed his input.

Lord Hague, the former Foreign Secretary, says that he received plenty of princely memos, but not about foreign affairs. 'I knew him well when I was Secretary of State for Wales. I used to get the black spider memos particularly about agriculture and the environment. I found them fascinating. I didn't find it inappropriate. He wasn't trying to override democratic process.' After a lifetime of diplomacy, the Foreign Office veteran, Sir Roger du Boulay, sees the Prince as a great asset. 'He's got his bees,' he says. 'Let them buzz.'

Chapter 13

THE FAMILY

THE DUKE

The Queen has always relied on members of her family to act, as David Cameron puts it, '*in loco reginae*'. As she herself has often said, 'I can't be everywhere and I can't do everything.' Throughout her reign, members of the family have had to stand in for her, none more so than the Duke of Edinburgh. His supporting role at the monarch's side has already been explored. For more than six decades, however, he would play a very important international role in his own right. During the early part of the reign, it was the Duke who undertook much of the heavy lifting on her behalf. In those initial years, when travelling took much longer and the priority was the Commonwealth, he would visit many of the remotest parts of the English-speaking world. Although the online royal drama *The Crown* might portray these trips as a glorified cruise, they had a groundbreaking diplomatic and scientific purpose, which is hard to convey to a twenty-first-century audience. Television viewers in 1957, however, were glued to his illustrated talks on the flora and fauna of the South Seas and the Indian Ocean.

The Duke would become the regular royal face at the Commonwealth Games when the Queen was unable to attend herself. It was he who pushed through the gradual change from the 'British Empire and Commonwealth Games' to the 'British Commonwealth Games' (as they became in 1970) to the 'Commonwealth Games' (from 1978).

As royal and Foreign Office priorities began to shift during the Sixties, the Duke would perform a similar sort of pathfinding role to that performed by the Prince of Wales a generation later. In 1960, the Queen was invited to tour Argentina and Chile, but declined, due to Commonwealth commitments and the arrival of Prince Andrew. Instead, she proposed sending the Duke of Edinburgh a little later, in 1962. The Foreign Office was in favour, for both commercial and political reasons. This was the height of the Cold War and no one wanted another Fidel Castro. An internal Foreign Office memo in 1961 notes that such a trip might deter 'further defections on the Cuban model'. In March 1961, the Duke's Private Secretary, Jim Orr, wrote to all the embassies in South America with a briefing that offers a useful insight into his approach to royal tours. Formal functions, he said, 'should be kept to a minimum' and 'return hospitality should not be encouraged'. All industrial visits 'should have a particular connection with Britain', and 'HRH would like to play polo whenever there is an opportunity'. Military events were extremely unwelcome. 'It is very much hoped that Service engagements are not included,' Orr added. 'In fact, HRH does not expect to take any uniforms with him.'

The Duke could always be usefully despatched to represent the Queen at events that might not be entirely appropriate for the monarch but which required a royal presence none the less. In 1971, after she was unable to attend the Commonwealth summit in Singapore, it would have been impossible for the Queen to attend the Shah of Iran's absurdly extravagant celebrations to mark 2,500 years of the Persian Empire. Nor would she have wanted to attend this eye-poppingly over-the-top four-day exercise in conspicuous consumption, staged in a purpose-built 160-acre tented city near the ancient capital of Persepolis. The Shah flew in Parisian caterers from Maxim's and a fake forest – plus genuine exotic birds to sit in its fake trees. A car-sized lump of ice would be delivered by helicopter each day, just to chill the champagne. The highlight was a five-hour banquet including quails' eggs stuffed with caviar, champagne sorbet and fifty roast peacocks. The whole event cost £275 million and triggered worldwide condemnation, not least from the exiled revolutionaries, who would use it as ammunition to foment revolution seven years later. The Shah was a British ally, however, and the House of Windsor needed to be properly represented at an event where all the world's other monarchies would be present. So the Queen sent the Duke and Princess Anne. The British photographer Reg Davis was there as the Shah's personal photographer. He recalls that the Duke was not best pleased to see him. 'What's he doing here?' he asked the Shah. 'He's working for me,' came the reply.

Over the years, the Duke's primary international role has been to accompany the Queen on her visits to most of the nations on Earth. Wearing his other hats – notably as international President of the World Wildlife Fund and President of the International Equestrian Federation – he would also be able to travel to places far off the beaten track, as far as official visits were concerned. His greatest global achievement, however, is surely the Duke of Edinburgh's Award, now in its seventh decade.

Yet all around the world, there have been thousands of people in positions of great authority – some have ended up running their countries – who have benefited from another of the Duke's bright ideas. At the end of the First World War, a pioneering clergyman called the Reverend Robert Hyde set up the Boys' Welfare Society 'to save young boys from degeneration'. It was his idea to bring together teenagers from poor backgrounds and from public schools at a series of summer camps. His work had the active support of the Duke of York before he became George VI. Hyde's movement evolved into the Industrial Society and, by 1952, it invited the Duke of Edinburgh to become its patron. He agreed as long as he could be 'of use'. He was particularly interested in the effect of modern post-war industry on the people it employed. The Duke decided to set up a conference of youngish leaders of the future – be they aspiring executives, union leaders or politicians. Together with the Industrial Society's rising star, a dynamic alumnus of Oxford and Harvard called Peter Parker,* he formed a board of eminent thinkers and, in 1956, the Duke of Edinburgh's Commonwealth Study Conferences (CSC) were born. The Duke deliberately chose the word 'study' so that no one felt compelled to reach a conclusion. Nearly 300 young leaders – one-third British, two-thirds Commonwealth – were invited to Oxford University to hear the Duke kick it all off with a televised speech in

* Peter Parker would go on to be chairman of, among other things, British Rail, Mitsubishi Europe, the National Theatre, British Airways and the British Tourist Authority. Knighted twice, he remained a trustee of the Commonwealth Study Conferences until his death in 2002.

which he urged them not to 'decide' anything, but to be 'more aware of what industry does to people'.

By royal standards, this was radical stuff. The delegates were split into mixed groups and taken all over Britain for a fortnight. It was an illuminating experience. One group found that workers' morale was ten times higher among London sewage workers than at the Savoy Hotel, purely because of different management styles. It worked so well that a second conference was organised in Canada in 1962. One team leader would later recall that his group included a rather cocky Australian union official who 'was always late, sauntering in five minutes after everybody else'. The union rep, a certain Bob Hawke, would go on to become Prime Minister of Australia, while the team leader ended up as the Defence Minister of Canada. The CSC would continue to attract a similar calibre of applicant. Alan Johnson, later MP and Home Secretary, has called it 'One of the most memorable events of my life ... It's not an exaggeration to say that the 1992 CSC enriched my life.'

Over time, the Duke would hand on much of his life's work to the next generation. The Princess Royal has followed him as patron of the Commonwealth Study Conferences and admits that no one, least of all the Duke, thought they would be going this long. 'The original concept was reconnecting the Commonwealth post-war in business, political and union terms,' says the Princess. 'I think he thought it was only going to be a couple of cycles and then it would probably not be necessary.' Like so many of the Duke's ideas, it would go on to exceed all expectation.

THE PRINCESS ROYAL, THE DUKE OF YORK AND THE EARL AND COUNTESS OF WESSEX

The Princess Royal has only the haziest memory of that first overseas tour, accompanying her elder brother in the Royal Yacht in 1954 towards the end of the Queen's round-the-world tour. She would start to learn the rudiments of royal diplomacy after her schooldays were over. She was with her parents and the Prince of Wales when the Queen performed that first walkabout in New Zealand in 1970. The Princess says her own first attempt took place a few days later in Melbourne, Australia. At the age of nineteen, she was not exactly thrilled by the prospect. 'What do you say when you walk up to a complete stranger? You learn by experience!' Her debut walkabout would have a bizarre twist, too. 'Almost the first person I stopped to talk to looked of contemporary age. I asked her where she came from. She came from Malta and she said: 'We've met before". I said: "Well it's first time I've been in Australia. How could that be?" And she said: "I was the floor maid in the hotel in Malta when you stayed in 1954". I didn't think she was much older than me! So even at that first attempt, you recognise how small that world is and how easily people move around the Commonwealth.'

She soon learned to enjoy the experience of walkabouts and says the Queen did, too. 'The people were so friendly and quite often came up with their own lines of communication. The chances were somebody would yell at you: 'My cousin's back in Perth!' It was that kind of conversation – lots of links that would come out of the crowd.'

Travelling with the Queen and Prince Philip, she also perfected another royal skill: waving: 'I remember going to King Constantine's wedding in Greece in Athens and being absolutely fascinated by Continental members of royal families and how they waved. It is completely different.' She laughs as she remembers the Australian students who presented the Queen with an inspired invention: a waving machine. 'They gave her a stuffed glove on a wooden lever so that you could tweak the end of the lever and this hand went to and fro. I think they thought it was rather cheeky but Her Majesty was thrilled.'

The Princess undertook her first solo engagements overseas a year later when she travelled to Kenya. Although she went there with Prince Charles, he would disappear on safari while she had planned a programme that would shape her work for years to come. On leaving school at Benenden, the Princess had decided to focus her attentions on a handful of charities. 'My father did suggest very strongly that you should only pick one or two that you really felt you could get involved with in the early stages,' she says. 'I think he felt that for both the Queen and himself, the expectation was that they take on all these things that had been done before. That way, you never really had the time to get under the skin of an organisation.' One of those she would embrace was Save the Children. 'I didn't choose it. They asked me,' she says.

Her visit to Kenya would be a chance to see the charity in action and to promote it. She was accompanied by a team from the children's television programme *Blue Peter*, and by presenter Valerie Singleton. This was a further piece of careful media management by the Palace press secretary, William Heseltine, the architect of the historic television documentary, *Royal Family*, the year before. If the public were to understand the nature of modern royal duties, they would need to see them being performed. The last thing the Princess wanted was yet another old-fashioned ribbon-cutting ceremony. During his days as Vice-Marshal of the Diplomatic Corps, Sir Roger du Boulay remembers receiving a draft programme for a visit by the Princess to Scandinavia. 'A perfectly respectable ambassador had sent a draft programme which consisted of babies. I tore it up and sent it back to him saying: "Take her anywhere cutting edge, technical and interesting. Take her to a car factory." She had a whale of a time.'

Heseltine's plans for the Princess's Kenyan tour had not gone down well with the Foreign Office, however. Sir Eric Norris, the British High Commissioner in Nairobi, regarded the presence of any media as a gross intrusion. He was of the FCO old school who seemed to regard his primary role as that of royal travel agent. The Prince and Princess, he informed his superiors in London, 'wished for a private visit with the minimum of publicity'. Heseltine's plan for the media, he warned, 'is hardly consistent with our contention that the object of the visit is to provide peace and quiet for Their Royal Highnesses'.

In the event, the Princess's trip would generate vast amounts of media coverage for both her work and for Save the Children. Sir Eric remained unimpressed. 'The gentlemen of the Press, more especially the photographers, were frequently importunate and not so well behaved as one would have wished,' he wrote in his despatch afterwards. 'A very difficult fortnight.' He was also sniffy about the *Blue Peter* team that was following the Princess. 'Most of the filming was with Miss Valerie Singleton, whose many accomplishments do not, I think, include the art of self-effacement.' The Princess, however, looks back on it all with great affection. Reviewing film footage of her visit, she instantly recognises the first school on her itinerary, explaining how, from a modest start, it has gone on to become one of the best schools in East Africa. She has revisited it many times.

On some tours with the Queen and the Duke, the host nation would arrange for the Princess to have a suitable 'companion' on tour. During the 1971 state visit to Turkey, she was entrusted to Belkis Versan, twenty-two, and the daughter of the director of protocol. The Foreign Office informed the Palace that she was 'an attractive, lively and sophisticated girl . . . well at ease with foreigners'. Although good at waterskiing, she had 'no particular knowledge of horses'.

Following the Princess's (first) marriage to Captain Mark Phillips in 1973, she would have no further need of companions. Her workmanlike approach to foreign visits has barely changed in years. She has long been one of the busiest royal travellers, often with a minimal entourage (or none at all, when touring outside the royal orbit as, for example, when she is travelling as a member of the International Olympic Committee). She has become the first member of the Royal Family to make an official royal visit to places like Mongolia, Vietnam and Madagascar. 'The great thing about the Princess Royal is she's very hardworking but she's also very efficient and very low-maintenance,' says Sir Simon Fraser, former head of the Diplomatic Service. 'She just does it.'

For ten years after leaving the Royal Navy in 2001, the Duke of York was an unpaid 'special representative' for British trade overseas. He relinquished the role in 2011 of his own volition, after headlines about some of his business contacts, notably a convicted American sex offender, became a distraction. Since then, he has focussed on promoting enterprise and new technology at home, while supporting the Queen in entertaining visiting world leaders. He has his critics inside the Foreign Office, where some remember being on the receiving end of his brisk manner, but the Duke has his fans, too.

Tom Fletcher, former Number Ten Private Secretary and Ambassador-turned-academic, says that he consulted the Duke for a review of Foreign Office strategy. 'He took a close interest in it. He has observed a lot of diplomats up close,' says Fletcher. 'He's pretty forthright on the strengths and weaknesses of the FCO. He gave me some good feedback which I was able to deploy, particularly in dealing with a region like the Gulf. The family have longer-term perspectives than governments. You need to invest in relationships which can carry weight across generations. He was very thoughtful about how do we ensure Prince William and Prince Harry have those long-term, load-bearing relationships that will be with them in fifty years' time.'

Like the Princess Royal, her younger brother, Prince Edward, the Earl of Wessex, decided early on to focus on a number of core projects. On the day he married Sophie Rhys-Jones in 1999, it was announced that he would, eventually, inherit the title of Duke of Edinburgh from his father. He has now taken on what will perhaps go down as the Duke's greatest creation, the Duke of Edinburgh's Award. In his youth, Prince Edward completed the bronze, silver and gold tiers of the award and now chairs its international operations as it continues to grow overseas. He also devotes a great deal of time to another international organisation that was once close to the Duke's heart, as vice-patron of the Commonwealth Games Federation.

The Countess of Wessex also places a strong emphasis on youth charities and young people. Internationally, one of her priorities has been the fight against avoidable blindness, the primary aim of the Queen's Diamond Jubilee Trust, of which the Countess is the vice-patron. She has followed its work all over the Commonwealth, but will never forget what happened during her 2017 visit to a remote part of Bangladesh, where she dropped in on a local health clinic. 'A lady sitting very close to me had a little baby sitting on her lap who was terribly sweet and I waved at him,' says the Countess. 'She immediately plonked him in my lap so I was playing with him. I turned him round to look at him and I noticed that he had a squint.' The Countess's own daughter, Lady Louise, had a similar eye condition as a baby. She recognised the symptoms in seven-month-old Junayed right away, being well aware of the importance of early intervention in strengthening eye muscles to prevent a 'lazy' eye. 'I could see that this baby definitely had a squint. So I asked the other professionals there if they would look at this child.' She was very conscious that this had to be done carefully. 'I probably put the fear of God into this poor mother. However, there were some very kind people there who made sure that the family were able to get the right kind of treatment. He's now being well cared for and he will be absolutely fine.'

DIANA, PRINCESS OF WALES

No royal ambassador would ever be quite like Diana, Princess of Wales. Her separation from the Prince in 1992 and her tragically short life as a divorcee, following the decree absolute in 1996, may have caused conniptions among the protocol departments both at home and abroad. Her post-marital modus operandi was never entirely clear. What exactly was Diana's royal status, as a semi-detached member of the family? Indeed, what was she trying to achieve on her occasional visits overseas, if they were not in the name of the Crown?

In the year following her separation, the Princess made her first solo visit overseas, with a trip to one of the poorest countries on Earth, Nepal. Only Diana could have attracted an international media entourage three times larger than the number of international phone lines out of Nepal. Even *Vogue* magazine despatched a team, complete with red 'Vogue' baseball caps, in the (vain) hope that the Princess would look at their lens before anyone else's. The government of the mountain kingdom was confused about how to welcome her. At the suggestion of the Foreign Office, there was no national anthem or formal welcome at the airport, prompting one British report of 'threadbare red-carpet treatment'. The Nepalese formally complained, pointing out that there was nothing threadbare about the length of red carpet that had been rolled out for the Princess.

The lack of pomp was put down to the fact that it was a 'working' rather than an 'official' visit, yet she was accompanied throughout by a Foreign Office minister, Lynda Chalker (by then elevated to the Lords as Baroness Chalker). They made a formidable diplomatic duo: the bountiful baroness bearing the British foreign aid cheque book, and the Princess bringing prestige and media attention to charities operating in some of the remotest parts of the world. Each learned from the other as they toured the Himalayan foothills by helicopter, Land Rover and on foot.

'I have a lovely picture of her and me,' says the Baroness. 'I am sitting in an old summer dress with a white collar and white sleeves – and the white ends were no longer white! I thought, this is not the dress to wear on a royal tour.' The minister was accompanied by her then husband, Clive. The Princess had her sister, Lady Sarah, in tow as lady-in-waiting. Yet it was a lean operation, by royal standards.

Lady Chalker was as fond of the Princess as she was of the Prince. 'You have to be able, in family break-ups, to be able to talk with both sides but, above all, to listen to both sides. So I did that,' she says. 'The Princess was finding her feet and it was a very strange period.' Even so, Lady Chalker's patience would be tested one night as she and her husband were asleep. 'We stayed in the house of the military attaché in the compound because there were only a limited number of rooms in the Ambassador's house,' she recalls. 'Suddenly I heard banging on the front door. It was the British Ambassador in a frantic state. He was saying: "Do you know where Her Royal Highness is?" I said: "Have you asked her sister?" ' The Ambassador had tried that. Lady Chalker could not help any further. 'I just said: "Well, ask the police!" It was not my job to keep her under lock and key.'

There was an awkward atmosphere at breakfast the following morning when the story unfolded. As Lady Chalker recalls, the Princess was 'a bit sheepish' as she explained where she had been. 'She went off with the Crown Prince. They had gone for a spin in his sports car. He had got the police to close off all the roads and they went through the centre of Kathmandu. I think Clive asked her if she put her seatbelt on at some point. She said the car didn't have seatbelts.'*

Had this been an official visit and had the Princess been a fully-fledged member of the Royal Family, then she would have been obliged to abide by ministerial advice. But what were the rules regarding a joyriding semi-royal Princess? Did she have to listen to the Baroness? 'She wouldn't – not if she didn't want to,' says Lady Chalker. 'But I was having to be more of a diplomat than a minister.'

The following year, Diana was in Zimbabwe, visiting projects involving those suffering from HIV/Aids and leprosy. Nearly 800 wealthy – mainly white – Zimbabweans paid handsomely to attend a glamorous charity reception in Harare and dressed accordingly. They

* Within eight years, tragedy would have befallen both the royal joyriders. Four years after the tragic death of the Princess in Paris's Pont de l'Alma tunnel, the Crown Prince massacred most of his family in a suicide shooting. It led to the end of the 240-year-old Nepalese monarchy soon afterwards.

were surprised and a little disappointed to find the Princess in a simple day-dress with no jewellery. As far as she was concerned, this was hardly a trip for dressing up. The local tourist board also expressed irritation that her itinerary focussed almost entirely on poverty and did not include famous landmarks like the Victoria Falls. Well aware of the dangers of 'compassion fatigue', she sent a note to her Private Secretary, Patrick Jephson, acknowledging the need to vary the nature of these trips in future. 'Change of diet is very important!' she wrote. With that in mind, she would soon be attending a fabulously glamorous fund-raiser in Paris and making her first (and last) trip to Moscow.

The British Ambassador to Russia at the time, Sir Brian Fall, says that the Princess had been wanting to come to Moscow for some time but the Foreign Office had wanted her to wait until after the Queen's 1994 state visit. 'Diana was a great problem to them. They'd been trying to stop her coming out, particularly before [the Queen], which was understandable,' he says. A date was fixed for June 1995, with the focal point being a children's hospital. The Foreign Office had only proposed a two-day visit, but Sir Brian was keen to offer longer, if that appealed to the Princess. He contacted the Palace and spoke to the Queen's Private Secretary, Robert Fellowes, who was also the Princess's brother-in-law, to explain what might be achieved by a slightly lengthier visit. Sir Brian's boss was furious. If anyone was going to decide where the Princess should go, it was the Foreign Secretary, Douglas Hurd. 'I committed a major crime,' chuckles Sir Brian. 'Douglas hit the roof and said he was the person who had the relationship with Diana and foreign policy and all that. What the hell was I doing?' The visit would be strictly limited to two days.

Sir Brian and his wife, Delmar, found the Princess 'an amazingly easy house guest', though she was wary of everyone, including the Embassy staff. 'You couldn't go into her room or even empty her waste paper basket,' says Lady Fall. The Ambassador took to her from the start. 'She arrived and on the way into the embassy we called in on Luzhkov [Yury Luzhkov, the long-serving Mayor of Moscow] who did his Soviet bit – on and on,' Sir Brian recalls. 'And he went on for forty minutes. Finally he drew breath and the Princess said: "Is this when I get to say something?" And I realised: "This is going to be alright as a visit!" Which indeed it was.'

When the Falls asked the Princess if she would make a detour to visit a centre for children with Down's syndrome, run by the wife of a British journalist, the Princess was delighted to oblige even though it was not on the schedule

Soon after the Princess's return from Moscow, there was a change of Foreign Secretary. Douglas Hurd was replaced by Malcolm Rifkind, and the Princess wasted no time in making contact. 'Out of the blue, I got a message saying "The Princess of Wales wonders whether you might possibly be free?"' says Sir Malcolm, chuckling at the idea that he might not have been able to find a gap in his diary. 'I realised I had not been invited for my wit. She was wanting to know what she could do abroad and she was very impressive in the way she handled people.' The Princess had just received an invitation that she knew was controversial. 'She'd been invited to Argentina and I explained why it had to be sensitive,' says Rifkind. A children's charity in Buenos Aires had asked her to attend a fund-raising event, although the request clearly bore the fingerprints of President Carlos Menem, a self-styled playboy figure. This would be the most high-profile British visit since the UK–Argentine war over the Falkland Islands thirteen years before. 'I said I could not see any obvious problem but it was a question of whether the Argentinians would try to use it. I was trying to be helpful because I thought she was a good asset,' says Sir Malcolm.

The Princess wanted to discuss her long-term plans, too. As Sir Malcolm recalls: 'It was a broad conversation: "What will be the constraints on my travel? I want to use my time and I do get a number of invitations". My personal view was that the whole world would want to meet her whether she was the Princess of Wales or not. I wrote to thank her and it crossed with a letter from her saying "I was so pleased you took time to see me. I know what a busy programme you have". I know it was just a pleasant courtesy, but what a way to charm. With all her problems, she had her own area of talent and ability.'

Travelling as 'K. Stafford' – an alias that would fool no one at all on her scheduled British Airways flight – the Princess flew to Argentina. There she attended a gala dinner and cabaret in the magnificent old Buenos Aires Post Office building where Eva Perón once had her headquarters. The Princess's hosts were mildly appalled when the (blind) orchestra decided to round off the cabaret with a jaunty version of 'I'm getting married in the morning', but the Princess found it hilarious. She also met – and towered over – the flirtatious President Menem (without discussing the Falklands war), had tea in a remote Patagonian town founded by Welsh migrants and went whale-watching, politely ignoring the directive to put an orange lifejacket over her pale-blue jacket. For all the diplomatic sensitivities, none of it would be anything like as controversial as the event that preceded her tour a few days before – that interview with the BBC's *Panorama*. In Britain alone, the audience of nearly twenty-three million set a new record for a factual television programme.

The programme would be the catalyst for divorce proceedings, but it left Diana feeling more confident about setting her own agenda. She accepted an invitation to Chicago to attend a 1996 charity ball for Northwestern University's Cancer Center, raising more than £1 million for cancer research in the process, and dancing with retired chat-show host Phil Donahue. She was also moved to tears meeting sick children at Cook County Hospital, the location for two of her favourite television shows, *Chicago Hope* and *ER*. The visit saturated national and international news media for two days.

There would be a similar trip to Sydney later in the year, again based around a major fund-raising gala evening, with some charity work bolted on. By now her divorce had been finalised and she was no longer HRH The Princess of Wales, but Diana, Princess of Wales. The 'HRH' style had been conferred on marrying into the Royal Family, the Palace explained, and it therefore disappeared on her departure from it. Regardless, the world would simply carry on calling her 'Princess Diana' – a title that she never had in the first place. It was clear that her star quality was undiminished. The Sydney trip caused anxiety within Buckingham Palace because the Princess set off for Australia midway through the Queen's state visit to Thailand. Many of the media covering the Queen were diverted from Bangkok to Australia. Although the Queen would never regard herself as being in competition with her ex-daughter-in-law, there was ill-concealed irritation inside both the Royal Household and the Foreign Office that a long-prepared official mission by the head of state should be eclipsed by the Princess's unofficial four-day trip to one of the Queen's realms.

Once again, the protocol was a source of endless concern to the Princess's hosts and of great fascination to the media. Her hosts, the Victor Chang Cardiac Research Institute, circulated a memo to staff explaining the Princess's new title. 'Under no circumstances is she to be referred to or called Princess Diana,' it explained. 'There is no requirement to curtsy.' The instructions were promptly ignored by genuflecting Australians, who called her 'Princess Diana' wherever she went. They also highlighted the uncertainties surrounding her semi-royal status. There was a motorcade to meet her at the airport, but it had nothing to do with the police or the Governor-General; it had been sponsored by a local Toyota dealer. Given that the Princess had arrived with just a lady-in-waiting and a secretary by way of an entourage, there was no need for a motorcade anyway.

The Australian press were obsessively interested both in the Princess's every move and in what the British press had to say. At the gala dinner, where 810 people paid A$1,000 a head for seared tuna and after-dinner entertainment from Sting, the Sydney *Daily Telegraph* had even given one reporter the task of monitoring the Princess's every move with her knife and fork: 'She ate one of three pieces of seared tuna, one half of roasted tomato, ignoring the squid ink-black noodles . . .'

Clearly aware that the timing of all this risked annoying the Queen, as the monarch's tour of Thailand disappeared from the news pages, the Princess went out of her way to include a Commonwealth dimension to her visit. While attending a lunch for Commonwealth charities (the Sydney *Daily Telegraph*'s royal food correspondent, still hard at work, observed that she had eaten 'none' of her smoked-emu carpaccio), the Princess suddenly started scribbling some notes during lunch. She then asked if she might say a few words and praised the Commonwealth for the way it 'gives a sense of belonging, one to another'.

Her hosts were determined to control every moment of this overtly corporate visit, right down to the exact route and timings of her post-prandial walkabout through the Sydney Convention Hall. Not even the Queen had scripted walkabouts. The Princess managed to inject some spontaneity into these sterile proceedings. 'Can I hug you because I really love everything you do?' asked Emma Jones, thirteen, who had lost half a leg to cancer. 'Of course. I love hugs,' the Princess replied, as Emma threw her arms around her.

From a charitable point of view, the visit had been extremely successful. However, the Princess was determined to be more than a royal (or partly-royal) figurehead and fund-raiser. At the time of her divorce she had shed her patronage of around a hundred charities. She wanted to use her position to do something more substantial. Among her aims was to shift international thinking on a pressing but divisive international issue: landmines. One of her former charities, the British Red Cross, was campaigning for a global ban on these lingering death-traps, left to maim and kill all-comers – especially children – long after wars had ceased. The Princess prepared to set off for Angola, a former war zone with one of the worst rates of landmine casualties in the world. Politically, this was more than sensitive. Her old friend, Baroness Chalker, the Minister for Overseas Aid, was very supportive. 'I went ahead of her, with the police, to set up the visit as an advance party,' she says. However, other sections of the British government were cautious, if not obstructive. In the Foreign Office there was plenty of opposition, not least from within the British Embassy in Angola. According to one royal source, the Ambassador was 'difficult' in the extreme. He did not want the Princess going anywhere near a minefield and made a complaint to the Foreign Secretary. The Ministry of Defence was unhappy, too. The British government not only had its own stores of landmines, but was reluctant to support a ban until there was international unanimity on the issue. One Defence Minister – later identified as Earl Howe – told *The Times*: 'We do not need a loose cannon like her.' Yet images of the Princess in protective mine-clearance kit, walking through an Angolan minefield, did more to highlight and popularise the issue than any publicity to date. She would make a similar trip to Bosnia that summer – and would create a similar impact. Here was a cause that was off-limits to the Royal Family, and one to which she was clearly making a substantial difference. Amid all the uncertainty in her private life, this appeared to be a solid, life-affirming base from which to develop that long-term modus operandi.

Diana never had the satisfaction of seeing 122 nations sign a new treaty eliminating the production and use of landmines later that same year. Nor did she live to see the International Campaign to Ban Landmines win the Nobel Peace Prize that winter. Her death in a Paris car crash would be met with appalled disbelief, even in countries that never knew her. The grief was global and profound, and the big anniversaries of it still resonate to this day, for her greatest twin legacies are now at the forefront of Britain's royal story, as formidable ambassadors in their own right.

THE DUKE AND DUCHESS OF CAMBRIDGE

Like their father and the Queen, both the Duke of Cambridge and the Duke of Sussex have shown a strong affinity for the Commonwealth. After leaving Eton, Prince William spent a 'gap' year that spanned army jungle training in Belize, farming in the UK and an Operation Raleigh project in a remote part of southern Chile. A television camera would be admitted to record the Chilean adventure, including the sight of the heir to the Heir to the Throne scrubbing a lavatory. However, it was the Prince's off-camera experiences in Africa that left the deepest mark. Once again, Kenya would play a central part in a royal rite of passage. For a few epiphanic months of 2001, the Prince worked as a ranch hand at the Lewa Wildlife Conservancy in northern Kenya. Tom Fletcher, embarking on a Foreign Office career after graduating from Oxford, was working at the British High Commission in Nairobi. As the office junior, and therefore the nearest in age to the teenage Prince, he was deputed to make the visit a success. He found the experience rather more enjoyable than Sir Eric Norris had found the same exercise with the Prince's father and aunt a generation before.

'The main thing was just trying to keep the whole thing secret and get him to Lewa,' says Fletcher. 'Once he was there, he was fine. Any press would have been shot or eaten. There was just a very small team – Jamie Lowther-Pinkerton [the Prince's Private Secretary] and the close-protection guys. Their role is always downplayed but they were incredibly involved.'

Fletcher would drop in now and then and tried to keep things as informal as possible – within reason. 'I think I called him "Your Royal Highness" a couple of times and then avoided it as much as possible. You might call him "William" in the third person in front of him.'

He remembers the Prince as 'very easygoing, quite shy' and keen to blend in. 'He was going off every day and mending fences with one of the Kenyan guys, doing what any other gap-year kid would have been asked to do.'

In this same area of Kenya, Prince William would end up dating the ranch owner's daughter, proposing to his future wife and spending his honeymoon. What is clearly going to be a lifelong passion for conservation stems from his early trips there. One of the first patronages that the Prince embraced was the wildlife charity, Tusk. Wary of the charge that these are the privileged concerns of an international safari set, the Prince has made African wildlife a central plank of his international work ever since. He has set up a taskforce to tackle both ends of the trade in animal parts and has recruited the former Tory leader, Lord Hague, as its chairman. Much of its work takes place behind closed doors beyond the gaze of the media. As an ex-politician, Hague remains in awe of the reach of royalty, pointing to Prince William's 2015 broadcast on Chinese television. This was especially sensitive territory, given that China drives the demand for animal parts and its President was about to pay a state visit to Britain. 'I doubt a British prime minister would get 300 million Chinese people to listen to a broadcast,' says Hague, 'and definitely no British Foreign Secretary. Maybe a president of the USA, or some immense Hollywood AAA-grade celebrity could get that. But no one else from this country.'

The Queen and the Prince of Wales were determined that Prince William should grow into his future role, not be pushed into it. Through his four years at St Andrew's University and the next four in the Forces – first, the Army (Blues and Royals), a short spell with the Royal Navy and then a formal transfer to the Royal Air Force – the Prince was largely left alone to lay the foundations for his royal future. There would be the occasional public/private overseas tour. One such was his 2005 visit to watch the British Lions rugby tour, while also attending commemorations to mark the sixtieth anniversary of the end of the Second World War. As ever, it was all closely discussed with the Queen.

There was a change of pace, though, after switching his commission to the RAF to pursue a new career as a pilot. Realising her grandsons' need for an independent presence in this formative stage of their royal careers, the Queen appointed one of Britain's most experienced diplomats to help both Prince William and Prince Harry map out their international future. In 2009, Sir David Manning, previously Britain's Ambassador to Washington, was appointed as senior adviser to the Princes, a role that continues to this day.

For his first official overseas tour, in January 2010, Prince William was asked by the Queen to open the new Supreme Court in Wellington on her behalf. New Zealand's Prime Minister at the time was John Key. Now Sir John, he explains that she had thought about opening it herself. Her decision not to was nothing to do with long-haul travel, but because she felt that the time had come to promote the younger generation. 'She could have come to open the Supreme Court because she came a year later to Australia,' he says. 'It wasn't that she couldn't have handled the flight. She really wanted to introduce the young royals to the Commonwealth. She had a very deliberate plan.'

The following year, Prince William was swift to return after a series of disasters across the continent. In New Zealand, the earthquake that hit Christchurch in February 2011 was one of the worst peacetime tragedies in the country's history, traumatising the handsome, rugby-mad city for years to come. It happened three months after the Pike River mining disaster, which killed twenty-nine. In Australia, too, the state of Victoria had suffered catastrophic flooding, the worst in living memory. The Queen wanted Prince William to extend her condolences to all of them. A few weeks before his wedding to Catherine Middleton – and his elevation to Duke of Cambridge – he arrived in New Zealand with a tiny entourage, including Sir David Manning, to undertake a tour that would require great sensitivity. Sir John Key recalls touring the devastated communities of South Island with him.

'We stayed at this hotel on the west coast and had dinner that night,' says Sir John. 'William had been there for a day at most. He looked exhausted and I said "You should go to bed". This hotel was right on the ocean and he had the room next to mine. In the morning, I was writing my speech on my balcony and he said to me from his balcony: "Do you think I could go for a walk – on my own?" I said: "Go that way". And he climbed down and off he went. That's the nice thing about New Zealand – you could do that.' The Duke was also astonished to see that Key was writing his own speech. He had assumed that politicians had people to do that sort of stuff for them.

It was a tour that would reinforce the same lasting affection for the 'Down Under' can-do resilience that the Prince shares with his father.

He would be back again three years later, by now as Duke of Cambridge, with both his wife and his son, Prince George. He was no longer a trainee but a fully-fledged royal ambassador. Sir Simon Fraser, then head of the Diplomatic Service, singles out two royal tours from that period. 'The most interesting and dramatic visit in my time was the Queen's state visit to Ireland but the other one that really struck me was when Prince William and Kate went quite early to the Far East. It really impacted. It was something which really made a big difference,' he says. Britain had just launched a new marketing push to coincide with the Queen's Diamond Jubilee and London 2012. 'We'd been running this thing called the "Great" campaign on the back of the Olympics. I thought that the contextualising of the campaign, the economic diplomacy and linking the royal visit to that was a very co-ordinated approach to the projection of the country. But these things have to be constantly reinvigorated and reinvented.'

The Duke of Cambridge's diplomatic skills would certainly be put to the test in 2015 during that trip to China, the most high-profile royal visit since the Queen's state visit almost thirty years before. In the intervening years, there had been bilateral strains over the Hong Kong handover and the Prince of Wales's well-documented admiration for the Tibetan spiritual leader, the Dalai Lama – very much *persona non grata* in Beijing. The Duke had his own issues with China in relation to endangered wildlife. Yet he knew that he was there to build bridges and not to lecture. As a result, his visit achieved a modest but undeniable hardening in Chinese policy against ivory imports. The fact that the Duke was invited to a Cabinet meeting with President Xi was similarly significant. Just six weeks earlier, the Foreign Office minister, Hugo Swire, had not even managed to secure a meeting with the chief executive of Hong Kong. Yet here was the Duke of Cambridge being granted a degree of access to the very top that was denied to many Western heads of state. If the Chinese leadership was happier meeting the heir to a hereditary monarchy than a democratically elected politician, Britain would simply play to its strengths. The Prince held court with twenty-five Chinese ministers for forty-five minutes. To make things even harder, the first five minutes were broadcast live on television.

Like his father and his grandmother, the Duke is now adept at sensitive diplomatic missions on the big stage. In June 2018, he became the first member of the Royal Family to pay an official visit to Israel. He is well aware, like his father, that the role of Head of the Commonwealth is not hereditary and must be earned. He has been keen to play his part in its affairs, taking a central role in the 2018 London CHOGM and holding several private one-on-one audiences with heads of government.

The Foreign Office has also deployed both the Duke and the Duchess of Cambridge as a sort of Brexit balm following the 2016 referendum vote to leave the European Union. 'Them going to Europe has been a deliberate policy of saying: "We still want the closest possible ties with you",' says a senior Foreign Office figure. 'Brexit has come at a time when the UK is very divided. At least we have one focus of national unity. The fact we have a Royal Family which is popular is an extraordinary asset. It can reaffirm links and bonds and friendship in a non-political way. So, in a way, the monarchy has found itself with a new relevance.'

No one seriously believes that Britain's tricky recalibration of its relationship with Europe will be swayed one way or the other by a few royal visits. The point is to keep the diplomatic mood-music warm, to underline the fact that the UK has not fundamentally changed, that certain pre-EU institutions will be unchanged in a post-EU Britain. It is a bilateral channel that operates at the highest level, but in a completely different atmosphere. It is why the Duke of Cambridge had a meeting with Chancellor Angela Merkel when he visited Germany in 2016, just weeks after the referendum upheavals, as he attended the seventieth anniversary of North Rhine-Westphalia. There was an even more important lunch the following year as the Duke returned with his family for a 'Brexit balm' tour of Poland and Germany. 'William is now able to go and play that role of serious interlocutor. He did it with President Hollande in Paris. He did it with Hillary Clinton and with the Obamas. He did it in Poland and he did it with Angela Merkel,' says a senior Foreign Office mandarin. 'Merkel had just come from the G20 summit which she had been hosting and which had been very demanding but she was charming and was keen to see William and Catherine.' The Duke, it seems, was careful to avoid offering an opinion. 'It was more interrogative on his side. But he is able to get across the message that the UK wants to stay friends, that there are good relations. I've seen a lot ministers in ministerial meetings and he is pretty good in comparison.'

Even Palace veterans were not expecting the sort of reaction that greeted the Cambridges in Germany. 'I was surprised by the levels of enthusiasm. Heidelberg had the sort of crowds we saw just after their wedding,' says one senior Palace aide. 'Back then, they were a sexy young couple. Now he's losing his hair, he's got three young children and yet the buzz is the same. What's the basis for that? Who knows? But it's there and it's very important.'

Such trips are also planned with an eye looking far beyond today's political cycle. So, in Poland, the British side was particularly keen on the Duke walking with Lech Walesa through the gates of the Gdansk shipyard, the birthplace of Poland's Solidarnosc movement. Walesa's place in world history is already assured, as the Nobel Prize-winning leader of the first independent trade union behind the Iron Curtain. Yet moments like this may, one day, help forge a connection with a generation as yet unborn. 'In fifty years, people in Poland will say of Prince William: "He met Walesa",' says Sir David Manning. It was one of the reasons why the Duke and his team were also keen to meet survivors of the concentration camp at Stutthof. It is a source of astonishment to large parts of today's world that the Queen once worked with Winston Churchill – a figure as remote to younger generations as Queen Victoria. Half a century from now there will be few, if any, public figures still in office who can say that they knew Angela Merkel, Lech Walesa, President Xi or President Obama or that they met Holocaust survivors in a concentration camp. Yet, an elderly King William V will be able to speak of these encounters with fondness and authority. That is the sort of continuity that royalty can provide.

THE DUKE AND DUCHESS OF SUSSEX

If carving out a relevant modern role has been a challenge for the Duke of Cambridge, it has been even more of one for his younger brother. 'The future is on tramlines for William and we know what has to happen,' says a senior member of the Royal Household. 'It's different for Harry. He has much more scope but there can be no entitlement and that is difficult. What is the point of a twenty-first-century Prince? Why have we got you? What are you supposed to be doing? He knows those are the questions.' As a result, the Prince has become perhaps the most internationally-focussed member of the Royal Family -and not merely in his choice of bride.

After leaving Eton in 2003, Prince Harry took a 'gap' year which followed a similar pattern to that of Prince William, with ranch-style work in Australia and Africa. It took him to the southern African hill kingdom of Lesotho and a meeting with Prince Seeiso, younger brother of King Letsie III, the Ampleforth-educated monarch whose boisterous coronation* had been attended by the Prince of Wales in 1997. Seeiso and Harry, though eighteen years apart in age, were younger royal brothers who had both lost their mothers and were keen to establish something to honour their memories. Aside from having the highest lowest point of any nation on Earth, Lesotho's other claim to a superlative was a grim one: one of the highest HIV/Aids infection rates in the world. It had left many children orphaned. The two Princes created the Sentebale charity – meaning 'forget me not' – to offer them a home, an education and hope. It has remained a core concern of Prince Harry ever since.

By the time it was up and running, Prince Harry had been through Sandhurst and was a second lieutenant in the Blues and Royals. Having risen to the top of the Combined Cadet Force at Eton, the Prince quickly proved a natural fit as a cavalry officer. His hopes of serving in Iraq in 2006 were frustrated by senior officers' concerns that he would be singled out by the enemy and would thus be a threat to his own men. His persistence was rewarded, though, in 2007 when he was sent on his first tour of Afghanistan, serving as a forward air controller in Helmand Province. It was only a media leak that forced an early return after ten weeks. He would then retrain as an Army Air

* It was King Letsie's second reign. He first became King when his father, Moshoeshoe II, was forced in to exile by the military in 1990. Letsie loyally abdicated when the old King returned in 1995, only to die in a car crash the following year. Lacking a big enough church for his four-hour coronation, Letsie was crowned (with leopardskin and feathered headband) in the national football stadium.

Corps helicopter pilot and proved to be one of the best in his intake, earning himself a place on the prized training course to fly the Apache attack helicopter. Friends say it was a turning point. 'Two things have made a key difference to him,' says a senior member of the Royal Household. 'One was when it turned out that he was an outstanding helicopter pilot. Being the pilot of an Apache – the top of the tree – was a very big thing. The other was finding he had this ability to mobilise people.'

He was back in Afghanistan in the autumn of 2012, fresh from representing the Queen at the closing ceremony of the London Olympics. This time he was at the helm of an Apache. Death threats from the Taliban did not prevent him from completing his tour, after which he qualified as an Apache commander in 2013 – a year that would be something of a turning point in many ways. By now, British casualties in Afghanistan had far exceeded those in the Falklands. The Prince was well aware that substantial numbers of wounded and damaged servicemen and women were in need of long-term support and new ways of delivering it. That same year, he joined a team of them on a trek to the South Pole with the charity Walking With the Wounded.

As he switched from the Army Air Corps to a staff officer role in London, he was well placed to work on a big new idea. It was in 2013 that he travelled to the USA to look at America's tournament for wounded Forces personnel. 'Harry went out to the Warrior Games and, when they finished, he just said: "We're going to have these in Britain",' recalls a member of his team. 'Then he spent nine months doing little else – boring things like sitting on committees and raising money and dealing with the Ministry of Defence. It was an extraordinary moment for him.'

The Invictus Games were an instant success. Blessed with a lot of goodwill and perfect timing – Britain was still enjoying the afterglow of London 2012 and a nearly-new Olympic Park – the first games drew 300 competitors from thirteen countries.

Those who have watched the Prince mature from shy teenager into one of Britain's best-loved public figures believe that his ten years in the Army have been the making of him (as he himself has acknowledged on several occasions) but, in 2015, it was time to move on.

He would now carve out a new career, one which would seek to show the point of a twenty-first-century Prince.

Invictus was almost a full-time job in itself. Unlike the Warrior Games, which rotate around different parts of the USA, Prince Harry wanted Invictus to move around the world. The next tournament, in 2016, took place in Florida, with the first lady, Michelle Obama, in a central role and bestowing the imprimatur of the White House. Even the Queen was recruited to help with a promotional video. Substantial international media coverage followed on both sides of the Atlantic. With a tried-and-tested formula, the event grew in size and moved on to Toronto in 2017, while Sydney was selected for 2018. By any standards – even royal ones – it was a major achievement to take a new and untried sporting event from a standing start to being an established, televised international fixture in under five years.

'Harry has shot the lights out with Invictus,' says David Cameron. The former US Ambassador to London, Matthew Barzun, agrees: 'What Prince Harry did with Invictus – I think you could see the best of his mother and his father in his natural connection with people. He is out there in his polo shirt being himself but also speaking out – and it's political with a lower case "p" – for these people who would otherwise be left behind.' Barzun remains impressed by Prince Harry's demeanour at these big occasions and by his 'modern, not too buttoned up' approach to the job. He recalls holding a large Invictus event at his official residence, Winfield House, with hundreds of wounded veterans and the Foo Fighters providing the music. 'I made a gaffe,' says the ex-Ambassador. 'In my excitement, I said: "Let's give a big hand to His Majesty, Prince Harry". As an American, the word "highness" is so strange, but you'd think I could say it. Anyway, I hand the microphone to Prince Harry just as it's dawning on me what I just said. He pats me on the shoulder and says: "Thanks for the promotion!" Which I thought was lovely.'

'He has come into his own in the last few years,' says Baroness Chalker who sits on the board of that first charity which Prince Harry created, Sentebale, and knows its Lesotho operations very well. The Prince, she says, is the ideal, hands-on patron. 'He is brilliant with children, absolutely brilliant.' Having accompanied their mother on her travels all those years ago, Lady Chalker first met both Princes as children. 'When I met Prince William a year or two ago, he said: "I remember you". I said: "Yes sir, you have sat on my knee!"' She sees so many parallels with the work of their father and of their late mother. 'I think they have broken the mould in a very appropriate way,' says the former minister. 'I think Diana would be jolly proud. I am sure she is. I mean, she broke the mould in my time when she decided she would go for the banning of landmines.'

The mould-breaking analogy extended very happily to his private life when, in 2017, Prince Harry announced his engagement to Meghan Markle, the first citizen of a foreign nation to become a British princess since the Duke of Kent married Princess Marina of Greece in 1934. The ease with which the star of the US television drama *Suits* was welcomed into the Royal Family was an illustration of the monarchy moving with the times. Almost a century before, there had been considerable excitement when a royal second son had married a 'commoner' for the first time. Lady Elizabeth Bowes-Lyon ended up as Queen because, back then, the Government and the Church of England of the day could not countenance Edward VIII marrying an American divorcee. Nor was Mrs Simpson an actress.

In twenty-first-century Britain, the fact that Ms Markle had been married before was of little more than passing interest. After all, the Prince of Wales was divorced and married to a divorcee. Having an American princess on the Palace balcony (even one who would take British citizenship in due course) could hardly be more timely at a moment when post-referendum Britain was being accused of succumbing to inward nationalistic urges. The monarchy was unquestionably looking outwards and welcoming the world – to the heart of the family. As for Ms Markle's acting credentials, these seemed a positive bonus, both in terms of handling the limelight and bringing added glamour to the institution. To many members of the public and to media commentators, particularly those from minority backgrounds, the most significant breakthrough was that a member of the Royal Family was marrying someone of mixed race. Ms Markle's mother was from an African-American family while her father was of Dutch-Irish descent. The future Duchess of Sussex had spoken openly and poignantly of her ethnicity. 'I wasn't black enough for the black roles and I wasn't white enough for the white ones, leaving me somewhere in the middle,' she had said. As far as the Queen and the Royal Family were concerned, however, the overarching view was quite simple: if Harry is happy, we are happy. The Queen gladly made small but telling indulgences not granted to previous royal brides-to-be, like inviting Ms Markle to join the Royal Family for Christmas and, indeed, using the term 'Ms' in a royal wedding announcement for the first time. For Prince Harry it also meant a welcome end to years of speculation, such as the excruciating if well-meaning remarks of the Prime Minister of Antigua, Gaston Browne, during the Prince's 2016 visit. 'I believe we are expecting a new princess soon,' the premier told the blushing Prince, long before any whiff of a royal engagement. 'You are very welcome to come on your honeymoon here.'

It did not go unnoticed at the Palace that, in their engagement interview, in which Prince Harry talked of 'the stars being aligned', the couple spoke enthusiastically about their hopes for the Commonwealth. The Prince was planning another major Commonwealth tour when wedding plans intervened. 'You know, with lots of young people running around the Commonwealth, that's where we'll spend most of our time hopefully,' Prince Harry told the BBC on the night of his engagement. A keen ambassador for the Queen's Young Leaders programme from its early days, the Prince played a leading role at the Commonwealth Summit in the month before his wedding. Freshly appointed to the role of Queen's Commonwealth Youth Ambassador, he made an opening speech in which he saluted her lifelong devotion to the cause and promised to do the same. 'My commitment will be to work with you to build better platforms for your leadership,' he told the summit's youth forum. 'I am also incredibly grateful that the woman I am about to marry, Meghan, will be joining me in this work.' His bride made that abundantly clear when she arrived at St George's Chapel, Windsor on the morning of 19th May 2018 wearing a Givenchy veil with the national flowers of every Commonwealth nation embroidered into the silk tulle. It was an inspired decision which not only touched many members of the Commonwealth – 'We were with her on that journey up the aisle,' says the Commonwealth Secretary-General, Baroness Scotland, proudly – but one which delighted the Queen. For her Coronation in 1953, the Queen's Norman Hartnell gown had been embroidered with the floral emblems of all four 'home' nations (the Welsh leek, Scottish thistle, English rose and Irish shamrock) plus those of the seven other nations which comprised the Commonwealth at that time. Yet here was Meghan Markle honouring no less than fifty-three nations, a beautiful hand-stitched reminder of how far the Commonwealth has come. No wonder it was a long veil.

Lady Chalker believes that the new Duke of Sussex can do things his elder brother cannot: 'I am sure that he will be a very worthy successor to the sort of action man role that Prince Philip had in his younger days. William will have too much of the governance and Harry can step into that role.'

With his easy manner, quick wit and natural rapport with young people, the Duke of Sussex has cast himself as the cheeky, irreverent, ultra-loyal 'spare' to the more serious 'heir'. Nor would royal life be quite as much of a culture shock to the Duchess as some commentators suggested. Long before she met Prince Harry, in her days as a television actress, Meghan Markle had a hands-on role in the charity sector. Her involvement went well beyond mere celebrity endorsements. It occasionally overlapped with the work of the Prince, such as her support for United Service Organizations (USO), the American forces charity which works closely with Prince Harry's Invictus Games. In 2014, Ms Markle joined a USO tour to entertain US troops all over the world, and ended up in Afghanistan. In other words, as they say in America, she has walked the walk.

The sight of the new Duke and Duchess of Sussex emerging on the steps of St George's Chapel, Windsor on 19th May 2018 was a joyful moment for the monarchy as it would be for any family. For the Queen, though, it also marked the start of a new chapter. In the space of a month, she had seen her eldest son endorsed as the next Head of the Commonwealth and now the next generation settled and eagerly looking to a future with the Commonwealth at the heart of their agenda. 'Team Windsor' had seldom seemed in better shape.

As the Queen well knows, nothing threatens the monarchy quite like complacency. Yet, on a day like this, as a large part of the human race sat glued to the latest instalment of the most enduring fairytale on Earth, who could argue that the contented matriarch quietly presiding over it all was not, after all, the Queen of the World?

APPENDIX

COMMONWEALTH TOURS BY THE QUEEN SINCE 1952

February 1952: Kenya (Nairobi, Treetops and Sagana Lodge, Kiganjo, where the Queen learned of her accession)
November 1953: Bermuda, Jamaica
December 1953: Fiji, Tonga
December 1953–January 1954: New Zealand
February–April 1954: Australia (New South Wales (NSW), Australian Capital Territory (ACT), Tasmania, Victoria, South Australia, Queensland, Western Australia)
April 1954: Cocos (Keeling) Islands, Ceylon (now Sri Lanka), Aden, Uganda
May 1954: Malta, Gibraltar
January–February 1956: Nigeria
October 1957: Canada (Ontario)
June–August 1959: Canada (opening of St. Lawrence Seaway, including one day in Chicago, Newfoundland, Quebec, Ontario, Alberta, British Columbia, Yukon, Northwest Territories, Saskatchewan, Manitoba, New Brunswick, Prince Edward Island, Nova Scotia)
January 1961: India*
February 1961: Pakistan*, India
March 1961: India
November 1961: Ghana*, Sierra Leone

December 1961: Gambia (departing via non-Commonwealth Senegal)
January 1963: Canada (overnight stay in Vancouver)
February–March 1963: Fiji, New Zealand, Australia (ACT, South Australia, Victoria, Tasmania, NSW, Queensland, Northern Territory, Western Australia)
October 1964: Canada (Prince Edward Island, Quebec, Ottawa)
February 1966: Barbados, British Guiana (now Guyana), Trinidad and Tobago, Grenada, St. Vincent, Barbados, St. Lucia, Dominica, Montserrat, Antigua, St. Kitts-Nevis, British Virgin Islands (Tortola, Beef Island, Virgin Gorda) and Turks and Caicos Islands (Grand Turk, South Caicos), The Bahamas (Nassau)
March 1966: Jamaica
June–July 1967: Canada (centennial celebrations and EXPO at Montreal)
November 1967: Malta
March 1970: Fiji, Tonga, New Zealand, Australia (NSW, Tasmania, Victoria, Queensland)
July 1970: Canada (Northwest Territories and Manitoba)
May 1971: Canada (British Columbia)
February 1972: Singapore*, Malaysia*, Brunei*
March 1972: Seychelles, Mauritius, Kenya* (Nairobi)
June–July 1973: Canada (Ontario, Prince Edward Island, Regina, Calgary)
July–August 1973: Canada (Ottawa Commonwealth Heads of Government Meeting, known as CHOGM)
October 1973: Fiji, Australia (ACT and Sydney for the opening of the opera house)
January 1974: Cook Islands (opening of Rarotonga International Airport), New Zealand (visit to Commonwealth Games)
February 1974: Norfolk Island, New Hebrides, Solomon Islands (San Cristobal, Honiara, Giza), Papua New Guinea, Australia (ACT – the Queen returned to the UK on 28 February for a General Election. The Duke of Edinburgh completed the tour)
February 1975: Bermuda, Barbados, Bahamas
April 1975: Jamaica (Kingston CHOGM)
May 1975: Hong Kong
July 1976: Canada (Nova Scotia, New Brunswick and Montreal for Olympic Games)

February 1977: Western Samoa (Apia, Tiafau), Tonga, Fiji, New Zealand
March 1977: Australia (ACT, NSW, Queensland, Tasmania, Victoria, South Australia, Northern Territory, Western Australia), Papua New Guinea
October 1977: Canada (Ontario), Bahamas, British Virgin Islands (Tortola, Virgin Gorda), Barbados, Antigua
July–August 1978: Canada (Newfoundland, Saskatchewan, Alberta for Commonwealth Games, Edmonton, accompanied by Prince Andrew and Prince Edward)
July 1979: Tanzania* (Arusha, Dares Salaam, Zanzibar, Kilimanjaro), Malawi* (Blantyre, Lilongwe, Zomba Plateau), Botswana* (Gaborone), Zambia* (Lusaka CHOGM, Kitwe, Ndola)
May 1980: Australia (Canberra, Sydney, Melbourne)
September–October 1981: Australia (Melbourne CHOGM, Tasmania, Western Australia, South Australia)
October 1981: New Zealand, Sri Lanka (Colombo, Anuradhapura, Kandy, Victoria Dam)
April 1982: Canada (Ottawa for Patriation of the Constitution)
October 1982: Australia (NWT, Queensland for Commonwealth Games, Brisbane, ACT, NSW), Papua New Guinea, Solomon Islands, Nauru, Kiribati, Tuvalu, Fiji
February 1983: Bermuda, Jamaica, Cayman Islands
March 1983: Canada (British Columbia)
November 1983: Cyprus (overnight stop), Kenya*, Bangladesh*, India* (New Delhi CHOGM)
March 1984: Cyprus (overnight stop)
September–October 1984: Canada (New Brunswick, Ontario and Manitoba)
October 1985: Belize, Bahamas (Nassau CHOGM), Little Inagua Island, St. Kitts-Nevis, Antigua, Dominica, St. Lucia, St. Vincent and the Grenadines, Barbados, Grenada
November 1985: Trinidad and Tobago
February–March 1986: New Zealand
March 1986: Australia (ACT, NSW, Victoria, South Australia)
October 1986: Hong Kong
October 1987: Canada (Vancouver CHOGM, British Columbia, Saskatchewan and Quebec)

April–May 1988: Australia (Western Australia, Tasmania, Queensland, NSW and ACT)
March 1989: Barbados (350th anniversary of Barbados Parliament)
October 1989: Singapore*, Malaysia* (Kuala Lumpur CHOGM)
February 1990: New Zealand (Commonwealth Games, Auckland, 150th anniversary of Treaty of Waitangi, Wellington, Christchurch)
June–July 1990: Canada (Alberta, Ontario, Quebec)
October 1991: Kenya (overnight stop), Namibia*, Zimbabwe* (Harare CHOGM)
February 1992: Australia (150th anniversary of founding of city of Sydney, ACT and Southern Australia)
May 1992: Malta*
June–July 1992: Canada (celebration of 125th anniversary of Confederation)
October 1993: Cyprus (Limassol CHOGM)
February 1994: Anguilla, Dominica, Guyana*, Belize, Cayman Islands
March 1994: Jamaica, Bahamas, Bermuda
August 1994: Canada (Nova Scotia, British Columbia, Northwest Territories)
March 1995: South Africa*
October–November 1995: New Zealand (Wellington, Christchurch, Dunedin, Auckland CHOGM)
June–July 1997: Canada (Newfoundland, Ontario, National Capital Region)
October 1997: Pakistan*, India*
September 1998: Brunei*, Malaysia*
November 1999: Ghana*, South Africa* (Durban CHOGM), Mozambique*
March 2000: Australia (ACT, NSW, Victoria, Tasmania, Northern Territory (Alice Springs), Western Australia
February 2002: Jamaica (Kingston and Montego Bay), New Zealand (Wellington, Christchurch and Auckland), Australia (South Australia and Queensland, including Coolum CHOGM)
October 2002: Canada (Nunavut, British Columbia, Manitoba, Ontario, New Brunswick and the National Capital Region)
December 2003: Nigeria* (Abuja CHOGM)
May 2005: Canada (Saskatchewan and Alberta)

November 2005: Malta* (Valletta CHOGM)
March 2006: Australia (Melbourne Commonwealth Games, Sydney), Singapore*
November 2007: Malta, Uganda* (Kampala CHOGM)
November 2009: Bermuda, Trinidad and Tobago* (Port of Spain CHOGM)
June 2010: Canada (Ontario, Manitoba)
October 2011: Australia (Canberra, Brisbane, Melbourne, Perth CHOGM)
November 2015: Malta* (Valletta CHOGM)

* Includes a state visit

Compiled from Royal Household lists and other sources.

STATE VISITS MADE BY THE QUEEN SINCE 1952

November 1953: Panama* – Colonel Jose Remon
May 1954: Libya* – King Idris
June 1955: Norway – King Haakon VII
June 1956: Sweden – King Gustaf VI Adolf
February 1957: Portugal – President Craveiro Lopes
February 1957: France – President René Coty
May 1957: Denmark – King Frederick IX
October 1957: USA – President Eisenhower
March 1958: Netherlands – Queen Juliana
February 1961: Nepal – King Mahendra
March 1961: Iran – Shahanshah Mohammad Reza Shah Pahlavi
May 1961: Italy – President Gronchi
May 1961: The Vatican – Pope John XXIII
November 1961: Liberia – President Tubman
February 1965: Ethiopia – Emperor Haile Selassie
February 1965: Sudan – Dr. El Tigani
May 1965: West Germany – President Lübke
May 1966: Belgium – King Badouin and Queen Fabiola
November 1968: Brazil – President da Costa e Silva
November 1968: Chile – President Frei Montalva
May 1969: Austria – President Jonas
October 1971: Turkey – President Sunay
February 1972: Thailand – King Bhumibol and Queen Sirikit
March 1972: Maldives – President Nasir
May 1972: France – President Pompidou
October 1972: Yugoslavia – President Tito

March 1974: Indonesia – President Suharto
February 1975: Mexico – President Echeverría
May 1975: Japan – Emperor Hirihito
May 1976: Finland – President Kekkonen
July 1976: USA – President Ford
November 1976: Luxembourg – Grand Duke Jean and Grand Duchess Joséphine
May 1978: West Germany – President Scheel
February 1979: Kuwait* – Emir Sheikh Jaber al-Sabah
February 1979: Bahrain* – Emir Sheikh Isa bin Salman Al Khalifa
February 1979: Saudi Arabia* – King Khalid
February 1979: Qatar* – Emir Sheikh Khalifa bin Hamad Al Thani
February 1979: United Arab Emirates* – Emir Sheikh Zayed
February/March 1979: Oman* – Sultan Qaboos
May 1979: Denmark – Queen Margrethe and Prince Henrik
April 1980: Switzerland – President Chevallaz
October 1980: Italy – President Pertini
October 1980: The Vatican – Pope John Paul II
October 1980: Tunisia – President Bourguiba
October 1980: Algeria – President Bendjedid
October 1980: Morocco – King Hassan II
May 1981: Norway – King Olav V
February 1983: Mexico* – President de la Madrid
February/March 1983: USA* – President Reagan
May 1983: Sweden – King Carl XVI Gustaf and Queen Silvia
March 1984: Jordan – King Hussein and Queen Noor
March 1985: Portugal – President and Senhora Eanes
February 1986: Nepal – King Birendra and Queen Aishwarya
October 1986: China – President Li Xiannian
July 1988: Holland* – Queen Beatrix
October 1988: Spain – King Juan Carlos and Queen Sofia
June 1990: Iceland – President Vigdís Finnbogadóttir
November 1990: Germany* – President von Weizsäcker
May 1991: USA – President George H. Bush
June 1992: France – President Mitterrand
October 1992: Germany – President von Weizsäcker
May 1993: Hungary – President Göncz
May 1994: France* – President Mitterrand

June 1994: France* – President Mitterrand
October 1994: Russia – President Yeltsin
March 1996: Poland – President Wałęsa
March 1996: Czech Republic – President Havel
October 1996: Thailand – King Bhumibol
April 1999: South Korea – President Kim Dae-jung
October 2000: Italy – President Ciampi
October 2000: The Vatican* – Pope John Paul II
May 2001: Norway – King Harald V and Queen Sonja
April 2004: France – President Jacques Chirac
November 2004: Germany – President Horst Köhler
October 2006: Lithuania – President Adamkus
October 2006: Latvia – President Vike-Freiberga
October 2006: Estonia – President Ilves
February 2007: Holland* – Queen Beatrix
May 2007: United States – President George W. Bush
May 2008: Turkey – President Gül
October 2008: Slovenia – President Türk
October 2008: Slovakia – President Gašparovič
November 2010: United Arab Emirates – Emir Sheikh Khalifa bin Zayed bin Sultan Al-Nahyan
November 2010: Oman – Sultan Qaboos
May 2011: Ireland – President McAleese
April 2014: Italy* – President Napolitano
April 2014: The Vatican* – Pope Francis
June 2014: France – President Hollande
June 2015: Germany – President Gauck

* Organised as an official or royal visit, rather than a full state visit

List compiled from Royal Household and other sources.

STATE VISITS RECEIVED BY THE QUEEN SINCE 1952

June 1954: Sweden – King Gustaf VI Adolf and Queen Louise
October 1954: Ethiopia – Emperor Haile Selassie
October 1955: Portugal – President Francisco Craveiro Lopes and Madame Craveiro Lopes
July 1956: Iraq – King Faisal II
May 1958: Italy – President Giovanni Gronchi and Signora Gronchi
October 1958: Germany – President Theodor Heuss
May 1959: Iran – Shahanshah Mohammed Reza Shah Pahlavi
April1960: France – President Charles de Gaulle and Madame de Gaulle
July 1960: Thailand – King Bhumibol and Queen Sirikit
October 1960: Nepal – King Mahendra and Queen Ratna
July 1962: Liberia – President William Tubman and Mrs. Tubman
October 1962: Norway – King Olav V
May 1963: Belgium – King Baudouin and Queen Fabiola
June 1963: India – President Sarvepalli Radhakrishnan
July 1963: Greece – King Paul I and Queen Frederica
May 1964: Sudan – President Ferik Ibrahim Abboud
July 1965: Chile – President Frei Montalva and Señora de Frei
May 1966: Austria – Federal President Franz Jonas and Frau Jonas
July 1966: Jordan – King Hussein
November 1966: Pakistan – President Ayub Khan
May 1967: Saudi Arabia – King Faisal
November 1967: Turkey – President Cevdet Sunay and Madame Sunay

April 1969: Italy – President Saragat and Signora Santacatterina
July 1969: Finland – President Urho Kekkonen and Madame Kekkonen
October 1971: Japan – Emperor Hirohito and Empress Nagako
December 1971: Afghanistan – King Mohammed Zahir Shah, Princess Bilqis and General Sardar Abdul Wali
June 1972: The Netherlands – Queen Juliana and Prince Bernhard
June 1972: Luxembourg – Grand Duke Jean and Grand Duchess Joséphine Charlotte
October 1972: Germany – President Gustav Heinemann and Frau Heinemann
April1973: Mexico – President Luis Echeverría and Señora de Echeverría
June 1973: Nigeria – Head of the Federal Military Government General Yakubu Gowon and Mrs. Gowon
December 1973: Zaire – President Mobuto Sese Seko and Madame Mobutu
April1974: Denmark – Queen Margrethe II and Henrik, Prince Consort of Denmark
July 1974: Malaysia – The Yang di-Pertuan Agong and The Raja Permaisuri Agong
July 1975: Sweden – King Carl XVI Gustaf
November 1975: Tanzania – President Nyerere
May 1976: Brazil – President Ernesto Geisel and Senhora Geisel
June 1976: France – President Valéry Giscard d'Estaing and Madame d'Estaing
June 1978: Romania – President Nicolae Ceauşescu and Madame Ceauşescu
November 1978: Portugal – President António Eanes and Senhora Eanes
June 1979: Kenya – President Daniel Arap Moi
November 1979: Indonesia – President Suharto and Madame Tien Soeharto
November 1980: Nepal – King Birendra and Queen Aishwarya
March 1981: Nigeria – President Shehu Shagari
June 1981: Saudi Arabia – King Khalid
March 1982: Oman – Sultan Qaboos bin Said al Said
June 1982: USA – President and Mrs Reagan*

November 1982: The Netherlands – Queen Beatrix and Prince Claus
March 1983: Zambia – President Kenneth Kaunda and Mrs. Kaunda
April 1984: Bahrain – Emir Sheikh Isa bin Salman Al Khalifa
October 1984: France – President François Mitterand and Madame Mitterand
April 1985: Malawi – Life President Hastings Banda
June 1985: Mexico – President Miguel de la Madrid and Señora de la Madrid
November 1985: Qatar – Emir Sheikh Khalifa bin Hamad Al Thani
April 1986: Spain – King Juan Carlos and Queen Sofia
July 1986: Germany – President Richard von Weizsäcker and Freifrau von Weizsäcker
March 1987: Saudi Arabia – King Fahd
July 1987: Morocco – King Hassan II
April 1988: Norway – King Olav V
July 1988: Turkey – President Kenan Evren
November 1988: Senegal – President Abdou Diouf and Madame Diouf
May 1989: Nigeria – President Babandiga and Mrs. Babangida
July 1989: UAE – President Sheikh Zayed bin Sultan Al Nahyan
April 1990: India – President Ramaswamy Venkataraman and Shri Venkataraman
October 1990: Italy – President Francesco Cossiga
April 1991: Poland – President Lech Wałęsa and Mrs. Wałęsa
July 1991: Egypt – President Hosni Mubarak and Mrs. Mubarak
November 1992: Brunei Darussalam – The Sultan Hassanal Bolkiah of Brunei Darussalam and The Raja lsteri
April 1993: Portugal – President Mário Soares and Senhora Soares
November 1993: Malaysia – The Yang di-Pertuan Agong and The Raja Permaisuri Agong
May 1994: Zimbabwe – President Robert Mugabe
July 1994: Norway – King Harald V and Queen Sonja
May 1995: Kuwait – Emir Sheikh Jaber al-Sabah
October 1995: Finland – President Martti Ahtisaari and Madame Ahtisaari
May 1996: France – President Jacques Chirac and Madame Chirac
July 1996: South Africa – President Nelson Mandela
February 1997: Israel – President Ezer Weizman and Mrs. Weizman

December 1997: Brazil – President Fernando Henrique Cardoso and Senhora Cardoso
May 1998: Japan – Emperor Akihito and Empress Michiko
December 1998: Germany – President Roman Herzog and Frau Herzog
June 1999: Hungary – President Árpád Göncz and Mrs. Göncz
October 1999: China – President Jiang Zemin and Madame Wang Yeping
February 2000: Denmark – Queen Margrethe II and Henrik, Prince Consort of Denmark
June 2001: South Africa – President Thabo Mbeki and Mrs. Mbeki
November 2001: Jordan – King Abdullah II and Queen Rania
June 2003: Russia – President Vladimir Putin and Mrs. Putina
November 2003: USA – President George W. Bush and Mrs. Bush
May 2004: Poland – President Aleksander Kwaśniewski and Mrs. Kwaśniewska
November 2004: France** – President Jacques Chirac and Mrs Chirac
December 2004: South Korea – President Roh Moo-hyun and Mrs. Roh Moo-hyun
March 2005: Italy – President Carlo Azeglio Ciampi and Signora Ciampi
October 2005: Norway* – King Harald V and Queen Sonja
November 2005: China – President Hu Jintao and Madame Liu Yongqing
March 2006: Brazil – President Luiz Inácio Lula da Silva and Senhora Lula da Silva
March 2007: Ghana – President John Kufuor and Mrs. Kufuor
October 2007: Saudi Arabia – King Abdullah bin Abdulaziz Al Saud
March 2008: France – President Nicolas Sarkozy and Madame Sarkozy
March 2009: Mexico – President Felipe Calderón and Señora Zavala
October 2009: India – President Pratibha Devisingh Patil and Dr. Devisingh Ramsingh Shekhawat
March 2010: South Africa – President Jacob Zuma and Mrs. Zuma
September 2010: The Vatican*** – Pope Benedict XVI
November 2010: Qatar – Emir Sheikh Hamad bin Khalifa Al Thani and Sheikha Mozah bint Nasser Al-Missned

May 2011: USA – President Barack Obama and Mrs. Obama
November 2011: Turkey – President Abdullah Gül and Mrs. Gül
October 2012: Indonesia – President Susilo Bambang Yudhoyono and Mrs. Yudohoyono
November 2012: Kuwait – Emir Sheikh Sabah al-Sabah
April 2013: UAE – Sheikh Khalifa bin Zayed bin Sultan Al-Nahyan
November 2013: South Korea – President Park Geun-hye
April 2014: Ireland – President Michael D. Higgins and Mrs. Sabina Higgins
October 2014: Singapore – President Tony Tan Keng Yam and Mrs. Tan Keng Yam
March 2015: Mexico – President Enrique Peña Nieto and Señora Angélica Rivera de Peña
October 2015: China – President Xi Jinping and Madame Peng Liyuan
November 2016: Colombia – President Juan Manuel Santos de Calderon
July 2017: Spain – King Felipe VI and Queen Letizia

* Official visit with a state banquet
** Official visit with a state banquet to mark the centenary of the Entente Cordiale
*** Papal visit with status of a state visit

Compiled from Royal Household list and other sources.

SOURCES AND BIBLIOGRAPHY

The Royal Archives

With the permission of Her Majesty The Queen, I have been granted access to the Royal Archives to view the unpublished official Tour Diary (Volumes I and II) of the 1947 Tour of South Africa (F&V/VISOV/SA/1947); selected speeches of His Majesty King George VI; and royal records relating to state banquets.

The National Archives

I have used the Open Government Licence to quote extensively from files held by The National Archives (TNA) and originating from the following departments:

The Prime Minister's Office (PREM)
The Cabinet Office (CAB)
The Foreign & Commonwealth Office (FCO)
The Commonwealth Relations Office (DO)
The Foreign Office (FO)

The Churchill Archives Centre, Churchill College, Cambridge

I have used material from the papers of Sir Alan Lascelles and from a memoir by Sir Roger du Boulay. I have also consulted the papers of Lord Soames.

The British Diplomatic History Programme

Also housed at the Churchill Archives Centre, this extensive collection of interviews with former diplomats includes material relating to many state and royal tours throughout the reign.

The Commonwealth Secretariat Archives

I have used material from internal memos, correspondence, cuttings, journals and books kept at Marlborough House.

Private Archives

I am most grateful to many of my interviewees for allowing me to see their own memoirs, diaries, scrapbooks, letters, cuttings and souvenirs of so many royal tours. Collectively they have been invaluable in conveying the scale of these royal expeditions and the depth of the affection for the Queen globally.

Additionally, I have consulted many official publications, including Hansard and *The Gazette*. I am also grateful to the editors of *Round Table*, the in-house journal of the Commonwealth. As important as any official source is what the press have had to say. Most royal stories from the early Nineties onwards are well documented online and in databases. For a full account of the first forty years of the Queen's reign, however, nothing matches traditional newspaper cuttings, and I have greatly enjoyed rummaging through piles of them, courtesy of the *Daily Mail*'s Reference Library and its excellent team of librarians. Throughout this book I have also drawn on my own notes, cuttings and files from the eighty-four royal visits to sixty-six countries and territories that I have covered as a journalist in the twenty-five years between 1992 and 2017.

All interviewees have been quoted and attributed directly, except for those who have requested anonymity. I have also drawn on the following books, which I commend to anyone examining the international role of the most-travelled monarch in history.

Allison, Ronald and Riddell, Sarah, *The Royal Encyclopaedia* (Macmillan, 1991)

Anderson, Ian and Ruimy, Joel, *Leadership in the Making: 50 Years of HRH The Duke of Edinburgh's Commonwealth Study Conferences* (Temple Scott, 2006)

Anyaoku, Emeka, *The Inside Story of the Modern Commonwealth* (Evans Brothers, 2004)

Bain, K. R., *The official record of the royal visit to Tonga: 19th–20th December, 1953* (Pitkin, 1954)

Bedell Smith, Sally, *Elizabeth The Queen* (Penguin, 2012)

Bradford, Sarah, *Elizabeth: A Biography of Her Majesty the Queen* (William Heinemann, 1996)

—— *George VI* (Weidenfeld & Nicolson, 1989)

Brandreth, Gyles, *Philip and Elizabeth: Portrait of a Marriage* (Century, 2004)

Connors, Jane Holley, *The Glittering Thread* (University of Technology, Sydney, 1996)

De Guitaut, Caroline, *The Royal Tour* (Royal Collection Enterprises, 2009)

Devon, Stanley, *The Royal Canadian Tour: The Complete Pictorial Story* (Pitkin, 1951)

Dimbleby, Jonathan, *The Prince of Wales: A Biography* (Little, Brown, 1994)

Fletcher, Tom, *The Naked Diplomat: Understanding Power and Politics in the Digital Age* (William Collins, 2016)

Goodsir, Sally, *Royal Gifts* (Royal Collection Trust, 2017)

Hardman, Robert, *Monarchy: The Royal Family at Work* (Ebury, 2007)

—— *Our Queen* (Hutchinson, 2011)

Heald, Tim, *The Duke: A Portrait of Prince Philip* (Hodder & Stoughton, 1991)

Howell, David, *The Commonwealth Transformed* (Book Printing UK, 2018)

—— *Old Links and New Ties: Power and Persuasion in an Age of Networks* (I. B. Tauris, 2013)

Jay, Antony, *Elizabeth R* (BBC Books, 1992)

Jephson, Patrick, *Shadows of a Princess* (HarperCollins, 2000)

Johnstone-Bryden, Richard, *The Royal Yacht Britannia: The Official History* (Conway Maritime Press, 2003)

Junor, Penny, *The Firm* (HarperCollins 2011)

Kielinger, Thomas, *Elizabeth II* (Verlag C. H. Beck, 2011)

La Grange, Zelda, *Good Morning, Mr Mandela* (Penguin, 2014)

Lacey, Robert, *Royal: Her Majesty Queen Elizabeth II* (Little, Brown, 2002)

Lascelles, Sir Alan (edited by Duff Hart-Davis), *King's Counsellor: Abdication and War* (Weidenfeld & Nicolson, 2006)

Longworth, Philip, *The Unending Vigil: The History of the Commonwealth War Graves Commission* (Pen & Sword Books, 2010)

McDonald, Sir Trevor with Tiffin, Peter, *The Queen and the Commonwealth* (Methuen, 1986)

McKinnon, Don, *In the Ring: A Commonwealth Memoir* (Elliott & Thompson, 2013)

Moore, Charles, *Margaret Thatcher: The Authorized Biography. Volume One, Not For Turning* (Allen Lane, 2013)

—— *Margaret Thatcher: The Authorized Biography. Volume Two, Everything She Wants* (Allen Lane, 2015)

Murphy, Professor Philip, *Monarchy and the End of Empire* (Oxford University Press, 2013)

Oliver, Brian, *The Commonwealth Games: Extraordinary Stories behind the Medals* (Bloomsbury Sport, 2014)

Owen, David, *Time to Declare* (Michael Joseph, 1991)

Pimlott, Ben, *The Queen* (HarperCollins, 1996)

Ramphal, Shridath, *Glimpses of a Global Life* (Hansib Publications, 2014)

—— *One World to Share* (Hutchinson, 1979)

Roberts, Andrew, *The House of Windsor* (Weidenfeld & Nicolson, 2000)

—— *The Royal House of Windsor* (Kindle edition, 2011)

Roche, Marc, *Elizabeth II: Une Vie, un règne* (Tallandier, 2016)

Rose, Kenneth, *Kings, Queens and Courtiers* (Weidenfeld & Nicolson, 1985)

Sebag Montefiore, Simon, *The Romanovs* (Weidenfeld & Nicolson, 2016)
Shawcross, William, *Queen and Country* (BBC Books, 2002)
—— *Queen Elizabeth, The Queen Mother* (Macmillan, 2009)
Smith, Arnold, *Stitches in Time: The Commonwealth in World Politics* (General Publishing, 1981)
Thomas, Wynford Vaughan, *Royal Tour, 1953–4* (Hutchinson, 1954)
Turner, Graham, *Elizabeth: The Woman and the Queen* (Macmillan, 2002)
Vickers, Hugo, *Elizabeth, The Queen Mother* (Hutchinson, 2005)
Wheeler-Bennett, Sir John, *King George VI : His Life and Reign* (Macmillan, 1958)
Wright, Patrick R. H., *Behind Diplomatic Lines: Relations with Ministers* (Biteback, 2018)

PICTURE PERMISSIONS

Picture section 1

1. Getty / Topical Press Agency
2. Getty / Rolls Press / Popperfoto
3. Getty / Paul Popper / Popperfoto
4. Getty / Fox Photos
5. Getty / Paul Popper / Popperfoto
6. Getty / Dmitri Kessel
7. Getty / Popperfoto
8. Getty / Fox Photos
9. Getty / Paul Popper / Popperfoto
10. Getty / Hulton Archive
11. Getty / Paul Popper / Popperfoto
12. Getty / Popperfoto
13. Getty / Bettmann
14. Getty / Hank Walker
15. Getty / Popperfoto
16. Getty / Popperfoto
17. Getty / Paul Schutzer
18. Getty / Rolls Press / Popperfoto

Picture section 2

1. Getty / Hulton Archive
2. Getty / Rolls Press / Popperfoto
3. Getty / DEUTSCH Jean-Claude
4. Getty / AFP
5. Getty / Doug Griffin
6. Getty / Keystone
7. Getty / Anwar Hussein
8. Getty / Fox Photos
9. Getty / Anwar Hussein
10. Getty / Popperfoto
11. Getty / Anwar Hussein
12. Getty / Anwar Hussein
13. Getty / William Campbell
14. Getty / Tim Graham
15. Getty / Georges De Keerle
16. Getty / Ronald Reagan Library
17. Getty / Anwar Hussein
18. Getty / Hulton Archive
19. Getty / AFP

Picture section 3

1. Getty / Tim Graham
2. Getty / Tim Graham
3. Getty / Princess Diana Archive
4. Getty / GERARD FOUET
5. Getty / Graham Wiltshire
6. Getty / Tim Graham Picture Library
7. Getty / Tim Graham
8. Getty / Julian Parker
9. Getty / AVENTURIER/BUU/HIRES
10. Getty / Tim Graham
11. Getty
12. Getty / Samir Hussein
13. Getty / Julian Parker
14. Getty / Independent News and Media

15. Getty / Morne de Klerk
16. Getty / ALASTAIR GRANT
17. Getty / The White House
18. Getty / WPA pool
19. Getty / WPA pool
20. Getty / Mark Cuthbert

INDEX

Abacha, Sani, 415
abdications, 80, 234–5, 238, 287, 531
Abdullah bin Abdulaziz, King of Saudi Arabia, 489
Abel Smith, Conolly, 351, 352, 353, 355–6
Aberconway, Lord, *see* McLaren, Henry
Aberdare National Park, Kenya, 12, 126, 128
Aboriginal Australians, 196, 201
Acland, Antony, 44, 48–9, 79–80, 251, 253–4, 271
Acland, John, 479
Adams, Gerry, 256, 460, 462
Adams, William, 61
Adamson, Colin, 101
Adeane, Helen, 73
Adeane, Michael, 28, 29, 73, 199, 282, 427, 431
Aden, 441
'Advance Australia Fair', 207
Afghanistan, 11–12, 528–9, 533
African tours
  1947 11, 19, 108–20, 137, 189–90, 273, 342, 346, 374, 403, 410, 411, 412
  1961 15, 18–19, 55, 135, 137, 142, 221, 307, 362
  1979 26, 30, 36, 57, 64, 307–40
  1997 498
African National Congress (ANC), 378, 379, 386–7, 400, 401, 402, 406, 408, 416
Ahidjo, Ahmadou, 21
AIDS (acquired immune deficiency syndrome), 498, 516, 528
Airlie, Countess of, 271
AK-47 rifles, 311
Akihito, Emperor of Japan, 79
al-Akiti, Afifi, 470
Alexander III, Emperor and Autocrat of All the Russias, 445, 450
Alexander, Harold, 1st Earl Alexander of Tunis, 220
Alexandra of Denmark, Queen consort of the United Kingdom, 100
Alexandra Feodorovna, Empress consort of All the Russias, 450
Algeria, 25, 166
Alice of Battenberg, Princess Andrew of Greece and Denmark, 426, 446
All Saints Church, Poplar, 177
Alleyne, Jonathan, 184
Allinson, Len, 313, 317, 321, 326, 332, 333, 334, 335
Altrincham, Lord, *see* Grigg, John
American Revolutionary War (1775–83), 120, 242, 243, 247, 264, 266, 268
Amery, Julian, 89, 98, 331
Amies, Hardy, 41, 291, 428
Amin, Idi, 23, 81–5, 86, 147, 329
Amnesty International, 401
Amos, Valerie Ann, 162
Amritsar massacre (1919), 158
Ananda Mahidol, King of Thailand, 39
Andamooka Opal, 21
Andover, *see* Hawker Siddeley Andover
Andrei, Stefan, 89
Andrew, Prince, *see* York, Duke of
Andrew of Greece, Princess, *see* Alice of Battenberg
Andrews, Julie, 248
Anglican church, 151–4, 340, 449, 484, 531
Anglo-Romanian Bank, 96
Angola, 483, 521
Anguilla, 20, 64, 170, 230–31
Anne, Princess, *see* Princess Royal
Annenberg, Walter, 241
annus horribilis (1992), 46, 75, 210, 250, 497
Anson, Charles, 406
Antarctica, 22, 183, 355–6, 529
Anthony, Douglas, 206
Anti-Apartheid Movement, 379
Antigua & Barbuda, 232, 532
Anyaoku, Emeka
  and *Britannia*, 370, 371
  and debt-relief strategies, 155
  gold mace gift (1992), 162
  and Edinburgh CHOGM (1997), 162–3
  on Francophonie, 168
  and Harare CHOGM (1991), 406, 407
  and Lusaka CHOGM (1979), 330, 338
  and Mandela, 402
  and Marlborough House CHOGM (1986), 400
  and Palestine, 166
  and racial inequality, 144
  and Singapore CHOGM (1971) 147
  and South Africa, 386–7, 390, 408, 409
apartheid (1948–94), 17, 119, 136, 146, 150, 172–3, 312, 316, 378–407, 413
Apprentice, The, 181
Arafat, Yasser, 166
Arctic convoys (1941–5), 451
Ardern, Jacinda, 217–18
Argentina
  Princess of Wales's visit (1995), 518–19
  Falklands War (1982), 155, 173, 245, 247, 377–8, 518, 519, 529
  Prince Philip's visit (1962), 508
  Queen's proposed visit (1968), 27–9
Argonaut, BOAC, 193
Argyll, Duke of, *see* Campbell, Ian
Armstrong, Robert, 242, 284
Armstrong-Jones, Antony, 1st Earl of Snowdon, 366
Ashanti, 11
Asia-Pacific Economic Cooperation (APEC), 146
Association of Commonwealth Universities, 141
Attenborough, David, 16
Attlee, Clement, 123, 124, 191–2, 346
Auckland British Empire Games (1950), 173
'Auld Lang Syne', 173, 341
Auriol, Vincent, 274
Australia, 4, 25, 30, 46, 59, 184, 188–218, 426
  1915 Gallipoli Campaign, 174
  1948 Ashes series, 45; Nationality and Citizenship Act, 190; Royal tour cancelled, 190–91
  1949 London Declaration, 124
  1953 Coronation, 193–4
  1954 Coronation tour, 11, 21, 40, 62, 127, 186, 188–9, 196–8, 350
  1956 Melbourne Olympics, 355
  1962 Perth Commonwealth Games, 173
  1963 Royal visit, 47, 49, 200–203

1966 Lyndon Johnson's visit, 203; Prince Charles studies at Geelong Grammar, 224, 473
1967 Harold Holt's funeral, 473
1970 withdrawal from Vietnam, 204; Royal visit, 34, 47, 56, 203–4, 345, 473, 510–11
1972 UK joins EEC, 205–6; Whitlam elected PM, 206–7
1973 Royal visit, 203
1974 Royal visit, 149
1975 constitutional crisis, 207; Papua New Guinea's independence, 233
1977 Royal visit, 207–9
1979 Zambia CHOGM, 337, 339
1981 Melbourne CHOGM, 161
1982 Brisbane Commonwealth Games, 173
1983 Royal visit, 209, 483
1985 Bahamas CHOGM, 384
1986 Australia Act, 209; Marlborough House CHOGM, 397
1991 Keating elected PM, 210
1993 awarded Olympic Games, 210
1994 Prince of Wales's visit, 211, 491
1996 Princess of Wales's visit, 519–21
1998 constitutional convention, 211
1999 republic referendum, 187, 211–12, 232, 498–9
2000 Royal visit, 47, 212–13; Sydney Olympics, 210, 213
2002 Royal visit 213
2011 Prince William's visit, 524; Perth CHOGM, 213–14
2015 Turnbull elected PM, 217
2018 Gold Coast Commonwealth Games, 174, 186; London CHOGM, 217–18; Invictus Games, 530
Australian Republic Movement, 215
Avram, Ion, 85
Ayub Khan, Mohammad, 40, 133
Azores, 366
Aztec civilisation, 470

Babangida, Ibrahim, 74
BAC 1-11 passenger jets, 90–91, 98, 102
Bader, Douglas, 309, 325
Bagehot, Walter, 44, 409
Bahamas, 55, 184–5, 232, 344, 383–7, 397
Balfour Declaration (1926), 121
Balmain, Pierre, 300
Balmoral Castle, Aberdeenshire, 30, 47, 60, 136, 210, 240, 258, 271, 336, 344, 376–7, 388, 451
Balogh, Tamás, 96
Banana, Canaan, 482
Band of the Royal Marines, 341, 345, 361, 368–9, 452
Banda, Hastings, 57–8, 143, 319, 320, 322, 329–30, 331, 337, 503
Bangladesh, 20, 106–7, 177–8, 381, 514
Bannister, Roger, 173
banquets, 72–8
Barbados, 232
barbecues, 47, 51, 354
Barber, Anthony, 386, 387
Barcant, Jonathan, 504
Barltrop, Roger, 313
Barotseland, 116
Barzun, Matthew, 4, 13, 261, 265, 268, 530
Bastawrous, Andrew, 152
Bathurst, Gambia, 19, 55
Battersby, John, 414
Battle of Britain (1940), 176, 320
Battle of Cape Matapan (1941), 31
Battle of El Alamein (1942), 298
Battle of Spion Kop (1900), 109, 115
Battle of Vimy Ridge (1917), 174, 175, 176
Battle of Waterloo (1815), 292, 430
Batwa Pygmies, 141
Bayeux Tapestry, 284
Beating Retreat, 361, 386, 452
Beaton, Cecil, 428
Beckett, Margaret, 7, 39, 77, 262
Bedell Smith, Sally, 50, 249, 399, 400, 419
beekeeping, 141
Behan, Brendan, 159
Beith, John, 27
Belgium, 45, 71, 93, 166, 273, 455
Belize, 47, 185, 232, 522
de Bellaigue, Marie-Antoinette 'Toni', 277
Benedict XVI, Pope, 66, 80
Benn, Anthony 'Tony', 208
Bennett, Ernest, 337
Bentley, 342
Bergen-Belsen concentration camp, 433
Berlin Olympics (1936), 173
Berlin University of Technology, 18
Berlin Wall, 246–7, 405, 424, 430–32
Bermuda, 194, 231, 242, 495
Bernhard of Lippe-Biesterfeld, Prince consort of the Netherlands, 256
Berryman, Frank, 193
Beston, Eric, 441
Bethell, Nicholas, 4th Baron, 104
Bethell Brothers, 435
Bhumibol Adulyadej, King of Thailand, 26, 38, 48, 63, 70
Bhutan, 492
Biggar, Nigel, 140
binnacle, 352
Birch, John, xxii, 64, 104, 486
Black Watch, 472, 496
Blair, Anthony 'Tony', 29, 86, 155–60, 237, 258, 370, 495, 500
Blair, Cherie, 495
Blenheim bombers, 472
Blitz (1940–41), 247
Bloch, Michael, 288
Bloody Sunday (1920), 457
von Blücher, Gebhard Leberecht, 430
Blue Peter, 512
Bluebottle, 348
Blues and Royals, 523, 528
Boer War (1899–1902), 11, 109, 111, 112, 113, 115, 225
Bolger, James 'Jim', 215
Bolsheviks, 445–6, 449–50
Bolt, Usain, 6, 171
Bomber Command, 176
Bongo, Omar, 168
Bonham-Carter, Christopher, 134
Bonner, Yelena, 448
Boothroyd, Betty, 77
Borel, Calvin, 263
Bosnia, 256, 521
Botha, Pieter Willem, 386, 387
Botswana, 105, 308, 319–20, 324, 331–2, 333, 387
du Boulay, Roger
African tour (1979), 64, 336
and Princess Anne, 512
Ceausescu's visit (1978), 90, 92, 93, 94, 100
on Prince of Wales, 506
on Foreign Office, 154
France visit (1972), 285, 293, 300–301
New Hebrides, Resident Commissioner of (1973–5), 345, 363
on Royal Visits Committee, 24

Bounty, HMS, 361
Bourgeois, John, 251
Bowen, Ivan and Ken, 196
Boys' Welfare Society, 509
Bradford, Sarah, 303
Bradford University, 91
Brandreth, Gyles, 198
Brazil, 21, 27, 59, 65, 278, 286, 364, 424, 478, 485
Brexit (2016–), 3, 6, 10–11, 16, 69, 167, 216–17, 269–72, 298, 462, 526
Brezhnev, Leonid, 24, 281, 293
Brighton hotel bombing (1984), 250, 376
Brind, Harry, 82
Brisbane Commonwealth Games (1982), 173
Britannia Royal Naval College, Dartmouth, 346
Britannia, HMY, 7, 20, 32, 39, 57, 341–73
  1953 launch, 348–9, 369
  1954 Libya visit, 350–51, Coronation tour homecoming, 127, 351–3; Canada visit, 353
  1955 Norway visit, 358; Caribbean cruise, 353; Scotland cruise, 353–4
  1956 Sweden visit, 358–9; Melbourne Olympics and Antarctica visit, 355–7
  1957 Portugal visit, 357; Denmark visit, 358
  1958 Netherlands visit, 358
  1959 Hong Kong visit, 345–6; North American tour, 221
  1961 West African tour, 19, 55–6, 362
  1963 Fiji visit, 235
  1964 Canada tour, 222
  1965 Germany visit, 431
  1968 South American tour, 28, 364
  1969 review of the Western Fleet, 368; Norway visit, 31
  1970 Australia tour, 203, 204, 345
  1971 Canada tour, 224; Pitcairn visit, 361
  1972 South East Asia tour, 38, 284; France visit, 35, 284, 304
  1973 Honeymoon of Princess Anne and Capt. Mark Phillips, 366
  1974 New Hebrides visit, 345, 363
  1975 Mexico visit, 365
  1976 Finland visit, 55; United States visit, 242, 243–4, 253, 365
  1977 Australia and New Zealand tour, 208
  1979 Middle East tour, 51, 53, 315, 363
  1981 Honeymoon of Prince and Princess of Wales, 366, 372; press reception, 56; Australia visit, 161
  1982 Tuvalu visit, 234, 370
  1983 United States visit, 247, 248, 249, 253
  1985 Nassau CHOGM, 384, 385, 386
  1986 Honeymoon of Duke and Duchess of York, 366; China visit, 365–6, 434–5, 437–8
  1990 Cameroon visit, 504
  1991 United States visit, 253, 254
  1992 France visit, 368
  1993 India visit, 366; Cyprus CHOGM, 54, 162
  1994 D-Day anniversary, 256–7, 368; Russia visit, 441–2, 451–3
  1995 South African visit, 409, 410
  1997 Hong Kong handover, 495; decommissioning, 261, 341, 369–71
Britannia, BOAC, 129
British Aerospace, 90
  BAe 146 plane, 342, 447, 457
British Aircraft Corporation (BAC), 90–91, 116, 102, 104
British Airways, 32, 33, 35, 38, 260, 384, 435, 440
British Broadcasting Corporation (BBC)
  Antarctica broadcast (1956), 356
  Ceausescu's visit (1978), 96
  Commonwealth Day coverage, 152
  Princess of Wales's *Panorama* interview (1995), 497, 519
  Elizabeth R (1992), 253
  India visit (1997), 159
  Jamaica visit (2012), 229
  Royal Family (1969), 46, 223, 241, 512
  United States visit (2007), 261
  Victoria Falls speech (1947), 117, 118
  World Service, 7
British Columbia, 22
British Commonwealth Games, 173, 507
British Diplomatic Oral History Programme, 14, 104, 486
British Empire, 1, 3, 17, 36, 85, 108–26, 141, 166, 183
British Empire and Commonwealth Games, 173, 507
British Empire Games, 173–4
British Invisibles, 365
British Lions, 523
British Museum, 18
British Nationality Act (1981), 230
British Overseas Airways Corporation (BOAC), 33, 34, 129, 193, 219, 228
British Overseas Trade Board, 365, 441
British Petroleum, 331
British Virgin Islands, 230
British West Indies, 227
Bronington, HMS, 477
brooches
  Flame Lily, 21, 116
  Maple Leaf, 219, 226
  Northern Star snowflake, 21, 227
  Wattle, 197
Brown, Gordon, 160–61, 264, 265
Brown, John, 348
Browne, Gaston, 532
Browne, Michael, 461
Brunei, 469
Bruni, Carla, 305–6
Brunswick, Duke of, *see* Ernst August
Buckingham Palace, London, 344
  Amin's visit (1971), 81
  banquets, 72–8
  Belgian Suite, 71, 87, 88, 97, 103, 417
  Blue Drawing Room, 1
  Bobo's residence, 40
  Bush's visit (2003), 259
  Ceausescu's visit (1978), 97–101, 259
  Commonwealth Fashion Exchange (2018), 170
  Commonwealth Heads of Government Meeting (1986), 389
  Commonwealth Heads of Government Meeting (2018), 1–3, 464
  Dadae's visit (2017), 233
  1844 Room, 1
  Fagan incident (1982), 210
  Felipe VI's visit (2017), 72, 74–6
  George, birth of (2013), 215
  gifts, 20
  Gustav VI's visit (1954), 69
  informal luncheons, 299–300
  McKenzie's visit (1975), 172
  Mandela's visit (1996), 416–17, 418, 451
  Margrethe II's visits, 78–9
  Mobutu's visit (1973), 86–7
  Olympic reception (2012), 5
  Orleans Room, 71
  Picture Gallery, 72, 105
  Queen's Commonwealth Trust reception (2018), 8–9

Queen's Young Leaders Awards, 14, 105–8
Ramaphosa's visit (2018), 421
Royal Household Hospitality Scholarships, 181–2, 184–5
Royal Library, 67, 268
Schmidt's visit (1977), 433
terrorist threats, 33
White Drawing Room, 15
Bukhara, Uzbekistan, 490
Bulawayo, Fines, 334
Bulgaria, 79
Bullard, Robin, 349, 369
Bunting, John, 233
Burlin, Terence, 95, 101
Burma, 122, 123, 472
Burmese (horse), 22, 246
Burns, Andrew, 91, 95
Bush, Barbara, 250
Bush, Barbara Pierce, 475
Bush, George Herbert Walker, 49, 250–52, 255
Bush, George Walker, 66, 252, 258–64, 266, 392, 475
Bush, Jenna, 475
Bush, Laura, 258
Buthelezi, Mangosuthu, 407
Butler, Richard 'Rab', 427
Butler, Robin, 97, 155, 167, 375, 377, 381, 392, 436, 473
Buxton, M. P., 431

Cable, John Vincent 'Vince', 270
Caesar, Julius, 120
Caine, Michael, 260
Callaghan, Leonard James 'Jim', 35, 156, 376
Amin's proposed visit (1977), 83, 84
Ceausescu's visit (1978), 89, 90, 96, 101–2
Silver Jubilee celebrations (1977), 208
Zambia CHOGM (1979), 312, 314
Cambridge, Duchess of (Catherine Middleton), 69, 76, 139, 170, 213, 220, 266, 457, 524, 526–7
Cambridge, Duke of (Prince William), 522–7
Army service, 523
Australia visits, 209, 483, 524
birth (1982), 483
and Botswana, 319
and Brexit (2016–), 69
British Lions tour (2005), 523
Canada tour (2011), 220
Commonwealth Day (2018), 164
at Eton College, 522
gap year (2000), 522
George, birth of (2013), 215
helicopter piloting, 33
holidays, 23
and Ireland visit (2011), 457, 462
Kenya trip (2001), 522–3
New Zealand visits, 524–5
Obama's visits (2011, 2016), 266, 269, 526
Olympic Games (2012), 5
Poland visit (2017), 527
Royal Air Force service, 457, 523
Royal Mail stamp (2016), 15
Royal Navy service, 523
Sentebale, 528, 531
and Tusk, 523
wedding (2011), 213, 232, 265, 457, 524
Cambridge University, 418, 474
Cameron, David, 7, 8, 10–11, 26, 68, 217, 507
and Australia, 213–14, 216
and banquets, 76, 283
and Brexit (2016–), 10–11, 216, 269
on Commonwealth, 165
D-Day anniversary (2014), 26
Germany visit (2015), 433
on Invictus Games, 530
Ireland visit (2011), 459
and Libya, 7
on McGuinness handshake (2012), 462–3
and Obama, 7, 265, 267, 269
RAF Voyager aircraft designation (2014), 32
and Saudi Arabia, 489
Sri Lanka CHOGM (2013), 501, 503
and succession, 213–14
on Thatcher, 383
Vanuatu CHOGM cancellation (2017), 161, 503
Xi Jinping's visit (2015), 70, 74
Cameroon, 9, 21, 503
Campbell, Alastair, 495
Campbell, Ian, 11th and 4th Duke of Argyll, 198
Campbell, John, 146
Canada, 4, 25, 40, 42, 47, 168, 184, 187, 218–27
1867 Confederation, 218, 221–2
1917 Battle of Vimy Ridge, 174, 175, 176
1923 halibut fishing treaty with US, 35
1930 Hamilton British Empire Games, 173
1939 Royal visit, 189, 227, 219, 227
1949 London Declaration, 222
1951 Royal visit, 4, 11, 192, 219–21, 342
1954 Vancouver British Empire and Commonwealth Games, 173, 353
1956 trumpeter swans gift, 22
1957 Royal visit, 221
1958 British Columbia centenary, 22
1959 Royal visit; St Lawrence Seaway opening, 149, 221, 357–8
1962 Commonwealth Study Conference, 510
1964 Royal visit; Confederation Conferences centenary, 221–2
1967 Royal visit, 149, 222, 225; de Gaulle's visit, 280; Expo 67 World Fair, 222
1968 Trudeau's UK visit, 223
1969 Commonwealth Prime Ministers' Conference, 222–3; Royal visit, 223
1971 Royal visit, 224
1973 CHOGM, 82, 148–50, 222
1976 Montreal Olympics; Royal visit, 5, 40, 224, 244, 316, 365
1977 Prince Andrew studies at Lakefield College, 224
1978 Edmonton Commonwealth Games, 172, 173
1982 Canada Act, 52, 224, 225
1983 Royal visit, 483
1985 Bahamas CHOGM, 384
1986 Marlborough House CHOGM, 396–7, 398, 399–400
1995 Quebec independence referendum, 225; Auckland CHOGM, 415
2011 Royal visit, 220
2015 Malta CHOGM, 48, 225
2017 sesquicentennial celebrations, 185–6, 225; Sapphire Jubilee gift, 21, 227; Invictus Games, 530
2018 London CHOGM, 225
Canterbury, Archbishop of
Carey, George, 67
Fisher, Geoffrey, 73
Ramsey, Michael, 151
Welby, Justin, 268
Williams, Rowan, 154
Cape of Good Hope, 355, 410, 413
Captain & Tennille, 243
Carey, George, Archbishop of Canterbury, 67
Caribbean, 184, 227–32
colonisation, 120

Caribbean (*Continued*)
Edinburgh Commonwealth Games boycott (1986), 389
honeymoons in, 366
hurricanes, 179, 231
national birds, 42
republicanism, 187, 150, 228–32
Royal Household Hospitality Scholarships, 181–2, 184–5
Royal visit (1955), 353
Royal tour (1994), 50, 229, 230–31
Royal tour (2000), 499
tax havens, 231
war memorials, 176
Windrush scandal (2018), 182–3, 227, 231
Carington, Peter, 6th Baron Carrington, 286, 307, 322, 325, 330, 337
Carlton Gardens, London, 8
Carpenter, Hugh, 450
Carter, James 'Jimmy', 25, 90, 244–5
Carthew, Anthony, 135
Cartledge, Bryan, 317
Casement, Roger, 458
Casson, Hugh, 348, 352, 372
Castle of Mey, Caithness, 354
Castro, Fidel, 232, 308, 331, 508
Cavendish, Andrew, 11th Duke of Devonshire, 136
Cayman Islands, 59, 495
Ceausescu, Elena, 88, 91–5, 99, 101–2, 104, 259
Ceausescu, Nicolae, 24, 87–104, 259, 270
Cecilie of Greece and Denmark, 426
Cenotaph, 176
Central Asia, 490–91
Ceylon (1948–72), 124, 127, 191, 193, 355
Chaban-Delmas, Jacques, 290, 304
Chalker, Clive, 516
Chalker, Lynda, 50, 53, 86, 415, 486–7, 515–16, 521, 530–31
Chamberlain, Neville, 343, 346
Changing the Guard, 127, 138, 258, 455
Channel Islands, 183
Channel Tunnel, 305
Charles I, King of Spain, 72
Charles II, King of England, Scotland and Ireland, 346
Charles, Prince, *see* Wales, Prince of
Charteris, Martin, 284, 286, 344
du Boulay, relationship with, 154
and France visit (1972), 284, 286, 295–6
and Germany visit (1965), 429
and Papua New Guinea independence (1975), 233
and South American tour (1968), 27
and Singapore CHOGM (1971), 148
and speeches, 57, 295, 242, 295–6
and United States visit (1976), 242
and West Africa tour (1961), 20
Whitlam, meeting with (1973), 207
Chartres, Richard, Bishop of London, 16
Chatham Islands, 356
Chelsea Flower Show, 176
Chequers, Buckinghamshire, 90, 432
Chicago, Illinois, 519
Chile, 27, 286, 364, 522
China, 24, 25, 135
1966 Cultural Revolution begins, 435
1972 Nixon's visit, 434
1979 support for ZANU in Rhodesia, 311
1982 Thatcher's visit, 436
1984 Joint Declaration on Hong Kong, 434
1986 Queen's visit, 24, 47, 365–6, 434–41
1989 Tiananmen Square massacre, 435, 441
1997 Hong Kong handover, 343, 441, 483, 494–6, 525
1999 Jiang Zemin's UK visit, 77, 441
2005 Hu Jintao's UK visit, 74, 441
2015 Duke of Cambridge's visit, 523, 525–6; Xi Jinping's UK visit, 68, 70, 74, 270, 441, 527
2018 Commonwealth summit, 167
Chirac, Bernardette, 78
Chirac, Jacques, 78, 305
Chona, Mainza, 334, 337
Chona, Mark, 333, 334, 336, 337
Choo, Jimmy, 471
Chrétien, Jean, 52, 225, 415
Christchurch British Commonwealth Games (1974), 173
Christianity, 151–4
Christmas broadcast, 57, 178–80, 191, 244, 356, 381–2
Christopher, Saint, 33
Church of England, 151–4, 340, 449, 484, 531
Churchill, Clementine, 293
Churchill, Mary, 281
Churchill, Winston, 109, 115, 127, 192, 220, 237, 280, 527
Battle of Spion Kop (1900), 115
and *Britannia*, 346
busts of, 264
Coronation tour homecoming (1954), 352
funeral (1965), 240, 422
de Gaulle, relationship with, 277
general election (1951), 192
KBO (Keep Buggering On), 493
Roosevelt, relationship with, 237
and special relationship, 259
Sutherland portrait, 293
and 'United States of Europe', 428
Cinema of Unease, 215
City of London, 75, 76, 151, 220
Civil Service, 24, 29
Clarence House, London, 67, 278, 488
Claridge's, London, 102
Clark, Helen, 216
Clarke, Kenneth, 155
Cleminson, James, 441
Clinton, Hillary, 256, 526
Clinton, William 'Bill', 255–7, 258–9, 418
Co-Ordination and Research Unit, 497
Coe, Sebastian, 23, 34, 171
Coetsee, Kobie, 386–7
Cohen, Samantha, 8
Cold War, 12, 24
Coldstream Guards, 67, 271
Coleman's Mustard, 441
Collins, Phil, 419
Colonial Office, 45, 154
Colonial Society, 151
Colville, John 'Jock', 275, 276
Colville, Richard, 44–6, 188, 190, 427
Common Market, *see* European Economic Community
Commonwealth, 8, 17, 33, 69, 138–80
and Amin, 81, 82, 83, 84
Anyaoku's secretariat (1990–2000), 144, 147, 155, 162, 166, 370, 402, 409
Association of Commonwealth Universities, 141
Burma's withdrawal (1948), 123
Beekeepers' Association, 141
Prince of Wales, succession of, 3, 217, 464–6, 498–506
debt-relief strategies, 155
Enterprise and Investment Council, 167
and Falklands War (1982), 155, 245, 377–8
Fashion Exchange, 170

Fiji's suspensions (1987–97, 2000–1, 2006–14), 164, 235
Gambia's withdrawal (2013–18), 164
Ghana's accession (1957), 178
and human rights, 141, 147, 153, 164, 167
Ireland's withdrawal (1949), 123
London Declaration (1949), 124–6, 127, 222, 350
Malaysia's accession (1957), 178
Maldives' withdrawal (2016), 164
Marlborough House HQ, 121, 143, 145, 152, 169, 311, 388–9, 395–400, 408, 474
McKinnon's secretariat (2000–8), 86, 156, 160, 499–500, 501
Mozambique's accession (1995), 166
and Nobel Peace Prize (2018), 17
Pakistan's suspensions (1999–2004, 2007–8), 164
Queen Elizabeth Diamond Jubilee Trust, 105, 514
Queen Elizabeth Scholarships, 179
Queen's Commonwealth Canopy, 9, 179
Queen's Commonwealth Essay Prize, 468–9
Queen's Commonwealth Trust, 8–9, 107
Queen's Young Leaders, 9, 14, 105–8, 468, 532
Ramphal's secretariat (1975–90), *see under* Ramphal, Shridath
Round Table, The, 401
Rwanda's accession (2009), 166
Scotland's secretariat (2016–), 126, 169, 504
Sharma's secretariat (2008–16), 56, 124, 125, 164, 501–2
Smith's secretariat (1965–75), 53, 81, 82, 143–5, 148–9, 152, 222, 311, 474
and South Africa, 344, 374, 378, 383–90, 395–401, 403–4, 408
Statute of Westminster (1931), 121
Study Conferences, 509–10
Trans-Antarctic Expedition (1956), 355
Victoria Falls speech (1947), 116–18, 119, 121, 126
War Graves Commission, 174–8, 206, 472
Youth Ambassador, 179
Zimbabwe's withdrawal (2003), 86, 164
Commonwealth Day, 151–2, 164, 501
Commonwealth Games, 171–4, 495, 507, 514
1930 Hamilton, 173
1950 Auckland, 173
1954 Vancouver, 173, 353
1962 Perth, 173
1966 Kingston, 172, 228
1970 Edinburgh, 507
1974 Christchurch, 173
1978 Edmonton, 172, 173, 507
1982 Brisbane, 173
1986 Edinburgh, 389, 394–5
2010 Delhi, 501
2014 Glasgow, 171, 174
2018 Gold Coast, 174, 186
Commonwealth Heads of Government Meetings
1971 Singapore, 81, 146–8, 222, 283, 313, 467, 474, 508
1973 Canada, 82, 148–50, 222
1975 Jamaica, 82, 150, 228
1977 United Kingdom, 82–4, 150
1979 Zambia, 36, 307–40, 377, 380
1981 Australia, 161
1983 India, 378, 380–81
1985 Bahamas, 185, 344, 383–7, 397
1986 United Kingdom, 388–90, 395–400
1989 Malaysia, 150, 406
1991 Zimbabwe, 155, 168, 403, 405–7
1993 Cyprus, 54, 162, 344
1995 New Zealand, 215–16, 414–16
1997 Scotland, 155–6, 162, 163, 420
1999 South Africa, 126, 420
2003 Nigeria, 35–6, 37, 62, 156
2007 Uganda, 21, 163
2009 Trinidad and Tobago, 160
2011 Australia, 213–14
2013 Sri Lanka, 501–3
2015 Malta, 48, 163, 225
2017 Vanuatu (cancelled), 161, 503
2018 United Kingdom, *see* London CHOGM
Commonwealth Ministerial Action Group (CMAG), 415–16
Commonwealth Prime Ministers' Conference
1948 London, 124
1949 London, 124
1961 London, 379
1964 London, 143
1965 London, 143–5
1966 Lagos, 145
1969 London, 222–3
Commonwealth Study Conferences (CSC), 509–10
Commonwealth Trans-Antarctic Expedition (1956), 355
Commonwealth War Graves Commission, 174–8, 206, 472
Como, Perry, 248
concentration camps, 433, 527
Concorde, 90–91, 253, 284, 342, 384
Congo, 45, 86–7, 168
Connors, Jane, 189, 190, 197
Constantine II, King of Greece, 511
Cook, James, 203, 204, 361
Cook, Robin, 157, 158, 160
Cook Islands, 170, 171
Cooke, Howard, 52–3
Cool Britannia, 155, 495
Cooney, Christy, 459
Cooper, Simon, 451
Copenhagen Climate Change Conference (2009), 160–61
Coq d'Or, Le, 77
Corbett, Jim, 128
corgis, 39, 73, 87, 268, 411
Cornwall, Duchess of (Camilla Parker Bowles), 69, 163, 186, 225, 467, 468, 479, 480, 483, 500
Cornwall, Duchy of, 466
Coronation (1953), 40, 127, 180, 193–4, 532, 348, 532
Coronation tour (1953–4), 11, 21, 62, 127, 186, 188–98, 228, 350, 354, 473, 510, 511
Coty, René, 280
Council of Europe, 206
Coventry, West Midlands, 92
Cowen, Brian, 456
Cowes Week, 367
Craig, Daniel, 5
Creswell, Michael, 27, 28
cricket, 45, 86, 139, 155, 182, 198, 209, 406, 413
crocodiles, 20, 21, 319
Croix de Guerre, 274
Croke Park massacre (1920), 457
Cromwell, Oliver, 454
Crosland, Anthony, 243
Cross, Jeremy, 470
Crown, The, 6, 14, 137, 240, 355, 507
Crusades, 487
Cuba, 232, 308, 331, 508
Cullinan Diamond, 111
Cultural Revolution (1966–76), 435
Cumming-Bruce, Francis, 200, 201–2
Cundy, John, 481
Cunningham, Andrew Browne, 31
Cyprus, 37, 54, 162, 344

Czech Republic, 37, 58, 423, 424
Czechoslovakia, 89

D-Day (1944), 26, 58, 176, 256–7, 306, 349, 368
D'Orsi, Lucy, 74
Dadae, Robert, 233–4
Daimler, 147
Dakar, Senegal, 19
Dalai Lama, 525
Dalí, Salvador, 72
Dalrymple-Hamilton, North, 358
Dargie, William, 40, 197, 198
Davis, Reginald, 33, 43, 55, 130, 429, 477, 509
Dawson, Bertrand, 1st Viscount Dawson of Penn, 289
Day, Derek, 316
Deakin, Charles, 467
Deane, Albert 'Dixie', 358, 360
Deane, William, 213
Deaver, Michael, 248
debt relief, 155
Deedes, William 'Bill', 308
Defender of the Faith, 153
Delhi Commonwealth Games (2010), 501
Delhi Durbar (1911), 130
Dempster, Nigel, 480
Dench, Judi, 16
Deng Xiaoping, 434, 436
Denmark, 74, 78–9
Dev, Kapil, 139
Devonshire, Duke of, *see* Cavendish, Andrew
Diamond Jubilee (2012), 9, 14, 15, 25, 47, 79, 105, 216, 501, 525
  and Commonwealth, 9, 14, 170
  in Jamaica, 187, 229
  Lambeth Palace reception, 153
  in Northern Ireland, 462
  in Papua New Guinea, 233
  Queen Elizabeth Diamond Jubilee Trust, 105, 514
  State Coach, 342
  Vogue survey, 43
diamonds, 111, 113, 117–19, 137, 319, 331, 411–12, 417
Diana, Princess of Wales, 362, 515–22
  Angola visit (1997), 521
  Argentina visit (1995), 518–19
  Australia and New Zealand visit (1983), 209, 483
  Canada visit (1983), 483
  charity work, 498, 516–17, 518, 520–22, 531
  Chicago visit (1996), 519
  death (1997), 47, 157, 159, 162, 211, 258, 496–8
  divorce (1996), 466, 497, 515, 519
  and Giscard d'Estaing, 305
  Hungary visit (1990), 486
  India visit (1992), 486–7
  Italy visit (1985), 484
  Nepal visit (1993), 515
  Panorama interview (1995), 497, 519
  Russia visit (1995), 517–18
  separation from Charles (1992), 466, 487, 494, 497, 515
  South Korea visit (1992), 486, 487
  Sydney visit (1996), 519
  telephone conversation leaks (1992), 210
  and United States, 250, 258, 485, 519
  wedding to Charles (1981), 366, 372, 478, 483
Dickson, E. J., 435
Diefenbaker, John, 221, 357
Digital Age, 12
Dimbleby, Jonathan, 445, 476
Dior, Christian, 275
Diplomatic Corps, 23–4, 144, 154, 282, 293, 294, 512
Diplomatic Reception, 484
Dire Straits, 268
Disraeli, Benjamin, 121
Dixon, Gwen, 197
Djibouti, 22
Donahue, Phil, 519
Dorchester Hotel, London, 44, 416, 419
Douglas-Home, Alec, 14th Earl of Home and later Lord Home of the Hirsel, 81–2, 134, 140, 147, 221, 282, 286, 296–7
Down's syndrome, 518
Downer, Alexander, 161, 205, 217
Downer, Alick, 200–201, 205–6
Downton Abbey, 16, 268
Dr No, 362
Dresden bombing (1945), 433
dresses, 39–43
  Amies, 41, 291, 428
  Coronation, 40, 127, 532–3
  France visit, 275
  Germany visit, 428, 431
  Hartnell, 40–41, 127, 221, 532–3
  Ireland visit, 458, 459
  Kelly, 458, 459
  Maple Leaf of Canada, 221
  Wattle, 40, 149, 198
Dreyer, Henry, 112
Duden, 18
Duff, Anthony, 316, 327
Dugdale, Katherine, 451
Duke of Edinburgh's Award, 17, 60, 179, 509, 514
Dunblane massacre (1996), 50
Duncan Smith, Iain, 479
Dyson, James, 468

Easson, Robert, 441
East Germany (1949–90), 431
East India Company, 120
Ecobescu, Nicolae, 95, 99, 100
economic crash (2008), 25, 265, 456
Eden, Anthony, 358
Edinburgh, Duke of (Prince Philip), 2, 507–10
  African tour (1979), 30, 331, 334, 335, 336
  Antarctica visit (1956), 355–6
  and Australia, 201, 209, 211, 345, 355
  barbecues, 47, 51, 354
  Battle of Cape Matapan (1941), 31
  and *Britannia*, 343, 347–8, 350, 353, 367, 368, 372
  and Canada, 219–20, 223, 224, 353
  and Ceausescu's visit (1978), 98, 100
  China visit (1986), 433, 436, 438–40, 441
  City of London luncheon (1992), 75
  and Common Market, 61
  Commonwealth Day (1966), 151
  Commonwealth summit (1965), 144
  Commonwealth Study Conferences (CSC), 509–10
  Coronation tour (1953–4), 189, 197, 198
  and Cowes Week, 367
  Czech Republic visit (1996), 37, 58–9
  D-Day anniversary (1994), 368
  and Dalí, 72
  Duke of Edinburgh's Award, 17, 60, 179, 509, 514
  Edward, Duke of Windsor, meeting with (1972), 302
  Finland visit (1976), 55
  France visits, 257, 273, 274, 275, 285, 299, 301–2
  gaffes, 59, 62, 433–4, 438–40, 441
  and Germany, 426, 427, 429
  golden wedding anniversary (1997), 163
  hip operation (2018), 2
  Hong Kong visit (1959), 345–6

India visits, 130–32, 157, 158
and International Equestrian Federation, 444, 509
and Industrial Society, 509
Iran visit (1971), 508
Kekkonen's visit (1969), 71
Kennedy memorial inauguration (1963), 240
on legacy, 15
Mandela's visit (1996), 418
Melbourne Olympics (1956), 355
and Mountbatten assassination (1979), 454
Nepal visit (1961), 134
Obama's visits, 265, 269
and *Oklahoma!*, 239
Pitcairn visit (1971), 361
Portugal visit (1957), 357
and press, 44
Russia visits, 443, 444, 445–6, 450, 451, 452
Saudi Arabia visit (1979), 53
Scottish cruise (1955), 354
South America tour (1968), 27, 65
speeches, 57, 58
Trump's visit (2018), 271
United States visits, 239, 241, 254, 255, 263
valet, 32
Vancouver British Empire and Commonwealth Games (1954), 353
vineyard, 2
wedding (1947), 44, 190, 273
West African tour (1961), 19
and World Wildlife Fund, 17, 59, 130, 509
Zambia CHOGM (1979), 309
Edinburgh, Scotland
CHOGM (1997), 155–6, 162, 163
Commonwealth Games (1986), 389, 394–5, 398
University, 433–4, 438–9
Edmonton Commonwealth Games (1978), 172, 173, 507
Ednie, James, 472
Edward the Confessor, King of England, 21
Edward VII, King of the United Kingdom, 12, 121, 299, 450
Edward VIII, King of the United Kingdom and Duke of Windsor, 122, 174, 238, 287–8, 302–3, 496, 531
Edward, Prince, *see* Wessex, Earl of,
Edwards, Blake, 248
Egypt, 24, 79, 355, 366
Sadat assassination (1981), 493
Suez Crisis (1956), 78, 198, 239, 355, 356
'Eight Centuries of British Life in Paris', 274
Eisenhower, Dwight, 129, 132, 221, 239–40, 257, 357
elections
1950 general election, 191
1951 general election, 191–2, 346
1974 general election, 149
1979 general election, 51, 308, 315, 320, 322
1997 general election, 370
Elizabeth I, Queen of England and Ireland, 120, 195, 437
Elizabeth II, Queen of the United Kingdom, *see* by nation, tour, host, guest, institution or organisation
Elizabeth, Queen Consort of the United Kingdom, Queen Mother
and bacon and eggs, 441
Britannia decommissioning (1997), 369
and Canada, 189, 219, 224
Castle of Mey, 354
death (2002), 225
Edward VIII's abdication (1936), 287, 531
and France, 276, 277, 278
and hot dogs, 266
Malawi visit (1957), 330
Mandela's visit (1996), 417
Parker Bowles, relationship with, 478–9
and Slater, 362, 363
and Sutherland, 293
Elizabeth Feodorovna of Russia, Grand Duchess, 446, 450
Ellison, John, 304
Eminent Persons Group, 384, 386–8, 400
Empire Day, 151
Empire Sports Meeting (1911), 173
English Speaking Union, 239
Entebbe raid (1976), 331
Entente Cordiale (1904), 78, 299
equerries, 20, 30–32, 49, 56, 71, 99, 190, 204, 224, 345, 349, 361, 363, 496
Erhard, Ludwig, 427
Ernst August, Prince of Brunswick, Prince of Hanover, 429
Ethiopia, 316
Eton College, Berkshire, 276, 420, 522, 528
European Economic Community (EEC)
and Australia, 149, 199, 203, 205–6, 426
and Christmas broadcast, 57
and Commonwealth, 10, 128, 148, 155, 198–206, 294, 296, 426, 476
and de Gaulle, 99, 137, 280, 297
and New Zealand, 198–9, 201–2, 203, 206, 426
and Royal visit to France (1972) 61, 280–87, 289, 294–9
and South Africa, 388
UK accession (1972), 149, 206
European Union (EU), 3, 10–11, 16, 17, 69, 142, 167, 420
Brexit (2016–), 3, 6, 10–11, 16, 69, 167, 216–17, 269–72, 298, 462, 526
Evans, Harold, 96
Evans, Richard, 435, 436, 437, 439
Ewart-Biggs, Christopher, 297–8
Expo
1967 Montreal, 222
1970 Tokyo, 474

Fabergé, Carl, 67
Fagan, Michael, 210
Faisal II, King of Iraq, 78
Falkender, Marcia, 91
Falkland Islands, 183, 231
and Royal visit (1968), 27–9
War (1982), 155, 173, 245, 247, 377–8, 518, 519, 529
Fall, Brian, 248, 249, 443, 444, 445, 447, 453, 488, 490, 517
Fall, Delmar, 450, 451, 452, 453, 488–9, 517
Farah, Mohamed 'Mo', 106
Farish, Sarah, 250
Farouk I, King of Egypt, 79
fashion, 170
Felipe VI, King of Spain, 48, 69, 70, 72, 75–6
Fellowes, Robert, 74, 255, 406, 517
Fergusson, Ewen, 88
Fermoy, Lady, *see* Roche, Ruth
Ferré, Gianfranco, 42
Festival of Britain (1951), 191
Fianna Fáil, 456
Field, Richard 'Dick' 341
Fiennes, Susannah, 485
Figgis, Anthony, 91
Fiji, 30, 34, 54, 164, 199, 234–6, 476
financial crash (2008), 25, 265, 456
Finland, 55, 71

First World War, *see* World War I
Fisher, Geoffrey, Archbishop of Canterbury, 73
Flame Lily brooch, 21, 116
Flanagan, Mark, 138
Fleming, Ian, 290
Fletcher, Thomas, 56, 214–15, 488, 513, 522
Fleur de Lys tiara, 76
Foale, Colin Michael 'Mike', 255
Foo Fighters, 530
Foot, Michael, 246
Forbes, Jared, 184, 185
Ford, Gerald, 241, 242, 243, 244, 253
Foreign and Commonwealth Office (FCO), 23, 25, 29, 32
  and African tour (1979), 312, 315, 316, 318, 319, 324, 327, 332, 336
  and Amin, 23, 81
  and Angola visit (1997), 521
  and Argentina, 508
  and banquets, 73
  and Brezhnev, 24
  and Brexit, 526
  and Ceausescu, 87–8, 93, 96, 97, 103
  and China visit (1986), 435, 440
  and Commonwealth, 139, 154, 156
  and Cuba, 508
  and D-Day anniversary (1994), 256
  and Diana, Princess of Wales, 515, 517, 519, 521
  and Duke of York, 513
  and Edinburgh Commonwealth Games (1986), 395
  and Edward, Duke of Windsor, 288
  and European Economic Community, 282, 287, 294, 295, 296, 297, 298, 476
  and France, 279, 281, 283, 284, 287, 289–91, 430
  and Frazier hug (1991), 252
  and Gandhi, 397
  and Germany visit (1965), 430, 431
  and Gulf War (1990–91), 49
  and Hawke, 397
  impact assessments, 62–3
  and India visit (1997), 159–60
  and Ireland visit (2011), 454
  and Jamaica visit (1994), 187
  and Kenya visit (1971), 477, 512
  and Kaunda, 397
  and media, 44–7
  and Middle East tour (1979), 35
  and Mulroney, 397
  and Nepal visit (1993), 515
  and Order of St Michael and St George, 49
  and Prince Philip, Duke of Edinburgh, 507–8
  and Prince of Wales, 475-6, 485, 486, 489, 508
  and Pindling, 397
  on Rama VIII, death of (1946), 39
  and Russia visits (1994, 1995), 443, 517
  and South Africa visit (1995), 412
  and South America tour (1968), 27–8
  and Sweden visit (1956), 359
  and speeches, 56–8, 61, 62
  and Turkey visits (1971, 1972), 36–7, 513
  and Turkmenistan, 491
  and United States, 475–6
  and Zimbabwean independence (1980), 481
Fountain of Honour, 17
Fox, Freddie, 41
France, 4, 25, 166, 168, 273–306
  1815 Battle of Waterloo, 292, 430
  1904 Entente Cordiale, 78, 299
  1917 Battle of Vimy Ridge, 174
  1938 Royal visit, 273
  1940 Dunkirk evacuation, 273, 277; German occupation, 205, 273, 277, 298; Vichy Statute on Jews, 278
  1944 D-Day, 26, 58, 176, 306, 349, 368
  1948 Royal visit, 273–6
  1957 Royal visit, 279–80, 426
  1958 Fifth Republic established, 280
  1960 de Gaulle's UK visit, 99, 137
  1962 de Gaulle's Germany visit, 432
  1963 de Gaulle vetoes UK EEC accession, 280, 425
  1965 Queen's Koblenz speech, 430; Wilson's visit, 293
  1967 de Gaulle visits Canada, 280; de Gaulle vetoes UK EEC accession, 280, 425
  1968 May protests, 289
  1969 Pompidou elected President, 280
  1970 death of de Gaulle, 476
  1972 Royal visit, 33–4, 35, 61, 281–305, 447; UK joins EEC, 206, 287
  1976 Giscard d'Estaing's UK visit, 291, 305
  1978 Queen's Huguenots comment, 432
  1982 G7 summit, 245
  1992 Royal visit, 368
  1994 Mitterrand's Turkmenistan visit, 490; opening of Channel Tunnel, 305; Mitterrand's South Africa visit, 409, 412; D-Day anniversary, 256–7, 368
  1995 nuclear tests, 415
  1998 World Cup, 278
  2002 presidential election, 305
  2004 Entente Cordiale centenary, 78
  2008 Sarkozy's UK visit, 305–6
  2009 Sarkozy attends CHOGM, 160
  2010 Sarkozy purchases Airbus, 489
  2014 D-Day anniversary, 26, 58, 306
  2017 Duke of Cambridge's visit, 526; Hollande's Malaysia visit, 471; Trump's visit, 270; Macron plans to replace Airbus, 489
Francis, Pope, 20–21
Francophonie, 168, 403
Fraser, Dawn, 213
Fraser, Malcolm, 207, 337, 339, 386
Fraser, Simon, 25, 68, 90, 165, 454, 513
Frazier, Alice, 252
Free France (1940–44), 205, 277, 278, 298, 290
Freeman, Simon, 391
Frei Montalva, Eduardo, 27
Frey, Roger, 290
Friends of the Earth, 60
Frogmore House, Windsor, 372
Fuchs, Vivian, 355

G7, 139, 141, 146, 245, 432, 489
G20, 139, 141, 146, 265, 526
Gabon, 168, 324
Gaelic Athletic Association (GAA), 457, 459
Gair, Vince, 196
Gallipoli Campaign (1915–16), 174
Gambia, 19, 36, 55, 164, 170
Gandhi, Indira, 381
Gandhi, Mohandas, 109, 129, 131, 138
Gandhi, Rajiv, 397, 398
Garnier, John, 366, 441
Gascoyne-Cecil, Robert, 3rd Marquess of Salisbury, 44
Gates, William 'Bill' 167
Gatwick Airport, West Sussex, 70, 98
de Gaulle, Charles, 290, 297–8, 301
  Canada visit (1967), 280
  death (1970), 476
  EEC vetoes (1963, 1967), 280, 425

Fifth Republic established (1958), 280
Foreign Office on, 289, 290
Free France (1940–44), 277, 278, 298, 290
Germany visit (1962), 432
Grand Trianon renovation (1963), 293
and manufacturing industry, 441
May protests (1968), 289
Soames, relationship with, 281
UK visit (1960), 99, 137
gazelles, 21–2
GCB (Knight Grand Cross of the Order of the Bath), 72, 100, 104, 285, 293, 411
GCMG (Knight Grand Cross of the Order of St Michael and St George), 383
Geelong Grammar School, Victoria, 224, 473
Geidt, Christopher, 8, 214
general elections, *see* elections
Georg of Hanover, 429
George Cross, 176, 204
George II, King of Great Britain and Ireland, 214
George III, King of Great Britain and Ireland, 49, 239, 242, 243, 244, 246–7, 266, 342
George IV, King of the United Kingdom, 1, 72
George V, King of the United Kingdom, 12, 16, 53, 121, 130, 173, 289, 445, 450, 454
George VI, King of the United Kingdom, 12, 39, 45, 67, 163
African tour (1947), 108–20, 189–90, 346, 374, 378, 403, 410, 411, 412
Australia and New Zealand tour cancellation (1948), 190–91
and Boys' Welfare Society, 509
Britannia Royal Naval College visit (1939), 346
Canadian tour (1939), 189, 219, 227
cancer diagnosis (1951), 192, 219
Commonwealth Prime Ministers' Conference (1948), 124
death (1952), 12, 193, 213, 244, 354
Edward VIII's abdication (1936), 287
Festival of Britain (1951), 191
France, relations with, 273, 277
Indian independence (1947), 121–3
London Declaration (1949), 124–6, 127
United States visit (1939), 189, 238, 252, 268
George of Cambridge, Prince, 15, 215, 269
George Washington, 257
Germany, 4, 16–18, 20, 25, 67
Berlin Wall, 247, 405, 424, 430–32
Brezhnev's visit (1972), 432–3
Dresden bombing (1945), 433
European Economic Community, 280, 282, 425
de Gaulle's visit (1962), 432
Heinemann's UK visit (1972), 282
Kennedy's visit (1963), 424
Nazi period (1933–45), 93, 173, 205, 273, 277–8, 298, 326, 346, 368, 388, 425, 433, 527
New Guinea protectorate (1884–1919), 233
Olympic Games (1936), 173
Presidency, 67
Queen, die, 18, 428
Queen's Lecture, 18
Reagan's visits (1982, 1987), 245, 246–7
reunification (1990), 433
Royal visit (1965), 16, 18, 342, 424–32, 433
Royal visit (1978), 432–3
Royal visit (1992), 433
Royal visit (2015), 18, 433
Royal visit (2016), 526–7
Schmidt's UK visit (1977), 433
Schmidt's Zambia visit (1978), 313
South-West Africa (1884–1919), 403, 404
World War I (1914–18), 177
World War II (1939–45), 205, 273, 277, 298, 346, 326, 368, 433
Gestapo, 278
Gevisser, John, 416
Ghafoor, Saj, 503
Ghana
1957 Independence, 135, 183; accession to Commonwealth, 178
1959 Nkrumah's UK visit, 136, 503
1961 Royal visit, 15, 135, 137, 142, 221, 307, 362
1964 Commonwealth Prime Ministers' Conference, 143
1965 Rhodesian UDI crisis, 145
1986 Edinburgh Commonwealth Games boycott, 389
1999 Royal visit, 62
2014 Mahama's UK visit, 68
2018 Commonwealth Day, 152; Commonwealth Fashion Exchange, 170
Gibraltar, 72, 76, 183, 366, 395, 495
gifts, 20–22, 48–9
Gillard, Frank, 117, 118
Gillard, Julia, 214
Girl Guides, 21, 116
Girls of Great Britain and Ireland tiara, 459
Giscard d'Estaing, Anne-Amoyne, 291
Giscard d'Estaing, Valéry, 97, 103, 290–91, 305
Giselle, 297, 447
Glasgow Commonwealth Games (2014), 171, 174
Glass, Leslie, 96–7
Gleneagles Hotel, Auchterarder, 150
Glittering Thread, The (Connors), 189
Gloucester, Prince Henry, Duke of, 361
'God Save the Queen', 207
Gold Coast (1867–1957), 135
Gold Coast Commonwealth Games (2018), 174, 186
gold disc, 17
Gold State Coach, 342
Golden Jubilee (2002), 15, 17, 38, 47, 53, 153, 187, 213, 216, 225, 305, 342
golden wedding anniversary (1997), 163
Goldfinger, Uriah, 253
Gonsalves, Ralph, 232
Good Friday Agreement (1998), 455
Gorbachev, Mikhail, 67, 72, 246, 253, 379, 387
Gorbacheva, Raisa, 67
Gordon, Charles, 11
Gordonstoun School, Moray, 473
Gore-Booth, David, 157–60
Gore-Booth, Paul, 27, 28, 431
Gore, Albert, 17
Gore, Michael, 59
Goronwy-Roberts, Goronwy, 96
Gorringe, David, 223
Gorton, John, 345
Gothic, SS, 127, 193, 194, 350, 353
Gow, Ian, 339
Grace, Princess of Monaco, 245
la Grange, Zelda, 421
Grant, Cary, 243
Grave of the Unknown Warrior, 99, 417, 457
Greece, 93, 168, 344, 361, 426, 446, 511, 531
Greenhill, Denis, 281–2
Greenpeace, 60
Grenada, 230, 232, 250, 380
Grenadier Guards, 98
Grenfell, Harry, 322
Grigg, John, 2nd Baron Altrincham, 198, 200
Guildhall, City of London, 151
Gulf War (1990–91), 49, 250, 252, 254

Gurkhas, 469, 492
Gustav V, King of Sweden, 63
Gustav VI, King of Sweden, 69–70, 72, 73, 75, 77, 100, 359

Hague, Ffion, 266
Hague, William, 5, 53, 58, 140, 214, 266, 505–6, 523
Hamilton British Empire Games (1930), 173
Hamilton, Alvin, 50
Hampton Court Palace, London, 16
Hankey, Robert, 63, 359
Hanks, Tom, 266
Hanseatic League, 295
Harald V, King of Norway, 256
Harare, Zimbabwe, 155, 168
Hardinge, Charles, 1st Baron Hardinge of Penshurst, 277
Hargrove, Charles, 291
Harlech, Lord, *see* Ormsby-Gore, William David
Harris, Kenneth, 392
Harrison, Alistair, 241
Harry, Prince, *see* Sussex, Duke of
Hart, Judith, 313
Hart Dyke, James, 485
Hartley, Ted, 239
Hartnell, Norman, 40–41, 127, 221, 532–3
Harvey, Oliver, 276
Haseler, Stephen, 15
Hassan II, King of Morocco, 48, 74
Hassanal Bolkiah, Sultan of Brunei, 469
Havel, Václav, 58, 423, 424
Hawke, Robert 'Bob', 155, 187, 209, 384, 397, 510
Hawker Siddeley, 96
  Andover, 320, 326, 334, 342
Heath, Edward, 8, 283
  and Ceausescu's visit (1978), 89
  de Gaulle's funeral (1970), 476
  and European Economic Community, 11, 280, 282, 283–4, 286, 287, 476
  and Mobutu's visit (1973), 86
  Nixon's visit (1971), 241
  and Singapore CHOGM (1971), 146–9, 283
  and South Africa, 81
  and Uganda, 82, 83
  and United States, 476
Hefford, Eric, 478–9
Heinemann, Gustav, 282
Heinz II, Henry, 243
Heisenberg, Werner, 101
helicopter piloting, 33, 360
Henderson, Nico, 246
Hennings, John, 187, 316
Herbert, Henry, 7th Earl of Carnarvon, 15
Heriot-Watt University, 91
Hermes, HMS, 477
Heseltine, Michael, 403
Heseltine, William 'Bill', 16, 29–30, 78
  and African tour (1979), 317, 320, 321, 326, 329, 334, 337
  and Amin's proposed visit (1977), 83
  and Australian tours, 203, 207–9
  and Canada tours, 222
  and Ceausescus, 87
  and China visit (1986), 436
  and Commonwealth Day (1972), 152
  and Fiji visits, 30, 235
  and France visit (1972), 35, 285
  and Germany visit (1965), 427, 429
  and India visit (1983), 381
  and Kenya visit (1971), 512
  and Marlborough House CHOGM (1986), 398–9
  and *Royal Family* (1969), 46, 512
  and speeches, 57
  and *Sunday Times* affair (1986), 391, 393
  and Thatcher, 376, 391
  and Turkey visit (1972), 46
Heuss, Theodor, 426
Hill, R. F., 285
Hillary, Edmund, 141, 196, 355
Hinduism, 153, 381
Hirohito, Emperor of Japan, 71, 474
Hitler, Adolf, 93, 173, 298, 425
Hodge, James, 63
Hollande, François, 26, 58, 306, 471
Hollywood, 248
Holocaust (1933–45), 278, 433, 527
Holroyd, William 'Bill', 15
Holt, Harold, 473
Holyoake, Keith, 199, 201
Hong Kong, 303, 343, 345–6, 434, 437, 440, 441, 483, 494–6, 526
Honolulu, Hawaii, 34
Hook, Neil, 491
Hope, Bob, 248
Hope for Children Cameroon, 9
Horse Guards Parade, London, 70, 85, 266, 416
horses, 17, 466
  Burmese, 22, 246
  Finland visit (1976), 55
  in Kentucky, 250, 255, 261, 263, 264
  Round Tower, 250
  Sefton, 455
  in Turkmenistan, 490–91
Hossain, Rahat, 106–7
hot dogs, 238, 266
Household Cavalry, 70, 455, 479, 483, 490
Howard, John, 211–12
Howard, Michael, 16
Howe, Geoffrey, 97, 385, 399, 436, 437, 438, 521
Howell, David, 8, 140, 142, 156, 166, 167, 172
Hu Jintao, 74
Hu Yaobang, 436
Hudson Bay Company, 223
Hughes, Hubert, 230–31
Huguenots, 432
Humboldt Forum, 18
Hungary, 14, 59, 60, 64, 96, 99, 100, 104, 486, 488
Hunt, John, 315, 317, 323
Hurd, Douglas, 361, 412, 453, 517, 518
hurricanes, 161, 179, 231, 503
Hutchinson, John, 331
Hyde, Robert, 509
Hyde Park and Regent's Park bombings (1982), 455, 479

Ibrahim, Mohammed 'Mo', 164
ICI, 96
Idris, King of Libya, 351
Ikimi, Tom, 415
Imperial War Graves Commission, 175
India, 120–25, 128, 138–9, 165, 176
  1857 Mutiny, 120
  1911 Delhi Durbar, 130
  1919 Amritsar massacre, 158
  1947 Independence, 108, 122, 123, 138, 183, 189, 191; Partition, 122, 130, 138; Queen's wedding, 138
  1948 Commonwealth Prime Ministers' Conference, 124
  1949 London Declaration, 124–5, 127, 222
  1953 Coronation of Elizabeth II, 127
  1961 Royal visit, 34, 40, 128–33, 137, 139, 142, 157

1983 Delhi CHOGM, 378, 380–81
1986 Marlborough House CHOGM, 397, 398
1993 Royal visit, 366
1997 Royal visit, 157–60
2010 Delhi Commonwealth Games, 501
2017 UK–India Year of Culture, 138–9, 142
2018 Charles' visit, 472; Modi's UK visit, 67, 473; Commonwealth Fashion Exchange, 170; London CHOGM, 67, 142, 467
Indonesia, 25, 68, 270
Industrial Society, 509
informal luncheons, 299–300
Ingham, Bernard, 390, 396
International Campaign to Ban Landmines, 522
International Equestrian Federation, 444, 509
International Monetary Fund (IMF), 155, 244
International Olympic Committee (IOC), 5, 513
Invictus Games, 529–30, 533
Invincible, HMS, 245
Iran, 100, 134–5, 508–9
Iraq, 49, 78, 250, 252, 254, 528
Ireland, 53, 68, 123, 151, 266, 298, 449, 453–62, 531
Irish Free State (1922–37), 454
Irish Guards, 48, 457, 471
Irish Republican Army (IRA), 250, 298, 326, 376, 400, 454–5, 462, 479
Islam, 152, 153, 469, 487
Islamabad, Pakistan, 133
Isle of Man, 171, 183, 353
Israel, 7, 319, 331, 526
Italy, 24, 25, 42, 47, 61, 67, 245, 256, 257, 426, 484
ITN, 96

jaguars, 21
Jamaica, 52–3, 150, 171, 172, 187, 194, 228–9, 232
James, C. M., 295
James Bond, 5, 33, 290, 362
Jamestown Colony (1607–24), 239, 260–61
Japan, 71, 79, 122, 166, 424, 468, 472, 473, 490
Jean, Grand Duke of Luxembourg, 48
Jean, Michaëlle, 47
Jebb, Gladwyn, 279
Jekyll, Gertrude, 175
Jenkins, Roy, 206, 418–19
Jephson, Patrick, 517
Jersey, 395
Jet Age, 12
Jiang Zemin, 77
Jinnah, Muhammad Ali, 122
Joan of Arc, 304
John Brown & Co., 347, 348
John Paul II, Pope, 66
Johnson, Alan, 510
Johnson, Boris, 7, 142
Johnson, Lyndon, 203, 238, 240
Johnston, David, 225
Johnstone-Bryden, Richard, 341, 348, 353
Joint Intelligence Committee, 315, 317
Jones, Emma, 521
Jones, Quincy, 419
Juan Carlos I, King of Spain, 80, 366
Jubilees
1977 Silver, 83, 150, 180, 207–9
1992 Ruby, 46
2002 Golden, 15, 17, 38, 47, 53, 153, 187, 213, 216, 225, 305, 342
2012 Diamond, 9, 14, 15, 25, 43, 47, 79, 105, 153, 170, 187, 216, 462, 501
2017 Sapphire, 21, 227
Judd, Frank, 35, 50, 51, 318, 363
Juliana, Queen of the Netherlands, 281

Kalashnikov rifles, 311
Kang, David, 491
Kashmir, 157
Kaunda, Kenneth
1979 Lusaka CHOGM, 308, 310, 313, 315, 318, 321–2, 325–8, 332–5, 337, 339–40
1985 Nassau CHOGM, 384, 385
1986 Marlborough House CHOGM, 397, 398
Kazakhstan, 490
KBO (Keep Buggering On), 493
Keating, Paul, 210–11
Keith, Kenneth, 92
Kekkonen, Sylvi and Urho, 71
Kelly, Angela, 39, 42, 43, 458, 459
Kelly, Grace, 245
Kennedy, Jacqueline, 21, 137, 240
Kennedy, John Fitzgerald, 221, 240, 404, 424
Kenny, Enda, 456
Kent, Prince Edward, Duke of, 98
Kent, Duchess of (Katherine), 98
Kent, Prince George, Duke of, 531
Kent, Duchess of (Princess Marina), 531
Kenya, 12, 21, 152, 170, 193, 264, 482
Moi's UK visit (1979), 26
Mau Mau Uprising (1952–64), 128, 264
Royal visit (1952), 12, 52, 126, 128, 193, 265, 317
Royal visit (1971), 477, 511–12
Prince William's trip (2001), 522–3
Zambia CHOGM (1979), 316, 322, 338
Kereama, Jude, 503
Kerr, John, 207, 208
Key, Bronagh, 173
Key, John, 10, 13, 171, 173, 217, 218, 502, 524, 525
Khalid, King of Saudi Arabia, 53
Khama, Seretse, 319–20, 332
Khartoum, Sudan, 11
Khrushchev, Nikita, 131, 137, 240, 246
Kielinger, Thomas, 4, 16, 424–5, 428, 431, 505
Kili handbag, 21
King and I, The, 70
King Steve, 224
King, Hilda, 292
King, John, 384
King, Julian, 456, 460, 461, 462
King's African Rifles, 81, 83, 330
Kingston British Empire and Commonwealth Games (1966), 172, 228
Kipling, Rudyard, 159, 175
Kirby, Simon, 434, 439
Kissinger, Henry, 17, 237, 241
Kite, Elizabeth, 106, 107, 108
de Klerk, Frederik Willem, 407
Knight of the Order of the Garter, 72
Knight of the Thistle, 202
Korean War (1950–53), 239, 487
Krizia, Mariuccia, 42
Kruzenshtern, 345
Kuwait, 68, 250, 315
Kwakiutl people, 22
Kyrgyzstan, 490

Lacey, Robert, 148
lady clerks, 32
'Lady Is a Tramp, The', 243, 252
Ladysmith Black Mambazo, 419
Lagos, Nigeria, 35
Lambert, David, 87–8, 91, 93, 95
Lambeth Palace, London, 153
Lancaster, Duchy of, 466
Lancaster House, London, 167, 222, 340, 478
Land Rover, 197, 269, 342, 355, 515

landmines, 498, 521–2
Landy, John, 173
Lange, David, 2, 210
Langkawi, Malaysia, 150
Lascelles, Alan 'Tommy', 45, 110–19, 238
Launer handbags, 42
Laurence, Timothy, 176
Lavery, John, 496
Le Pen, Jean-Marie, 305, 306
League Against Cruel Sports, 131
Learmonth, James, 190
Lebanon, 488
Lee Kuan Yew, 147, 309, 316, 468
Lee, Caspar, 14
Légion d'honneur, 274, 293, 301
Leibovitz, Annie, 279
Leigh-Pemberton, Robin, 92
Lenin, Vladimir, 446
Leopold I, King of the Belgians, 71
Lesotho, 114, 528, 530–31
Letizia, Queen consort of Spain, 48, 72, 76
Letsie III, King of Lesotho, 528
Levin, Bernard, 98, 103
Lewa Wildlife Conservancy, Kenya, 522
Li Xiannian, 435, 436–7
Liberia, 19, 362
Liberty Bell, 242
Libya, 7, 193, 269, 350–51, 390
Life of Brian, 140
Lindström, Ulla, 63
Littlejohn Cook, George, 45, 46
Liverpool University, 91
livestock, 17
Livingstone, David, 11, 330
Lloyd Webber, Andrew, 259
Lloyd, Ian, 312–13
Loch Ness monster, 277
Lomawa Ndwandwe, Queen mother of Swaziland, 114
London CHOGM (2018), 1–3, 167, 169–70, 179, 180, 464–6, 503
  and Australia, 217
  and Cambridge, Duke of, 526
  and Canada, 226
  and Charles, succession of, 3, 217, 464–6, 503
  and Enterprise and Investment Council, 167
  and Prince Harry, 532
  and India, 67, 142, 467, 472
  and South Africa, 421
  and Windrush scandal (2018), 182, 227
London Declaration (1949), 124–6, 127, 222, 350
London Fashion Week, 170
London Zoo, 20, 21
Longford, Elizabeth, 275
Lord Chamberlain's Office, 45–6, 73, 285
Lord Chancellor, 29
Louis of Cambridge, Prince, 216
Louise, Queen consort of Sweden, 69, 100
Lover's Knot tiara, 76
Lowther-Pinkerton, Jamie, 522
Lübke, Heinrich, 428, 429
Lusaka CHOGM (1979), 36, 307–40, 377, 380, 491
Lutyens, Edwin, 159, 175
Luxembourg, 48, 55
Luzhkov, Yury, 448, 517
Lyon, Tom, 441

MacDonald, Margaret 'Bobo', 39, 42, 292, 358
Macedonia, 168
MacGregor, Neil, 36
Macmillan, Harold, 136, 149, 239, 331, 378
Macron, Emmanuel, 270, 489
Madagascar, 176, 513
Magpie, HMS, 353
Major, John, 4, 16, 50
  Auckland CHOGM (1995), 415
  and *Britannia*, 347, 370
  and Bush election campaign (1992), 255
  Charles and Diana's separation (1992), 487
  Clinton, relationship with, 255–6
  and cricket, 155, 406, 413
  Harare CHOGM (1991), 155, 406
  and income tax, 497
  leadership election (1990), 401
  Malaysia CHOGM (1989), 406
  Mandela's visit (1996), 418
  and Queen's Young Leaders, 106
  South Africa visit (1994), 409
  Turkmenistan visit (1993), 490
Makwara, Ransford, 481
Malan, Daniel 'DF', 124
malaria, 144, 339
Malawi, 57–8, 143, 319, 320, 322, 329–30, 331, 503
Malaysia, 36, 150, 178, 183, 355, 406, 470–472
Maldives, 164
Mali, 25
Mallaby, Christopher, 279
Malta, 48, 163, 225, 350, 504, 511
Mandela, Nelson, 86, 375, 400–422, 443, 494
  arrest (1962), 379
  Prince of Wales's visit (1997), 498
  death (2013), 421
  general election (1994), 402, 407
  George VI's visit (1947), 378
  Harare CHOGM (1991), 406–7
  imprisonment (1964–90), 86, 379, 380, 383, 386–7, 400–401
  Mitterrand's visit (1994), 409, 412
  'Nkosi Sikelel' iAfrika', 113
  Order of Merit (1995), 375, 411, 417
  Queen's Counsel appointment (2000), 420–21
  release from prison (1994), 401–2, 403
  Royal visit (1995), 343, 409, 411–14, 443
  Thatcher, meetings with (1990, 1996), 402–3, 420
  UK visit (1996), 416–20, 451
Mandela, Winnie, 411
Mandela-Dlamini, Zenani, 416, 418
Mangwende, Witness, 36
Manley, Michael, 150, 228
Manning, David, 141–2, 260, 264, 524, 527
Mansell, Benjamin, 11
Maoris, 152, 195–6, 199, 200, 209–10, 216, 363
Maple Leaf brooch, 219, 226
Maple Leaf of Canada dress, 221
Mara, Kamisese, 30
Marcos, Ferdinand, 24
Margai, Albert, 145
Margaret, Princess, Countess of Snowdon, 73, 109, 190, 228, 277, 366, 410, 441, 476
Margrethe II, Queen of Denmark, 74, 78–9
Marina of Greece and Denmark, *see* Kent, Duchess of
Markle, Meghan, *see* Sussex, Duchess of
Marks & Spencer, 493
Marland, Jonathan, 167
Marlborough House, London, 121, 143, 145, 152, 169, 311, 388–9, 395–400, 408, 474
Marley, Robert 'Bob', 483
Marr, Andrew, 10
Marriott, John Willard, 243
Marshall Islands, 21
Marshall, Peter, 125, 141

Marten, Henry, 276–7
Marxism, 86, 149–50, 230, 232, 309, 311, 398, 446
Mary of Teck, Queen Consort [CAPC] of the United Kingdom, 121, 276, 417, 459
Masefield, Thorold, 440
Masekela, Hugh, 419
Mason, Frederick, 27
Mau Mau Uprising (1952–64), 128, 264
Maximilian, Margrave of Baden, 429
Maxwell, Robert, 395
May, Theresa, 161, 169, 182, 227, 270, 271, 283, 465, 504
Maya civilisation, 470
Mayall, Lees, 61, 82, 282, 283
Mayflower Primary School, Poplar, 177–8
Mbeki, Thabo, 420
McAleese, Mary, 455, 456, 458, 460
McCartney, Stella, 170
McCorquodale, Sarah, 516
McDonald, Trevor, 210
McGuinness, Martin, 462–3
McKenzie, Precious, 172–3
McKinnon, Donald, 86, 156, 160, 416, 499–500, 501
McLaren, Henry, 2nd Baron Aberconway, 348–9
McLeod, M. G., 118
media, 43–7
Melbourne, Victoria, 161
Mellon, Paul, 239
Mendi, SS, 413
Menem, Carlos, 518–19
Menin Gate, Ypres, 206
Menzies, Pattie, 49
Menzies, Robert, 46, 49, 197, 199, 202, 503
Mercedes, 147, 441
Merino sheep, 49
Merkel, Angela, 18, 526–7
Metropolitan Police, 301
Mexico, 24, 25, 68, 168, 247, 365
Meyer, Christopher, 258
Michael, King of Romania, 79, 104
Middle East tours
  1979 35, 50, 53, 363, 424
  1997 366
Miklaszeski, James 'Jim', 251
Miliband, David, 8
Milton, Derek, 187, 229
miners' strike (1984–5), 390
Mintoff, Dom, 502–3
Mirzoeff, Edward, 253
Misérables, Les, 78
Mitterrand, François, 256, 305, 368–9, 409, 412
Mo Ibrahim Index, 164
Mobutu Sese Seko, 86–7, 93, 168
Mobutu, Marie-Antoinette, 86–7
Modi, Narendra, 67, 472
Mogotsi, Joe, 417
Mohammad Reza Pahlavi, Shah of Iran, 100, 508–9
arap Moi, Daniel, 26, 338
Mole, Stuart, 150, 152, 153, 155–6, 162, 386, 391, 494
Monday Club, 89
Mongolia, 22, 513
Montefiore, Simon Sebag, 446
Montejo, Michelle, 184
Montreal Olympics (1976), 5, 40, 224, 244, 316, 365
Monty Python, 140, 492
Moon, Peter, 64, 318
Moore, Charles, 339, 340, 375–6, 377, 380, 383, 384, 436
Moore, Dudley, 248
Moore, Jon, 41
Moore, Philip, 64, 148, 317, 335
Morgan, Peter, 14
Morgan, Piers, 272
Morocco, 48, 74
Morrow, Anthony, 244, 343, 362, 363, 366, 368, 495
Morton, Andrew, 487
Moshesh, Jeremiah, 113
Moshoeshoe II, King of Lesotho, 528
Mostert, Cornelius, 114
Mother Teresa, 381, 411
Motherwell, Jim, 49
Mountbatten, Lord Louis, 69, 84, 123, 124, 361, 363, 454, 460, 468
Mountbatten, Lady Pamela, 195–6
Mozambique, 166, 311, 326
Mr Scarborough's Family, 110
Mtirara, Rochelle, 411
Mugabe, Grace, 85
Mugabe, Robert, 85–6, 164, 311, 326, 398, 405–7
  Blair, relationship with, 86
  Commonwealth withdrawal (2003), 86, 164, 169
  general election (1980), 478–9, 482
  Grace, marriage to (1986), 85
  Harare CHOGM (1991), 405, 406, 407
  Independence (1980), 482, 483
  Marlborough House CHOGM (1986), 398
  Rhodesian Bush War (1964–79), 311, 326
  and Strasser, 54
  UK visit (1994), 54, 85–6
Mugabe, Sally, 85
Muggeridge, Malcolm, 158
Muhammad V, Sultan of Kelantan, 470
Mulchrone, Vincent, 205
Muldoon, Robert, 309, 316, 323, 325, 326
Mullin, Chris, 62
Mulroney, Brian, 384, 396–7, 398, 399–400
Murdoch, Gaye, 365
Murdoch, Rupert, 382
Mureithi, Nahashon, 128
Murphy, Philip, 44, 136, 222, 227
'Musical Fairy Tale, The', 363
'Muskrat Love' (Captain & Tennille), 243
Muzorewa, Abel, 325, 328, 338

Naiad, HMS, 364
Naisali, Henry, 234
Naked Diplomat, The (Fletcher), 488
Namibia, 31–2, 43, 403–5, 409
Nandi, Fiji, 34
Napoleon I, Emperor of the French, 119, 120, 430
Napoleon III, Emperor of the French, 8
Napoleonic Wars (1803–1815), 292, 430, 487
Narayanan, Kocheril Raman, 159
Nassau CHOGM (1985), 185, 344, 383–7, 397
Nasser, Gamal Abdul, 131
National Aeronautics and Space Administration (NASA), 255, 263
National Archives, 294
National Council for Scientific Research, 101
National Gallery, London, 468
National Westminster Bank, 92
Nauru, 171–2
Nazi Germany (1933–45), 93, 173, 205, 273, 277–8, 298, 326, 388, 425, 527
Nazrin Shah, Sultan of Perak, 471
Nehru, Jawaharlal, 122, 124, 125, 127, 129, 143, 179
Neil, Andrew, 390, 391, 393
Neill, Sam, 215
Nelson, Horatio, 1st Viscount Nelson, 17
Nepal, 23, 129, 134, 492, 515–16
Netflix, 6, 14, 137, 240, 355, 507
Netherlands, 256, 273, 281, 358, 531

New Hebrides, 345
New Law Journal, 102
New Zealand, 2, 10, 13, 25, 184, 188, 211, 426
 1840 Treaty of Waitangi, 195, 199, 216
 1930 Hamilton British Empire Games, 173
 1948 George VI cancels tour, 190–91
 1949 London Declaration, 124
 1950 Auckland British Empire Games, 173
 1953 Coronation tour, 21, 127, 186, 189, 193–6, 350
 1956 Royal visit, 356
 1963 Royal visit, 43, 49, 199–200, 201
 1970 Royal visit, 52, 204–5, 473, 510
 1972 UK joins EEC, 206
 1974 Christchurch British Commonwealth Games, 173
 1976 All Blacks tour South Africa, 316
 1977 Royal visit, 208
 1979 Zambia CHOGM, 309, 315–16, 323, 325, 326
 1982 Falklands War, 378; Prince Edward studies at Wanganui Collegiate School, 224
 1983 Royal visit, 483
 1986 Royal visit, 209–10
 1995 Auckland CHOGM, 215–16, 414–16
 2010 Prince William's visit, 524
 2011 Christchurch earthquake, 524; Pike River mine disaster, 524; Prince William's visit, 524–5
 2016 new flag referendum, 218
 2018 Commonwealth Day, 152; London CHOGM, 217–18
Newman, Adrian, Bishop of Stepney, 177
Nhongo, Rex, 482
Nicholas I, Emperor and Autocrat of All the Russias, 445
Nicholas II, Emperor and Autocrat of All the Russias, 445–6, 450
Nicholas, John, 4
Nigeria, 155, 178, 499
 1956 Royal visit, 40, 56
 1966 Commonwealth Prime Ministers' Conference, 145
 1979 Rhodesia trade ultimatum, 326; nationalisation of British Petroleum, 331; Lusaka CHOGM, 337
 1986 Edinburgh Commonwealth Games boycott, 389
 1989 Babangida's UK visit, 74
 1990 Commonwealth foreign ministers meeting, 402
 1995 Saro-Wiwa execution, 415–16
 2003 Abuja CHOGM, 35–6, 37, 62, 156
Nigeria, HMS, 118
Nightingale, Florence, 381
Nixon, Richard, 240–41, 242, 434, 475
Nixon, Tricia, 475
Niyazov, Saparmurat, 490–91
Nkomo, Joshua, 311, 315, 322, 323, 328, 332, 333, 478–9, 481–2
'Nkosi Sikelel' iAfrika', 113
Nkrumah, Kwame, 15, 19, 135–7, 143, 362, 503
Nobel Prize, 17, 60, 381, 419, 522, 527
Nobel, Alfred, 17
Norfolk Island, 171
Norman Conquest (1066), 3, 276, 284
Norman, Jessye, 252
Norman, Richard, 95, 101
Normandy landings (1944), 26, 58, 176, 256–7, 306, 349, 368
Norrell, Ellis 'Norrie', 359, 360
Norris, Eric, 477, 512
North Atlantic Treaty Organization (NATO), 245, 432, 433
North Korea, 465
North Sea ferries, 347
Northern Ireland, 33, 256, 298, 326, 376, 382, 400, 454–6, 460, 461–3
Northern Rhodesia (1924–64), 116, 310, 424
Northwestern University, 519
Norway, 24, 31, 34, 79, 256
Not Forgotten Association, 497
Nottingham University, 470
Nujoma, Sam, 32
Nyasaland (1907–64), 319
Nye, Joseph, 24, 26, 165
Nyerere, Julius, 64, 81, 84, 318, 329, 338, 339

'O Canada', 220
O'Connell, Pat, 461
O'Neill, Con, 206
Obama, Barack, 7, 13, 17, 68, 264–70, 306, 471, 526, 527
Obama, Michelle, 265, 530
Obasanjo, Olusegun, 386, 499
Oberon, Merle, 243
Obote, Milton, 81, 82, 147
Odd Man Out, 110
Oklahoma!, 239
Old Links and New Ties (Howell), 142
Olisa, Kenneth, 178
Oliver, Brian, 172
Oliver, William, 200, 202
Olympic Games, 171, 172, 513
 1936 Berlin, 173
 1956 Melbourne, 355
 1976 Montreal, 5, 40, 224, 244, 316, 365
 2000 Sydney, 210, 213
 2012 London, 5–6, 33, 171, 529
Onslow, Robin, Countess of, 349, 369
Operation Raleigh, 522
Order of Good Hope, 411
Order of Merit, 293, 375, 381, 403, 411, 417
Order of Socialist Romania, 100
Order of St Michael and St George, 49, 383
Order of the Bath, 72, 100, 104, 285, 293, 411
Order of the Companions of Honour, 16
Order of the Garter, 72
Order of the Mosquito, 144
Organization of the Petroleum Exporting Countries (OPEC), 141, 146
d'Ormesson, Jean, 300
Ormsby-Gore, William David, 5th Baron Harlech, 326
Orr, Jim, 508
Orwell, George, 93
Osborne, George, 16, 456
Owen, David, 11, 12, 16, 38
 and African tour (1979), 314–15, 319–20
 and Amin's proposed visit (1977), 83, 84
 and Ceausescu's visit (1978), 88, 91, 93, 97, 103
 and Prince of Wales, 180, 478
 and Juan Carlos of Spain, 80
 and Middle East tour (1979), 50, 53
 on rum ration, 351
 and *Sunday Times* affair (1986), 394
Oxfam, 35, 318
Oxford University, 140, 418–19, 426, 469, 509

Page, Peter, 317
Pakistan, 165
 Bangladeshi independence (1971), 20
 Coronation of Elizabeth II (1953), 127

  Independence (1947), 123, 124, 138, 191
  London CHOGM (2018), 1–3, 67, 142, 503
  Royal visit (1961), 20, 40, 129, 133
  Royal visit (1997), 20, 157–60
  suspensions from Commonwealth (1999–2004, 2007–8), 164
Palestine, 166
Palliser, Michael, 315
Panorama, 497, 519
Papua New Guinea, 36, 106, 233–4, 355, 475
Paraguay, 59
Parker Bowles, Andrew, 455, 479–83, 504–5
Parker Bowles, Camilla, *see* Cornwall, Duchess of
Parker, Michael, 357
Parker, Peter, 509
Parker, Robert, 193
Parvin, Stewart, 42, 43
Paterson, James, 322
Patil, Pratibha Rao, 501
Patten, Christopher, 343, 496
Patterson, Percival 'P. J.', 187
Paul, King of Greece, 361
Paul VI, Pope, 90
Payne, Keith, 204
Payne, Liam, 152
Pearson, Lester, 125, 145, 221, 222
Pelé, 65
Peres, Shimon, 7
Perkins, Albert, 301
Permanent Royal Yacht Service (PRYS), 359
Perón, Eva, 518–19
Persian Gulf tour (1979), 51, 53, 315, 363
Perth Commonwealth Games (1962), 173
Pétain, Philippe, 278
Philip, Prince, *see* Edinburgh, Duke of
Philippines, 24
Phillips, Mark, 366, 513
Photographer of the Year awards, 43
Picasso, Pablo, 469
Pick, Hella, 98
Picture Gallery, 72
Pike River mine disaster (2010), 524
Pilgrims of Great Britain, 475–6
Pindling, Lynden, 385, 397
Pitcairn Islands, 361
Plunket, Patrick, 427
Poland, 257, 488, 527
Polytechnic of Central London, 95, 97, 101
Pompidou, Claude, 291, 292, 293, 303
Pompidou, Georges, 35, 274, 280–82, 284–9, 291–3, 297–8, 303–4
Pope
  Benedict XVI, 66, 80
  Francis, 20–21
  John Paul II, 66, 246
  Paul VI, 90
Poplar, London, 177–8
Porchester, Lord, *see* Herbert, Henry
Portillo, José López, 24
Portugal, 166, 311, 357
Powell, Colin, 259
Powell, Enoch, 382
Prada, Miuccia, 42
Prague, Czech Republic, 37, 58
Prasad, Rajendra, 129
President and the Princess, *The* (Giscard d'Estaing), 305
press, 43–7
Prichard, John, 345
Priestley, Raymond, 355
Prince's Trust, 8, 179, 470, 471, 504
Princess Royal (Princess Anne), 46, 220, 224, 510–13
  Australian tour (1970), 203, 345, 473, 510–11
  Bangladesh visit (1983), 381
  birth (1950), 239
  birthday party (1971), 343
  and *Britannia*, 341, 350, 351, 366, 369, 372
  Canada tour (1951), 220
  Ceausescu's visit (1978), 98
  and Commonwealth cemeteries, 175–6
  Commonwealth Games (1966), 172
  and Coronation tour (1953–4), 194–5, 350–51, 473, 510, 511
  D-Day anniversary (1994), 257
  Greece visit (1964), 511
  Iran visit (1971), 508
  Kenya visit (1971), 477, 511–12
  Montreal Olympics (1976), 224
  New Zealand tour (1970), 205, 510
  and Nobel Peace Prize, 17
  and Save the Children, 17, 381, 476, 511–12
  Scottish cruise (1955), 354
  Turkey visit (1972), 513
  United States visit (1970), 241, 475
  wedding (1973), 366, 513
Privy Purse, 25
Putin, Vladimir, 68–9, 444, 451
Pym, Francis, 248

Qatar, 68
Quebec, 219, 222, 225, 280
Queen, die, 18, 428
Queen Elizabeth, 348, 349
Queen Elizabeth Canadian Research Fund, 22
Queen Elizabeth Commonwealth Scholarships, 179
Queen Elizabeth Diamond Jubilee Trust, 105, 514
Queen Elizabeth Land, Antarctica, 22, 183
Queen Elizabeth Prize for Engineering, 17–18
Queen Mary tiara, 263
Queen Mary, 348
Queen's Commonwealth Canopy, 9, 179
Queen's Commonwealth Essay Prize, 468–9
Queen's Commonwealth Trust, 8–9, 107
Queen's Lecture, 18
Queen's Young Leaders, 9, 14, 105–8, 468, 532

Rabuka, Sitiveni, 235
Rajapaksa, Mahinda, 501
Rajpipla State (1340–1948), 122
Raleigh International, 522
Rama IV, King of Thailand, 38
Rama VIII, King of Thailand, 39
Rama IX, King Bhumibol of Thailand, 26, 41, 48, 63, 70
Rama X, King of Thailand, 48, 63
Ramaphosa, Cyril, 421
Ramphal, Shridath 'Sonny', 10, 12, 53
  and Amin's proposed visit (1977), 83, 84, 85
  and Blair, 156
  and Christmas broadcast (1983), 382
  and Edinburgh Commonwealth Games (1986), 395
  and George VI, 125
  and Gonsalves, 232
  and Kenya visit (1952), 12
  and London CHOGM (1977), 150
  and Lusaka CHOGM (1979), 313, 325, 326, 328, 333, 337–9, 380
  and Mandela, 402
  and Manley, 150, 228
  and Marlborough House CHOGM (1986), 389–90, 396, 398, 399

Ramphal, Shridath 'Sonny' (*Continued*)
and Melbourne CHOGM (1981), 161
and Nassau CHOGM (1985), 384, 385, 386
and Nyerere, 318
retirement (1990), 155
and Rhodesian UDI (1965), 145
and Singapore CHOGM (1971), 147
and Thatcher, 155, 380, 384, 386, 394, 400, 401
and Trudeau, 222–3, 224
Warwick University chancellorship (1989–2002), 418
Ramsey, Michael, Archbishop of Canterbury, 151
Ratiu, Ion, 102
Rawlinson, Ivor, 93
Rayne shoes, 42
Reagan, Nancy, 245, 248, 249, 250, 263
Reagan, Ronald
Botha, relationship with, 386
on Commonwealth, 167
and Falklands War (1982), 245
Grenada invasion (1983), 230, 250, 380
Libya bombing (1986), 390
Royal visit (1983), 247–50
Royal visit (1985), 485
Royal visit (1991), 253–4
Soviet Union, relations with, 101
Star Wars programme, 101
Thatcher, relationship with, 167, 237, 246, 380, 386, 390
UK visit (1982), 66, 244–7, 267, 418
Red Cross, 521
Reed-Purvis, Henry, 326–7
Rees, Merlyn, 84
Regan, Gaynor, 159
Rehse, Karl-Ludwig, 42
Remembrance Sunday, 176
Renwick, Robin, 402, 419
republicanism, 14, 15, 44, 63, 136, 146, 162, 186–7, 505
Australia, 149, 187, 202, 206–17, 498–9
Bulgaria, 79
Canada, 186, 223–4
Caribbean, 187, 150, 228–32
India, 123–5, 127, 131, 222
Jamaica, 150, 186, 228
New Zealand, 211, 216–17
Papua New Guinea, 233
Romania, 79
South Africa, 109, 136, 379, 408
Tuvalu, 234
Reynolds, Albert, 449
Rhédey, Claudine, 100
Rhodes, Cecil, 117, 140, 322
Rhodes, Margaret, 14
Rhodesia, *see* Northern Rhodesia; Southern Rhodesia
Rhys-Jones, Sophie, *see* Wessex, Countess of
Richards, Chris, 400–401
Richards, Francis, 31–2, 404–5, 444, 448, 453
Rifkind, Malcolm, 37, 60, 166, 389, 395, 401, 484, 490, 518
Ritchie, Lewis, 109–10, 111, 112, 113, 114, 115, 116, 118
Roberts, Frank, 425, 428
Roberts, Philip and Hannah, 201
Robertson, Patsy, 83, 145, 150, 228, 333, 385
Roche, Marc, 168, 278, 305, 306
Roche, Ruth, Baroness Fermoy, 362
Rochon, Steve, 261–2
Rodgers and Hammerstein, 70
Rohingyas, 472
Rolls-Royce, 53, 90, 132, 147, 342, 397, 445, 486
Romania, 24, 79, 87–104, 270
Romanov, House of, 445–6, 450
ROMBAC, 104
Roosevelt, Franklin, 237, 252
Roosevelt, Theodore, 95
Ross, Diana, 485
Rostropovich, Mstislav, 448
Round Table, The, 401
Round Tower (horse), 250
Rouse, Philip, 440
Royal Air Force (RAF), 457, 469
Andover, 320, 326, 334, 342
Blenheim bombers, 472
Czech Republic visit (1996), 37
France visit (1972), 33–4, 286
Lusaka CHOGM (1979), 308, 320, 326
Royal Squadron, 447
Shackleton seaplanes, 193
Spitfires, 310
Vickers VC10, 33, 34, 39, 286, 331, 342, 381, 384, 404–5
Voyager, 32, 469
William's service, 457, 523
World War II (1939–45), 176, 310, 320, 472
Royal Albert Hall, London, 419, 473
Royal Archives, 266, 424
Royal Ascot, 182
Royal Barge, 359, 368
Royal Canadian Mounted Police, 22
Royal Chef, 1, 138
Royal Collection, 20, 40, 266, 268
Royal Commonwealth Society (RCS), 151, 152, 153, 469
Royal Dutch Shell, 415
Royal Family, 46, 223, 241
Royal Gallery, 246, 418
Royal Gurkha Rifles, 134
Royal Horse Guards, 478
Royal Household Hospitality Scholarships, 181–2, 184–5
Royal Institute of Chemistry, 95, 101
Royal Library, 67, 72, 225–6, 268
Royal Mail, 15
Royal Marines, 341, 345, 361, 368–9, 452
Royal Mews, 70, 342
Royal National Lifeboat Institution (RNLI), 454
Royal Navy, 385, 441
and Prince Andrew, Duke of York, 245, 513
Arctic convoys (1941–5), 451
and *Britannia*, 244, 346–7, 349–50, 359–60, 367, 369, 371, 385, 441
and Prince of Wales, 8, 245, 302, 466, 477–8, 496
Falklands War (1982), 245, 378
Faslane submarine base, 360
and Prince Philip, Duke of Edinburgh, 11, 31, 274, 367
piping aboard, 244
rum ration, 351
and South Yemen Civil War (1986), 441
Prince William's service, 523
Royal Opera House, London, 77
Royal Society, 91
Royal Train, 70, 98, 219–20, 238, 342, 428
Royal Victorian Order, 49
Royal Visits Committee, 23–4, 435, 489
Royal Yacht, see *Britannia; Vanguard*
Royal Yacht Service, 350, 359
Ruby Jubilee (1992), 46
Rudd, Amber, 183
rugby, 316, 523

rum ration, 351
Russell, John, 65, 92, 364
Russian Federation, 20, 68–9, 441–53, 488, 517
Russian Fringe tiara, 100, 130, 417
Rwanda, 2, 21, 166

Sadat, Anwar, 24, 366, 493
Sakharov, Andrei, 448
salad dressing, 47
Saleha, Raja Isteri of Brunei, 469
Salisbury, Lord, *see* Gascoyne-Cecil, Robert
Sālote Tupou III, Queen of Tonga, 107
Samarkand, Uzbekistan, 490
Samoa, 2
Sandhurst, Berkshire, 528
Sandringham, Norfolk, 30, 126, 344, 356
Sandys, Duncan, 143, 200, 206
Sapphire Jubilee (2017), 21, 227
Sargent, Emma, 485
Sarkozy, Nicolas, 160, 305–6, 489
Saro-Wiwa, Kenule, 415
Saudi Arabia, 21, 53, 167, 270, 315, 487, 489
Savalas, Aristotelis 'Telly' 243
Save the Children, 17, 381, 476, 511–12
Saxe-Coburg-Gotha, House of, 177, 426
Scarf, Arthur, 472
Schmidt, Helmut, 313, 433
Schumann, Maurice, 281, 290
Schwarzkopf, Norman, 254
Scotland, 23, 225, 270–71, 277
  Balmoral Castle, 30, 47, 60, 136, 210, 240, 258, 271, 336, 344, 376–7, 388, 451
  and Banda, 330
  and *Britannia*, 347–50, 345, 353–4, 367, 371, 372
  Castle of Mey, 354
  CHOGM (1997), 155–6, 162, 163
  Commonwealth Games (2014), 171, 174
  Dunblane massacre (1996), 50
  Edinburgh Commonwealth Games (1986), 389, 394–5, 398
  and France visit (1948), 275–6
  Gleneagles Hotel, 150
  Gordonstoun School, 473
  John Brown & Co., 347, 348
  Loch Ness monster, 277
  Royal cruises, 345, 353–4, 367, 371
  St Andrew's University, 139, 155, 523
  and Trump, 270–71
Scotland, Patricia, 126, 169, 504
Scots Guards, 267, 479
Scott, Kenneth, 92, 93, 94–5, 96, 444
Scott, Michael, 57–8, 319
Scott, Peter, 22
Scott, Robert, 355
Scouts, 497
Seago, Edward, 355
Second World War, *see* World War II
Secondé, Reginald, 92, 93, 94, 96, 102, 103
Seeiso of Lesotho, 528
Sefton (horse), 455
Senegal, 19, 25
Sentamu, John, Archbishop of York, 136, 154
Sentebale, 528, 530–31
September 11 attacks (2001), 237, 258
Serbia, 80
Shackleton, Ernest, 355
Shackleton seaplanes, 193
Shakespeare, William, 4, 267, 318, 329, 417
Shand, Camilla, *see* Cornwall, Duchess of
Sharma, Kamalesh, 56, 124, 125, 150, 164, 165, 168, 180, 501–2
Sharpeville massacre (1960), 379
Shave, Alan, 64, 231
Shawcross, William, 223, 244, 248, 258, 340, 401, 436
Shea, Michael, 329, 382, 390, 391, 393–4, 436
Shell, 96
Shetland Isles, 31, 356
Shore, Peter, 294
Shultz, George and Charlotte, 263
Sierra Leone, 19, 54, 106, 144, 170
Sikorsky helicopters, 33
Silk Road, 490
Silver Jubilee (1977), 83, 150, 180, 207–9
Simeon II, King of the Bulgarians, 79
Simpson, Wallis, *see* Windsor, Duchess of
Simpson-Miller, Portia, 229
Sinatra, Frank, 248
Singapore
  1956 Chinese middle schools riots, 355
  1971 First CHOGM, 81, 146–8, 222, 283, 313, 467, 474, 508
  1979 Lusaka CHOGM, 309, 316
  2018 Prince of Wales's visit, 467–9
Singleton, Valerie, 512
Sinn Fein, 256, 460, 461
Sir Edmund Hillary Fund, 141
Sirikit, Queen consort of Thailand, 48
Sirindhorn, Princess Royal of Thailand, 48
Slater, John 'Jock', 19–20, 30–31, 56, 71, 204, 224, 349, 361–3
Smith, Arnold, 53, 81, 82, 143–5, 148–9, 152, 222, 311, 328, 474
Smith, Edward, 476
Smith, Eve, 144
Smith, Ian, 310, 314, 322, 338, 478
Smith, Margaret 'Maggie', 15, 268
Smuts, Jan, 109, 111, 115, 119, 124
Snow, Peter, 96
Snowdon, Earl of, *see* Armstrong-Jones, Antony
Soames, Christopher
  France, ambassador to (1968–72), 35, 281–2, 286, 288–9, 292, 294–7, 299–301, 303
  Southern Rhodesia governor of (1979–80), 85, 478, 482
Soames, Emma, 483
Soames, Nicholas, 85, 288, 292, 304
Sobchak, Anatoly, 444, 451
Sobhuza II, King of Swaziland, 114
soft power, 6, 8, 165, 370
Solomon Islands, 234, 337
Somalia, 176
Somerville, Philip, 42
Sophia, Queen consort of Spain, 361, 366
South Africa, 14, 17, 82, 108–115, 374–5, 378–422
  All Blacks tour (1976), 316
  apartheid period (1948–94), 17, 119, 136, 146, 150, 172–3, 312, 316, 378–407, 408, 413
  arms sales to, 81, 146–7
  Bahamas CHOGM (1985), 344, 383–7, 397
  bombing raids (1986), 387
  British Empire Games (1934), 173–4
  Commonwealth Prime Ministers' Conference (1961), 379
  diamonds, 111, 113, 117, 118, 119, 137, 411–12, 417
  Durban CHOGM (1999), 126, 420
  Eminent Persons Group (1985–6), 384, 386–8, 400
  George VI's visit (1947), 108–119, 137, 189–90, 273, 374, 378, 410, 411, 412
  general election (1994), 402, 407

South Africa (*Continued*)
London Declaration (1949), 124–5
Macmillan's 'Wind of Change' speech (1960), 136, 378
Major's visit (1994), 409
Malawi, relations with, 319
Mandela presidency (1994–9), 86, 113, 343, 375, 407–20, 443
Mitterrand's visit (1994), 409, 412
Ramaphosa's UK visit (2018), 421
Republic referendum (1960), 136, 379, 408
Royal visit (1995), 343, 374, 409–14, 443
sanctions on, 379–80, 383, 388, 389, 399
Sharpeville massacre (1960), 379
South-West Africa (1915–90), 403, 404
South Africa House, London, 416, 419–20
South America tours
1962 508
1968 26–8, 65, 364
South Korea, 68
South West Africa (1915–90), 403, 404
South Yemen Civil War (1986), 441
Southampton University, 91, 93
Southern Rhodesia (1923–80), 85, 149, 228, 335
Air Rhodesia Flight 825 shot down (1978), 312
Bush War (1964–79), 309, 310–12, 314–15, 320, 322–9, 331–3, 338–40, 377, 478
general election (1979), 325, 331
general election (1980), 478–9, 481
Geneva peace conference (1976), 314
Lancaster House Agreement (1979), 340, 377, 478
Royal visit (1947), 20, 21, 116–17, 118, 403
sanctions on, 50, 311
Thatcher, relations with, 315, 322, 338–40, 377, 478
Unilateral Declaration of Independence (1965), 144–5, 310–11
Sovereign Grant, 465
Soviet Union (1922–91)
and Berlin Wall, 246, 430
Brezhnev period (1964–82), 24, 281, 293, 432–3
Czechoslovakia invasion (1968), 89
dissolution (1991), 443
Ghana relations with, 135, 137
Gorbachev period (1985–91), 67, 72, 246, 253, 379, 387, 442–3
India, relations with, 124
Khrushchev period (1953–64), 131, 137, 240, 246
Reagan, relations with, 101, 380
Zimbabwe African People's Union, relations with, 311, 322
Space Age, 12
Spain, 48, 69, 70, 72, 75–6, 79–80, 361, 366
'special relationship', 7, 237–8, 259
speeches, 56–62
Spencer, Charles, 9th Earl Spencer, 498
Spice Girls, 498
Sri Lanka, 4–5, 337, 342, 492–3, 501–3
St Andrew's University, Scotland, 139, 155, 523
St George's Chapel, Windsor, 152, 533
St George's Hall, Windsor Castle, 78
St Helena, 119, 231, 357
St Kitts & Nevis, 232
St Lawrence Seaway, 221, 357–8
St Lucia, 232
St Martin-in-the-Fields, London, 151
St Paul's Cathedral, London, 84, 240, 422
St Vincent & the Grenadines, 232
stamps, 15, 225
Star Wars programme, 101
'Star-Spangled Banner', 237, 258
State Coach, 342
Statute of Westminster (1931), 121, 183
Steel, David, 103, 270
Stephen, Marcus, 171–2
Stephens, Caroline, 375
Stevens, Siaka, 144
Stewart, Michael, 432
Steyn, Colin, 113
Sting, 520
Strasser, Valentine, 54
Stratocruiser, BOAC, 219
Straw, Jack, 6, 35–6, 37, 60, 68–9, 166, 259, 488
Stroessner, Alfredo, 59
succession, 3, 169, 180, 186, 213–15, 217, 464–6, 498–506
Sudan, 11
Suez Crisis (1956), 78, 198, 239, 355, 356
Sugar, Alan, 181
Suits, 531
Sunay, Cevdet, 36–7
Sunday Times affair (1986), 390–92, 395
supermarket, first visit to, 239
Sussex, Duchess of (Meghan Markle), 6, 180, 216, 238, 319, 397, 531–3
Sussex, Duke of (Prince Harry), 527–33
Afghanistan War, service in, 528–9
Antarctic trip (2013), 529
Antigua visit (2016), 532
Australia visit (2003), 528
birth (1984), 484
Army service, 528–9
and Botswana, 319
as Commonwealth Youth Ambassador, 179
at Eton, 420, 528
and Felipe VI, banquet for (2017), 75
gap year (2003), 528
helicopter piloting, 33
holidays, 23
Invictus Games, 529–30, 533
Jamaica visit (2012), 187, 229
and London CHOGM (2018), 532
Obama's visit (2011), 269
and Olympic Games (2012), 5, 529
and Queen's Commonwealth Trust, 8
and Queen's Young Leaders, 106, 532
and Royal Household Hospitality Scholarships, 184–5
and Sentebale, 528, 530–31
South Africa visit (1997), 498
Warrior Games (2013), 529
wedding (2018), 6, 180, 216, 238, 397, 531–3
Sussex University, 91
Sutherland, Graham, 292–3
Suzman, Helen, 383
Swan, John, 231
Swaziland, 114–15
Sweden, 24, 63, 69, 72, 73, 75, 77, 100, 358–9
Swire, Hugo, 525
Sword of Stalingrad, 67
Sydney-Davies, Euphemia, 170
Syria, 69

Taliban, 12
Tall Ships Race, 345
Tamar, HMS, 495
Tambo, Oliver, 408, 421
Tambo, Thembi, 421
Tanzania, 20, 64, 81, 84–5, 145, 318, 320, 329, 338, 339
Tartar, HMS, 365
tax havens, 231

Teresa, Mother (Saint Teresa of Calcutta), 381, 411
terrorism, 33, 128, 179, 237, 269, 432
  and African National Congress, 400
  Brighton hotel bombing (1984), 250, 376
  Hyde Park and Regent's Park bombings (1982), 455, 479
  Irish Republican Army, 250, 298, 326, 376, 400, 454–5, 462, 479
  Mau Mau Uprising (1952–64), 128
  Mountbatten assassination (1979), 454, 460
  Rhodesian Bush War (1964–79), 312, 326, 339
  September 11 attacks (2001), 237, 258
Thailand, 26, 38–9, 41, 48, 63, 70, 78, 284, 286, 471, 519–20
Thatcher, Denis, 77, 339, 380–81, 383
Thatcher, Margaret, 8, 24, 50, 51, 167, 283, 320
  Balmoral meetings, 376–7
  Brighton hotel bombing (1984), 250, 376
  China visit (1982), 436
  death (2013), 421–2
  Edinburgh Commonwealth Games (1986), 389, 394–5
  Falklands War (1982), 155, 377
  Fiji abdication (1987), 235
  general election (1979), 51, 308, 315, 320, 322
  Gorbachev, relationship with, 67, 387
  Hungary visit (1990), 14
  Jiang Zemin's visit (1999), 77
  Joint Declaration on Hong Kong (1984), 434
  Lusaka CHOGM (1979), 308–9, 312–15, 322–9, 330, 332–4, 337–40, 377, 380
  Malaysia visit (1989), 150
  Mandela, meetings with (1990, 1996), 402–3, 420
  Marlborough House CHOGM (1986), 395–400
  miners' strike (1984–5), 390
  Nassau CHOGM (1985), 383–5
  Order of Merit (1990), 375, 403
  Reagan, relationship with, 167, 237, 246, 380, 386, 390
  resignation (1990), 403, 405
  Rhodesia, relations with, 315, 322, 338–40, 377, 478
  and royal protocol, 375–6
  South Africa, relations with, 380, 383–5, 388, 389, 390–403, 412
  Sunday Times affair (1986), 390–94, 395
  Zimbabwean independence (1980), 483
Thin, Jean, 288, 302
Thoreau, Henry David, 252
Thuillier, Raymond, 301
Tiananmen Square massacre (1989), 435, 441
tiaras, 40, 52, 67, 72
  Cullinan Diamond, 111
  Fleur de Lys, 76
  Girls of Great Britain and Ireland, 459
  Lover's Knot, 76
  Queen Mary, 263
  Russian Fringe, 100, 130, 417
  Vladimir, 40, 428
Tibet, 71, 525
tiger hunting, 23, 130–34, 134, 135
Tikolevu, Jitoko, 236
Timbertop School, Victoria, 224, 473
Timbuktu, Mali, 25
Tito, Josip Broz, 131, 326, 434
Togo, 166
Tonga, 106, 107, 108, 337, 355, 503
Torres Straits Islanders, 196
tot, 351
totem pole, 22
Townsend, Peter, 190
Transparency International, 164
Transylvania, 104
Travers, Barbara, 482
Travolta, John, 485
Tre Kronor, 69
Treadell, Victoria, 471
Treaty of Waitangi (1840), 195, 199, 216
Treetops, Aberdare National Park, 12
Trevor-Morgan, Rachel, 42
Trinidad and Tobago, 160, 227, 232, 504
Tristan da Cunha, 186, 357
Tristar, 435, 441
Trollope, Anthony, 110
Trooping the Colour, 22
Trudeau, Justin, 48, 174, 224, 225–6
Trudeau, Margaret, 224
Trudeau, Pierre, 48, 52, 148–50, 222–4, 225, 226, 503
Truman, Harry, 219, 239, 269
Trump, Donald, 25, 181, 270–72
Trump, Ivana, 261
Trump, Mary, 271
trumpeter swans, 22
tuberculosis, 347
Tubman, William, 19
Tully, Mark, 159
Tunisia, 362
Turing, Alan, 48
Turkey, 36–7, 46, 68, 286, 344, 513
Turkmenistan, 490–91
Turks and Caicos Islands, 230
Turnbull, Malcolm, 217, 218
Turnbull & Asser, 54
Turner, Graham, 207, 396
Turner, Wilfred, 320
Tusk, 523
Tutu, Desmond, 388, 408, 411
Tuvalu, 234, 370, 424

Uganda, 21, 23, 81–5, 136, 141
  1962 Independence, 81, 82
  1971 Singapore CHOGM, 81; Amin coup, 81, 147; Amin's UK visit, 23, 81–2, 86
  1972 expulsion of Asians, 82
  1976 Entebbe raid, 331
  1977 London CHOGM, 82–4
  1978 invasion of Tanzania, 84–5
  1979 Tanzanian invasion; ousting of Amin, 85, 329
  2007 Kampala CHOGM, 21, 163
UK Trade and Investment, 25
Ukraine, 69, 168
Ulster Unionist Party (UUP), 382
United Arab Emirates, 68, 424
United Nations, 146, 150, 160, 169, 216
  Charter, 109
  Climate Change Conference (2009), 160–61
  Falklands War (1982), 378
  Human Development Index, 79
  Queen's address (1957), 239
  South African re-admittance (1994), 408
  World Tourism Organisation, 234
  Zimbabwean independence (1980), 482
United Service Organizations (USO), 533
United States, 4, 237–72
  Bush Jr administration (2001–9), 66, 237, 258–64, 266, 392, 475
  Bush Sr administration (1989–93), 49, 250–55
  Carter administration (1977–81), 25, 90, 244–5
  casinos, 55
  Clinton administration (1993–2001), 255–7, 418
  D-Day anniversaries (1994, 2014), 256–7, 306
  Declaration of Independence (1776), 242

United States (*Continued*)
Eisenhower administration (1953–61), 129, 221, 239–40, 257, 357
Ford administration (1974–7), 241–4, 253
George VI's visit (1939), 189, 238, 252, 268
Grenada invasion (1983), 230, 250, 380
Gulf War (1990–91), 49, 250, 252, 254
halibut fishing treaty (1923), 53
Invictus Games (2016), 530
Johnson administration (1963–9), 203, 238, 240
Kennedy administration (1961–3), 21, 137, 221, 240, 404, 424
Korean War (1950–53), 239
Libya bombing (1986), 390
Nixon administration (1969–74), 240–41, 242, 434, 475
Obama administration (2009–17), 7, 13, 17, 68, 264–70, 306, 471, 526, 527, 530
Reagan administration (1981–9), 66, 101, 167, 230, 237, 244–50, 267, 380, 386, 390, 418, 485
Revolutionary War (1775–83), 120, 242, 243, 247, 264, 266, 268
Roosevelt, Franklin administration (1933–45), 237, 252
Roosevelt, Theodore administration (1901–9), 95
Royal Commonwealth Society (RCS), 151, 239
Royal visits, *see* United States, visits to
and Royal wedding (2018), 6, 238, 531–3
September 11 attacks (2001), 237, 258
St Lawrence Seaway opening (1959), 221, 357–8
Truman administration (1945–53), 219, 239, 269
Trump administration (2017–), 25, 270–72
Vietnam War (1955–75), 204, 240
Watergate scandal (1972–4), 186, 242
Wilson administration (1913–21), 66
United States, visits to
1939 189
1951 192, 219, 239
1957 21, 221, 239, 260
1970 475
1976 241–4, 365
1983 247–50, 263
1984 250
1985 485
1986 250
1989 250
1991 49, 250–55
2007 260–64, 392
University of Bradford, 91
University of Cambridge, 418, 473
University of Edinburgh, 433–4, 438–9
University of Liverpool, 91
University of Nottingham, 470
University of Oxford, 140, 418–19, 426, 469, 509
University of Southampton, 91, 93
University of Sussex, 91
University of the Oceans, 371
University of Warwick, 54, 418
University of York, 93, 95
Upham, Charles, 205
Urquhart Irvine, Oliver, 72, 225–6
Uruguay, 27, 168
Uzbekistan, 490

Vajiralongkorn, King of Thailand (as Crown Prince), 48, 63
Vajpayee, Atal Bihari, 124
Valenti, Jack, 248
Vancouver British Empire and Commonwealth Games (1954), 173, 353
Vanguard, HMS, 109, 110, 118, 119–20, 190, 346, 349, 353
Vanity Fair, 278–9
Vanneck, Peter, 94
Vanuatu, 161, 503
Vatican, 484
Veeraswamy, London, 138
Vella, Roland, 504
Veniard, Ernest, 49
Versan, Belkis, 513
Verwoerd, Hendrik, 136, 378, 379
Vichy France (1940–44), 278
Vickers VC10, 33, 34, 39, 286, 331, 342, 381, 384, 404–5
Victor Chang Cardiac Research Institute, 520
Victoria Cross, 176, 204
Victoria Falls, 116–18, 119, 324, 517
Victoria Station, London, 70, 85, 98
Victoria, Queen of the United Kingdom, 12, 15, 71, 261, 276, 527
Canadian Confederation (1867), 218, 226
Empire Day, 151
as Empress of India, 121, 122
Germany visit (1845), 428
holidays, 23
as Monarch of the Fijians, 238
Rama IV, relationship with, 38
and slavery, 229
Treaty of Waitangi (1840), 199, 216
US presidents, letters to, 266
Victoria and Albert, 346, 359
Vietnam, 204, 240, 513
Vimy Ridge, battle of (1917), 174, 175, 176
Virginia Tech shooting (2007), 260
Vladimir tiara, 40, 428
Vogue, 43, 170, 515
Volcker, Paul, 365
Vunipola, Billy and Mako, 503

Waddington, David, 231
Wade, Hunter, 148
Waldheim, Kurt, 482
Wales, 353, 420, 473, 519
Wales, Prince of (Prince Charles), 24, 26, 464–506
airliner, 489
and architecture, 468, 488
Asian tour (2018), 467–72
Australia visits, 203, 209, 224, 473, 475, 491
Bahamas independence (1973), 385
birth (1948), 190, 191, 274
and Brexit (2016–), 69
and *Britannia*, 341, 350–51, 353, 363, 366, 371
Cambridge, studies at, 473
Camilla, relationship with, 226, 479, 480, 482, 500
Canada visits, 186, 225, 484
Caribbean tour (2000), 499
Ceausescu's visit (1978), 93, 98, 100
Central Asian tour (1996), 490–91
charity work, 500
CHOGM (2007), 163
CHOGM (2018), 1, 167, 217, 464–6
Commonwealth Day (2018), 164
and Coronation tour (1953–4), 194–5, 341, 350–51, 473
'Defender of Faith' remark (1994), 153
Diana, relationship with, 366, 372, 466, 479, 483, 487, 494, 496–8
Dimbleby's biography (1994), 445, 476
divorce (1996), 466, 497, 515, 519
Duke of Windsor, meeting with (1972), 288, 302
and European Economic Community, 476

France visit (1972), 288, 302
de Gaulle's funeral (1970), 476
Geelong Grammar, studies at (1966), 224, 473
Gold Coast Commonwealth Games (2018), 174, 186
Gordonstoun School, studies at, 473
helicopter piloting, 33, 360
Hong Kong handover (1997), 483, 494–6
Hungary visit (1990), 486
India visits, 472, 486–7
and Islam, 487–8
Italy visit (1985), 484
Japan visits, 489–90
and Kenya, 52, 476–7, 511
Letsie III's coronation (1997), 528
Mandela, relationship with, 418, 421
Marlborough House, day at (1970), 474
'Musical Fairy Tale, The', 363
on National Gallery, 468
Nepal visit (1998), 492
Nixon, meetings with, 240, 475
Papua New Guinea visits, 233, 475
Pilgrims of Great Britain speech (1970), 475–6
Prince's Trust, 8, 179, 470, 471, 504
Reagans, relationship with, 245
Romania visit (1998), 104
Royal Mail stamp (2016), 15
Royal Navy service, 8, 245, 302, 466, 477, 496
Russia visit (1993), 443, 444, 488
Sarkozy's visit (2008), 306
and Saudi Arabia, 487, 489
separation from Diana (1992), 466, 487, 494, 515
South Africa visit (1997), 498
South Korea visit (1992), 486, 487
Sovereign Grant, 465
Sri Lanka visits, 492–3, 501
succession, 3, 169, 180, 186, 217, 464–6, 498–506
Sydney speech (1994), 211
and Tibet, 525
United States visits, 241, 475, 485
Victoria and George Cross events, 177
Vimy Ridge Day (2017), 174
Wales visit (1955), 353
wedding to Camilla Parker Bowles (2005), 47, 500
wedding to Lady Diana Spencer (1981), 366, 372, 478, 483
Prince William, birth of (1982), 209
Woodard's tutoring, 360, 477
'Youth and the Commonwealth' speech (1970), 474
Zimbabwean independence (1980), 478–83
Walesa, Lech, 257, 527
walkabouts, 58
1970 New Zealand, 52, 205, 474, 510
1977 New Zealand, 208
1979 Malawi, 330
1995 South Africa, 411, 413
2007 United States, 263
Walker, Karen, 170
Wall, Michael, 135
Walton, William, 251
'Waltzing Matilda', 173, 207
Ward, John, 484
Ware, Fabian, 175
Waring, Fred, 239
Warrior Games, 529, 530
Warsaw Pact, 89
Warwick University, 54, 418
Watergate scandal (1972–4), 186, 242
Waterloo Chamber, Windsor Castle, 78
Waterloo, battle of (1815), 292, 430
wattle brooch, 197
wattle dress, 40, 149, 198
Way Ahead Group, 497
weddings
1934 George and Marina, 531
1937 Edward and Wallis, 287, 531
1947 Elizabeth and Philip, 44, 190, 273
1973 Anne and Mark, 366, 513
1981 Charles and Diana, 366, 372, 479, 483
1986 Andrew and Sarah, 366, 390
1999 Edward and Sophie, 367, 514
2005 Charles and Camilla, 47, 500
2011 William and Catherine, 213, 232, 265, 457, 524
2018 Harry and Meghan, 6, 180, 216, 238, 397, 531–3
Welby, Justin, Archbishop of Canterbury, 268
Wellesley, Arthur, 1st Duke of Wellington, 292, 430
Wessex, Countess of (Sophie Rhys-Jones), 42, 170, 219, 367, 514
Wessex, Earl of (Prince Edward), 45, 172, 173, 221, 224, 240, 367, 514
West Cape Welsh Corgi Club, 411
West Germany (1949–90)
Berlin Wall, 247, 405, 424
Brezhnev's visit (1972), 432–3
European Economic Community, 280, 282, 425
de Gaulle's visit (1962), 432
Heinemann's UK visit (1972), 282
Reagan's visits (1982, 1987), 245, 246–7
Royal visit (1965), 16, 18, 342, 424–32, 433
Royal visit (1978), 432–3
Schmidt's UK visit (1977), 433
Schmidt's Zambia visit (1978), 313
Westlife, 461
Westminster Abbey, London, 99, 152, 408, 417, 457
Westminster Hall, 246, 267, 418
Whistler, Laurence, 349
Whitlam, Gough, 206–7, 233
Whitlam, Margaret, 207
Whittle, Frank, 23
Wicks, Nigel, 391
Wiggin, Charles, 283
William I 'the Conqueror', King of England, 284
William, Prince, *see* Cambridge, Duke of
Williams, Austen, 151
Williams, Rowan, Archbishop of Canterbury, 154
Wilson, Harold, 35, 146, 149, 156, 376
France visit (1965), 293
Germany visit (1965), 427, 432
Lagos Commonwealth summit (1966), 145
Rhodesian UDI crisis (1965), 310–11
and Romania, 89, 90, 91
Soames affair (1969), 281
and Vietnam War, 240
Wilson, Mary, 473
Wilson, Woodrow, 66
'Wind of Change' speech (1960), 136, 378
Windrush scandal (2018), 182–3, 227, 231
Windsor Castle and Estate, Berkshire, 30, 66, 344
bonsai jasmine tree, 440
Commonwealth gifts, 163
Crimson Drawing Room, 272
dine and sleep, 268
Entente Cordiale centenary (2004), 78
fire (1992), 47, 75, 162, 210, 497
Frogmore House, 372
Kennedy memorial service (1963), 240
Kwakiutl totem pole, 22
Oak Room, 271
Reagan's visit (1982), 66, 246
schoolroom, 276

Windsor Castle and Estate, Berkshire (*Continued*)
St George's Chapel, 152, 533
Trump's visit (2018), 271–2
vineyard, 2
Windsor, Duchess of, 287-288
Windsor, Duke of, *see* Edward VIII
wine, 34–5, 75–6, 99, 266, 276, 292, 297, 300–301, 417
Winfield House, London, 530
Winskill, Archibald, 286, 317, 320, 321, 326, 334
Wintour, Anna, 170
Woodard, Robert, 344, 360, 362, 367
on barbecues, 354
on Cowes Week, 367
Cyprus CHOGM (1993), 54, 162
D-Day anniversary (1994), 257, 368
France visit (1992), 368–9
on lifejackets, 360
piloting, 360
Prince of Wales, tutoring of, 360, 477–8
Russia visit (1994), 442, 447, 451, 452–3
South Africa visit (1995), 409, 410
on speeches, 57
United States visit (1991), 253, 254–5
World Bank, 155
World Cup, 278
World War I (1914–18), 11, 109, 174–8, 413, 426, 428, 455, 458
World War II (1939–45)
Abel Smith's service, 355–6
Arctic convoys (1941–5), 451
Australian Armed Forces, 176, 205, 426
Battle of Britain (1940), 176, 320
Battle of Cape Matapan (1941), 31
Battle of El Alamein (1942), 298
Blitz (1940–41), 247
Bomber Command, 176
du Boulay's service, 90
Burma Campaign (1942–5), 122
Bush's service, 250
Canadian Armed Forces, 176, 219
D-Day (1944), 26, 58, 176, 256–7, 306, 349, 368
Dresden bombing (1945), 433
Dunkirk evacuation (1940), 273, 277
Elizabeth's service, 11, 50
France, fall of (1940), 205, 273, 277, 298
Free France (1940–44), 205, 277, 278, 298, 290
Holocaust (1933–45), 278, 433, 527
Japanese surrender (1945), 468
Malayan Campaign (1941–2), 472
memorials, 176, 263, 523
New Zealand Armed Forces, 176, 205, 426
North African Campaign (1940–43), 298, 351
Philip's service, 11, 31, 274
refugee monarchies, 79, 277
Sword of Stalingrad, 67
Tito's resistance (1941–4), 326
Vichy France, 278
UK declares war on Germany (1939), 346
World Wildlife Fund, 17, 60, 130, 509
Wright, Patrick, 74, 383

X-rays, 347
Xi Jinping, 70, 71, 74, 525, 527

Yee, Anthony, 469
Yeltsin, Boris, 20, 442–53
Yeltsin, Naina, 447
Yimbesalu, Joannes, 9
York, Sarah, Duchess of, 250, 366, 390
York, Duke of (Prince Andrew), 513
African tour (1979), 317, 320, 325, 331, 336
birth (1960), 128, 221, 508
and Commonwealth Games, 172, 173
Falklands War (1982), 245
helicopter piloting, 33, 360
Lakefield College, studies at (1977), 224
Royal Navy service, 245, 513
as special representative for trade, 513
wedding (1986), 366, 390
York University, 93, 95
Youde, Edward, 303
Young, Hugo, 388
'Youth and the Commonwealth' speech (1970), 474
Yugoslavia, 131, 326, 424, 444

Zaire (1971–97), 86–7, 168
Zambia, 4, 12, 83, 116, 307–17
1979 Lusaka CHOGM, 30, 36, 307–40, 377, 380, 491
1985 Nassau CHOGM, 384, 385
1986 South African bombing raid, 387; Marlborough House CHOGM, 397, 398
1990 Mandela's visit, 402
Zanzibar, 329
Zayed bin Sultan, Emir of Abu Dhabi, 424
Zhao Ziyang, 437
Zimbabwe, 20, 36, 54, 85–6, 116, 118, 164, 478–83
Princess of Wales's visit (1994), 516–17
Edinburgh Commonwealth Games boycott (1986), 395
Harare CHOGM (1991), 155, 168, 403, 405–7
Independence (1980), 377, 379, 478–83
Marlborough House CHOGM (1986), 397, 398
Mugabe's governance (1980–2017), 54, 85–6, 169, 398, 405–7
South African bombing raid (1986), 387
Commonwealth withdrawal (2003), 86, 164, 169
Zimbabwe African National Liberation Army (ZANLA), 480, 482
Zimbabwe African National Union (ZANU), 311, 326, 478–9, 481
Zimbabwe African People's Union (ZAPU), 311, 315, 322–3, 325–6, 328, 332, 333, 478–9, 481
Zimbabwe-Rhodesia (1979), 325, 328, 331, 332, 338
Zulus, 115, 407, 413

Different titles and rank may often apply to the same person at different times in the course of this book. Therefore, with the exception of hereditary and courtesy titles, the index lists individuals without honours, rank or honorifics.